CRAFTSMEN AND
INTERIOR DECORATION IN ENGLAND
1660–1820

CRAFTSMEN
AND
INTERIOR DECORATION
IN ENGLAND
1660–1820

Geoffrey Beard

JOHN BARTHOLOMEW & SON LIMITED

EDINBURGH

1981

First published in Great Britain 1981 by
JOHN BARTHOLOMEW AND SON LIMITED
12 Duncan Street, Edinburgh EH9 1TA

© Geoffrey Beard, 1981

ISBN 0 7028 8430 8

Typography and binding design by Douglas Martin Associates, Leicester
Set in 'Monophoto' Ehrhardt 12/15, 9/10½ pt.
Typesetting, black and white reproduction and printing by
BAS Printers Limited, Over Wallop, Hampshire.
Colour printing by John Bartholomew and Son Limited
Edinburgh.

British Library Cataloguing in Publication Data
Beard, Geoffrey
Craftsmen and interior decoration in England, 1660–1820.
1. Decoration and ornament, English
2. Decoration and ornament, Architectural
I. Title
729'.3   NA3544.A1

CONTENTS

ILLUSTRATIONS

Figures

Ornaments

The ornaments on the prefatory pages (iii, xiii, 1, 113 and 239) have been taken from the three volumes of *The History of the Rebellion and Civil Wars in England Begun in the Year 1641. With the precedent Passages and Actions that contributed thereunto, and the happy End, and Conclusion thereof by the Kings blessed Restoration and Return upon 29th of May in the Year 1660*, written by Edward, Earl of Clarendon and printed in Oxford at the Theater, 1704. These engraved ornaments were executed by M Burghers, sculptor to the University of Oxford.

TO THE MEMORY OF
EDWARD CROFT-MURRAY
1907–1980

ACKNOWLEDGMENTS

In my work I have been assisted by many people: by the owners of houses, librarians, archivists, museum and art gallery staffs, many clergymen and by several of my former and present colleagues and students. I am deeply indebted to them, and hope they will accept this general but inadequate expression of my thanks for their help. At the same time a few friends have rendered me especial help and should be mentioned individually. I have been instructed, as so many others, by the distinguished contributions about architects, the range of activities of the King's Works, sculptors and decorative painters made by Dr Howard Colvin, the late Rupert Gunnis and the late Edward Croft-Murray. I regret that Rupert Gunnis never saw my plasterwork book in print, but I was privileged to dedicate its pages to our mutual friend Howard Colvin. It gave me equal pleasure that Edward Croft-Murray had accepted the dedication of this present book. It was a token to acknowledge what he had imparted, generously, to me and others by his own two volumes on decorative painters in England. Sadly, he died in September 1980, when this book was in the press.

I have been able to benefit on many occasions from the special knowledge of John Cornforth, Dr Terry F Friedman, Dr Eric Gee, John Harris and Dr Peter Willis. I have also been helped with many problems by Barbara Fisher, Christopher Gilbert, Dr Andor Gomme, Nicholas and Judith Goodison, Helena Hayward and Alison Kelly. Anthony Kersting, FRPS, has provided me with excellent photographs for books and articles over the past 25 years; he has likewise enhanced this book by providing about half the illustrations. The Leverhulme Trust, The Twenty-Seven Foundation, The British Academy and The Marc Fitch Fund have supported my researches and travels on various occasions since 1958; I have again been assisted in the considerable travels for this book by The British Academy Humanities Research Fund. Some of my findings were set out in 1975 during six Rhind Lectures on 'Interior Decoration in Great Britain'. These were delivered in Edinburgh during Architectural Heritage Year, and I am grateful to the President and Council of the Society of Antiquaries for Scotland for the opportunity to work on the subject. I also benefited from the wide range of information proffered in 'after-lecture' conversations.

Finally, my wife and daughter have endured my preoccupied presence and frequent absence with cheerful understanding, and have in addition given much practical help.

Geoffrey Beard
University of Lancaster, September 1980

TO THE READER

In this prefatory note I want to explain the scheme of this book, and also say a little about the reasons for undertaking it. After a short Introduction the text is divided into three parts, each of which emphasises the contribution craftsmen made to interior decorations. It is not, however, a history of stylistic change. The first part deals with patrons, with the training and methods of work of craftsmen, and the materials used. The second part outlines many commissions, chosen to illustrate particular points in the careers of architects and craftsmen. They are but a selection from the wide range available in the period 1660 to 1820. I have concentrated mainly on private commissions, in that the important volumes on the *King's Works*, edited by Dr H M Colvin, have rendered further comments on those commissions less necessary. The third part is a select dictionary, arranged alphabetically by the craftsman's surname. This excludes certain categories of workers, either because they were not involved primarily with interior decoration, or because comprehensive lists are in existence or in preparation. There is, therefore, little listing of masons, plumbers, wrought-iron workers, decorative painters and sculptors. I have for convenience included brief entries for the painters Verrio, Laguerre and Thornhill, as they are often mentioned in the text.

My aim in Part III has been also to avoid duplication of lists other than my own. Those which appeared in 1966 and 1975 were in my books on *Georgian Craftsmen* and *Decorative Plasterwork*, and these are now out of print. I have revised the lists and have added many new names and commissions to them. A system of abbreviations for titles in frequent use is followed in the lists and the notes to the text and plates. It has been satisfying to add several new facts—the plasterers at Warwick Castle and some details about Houghton, for example—and amusing to find a new but all-too-rare research source: it proved possible to work out the time taken at Houghton in 1726 by the Italian *stuccatore* Giuseppe Artari and his team by their daily consumption of red wine; the gift of each bottle was recorded faithfully by a member of Sir Robert Walpole's household staff!

In selecting illustrations I have given more emphasis to those which depict details of rooms rather than the whole setting. The former are often unaltered (as, for example, in the case of the staircase from Cassiobury, pl. 28), even when their locations are disturbed. An exception has been that almost all the 16 colour plates show a substantial part of a fine room—the drawing together of the component parts.

Finally, I have tried to give the sources for all statements and quotations, and to list in the Bibliography some of the books which have been useful in giving instruction to craftsmen, and less committed readers, alike. The book is concluded with three indexes: one of persons, one of places, and another for subjects.

My researches into the history of interior decoration began in 1952 at the behest of the late Margaret Jourdain. She urged me, at one of a number of meetings at which she imparted information with typical generosity, to give some substance to the aspect she had been unable to deal with in her *English Decorative Plasterwork of the Late Renaissance* (1926). This was to identify and list work by plasterers and stuccoists. I pursued the subject spasmodically for several years as its very anonymity was too frustrating. Finally my book, entitled *Decorative Plasterwork in Great Britain*, appeared in 1975, with the generous support of the Paul Mellon Centre for Studies in British Art. I had been concerned in the interim with Georgian craftsmen alone and with pioneer and often frustrating research in bank archives to supplement those in more usual repositories. Of recent years I have become more interested in methods of work used by craftsmen; along with this, and by revising and expanding my lists, there seemed room for this present book. I offer it in the hope that its facts and illustrations may win a few more to appreciate, and help to preserve, fine examples of craftsmanship in English houses and churches.

Colour plate 1 CHATSWORTH, Derbyshire. The State Drawing Room, 1689–94 (photograph: A F Kersting).

The State Rooms at Chatsworth, on the 2nd floor of the S. front, were ready for the joiners in the summer of 1690. In October wainscot wood was brought from Hull, and the rooms were plastered. The carvers Joel Lobb, Roger Davis and Samuel Watson signed agreements in September 1692 to carve ornaments in lime wood. The Mortlake tapestries (woven *c* 1630) depict 'The Healing of the Lame Man at the Gate of the Temple'. The 6th Duke of Devonshire provided new mouldings around the tapestries. The one portrait, an oval in the carved work, is of the patron, the 1st Duke of Devonshire.

The ceiling painting by Louis Laguerre depicts in oil on plaster an 'Assembly of the Gods' and, in the covings, the 'Forge of Vulcan' and 'Vulcan discovering the loves of Mars and Venus'.

ABBREVIATIONS

Arch Rev	*Architectural Review*, monthly periodical
Baker, 1949, *Brydges*	C H C and M I Collins Baker, 1949, *The Life and Circumstances of James Brydges, 1st Duke of Chandos*
Beard, 1966, *Craftsmen*	Geoffrey Beard, 1966, *Georgian Craftsmen and their Work*
Beard, 1975, *Plasterwork*	Geoffrey Beard, 1975, *Decorative Plasterwork in Great Britain*
Beard, 1978, *Adam*	Geoffrey Beard, 1978, *The Work of Robert Adam*
Bolton, 1922, *Adam*	Arthur T Bolton, 1922, *The Architecture of Robert and James Adam*, 2 vols.
BL Add. MSS	British Library, Additional Manuscripts
Burl Mag	*Burlington Magazine*, monthly periodical
CUL(CH)	Cambridge University Library, Cholmondeley (Houghton) Archives
Colvin, 1950, *Arch Rev*	H M Colvin, March 1950, 'Fifty New Churches', *Architectural Review*, pp. 189–96
Colvin, 1954, *Dictionary*	H M Colvin, 1954, *A Biographical Dictionary of English Architects, 1660–1840*
Colvin, 1978, *Dictionary*	H M Colvin, 1978, *A Biographical Dictionary of British Architects, 1600–1840*
Colvin, 1976, *King's Works*	H M Colvin (ed.), 1976, *The History of the King's Works, V, 1660–1782*
Croft-Murray, 1962, 1970, *Painting*	Edward Croft-Murray, *Decorative Painting in England*, 1 (1962), 2 (1970)
Crook and Port, 1974, *King's Works*	J Mordaunt Crook and M H Port, 1974, *The History of the King's Works, VI, 1782–1851*
C Life	*Country Life*, weekly periodical
CRO	County Record Office
dest	destroyed
Fleming, 1962, *Adam*	John Fleming, 1962, *Robert Adam and his Circle in Edinburgh and Rome*
Gibbs, 1728, *B of A*	James Gibbs, 1728, *A Book of Architecture*
Goodison, 1974, *Ormolu*	Nicholas Goodison, 1974, *Ormolu: The Work of Matthew Boulton*
Gunnis, 1953, *Dictionary*	Rupert Gunnis, 1953, *Dictionary of British Sculptors, 1660–1851*
Harris, 1962, *Furniture*	Eileen Harris, 1962, *The Furniture of Robert Adam*
Harris, 1970, *Chambers*	John Harris, 1970, *Sir William Chambers: Knight of the Polar Star*
Hussey, *ECH*	Christopher Hussey, 1965, *English Country Houses: Early Georgian*; 1956, *English Country Houses: Mid-Georgian*; 1958, *English Country Houses: Late Georgian*
Jourdain, 1926, *Plasterwork*	Margaret Jourdain, 1926, *English Decorative Plasterwork of the Late Renaissance*

Colour plate 2 BURGHLEY HOUSE, Northamptonshire. Ceiling of the Dining Room (4th George Room), *c* 1692 (photograph: The Marquess of Exeter, and the Governors of the Burghley House Preservation Trust).

The extensive painted work on walls and ceilings in the Burghley State Rooms in the 1690s by Antonio Verrio and his assistants is noted elsewhere in this book (Part II). This ceiling displays a Banquet of the Gods.

Little, 1955, *Gibbs*	Bryan Little, 1955, *The Life and Work of James Gibbs*
Mortimer, 1763	Thomas Mortimer, 1763, *Universal Director* (copy in Guildhall Library, London)
NLW	National Library of Wales
NRA	National Register of Archives
PCC	Prerogative Court of Canterbury (Wills and Administrations filed at PRO, London)
PRO	Public Record Office, London
RA	Robert Adam, architect (1728–92)
RABA	Robert Adam's bank account (1764–92) (Drummonds Branch, Royal Bank of Scotland, London)
RCHM	Royal Commission on Historical Monuments
RIBA Library	Royal Institute of British Architects Library (British Architectural Library and Drawings Collection), London
Stillman, 1966, *Adam*	Damie Stillman, 1966, *The Decorative Work of Robert Adam*
Thieme–Becker	Ulrich Thieme and Felix Becker, 1907–50, *Allgemeines Lexikon der Bildenden Kunstler von der Antike bis zur Gegenwart*, 37 vols., Supplement (1953–62), (continues)
VCH	Victoria County History
Walpole Soc	Walpole Society
Willis and Clark, 1886, *Cambridge*	R Willis and J W Clark, 1886, *Architectural History of the University of Cambridge*, 3 vols.
Wren Soc	*The Wren Society*, 20 vols. (1924–43), Index in XX

INTRODUCTION

The shattering effects of the Civil War in England had many restrictive repercussions other than those of hindering material and social progress. While the arts were not suppressed completely, the achievements of Inigo Jones were sealed off effectively from a later generation, and many craftsmen who had trained under him in the Office of Works had died or were elderly and out of touch. His nephew, the talented architect John Webb, was prevented from obtaining his correct position as Surveyor-General to the Office of Works at the Restoration of Charles II in 1660, and was again passed over in 1668 when Christopher Wren succeeded Sir John Denham. Sir Roger Pratt, who had come to maturity in the lifetime of Inigo Jones (1573–1652), had been out of England since the death of Charles I, and during the Commonwealth he was content to read, enlarge his architectural library, write his architectural notebooks and act as advisor to his cousin, soon to be building at Coleshill.

English architecture at 1660 had therefore suffered a setback: skilled craftsmen were in short supply, and the revival of intellectual interests in patron, architect and scientist had to reckon with the attitudes of the old Caroline court. The king, back from exile, understood France and Holland best, and his patronage placed them quickly as alternative sources of inspiration to Italy. The Royal Society held its first meeting under its royal charter in 1662, and Wren, appointed Savilian Professor of Astronomy at Oxford in the previous year, was encouraged towards architecture by the invitation in 1663 to consider the repairing of Old St Paul's Cathedral. He also visited Paris in 1665 to survey 'the most esteem'd Fabricks'. It was a visit which coincided with that of the great Italian architect and sculptor Bernini, who was preparing his designs for the east front of the Louvre. Wren found, however, that 'works of Filgrand and little Knacks are in great vogue'; he preferred the solidity of English mason tradition to the spirited verve of Continental baroque, even if he did come as near to adopting that heady style as any of his later adherents. The English apprenticeship system of training craftsmen was slow to adapt to new techniques and materials, and much of the work created lacked the vitality and discipline of foreign achievements. The portrait painters were busy, but there were none of native talent who could fresco the ceilings of Wilton, or create a figure with the dramatic stance of Bernini's *David*. Craftsmen such as joiners and carpenters struggled to take each other's livelihoods but were rarely adept, even if allowed, to practise satisfactorily both skills. Wren's great task was to 'bred up' in the best way a team of craftsmen who could achieve his schemes and, by their example, encourage innovation and better standards.

Even so, and with the notable exception of Sir James Thornhill, mural painting remained largely the province of foreign craftsmen such as Antonio Verrio and Louis Laguerre. Grinling Gibbons led a school of imitators in woodcarving who could only rarely achieve his own considerable skills, and the French smith Jean Tijou worked 'Iron in perfection and with Art', a maxim he set forth on the title page of his *A new Booke of Drawings* . . . in 1693. He was to dominate the craft into the early eighteenth century. Meanwhile, the joiner and carpenter could provide what they understood—timber framing, wainscoting, panelled doors and bolection moulds—but to the very strict requirements of the Act of 1667 regulating the rebuilding of London after the Great Fire. The ill wind which fanned destruction brought with it the opportunity for considerable work, the hastening forward of the more rigid application of building standards, and the patronage of the many City Companies intent on rebuilding the Livery Halls. The trading community was busy with the creation of wealth to finance the work, and Parliament helped with the City churches by the application of a 'sea-coal tax' levied on coal brought into London by sea. For craftsmen, with the promise of work in London in abundance, the results were important; some, like Edward Jerman, who belonged to a family who had been carpenters since the sixteenth century, became adept at surveying and rebuilding many Company Halls. Those who worked for Wren on the churches were content to stay in their trades and leave all the architectural lines to him; they provided woodwork and richly foliated plaster ceilings—the destruction of many halls and City churches in the Second World War has rendered it more difficult to appreciate the nature of their achievements—but it was not always of a consistent standard, and was occasionally old fashioned, however durable. It was the late 1680s before Wren's team was adept and as good as those who understood the Italian ways of Inigo Jones, 60 years earlier.

The rebuilding of St Paul's Cathedral (Wren's major achievement) took almost 35 years, and its dome combined the best characteristics of High Renaissance style. It brought his craftsmen to high levels of attainment, but they had serious competitors. Hugh May's important baroque interiors at Windsor Castle, fashioned with the king's lavish financial support, brought forward the first great painted staircase in England. As it was entered through a low, columned vestibule, its effect was undoubtedly overwhelmingly dramatic and did much to introduce those working alongside Verrio and Gibbons to new standards of spatial organisation. It was an Italianate conception, however, which Wren turned away from, and his secular buildings of the 1680s and 1690s, using brick with stone dressings, were if anything more dependent on French pattern and English solidity. In the one fervent building on which the Catholic James II imposed his will, the Whitehall Chapel, the work of Verrio in 'the Assumption of the Blessed Virgins according to their tradition, with our Blessed Saviour, and a world of figures . . .' made it a Popish chapel despite Wren's reticent styling.

The country houses, likened early in the seventeenth century by Ben Jonson to 'proud, ambitious heaps and nothing else', were being created in two opposing styles. The cautious favoured those with hipped roofs, a design which owed much to Pratt's Coleshill House, Berkshire, begun in 1649 and finished with John Grove's rich ceilings by 1662. The fashionable, such as Ralph, 1st Duke of Montagu, and the 6th 'Proud' Duke of Somerset, welcomed grand baroque ideas and patronised a large company of talented foreigners at Montagu House, Boughton and Petworth. The best of English work was put into houses such as Belton, Hampstead Marshall, Combe Abbey and Buckingham House built from the 1670s under the casual superintendence of Captain William Winde. Born in Holland of English parents, and a godson of his principal patron, the 1st Earl of Craven, he employed 'the beste master in England in his profession', Edward Goudge, as plasterer and the equally talented Edward Pearce as carver. There were no grand colonnaded painted rooms such as Verrio created at Burghley House in the 1690s, and the internal arrangements were staid and practical with an emphasis on a great staircase with wreathing acanthus in foliated panels, or set with richly carved balusters. More mysterious even than Winde, who anyway had his army career to attend to, was the architect William Talman. He quarrelled with many of his patrons, with Wren and Sir John Vanbrugh, and yet remained one of the most considerable talents at the turn of the eighteenth century. His south front for Chatsworth, with its acknowledgment to Bernini's design for the east front of the Louvre, was an important point in English architecture and betokened an architect of great competence. But behind the façade, and despite rich interiors, was what so often hindered innovation and encouraged mediocrity, an Elizabethan house altered and patched by its owner. It says much for Talman that he contrived an impressive staircase, set with Tijou's balustrade and flanked by painted schemes worthy of a major suite of baroque staterooms. All the principal painted decoration was by foreigners, although Edward Goudge surrounded Verrio's paintings with scrolled and gilded plasterwork, and a team of English woodcarvers came on to the house from Burghley.

In the late seventeenth century, interiors for a fashionable few were influenced by the Dutch styles introduced by William III and by the Huguenot designer Daniel Marot (*c* 1660–*c* 1752). But the diplomatic journeys of the Duke of Manchester in 1707 were, with Vanbrugh's approval, to bring back Venetian painters such as Pellegrini and Marco Ricci. They came intent on also trying to wrest the forthcoming commission for the decoration of the dome of St Paul's (1709) away from Thornhill—to whom it was given—and to work meanwhile at Kimbolton and Castle Howard. They were followed shortly by the *stuccatori*—Giovanni Bagutti was at Castle Howard by 1709, and new evidence suggests that Francesco Vassalli and one of the Artari family were working for the gentleman architect William Wakefield in Yorkshire by 1715. England, however, had an unfavourable climate for those who loved the sun and conveyed it brightly in the colours and allegories of their paintings; Ricci and Pellegrini had gone by 1717 and 1721 respectively, and their activities had done little to disturb the slow and magisterial work of Thornhill at St Paul's Cathedral and in the Painted Hall at Greenwich.

The younger architects such as Vanbrugh and Hawksmoor, who owed much to Wren, were ready to encourage English as well as foreign talent, and the commissions at Castle Howard and Blenheim in the first few years of the eighteenth century provide adequate evidence of this. James Gibbs and Colen Campbell were, equally, ardent supporters of the *stuccatori* as well as of London carvers of the calibre of James Richards. William Kent was always intent while in Italy (1709–19) on becoming a painter and was patronised lavishly by the 3rd Earl of Burlington; he provides the most important example of one who, as architect, painter, landscape gardener, book illustrator and designer of silver and furniture, blended the rhythms of foreign pattern with the abilities of his English executants. It was James Richards who carved Kent's barge for his royal patron, Frederick, Prince of Wales, and it was Robert Dawson who plastered the Kent ceilings in Henry Pelham's house in Arlington Street. It was Kent, however, who assisted in the design and decoration of Houghton, and his work at Kensington Palace is of prime importance.

Such work demanded good materials, and the more one examines house archives, the more apparent it becomes that a large and complex organisation provided them. London, Hull and Bristol importers handled timber—mahogany became a most important requirement from its introduction about 1715—and this was sent along the rivers or by road carriers to merchants who delivered it to the site. Various account books for the building of Sir Robert Walpole's large house at Houghton, Norfolk, document its supply from Jamaica as well as the normally unconsidered tasks of lime-burning, brick-making, the providing of nails, hinges, scaffolding, ropes, stair cramps, lead and pantiles—the many minor requirements at any building venture and without which it could not proceed towards completion.

It is also apparent, although more difficult to establish, that craftsmen of various trades visited the house in a defined sequence. The plasterer worked usually from a staging set beneath the ceiling area but before the floorboards or wooden wainscoting were in place; in this way his wet and messy debris did not harm other expensive parts of the rising structure. It is possible to establish this sequence on occasions not only from manuals of instruction but from such humdrum listings as those of riding charges, stabling of horses of various craftsmen, and, in the case of the Italian *stuccatori* working at Houghton, from their daily consumption of red wine. It was, however, work that was usually paid for by the patron tardily and, in some cases, many years late. An interesting exception, one of very few noted, was when Stiff Leadbetter was supervising work in progress from 1758 to 1765 at Shardeloes, Buckinghamshire. He was working under the overall direction of Robert Adam. His careful accounts include many payments phased at weekly, fortnightly or monthly intervals but, over six and a half years or so of building activity, an interest payment at 5 per cent was added to each amount paid; to a total expenditure of £15 484. 14s. 5d., an additional £2163. 17s. 6d. was added in interest payments, and it is possible to establish the precise duration of each craftsman's stay on the site from the itemised interest due.

Such generous systems were, however, far from general practice, and many architects concerned themselves more with the elevations and sections than with accounting complexities. The mid-eighteenth century was a time when English interior decoration was undergoing swift and stylistic change; architects and craftsmen needed to give extra attention to what patrons demanded. The upheavals were caused by the acceptance and intermingling of chinoiserie, rococo and a revival of Gothic styles. To satisfy whims as well as a need for practical information, a number of architects, surveyors and engravers issued a wide variety of pattern books and manuals of instruction. James Gibbs had reinforced the constant demand for drawing instruction by issuing his *Rules for Drawing the Several Parts of Architecture* in 1732; it was a popular book and went into two further editions in 1738 and 1753. Isaac Ware published volumes on the designs of Inigo Jones (c 1733), on the plans, elevations and sections of Sir Robert Walpole's great house at Houghton (1735), and a translation of Palladio's *Four Books of Architecture* (1738). But it was the smaller manuals which found their way more readily to the workbench; Batty Langley's *The Builder's Complete Chest Book* (1738) and the many publications by William Halfpenny and William Pain, for example, instructed those whose apprenticeship had been based on earlier methods. Langley also provided in 1747 a very comprehensive manual on Gothic architecture 'improved by Rules and Proportions in many Grand Designs of Columns, Doors, Windows, Chimney-Pieces, Temples and Pavillions . . .'. Those craftsmen who had been brought up on the classical orders found it, presumably, of much use. They also acquired as many engravings and books showing new patterns as possible to satisfy the requirements of patrons desiring to be up to date.

The demands imposed on English craftsmen by these stylistic changes were varied, and some rose to the challenge and could compete satisfactorily with foreigners. A group of young architects led by James Paine and Isaac Ware concerned themselves especially with interior arrangement and decoration; Paine claimed in his book on the ornaments of the Mansion House he had designed at Doncaster (1751) that the stucco ornaments by Thomas Perritt of York and his apprentice Joseph Rose, senior, were equal to the best work by the Italians. There is, however, evidence that foreign stuccoists were in English teams: Charles Stanley from Denmark assisted Thomas Roberts of Oxford, Patroli worked with the Rose family, and Vassalli seems to have worked in Scotland with Thomas Clayton and on early Robert Adam commissions (Croome Court). Some, such as Giuseppe Cortese, settled in England; he did much work for the York architect John Carr. When he died in 1778 at Wakefield, his executors were Carr's favourite plasterer James Henderson and the Yorkshire cabinet-maker Edward Elwick.

In the early 1750s William Chambers, James Stuart and Robert Adam were abroad travelling in Italy or Greece and, with contacts among the *literati* of the academies, they were learning the tricks by which to revive the Roman and Greek forms. Upon their return to England (with, in Chambers's and Adam's case, patronage from George III), they all issued grand folios—on the antiquities of Athens, on the ruins of Diocletian's Palace at Spalato, and on Chinese and Civil architecture. Several craftsmen subscribed to them as they needed to come to terms both with architects who knew what they were about and with patrons such as the 1st Duke of Northumberland. He was one of many who knew unerringly when mouldings had been ill-executed, and could command their amendment until he and his architect were finally satisfied with the result. In Adam's case, a large team of craftsmen was well controlled; quality of work and costs were assessed carefully, but much was created which was too similar. Adam ceilings are colourful and well fashioned in composition plaster, but comparing them is a weary business and differences are often minimal; only those which incorporate painted roundels, often of cloying subject matter, give some variety to the whole. The Adam achievement was nevertheless considerable and drew forth from workers in metal, wood, wire, plaster and paint components of regular and lasting quality.

Adam's own career attracted many contemporary critics and several distinguished rivals. It is fascinating to see how the major commissions of Chambers and Adam were completed to the highest standards by separate teams; Adam almost invariably used the Rose family for his plasterwork, Chambers the services of Thomas Collins, but some, such as the carver Sefferin Alken, worked for both. It is a tribute to the cautious apprenticeship scheme, grounded as it was in long and safe precedent, that enough craftsmen could satisfy the demand made on their abilities. Chambers also fancied himself as 'a very pretty connoisseur in furniture', and was not above trying to correct Thomas Chippendale as cabinet-maker. He was, however, overruled by his patron, Lord Melbourne, who again demonstrated a knowledge inherent to his status which allowed him to state that 'the Elegance of that Room is from the lightness of well-disposed, well-executed Ornaments', and that he was averse to admitting any gilding whatever in the furniture.

A late eighteenth-century revival of interest in Gothic architecture benefited Wyatt and the foreign stuccoist Francesco Bernasconi. He worked for Wyatt at Blithfield and elsewhere, and also had extensive employment in buildings by Sir Jeffry Wyatville and in the great soaring interiors of Sir Robert Smirke's medieval-style castles at Eastnor, Lowther and elsewhere.

Much of what was created in the late years of the eighteenth century and within the reign of George IV to 1820 was worked, however, by machinery and in new compositions. Patents abounded for improvements to sawing and planing machines, moulds were made in gelatine, and ornament was fashioned in papier mâché or in materials such as 'plastic wood' (which could be poured into moulds). They eased the craftsman's task and allowed more efficient repetition. He worked either as a small part of a large building team (such as that assembled by Thomas Cubitt) and had no responsibility for the flow of materials and cash to the business, or as a large employer himself with little direct contact with the practical benchwork.

These considerations were less applicable in earlier years, and it says much for the ability of craftsmen that they countered difficulties and rose on many occasions beyond mere competence to near virtuosity. Much of what they created has not failed structurally at any later time. Modern techniques of varnish removal and strengthening with non-ferrous metals have also frequently restored a damaged work and shown again how it looked in the splendour of its first creation. This book is about the more significant examples—the methods by which they were fashioned and the names of those who became adept at a whole variety of skills, worked out to make incomparable settings.

PART I

Masters, Men and Materials

'If you are not able to handsomely contrive it
yourself, get some ingenious gentleman who
has seen much of that kind abroad . . . to do it
for you.'

Notebooks of Sir Roger Pratt, 1660
(cited by R T Gunther, 1928,
The Architecture of Sir Roger Pratt, p. 60)

[1]
The Talented Host

The Patron

From the Elizabethan period onwards there had always been those titled noblemen in England who earned money by their abilities and were then forward in architecture and building. The 9th Earl of Northumberland in the late sixteenth century was assiduous about his buildings at Syon, and he possessed foreign architectural books.[1] Sir John Thynne at Longleat and the 1st Lord Burghley at Theobalds and Burghley House were equally active in the late years of Elizabeth's reign in building grand houses.[2] In the early seventeenth century Sir Arthur Ingram, as Secretary to the Council of the North, gathered a large fortune by the granting to him of monopolies by James I and became one of the ablest and most unscrupulous financiers of the period; he founded the fortunes of the family who lived at Temple Newsam, Leeds, for the two and a half centuries after he had acquired it in 1622 for £12 000.[3]

Twenty years later Sir John Banks amassed a fortune from his financial operations, commerce and land-owning,[4] and in 1670 he made considerable alterations to the Carthusian Priory at Aylesford, Kent. Sir Richard Newdigate, who was appointed Chief Justice in 1660, the auspicious year of the Restoration of King Charles II, was a successful lawyer; so lucrative was his practice that he managed to buy back the family's former seat at Harefield, and he also bought Astley Castle as well as owning Arbury, Warwickshire.[5] Ferdinando Gorges, who bought Eye Manor, Herefordshire, in 1673 was a Barbados merchant trading in sugar and slaves,[6] and Thomas Foley, who completed Stoke Edith, Herefordshire, by 1702, was a prominent ironmaster. His father, Paul, who acquired the estate from the Lingen family (who were impoverished in the Royalist cause), was later Speaker of the House of Commons, and son of an earlier Thomas, also a prominent ironmaster.

While the demands of building took their toll of finances—Lord Conway wrote to his cousin Sir Edward Harley in 1677 of his Warwickshire home, Ragley: 'Here you find me playing the foole in laying out money upon building, having cheefely undertaken it because I finde my grandfather designed to build heere; yet I am not satisfied with myselfe'[7]—similar patterns[8] of

1. G R Batho, 1956, 'Syon House, the First Two Hundred Years', *London and Middlesex Archaeol. Soc., Transactions*, XIX, p. 13.
2. Eric Mercer, 1962, *English Art, 1553–1625*, pp. 12–16; Mark Girouard, 20 September 1956, 'New Light on Longleat', *C Life*, CXX pp. 594–97.
3. A F Upton, 1961, *Sir Arthur Ingram, c 1565–1642*.
4. D C Coleman, 1963, *Sir John Banks, Baronet and Businessman*.
5. Warwickshire CRO, Newdigate Archives, A2, 26.
6. Christopher Sandford, 1952, 'Eye Manor', *Woolhope Club, Transactions*.
7. Historical Manuscripts Commission, XIV, Appendix 2, p. 357.

8. Lawrence Stone, 1965, *The Crisis of the Aristocracy, 1558–1641*, chs. IV and VII; 1973, *Family and Fortune, Studies in Aristocratic Finance in the Sixteenth and Seventeenth Centuries*; Alan Simpson, 1963, *The Wealth of the Gentry, 1540–1660*; Ray A Kelch, 1974, *Newcastle, A Duke without Money: Thomas Pelham-Holles, 1693–1768*, Univ. of California Press. Theses: A M Minardière, 1963, 'The Warwickshire Gentry, 1660–1730', MA, Univ. of Birmingham; H D Turner, 1964, 'Five Studies of the Aristocracy, 1689–1714', M Litt, Univ. of Cambridge; D R F Davies, 1971, 'The Dukes of Devonshire, Newcastle and Rutland, 1668–1714, A Study in Wealth and Political Influence', D Phil, Univ. of Oxford.

office-seeking to help in the restoration of 'cash to hand' continued throughout the eighteenth century. The 1st Duke of Chandos became rich through office and adroit corruption,[9] and the 2nd Earl of Nottingham made a clear profit of over £50 000 while Secretary of State at the start of the century. Even more remarkable in terms of audacity was John Aislabie who, as Chancellor of the Exchequer at the time of the South Sea Bubble troubles in 1720, was accused of making large profits; he had been building his house, Studley Royal, Yorkshire, at the time, but this halted when the Bubble burst with disastrous results. It has been established[10] that he invested profits gained by his foreknowledge of stock movement in his estate. He was finally brought to account, his estates forfeited (reported in 1729 at nearly £2 million) and work on his house halted while he served imprisonment in the Tower.

The 3rd Earl of Burlington, who in 1717 had debts estimated at £23 000, tried a safer method of raising money. He submitted a bill to the House of Lords to free him from irksome restrictions in his father's will and to permit him to grant building leases on land near his London home, Burlington House, Piccadilly. He had position and did not need to grovel for sinecures but needed, as did most of his contemporaries, money to build. From his account at Hoare's Bank he drew some £20 000 in the years 1721–26. His House of Lords bill had received Royal Assent a year or two earlier, in 1718, but financial problems and lawsuits[11] against his agents were to occupy Burlington well into the 1730s. He went on building, however, at Burlington House and Chiswick and patronised not only craftsmen but Handelian opera and singers. In his green account book (at Chatsworth), he recorded in meticulous detail the vagaries of his South Sea stock, the assignment of mortgages and the fluctuating, ever critical balance of money 'to hand'. His banker obtained lottery tickets for him regularly and, as with all London bankers, advice was freely available to him on the raising of mortgages at fair interest rates. The banker Richard Hoare was always on the look-out for good mortgages and, when not in a position to take them up himself, would pass them on to his customers;[12] the bank's ledger of 'Money lent on Bond and other Securities, 1696–1718' shows a singularly healthy blend of available finance and banking acumen for the ever-present and hard-pressed customers.

Reward for attendance and skill to a variety of offices and enterprises continued as a pattern throughout the later years of the eighteenth century. The sale and use of land, the seeking of office or the management of a trade or profession remained the main sources of the nobility's wealth. They displayed greatness in a variety of ways, and not least in the building of houses. The pursuit was so entrenched that, by the early eighteenth century, George Dodington instructed his executors to use £1800 per annum from his estate for the completion of his house at Eastbury, designed by Sir John Vanbrugh and completed after the architect's death in 1726 by Roger Morris. This move to make money available for steady expenditure had been made necessary by Dodington's losses in the South Sea fiasco, which postponed building operations and may also have curtailed the design of Eastbury.[13]

9. Godfrey Davis, November 1951, 'The Seamy Side of Marlborough's War', *Huntingdon Library Quarterly*, XV, No. 1, pp. 21–44.

10. Kenneth Darwin, 1950, 'John Aislabie, 1670–1742', *Yorkshire Archaeological Society, Transactions*, XXXVII, pt. 147, pp. 318–19.

11. Chatsworth MSS, Private Account Book, Lord Burlington; 1966, *Survey of London*, XXXII, p. 210; James Lees-Milne, 1962, *Earls of Creation*, p. 149.

12. H P R Hoare, 1955, *Hoare's Bank, A Record*, p. 26.

13. Laurence Whistler, 1954, *The Imagination of Vanbrugh and his Fellow Artists*, p. 156.

Others avoided investment in the South Sea Company. In the years 1720–25, when the 3rd Lord Leigh was building at Stoneleigh, his average income was £5091 a year; his expenditure on his house, excluding furnishings, remained at a comfortable 11 per cent of his income during the period. Others had to struggle a little more: when George Lyttelton came to build at Hagley, Worcestershire, in 1754—the year in which he was made Cofferer of the Royal Household—he wrote to his architect, Sanderson Miller, that his income was 'a good £2200 per annum, all Taxes deducted, and if I hold it three or four years will build my new House with the help of my Falls of wood without my being obliged to borrow any money'.[14]

The post of Chancellor of the Exchequer, which Lyttelton held in 1755–56, was also lucrative and his disappointment at being excluded from office after 1756 was no doubt due in part to the loss of income. He sold a piece of land near Birmingham for £20 000 to help pay for the house, and his brothers Charles and William Henry loaned money and helped in other ways.[15] The total cost of the house, including furnishings, was said to have been £34 000.[16] While Lyttelton was a comparatively undistinguished politician, he had moved in the correct circles from the late 1720s when he had been Secretary to Frederick, Prince of Wales. His years were those of the political and social supremacy of the Whigs; it was possible for their stewards to capitalise on the increasing value in land by the sale of building leases—as Burlington did—and to increase rents, particularly of those properties in London[17] and the large towns.

It was also open for owners to extend and diversify their own entrepreneurial skills, and to marry well: when Lord Aylesford's son married the younger daughter of the Duke of Somerset in 1750, the match was said to have brought him £50 000. The Birmingham button manufacturer John Taylor employed his own abilities to amass a fortune of £200000, out of which he built a large house at Bordesley, near Birmingham.

By the late eighteenth century—at 1790 or thereabouts—many of the 400 or so great landlords owed not a little of their income, averaged at £10 000 each, to skill in industrial and commercial enterprises.[18] By the time the nineteenth century was under way, a South Yorkshire ironmaster such as Walter Spencer Stanhope[19] could add a new wing to his home in 1804, designed by John Carr, and paid for from industrial investment. Coal and iron produced money for many others to emulate him.[20] House building was described by Maria Edgeworth in *Vivian* as one of 'those objects for which country gentlemen often ruin themselves'. Only the long national purse could attempt to sustain building expenditure on the scale employed by

14. Warwickshire CRO, Miller MSS, Lyttelton to Miller, April 1754. Lyttelton borrowed £10 000 in 1765 from Hoare's Bank (Bank Loans Ledger).

15. Hagley MSS, II, pp. 313–16 (dispersed by sale, Sotheby's, December 1978); cited Rose M Davis, 1939, *The Good Lord Lyttelton*, p. 257, Bethlehem, Pa., USA.

16. T R Nash, 1782, *History of Worcestershire*, II, Supplement, p. 35.

17. At the accession of the 4th Duke of Bedford in 1732 the total rental of all his estates was £32 545, of which nearly a third came from his Bloomsbury and Covent Garden property, Gladys Scott Thomson, 1940, *The Russells in Bloomsbury, 1669–1771*, p. 301; *see also* Donald J Olsen, 1964, *Town Planning in London, the 18th and 19th Centuries*, Appendix 1, pp. 219–23, Yale;

H J Habbakuk, 1939, 'English Landownership, 1680–1740', *Economic History Review*, X, pp. 1–20.

18. Vicary Gibbs (ed.), 1910, GEC, Complete Peerage I, p. 365 (Lord Aylesford); G C Tyack, 1970, 'Country House Building in Warwickshire, 1500–1814', BA thesis, p. 98, Univ. of Oxford (John Taylor); G E Mingay, 1963, *English Landed Society in the Eighteenth Century*, p. 26 (owners' incomes).

19. Ruth Simpson, 1959, 'Walter Spencer-Stanhope, Landlord, business entrepreneur and Member of Parliament of the 18th Century', BA thesis, Univ. of Nottingham.

20. David Spring, 1951, 'The English Landed Estate in the Age of Coal and Iron, 1830–80', *Journal of Economic History*, XI, pp. 1–23.

George IV in transforming Buckingham House. The 1st Marquess of Ailesbury was one contender by spending about £250 000 on Tottenham House,[21] and the 6th Duke of Devonshire lavished a considerable fortune on Chatsworth,[22] as his predecessors had done.

Some of this money came from town property which had increased in value and by the expansion of the estate, which put more names on the rent roll. The Bedford London estates in 1819 brought in a total of £48 413 in rents, but by the following year, due to increases on the Covent Garden area of the estate, payments had risen to £101 259.[23] The Earl of Verulam more modestly added wings to Gorhambury House at an expense of £11 000 raised by the estate steward;[24] Verulam had six sons and four daughters to accommodate. The expenditure by Sir Robert Smirke on Eastnor Castle, Herefordshire, building from 1812 to final works in 1820, is a good example of controlled outlay; Smirke estimated the castle would cost £82 000, of which sum £13 000 was for the 'Masonry, including the expenses of the carriage of the stone, quarrying, lime, sand, etc.'. Expended year by year, the work exceeded the estimates by at least £18 000 before all was done. As the expenditure was set down (with the estimate also surviving) in 17 detailed account books, every penny can be traced; it is summarised later in this book (p. 227) as an indication of what a patron needed to gather to build on a grand scale, and the proportions in which it was disbursed to a host of craftsmen, albeit tardily.

Training the Men

The architectural profession, from the Restoration of the monarchy in 1660 to the early years of the eighteenth century, was represented by a considerable number of competent men, with a few who were outstanding in ability and originality. They were the important founders of a profession, although few of them had had an education which instructed them specifically in architecture. The Office of Works played the most important role in focussing English architectural activity and 'maintaining the tenuous thread of architectural experience'.[25] For the most part, however, the design of buildings in the mid-seventeenth century was still being carried out by master craftsmen who provided 'platts and uprights' as required. While they may

21. Earl of Cardigan, 1949, *The Wardens of Savernake Forest*, p. 297.
22. F Thompson, 1949, *A History of Chatsworth*, Ch. IX; David Spring, 1963, *The English Landed Estate in the Nineteenth Century: Its Administration*, Baltimore; F M L Thompson, 1963, *English Landed Society in the Nineteenth Century*.
23. D J Olsen, 1964, *Town Planning in London*, p. 221, op. cit., (17).
24. J C Rogers, 1933, 'The Manor and houses of Gorhambury', *St Albans and Herts. Architectural Society, Transactions*, VIII pp. 105–6.
25. Colvin, 1978, *Dictionary*, p. 30; Colvin, 1976, *King's Works*, V, pp. 3–18.

Colour plate 3 TRINITY COLLEGE, Oxford. The Chapel, 1691–95 (photograph: A F Kersting).

The design of this fine building is attributed to Henry Aldrich (1648–1710), an 'able judge in architecture', and Dean of Christ Church, Oxford, from 1689. The college authorities at Trinity took his advice before rebuilding, and a design was submitted for Sir Christopher Wren's approval.

Two letters (Bodleian Library, Corpus Christi) establish that the carving, other than the reredos (which may be by Grinling Gibbons), was by Jonathan Maine of Oxford. He worked at the college with the joiner Arthur Frogley, and principally at St Paul's Cathedral, London, 1696–1709.

Lit: Colvin, 1978, *Dictionary*, p. 63; *C Life*, 31 December 1948.

have known little of the splendid, disciplined form of Palladio's buildings (even through their publication in 1570 in his *I Quattro Libri Dell' Architettura*), they would know the durability of Ketton stone, the current prices of timber and the varying thicknesses of sash-bars.

The relationship of architect and builder has become more defined in recent years.[26] Sir Christopher Wren maintained long association with many families of craftsmen, but was not beyond issuing a sharp reminder of their negligence by making them view the fallen buildings at Hampton Court in 1689. Some consideration was shown to those injured by the fall by the payment of the 'chirugion' who attended them, and Wren often interceded on behalf of those in his employ for arrears due to them, or to suggest them for work which he felt they were capable of undertaking.

Architects, however, had to take heed of owners who might feel disposed to dispense with their services altogether, using the best workmen of all trades under their own supervision. Most gentlemen travelled abroad and took a keen interest in architecture, and some, like the 2nd Duke of Argyll, had a very extensive library[27] of architectural books with works ranging from a 1552 edition of Vitruvius to *The Builder's Pocket Companion* of 1731. A mode of learning by travel and observation which was good enough for a duke was also good enough for architects, or those who pretended to the title. Both James Gibbs and William Kent trained in Italy, Thomas Archer travelled there, and many persons abounded in Rome and elsewhere qualified to instruct, assist and occasionally delude the visitor. He spent his time inspecting ancient remains of architecture and making drawings of what he had seen, or thought he had seen.

In these processes of instruction by foreign example added to eager curiosity, craftsmen rarely followed suit. The reasons for this may be found in the inflexibility of the apprenticeship system, and the action of patrons who kept them short of money. When the 1st Duke of Devonshire, the great builder of Chatsworth but a great gambler, died 'deep in debt' in 1707, John Macky recorded that he was of 'nice honour in everything, but the paying his tradesmen'. The magisterial statement of Sir Edward Knatchbull in 1771 about paying his tradesmen once a year because he received his rents once a year, was also typical of many[28] made by those who

26. Frank Jenkins, 1961, *Architect and Patron*, pp. 120–59; H M Martienssen, April 1964, 'Chambers as a professional man', *Arch Rev*, CXXXV, pp. 277–83; Malcolm Airs, 1975, *The Making of the English Country House, 1500–1640*, pp. 53–64; Colvin, 1978, *Dictionary*, pp. 18–25.

27. 1758, *Catalogus Librorum*, Glasgow.
28. Sir Edward Knatchbull to Thomas Chippendale, 23 January [1771], C G Gilbert, 1978, *The Life and Work of Thomas Chippendale*, I, p. 225; John Macky, 1714, *A Journey through England, in Familiar Letters, from a Gentleman Here to his Friend Abroad*, p. 42.

Colour plate 4 CASTLE HOWARD, Yorkshire. The Hall, *c* 1706–10 (photograph: A F Kersting).

This great room, 70 ft high and 52 ft square, is at the centre of the first house designed by Sir John Vanbrugh, for the 3rd Earl of Carlisle. The conjoined square columns carved by Samuel Carpenter support the dome and cupola, which were painted, as are also the pendentives, by the Venetian painter Giovanni Antonio Pellegrini, whom Carlisle's friend, the 1st Duke of Manchester, had brought back to England with the painter Marco Ricci. The stucco fireplace (1709–10), facing a scagliola niche, was the work of the Italian *stuccatori* Giovanni Bagutti and Plura, and is their first recorded work in England. The black and white floor was provided by John Thorp of Bakewell, Derbyshire, and the wrought-iron balcony by John Gardom from Baslow, a pupil of the French smith Jean Tijou, whom he assisted at Chatsworth (*see* pl. 31).

rewarded industry tardily, if at all. In consequence, ability as a craftsman sometimes had to take second place to a greater ability to extend credit to those well able to make payments more promptly. Occasionally the record was set straight, as in the case of the building of the Radcliffe Camera at Oxford, designed by James Gibbs; in the preface to his *Bibliotheca Radcliviana*, 1747, Gibbs thanked the Trustees on behalf of 'all Persons employed by you' who 'honour you for your punctual payments'.

The methods of work craftsmen used have received less attention than they deserve and are treated in later pages. One of the prime functions of architects and craftsmen was to use, to contort and to exploit materials in embellishing buildings. Although the varied styles they used found favour for a wide range of decorative functions, the general run of patrons and architects was true to the classical system of proportions and orders. This caused problems for the compilers of pattern books and manuals of instruction; for their publications to succeed, they had to continue to appeal to the underlying conservative system while applying the fashionable flourishes of a contemporary but more bizarre style. In this ambition they succeeded but rarely, mainly because they had little real understanding of the manner in which such styles had originally been used. It was perhaps a failure of the methods by which craftsmen trained, and an indication that our native workmen lacked the innovative flair and fluency of techniques found readily enough in work by the many foreign artists active in England and Scotland.

Guilds and Apprentices

The apprenticeship system, set by statute (5 Elizabeth, ch 4), allowed masters to take apprentices for periods of instruction of seven to eight years. The virility of the local centres, apart from London, may be indicated by the number of apprentices at York put to the joinery and allied trades in the period 1660–1720: there were 136 joiners, 210 carpenters and 6 carvers under training, forming a small but important part of a total of 2659 apprentices in all trades in the city in the same period.[29] At Durham, Bristol, Newcastle and Edinburgh during the seventeenth century, the various trade guilds also occupied important positions in social life.

Having sought out a suitable master, the parents of an intended apprentice paid an apprenticeship premium, were issued with an indenture setting out the conditions of training, and the boy or girl moved into the family circle. It was hoped that, during their seven years of training, they would not only be taught their master's trade, but be set an example of good workmanship. They assisted on commissions and, as they progressed in ability and knowledge in the several branches of their 'mystery', they were entrusted with more specialised tasks. Many were allowed to measure work, make out accounts and sign receipts against payments made, through them, from patrons to their masters.

When the apprenticeship was finished, the test work undertaken was examined carefully by representatives of the Livery Company. Then, at three successive meetings, the apprentice was 'called'; if no one objected to his election, he was sworn in as a member of his guild—before the mayor at the borough court in the case of Durham freemen.[30]

29. VCH, 1961, *The City of York*, ed. P M Tillott, pp. 167 and 217.

30. C E Whiting (ed.), 1945, Durham Civic Memorials, *Surtees Society*, CLX, p. xvii.

The ordinances of most guilds were very similar. Those at Durham and York give guidance as to the regulations to which a master needed to adhere: he was not to absent himself from guild meetings and was to see that apprenticeship indentures were available to the 'searchers'; he could be put out of his occupation and not be allowed to work within the city if he took or used any goods which did not belong to him; he could take no apprentices until he had been a freeman or brother of the 'mystery' himself for seven years and, after, he was not allowed to take apprentices for a term less than seven years. There were also fines for default in workmanship and for the use of inferior materials. Whilst it could be claimed that the system had the framework for a rigid oversight of men and work, a great deal depended on the integrity of the guild officers. The seventh injunction, also found in those regulating London Companies, 'not to have any more Apprentices but two' was openly disobeyed;[31] to take undue notice of it would have limited the capacity of a business to expand and become more efficient. However, training more than two apprentices at a time was a difficult task.

Competition from Foreign Craftsmen

Thus guild members were ill-equipped for competition from foreign craftsmen, who enjoyed more freedom to learn by example and experiment and could travel to train in sophisticated centres of artistic activity, such as Rome. When Charles II returned from exile abroad, it was a signal for a number of foreign artists, the decorative painter Antonio Verrio and the carver Grinling Gibbons among them, to come to seek employment in England; the chapels at Windsor, St James's and Whitehall were to be examples in England of the best found in France and Italy. But the subsequent flight of James II and the introduction of the Dutch ideas of William III did much to sweep away the French influence which had been so important to the court of Charles II. It was not until the Peace of Ryswick in 1697 that William's principal supporters felt able to revive their interest in French painting and architecture.

While war and intrigue were no help in forwarding the rival claims of craftsmen, native or foreign, to a patron's attention, he for his part had the freedom of choice. The Worshipful Company of Plaisterers petitioned the government on three occasions in the late seventeenth century[32] about foreign painters coming into England and taking over the decorative schemes which they might otherwise have covered with plaster.

Rebuilding after the Fire of London focussed attention on the restrictive attitudes of the trade guilds. With many Livery Company Halls needing rebuilding, and many houses, both of quality and quantity, in urgent need of attention, there was work in abundance. It was hopeless to expect that the city could be rebuilt solely by freemen of the London Companies; it was necessary in the Act of 1666 to allow all tradesmen from whatever part to work for the space of seven years and to enjoy the same liberty as the freemen. The monopoly of the guilds was broken and craftsmen of all trades could flock to London and seek work.[33] Many were also known as 'foreigners'—anyone not a brother of a London Company.

31. Whiting, *Memorials*, p. xviii; York Minster Library, MS BB5; London, Guildhall Library, MS 6132.

32. London, Guildhall Library, MSS 6132–3.

33. N G Brett-James, 1935, *The Growth of Stuart London*, p. 300; Colvin, 1978, *Dictionary*, p. 459.

The records of this 'immigration' are not easy to trace. The authorities were too busy, and the Companies did not fill the gap. The records of the Worshipful Company of Carpenters[34] mention journeymen who came from Leicester, Beaumaris and Carmarthen. Master masons came from Taynton and Burford, the quarry districts in Oxfordshire, and from the Isle of Portland.[35] By 1670 the building trades complained that 'foreigners' had come in from all parts of the kingdom. As well as the Plaisterers, the Companies of Carpenters, Masons, Bricklayers and Joiners presented a joint petition against foreigners working on the rebuilding of London without the necessary qualifications of apprenticeships.[36] They also squabbled among themselves and, by 1672, the old quarrels about the allocation of tasks between joiner and carpenter had broken out again.[37]

The official policy, however, of expanding English trade led to tolerant naturalisation orders; all the protests went unheeded. Even the powerful Goldsmiths' Company could do little about the inrush of Huguenot goldsmiths leaving the Continent: in the 25 years before 1710, some 120 French goldsmiths came to London.[38] The new styles and engravings they brought with them fitted alongside the growing acceptance by English craftsmen of pattern books and practical manuals of all kinds.

In the late seventeenth century, Joseph Moxon (1627–1700), author of a number of such books, and in particular of *Mechanick Exercises*, applied to a number of trades, suggested that craftsmen should study architectural books. He listed a number he considered suitable—Serlio, Palladio and Vignola, as well as Sir Henry Wotton's important *Elements of Architecture* (1624). With this sort of reading, he predicted, there would seen be more 'Master-Workmen that will contrive a Building, and draw the Designs thereof, as well, and as curiously, as most Surveyors . . . especially those Workmen who understand the Theorick part of Building, as well as the Practick'.[39]

There is no doubt that, while foreign competition was disliked by English craftsmen, they needed to come to terms with it and to analyse its success. Some of the reasons were not hard to trace: there was an understanding, bred of long observance of skills such as fresco painting, which put the itinerants ahead; they were also more daring in the use of colour, they were better versed in the niceties of architectural style, could contort it to their uses in an able way, and they had been exposed to a wider repertory of engraved ideas and motifs.

The rivalry taught our own craftsmen, albeit slowly, to be competitive and to learn from example. They had to master the art of carving with dexterity in softwood and pin the work together in trophies and swags, learn how to manage the hard-setting Italian stucco or the more involved aspects of rustication on stonework, the cutting and dressing of brick, and the veining and marbling of paint to simulate more exotic materials. The apprenticeship system covered

34. London, Guildhall Library, MSS 8332–4; Bower Marsh, 1913, *Records of the Worshipful Company of Carpenters*, p. xi.
35. D Knoop and G P Jones, 1935, *The London Mason in the Seventeenth Century*, pp. 35 and 45.
36. T F Reddaway, 1940, *The Rebuilding of London after the Great Fire*, p. 119.
37. E B Jupp and W W Pocock, 1887, *An Historical Account of the Worshipful Company of Carpenters*, pp. 303–6.
38. Joan Evans, 1933, 'Huguenot Goldsmiths in England and Ireland', *Proceedings of the Huguenot Society*, XIV, p. 496; W C Scoville, 1952, 'The Huguenots and the Diffusion of Technology', *Journal of Political Economy*, 60, p. 29.
39. Joseph Moxon, 1703, *Mechanick Exercises*. Published by Praeger Reprints, 1970, New York, with an excellent introduction by Benno Forman, p. 253.

only a small part of this, and there is little doubt that foreign intervention hastened forward the intricate process of learning new tricks. By the mid-eighteenth century, foreign artists were frequently part of an English team of decorators.

Abilities and Travel

Some, however, still doubted the ability of English craftsmen to improve themselves in these ways. In a long statement in 'An Account of Architects and Architecture' which John Evelyn appended in 1664 to his translation of Fréart's *Parallèle de l'Architecture . . .*, he wrote that he thought English 'mechanicks' impatient at being directed and unwilling to recognise faults; there was a current arrogance, he thought, which implied that craftsmen were unwilling to be taught their trade further when they had served an apprenticeship and worked for gentlemen who were satisfied with their endeavours. He did admit that our craftsmen were capable of exceeding 'even the most exquisite of other countries' when they set their minds to it, and that English smiths and joiners excelled beyond those 'of all other Nations whatsoever'.

There is some slight evidence to suggest that a few craftsmen improved themselves by study on foreign travels in the late seventeenth century; bred up by their fathers in the way of apprenticeship, the occasional man of the calibre of Edward Pearce (*c* 1630–95), a talented woodcarver and sculptor, may have travelled abroad. If his work was known only in England, it is difficult to account for a letter written by John Talman from Rome in 1711 to his father, William Talman, in England[40] in which he describes an entertainment he gave in Rome; writing about the decoration of one of the banqueting rooms, he says: 'Round the room were twelve heads painted representing Vitruvius, Fabris the painter, Glycon the sculptor, opposite were Palladio, Raphael and Bonarota [Michelangelo], on another side Inigo Jones, Fuller and Pierce.' Pearce (or Pierce) is thus given the honour of representing English sculpture in this great gallery and may mean he was known in Rome. His accomplished bust of Sir Christopher Wren (Ashmolean Museum, Oxford) suggests association with Bernini and his school.[41]

When William Kent came out of his apprenticeship to his father, a coach-painter at Hull, about 1705, and at a time when he could hardly have shown great promise or virtuosity, some latent talent was recognised in him. Burrell Massingberd, Sir John Chester and Sir William Wentworth sent him to study as a painter in Italy. In 1713 he won the Pope's prize for painting. The Yorkshire historian, Ralph Thoresby, recorded the event in delight at the honour it had brought to their native county.[42]

For the most part, however, native craftsmen at work in England were of humbler abilities, even if in special cases, such as John Etty and William Thornton of York, their skills were beyond those of their contemporaries. Etty's tombstone of 1707/8 in All Saints' Church, York, records that he had 'acquired great knowledge of Mathematics, especially Geometry and

40. *Wren Soc*, XVII, p. 4. *See also* Vertue, 1930, *Notebooks* (*Walpole Soc*), XVIII, p. 69; Terry Friedman, December 1975, 'The English Appreciation of Italian Decoration', *Burl Mag*, CXVII, p. 841.

41. M D Whinney, 1964, *Sculpture in Britain, 1530–1830*, p. 47.

42. Ralph Thoresby, 1715, *Ducatus Leodensis*, p. 494; Edward Croft-Murray, 1950, 'William Kent in Rome', *English Miscellany*, I, pp. 221–29; U Middeldorf, April 1957, 'William Kent's Roman Prize in 1713', *Burl Mag*, XCIX, p. 125; Geoffrey Beard, August 1970, 'William Kent and the Royal Barge', *Burl Mag*, CXII, p. 488.

Architecture in all its parts far beyond any of his Contemporaries in this City'. Thornton was said by the York historian Francis Drake[43] to be regarded as the 'first artist' in England in joinery. He died in 1721 and is also buried in York.

The humbler abilities of the majority were pin-pointed by Sir Christopher Wren. Writing in 1694 to the Treasurer of Christ's Hospital, he indicated the fundamental weakness in English training: what was wrong was the lack of education in designing or drawing. Craftsmen were capable of copying a foreign pattern so well that often they excelled the original, but they could not measure against the common training 'which everybody in Italy, France and the Low Countries pretends to more or less'. Wren's words were heeded by the school at least and Bernard Lens was appointed as drawing master. In the eighteenth century, apart from the important role of the London coffee-houses as centres in which scientific and practical knowledge was disseminated, there were many academies.[44] These were served by loosely knit groups of artists, but in 1789 the architect Peter Nicholson set up a 'Philosophical Institute' in Soho where he established evening classes for mechanics, joiners and carpenters. To this activity he added the equally demanding one of writing practical instruction manuals, such as *The Carpenter's and Joiner's Assistant* (1797).

Another important stabilising influence from the middle of the eighteenth century was the Society of Arts, founded from coffee-house beginnings in 1754. It played the same part in forwarding the interests of arts and manufactures as The Royal Society had done for the sciences from its earlier start in 1662. It seems, however, improbable that English interior decoration and monumental sculpture would have demonstrated much of true interest without further stimulus from patrons who travelled abroad to see and to acquire, and by foreign craftsmen coming here to work.

Agreements to Work

Having set out a little about the methods by which craftsmen were trained, in the seventeenth century in particular—that is, by serving an apprenticeship—it is appropriate to describe how agreements and formal contracts to work were applied. Writing to the Bishop of Oxford on 25 June 1681, Wren instanced the current methods of building agreement: '. . . there are 3 ways of working: by the Day, by Measure, by Great . . .'.[45]

The first method supposes the direct employment of the builder on time rates, and Wren wrote that by this method he could tell when the workmen were lazy. At the other extreme, building 'by the Great' meant that the builder agreed to erect the house at a fixed price. A sure bargain could be made through this method, which hurt neither side, except that a workman might neglect the work if he found unexpected expense in tasks he was unfamiliar with. Wren preferred 'work by measure' according to prices agreed by a previously submitted estimate; the work would be measured on completion by independent but competent tradesmen. It was common for workmen contracted to the Office of Works to be paid a daily rate, but there seems

43. Francis Drake, 1736, *Eboracum*, p. 210, York.
44. *Wren Soc*, XI, p. 74; the academies are discussed by

N Hans, 1951, *New Trends in Eighteenth Century Education*.
45. *Wren Soc*, V, p. 20.

no record of any house raised entirely by day payment. Kiveton, the Duke of Leeds' house in Yorkshire (demolished *c* 1810), was a good example of erection 'by the Great', but with all its joinery, painting, plastering and other interior work done by measured rates (*see* p. 142).

Working to rates agreed against a previous estimate, and measured on completion, gradually took over from the other methods. Sir Roger Pratt warned his readers in the 1650s against working 'by the Great', which he argued would be prejudicial to building and be a system abused and overreached by the workmen.[46] When the method had, however, been chosen in consultation with the architect or surveyor (if one was being used), it was necessary to appoint a competent clerk of works, arrange contracts with craftsmen, and have drawings and a model of the intended building made. Attention was also given to the availability and supply of building materials.

At Kiveton, Yorkshire, while advice was taken in the early 1690s from the architect William Talman, the actual erection was supervised (seemingly without any further intervention by Talman) by a typical clerk of works, Daniel Brand of Westminster. He received £1000 in six payments for his work, but additional sums were given to him for extra responsibilities such as visits with the carpenters to choose flooring materials and to quarries away from the estate. Brand agreed all the payments to workers on a joint signature with the Duke of Leeds' steward.

Drawings and Models

An examination of architectural drawings of the seventeenth century shows, as expected, that Inigo Jones was by far the most accomplished draughtsman. There is also no shortage of drawings for most of the major architects and surveyors of the seventeenth and eighteenth centuries. Those like Sir Balthazar Gerbier provided only rough, crude sketches, and Sir Christopher Wren was assisted by highly skilled draughtsmen such as Edward Woodroffe and William Dickinson. William Winde relied on his craftsmen to submit their own designs (*see* pl. 61) for decorative features such as plasterwork, joinery and marquetry.

In the disputes which arose at the beginning of the eighteenth century over William Talman's designs for Castle Howard, some information is gleaned of the procedure for providing drawings. Talman demanded a higher price for his work than Lord Carlisle was prepared to pay, and the architect proceeded finally to law against the earl.[47] Sir John Vanbrugh was called to give evidence before Lord Chief Justice Trevor and indicated that most architects followed the practice of not charging for sketches drawn quickly to show ideas for a house, as Talman's had been for Castle Howard, but that when a design was chosen and followed it must be paid for, together with those necessary for the workmen to follow, drawn 'at large'. The judge and jury agreed with his opinion and dismissed Talman's plea.

By the 1720s the architect's control of the design extended to the preparation of detailed drawings. The meticulous plans and elevations by Colen Campbell and James Gibbs[48] indicate

46. R T Gunther, 1928, *The Architecture of Sir Roger Pratt*, p. 48.

47. L Whistler, 1954, *The Imagination of Vanbrugh and his fellow artists*, pp. 34–35.

48. RIBA, Drawings Catalogue, *Colen Campbell*, ed. J. Harris, 1973; Ashmolean Museum, Oxford, Gibbs drawings (Italian), I.

some diversity in their training. Campbell was in some way associated with James Smith, the Surveyor of the Royal Works in Scotland, but had started life as a lawyer. At some point in his early life, as with Smith, he visited Italy but, unlike Gibbs, did not train there. The latter entered Carlo Fontana's studio in Rome in 1704 and stayed there for five years. His drawings from these years, spirited works in red crayon, are accomplished and informative as to his ability.

Use of an architect's drawings was supplemented by reference to a model,[49] usually made in wood (*see* pls. 6 to 9). Sir Roger Pratt advocated their use in the 1660s in order that all the parts of a building could be seen exactly and in their due proportions. Those prepared for Sir John Vanbrugh's use at Castle Howard and Blenheim probably owed much to Nicholas Hawksmoor's intervention; he was a firm believer in models and those he used for Easton Neston (*see* pl. 7), King's College, Cambridge, and the Radcliffe Library, Oxford, survive.[50] Vanbrugh's Castle Howard model was also sent to Kensington for King William's view upon it.[51] James Gibbs also used models to advantage, and those for St Mary-le-Strand and St Martin-in-the-Fields (*see* pls. 8 and 9) are in existence. Once the method by which work would be undertaken was agreed, and drawings and a model made, it was time to enlist craftsmen and make agreements with them.

Contracts

With the master craftsmen it was usual to draw up separate and exact contracts with each one. These safeguarded the patron to a greater degree than the craftsman, and established the rates of payment for measured work, the use and cost of old and new materials, and set out a timetable for the work's progress. Not infrequently the contracts specified that certain work was to be carried out in the style of some chosen example.[52] Defects in workmanship had to be remedied free of charge; in case of default in this direction a clause was inserted by which £20 was held back for 12 months after the time for finishing for making good deficiencies which, by then, would have appeared. The contracts were sealed by both parties before three witnesses.

For work on Kensington Palace in 1689, a 'Palace Contracts Book'[53] was started by Nicholas Hawksmoor. The five contracts therein, two with bricklayers and three with carpenters, were signed in Hawksmoor's presence. They not only included the usual clauses but one which specified that the floors in the queen's rooms were to be made 'extraordinary cleane'. On large tasks like that undertaken by the Office of Works at Greenwich, Hawksmoor and John James were ordered in 1712 to draw up schemes for the contracts in such a way that the undertakers would put in their prices but blanks would be left for the directors to insert times for finishing and penalties for non-performance.[54] Notices were also frequently inserted in the *London*

49. John Wilton-Ely, July 1967, 'The Architectural Model', *Arch Rev*, CLXII, pp. 26–32; University of Nottingham, Department of Fine Art, 'The Architect's Vision': Exhibition Catalogue of 19 models, March 1965.
50. The Oxford model was made by a Mr Wartwell and is illustrated by S Lang, April 1949, 'By Hawksmoor out of Gibbs', *Arch Rev*, CV, p. 183.
51. Geoffrey Webb, ed., 1928, *The Works of Sir John Vanbrugh. IV The Letters*, p. 18.
52. Colvin, 1978, *Dictionary*, p. 22.
53. PRO, Works, 5/146.
54. *Wren Soc*, VI, p. 67.

Gazette inviting craftsmen to submit their intentions and prices for listed work. In accepting contracts with the Office of Works, craftsmen were advised that they had to abide by the final decision of the officers of the works.[55]

Vanbrugh, as Comptroller of the Works (1702–26), became troubled by Wren's easy practice of allowing Office of Works tradesmen to accept contracts and to do the work themselves when they were salaried employees of the Crown. In an important letter,[56] he indicated to Lord Godolphin, Queen Anne's Lord High Treasurer, that he had prevailed upon Wren that this was a practice utterly against common sense and contrary to the Board's rules.[57] Wren owned to the correctness of this but had not acted to see it observed.

A point which usually led to trouble in both government and private dealings was to draw up contracts with different craftsmen of the same trade, but pay different rates for the same kind of work. When John James was Assistant Clerk of Works at Greenwich (from 1705), one of his duties was to make all the measurements; his enquiries revealed that the bricklayers' contracts allowed different prices and that this was troubling the craftsmen. He informed his committee that, in private work, it was customary to allow 20 to 21 shillings a rod ($5\frac{1}{2}$ yards) for brickwork, and the thicker the work, the cheaper it should be. He instanced the bricklayer Thomas Hughes being paid at 30 to 32 shillings a rod, while Richard Billinghurst, who seemed equally competent, was receiving 5 shillings less. For his part, Hughes was making a profit of about 20 shillings for every rod laid.

The committee visited Greenwich but, finding that Hughes was working precisely to his contract, took no steps to reduce his profit. For once the supervision by the officers of the works may have been lax, as James admitted that certain work had not been according to the contracts, which he had not previously seen. They also had little excuse for such laxity as there was always a clause in contracts, usually relating to the time payments were to be made, which said:

> And when the said severall works shall be well and sufficiently done, & approved of, then the said [name of craftsmen], his Exors or Assigns shall receive [sum of money] as the said work upon a Just measurement thereof had & made shall Justly amount unto, after the Rates and Prices above mentioned.[58]

The building of Somerset House in the late eighteenth century (1776–95) under the supervision of Sir William Chambers was one of the last great occasions of paying workmen by measure at agreed rates; no contracts 'by the Great' were entered into. Measured work required close supervision and Chambers devoted his whole energies to the project, to the detriment of his income. In the early nineteenth century, the successful builder and housing speculator Thomas Cubitt (1788–1855) pioneered a system of competitive tendering which did away with individual contracting. It led to acceptance of the lowest tender and this in turn led to the need to safeguard standards in towns by the application of building regulations. It was, however, a time to accept new methods, and Cubitt's final vindication was to build Osborne House, Isle of

55. *Wren Soc*, VII, p. 28.
56. Webb, *Vanbrugh*, VI, pp. 11–13.
57. 'No officer to take upon him more than is incident to his own charge or shall hereafter be appointed', PRO, Works, 6/368, f. 2.

58. *Wren Soc*, XVI, p. 7; for Victorian contracts, M H Port, 1967, 'The Office of Works and Early 19th Century Building Contracts', *Economic History Review*, XX.

Wight, for Queen Victoria and the Prince Consort (1845–48), and, almost in the same years, the new east front of Buckingham Palace.

Measurement

No researcher in seventeenth and eighteenth-century archives relating to building activities reads far before he encounters the charges for measuring the work. The most succinct account of the terminology involved was given by Batty Langley in Lecture XI in his *The Builders' Chest Book* (1727). The dialogue was set down as questions and answers between Master (M) and Apprentice (P):

> M. How many kinds of measures are used in Building?
> P. Three, viz., Lineal, Superficial and Solid.
> M. What is Lineal Measure?
> P. Lineal Measure is the measuring of any thing that hath length only, as a Line &c.
> M. What is Superficial Measure?
> P. Superficial Measure is the measuring of any substance that hath Length and Breadth only, as Land, Pavement, Painting, Plastering &c.
> M. What is Solid Measure?
> P. Solid Measure is the measuring of any quantity that hath Length, Breadth and Depth, as a Stone, Timber &c.
> One Superficial foot = 144 inches (12 × 12 in.).
> Solid or cubical foot, each side 12 in. = 1728 in.
> Carpenters have the Square of ten feet, viz Ten Feet every way, the whole Square being equal to 100 Feet, and by this Measure Carpenters measure their Carcase, Framing, Roofing, Partitioning, Flooring.

Measurement of wainscoting was usually rated as Single Measure 'taking the Length by the Perpindicular Height from the Top rail to the Bottom'. It was sometimes measured 'once and a half, per yard Superficial'. The measurer was often another craftsman of the trade involved, but in the latter half of the eighteenth century it became a profession in its own right, with several manuals of guidance (*see* Bibliography pp. 297–302).

1 (*left*) HAMPTON COURT, Middlesex. A design for a ceiling decoration in paint and plaster by Daniel Marot (1661–1751), probably intended for Hampton Court, *c* 1692. *London, RIBA, Drawings Collection* (photograph: RIBA, Library).

The work is not known to have been carried out, and the drawing was mistakenly attributed by the late Professor A E Richardson as for the ceiling of the Royal Barge designed by William Kent (1732) for Frederick, Prince of Wales (RIBA Journal, 24 January 1931, pp. 172–76).

Marot was summoned to England in the 1690s 'to design the parterre' at Hampton Court, the Delft-lined dairy, and probably the entire interior of the Queen's Water Gallery apartments, later demolished. (Gervase Jackson-Stops, *Apollo*, May 1977, p. 327.)

2 (*below*) WENTWORTH CASTLE, Yorkshire. Jean de Bodt's lateral and longitudinal section of the Gallery (as originally projected) in the N.E. front, *c* 1708. Pen, ink and watercolour, *Victoria and Albert Museum, London.* Inv. No. E 307–1937 (photograph: V&A).

By 1703 Thomas Wentworth, Lord Raby, was in Berlin as Ambassador to the Court of the King of Prussia. About 1708 he acquired a set of plans for his Yorkshire house from Jean de Bodt, the king's architect. Bodt's suggestions for the interior decoration were not proceeded with. James Gibbs supplied a design for the Gallery and his joiner Charles Griffiths and the Yorkshire joiner William Thornton worked at the house.

3 (*above*) STAMP BROOKSBANK'S HOUSE, Hackney, London. Section of the Saloon by Colen Campbell, *c* 1727. *Inscr*: 'The Section of the Salon at Stamp Brooksbanks at Hackney/c.c.' Ink and pencil, *London, RIBA, Drawings Collection* (photograph: RIBA, Library).

This drawing shows the treatment of a room by Campbell in which a carver such as James Richards would have executed the door-case, and the Italian *stuccatori* the figures over the door, in the cove and wall-panels. The house was demolished *c* 1792.

4 KIRTLINGTON, Oxfordshire. Drawing for the four walls and ceiling of the Dining Room, *c* 1748. *Metropolitan Museum of Art, New York* (photograph: museum).

The building history of Kirtlington is confused despite the survival of Sir Francis Dashwood's account book. William Smith was in charge and made many of the payments to craftsmen.

5 WARDOUR CASTLE, Wiltshire. Design by James Paine for the Central Hall, *c* 1770. Pen, ink and watercolour, *Victoria and Albert Museum, London*. Inv. No. 8416.3 (photograph: V & A).

Henry, 8th Lord Arundell of Wardour, began the rebuilding of Wardour Castle about 1769 — his mind had been toying with schemes for years before and he employed many amateurs to prepare them. In the autumn of 1769 he accepted James Paine's designs for his mansion and by 1776 it was complete. His work included a fine Roman Catholic chapel, with an altar provided from Rome by Giacomo Quarenghi.
Lit: C Life, 22–29 November 1930, 10 October 1968.

ARCHITECTURAL MODELS

6 St Paul's Cathedral, London. Interior of the Great Model, 1673–74. *St Paul's Cathedral, Model Room* (photograph: Courtauld Institute of Art).

In 1669 William Cleere, a London joiner, made a model of Wren's design for the new St Paul's Cathedral. It was not, however, much admired: it was criticised by Sir Roger Pratt as unlike any cathedral in the world. Wren defended himself (and the text of this is given by the younger Wren in *Parentalia*), but submitted further drawings. When, in November 1672, Charles II approved the rebuilding, a new model was in preparation, known now as the Great Model. Twelve joiners worked on it and Richard Cleere cut more than 350 capitals, as well as festoons and cherubims' heads. John Grove I plastered the interior and Robert Streeter, the Sergeant-Painter, was paid for gilding. It cost over £500 to make and is 18 ft long.

7 Easton Neston, Northamptonshire. The Model, *c* 1690. *London, RIBA, Drawings Collection* (photograph: A F Kersting).

This model may represent the building which was planned by Wren's office and executed by Nicholas Hawksmoor, or a scheme for rebuilding the house *c* 1695–1700. Professor Kerry Downes has pointed out that the model differs from the house in several respects. In 1692 Sir William Fermor, its builder, acquired the barony of Lempster and married the daughter of the Earl of Danby, later 1st Duke of Leeds; her dowry, reported at £10 000, was useful for building.
Lit: Kerry Downes, 1969, *Hawksmoor*, pp 33–34; Colvin 1978, *Dictionary*, p. 403; *C Life*, 15 October 1970.

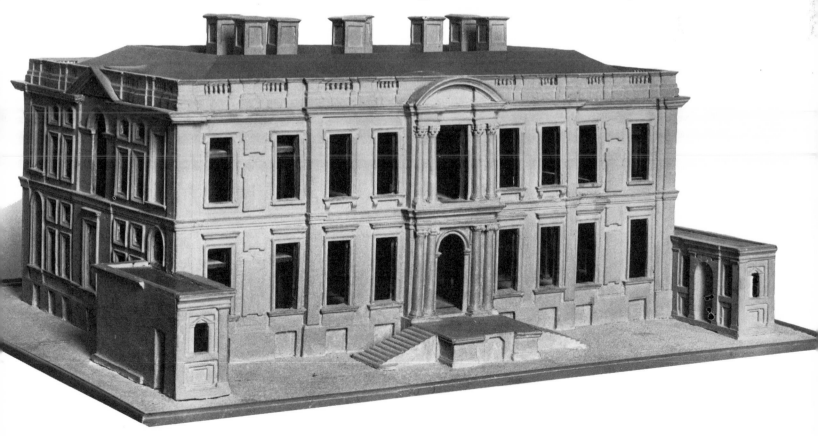

8 and 9 ST MARTIN-IN-THE-FIELDS, London. Exterior and interior of the Model, *c* 1720. *London RIBA, Drawings Collection* (photographs: National Monuments Record).

In 1720, as the parishioners of St Martin-in-the-Fields wished to replace their medieval church, Commissioners were appointed by Act of Parliament to carry out the task. James Gibbs was chosen as architect and this display model was prepared at a cost of £71. The steeple of the model varies from that built, but, as Gibbs included at least six versions in his 1728, *B of A* (pls. 29–30), it is likely that other variations were available which are now lost. The interior (*see* pl. 9) shows that, despite Gibbs's reluctance, he gave maximum space to accommodating a large congregation by the use of galleries upon three sides of the nave. The church was consecrated on 20 October 1726.

[2]
Machines and Materials

Machines

One of the most complicated tasks which faced any craftsman was to keep ahead of technical innovation within his trade, and to make use of many machines, devices and tools for easier working and greater efficiency. House building and decoration, and the erection of churches, public buildings and monuments, created their own special structural problems. None was more demanding than the raising or lowering of heavy weights—of stone, baulks of timber, bricks and so on. Medieval references to cranes, hand- and tread-mill wheels and other weight-lifting devices abound,[1] and there is no reason to think that seventeenth and eighteenth-century cratsmen did not use similar, and occasionally improved devices. They also looked abroad for ideas which had come down in unbroken line from the writings of Vitruvius, through the refinements of Renaissance engineers.

In 1617 Octave de Stradaa Rosberg issued at Frankfurt *Desseins Artificiaulx de Toutes Sortes des Moulins* in which he depicted various machines suitable for raising and lowering weights. In some of these, a trundle was mounted upon an axis turned by a handle and giving motion to a large wheel having pins or teeth on its circumference. The latter was fixed upon the axis of a drum to which the rope was connected that was to raise or lower the weight; the rope passed through blocks, the pulleys of which were in several instances set one below the other to provide greater control.

Another influential volume was that which Vittoria Zonca issued at Padua in 1656 entitled *Novo Teabodi Machine et Edificii*. It included illustrations of various kinds of horse-gin applied to raising materials for building purposes. The tethered horse would walk a prescribed route, often turning a geared windlass on to which a rope would wind or unwind, raising or lowering the weight. Another of Zonca's illustrations showed the application of worm and worm wheel to drive the barrel of a windlass or crane; improvements were made in the eighteenth century to the windlass by the addition of pawls to prevent the barrel running backwards under heavy load.

In the late seventeenth century, knowledge of hydraulics and the use of water power had reached the stage of very effective application. In 1692 Joseph Williams patented a new engine consisting of screws, wheels and wrenches whereby the operative was able to draw and raise great weights with ease. The following year three inventors combined to patent their engine of screw wheels and long timbers to raise and let down weights; it was said to be capable of 'raising the heaviest stones to the top of the highest buildings'.[2]

The crane developed considerably during the eighteenth century, with a number of patents

1. L F Salzman, 1967, *Building in England down to 1540: A Documentary History*, pp. 318–29.

2. *Patents of Invention*: Joseph Williams, 2 December 1692, No. 306; George Nation, John Dewee and Thomas Puckle, 17 January 1693, No. 311.

being filed for those that floated, or had swinging booms, or which could lift entire coal waggons for tipping and emptying. Something similar to that invented by Edward Cox in 1757 must have been used for work at Greenwich Hospital Chapel. The architect James 'Athenian' Stuart wrote on 10 July 1764 to his patron Thomas Anson, on whose Staffordshire house of Shugborough he was working, that, despite a violent cold, he had to attend at Greenwich 'to survey the Crane by which the materials for building the Infirmary are to be raised out of the lighters'.[3]

The artisans who worked on the exterior and interior of all kinds of buildings benefited greatly from machines. In 1718 Marshall Smith invented a machine or engine which could both polish marble and grind colours for paints. The Birmingham printer John Baskerville turned his attention in 1742 to making thin metal plates for mouldings, and there were many patents filed for improvements to machines and for products which resembled something else — ornaments in paper to resemble woodcarving and, in 1693, a composition to run liquid into moulds as 'artificial wood'.[4]

The carpenter and joiner both needed to cut wood in bulk. While Henry Bullock had invented a machine in 1629 for cutting timber into plank or board and other squares; machinery for cutting timber generally belonged to the period when steam power replaced the waterwheel, with two further exceptions: in 1683 John Booth had invented an engine for sawing timber, and George Sorocold, a hydraulics engineer from Derby, invented a horse or water-powered sawing machine in 1703. There were also early seventeenth-century engines (1635–38) for cutting thin veneers.[5]

There were also many inventions which were the work of foreigners resident in England: the first paper-making machine by the Frenchman Louis Robert and the Fourdrinier brothers, roller spinning by the French Huguenot, Lewis Paul, and silk-throwing by the Lombe brothers. John Farly, an engineering consultant, set it out eloquently to the Committee on Patent Laws in 1829:[6]

3. Staffs CRO, D 615/P(S), 1/6.
4. *Patents of Invention*: Marshall Smith, 23 May 1718, No. 421 (marble); John Baskerville, 16 January 1742, No. 582 (metal plates); Marshall Smith and Thomas Puckle, 7 March 1693, No. 317 (artificial wood); John Pickering, 20 December 1773, No. 1058 (paper ornaments).
5. *Patents of Invention* (timber cutting engines): Hugh Bullock, 2 January 1629, No. 45; John Booth, 27 November 1683, No. 230; George Sorocold, 1 January

1703, No. 369. For Sorocold *see* A E Musson and E Robinson, 1969, *Science and Technology in the Industrial Revolution*, pp. 43–44; *Patents of Invention* (cutting veneers): 31 October 1635, No. 87, and 20 October 1638, No. 120.
6. Parliamentary Papers, 1829, III, p. 153, cited by Musson and A E Robinson, *Science and Technology*, pp. 63–64. *See also* W C Scoville, 1952, 'The Huguenots and the Diffusion of Technology', *Journal of Political Economy*, 60.

Colour plate 5 DITCHLEY HOUSE, Oxfordshire. Entrance Hall Door-case, *c* 1725 (photograph: A F Kersting).

This important house, designed by James Gibbs and erected under the supervision of Francis Smith, was the first at which all the Italian *stuccatori* gathered. Their bill of 1725, submitted by Francis Vassalli on behalf of 'me and my partners', included 'for doing the six Images over the pediments £21' (two are shown in this view). Francesco Serena charged £21 for the 'Basso relievos done in the Hall'—the panels of mythological ornament. The door leads to the Saloon (*see* pl. 67).

Clocks and watches, the coining press, the windmill for draining land, the diving bell, the cylinder paper machine, the stocking frame, figure weaving loom, silk throwsting mill, canal-lock and turning bridge, the machine for dredging and deepening rivers, the manufacture of alum, glass, the art of dyeing, printing, and the earliest notions of the steam engine were all of foreign origin.

The last half of the eighteenth century saw several developments in woodworking machinery: planing and fluting machines, those for making joints and for grooving and tonguing floorboards. There was also a close connection between the development of machines for wood and for metalworking, occasioned by early machines being constructed in part of wood. The engineer James Stansfield and the locksmith Joseph Bramah led the way with many innovative ideas:[7] an improved sawmill, a door lock, a flushing water-closet, apart from anything requiring the application of a machine to supersede mere manual dexterity.

Side by side with mechanical contrivances which were at a considerable level of ingenuity and purpose in such great manufacturing centres as Matthew Boulton's Soho manufactory in Birmingham were simpler devices common to all the building trades. The most essential was 'scaffolding', which was erected, moved or dismantled completely by the carpenter.

Scaffolding

The wooden scaffolding in use from early medieval times until the advent of that made from tubular steel seems to have varied little over the years. After raising a wall from ground level to a height of about 4 ft 9 in, a workman required a platform to continue raising the work. This was usually managed by a series of upright wooden poles supporting horizontal timbers (*ledgers*) fixed at about 3 or 4 ft from the walls, carrying putlogs (*putlocks*) on which planks were fixed for the passage or platform of the craftsmen. The poles were usually between 20 and 30 ft or more long, and from 6 to 9 in at the butt end. The putlogs were poles about 4 in diameter and about 6 ft long, chopped square to prevent them from rolling, the ends being squared to about $2\frac{1}{4} \times 3\frac{1}{2}$ in, in order that they might fit into the space of half-a-brick. Lashings of $1\frac{1}{2}$-in rope, each about 18 ft long with wooden wedges to tighten the lashings, were required. The planks, of

7   R Willis, 1852, 'Machines and Tools for Working in Metal, Wood and other Materials', *Lectures on the Results of the Great Exhibition*, pp. 291–320; D Hudson and K W Luckhurst, 1954, *The Royal Society of Arts*, p. 118.

Colour plate 6 HOUGHTON HALL, Norfolk. The Saloon, *c* 1728 (photograph: *English Life*).

The Saloon adjoins the Stone Hall in the double-pile thickness of the house. It is entered through James Richards's splendid door-case of carved and gilded mahogany, and from beneath William Kent's ceiling. In the central octagon he painted 'Phaeton driving the chariot of the Sun, watched by Jupiter'. The deep cove is painted in gold monochrome with animals of the chase and borders with feigned busts on grounds of gold scales. The chimneypiece of black, gold and white marble, allegedly to Kent's design, was probably obtained through the mason-contractor Christopher Cass. The walls are lined with crimson wool damask (*see* pl. 51 for the window side of the room).

12 to 14 ft long by 1⅓ in thick, were usually hooped at the end to prevent them splitting, and laid across the putlogs.

The extensive citations of scaffolding in fabric rolls and other archival sources for the medieval period have been noted.[8] A late eighteenth-century use is depicted in a painting by George Garrard (1760–1826) of the rebuilding of Southill Park, Bedfordshire, about 1796.[9] This shows the use of diagonally placed poles to act as bracing, and transverse struts which were added in high buildings to prevent the line of scaffolding from separating at the top.

Scaffolding was expensive to acquire and, when the Master Plasterer John Grove I died in 1676, he left to his son, John, his 'Scaffolding Boards & Poles'.[10] For external working the scaffolding was often cased in wattlework to act as some protection against the weather. A scaffold of wickerwork was erected in 1776 by Thomas Birch for £20 around the spire of Islington Church, London, within which was a spiral staircase from the tower to the vane. Alderman Sir William Staines is said to have contrived such a scaffold to the spire of St Bride's Church, Fleet Street, damaged by lightning in 1764; this was improved by Birch in repairing the steeple at St Alban's, Wood Street, London, and perfected by him at Islington.[11]

The citations in late seventeenth-century accounts of payments for erecting a 'Great Scaffold' imply that painters and plasterers varied their work between that done from a large structure, fixed for a long period, and a 'Little' or movable scaffold, some 20 ft square, for working within an arch or on a particular area of wall or ceiling. The need for many scaffolds, or for frequent moving of those in use, is instanced in the building accounts for many large houses such as Chatsworth and Audley End. Henry Winstanley, Clerk of Works at Audley End, paid the carpenters in 1687 for making a frame for a moving scaffold to mend the ceiling of the Great Hall; the following year the carpenter took it down and moved it so that the ceiling of the Great Staircase could be whitened. At Chatsworth in 1692 the carpenter was paid for 'taking down scaffolds in ye Chappell', and in the same year he was also 'putting up tressells for ye carvers'.[12] In the last quarter of 1693 the carpenters were again paid 'for putting up a Scaffold in ye Hall for Mr Ricard, and removeing it severall times';[13] in the third quarter of that year they had also dismantled 'the great scaffold', and 'a moving scaffold' was set up in its place for use by the painter Ricard.[14] Again, they had erected a 'scaffould for Mr Varyo to paint ye troses' on the Great Stairs (1690)—perhaps the trusses or the wall spaces below the cornice—and in the first quarter of 1693 the invaluable estate carpenters were paid 'for making a step ladder for Mr Vitti to stand on to gild the Iron work, takeing downe the great Scaffold in the Staircase, and putting up a little one to finish the gilding'.[15]

There seems little reason to assume that most craftsmen worked in other than a standing or kneeling stance from scaffolding. While Renaissance artisans are held to have erected hammock-like cradles to work in, there is seemingly no evidence in English archives of work

8. L F Salzman, 1967, *Building in England down to 1540: A Documentary History*, pp. 318–29.
9. John Steegman and Dorothy Stroud, 1949, *The Artist and the Country House*, pl. 54.
10. Grove's will, PCC, 29 March 1676 (PRO).
11. *European Magazine*, 1812, lii, p. 338; Nelson, 1811, *History of Islington*, p. 312; PRO, Works, 5/41,

September 1687; 5/42, May, June 1688 (Audley End).
12. Chatsworth, *Building Accounts*, II, p. 104. I am indebted to the late Mr Tom Wragg for much help in their elucidation.
13. *ibid.*, II, pp. 148 and 156.
14. *ibid.*, II, pp. 131 and 135.
15. *ibid.*, II, pp. 92 and 116.

being done other than from scaffolding, and that from a non-recumbent position. It will be obvious that only detailed work over a small area could be done from a reclining position; running a profile plaster mould required concentration on the ceiling ahead, and an unhindered walk along many yards of platform—the 'great scaffolds' mentioned in accounts.

An alternative form of scaffold to that which had poles bearing on the ground was that used in the construction of many Renaissance buildings, especially those with domes such as Brunelleschi's Duomo in Florence and the great Basilica of St Peter's in Rome. This sprang in slightly arched form from a convenient high-level ledge. The engravings in an important book by Niccolò Zabaglia (1664–1750) of 1743—entitled *Castelli e ponti di Maestro Niccolò Zabaglia con alcune ingegnose practiche . . .*—on the scaffolding and other devices used in the repair of St Peter's, Rome, from 1703 allow us to assume that the English examples were little different, except in scale. While there is no documentary evidence, similar constructions must have been in use at great houses such as those erected by Vanbrugh for construction and decoration of drums and domes. They were employed when the building had great height and when suitable access to the scaffolding platforms was possible from adjacent staircases, or from ladders. The various galleries and access points to the inner domes of St Paul's Cathedral, London, would allow use of 'sprung' scaffolding. Zabaglia's important but rare book on the devices in use at St Peter's does, however, show ladders of great length of 70 rungs or more, able to reach heights of over 60 ft. Unfortunately, England's major buildings lacked the large team of trained craftsmen, the *Sanpietrini* whom Zabaglia trained to maintain the St Peter's fabric. The nearest approach to them was the talented group, especially of stonemasons, used by Sir Christopher Wren, and the many craftsmen working on the royal palaces for the Office of Works.

When the extensive repairs were carried out to the Banqueting Hall, Whitehall, in the 1720s, the Board of Works had erected conventional scaffolding. Some of this was used for inspection of the painted ceiling, some for support, and some for restoration work on the Rubens' ceiling paintings carried out by William Kent. In January 1734, George II and his queen inspected the paintings from the 40 ft high scaffolding, and Kent was complimented by them on his work.[16] Erection of scaffolding for the restoration of the Greenwich Hospital Painted Hall in 1958 allowed a reasonable deduction to be made from the nature of the painted surface that the painters worked in a standing position with very little chance to visualise the effect from below.[17] By the 1840s there were many adjustable, and even revolving scaffolds which were used by Sir Charles Barry as he rebuilt the Houses of Parliament, 1837–50, and on large structures such as Nelson's Column, Trafalgar Square, London.[18]

16. Colvin, 1976, *King's Works*, V, p. 301.
17. I am indebted to Dr Maurice Craig for this information, and for being allowed to ascend the scaffolding to the ceiling in 1957. William Kent wrote to Burrell Massingberd from Rome on 15 September 1717: 'my Ld Burford did me ye honour with other Gentlemen to come upon ye Scaffolds to see me paint' (London, Society of Genealogists, William Kent MSS).
18. References are cited under 'Scaffolding' in Wyatt Papworth, ed., 1852–92, *The Dictionary of Architecture*, 8 vols., Architectural Publication Society. *See also* Crook and Port, 1974, *King's Works*, VI, p. 606, pl. 32.

Materials

Of recent years there has been increased interest in the nature and source of materials used in house building and interior decoration, with welcome additions to the sparse literature. A brief account of some of the materials most in use follows. It has been included so that there can be a better understanding of terms and items in the discussion of craftsmen's work and methods in chapters 3 and 4.

While most craftsmen were ready to choose good materials, the owner and architect needed to control as far as possible the price and quality. Within the Office of Works it was even more necessary to see that materials were properly used and accounted for. The chief officers were required jointly to make out warrants to the Purveyor specifying quantity and quality of materials; he then obtained them at as competitive a price as possible.[19] Reuse of materials was encouraged (and included frequently in contracts). Wren noted, however, that the demand for houses to be erected after the Fire of London had debased the value of materials; good bricks were scarce due to shortages caused by war and of money to pay for them, and by 1711 a very low level of building was being experienced.[20] Yellow deal was also in short supply, tiles were ill-made, slate not properly riven, and craftsmen had to charge for many extra journeys to timber yards and quarries to choose materials.

STONE AND BRICK

By the beginning of the seventeenth century, it was becoming more necessary to build in stone and brick due to the growing shortage of timber. The spasmodic despoliation of innumerable unused abbeys and priories after the Dissolution, for their stone, was a haphazard and uncontrolled source, replaced as many quarries were opened in various parts of the country. A large part of the cost of masonry had always been in the carriage of the stone; while there was a natural tendency to use easily available—and often unsuitable—stone on the owner's estate, those concerned for prestige and eventual economy opted for stone from a good, established quarry. This guaranteed regular supplies of stone at similar quality and price. If this lay at a distance from the site, it was more usual to buy the stone ready cut to convenient sizes. Final tooling would take place on the site.

The demand for varieties of stone known to be satisfactory made the Northamptonshire quarries justly celebrated.[21] London could draw on supplies in Kent and Surrey, and use the Medway for carriage of the Kent stone. East Anglia could turn to the Northamptonshire quarry at Barnack, the durable stone used to build both Ely and Peterborough cathedrals and Burghley House. Other good quarries in Oxfordshire and Yorkshire served their areas, and on occasion stone was sent farther afield; Aislaby sandstone from near Whitby was sent down the coast to be used at Sir Robert Walpole's house at Houghton, 1722–25. Wren remarked on the dearness of stone unless the quarries lay near the sea; he favoured Portland or Roche Abbey stone, but even those had their faults. Portland stone was used extensively in the rebuilding of London after the Fire.

19. PRO, Works, 6/386, f. 2.
20. J Parry Lewis, 1965, *Building Cycles and Britain's Growth*, pp. 10–16.
21. J M Stearne, 1967/68, 'Building Materials used in Northamptonshire and the area around', *Journal, Northants., Record Society*, IV, No. 2, pp. 71–82.

Bath stone had long been recognised as good, but was not fully used until Ralph Allen introduced it to London in the 1730s at St Bartholomew's Hospital, then being erected to the designs of James Gibbs. The high cost of stone—the cost of that used at St Paul's Cathedral from 1675 to 1710 was over £90 000, of which about a third was for Portland stone[22]—seems to have encouraged a revival in the popularity of brick. Also, ships carrying the Portland stone to London were occasionally seized during time of war.[23]

While the cost of the stone is sometimes recorded in family archives, it usually has to be reckoned as part of the payment made to the masons; their work accounted for the greatest expenditure. At Kiveton, Yorkshire, building for the Duke of Leeds, 1694–1704, the masons were paid £1330. 14s. 5d., and £253. 10s. 6d. was expended for 'slitting stone'.[24] At Wrest, Bedfordshire, where both Thomas Archer and Giacomo Leoni worked for the Duke of Kent in the early eighteenth century, the stone came from Ketton, near Stamford, at 1s. 6d. per foot, with the carriage per ton from Bedford at 8s. 0d.[25] At Studley Royal, Yorkshire, the Plumpton stone was provided at '2½d. per superficiall foot'[26] in the years 1716–40.

Two examples show the difficulties of transporting stone over a great distance. Firstly, the efforts of Ralph Allen in bringing Bath stone to London for the first time and, secondly, in the early nineteenth century, the transporting of stone from the Ruardean quarries in the Forest of Dean by the Herefordshire and Gloucester Canal Company to Eastnor Castle, Herefordshire.

Bath stone was cheaper than Portland stone,[27] and this fact may have persuaded the Governors of St Bartholomew's Hospital, London, to agree to its use for their building works. The detailed negotiations dragged on for many years,[28] the Building Committee deciding at its meeting on 29 June 1730 to use Bath stone. The clerk, William Tims, entered into correspondence with Ralph Allen, draft contracts were prepared and meetings arranged. Within a month, alterations in the estimates were being proposed because of the differences between the plan of the buildings drawn by Gibbs and the printed plan, but Allen agreed to stand by his offer of £1700 as a low price. The negotiations continued on over many years for various phases of the building and are explained at length in a very long letter from Allen of 7 February 1746.[29] He indicated the difficulties of supplying stone during the time when England was at war with Spain in 1739, with the complications of the French intervention in 1744, and the Jacobite rebellion of 1745. Ships were expensive to come by, having to wait for escorts from Portsmouth, and could only make one journey a year to a former three. Allen concluded in grim fashion: 'I have not sold so much as one Tun of Stone in London Since ye Commencement of the War. . .'.

At Eastnor, building from 1812, the stone was carried from Ruardean by canal. At the site it travelled over railroads laid about the works by John Jones, who was also superintending the obtaining of additional stone from the local Eastnor quarry. The masonry had been estimated

22. *Wren Soc*, XV, p. xvi.
23. *Wren Soc*, XV, p. 144.
24. Yorkshire Archaeological Society, Duke of Leeds MSS, Box 33, 'Analysis of Expenditure, 1694–1704'.
25. Melbourne MSS, Thomas Coke's Garden Notebook, 1706, 'Prices of building att Wrest in Bedfordshire, Duke of Kent'.
26. Leeds Archives Dept., Studley Royal Archives, Parcel 286.
27. Sir Christopher Wren remarked on the dearness of stone 'unless the quarries lie near the sea', and said 'the best is Portland, or Roche Abbey stone but these are not without their faults . . .', *Wren Soc*, IX, p. 16.
28. London, St Bartholomew's Hospital, MS, HA/19/29.
29. *ibid.*, HA/30/7.

by Smirke at £13 000, but expenditure overall exceeded the estimates by some £8700 before all was done in 1820 (*see* p. 227). It may be assumed that the stone, with carriage, lime, and other materials cost some £2000 extra to the amount allowed.

Ornamental brickwork and its elaboration had achieved its peak by the late years of the seventeenth century. The process of carving the brick involved cutting and rubbing it with various abrasive tools. Sir Balthazar Gerbier, writing in 1662[30] at a time when cut-brickwork techniques were evolving, wrote that brick made a good union with Portland stone, but his idea does not seem to have been practised to any large extent until the early eighteenth century, when many houses were built with stone quoins flanking red brick. Some costs[31] over the years are:

1659–65 17s. to 21s. per 1000 at Cambridge.

1676   'Now somewhat dear, about 18 or 20s. a thousand.'

1706   At Wrest: 12s. per 1000, and carriage at 1s. 0d. for a load of 300.

1722   1s. per 1000 to Lord Chandos for building at Bridgewater, Somerset. (This is a surprising contrast to the Wrest price, but perhaps the order for half a million bricks helped to reduce the price.)

1734   16s. per 1000 for erecting a fabric 20 × 44 ft.

1741–42 163 000 bricks at 6s. 6d. per 1000 for Cusworth Hall, Yorkshire.

1748   Place Bricks 14s.; Grey Stocks 18s.; Grey Stocks, especially chosen for uniformity of colour, 20s. or 22s.; Red Stocks 30s.; Cutting Bricks 60s. per 1000.

The number of bricks required in building a large country house is difficult to ascertain, but some guide may be given by the reference of 1688 in the steward's account book at Belton House, Lincolnshire (1684–86): 'Sam Truman for digging clay for 420 000 bricks, £20'. Tradition also asserts that Thomas Cole used three million bricks in building Mersham-le-Hatch, Kent (1762–65), to Robert Adam's design.[32]

TIMBER

Apart from stone and brick, the other main requirement in building and decoration was timber for flooring and panelling. Wren, in writing 'something of the Materials for Public Fabricks', said: '. . . as to Roofs good oak is certainly the best because it will bear some negligence. Next to oak is good yellow deal . . . our sea-service for Oak, and the Wars in the North-sea, make timber at present of excessive price.'[33] In Scotland, growing timber of any size was in any case excessively rare, a situation which affected price and the nature of work undertaken, and which did not improve until late in the eighteenth century.[34]

30. Sir Balthazar Gerbier, 1662, *A Brief Discourse . . . on Magnificent Building*.

31. Sources in order of examples cited: J E Thorold Rogers, 1888, *A History of Agriculture and Prices in England*, VI, pp. 518–19; H Philippes, 1676, *The Purchaser's Pattern*, 5th edn.; Melbourne MSS, Thomas Coke's Garden Notebook, 1706; C H C & M I Baker, 1949, *The Life and Circumstances of James Brydges . . .*, p. 222, fn. 1; William Leyburn, 1734, *The Mirror of Architecture*, 7th edn., pp. 91–92; Leeds

Archives Dept., Battie–Wrightson Archives, BW/A/23; Batty Langley, 1748, *The London Prices of Bricklayer's Materials and Works*.

32. Beard, 1978, *Adam*, p. 44, pl. 89.

33. *Wren Soc*, IX, p. 16.

34. The Royal Society of Arts encouraged planting from 1758 to 1835 by making awards of gold and silver medals—D Hudson and K W Luckhurst, 1954, *The Royal Society of Arts*, pp. 86–89.

The largest source of timber supply to England and Scotland in the early eighteenth century was Norway. In December 1666 the Privy Council referred to its rebuilding committee the possible replacement of fir for oak, and it was said that 'the Norwegians warmed themselves comfortably by the Fire of London'.[35] Wren knew also that, in due course, he would need to have 'recourse to the West-Indies where most excellent timber may be had for cutting and fetching'.[36] This trade came into Bristol, while that from Scandinavia came to London, Hull and Leith. When timber was required for the building of Burley-on-the-Hill, Rutland, at the turn of the eighteenth century, Norwegian deal was brought in the ships of John Landells to London and then sent up the east coast by ship to Boston and Spalding. Then it went by road to Burley. On 7 November 1730, the Bath architect John Wood wrote from London to the Duke of Chandos's cousin, William Brydges (for whom he was building at Tibberton Court, Herefordshire):

> Sir, I am here making draughts &c., for a new Bank and have a ship loading for Bristol, if you would have some Norway Oak for your stairs I can get you some that is very good . . .[37]

In whatever way and at whatever cost, the timber arrived and was used to create floors, stairs and wainscot. The class of imports known as 'deals' was defined by customs regulations as sawn boards up to $3\frac{1}{4}$ in thick, from 7 to 11 in wide and 8 to 20 ft in length. Boards of narrower width, but otherwise of the same dimensions, were styled 'battens' and lower duty was paid on them. A width above 11 in placed the timber in the category of 'planks', on which the highest rate of duty was paid. When duties were low it was advantageous to import $\frac{1}{2}$-in deals for walls and panelling, $1\frac{1}{4}$-in for flooring and $2\frac{1}{2}$-in for general joinery work. Norway deals were generally 10 to 12 ft long and Baltic and White Sea deals 14 to 20 ft. Deals were reckoned by the long hundred or six score: thus a 'standard' of deals consisted of 120 lengths of 12 ft $\times$ $1\frac{1}{2}$ in $\times$ 11 in timber. Trade was not often affected by war, although the Napoleonic Wars in the early nineteenth century disrupted trade seriously. When building was very active from 1750 to 1770, an average of 20 000 to 25 000 loads of timber were being landed each year.

The landing of some of this material in the north-east can be traced in the Hull Port Books.[38] These are arranged in sections for inward and outward trade, and the daily entries give such information as 'name of ship, port of origin, quantity and nature of cargo'. The only totals given are quarterly values of all the cargoes, with no analysis of particular commodities, or the importers' names. The Hull records at their commencement in 1706 show oak planks, spruce deals and deals coming in — with much else — and malt, lead, woollen goods, red lead, leather and wine going out. It was a similar pattern at Bristol and Lancaster: in 1700 some 240 ships arrived in Bristol, some carrying cedar planking from South Carolina.[39] The Gillow family at

35. H S K Kent, 1955, 'The Anglo-Norwegian Timber Trade in the Eighteenth Century', *Economic History Review*, 2nd series, VIII, pp. 62–74; H L Faber, 1926, *Caius Gabriel Cibber, 1630–1700*, p. 61.

36. *Wren Soc.*, IX, p. 16.

37. Leicestershire CRO, Finch MS, D9/7/1/129 (Burley-on-the-Hill). The Wood letters were found *c* 1952 by W Sydie Dakers and quoted in his *John Wood and His Times* prepared for the Bath Assembly, 1954, p. 13.

They are now at Hereford CRO as part of the Brydges Collection.

38. PRO, E190/341, 6.

39. W E Minchinton, 1957, 'The Trade of Bristol in the XVIIIth Century', *Bristol Record Society*, XX; Kenneth Docton, 'The Lancaster Custom House', Collected Papers (Lancaster Public Library). Based on Lancaster Port Books (Lancaster Reference Library).

MOULDINGS AND PANELLINGS

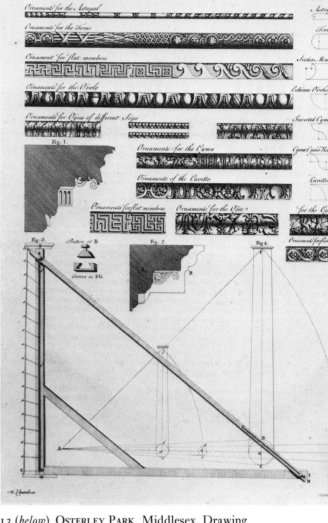

10 (*right*) Sir William Chambers (1723–96). 'REGULAR MOULDINGS WITH THEIR PROPER ORNAMENTS', facing p. 3 in Sir William Chambers, 1759, *A Treatise on the Decorative Part of Civil Architecture* (photograph: Victoria and Albert Museum).

Chambers's important *Treatise* appeared in the spring of 1759 and was accorded a good welcome in London and Paris. He was able to draw on his experiences and learning to set out the form of the orders and all the decorative accompaniments, as well as to declare himself on Greek studies, Gothic, Proportions and Beauty. His plate of 'Regular Mouldings' depicted those suitable for the Astragal, the Torus, flat members, the Ovolo, Ogees of different sizes, the Cyma and the Cavetto.

The *Treatise* appeared in a 2nd edition in 1768. *Lit*: 'The Treatise on Civil Architecture' in Harris, 1970, *Chambers*, pp. 128–143.

11 (*left*) HAMPTON COURT, Middlesex. King William's State Bedroom. Door-frame carving by Grinling Gibbons, *c* 1699 (photograph: National Monuments Record).
In 1698 the fire at Whitehall caused William III to revive his interest in Hampton Court, and in April 1699 Wren submitted an estimate for finishing the state apartments, on which work had ceased at Queen Mary's death in 1694. Gibbons and his assistants were much involved with woodcarving, including elaborate mouldings to door-cases, cornices and chimneypieces.

12 (*below*) CASTLE BROMWICH HALL, Warwickshire. A sketch for veneering the closet floor submitted by Captain William Winde, *c* 1688. *Inscr*: 'A. The Floor of ye closet B Fenering of walnute Tree C Fenering of Cedar, or Cypres.' *Earl of Bradford's Archives* (photograph: Geoffrey Beard).

Captain William Winde was a cousin to Lady Mary Bridgeman, who, with her husband Sir John, remodelled Castle Bromwich Hall with his assistance, 1685–90. A talented team of decorators was assembled, including the plasterer Edward Goudge and the carver Edward Pearce. While some 80 letters survive from Winde, this is the only sketch which relates to the extensive alterations.

13 (*below*) OSTERLEY PARK, Middlesex. Drawing Room, mouldings *c* 1773 on the chair rail, window architrave and (at left) a pier-glass and commode. *Victoria and Albert Museum* (photograph: V & A).

The chair rail moulding, with its intertwined continuous pattern (called *guilloche*), derived from a frieze enrichment in classical architecture. It was revived in the mid-sixteenth century and used extensively by neoclassical architects from the 1760s. The architrave moulding (rising vertically at the right of the illustration) uses a form of stylised acanthus leaf for its decoration. The moulding to the pier-glass uses at the inner edge to the brocade the palmette motif found on friezes at the Forum of Trajan in Rome (2nd century A.D.) and elsewhere. Among the volumes of Adam drawings at Sir John Soane's Museum, London, one (volume 53) is devoted almost exclusively to drawings of friezes.

14 (*right*) PETWORTH HOUSE, Sussex. The Marble Hall, 1692 (photograph: A F Kersting.)

The design of this room is attributed to Daniel Marot, with carving by John Selden, joinery by Thomas Larkin, plasterwork by Edward Goudge and David Lance, bolection-moulded chimneypiece by Nicholas Mitchell, and the marble paving by a 'Mr. Stroud'.

The huge bracketed frieze rests on an 'egg and dart' moulding. The chimneypiece (one of two) has a round-topped frame breaking into a segmental pediment, and there is a giant acanthus moulding round the doors and overdoor frames. The wainscot panels are bevelled, or 'fielded'.

15 (*below*) CHEVENING, Kent. Dining Room panelling, gilt lead capital, *c* 1721 (photograph: Courtauld Institute of Art).

In 1721 Captain Nicholas Dubois (*c* 1665–1735) was invited by Lady Stanhope to supervise alterations at Chevening, and may well have directed the erection of the staircase. The cabinet-maker William Bradshaw was also involved in joiner's work at the house. However, lead capitals were unusual and contrast with those normally found fashioned in wood or in stucco (*see* pl. 66).

16 (*above*) SUTTON SCARSDALE, Derbyshire. First Oak Room, *c* 1724. *Philadelphia Museum of Art* (re-erected 1928) (photograph: museum).

A lead rising-plate at the house (now lost) recorded that the joiner at Sutton Scarsdale was Thomas Eboral of Warwick, and Edward Poynton of Nottingham was the carver. Poynton died in 1737 and left a small bequest to Eboral and to a London carver, William Watts. The room is of oak with tall pilasters, fielded wainscoting, and carvings in lime wood. Two other rooms from Sutton Scarsdale, a second Oak Room and one in painted deal, were also re-erected in Philadelphia.

Lancaster, important cabinet-makers throughout the eighteenth century, exported rum, clothes and other commodities to balance their extensive West Indies trade in exotic timbers, particularly mahogany.[40]

House archives often contain mention of visits to choose timber. In 1694 Thomas Young was paid 'for going to Hull to buy Deels, for his horse hire charges & some dayes work at Kiveton £002.02.00.'.[41] When Castle Howard was building, a few years after Kiveton, the joiner Sabyn was paid in 1702 for '2 days at Yorke choosing out deals for floore' which had come from Mr Perritt at Hull.[42] Both Young and Sabyn were competent men, anxious to choose the correct materials for the job; this involved knowledge of most of the timbers available as well as a concern for seeing it was well seasoned, straight and free from the knots and blemishes which would weaken, particularly in oak.

The knowledge of the properties of timber determined its use within the structure. Walnut was scarce, brittle and of a cross-grained texture which rendered it too expensive and unsuitable for the main timbers of a building. It was, however, like cedar, little affected by worm, and was used in panelling and in cabinet-work. Cedar was highly desirable for panelling by reason of its durability, straightness of grain, easy working and ready splitting. Chestnut, used in the roofs of Westminster Hall and King's College, Cambridge, vied with oak for durability, although, as John Evelyn observed,[43] it was often well-looking outside when rotten and decayed within. For lightness and stiffness, however, little could rival the red or yellow fir[44] for bearers, joists, rafters and framing, and craftsmen used it in abundance.

GLASS

The two main types of glass for windows were cylinder glass and crown glass. The earliest glass was blown in cylinders and, as these cooled, they were gradually opened and flattened. Most of the window glass used in the eighteenth century was blown in large bubbles which were flattened on a revolving circular table. As the glass reacted to centrifugal force, the centre remained thick and the best glass was that cut from the thin edges. Gradually it drove from the market the broad glass popularised in the early seventeenth century by the Lorraine glass-makers working in the Midlands.[45] The brightness of crown glass was the one quality by which it excelled over broad glass. The Newcastle and Stourbridge glass-makers turned to producing it, but faults remained—it was noted in 1703[46] that the crown glass most in use in England had specks, blemishes and streaks within it and was of an ash colour.

40. Spanish mahogany, introduced into England about 1724—and used by William Kent at the Treasury in 1733—was imported from Cuba, Jamaica, Hispaniola and St Domingo and was held to be superior to Honduras mahogany. The latter, which held with glue better than any other wood, was popular for general building purposes (such as stair handrails, sashes) and in cabinet-making: Joseph Gwilt, 1894, *An Encyclopedia of Architecture*, revised by Wyatt Papworth, p. 499; W A Thorpe, April 1951, 'The Sea and the Jungle in English Furniture', *Chartered Auctioneers' Journal*, LXXVII, pp. 12–20.

41. Yorkshire Archaeological Society, Duke of Leeds Archives, Box 32.

42. Castle Howard Archives, Masons and Carpenters Book, 1702–08.

43. John Evelyn, 1670, *Sylva, or a Discourse of Forest Trees*, p. 24.

44. *Pinus sylvestris*. A variety often noted in house archives was the White fir (*Pinus abies*) imported from Christiana, Norway, as 'Christiana deals'.

45. D R Guttery, 1956, *From Broad Glass to Cut Crystal*, pp. 44–45.

46. Richard Neve, 1703, *Builder's Dictionary*, p. 20.

The *London Gazette*, in a series of advertisements from 1710 to 1717,[47] recorded the breakdown in broad-glass manufacture, and it is crown glass which is mentioned in most house archives.

The costs of using crown glass in earlier periods were not excessive in relation to the total cost of building: £47 in 1700 at Kiveton and £52 in 1692 at Dyrham, with £1109 being needed for that supplied for St Paul's Cathedral.[48] Glass was sent throughout the country from London, Stourbridge or Newcastle, or, rarely, as in the case of Wentworth Castle, Yorkshire, from a local glasshouse such as Bolsterstone. By the early eighteenth century, when wooden sash-bars were in use, William Thornton, the York joiner, could write to Lord Stafford that 'the bigness of glass for fourteen lower windows (at Wentworth Castle) was $17\frac{3}{4} \times 16$ inches if into three panes to the width, and $17\frac{3}{4} \times 11\frac{3}{4}$ inches if four panes to the width'.[49] For Castle Howard, where Thornton worked, he told his patron that Lord Carlisle's windows were '$18\frac{1}{2} \times 11\frac{1}{2}$ inches', and that Lord Bingley at Bramham Park, also in Yorkshire, had used glass '$16\frac{1}{2} \times 10$ inches'.

The price of glass is, of course, often hidden in payments to the glaziers. In London, Richard Cobbett was a glazier well used by William Kent and others: he was paid £142 in 1742 for glazing Henry Pelham's house in Arlington Street, and with his son, John, 30 to 40 years later received (from 1776 to 1795) some £3699. 8s. 1d. for glazing Somerset House.[50] William Cobbett charged £477. 10s. 11½d. for glazing Kedleston, Derbyshire, under Robert Adam's supervision in the 1760s.[51] In 1774, the York architect John Carr reckoned that 'glazing sashes with Crown Glass, 12d. p. Foot'[52] was a fair price, but the job at Serlby to which the document relates was given to James Paine and the price he obtained is not recorded.

In 1765 the Royal Society of Arts awarded a first premium to Jeremiah Burrows of Southwark for a machine for the grinding and polishing of plate glass.

It was not until 1824, when Robert Lucas Chance purchased the British Crown Glass Company's works at Smethwick, that 'sheet glass' was introduced in quantity by his French and Belgian workers. Its great advantage was that it could be made into plates of larger dimensions; it also avoided the waste arising from the circular form of the crown tables, and the knob or bull's eye in the centre. The surface was, however, less brilliant than crown glass, but by 1838 Chance's had effected improvements in thickness and quality. The London market was also organised with warehouses like that of Western Crown and Sheet Window Glass, inserting advertisements in journals like *The Builder* (1843). Demand became near universal, the more so after the successful use of sheet glass at the Crystal Palace in 1851.

IRON AND LEAD

After the Restoration the manufacture of iron was in four stages: the smelting of ore into pig or cast iron, the refining of pig iron in 'finery' forges, 'chafery' forges for hammering the product

47. *London Gazette*, 27 July 1710, 10 January 1712 and 4 January 1717, record cuts in price and the availability of broad-glass workmen to work as journeymen anywhere within the United Kingdom.
48. Yorkshire Archaeological Society, Duke of Leeds Archives, Box 32 (Kiveton); Gloucestershire CRO, Blathwayt Archives, B13/2 (Dyrham); *Wren Soc*, XV, p. xxxi.
49. BL Add. MS, 22, 238, ff. 145, 146, 150.
50. London, RIBA, Library MS, 728.3 (42.13A), Pelham; PRO, AO3/1244.
51. Kedleston Archives, Account Book, 3R.
52. Nottingham University Library, Galway Archives, 12415.

into wrought-iron bars, and slitting mills where certain types of bar-iron were rolled and cut into rods.[53] Most of these products were sent to Birmingham and the industrial towns and villages of the adjacent coalfield. Here, the finishing iron trades flourished: blacksmiths, whitesmiths, locksmiths, edge-tool makers, gunsmiths and, outnumbering them all, the nailers.[54] The bar-iron was worked by the smiths for the provision of elaborate gates to houses and churches; its other minor uses were included in bills for ironwork and locksmithing.

The fourth charter of 1685 granted to the Worshipful Company of Blacksmiths heralded the beginning of their great prosperity. This was encouraged by the refurbishing of the City churches after the Great Fire of London. By the beginning of the eighteenth century, however, there was also some architectural use of cast iron. While more brittle and granular, cast iron is durable and resistant to rusting; Wren used it (against his better judgment, however) at St Paul's in 1714. Its continued use led to a gradual decline in blacksmithery. The craft suffered a serious set-back when the contents of the Worshipful Company's Hall were sold in 1785. The later revulsion against cast iron[55] owed much to Pugin, Morris and Ruskin, prophets, variously, of the Gothic revival and exponents of a revival of the medieval concept of the craftsman's role in society.

Casting, which became almost universal in the Victorian period, was the process used until the end of the seventeenth century to fashion lead. It was obtained by the plumber in the lump and cast into sheets by him at or near the building in progress. This was done on an oblong table, originally of wood but in the nineteenth century of cast iron, with a rising edge all round it; the table was covered with fine, damp sand and into this it was possible to press models of letters, numerals or ornaments. When the table had been made ready in this way, molten lead was poured over it and immediately levelled to the raised rim of the table. At Wentworth Woodhouse, Yorkshire, the sheets are 17 ft long by some 16 ft wide, implying a very large casting frame.[56]

Milled lead was produced during the last quarter of the seventeenth century. It was 'rolled' into lengths of 34 ft, twice the length of a casting table, and at first was rolled too thin. At Greenwich Hospital, which had been covered with milled lead, it rained in badly in 1700, and Parliament instructed the Master and Wardens of the Plumbers' Company to view the faulty work. They declared that the milled lead was not fit to remain on the buildings.[57] The prejudice against it lingered until the nineteenth century, and most of the houses mentioned in this study were covered with cast lead.

The material was unfortunately expensive, and this was always a restraining influence on its widespread use. For a modest rebuilding of a house at Meriden, Warwickshire, in 1720, supervised for Martin Baldwin by Francis Smith, the Warwick architect, the cost of the lead

53. B L C Johnson, 1952, 'The Iron Industry at the end of the Charcoal Era', *Economic History Review*, IV, p. 331.

54. W H B Court, 1938, *The Rise of Midland Industries, 1660–1838*.

55. Richard Sheppard, 1945, *Cast Iron in Building*; John Gloag and Derek Bridgwater, 1948, *A History of Cast Iron in Architecture*; J E Stephens, 19 May 1966,

'Wrought Iron's 19th Century Revival', *C Life*, CXXXIX, pp. 1277–80.

56. I am indebted to the estate maintenance staff at Wentworth Woodhouse for enabling me to inspect the roofs, and for explaining lead-casting. *See also Patent of Invention*, Sir James Creed, 13 December 1749, No. 651.

57. *Wren Soc*, VI, p. 82.

and the carriage amounted to £162 out of a total expenditure of £860.[58] The use of lead for decorated rain-heads (often a useful guide to approximate building dates when monograms of owners' initials or dates are moulded in the decoration) and fall-pipes was common in the sixteenth and seventeenth centuries. With the use of Palladianism in revived form in the early eighteenth century, English ornamental leadwork was in sharp decline, unable to compete with the transplanting of severe proportion to great houses.[59] Lead continued to be used by a number of sculptors, particularly John van Nost at the turn of the eighteenth century, for garden statuary.

By the 1830s, lead mixed with antimony had been introduced into England from Germany and was adapted to all purposes to which lead was usually put. Its advantages were greater malleability, tenacity, elasticity and resistance to acids, oxidation and the action of the sun and the atmosphere. The roof of the Royal Polytechnic Institution was covered with it in the form of 'Wetterstedt's Patent Marine Metal' in 1838, and 60 years later was still in perfect condition.[60]

PLASTER AND STUCCO

In the wide range of decoration in interiors, the plasterer played an important part.[61] The composition he used was made of lime, sharp sand, animal hair and water, and built up in some three layers, each finer than the underlying one. What was called the 'fine stuff' was made of pure lime slaked with a small quantity of water and, afterwards, without the addition of any other material, saturated with water and, in a semi-fluid state, placed in a tub until the water had evaporated. In some cases, for better binding of the work, a small quantity of hair was added. For interior work, three parts of fine stuff was mixed with one part of very fine washed sand. It made a proper surface for receiving painting. Work which consisted of three coats was *floated*, taking its name from the float or rule which was moved in every direction while the plaster was soft to give a perfectly smooth surface.

In making coves and cornices as light as possible, gypsum or plaster of Paris was largely used, often over *bracketing* of wood which was formed in the approximate profiles required. A variation of plaster, much used in the baroque churches of Italy and Germany, was stucco. This again was in three coats, with a coarse first one to form the rendering. The second coat was much finer and, containing a larger proportion of lime, brought the work up to an even grain. The final coat was composed of rich lime, well slaked, sieved and allowed to stand for several months in order that every particle was reduced to a hydrate. When great perfection was required, pounded white Carrara marble was mingled with it.

The *stucco-marmor* practised by the Italian *stuccatori* consisted of filling the pores in the plaster surface with gum or size dissolved in lukewarm water. The colours obtained from metallic oxides were then mixed with gypsum and lime water, worked like dough into balls, combined into a 'sausage' form, rolled like pastry on to glass and then applied to the surface. When the whole surface had dried, it was rubbed with grit stone and polished up with rubbers, much in the same way as real marble. The rarer *stucco-lustro* consisted of trailing colours across

58. Birmingham Reference Library, Digby Archives, 7313L, No. 98.

59. Sir Lawrence Weaver, 1909, *English Leadwork*, p. 27.

60. Joseph Gwilt, 1894, *An Encyclopedia of Architecture* (revised Wyatt Papworth), p. 517.

61. Beard, 1975, *Plasterwork*.

a wet lime surface which was subsequently heated with a flat iron to fix the effect of variegated marble. As a more delicate finish, it was used much less than the cold and more durable *stucco-marmor*.[62] The techniques have remained virtually unchanged since the early eighteenth century. In England *stucco-marmor* was known as *scagliola*.

MARBLE, ALABASTER AND SCAGLIOLA

The name of marble is applied to all stones harder than gypsum, that are found in large masses, and are susceptible to a good polish. On this principle, under the head of marble are included many varieties of limestone, porphyry, and even granite and fine-grained basalts. The word, however, has for most observers a more restricted sense, being confined to those varieties of compact and granular limestone that are capable of receiving a good polish.

Marble is more or less translucent, is brittle and occurs through a wide colour range with spots, dots, stripes and veins prominent. Carrara marble from Tuscany, in quarries celebrated from an early period, has been a well-known source to statuary sculptors of the late seventeenth and eighteenth centuries through to the contemporary sculptures of Henry Moore and others. Most of the variations are all found in quarries in the immediate neighbourhood of Carrara, or in Lucca. The Ravaccione, or so-called Sicilian marble, was expected to resist the action of an English atmosphere longer than Italian veined or white Carrara marble. The beautiful species of yellow marble obtained from quarries near Siena in Italy, and known in England as Siena marble, was used extensively by good sculptors of the calibre of the Cheere family, Joseph Wilton and Thomas Carter and his son.

The English marbles from Kent and Sussex, and in particular from Purbeck, were used in the medieval period, polished and unpolished. Those found in Derbyshire, some black, were used at Chatsworth, and John Thorp of Bakewell provided this kind of marble for squares in the hall floor at Castle Howard in 1708.

Like marble, alabaster takes a good polish, and is a white, semi-transparent variety of gypsum, or calcium sulphate. Of all building materials it is about the least porous or absorbent. It occurred commonly in Derbyshire and Staffordshire, and was used for ornamental purposes such as screens, panels and columns. It can be seen notably in the great halls at Kedleston and Holkham (*see* pl. 143).

Scagliola is an imitation of real marble, a species of plaster or stucco said to have been used first in Italy by Guido Sassi in the early seventeenth century. It was not, however, until the middle of the eighteenth century that the art of making scagliola was brought to perfection. Pure gypsum was broken into small pieces and calcined; as soon as the largest fragments lost their brilliancy, the fire was withdrawn, the powder passed through a fine sieve and mixed up with sand, a glue and isinglass solution. In this solution the colours required to imitate the marble were diffused and, like *stucco-marmor*, mingled and incorporated in the gypsum surface. This was then polished and finished with various oil mixtures and pure oil.[63]

62. Conversations, 1979, with the restoration teams of Anton Fuchs of Würzburg, W. Germany, and more details of these techniques will be given in my forthcoming book, *Stucco in Europe*.

63. *The Builder*, 11 January 1845 and 28 November 1863, list examples of scagliola work, and these mentions have been extended and several illustrations provided by R B Wragg, 10 October 1957, 'The History of Scagliola', *C Life*, pp. 718–21.

PAINT

The 'whiting' of walls, plaster surfaces and decorations occurred throughout the seventeenth and eighteenth centuries. The distemper was made from Spanish white or 'whiting' broken into warm water, to which was added strong size. On cooling it appeared as a thin jelly and was brushed on in at least two coats.

It was, however, the art of painting interiors with pigments ground in oil which preoccupied owners and artisans from the Restoration onwards. The mysteries of the ground pigment, the medium to render the colour fluid, and various additives to help drying were set out in a wide variety of manuals with extensive directions on methods. Ready-mixed paint was also available in the eighteenth century, such as white lead and Prussian blue ground into oil by laborious manual work, or by the use of a horse-mill.[64]

The wide range of colours needed by the painter of decoration is instanced in René Cousin's bill[65] for materials used at Burghley House, Northamptonshire, in 1692. As Verrio's gilder, he assisted at the grand decorative schemes at that house (*see* p. 133).

12 [lb?] white lead 8/-; $\frac{1}{2}$ of fine lake £1. 12*s*; $\frac{1}{4}$ of holland lacca 5/-; 3 oz fine lacca, 9*s*; $\frac{1}{4}$ of Common lacca 6*s*; 1 of Italian green earth 3/6*d*; 2 of yellow ocre 8*d*; 2 of Ombre earth 6*d*; $\frac{1}{2}$ of pink 9*d*; 2 of vermilion 9*s*; 4 of Enamell 12*s*; 3 quarter of oyl of Lin[seed] 2*s*; 2 quarters of oyles of Nuttes 10*s*; 2 quarter of oyl of Turpentine 8*s*; for bruiches and pencills £1. 5*s* 8*d*; for the two boxes, cords and porters 3*s*. Somme totale £6. 15. 1.

Alexander Emerton was charging 4*d*. per pound in 1734 for 'Best White Lead, ground in oil',[66] and in the early 1740s it was a little under 4*d*. per pound if taken at the hundredweight,[67] costing 36*s*. It formed the principal basis of many colours.

By the early nineteenth century there was an additional emphasis on varnishing over the paint, and model specifications included words such as:

All the wrought woodwork (except the floors, and the work executed in oak) to be stained, once coated with linseed oil, and twice varnished with the best copal varnish.[68]

The varnish was formed from different resins in a state of solution, of which the most common were benzoin, copal and amber dissolved in essential oils or alcohol.

PAPER

Painting is often connected with the practice of paper-hanging by the same artisan, but in the

64. John Fowler and John Cornforth, 1974, *English Decoration in the Eighteenth Century*, pp. 174–75; Ian Bristow, April 1977, 'Ready-Mixed Paint in the Eighteenth Century', *Arch Rev*, CLXI, pp. 247–48.

65. First noted by Croft-Murray, 1962, *Painting*, I, pp. 58–59. Mr Croft-Murray kindly loaned me his transcript of the extensive Verrio/Burghley archive which includes 333 receipts and receipted bills,

1687–98.

66. Bristow, 'Ready-Mixed Paint', p. 247 *op cit. (64)*.

67. 1734, *The Builder's Dictionary*, copy with contemporary annotations, Metropolitan Museum, New York (Print Room, 41.100.77); first noted by Dr Eileen Harris.

68. W Pewtner, 1870, *Comprehensive Specifier: A Guide to Practical Specifications*, ed. W Young.

eighteenth century there were a number of skilled firms specialising in paper supply and hanging, such as those of John Baptist Jackson, Thomas Bromwich (later Bromwich and Leigh), J Duppa and Cowtan & Sons, whose wallpaper order books for the whole of the nineteenth century survive.[69] Papers were hand-blocked or machine-printed with many exotic variations; those in embossed flock were formed from wool ground to a fine powder, being fixed to the paper by a sticky oil. Papers simulating stucco and ornaments fashioned in papier mâché were common by the middle years of the eighteenth century. Horace Walpole, writing to Horace Mann on 4 March 1753, told him that the high price of some of the papers was due to the fact that they were hand-painted. The kinds chiefly in use were those known 'as stucco paper and Gothic paper'.[70] The earliest reference to the former seems to be in a letter from Lady Luxborough to William Shenstone, 13 February 1750/1:

> Moore (who has lately been at London) talks to me of a sort of stucco paper, which I have never heard of; and says Lord Foley has done his chapel in Worcestershire[71] with it (the ceiling at least). By his description the paper is stamped so deep as to project considerably, and is very thick and strong and the ornaments are all detached, and put on separately. As suppose for example, it were the pattern of a common stucco-paper, which is generally a mosaic formed by a rose in a kind of octagon, it seems in this new way one of the roses is to be bought singly; so you have as many in number as the place requires, which are pasted up separately, and then gilt.[72]

Mrs Delany, writing to her sister Mrs Dewes on 11 January 1752, indicated that, if her sister were to have her parlour stuccoed, thought she 'should rather hang it with stucco paper [and]

---

69. Victoria and Albert Museum MSS (National Register of Archives list, 13466).
70. Paget Toynbee, ed., 1927, *Strawberry Hill Accounts, 1747–1795*, pp. 5, 39 and 42; other references are given by E A Entwisle, 1954, *The Book of Wallpaper*, and 1960, *A Literary History of Wallpaper*; for work in Ireland *see* A K Longfield, 1948, 'The Manufacture of Raised Stucco or Papier-Mâché papers in Ireland', *Journal, Royal Antiquarian Society of Ireland*, LXXVIII, pp. 22–43.
71. Great Witley Church, Worcestershire. Lord Foley acquired a ceiling stuccoed by Giovanni Bagutti at the Canons sale of 1747 and inserted it in the church. He obviously made good certain ornaments with gilded papier mâché, which were noticed during the extensive restorations at the church in the late 1960s. In 1971 the removal of one 'boss' as a pattern revealed a paper with eighteenth-century German black-letter printing.
72. Marjorie Williams, ed., 1939, *The Letters of Willian Shenstone*, p. 110.

Colour plate 7 CHISWICK HOUSE, London. The Gallery, looking N. *c* 1728 (photograph: A F Kersting).

Chiswick was created as a villa and 'temple of the arts' by Richard Boyle, 3rd Earl of Burlington. Started in 1725, it was complete by 1729 and owed much in its conception to the earl's interest in the architecture of Palladio and Inigo Jones. Many of the interior detail drawings are signed by Burlington, although he was helped by William Kent, who also painted some of the ceilings.

The Gallery is divided into three parts. This view shows that gained when a visitor has entered at the far end, traversed the centre section and is ready to return. Entry is made from the octagonal segment through a round-headed arch into a central rectangular apartment which has an apse at each end. There are statues in niches and a ceiling painted by Kent. The farthermost part of the Gallery is circular rather than octagonal. Much of the gilded carving and stucco-work was executed, presumably, by those who worked for Lord Burlington at his Piccadilly house: James Richards, John Hughes and Isaac Mansfield.

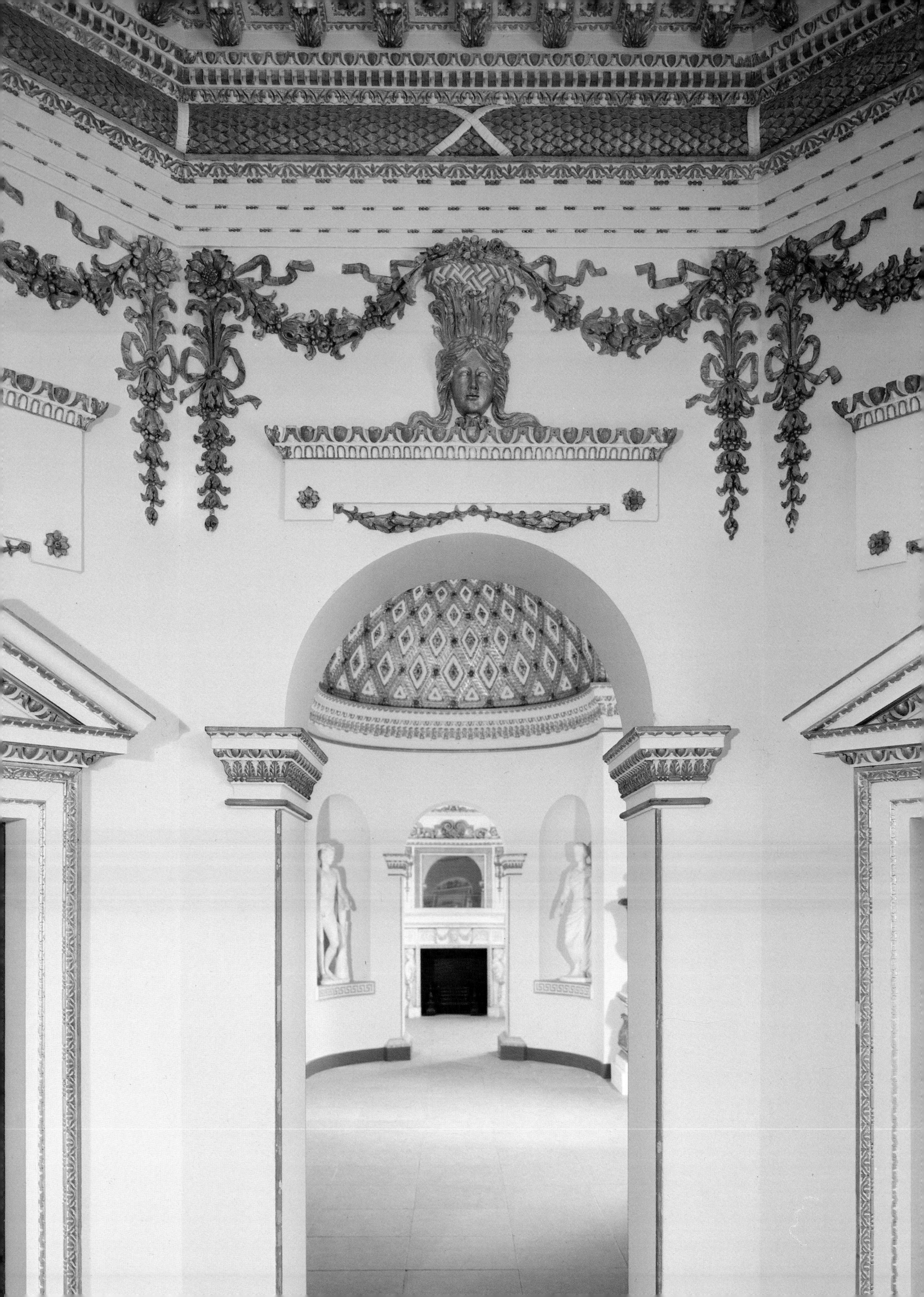

must have plugs of wood . . . to hang pictures to fix nails in'.[73]

In 1754 John Baptist Jackson, who had worked in Paris in the 1720s with the wood-engraver Papillon, issued a book *An Essay on the Invention of Engraving . . . and the Application of it to the making Paper Hangings of Taste, Duration and Elegance.* He set up a paper-hanging factory at Battersea, and some of his Venetian prints found their way on to Walpole's walls at Strawberry Hill. Colouring was applied by hand by 'paper-stainers' (who had their own Livery Company). Matthew Darly, who engraved some of the plates in Thomas Chippendale's pattern book *The Director* (1754), issued a trade card on which he advertised 'The Manufactory for Paper Hangings, Painted or Printed from Copper Plates or Wood', describing himself as 'Painter, Engraver & Paper Stainer'.[74]

There were also extensive efforts in the 1750s to imitate expensive Chinese papers. Some claimed that they could make them 'not distinguishable from rich India paper . . . beautifully coloured in pencil work and gilt'.[75] Robert Dossie in his invaluable *Hand Maid of the Arts* (1764) described their production, noting that the outlines were made by printing. On the back of most of the papers an impressed duty stamp was placed under the terms of an Act of 1712. This imposed a duty of 1*d.*, increased in 1714 to 1½*d.* It persisted until 1836.

Anglo-Chinese papers bearing similar stamps were still popular in the early nineteenth century and there are splendid examples at Temple Newsam House, Leeds (said to have been presented by George IV to Lady Hertford and hung there *c* 1806), Weston Hall, Staffordshire, and Tregothnan in Cornwall. A favourite supplier of paper and heraldic stained glass and ornaments to the nobility at this time was Thomas Willement; he was employed at Charlecote, Penrhyn and Scotney Castle and his 'Syrian damask' flock and metal papers were in great demand.

In the nineteenth century, wallpaper had to stand competition from the use of tiles and from ornamentation in papier mâché. In 1833 Wright of Shelton obtained a patent for making inlaid tiles, which was bought out by the Staffordshire potter Herbert Minton. He improved on it and his 'encaustic tiles', in which the pattern was inlaid rather than impressed, were used extensively in church decoration.

73. Toynbee, *Strawberry Hill Accounts*, p. 39, *op cit. (70)*.
74. Sir Ambrose Heal, 1925, *London Tradesmens Cards of the 18th Century*, pl. LXX; E A Entwisle, 1960, *A Literary History of Wallpaper*, p. 53; Christopher

Gilbert, 1975, 'The Early Furniture Designs of Matthias Darly', *Furniture History*, XI, pp. 33–39.
75. *London Evening Post*, 8 January 1754.

Colour plate 8 MOOR PARK, Hertfordshire. The Hall, *c* 1730–32 (photograph: A F Kersting).

This two-storey hall, a 40 ft cube, was created for Benjamin Styles. Four large paintings in gilt frames—of which two can be seen in this view— are by the Venetian painter Jacopo Amigoni. They are flanked by great door-cases topped by stucco figures by Giovanni Bagutti, and oak swags. The painter of the *chiaroscuro* figures in niches on the gallery walls and the *trompe l'oeil* dome (of which only the rim can be seen here) was probably Francesco Sleter, who signed work on the adjacent staircase in 1732. His work is again surrounded by Bagutti's stucco trophies. While his presence at the house is attested by a drawing addressed to him there (Ashmolean Museum, Oxford, Gibbs drawings IV, 24), Sir Edward Gascoigne, a Yorkshire traveller, noted work at Moor Park by the two Artaris in his travel-diary, and invited them to work at his own Yorkshire home, Parlington Hall.

Lit: T P Hudson, November 1971, 'Moor Park, Leoni and Sir James Thornhill', *Burl Mag*, pp. 657–59.

CEMENTS

For interior use the cements known as Martin's, Keene's and Parian were largely in use in nineteenth-century buildings. In reality they were forms of plaster capable of being worked to a hard, fine surface, and able to take paint within a short time of setting. In exterior use, that known as Parker's or Roman cement, discovered in 1796 by James Parker, was superior.[76] Its use was lessened from about 1843 when Portland cement became a more effective substitute. Martin's cement was capable of taking a fine polish, although it was more usual to mix in metallic oxides to produce a coloured cement. At the rebuilding of the new Palace of Westminster (1837 f.), Parian cement in 'Keatings patent' form was used for internal stucco; it had the advantages of being immune to efflorescence (when, due to nitrification, minute crystals work from the interior to the exterior of the stone), and took paint or paper in 48 hours.[77]

A variation of cement for ornamental use was 'composition' used in various patented forms from the 1760s.[78] In the nineteenth century it consisted of powdered whiting, glue in solution and linseed oil, mixed together and heated. After heating it was laid upon a stone covered with powdered whiting, and beaten to a tough and firm consistency. It was then covered with wet cloths until ready to be put into moulds and pressed. It found ready use as circular medallions and the other complex ornaments of nineteenth-century ceilings and friezes.

76. A P Thurston, 1938, 'Parker's Roman Cement', *Transactions of the Newcomen Society*, XIX, pp. 193–206.
77. Joseph Gwilt, 1894, *An Encyclopedia of Architecture*, revised by Wyatt Papworth, p. 711.
78. Beard, 1975, *Plasterwork*, pp. 72–74. About 40 cements and mastics were patented in the period 1760–1840.

17 (*below*) CHATSWORTH, Derbyshire. The Painted Hall, 1692–94, Staircase and Gallery rebuilt 1912–13 (photograph: A F Kersting).

The Elizabethan Great Hall of the first Chatsworth stood on the site of the present two-storey Painted Hall. Louis Laguerre and his assistant Ricard painted the walls and ceiling, 1692–94, with scenes from the life of Julius Caesar. The stone screen at the head of the stairs incorporates trumpeting *putti* over the arch carved by Samuel Watson. It leads to the Great Staircase, with its ironwork by Jean Tijou (*see* pl. 31).

18 (*above*) TWICKENHAM, Middlesex, The Octagon Room, 1720 (photograph: A F Kersting).

The Octagon Room was designed by James Gibbs for James Johnston, Secretary for Scotland. It stood in the grounds of Orleans House, demolished in 1927. The stucco decoration was the work of Bagutti and Artari—a fact noted by the architect in his 1728, *B of A*, p. xix—and the elaborate carved overmantel was carved by the London joiner Charles Griffiths. This fine room is now attached to an art gallery.

20 (*facing page*) SHUGBOROUGH, Staffordshire. The Library, 1748 (photograph: A F Kersting).

Writing in 1748 of recent improvements at Shugborough, Lady Grey stated that 'the house has some fine rooms lately added to it, and one exceedingly odd and pretty that is the Library.' It is built in two parts: one in the central block of the house, with the other in the link to the S. pavilion. They are joined by the flattened arch burrowed through the thickness of the outer wall of the older house. It is 5 ft deep and 8 ft high and carried on small Ionic columns. The rococo plasterwork decoration was executed by Francesco Vassalli, presumably under the supervision of Thomas Wright. (*C. Life*, 2 September 1971, pp. 546–8)

21 (*facing page*) STRAWBERRY HILL, Middlesex. The Library, 1754 (photograph: A F Kersting).

Horace Walpole had extensive collections of prints, coins and classical antiquities, and a library of about 8000 books. In his extensive rebuildings from 1750, a library was set in the N.E. corner on the 2nd floor. The books were set within Gothic arches of pierced work based on a plate of the side-door to the choir in old St Paul's Cathedral in Sir William Dugdale's 1658, *History of St. Paul's Cathedral*. The tracery was hinged to give access to the shelves. The ceiling was painted by J F Clermont with heraldic shields on a mosaic ground after a design by Walpole and Richard Bentley. The chimneypiece was based on the tomb of John of Eltham at Westminster Abbey, and the stonework above from that of the Duke of Clarence at Canterbury. Its cusps originally framed a fifteenth-century painting of the marriage of Henry VI. On the wall spaces above were oval portraits of friends and ancestors. Walpole's possessions at Strawberry Hill were dispersed in a 32-day sale in 1842.

19 (*above*) ALL SOULS COLLEGE, Oxford. Codrington Library, 1716–35 (photograph: A F Kersting).

In 1710 Christopher Codrington died and left money to build a library at All Souls to house his books. George Clarke, a fellow of All Souls and a man well versed in architectural matters, was involved in much building at his college and in Oxford. He was deeply involved (until his death in 1736) with plans for a new northern quadrangle (to include the Library), which were carried out by Nicholas Hawksmoor. 'The Library was not fitted up in Hawksmoor's lifetime, or according to his intentions'; the ceiling pattern was altered also, but it still encompasses a very fine room. The statue of Christopher Codrington (1732) is by Sir Henry Cheere.

23 (*below*) SYON HOUSE, Middlesex, The 'Round Closet' at the corner of the Gallery, *c* 1766 (photograph: A F Kersting).

From either end of the Gallery at Syon a closet opens in a corner tower, one round and one square. One was hung with Chinese paper, while that shown here was decorated by Joseph Rose & Company in rich, classical composition stucco. It snakes up the columns, across the frieze and cornice and within the compartments of the circular domed ceiling.

22 (*above*) WOBURN ABBEY, Bedfordshire. Queen Victoria's Dressing Room, *c* 1755 (photograph: A F Kersting).

This room adjoins the Bedroom (*see* col. pl. 11) which was used by Queen Victoria on her visit to Woburn with the Prince Consort in 1841. It is one of the series of state rooms created originally by the 4th Duke of Bedford from 1747 to 1761 under the direction of Henry Flitcroft. The architect's bank account shows his dependence on a talented team of craftsmen, most of whom are listed in an extensive archive about the work.

The chimneypiece was again supplied by John Devall, although others in the house (*see* pl. 141) are by John Michael Rysbrack, who also enhanced one by Devall in the Saloon with a panel (*see* pl. 142).

24 (*facing page*) KEDLESTON, Derbyshire. The Saloon, 1761–62 (photograph: A F Kersting).

This room, with its coffered dome and niches, is the most Roman of Robert Adam's interiors and compares with the oval saloon at Stowe. It is a circle 42 ft in diameter and 55 ft high to the top of the dome. William Hamilton provided the paintings of ruins, Biagio Rebecca the grisaille panels, Domenico Bartoli the pilasters of verd–antique scagliola, and the Carron Ironworks the cast-iron altar stoves. The doors and frames are shaped to the curve of the walls.

25 (*above*) WIMPOLE, Cambridgeshire. The Book
Room, *c* 1791–93 (photograph: A F Kersting).

26 (*below*) STOURHEAD, Wiltshire, The Library,
looking N., *c* 1796 (photograph: A F Kersting).

Adjacent to the Great Room at Wimpole which
was built to house the library formed by Edward
Harley, 2nd Earl of Oxford, early in the eighteenth
century, is an attractive book room. It was added
to the house by the architect Sir John Soane. He
made alterations and additions to Wimpole in the
early 1790s, including a Yellow Drawing Room,
for the 3rd Earl of Hardwicke. The repeat of
shallow arches, each dominated by circular plaster
motifs (probably by John and Joseph Baily), gives
a particularly satisfying unity to the room.

The Library is designed as a composition of
segmental curves and squares from its ceiling to its
'mosaic floor' patterned in Wilton carpeting of
yellow on green. The doors are surmounted by
ovals containing busts of Dryden and Pope by
Rysbrack from an earlier library. Built as a great
Palladian house by Colen Campbell in the early
1720s, Stouhead was added to by wings which
contain the Picture Gallery and Library. The early
Georgian chimneypiece of carved wood,
surmounted by a plaster relief, was originally at
Ranelagh House and was moved to Stourhead only
about 70 years ago.

[3]
The Woodworking Craftsmen

The Carpenter

The working relationship between carpenters and other craftsmen of the building trades was a close one which led frequently to common allegiance to the same provincial guild.[1] In London they had organised as early as the thirteenth century and, in a period when buildings were largely constructed to timber, they found good employment not only in the City but from residing in the provincial towns. To obtain variety of work and participate in important commissions, however, entailed travel.[2] Nonetheless, what they had to do varied little with the passage of time.

The division of labour in the woodworking trades was a complex and easily disturbed one. In 1632 the Carpenters' Company imprisoned several joiners for interference in carpenters' work; Articles were drawn up to settle the differences. This document[3] divided the work of joiners and carpenters as follows. It has been abbreviated, and petty and minor differences have been avoided. It is, however, relevant because staircases, which are not mentioned specifically, could have wainscot panels on the wall side by a joiner, balusters provided by a turner and applied decoration by a carver (*see* pls. 32, 36 and 39).

Carpenters

All Drapers tables, Tables for Taverns, etc., all tables made of Deal, Elm, Oak, Beech, nailed together without glue. All Stools headed with the above-named woods.

All sorts of frames made of the above-named woods.

The laying of floors of Elm or Oak except those that are grooved.

Dividing of ware-houses and chambers unwainscoted.

Shelving of rooms as above.

Sign boards not made of wainscot or glued or carved.

Setting up 'Pillars or ballasters' for lights in a partition.

Joiners

All sorts of Bedsteads, Chairs and Stools made with mortice and tenon joints.

Tables of wainscot walnut. Forms framed with sides pinned or glued. Chests with dovetailed joints, pinned or glued.

Cabinets or Boxes constructed as above.

Cupboards constructed as above.

All sorts of presses for weareing apparell, constructed as above.

All sorts of 'wainscott and sealing of Houses'.

All sorts of shop windows 'that are made for ornament or beautie'.

All sorts of Doors, framed, panelled or glued.

All hatches, constructed as above.

1. York Minster Library, MS, BB/5, Ordinances of a Company of Builders, Tilers and Plasterers.
2. L F Salzman, 1967, *Building in England down to 1540: A Documentary History*, p. 34.
3. London, Guildhall Library MS, 8332, cited by E B Jupp and W W Pocock, 1887, *An Historical Account of the Worshipful Company of Carpenters*, pp. 295–99.

Carpenters—contd.

All Galleries in Churches and other places unless of wainscot, panelled or carved.

Shelving in Kitchens.

Laying of floors in Church Pews.

Screens for halls not made of wainscot, or glued or carved.

Joiners—contd.

All pews, pulpits, and seats constructed as above.

All sorts of frames upon Stalls framed or glued.

All picture frames.

All lining of walls.

All sign boards of wainscot or carved.

All work made with the use of all manner of nails.

All carved works either raised or cut through or sunk in with the ground taken out, being wrought and cut with carving tools without the use of plains.

In addition, joiners constructed coffins made of wainscot, but if they were of other wood they could be made by either joiners or carpenters.

The divisions of labour were set out with exactitude but, in practice, they were almost impossible to adhere to. The two Companies faced many controversies through the years. The matter came to a head again in 1672 when the joiners tried to enforce the rules agreed 49 years earlier, and at a time when there was considerable work following the Great Fire of London. The Court of Aldermen's decision, as set out in the list of duties noted above, meant that the carpenters were to be limited to plain work, and the craft of the joiner edged into a commanding position. There were, of course, occasions when they worked amicably together: John Brasse, a Durham joiner, and Abraham Smith, a carpenter, agreed in 1663 to erect an 11 ft high screen in the chapel at Bishop Auckland. For every yard of work 11 ft high they were to receive 40*s*.[4] Certain tasks the carpenter made his own, however.

THE FRAMING

When a building had proceeded to the foundation stage, it was the carpenter's job to set the framing for the floors. He laid ground-plates on the foundations, in a square or rectangular form as required. These 'plates' were made of oak planks (*see* fig. 1, AB–CD), framed together at the corner by mortice and tenon joints (with oak pegs driven through to keep the joint true), laid on to the brickwork some 8 to 20 in, in breadth and 6 to 10 in, in depth. These mighty baulks of timber had to be drilled with an auger and tenoned for all the joists, and were not set finally into position as a frame until they were squared and true. This was done by supporting them on temporary piers a few inches above the foundation or brickwork on which they would ultimately lie, checking at each jointed corner with a square to establish a right angle, then pinning the joint with an oak peg to prevent movement; finally, the frame was lowered into position by removal of the temporary piers.

4. 'Correspondence of John Cosin, Bishop of Durham' *Surtees Society*, 1872, Vol. 55, II, pp. 369–70.

In order that there should be less tendency for the frame to move out of true over its length, a 'summer' or intermediate lateral support (EE) was inserted at about its half-way point. The broadest dimension was placed uppermost and this in turn was pinned; there were also 'girders' pinned at its centre (FG–GH).

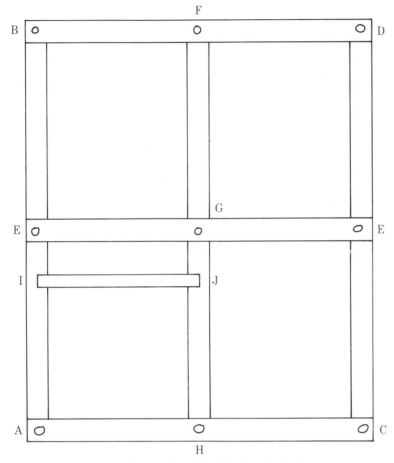

Figure 1 Construction of the framing for the floors.

Into this construction, prior to its final pinning, were inserted the joists (IJ), each one tenoned into the outer frame, with 'trimmers' or subsidiary frames marking the staircase and chimney positions. The joists, usually of 7 in deep and 3 in broad, were set with the narrower dimension on top and supported laterally on the 'girder', or bearing wall, at no more than 8-ft centres. Their relationship one to the other was checked with a level, and, this proving satisfactory, it was possible to set up the 'carcase' above it.

This was given a unifying basis in the vertical by the erection of four corner-posts of the same dimension timber as the ground-plates; for example, a usual size in seventeenth- and eighteenth-century building was 8 in wide by 6 in thick. These heavy timbers, each of one piece, had to reach up to the 'beam' or 'raising-plate' of the roof. The lower end of each was tenoned into a mortice near the corner of the ground-plate frame. Its upper end was also tenoned to fit into a mortice on the raising-plate.

At the height of the first storey, these principal posts were again morticed to receive the tenons on the 'girders' supporting the joists and boards of the upper floors; confusingly, the girders at these levels were called 'bressummers' or 'interduces'. The process was repeated at the second storey. Each corner-post was so jointed and, after being set upright by use of a plumb-line, was kept exactly vertical at this stage by diagonal braces of timber tacked to it and to some convenient floor member.

With the principal posts and the frame structures in position, several more posts were set up within the height of each storey and the whole structure pinned with pegs. While the sizes of timber chosen could vary, minimum standards had been set down by the Act of 1666 for rebuilding the City of London after the Great Fire.

This Act also required that no timber was laid in London houses within 12 in of the front of chimney jambs, and that joists on the back of any chimney should be set at 6 in distance from it. No timber was to penetrate the structure of the chimney itself upon penalties ranging up to 10 shillings, with a further 10 shillings a week fine if the work remained uncorrected. It also set out tolerances for the setting of joists and other structural members so that they were within a safe capacity, and advised that the ends of timber lying in walls should be treated with pitch and be set in loam, to prevent the mortar corroding and rotting it. It was a useful standard for others to work to for, as Moxon states, able workmen—presumably from the Office of Works—had checked all the suggested measurements before they were put into the Act.

The carpenter's first work on the carcase of the house was now complete and, in sequence, he turned his attention to the roof, flooring of rooms, stairs and hanging of doors. It is obvious that some of these tasks awaited the tiling over the roof timbers, otherwise wet weather would have damaged floors and other finer woodwork; they were also not done until the plasterer had completed the walls and ceiling so that the watery mess, fragments of discarded moulds and ornamentation dropped through the joists rather than on to floors.

THE ROOF

A principal task was the construction of the timber part of the roof. The first and obvious consideration was the width of the structure, as it was not always possible to find timber in sufficient lengths to stretch across the void to be covered. It was necessary for the carpenter to know how one piece of timber could be joined to another, for the purpose of lengthening it, so that the two pieces would be as near as possible equal in strength and dimensions to one whole piece of timber. This operation was known as *scarfing*. To perform it, the joints were indented (*see* fig. 2, AB) and bolts passed through the pieces within the length of the indents.

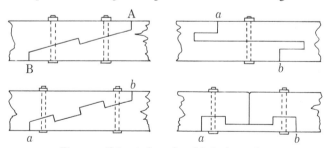

Figure 2 Joists indented and bolted together.

There were several forms of indent which enabled the length of the timber to be increased. It was necessary to be accurate, for if the indents did not bear equally, the greater part of the strength was lost. This precluded complicated forms for the indent.

The pieces of timber required for certain roof areas and for partitions and frames were joined to one another by the aid of mortice and tenon joints, and by iron straps and bolts. Other general factors which entered into roof construction were the pitch or slope to be given to it, the strains it had to bear and those it exerted, and its appearance, both external and internal.

Isaac Ware, in his *A Complete Body of Architecture* (1756), wrote: 'There is no article in the whole compass of the architect's employment that is more important or more worthy of a distinct contribution than the roof.' As a Warden, and later Master, of the Carpenters' Company, as well as being a good architect, Ware advocated that roofs which were not 'massy' enough (through too little timber being used) could not perform. There was a balance to be struck between inadequate members and too much load on the walls. To see that the walls remained perpendicular, which the thrust of the rafters tended to derange, a system of framing was necessary. This had undergone various complex amendments from medieval times. In simple form (*see* fig. 3), the rafters AB–BC are tied or confined at their feet by a *tie beam* AC; if the tie *ac* is introduced above the level of the walls, it is called a *collar beam*.

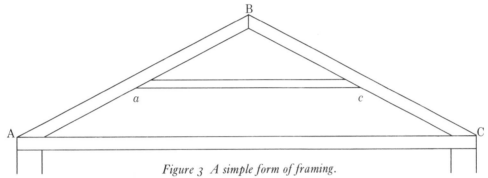

Figure 3 A simple form of framing.

The tie beam by its own gravity, especially in a large opening, has a tendency to sag or bend in the middle. To prevent this, a fresh tie is introduced called a *king-post* (*see* fig. 4, DB). The beam is tied or slung up to the apex of the principal rafters. This combination of a pair of rafters, a tie beam and king-post is called a *truss*; it was the most important assemblage the carpenter produced. When the rafters were of such length that they would be liable of themselves to sag down, supports *aa* were introduced at the points where such failures would occur. These *struts* were set in a direction perpendicular to the slope of the rafters. They could be introduced in strategic positions and set into various patterns depending on the span being covered.

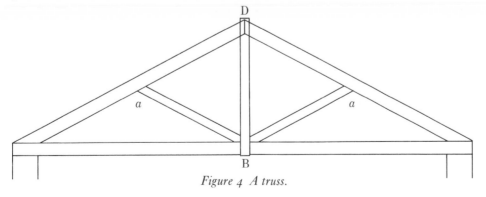

Figure 4 A truss.

The trusses, however framed, were placed apart at no more than 10-ft intervals. They bore the weight of the 'common rafters' and that of the covering, as well as suspending the tie beam by which the walls were kept together. The rafters so framed in a truss are called 'principal rafters'. The *purlins*, lying horizontally throughout the roof's length on the principal rafters, were made to bear all the superincumbent load; they were received at their feet on a *pole-plate* and at their summits on a *ridge-piece*.

Three examples may serve to bring the various component parts together. At St Paul's Cathedral, Wren's carpenters had to encompass an ambitious scheme. The external dome is supported on a timber frame while the internal dome is of brickwork, two bricks thick. The dome was constructed from a centre—the temporary woodwork or framing from which any vaulted work is built. It rested on the projection at its point of springing, without any support from below, and was afterwards left for use by Sir James Thornhill and his assistants when painting the dome's inner surface. The various structures coming together at this springing part were banded together with iron provided by Jean Tijou, and the Portland stone lantern, 64 ft high and 21 ft in diameter, stands on a brick cone, strengthened by a great encircling chain also provided by Tijou.

On this cone is supported the timberwork which carries the external dome. The four hammer beams are tied into corbels with iron cramps, which are well bedded in with lead and bolted to the hammer beams. The stairs which lead to the Golden Gallery on top of the dome are carried between the trusses of the roof. The dome is boarded from the base upwards, hence the ribs are fixed horizontally at near distances to each other. The 'scantling' (or dimensions of timber in breadth and thickness) of the curve rib of the truss is $10 \times 11\frac{1}{2}$ in at the bottom and 6×6 in at the top. The whole combination was an admirable example of Wren's mathematical skill and judgment and the skill of his craftsmen. It was one they had also shown in his 68 ft-span roof at the Sheldonian Theatre at Oxford, designed in 1663.[5]

At Gibbs's St Martin-in-the-Fields, London, the timber erred on the generous side in dimensions for the loads to be carried. The width of the church with its two aisles is 69 ft—the middle aisle, 39 ft 11 in.

This all came into the province of the appointed carpenters, Benjamin Timbrell and Thomas Phillips. As the rafters were erected, they provided a temporary timber covering to protect the walls from the weather. They also provided timber centring for arches, flooring, deal boarding, deal guttering on oak bearers, door-cases with doors ledged and tongued (16s. each), moulds for the smith to make the metal windows, erected and moved the plasterers' scaffold and 'firing out' various projections for him apart from bracketing for the cornice.

---

5. Wren took as his model the ancient theatre of Marcellus in Rome (11 B.C.), which was open to the sky. His Oxford building, enclosed against an English climate, had a span of 68 ft, and it was necessary to create trusses composed of timbers dovetailed and tenoned into each other. The principles of this had been set out by Philibert de L'Orme in his *Nouvelles Inventions pour bien bastir et à petits frais* (1561), a book which Wren may have seen. The use of the tie beam was avoided, and de L'Orme claimed to be able thus to roof any space up to 300 ft wide: Charles Singer *et al.*, eds., 1968, *A History of Technology*, III, pp. 253 and 265. For Wren's carpentry supervision, *see also* H M Fletcher, 1923, 'Sir Christopher Wren's Carpentry: A Note on the Library at Trinity College, Cambridge', *RIBA, Journal*, 3rd ser. XXX, pp. 388–89.

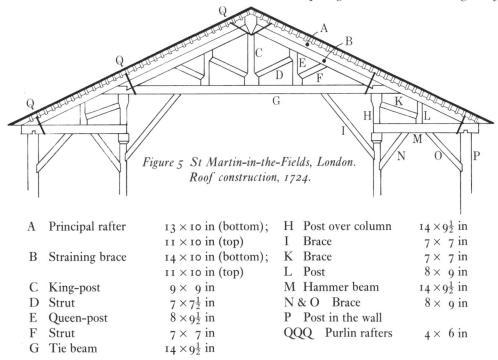

*Figure 5 St Martin-in-the-Fields, London.
Roof construction, 1724.*

A	Principal rafter	13 × 10 in (bottom); 11 × 10 in (top)	H	Post over column	14 × 9½ in
			I	Brace	7 × 7 in
B	Straining brace	14 × 10 in (bottom); 11 × 10 in (top)	K	Brace	7 × 7 in
			L	Post	8 × 9 in
C	King-post	9 × 9 in	M	Hammer beam	14 × 9½ in
D	Strut	7 × 7½ in	N & O	Brace	8 × 9 in
E	Queen-post	8 × 9½ in	P	Post in the wall	
F	Strut	7 × 7 in	QQQ	Purlin rafters	4 × 6 in
G	Tie beam	14 × 9½ in			

Much of this work involved exhibiting models to the Board of Commissioners, appearing before them to answer questions, and having their work measured prior to payment. They worked continuously, 1720–25, and received almost £5600.

At Greenwich Hospital Chapel, *c* 1785, James Stuart, assisted by William Newton, designed a timber structure to span 51 ft. He placed his trusses at 7-ft intervals and secured all joints by iron straps. His tie beam, 57 ft long by 14 × 12 in, was supported by an iron king-post, two timber queen-posts, various struts and straining beams.

THE FLOORS

While the roofing was going ahead, the carpenter was also considering the flooring of the rooms beneath. At an early point he had rough-planed his boards and laid them aside in a covered shed to season; when they were needed, they were first checked for straightness and splits, and one was chosen of average thickness. After testing the framing of the floor with a level (in case in the interval between laying and flooring it had risen or settled slightly), the carpenter then corrected irregularities with an adze and laid the chosen board close against one side of the room and 'athwart', or running in a contrary direction to the joists; it was then nailed firmly with two nails hammered 1 to 1½ in within the edge of the board, and at each point where the board crossed a joist. A second board was then laid close to the first, tested for level and closeness of point and likewise nailed. If the boards were not dry, they would shrink further after laying; to compensate for this (although the best solution was dry, well-seasoned timber), a gap slightly smaller than the width of two boards was left after the first had been nailed. A fourth board was nailed in position and, by placing boards 2 and 3 together at a slight angle, it was possible by walking or jumping on the join to force them into the predetermined gap. This process was helped by bevelling the under-edge of each of the boards. It was also essential that the boards were cut to equal length in order that further lengths could be abutted (or laid against them, if in a contrary direction) in what was called a close 'beaking joint'. When the whole room was boarded and nailed, any irregularities were removed with the plane, one of the oldest tools in the carpenter's chest.

Variations in the method of flooring have, of course, been noticed. At Audley End, Essex, and Osterley, Middlesex, houses which were remodelled by Robert Adam in the 1760s, some rooms have the widest boards at the centre, decreasing in width either side towards the walls, are pegged with wooden dowels, and 'secret nailed' diagonally into each other. Tongued and grooved boards appear to have been used from the mid-1820s and, in 1827, a Mr Muir of Glasgow patented a machine for working floorboards.

HANGING DOORS

The floors being boarded and stairs inserted, the next work was to hang the doors. Most fine rooms had door-cases comprised of moulded architraves formed of an upper part or lintel, called the *traverse*, and two sides or *jambs*. The carpenter needed to see that the jambs were exactly perpendicular (by use of a plumb-line), and that the traverse or head of the case was fitted exactly square to the jambs. Consideration was then given to the sort of hinges best suited to the door, and that they would be strong enough. In the 1670s, hinges were often nailed to doors or, where the hinge was a long one, riveted so that the head of the rivet, sometimes ornamented, was on the outside of the door.

BRACKETING

Examination of archives brings frequent mention of 'bracketing', another task of the carpenter. The pieces of wood which sustained the laths of cornices, coves and the like were called brackets; they were formed as far as possible in the shapes to which they were to be finished and were often complex exercises in applied geometry, especially at angles and corners. The bracketing was covered usually by plaster, moulded or 'run' in profile form *in situ*.

Much more complicated was the formation of the timber cradling for domes and pendentives. If a hemisphere or other portion of a sphere is intersected by cylindrical or cylindroidal arches, vaults are formed which are called *pendentives*. The termination of these at the top will be a circle whereon may be placed a dome, or an upright drum which, if necessary, may be terminated by a dome. The illustration looking up to the dome and lantern at Castle Howard (*see* col. pl. 4), created by Sir John Vanbrugh and painted in 1708–09 by Giovanni Antonio Pellegrini, shows the 'Four Elements' on the pendentives and the 'Fall of Phaeton' on the inner dome above the drum. Beneath the painted surface is an intricate timber construction between the inner and outer domes and behind the pendentives.

WINDOWS

Finally, amid a multitude of smaller tasks, the carpenter set into the carcase the window frames, although he did not always make them. The more sophisticated they were, with sliding sashes, multiple openings or of intricate, architectural form, the more they became the province of the mason (in stone) and the joiner (in wood). The sash window (the French term for a window frame is *chassis*) was used in France from early in the seventeenth century, and not known in

England until its use in the 1670s at Ham House, and by Wren at Windsor and elsewhere 10 years later.[6] By the early eighteenth century, their use had extended but, by a statute of Queen Anne's reign, it was enacted that in London, after 1 June 1709, 'no door frame, or window frame of wood to be fixed in any house or building, within the cities of London etc., shall be set nearer to the outside face of the wall than four inches'. This law overcame the old practice of setting the frame flush to the face of the wall. By 1840 Sir Joseph Paxton had invented a machine for making sash-bars, which had previously been thick and time-consuming to make; it was first used for the sash-bars of the 1851 Great Exhibition building.[7]

The growing dominance of the smith, who produced in metal what the carpenter made in wood (chests, bedsteads, doors and gates, etc.), had started to have an effect from the late seventeenth century onwards. The introduction of iron, cast iron and steel in the eighteenth century hastened the process, and the wide use of concrete in the nineteenth century took many tasks away from the carpenter. Cast-iron girders were used in the Albion Mill at Blackfriars built by Samuel Wyatt in 1783–86, and a patent of 1811 (granted to T Pearsall) was for cast-iron rafters, joists and skeletons of staircases. The carpenter, with his simple tools, had few effective answers.

TOOLS

The tools used by the carpenter did not alter much with the passage of time. A Roman plane did not look dissimilar to its wooden counterpart in the nineteenth century except in size, weight and the masking of the essential shape into a wood rectangle.[8]

The carpenter's principal tools were the adze, axe, various chisels, commander, crow, draw-knife, hook-pin, jack, level, plumb-line and saw. In addition he had a hammer and various lifting devices such as the block, crab, drug, levers and snatch-block. They are illustrated in figs. 7 and 8 following Moxon's depiction of them in his *Mechanik Exercises* in 1703. The *adze* and *axe* acted as wood-shaving and cutting implements wielded with different swinging actions— the adze as a pendulum swings, the axe in a near circular motion. The axe was wedge shaped to both cut and split at the same time. The sharp-bladed *chisels* were struck with a mallet. The *commander* (or 3-ft, long-handled mallet) was used to drive in wooden piles and set frames into position. The carpenter in particular used a 'ripping chisel', with a wide, bevelled blade. The 'socket chisel' had a hexagonal metal socket and a broad, triangular blade; a solid wooden head of the same shape as the socket was inserted so that it could be struck heavy blows with a mallet. The advantage of this was the need to replace the blade and socket less frequently as the head took the main hammer impact.

The *crow*, made of iron, was to remove heavy timber. It acted as a strong lever and had one pointed end for insertion under planks and joists, and one which was flared, or bifurcated, for

6. The introduction of sash windows is summarised by Peter Thornton, 1978, *Seventeenth Century Interior Decoration in England, France & Holland*, pp. 82–84.

7. Wyatt Papworth ed., 1852–92, *The Dictionary of Architecture*, 8 vols, s.v. 'Sash', 'Sash-bar', Architectural Publication Society.

8. Norman Davey, 1961, *A History of Building Materials*, Appendix, 'Building Tools', p. 230; Kenneth D Roberts, 1976, *Tools for the Trades and Crafts*, Fitzwilliam, New Hampshire, Roberts Publishing Co., USA.

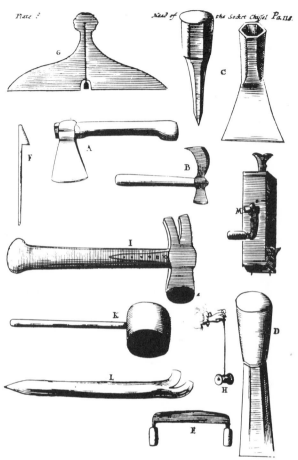

Figure 6 (left) A Corinthian Door for a Room of State. Batty Langley, 1729. A Sure Guide to Builders, pl. 48.

Figure 7 (above) The carpenter's principal tools, (after Moxon).

A Axe
B Adze
C Socket chisel with head
D Ripping chisel
E Draw-knife
F Hook-pin
G Level
H Plumb-line
I Hammer
K Commander
L Crow
M Jack

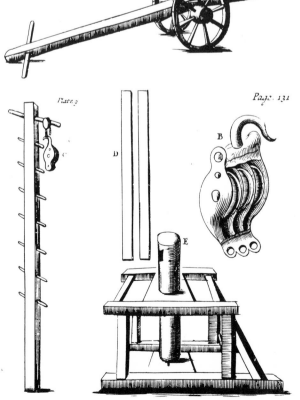

Figure 8 (left) Lifting devices, (after Moxon).

A Drug
B Block
C Snatch-block
D Levers
E Crab

inserting under the heads of nails. The *draw-knife* (or 'spoke-shave') was a blade with one cutting edge mounted between two wooden handles; it could shave thinly by applying pressure as it was drawn along the wood. The *hook-pin*, pointed at one end and with a triangular section at the other, could be driven into floor or roof frames or wherever a fastening point was needed; it was sometimes knocked out and wooden pins set in its place. The *level*, with its own small plumb-line, had a broad, wide blade from 2 to 10 ft wide which could be set on surfaces and moved to a right-angle by observation of the plumb-line, so enabling variations in surface to be detected. A modern analogy would be that of putting a long-straight-edge over concrete or earth to detect hollows and raised sections.

The *jack*, which could by simple gearing raise timber, was described by Moxon as 'an Engine used for the removing and commodious placing of great Timber'. In addition to using the jack for such work, the *crab* was a sturdy trestle which had at its centre a socket into which a pole with pegs at various heights could be inserted. A pulley could be attached to one of the pegs and, by a simple 'block and tackle' action, large timbers could be winched into different positions. Long pieces of timber were moved on a two-wheeled handcart with a long pulling handle called a *drug*.

One of the tasks the carpenter needed to undertake was that of sawing his timber to the required length and thickness. For ordinary lengths of timber he used his saw, which in the late seventeenth and most of the eighteenth century was made from iron, hammer hardened. For considerable quantities of timber a sawyer's services would be used, and large logs needed the use of a saw pit. This was sometimes lined with timber across which, level with the surface, were fixed two or more beams on which were placed the logs to be sawn through. One man stood in the pit to assist in working the long saw up and down, while the 'top-sawyer' directed the saw along the line marked on the log or timber. The saw bench with a mounted steel circular saw—in use from the late eighteenth century—superseded the ancient operation of the saw pit.

The Joiner

The joiner's task, among many which were claimed from time to time by carpenters, was to frame or *join* together wood for the external and internal finishings of houses. This included lining walls with wainscoting or panelling, putting together doors, windows and stairs, and required more accurate and better-looking workmanship than most carpenters produced. The surfaces needed to be smooth and well wrought, with joints of great precision.

The disagreement of 1632 between carpenters and joiners (*see* pp. 47–48) indicated, in the opinion of the carpenters, 'that without question the Joyners trade before their incorporacion was chiefly to make and sell joyned ware'.[9] The Great Fire of London, with the rebuilding of the City, encouraged greater sophistication and comfort inside houses; it also encouraged many foreign craftsmen to come to England (particularly from Holland) to tempt patrons away from the use of English joiners. John Evelyn wrote in his *Diary* (4 February 1685): 'Charles II loved planting and building, and brought in a politer way of living which passed to luxury and intolerable expense.'

9. London, Guildhall Library, MS, 8332.

Celia Fiennes, indefatigable traveller through England on horseback in the reigns of William III and Queen Anne, wrote of the additions at Chatsworth; they characterise much in the province of the joiner.

The Hall is very lofty, painted top and sides with armory and there is 18 steps on Each side goes up as an arch, with Iron Barristers tipt with gold wch Meetes on ye top Large steps of Stone. Thence you enter a dineing-roome, two drawing roomes, a bed Chamber and Closet . . . ye floores of ye Roomes are all finely Inlaid, there is very curious Carving over and Round the Chimneypieces and Round the hooking-glasses . . . and fine Carv'd shelves or stands on Each side of ye glass. Each roome is differing work and all fine Carving and over ye Doores some of it is of ye Natural Coullr of ye wood and varnished only—others painted. Ye Duchess's Closet is wainscoated with ye hollow burnt Japan, and at each corner are piers of Looking glass.[10]

WAINSCOTING

From this description it can be seen that the wainscoted walls and inlaid floors were important—reference to a simple diagram (fig. 9) will make discussion of the component parts of wainscoting more intelligible.

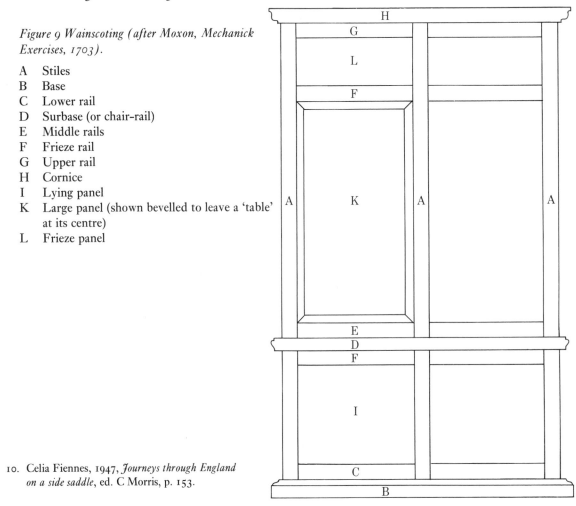

Figure 9 Wainscoting (after Moxon, Mechanick Exercises, 1703).

A   Stiles
B   Base
C   Lower rail
D   Surbase (or chair-rail)
E   Middle rails
F   Frieze rail
G   Upper rail
H   Cornice
I   Lying panel
K   Large panel (shown bevelled to leave a 'table' at its centre)
L   Frieze panel

10. Celia Fiennes, 1947, *Journeys through England on a side saddle*, ed. C Morris, p. 153.

In rooms under 10 ft high, two heights of panel were used; if 11–12 ft and over, three panels. In proportion the frieze rail (F) had the same breadth as the stiles (A), and the middle rail (E) was commonly twice the breadth of the stiles; the upper and lower rails (G and C) were also of the same breadth as the stiles. In the late seventeenth century, skilled joiners started to bevel the edge of the panels (I, K and L) to leave a raised 'table' in the middle. The oblong panels were usually 4–5 ft in width, and as tall, and dignified with the simplest of mouldings. Enrichment was the province of the carver.

The wood used for wainscoting varied with a patron's ability to pay and the joiner's competence to work it. Oak was in frequent use but, in many City Company Halls and Oxford and Cambridge colleges, cedar and walnut were worked with great competence. The wood was usually cut to show the attractive radiating medullary rays of the tree, so displaying the largest amount of grain. Celia Fiennes described the hall at Chippenham Hall, near Newmarket, as 'wainscoated with walnutt tree, the panels and Rims round with Mulberry tree yt is a Lemon Coulleur, and ye moldings beyond it round are of a sweete outlandish wood not much differing from Cedar, but of a finer graine'.[11] Sometimes a heavy, expensive timber such as oak was substituted with painted fir, and John Evelyn noted that, at Euston Hall in 1677, 'The wainscott, being of fir and painted does not please me so well as Spanish oak without paint.'[12]

The fir came to England as part of the extensive Norwegian timber export trade, and many effects of exotic timbers were obtained by painting it in various ways. Two important letters touching on this subject are those written by William Winde to Lady Mary Bridgeman on 6 September 1690 and 3 August 1700. They show the materials in use and the interest in viewing and varnishing. The 1690 letter reads:[13]

Madam

You Ladyp Leter of ye 1 instant, I have received and have ordered Mr. Symes (my Lord Joyner) to make use of his skill, to have good stuffe, and ye best wainscot that can be made, is of Dansike oake, wch is ye best and will not easily change, but ye greattest difficulty will bee ye transportation of them, wch I feare must bee by yr Ladysp carrier, for it is not safe to send them by any other, as when yr Ladysp mentions of ye varnishing of ye wainscot, if it be faded, or turned from its natural color, to varnish it then will be to no purpose, but if ye wainscot lookes bright, and ye Rooms or places bee dampe, then varnishing will doe good and will keep ye wainscot of ye same color, it was . . . ye prices of varnishing by ye yard, I will sent yr Ladyp by ye next Letter, of a price of varnishing ye bedchamber of Englis oake, & ye graze Walnut tree in yr Ladp closet will doe very well, onely Mr. Holmes muste vayne itt very sofft, and let him make as mucht use of his pencill As of his brushe wch will make it looke ye better, yr Ladyp stayre case can not well hee compleat withe out ye starye case be so finished with wainscot. I have nothing Else at present, to give yr Ladyp an account, but of my being withe great deale.

In 1700 Winde enclosed some patterns for painting wainscot, and continued:

11. *ibid.*, p. 124.
12. John Evelyn, 1955, *Diary*, ed. E S de Beer, **I**, p. 29.
13. Staffs CRO, Earl of Bradford's Archives, 18/4.

Madam,

I could have wished them Larger but the[y] whoud not then suit the compas of a Letter as I intended, yr Ladp's painter if an able one (as I suppose he is), will easely by them make others wch may be used in sucht places as yr Ladp shall think fitt the 3 first paterns A B C are moste in use and I prefer that of B, ye properest for a Bedchamber, if well peformed (withe the pencil), and not tou mucht withe a brushe as is the common way, it will requier moor skill to paynes & will coste the moor, it represents a Light wall-nut tree color as I have seen some cabinets, and is proper for Antirooms & Bedchambers, the other A is a dark wallnut tree & will requier a glossey varnishe, and is very proper in Light chambers—C is a wainscot color muche in voge (since wright wainscot is subject to groe darke and in spotts,) and generally speaking ye use at present is a flate color that of torteschall & the mouldings being vayned marble etz is mucht out of use except in Banketing houses as somer parlors for these requier a highe varnishe and are soone spoyled [either] by ye moistues of the ayre or hott sun.

Winde's advice was precise and many owners of great fine houses must have received similar information from their architects, and master joiners too, if equal to their job.

One who was well practised in the art was the London joiner John Chaplin of St Anne's, Westminster. He entered into agreement in 1697 to do the joinery work at Kiveton for the 1st Duke of Leeds. His agreement[14] set out that, for fitting up old wainscot, he would charge '10½d. p. yard for every square yard' and find nails and glue as well as workmen. For new wainscoting with whole or slit deal, having base, surbase and cornice, nails and workmen provided, he was to receive 17d. per square yard. Whole deal was usually 1¼ in thick, and slit deal half that thickness. Beadwork was set at 20d. a square yard and bolection mouldings at 24d. Measurement was to be carried out by John Fitch, and Chaplin was to have 40s. a journey from London to Kiveton in Yorkshire and subsistence at the rate of 5s. a man. After four rooms had been finished, measurements were to be taken. The Duke had the right to retain £20 for 12 months after all the work was finished to make good deficiencies which might arise. In all Chaplin received £706 14s. 8d. out of a total bill of a little over £15000.

In 1721, when work was proceeding at Chevening, Kent, partly under the direction of the architect Nicholas Dubois, the joiner Robert Matthews submitted an account of 'what Materials are here and for what uses they are':[15]

Three hundred of ten foot Christiana Deals
One hundred of ten foot Single Yellow Dram* Deals
One hundred of ten foot Duble D°
1229 foot of Clean Deals
5 Inch and quarter Wainscotts
2 Inch and half
1 Two Inch | Wainscotts
1 Four Inch

14. Yorkshire Archaeological Society, Library, Leeds.
    Duke of Leeds Archives, Box 32.

15. Kent CRO, MS U1590 E 26/2.
    *   See Glossary

60 Pieces of firr Timber

1 Bagg of 20 penny
1 Bagg of 10 penny ⎱ Nails
1 Bagg of 6 penny

1 Thousand of Inch
3 Thousand of Inch & half ⎱ Brads
3 Thousand of two Inch

The above Materials were for 'Wainscotting the Stair Case, finishing the halls, Making Doors where Wanting, Laying the floors in the Closets, Covered Way and Roof Their, and Carrying up a Stair Case in the Kitchen Offices etc'.

STAIRCASES

The selection of the place in which the staircase—often the best feature in a house—was to be placed required great judgment, and was one of the most difficult tasks in the formation of a plan. Palladio had indicated that they needed to be placed so that no part of the building 'should receive any prejudice by them'.[16] He noted that three openings were necessary to any staircase: the doorway leading to it, the windows by which it was lighted, and the landings by which one entered upper rooms. In the satisfaction of these requirements many splendid drawings of great mathematical complexity (*see* p. 62) adorned manuals of practical instruction, such as that by Abraham Swan. Entitled *The British Architect: or the Builder's Treasury of Staircases*, it was first issued in 1738 and went through at least four English and American editions before the end of the eighteenth century.

While Swan's publication was informative and influential, his book was one of many, and the more important of these are noted in the first section of the Bibliography at the end of this book. In particular, those manuals by Batty Langley and William and James Pain had a wide circulation in the latter half of the eighteenth century.

Staircases are basically of two sorts, straight or winding. In proceeding with the house design, the architect, often in consultation with a master carpenter, had to ensure that the person ascending had enough 'headway', the distance between any step or landing to the underside of the ceiling or other part immediately above it. It was also necessary in the case of all staircases to decide about the *newel*—in a winding staircase, the upright cylinder or pillar round which the steps turn and are supported from the bottom to the top is so called. When the steps ascend in geometrical flights, being pinned into the wall at left or right and there is no central pillar, the staircase is said to have an *open newel*.

The next important decision was to settle the proper relation between the height and width of steps. These were set out with some exactitude by the French engineer and mathematician François Blondel (1617–86) in the series of his lectures published as *Cours d'Architecture* between 1675 and 1698. They were followed by most pattern-book publishers, on the following basis:

16. Andrea Palladio, 1570, *I. Quattro Libri Dell' Architettura*, Book I, Ch. XXVIII.

Figure 10 Side elevation of balusters. Abraham Swan, 1738, The British Architect, or The Builder's Treasury of Stair Cases, pl. 34.

Figure 11 The geometrical construction of banisters and balustrades. Batty Langley, 1738, Builders' Chest Book pl. 68.

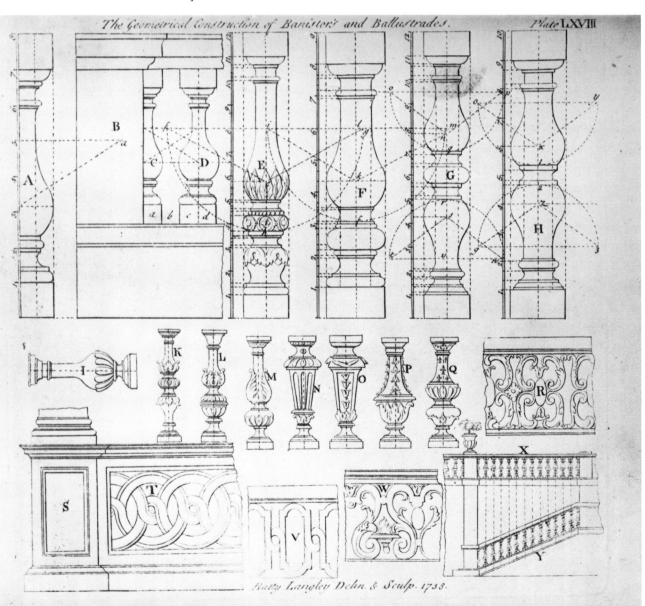

Let x equal the spaces over which a person walks with ease upon a level plane, and z the height a person could with equal ease ascend vertically. Then if h be the height of the step, and w its width the relation between h and w must be such that when $w = x$, $h = o$, and when $h = z$, $w = o$. These conditions are fulfilled by equations of the form $h = \frac{1}{2}(x - w)$ and $w = x - 2h$.

Blondel assumed 24 (French) inches for the value of x, and 12 for that of z. If these values were substituted in the equation $h = \frac{1}{2}(24 - w)$, and $w = 24 - 2h$, then, if the height of a step is 5 in, its width should be $24 - 10 = 14$ in. Eighteenth-century architects seemed to rely on this theory, and experiments which led to reducing the height of the risers without giving a corresponding width of tread to the step only led to inconvenience and an unpleasant feeling to the user. Furthermore, 11 to 13 steps were considered sufficient for a flight before the need for a landing.

Help with construction would usually be given by a carpenter with those parts which were hidden from further view—the 'carriage' or framework on which the steps of a wooden staircase were supported. These massive timbers, laid parallel to each other, were pinned into the joists and wall where necessary to allow for the construction of flights at a different angle and for the landings. This timber construction was overlaid with 'treads' (horizontal steps) and 'risers' (the upright face of a step from tread to tread). The riser was dovetailed into the step. The nosing of each tread was rounded and, at the well edge, the steps were set into a 'string board'. The face of this followed the direction of the well-hole, whatever the form; when curved it was formed usually in thicknesses glued together, although examples worked out of the solid are encountered. Carvers embellished the string board with all forms of scrolled ornamentation, representations of tools (*see* pl. 39) and of the arts. Above the string board, the balusters (*see* pl. 36) were set into part of the carriage. Alternatively, in the years from about 1650 to 1675 balusters were supplanted by panels of carved softwood ornamentation representing foliage (*see* pls. 27 and 28). This part of the staircase was finished by a handrail into which the upper part of the balusters or panels was fitted. In the years from about 1750, however, wood balusters were often replaced by wrought or cast-iron ones, although splendid iron balustrades by Jean Tijou (*see* pl. 31) and others survive from the 1690s.[17]

The practical manuals abounded in suggestions: the number of balusters to each tread, the distance between them not to exceed half their respective diameters (which was also equal to the shorter side of the square part at the top); the height of the baluster from nose of step to underside of rail not to exceed 2 ft 2 in; and hints on embellishment with knops and carving. The production of balusters became the especial province of the turner, who demonstrated his great dexterity with the lathe in fashioning them. The wall side of a staircase, as opposed to the open well side, was usually wainscoted or painted (*see* pls. 88 and 96). The rail and rail mould also received the attention of assiduous authors. Its height, sweeps on the bottom step and its embellishment demanded excellent materials, good application of geometrical knowledge and skill in carving from the solid. It was often inlaid, steam-bent (in the later eighteenth century) and demanded precision in its surface finish and in fitting it to the balusters.

The various craftsmen who worked on the embellishment of the 12 churches which were built as a result of the 1711 Act for '50 new churches' in London worked to precise contracts and

17. John Harris, ed., 1960, *English Decorative Ironwork from Contemporary Source Books, 1610–1836*.

their charges for work done are available.[18] John Mead, the carpenter at St George, Hanover Square, estimated in March 1722/23 for:

Steps of Stairs One Inch & half thick Wainscot with String & Bearers of Oak at p. foot runing	o. 3s. od.
Half Paces of Oak Timber, Boarded with Inch & half Wainscot at p. foot Superficial	o. 1s. 6d.
Raile & turnd Ballisters of Wainscot, the Raile four inches Square with a Wainscot String p. foot runing	o. 4s. od.

All work was to be done 'with the best Stuff free from Stains and other Defects, and wrought after the best Manner'.

The same group of archives, but relating to Nicholas Hawksmoor's church of Christchurch, Spitalfields (1723–29), record an 'Abstract of Joiners' Proposals'.[19] The charges for various classes of work are listed in the accompanying table.

Nature of work	Measure	John Lane and William Beaverstock Rate	Price £ s d	Gabriel Appleby Rate	Price £ s d	John Simmons Rate	Price £ s d
Fronts of pews	390 yd	6/6d.	126 15. 0.	7/6d.	146 5. 0.	7/6d.	146 5. 0.
Partitions	610 yd	5/6d.	167 15. 0.	5/6d.	167 15. 0.	6/9d.	205 17. 6.
Desk boards	100 yd	4/od.	20 0. 0.	4/od.	20 0. 0.	6/od.	30 0. 0.
Cap mouldings	980 ft	9d.	36 15. 0.	4½d.	18 7. 6.	9d.	36 15. 0.
3-in doors	185 ft	3/3d.	30 1. 3.	3s.	27 15. 0.	3/od.	27 15. 0.
Pilasters	590 ft	1/8d.	49 3. 4.	2s.	59 0. 0.	1/9d.	51 12. 6.
Mouldings	8870 in	2½d.	92 7. 11.	2d.	73 18. 4.	3d.	110 17. 6.
Circular mouldings	760 in	6d.	19 0. 0.	5d.	15 16. 8.	6d.	19 0. 0.
Modillion cornice	2200 in	8d.	73 6. 8.	7½d.	68 15. 0.	9d.	82 10. 0.
Benches	1100 in	6d.	17 10. 0.	6d.	27 10. 0.	6d.	27 10. 0.
Totals			£642 14. 2.		£625 2. 6.		£738 2. 6.

The lowest estimate, Gabriel Appleby's, was agreed by Hawksmoor and accepted. The list gives guidance as to the nature of ecclesiastical work undertaken, and the full records are supplemented by those for St Martin-in-the-Fields. On acceptance of his estimate for the latter church in 1725 by its architect James Gibbs, Charles Griffith proceeded to frame the front of the galleries and pew doors with fir, and spent 12 days cutting away the floor in the lower part of the church to put the wainscot up. This involved seeing that the timber frame for the wainscoting formed a tight join with the floorboards. He then worked on three patterns of banisters in cedar wood, turned and fluted for various staircases, and also submitted a deal one. He 'firred-out' the

18. Lambeth Palace Library, MSS, 1690/170, calendared by E G W Bill, 1980, *Queen Anne's Churches: Commission for Building Fifty New Churches in London and Westminster, 1711–1759*. This contains a revised introduction by Dr H M Colvin based on his pioneer article (*Arch Rev*, March 1950).

19. Lambeth Palace Library, MS, 2713, f. 41.

organ loft and several doorways, made the fine pulpit and sounding boards, and set out a pattern in Virginia walnut tree for the altar rail. He eventually provided 25 ft of this in a $4 \times 3\frac{1}{2}$ in square form at 2s. 4d. per ft. It capped Thomas Goff's wrought-iron rail.

Some of Griffith's duties overlapped those of the carpenter in that he made a large scaffold for use in gilding the altar, and he filled in various 'air holes' and holes made by the insertion of scaffolding poles. He finished his work by fluting and carving various Ionic and Doric columns, inserted iron bars in them and shored up the gallery while they were positioned. The four supporting the organ loft are presumably of this series, although marks on the gallery soffits indicate the former position of many more. Finally, he set up the splendid (surviving) pulpit (ready for embellishment by the carver Thomas Bridgewater) for £80.

TOOLS

For the variety of finer work undertaken by joiners a large assemblage of tools was needed (*see* fig 12). Many of these have not altered in form or purpose over the years. The joiner worked at a bench which had a rising hook or stop incorporated so that the ends of planks could be butted against it to prevent sliding during planing or shaping. The bench also had a side vice. He also used a mallet, chisels, gouges, a variety of planes for jointing, forming mouldings or shaving surfaces, squares to form angles, many saws, augers, pierces and kettles for boiling glue.

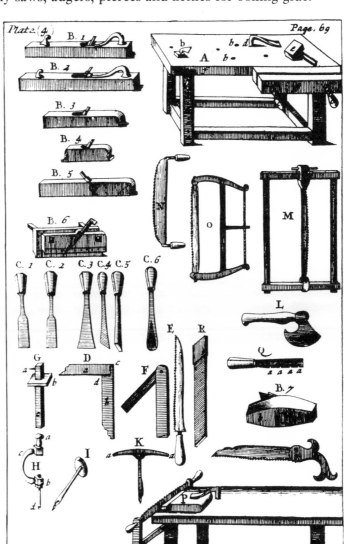

Figure 12 Joiner's tools, (after Moxon).

A	Work-bench
B	Planes
C	Chisels
D	Square
E	Compass saw
F	Bevel
G	Gauge
H	Piercer
I	Gimlet
K	Auger
L	Hatchet
M	Pit saw
N	Whip saw
O	Bow saw
P	Whetting block or rub stone
Q	Saw rest or set
R	Mitre square

The Carver

The craftsmen who were able to both pierce wood and fashion it so that it resembled other materials and natural forms were the carvers. They were usually skilled joiners who had specialised in that they had no trade guild of their own. Frequently they were adept at carving in both stone and wood, and surviving accounts are not always informative about the choice of material. Carving in wood appears synonymous in the late seventeenth century with the achievements of Grinling Gibbons (1648–1721); however, he was also an accomplished statuary and there were several woodcarvers, such as Jonathan Maine of Oxford (*see* pls. 112 and 113) and Edward Pearce (*see* pls. 27 and 46), who were almost his equal. The materials and tools the carver used were more specialised than those of carpenters and joiners—they were embellishers and therefore moved in to a house at a late stage when its carcase and wainscoting were done.

The principal wood in use by carvers was lime, laminated with glue into two or three layers.[20] However, they also worked in oak, box, mahogany and in fruitwoods such as pear. The grain needed to be carefully observed as it was worked with a wide range of gouges, veiners, chisels, points and fine saws. The work was assembled into its pattern by fixing with glue and iron pins. These pins have, in many cases, rusted over the years and woodworm has taken a savage toll, yet enough pieces survive in reasonable condition to demonstrate the art was a considerable one (*see* pls. 106–111).

When the provision of such elaborately carved and pierced additions to overmantels and cornices died away in the early years of the eighteenth century, the carver rose again as a specialist joiner who enriched fixtures with a variety of mouldings (*see* pl. 13). The post of Master Carver to the Crown ceased at the death of James Richards in 1759. When Sefferin Alken worked in stone and wood at Croome Court, Worcestershire, in 1763, his work in the Tapestry Room there included:[21]

	£	s	d
Plinth Base. 2 Members Carved at 2/3½d.	10.	10.	0.
Surbase. 4 Members Carved at 3/6d.	16.	2.	0.
2 Friezes in Symmetry, Richly Carved Demi-Boys & foliage (£6. 12. 6.)	13.	5.	0.
Architrave to 2 Doors, 3 Members Carved (at 3/1d.)	6.	1.	9.
30 Modillions to Cornice at 3/6d.	5.	5.	0.
Upper Ogee very richly carved to Cornice, at 3/10d.	2.	11.	7.
Upper Ovolo to Cornice at 1/-	—	13.	0.
Bottom Ogee, with small Ogee to Capping of Modillions at 6d.	2.	11.	7.
Architrave of 2 windows carved as the Doors at 3/1d.	7.	8.	0.

Alken also carved capitals to pilasters and columns in rooms and on bookcases, the font, pulpit, sounding boards and desks in the church and various ornaments in stone. For the pediment of the house, he provided in 1761 'My Lords Arms' and supporters (10 ft × 5 ft high) for £27. 15s., with £1. 18s. for a model in lime wood. The elegant surviving greenhouse was also

20. David Green, 1964, *Grinling Gibbons*, pp. 178–79.   21. Croome Court Archives, Building Bills No. 35.

enhanced with Alken's large stone carving (£35. 10s.) in its pediment of a large basket of flowers and festoons.

The Turner

In London turners had formed themselves into a City Company in the sixteenth century; their account books survive from 1593 and court minutes from 1633.[22] Their principal task was to turn on a lathe items in soft and hard woods, ivory, brass and iron. This was done by directing various cutting tools such as hooks, grooves, gouges and chisels on metal rests against the revolving material. Screw threads could be produced, stair balusters, chair and table legs in quantity, and, in certain cases, elaborate items such as tapered wood columns.

Like the carvers, the turners fashioned a great deal of work in softwood (maple, alder, birch, fir) on their treadle lathes or on those which, for heavier work, incorporated a pulley over a great wheel. Moxon's description (1703) of their activities is fulsome:

> Having thus fitted it [the work] into the Lathe they begin to work with the Sharp-pointed Grooving Tool, or else with the Triangular Grooving Tool, and with the point of either of these Tools break the Grain of the Wood, by laying small Grooves upon its surface, till they have pretty well wrought away Extuberances, and brought the Work tolerably near an intended shape . . .
>
> Afterward they cut down and smooth . . . and bring the work into a perfect shape . . .
>
> Lastly they polish with Bees-wax . . . and set a gloss on it with a very dry woollen rag, lightly smeared with salad oil. Ivory they polish with Chalk and water.[23]

When it is recognised that one imposing staircase of three flights used between 100 and 140 balusters (depending on the number to each tread and the length of the landing), the turner's work seemed assured. They have, however, remained a largely anonymous group in the decorating of a country house with their work being provided through the joiner's account.

---

22. London, Guildhall Library, MS, 3297, Account Books, 1593–1758; MS, 3295, Court Minutes, 1633–88.

23. Joseph Moxon, 1703, *Mechanick Exercises* (ed. Benno Forman, 1970), pp. 167–236.

STAIRCASES

27 SUDBURY HALL, Derbyshire. The Great Staircase, carved by Edward Pearce, 1675 (photograph: A F Kersting). *See also* pls. 46 and 60.

This is one of the finest staircases of its date *in situ* in an English country house. Edward Pearce, who had also carved one at Wolseley Hall, Staffordshire, received £112. 15s. 5d. for his spirited work. The balustrade is pine and this photograph shows the staircase prior to its being painted white in 1969—traces of white had been found in paint-scrape tests. When Celia Fiennes saw the Cassiobury staircase (*see* pl. 28) in the mid-1690s, she observed that it was 'all white natural wood without varnish', and it is now so displayed. Whatever the truth at Sudbury of the original decoration—and I do not believe the foliated panels were painted white—the removal of old brown paint and varnish effected an improvement. Its subsequent repainting does little to detract from its great splendour and, in some opinions, may improve it.

Lit: C *Life*, 22–29 June 1935; 10 June 1971 (colour views of repainted rooms).

28 CASSIOBURY, Hertfordshire. Panel by Grinling Gibbons from a staircase carved between 1677 and 1680 (now re-erected *Metropolitan Museum of Art, New York*, Rogers Fund, 1932) (photograph: musem).

This ash and pine staircase, with its lavish foliated panels, was commissioned from Gibbons by Arthur, 1st Earl of Essex. He was in Ireland as Lord Lieutenant from 1672 to 1677, and conducted the progress of his house, erecting under Hugh May, by letters to his brother. John Evelyn visited it when complete on 18 April 1680, and recorded in his *Diary* that 'there are divers fair and good rooms, and excellent carving by Gibbons'.

The staircase, now reassembled from these component parts in New York, is built up from three principal woods—pine for the handrail and oak-leaf and acorn string, solid ash for the scrollwork balustrade and pine-cone finials, and oak for the risers, treads and landings. It was left unvarnished and unpainted by the carver, who may have drawn some of his design inspiration from French engravings (*see* pl. 29).

Lit: James Parker, June 1957, 'A Staircase by Grinling Gibbons', Metropolitan Musem of Art, *Bulletin*, pp. 228–36.

29 ENGRAVING OF FOLIATED FRIEZES, c 1670, Jean
Le Pautre (1618–82) (collection and photograph:
Geoffrey Beard).

The many engravings by Jean Bérain (1640–1711),
Jean Le Pautre and his eldest son Pierre
(1649–1716) did much to create the early years of
the rococo style in France. Their inventive
arabesques, friezes and designs for all forms of
architectural decoration were widely distributed.
They were probably used as background
illustrative material by carvers such as Gibbons for
staircase panels and friezes.
Lit: David Green, 1964, *Grinling Gibbons*, pls. 90,
101; Fiske Kimball, 1943, *The Creation of the
Rococco*, pp. 62–64; R A Weigert, 1960, *Louis
XIV: Faste et Décors*, Paris, Musée des Arts
Décoratifs, Introduction.

30 ASHDOWN HOUSE, Berkshire. Staircase at the
1st landing, c 1675 (photograph: A F Kersting).

Soon after the restoration of Charles II, the 1st
Earl of Craven, a friend and supporter of Queen
Elizabeth of Bohemia, the sister of Charles I,
started to rebuild several of his houses. He owned
Ashdown, Hampstead Marshall, also in Berkshire,
and Combe Abbey in Warwickshire. He may have
used at first the elderly Sir Balthazar Gerbier (but
he died c 1663), or Gerbier's pupil William Winde,
to assist him with the design. Ashdown, a pleasing
symmetrical house with a dominant cupola, has
internal joinery of great solidity. The staircase,
with its robust balusters, huge newels and wide,
moulded handrail, follows those (as at Cassiobury,
see pl. 28) in which the use of balusters was
prefaced by panels of carved wood.

31 (*facing page*) CHATSWORTH, Derbyshire. The Great Staircase, 1688–91 (photograph: A F Kersting).

In 1688–89 Jean Tijou, the French smith, received £250 for the iron balustrade, but it was not fitted until his second visit to the house in October 1691. During his period at Chatsworth and Kiveton, Tijou trained the Derbyshire smith John Gardom, and he did excellent work in the W. wing at Chatsworth. The feigned relief panels on the walls were probably painted under Verrio's supervision by a Huguenot painter, Nicolas Heude. The brass vase shown on the 1st newel may be one of 17 supplied by Josiah Ibeck.
Lit: Francis Thompson, 1949, *A History of Chatsworth*, pp. 123–25.

32 and 33 (*below and right*) HANBURY HALL, Worcestershire. The Staircase (32) and a detail of the balusters (33), *c* 1705 (photographs: A F Kersting (32), National Monuments Record (33)).

Hanbury is dated '1701' in the centrepiece of the E. front, and was finely built in red brick, with stone dressings, for Thomas Vernon. The Staircase Hall is entered directly from the porch, and the staircase with its oak balusters rises in two left turns past the wall paintings by Sir James Thornhill. Preparatory drawings for them are in the British Museum, London, and in New York (Cooper Hewitt Museum, Smithsonian Institution). They illustrate scenes in the life of Achilles, while those on the ceiling contain the usual vast horde of classical deities; here, Mercury points to a small portrait of Dr Sacheverell, who was impeached for seditious treason in February 1710. The ceiling must be a little after this date and Thornhill signed it on a scroll held by a cupid. The staircase and hall were restored by Mr Michael Gibbon in 1954–55, when the house transferred to the ownership of The National Trust.

34 (*left*) EASTON NESTON, Northamptonshire. The Staircase, *c* 1700 (photograph: A F Kersting).

As at Hanbury (*see* pl. 32), Thornhill worked on the walls of the Easton Neston staircase with subjects from the history of Cyrus. The house was designed by Nicholas Hawksmoor, and the wooden model survives (*see* pl. 7). The craftsman of the fine iron balustrade is unknown but may well have been Tijou or John Montigny. It incorporates an intertwined 'L' monogram for its owner, Lord Lempster, in the newel on the principal turn at the 1st landing, and again in the panel at the head of the stairs. They are similar to those depicted in Tijou's 1693, *A New Booke of Drawings* and Charles D'Avilier's 1710, *Cours D'Architecture*, Paris.

35 (*facing page*) STONELEIGH ABBEY, Warwickshire. The Staircase, *c* 1725 (photograph: A F Kersting).

Francis Smith of Warwick contracted in 1714 to the 3rd Lord Leigh to erect Stoneleigh for the comparatively small sum of £545. What Lord Leigh got exactly is not certain, as some rebuilding was involved and much re-use of materials already on the site. Work went on for the next 20 years, including the insertion of a typical Smith staircase—three balusters to a tread, and with fluted columns in the angles and at the centre of the landing rail. Similar examples are found at Chicheley, Hinwick and Lamport—houses in which Smith was involved. The joiner at Stoneleigh was probably Thomas Eboral of Warwick, who was named on the rising-plate for Sutton Scarsdale which Smith had erected by 1724.

Lit: Andor Gomme, 1971, *Archaeological Journal*, CXXVII, pp. 247–50.

36 DAVENPORT HOUSE, Shropshire. The Staircase balusters, *c* 1726 (photograph: Courtauld Institute of Art).

Davenport is another of the Midland houses erected by Francis Smith, and some of its interior marquetry decoration has affinities with Mawley Hall nearby. The staircase occupies both storeys in the N.W. corner of the house. The stairs are of oak, with the risers inlaid in a darker wood; the handrail is of veneered mahogany. Three patterns of baluster are in use and, as at Stoneleigh, the newels are columns. The space under the lower flight and the wall side are enclosed with wainscoting. In the upper flight the treads are moulded to the profile of the carved brackets. The lead rainwater heads on the house are dated '1726'.

37 COMPTON PLACE, Eastbourne, Sussex. The Staircase, 1728–29 (photograph: *C Life*).

Colen Campbell submitted designs for this house to Spencer Compton, Lord Wilmington, in 1726, and detailed accounts survive at the house of the work done by a team of craftsmen. These included the carver James Richards, who was responsible for the staircase and door-cases. The richly carved balusters may be compared with those on the staircase at Houghton Hall, Norfolk, also by Richards (Hussey, 1965, *ECH: Early Georgian*, pl. 106).

Letters from the gardener, William Stuart, to his master detail progress on the house. On 8 April, 1728 Stuart noted that 'the Carpenters and Joyners continue the same worke, on ye Stairs, preparing for ye floors etc in ye New Building'. By 10 March 1728/29, the plasterers were at work on the great staircase and gallery ceilings; they were still there on 7 April, and more work was in progress on 2 June 1729. James Richards was paid £100 on 20 December 1729, and £190. 10*s*. 'in full' on 9 August 1731.

38 and 39 MAWLEY HALL, Shropshire. Upper landing of the Staircase (38) and carving on the string of the upper landing (39), *c* 1730 (photographs: Courtauld Institute of Art).

Mawley Hall possesses one of the finest interiors (with work by the Italian *stuccatori*) of any house worked on by Francis Smith. Some evidence survives that the design was provided by the owner himself, Sir Edward Blount. No documents survive, and Smith's involvement is based on stylistic similarities to his other work. The staircase rail, with its undulating movement, ripples from the tail (pl. 38) down the three flights to end in a dragon's head. The faces of the strings are carved in relief with arrangements of tools (pl. 39) and symbols of painting, gardening and music. One assumes that Smith's team of craftsmen (we know the names of those who worked for him at Sutton Scarsdale in 1724) worked at Mawley. The staircase rail is of excellent workmanship, however, and finds no parallel in other Smith houses. The lead rainwater heads are dated '1730'.

40 (*left*) 44 BERKELEY SQUARE, London. Staircase, 1st floor landing, *c* 1742 (photograph: A F Kersting).

William Kent designed this town house for Isabella, Lady Finch, and provided it with a superb double staircase, excellent woodwork and good painted ceilings. The accounts survive (Sir John Soane's Museum, London) and show that John Marsden was responsible for the carpentry and joinery, Robert Dawson for the plasterwork, and Benjamin Holmes (who appeared often in Henry Flitcroft's bank account) did the 'rich ironwork to railing the great stairs'. Horace Walpole declared the staircase to be 'as beautiful a piece of scenery, and, considering the space, of art, as can be imagined', (1798, *Anecdotes of Painting*, III, p. 80). The commission probably came to him through Lady Burlington, a niece of Lord Winchelsea, Lady Isabella Finch's father.

Kent left Lady Isabella four busts of Newton, Clarke, Locke and Wollaston in his will.

41 (*right*) CLAYDON HOUSE, Buckinghamshire. Staircase, 2nd floor landing, *c* 1768 (photograph: A F Kersting).

In July 1768 Sir Thomas Robinson, who was designing work for Ralph, 2nd Earl Verney, at Claydon, wrote that Luke Lightfoot, the talented but erratic carver, was retarding the staircase by not sending instructions to Joseph Rose, the plasterer. 'The Staircase', he continued, 'will be very Noble and Great . . . and will be one of the great works of Claydon.'

The Staircase has mahogany treads and risers (also the landing floors), and these are inlaid with holly, ivory and ebony in repeating geometrical patterns. The balustrade is in delicate rococo metalwork by an unknown smith; specimens of carved balusters by Lightfoot are mounted as library steps. His involvement in a Chancery suit brought against him by Lord Verney is noted in the Dictionary entry in Part III.

42 DODINGTON PARK, Gloucestershire. The Staircase Hall, looking S. *c* 1812 (photograph: A F Kersting).

As with the staircase at Belton (*see* pl. 43), that at Dodington is built up of parts of different dates. The balustrade and the staircase arrangement were designed to accept wrought-iron work from Fonthill House (1756–65). As James Wyatt, Dodington's architect, was building the Gothic Abbey at Fonthill for the younger Beckford (1796–1807), he may well have decided to use the ironwork from the mid-Georgian Fonthill at

Dodington from an early stage in his work. His drawings are dated 1812, but five carriages had been sent to Dodington 'and a second time with six carriages' to bring the Grand Staircase from Fonthill. In 1810 Richard Beckett was paid 'for taking down the Grand Staircase at Fonthill brought to Dodington £20'. The 'railing of the best staircase' and fanlights for the staircase were supplied in 1812 by a Mr Browne, possibly Joseph Browne, a marblework contractor at Buckingham Palace and for the Marble Arch.

Lit : C Life, 29 November 1956, p. 1232.

43 COUND HALL, Shropshire. 'The Flying Staircase' *c* 1800 (photograph: Courtauld Institute of Art).

Cound is an early eighteenth-century house which has undergone extensive internal remodelling. It passed from the Cressett family—it was built, as the date on the N. front indicates, in '1704' for Richard Cressett—to the Pelhams in the 1770s. They inserted the staircase into the hall. The name derives from the 'flyers'—steps in a flight of stairs that are parallel to each other.

44 BELTON HOUSE, Lincolnshire. The Staircase Hall, *c* 1686, amended 1809–20 (photograph: A F Kersting).

The late seventeenth-century building history is noted under pl. 62. From about 1809 Sir Jeffry Wyatville was engaged in various works for Lord Brownlow. While the walnut treads and panelled risers of the staircase are those put in the mid-1680s house, the balusters were renewed and a brass rail and knobs let into a new balustrade under Wyatville's supervision. The staircase well ceiling is a fine one of *c* 1687 by Edward Goudge (*see* pl. 62).

46 SUDBURY HALL, Derbyshire. Door-cases to the Queen's Room, *c* 1675 (photograph: A F Kersting).

The building history of Sudbury and the work on the Great Staircase by Edward Pearce, the London carver, is noted under pl. 27. Pearce was also responsible for the door-cases at the head of the stairs. The carved pediments are on broken entablatures, with sprays of olive and palm. They are surmounted by plasterwork by Robert Bradbury and James Pettifer (*see* pl. 60).

45 THORPE HALL, Northamptonshire. Design for door-cases and doors in the former Great Parlour, *c* 1658. *Victoria and Albert Museum, London*, Inv. No. 1833–85 (photograph: museum).

A year or two before Charles II was restored to the throne, Peter Mills designed Thorpe Hall for Oliver St John, Chief Justice to Oliver Cromwell. This important fact (established by Dr H M Colvin) tempts one to assume that the actual door-case, of which this is the drawing, was worked by Thomas Whiting, joiner, and Richard Cleere, the carver who worked for Wren on the Great Model of St Paul's Cathedral (*see* pl. 6). They worked in the early 1660s at Cobham Hall, Kent, under Mills's supervision.

The door-case and panelling from the Great Parlour (or Library, as it was later called) were removed *c* 1920 and inserted into Leeds Castle, Kent. *Lit:* Dr H M Colvin, 6 June 1952, 'The Architect of Thorpe Hall', *C Life*; Peter Mills and Cobham Hall: 1970, *The Country Seat*, ed. Colvin and J Harris, p. 45; door-case *in situ* at Thorpe, *repr.* Oliver Hill and John Cornforth, 1966, *English Country Houses: Caroline*, p. 109.

47 (*facing page*) CHATSWORTH, Derbyshire. Door-case in State Drawing Room, *c* 1692 (photograph: National Monuments Record).

The carvers Joel Lobb, Roger Davis and Samuel Watson signed agreements in September 1692 for work in this room (*see* col. pl. 1). Samuel Watson's Account Book (Chatsworth Archives) includes sketch designs for overdoors, intended as preliminary sketches for the 1st Duke of Devonshire's approval.

48 (*below*) BLENHEIM PALACE, Oxfordshire. Door-case in the Gallery, N. side, *c* 1725 (photograph: A F Kersting).

Two competent Oxford master-masons, William Townesend and Bartholomew Peisley Junior, erected this fine marble door-case in the centre of the N. wall of the Gallery or Long Library at Blenheim. They also contracted for other work including the erection of the Woodstock Gate and the Column of Victory.

49 (*above*) DITCHLEY HOUSE, Oxfordshire. Pedimented niche in Entrance Hall, *c* 1725 (photograph: A F Kersting).

The two-storey hall at Ditchley, decorated by the Italian *stuccatori* (*see* col. pl. 5), has this well-carved niche on one wall, facing a chimneypiece and overmantel by Edward Stanton and Christopher Horsenaile. The over-pediment figures are two of the six for which Francesco Vassalli charged £21. The names of the joiner and carver are not known, but James Richards (*see* pls. 50–52) may be suspected.

50 MEREWORTH CASTLE, Kent. Door-case in the Gallery, looking through to the Rotunda, *c* 1726 (photograph: A F Kersting).

There is no documentation for the joinery and carving at Mereworth but, as its architect had used James Richards at several houses before and after Mereworth (1722–25), this splendid white and gilded door-case of the highest quality may be attributed to him (*see also* pls. 37, 51, 52).

51 (*above*) HOUGHTON HALL, Norfolk. The W. (or window) side of the Saloon, *c* 1728 (photograph: *C Life*).

This mahogany and gilded window case faces an equally splendid door-case (*see* col. p. 6). The Houghton archives support, by indication of his presence, the attribution of the carved work and staircase to James Richards, Master Carver to the Crown.

52 (*below*) CHISWICK HOUSE, London. Door-case in the Red Velvet Room, *c* 1728 (photograph: A F Kersting).

The name of James Richards as joiner and carver is attached to work in many houses designed by Colen Campbell and William Kent. His name appears in Lord Burlington's green account book (Chatsworth Archives) for work at Burlington House and Chiswick. The pulvinated frieze with crossed ribanding was followed by many joiners, but close scrutiny of those at Chiswick and Mereworth show identical mannerisms.

53 CLAYDON HOUSE, Buckinghamshire. The
North Hall, S. wall, carved niche and door-case,
c 1769 (photograph: A F Kersting).

The Great Eating Room at Claydon (now known
as the North Hall) has spirited woodcarving by
Luke Lightfoot on its ceiling (*see* pl. 126), and
possibly on the niche and door-case shown here.

Lord Verney and his architect Sir Thomas
Robinson, however, were becoming disaffected
with Lightfoot, who may have used other talented
carvers of the skills of Thomas Johnson in his
team. Whatever the truth, Lightfoot's work at
Claydon, hovering between baroque and rococo in
mood, is unparalleled in an English house (*see also*
pl. 41).

54 (*top left*) CLAYDON HOUSE, Buckinghamshire. Detail of a panel in one of the Saloon doors, *c* 1768 (photograph: A F Kersting).

The Saloon doors and door-cases at Claydon are the work of a very skilled joiner. The doors are of mahogany with rosewood carving set over inlays of ebony and ivory, edged with satinwood.

55 (*centre left*) OSTERLEY PARK, Middlesex. Detail of panel in the frieze of the Drawing Room door-case, *c* 1772. *Victoria and Albert Museum, London* (photograph: museum).

This small neoclassical detail of griffins flanking a classical head emphasises the quality of decoration at Osterley; the room earned the high praise of Horace Walpole as one 'worthy of Eve before the Fall'. The frieze is supported on console brackets terminating in gilded wood rams' heads.

56 (*lower left*) SALTRAM, Devon. Door furniture in the Saloon, *c* 1768 (photograph: Tom Molland).

While it is often assumed that Matthew Boulton supplied ormolu door furniture to Robert Adam's clients, there is ample evidence that the architect turned mostly to Thomas Blockley of Birmingham. There is no archival evidence that he did so at Saltram but, as he provided those at Croome (1760, 17*s*. 6*d*. a pair), Shardeloes (1764–65), 20 St James's Square, London (1773), and Harewood House (1773), it may be assumed. *Lit:* Goodison, 1974, *Ormolu*, p. 130, pl. 48.

57 (*below*) SYON HOUSE, Middlesex, Door-case and doors, Red Drawing Room, *c* 1766–67 (photograph: A F Kersting).

The Syon accounts at Alnwick Castle (Beard, 1966, *Craftsmen*, p. 81) show that the ormolu decoration on the door-case was the work of Diederich Nicolaus Anderson (Goodison, 1974, *Ormolu*, pls. 65–72). That on the door was by 'Mr Bermingham'. This may have arisen through Anderson's death in 1767. Bermingham has been tentatively identified as Nathaniel Bermingham, who advertised his ability at cutting out patterns in Mortimer's 1763, *London Directory* (see Dictionary, Part III).

[4]
Wrought in Lime, Paint and Marble

The Plasterer

When the London and York plasterer Isaac Mansfield submitted his proposals in 1718 for plastering Christchurch, Spitalfields, he was working to a contract which spelled out precisely the nature of his work. It provides us with a succinct statement of how a plasterer proceeded. It merits quotation in full:

> For Lathing and Plastering work done with extraordinary heart Lath, and lathed with good 3*d*. Nails of 3 lb. weight to the 1000. The first coat to be lathed and scratched in order to make good key for the 2nd which is to be tried with a 10 or 12 foot Rule and floated: both which Coats are to be of good Stuff well turned up and wrought in the best manner and finished with a good coat of white nacred Stuff upon the two former at per yard £0. 1*s*. 1*d*. . . .
>
> The above mentioned work to have no more than one load of Sand to one hundred of Lime and not less than Ten Bushell of good black hair to the same, the Sand to be good Sharp Pit Sand, and not the white Sand dug upon Black Heath. The Lath and Nails to be according to a specimen produced for the approbation of the Honourable Commissioners or their Officers.[1]

MATERIALS

The best kind of plaster was obtained from burning gypsum or plaster of Paris. In this and various other forms, it was added to sand and water; animal hair was also added to give tensile strength and to act as a binding agent. This was then applied in successive coats over a ceiling which had been prepared by having oak or other laths nailed to the joists. I have discussed these matters in detail elsewhere.[2]

Batty Langley in *The Builders' Chest* (1727, Lecture VIII) is more explicit than Mansfield about the kind of *laths* available:

> The sorts of Laths . . . are principally of two sorts, the one five Feet long, and the other four Feet long. Those of five Feet long have five score or one hundred in the Bundle, the other of four Feet have six score, or 120 in the Bundle; their breadth ought to be one Inch and half, and thickness half an inch, and of both these lengths there are three sorts:
> First: Heart of Oak   Second: Sap-laths
> And Lastly, Deal-laths.

1. Lambeth Palace Library, MS, 2703, ff. 74–75.   2. Beard, 1975, *Plasterwork*, pp. 9–22.

The need for different lengths and qualities was then explained by Langley: 'Because that all Rafters upon which they are nailed, are not placed at equal Distances'.

The quality was related to the place where they were to be used. Heart of oak laths were the best and necessary for roofs supporting tiling. Sap laths were best for plastered walls, and those in deal for ceilings.

The *hair* added to give toughness to the plaster was usually taken from cows and bullocks, and, for finer work in the final coat, from goats. The *sand*, as Mansfield noted, was to be sharp (composed of angular grains) and free from any impurities which would stain the hands when rubbed together. The handmade lath *nails* were used in the proportion of 500 to a bundle (100) of 5-ft laths, and 600 to a bundle (120) of the 4-ft laths—that is, five to each lath. Every 'hundred' of nails contained 'six score' (120). A further preparation prior to the scratched first coat is noted in the building accounts for St Martin-in-the-Fields, London (*see* p. 177). Here the plain work was by Chrysostom Wilkins, who had submitted a lower tender than Isaac Mansfield. The mason Christopher Cass set some labourers to work over seven days in 1724 (2s. a day), to: 'making Holes in the Freestone & Portland Stone Inside of the Church in the Peers & windows the better to make the Plastering Stick'.

Wilkins, as Mansfield, used 4 bundles of oak laths, 2000 nails, 21 hods of lime and hair, and made use of the scaffolding erected for the stuccoist, or 'frettworker', Giovanni Bagutti.

Since my previous writings in 1975 on plasterwork in Great Britain, important evidence on plastering techniques in the 1760s has been made at Audley End, Essex. The excavations (1977–79) under the floors of certain rooms by members of the Chichester Excavation Committee[3] have uncovered debris; it is obvious that the plasterers were using the covered rooms as a workshop and various spoiled pieces were thrown down into the foundations before the floorboards were laid. Mould fragments in plaster, wax and stucco have been recovered as well as pieces in plaster composition and stucco of both the Adam period ornament and that used at the same time in repairing the neo-Jacobean Vanbrugh work of *c* 1708. The main impression provided by the bulk of the material is of the variety of moulded work, of pieces scratched at the back to give a key to other surfaces, and of one mould used to provide small stucco dentils or drops into which a lath nail had been placed to provide an 'armature' or support.

METHODS

It was essential for plasterers to work from scaffolding or tressels; there is no evidence, even for the Italian *stuccatori*, of working from cradles slung beneath a ceiling. The architect James Wyatt is said to have daringly practised something akin to this when in St Peter's in Rome

3. I am indebted to Mr Paul J Drury, Surveyor to the Committee, for showing me this material, which will be eventually published with supporting drawings and chemical analyses. *See also* Paul J Drury, 1980, 'The evolution of Audley End, 1605–1745', *Architectural History*, XXIII, pp. 1–39.

(*c* 1764)—'lying on his back on a ladder slung horizontally without cradle or side-rail, over a frightful void of 300 feet'.[4] What, however, seemed more normal, even for the stuccoists, was to work from the usual scaffolds or planks across two-legged 'great trussels'. At St Martin-in-the-Fields, London, where Bagutti was working in 1724–25, the carpenters (Benjamin Timbrell and Thomas Phillips) charged as follows:

August 1724	For the use of Mr. Bagutty.	
	4 ft of Firr, 5 × 4, for Trussels	o. 13*s*. 8*d*.
	By 64 ft Do., 3 × 2, for Legs.	
	7 whole Deals for Mortar Boards	o. 14*s*. 8*d*.
September 1724	For Mr. Bagutty for Trussells	
	By 8 ft of Firr, 5 × 4, 20 ft. Do.	
	3 × 2. 4 10 ft Deals.	o. 9*s*. 2*d*.

They also charged for moving 'Mr. Bagutty's Scaffold Boards' and, on 29 January 1725, for 'Strikeing [taking down] Mr. Bagutty's Scaffold'.[5]

The use of a cradle could only be envisaged for detailed work on one figure, but the evidence again suggests a scaffold set within 7 to 8 ft of the surface to be plastered. One of the plasterer's frequent tasks was to 'run' a moulding by pushing a tool with a cut-out profile of the shape required against the soft plaster adhering to the ceiling. This required freedom to walk forward unhindered for several yards across the scaffolding boards.

Frequent confusion arises over the use of moulds and modelling work *in situ*. There were some ornaments which were more quickly and accurately realised by turning them out from a mould on a table at ground level. The usual division of labour was for repetitive work to be moulded, and single features such as coats-of-arms, full-size figures or *putti* to be modelled *in situ*. Complicated ornamentation could not be created in some moulds because a great deal of undercutting was needed, but I believe the ratio of moulded work to free modelled to be something in the order of 3 : 1. The boring jobs were to create the yards of 'ovelo with eggs and anchors', the roses, leaves and paterae, and, at about 1*d*. a yard, to wash, stop, whiten, size, black or colour the work where required.

From the early 1760s there was a growing tendency to model most work, and plasterers' premises sometimes contained 'Cast Rooms' for patterns and a 'Wax Room' (where the moulds were made and, if not required as stock, melted down after use); if needed, they were stored in the 'Mould Room'.[6] All the impedimenta of a plasterer working in one of the new patent stuccoes was kept here—the vases, crests, medallions, masks, figures, griffins and paterae necessary for a dominant share of the active market for neo-classical motifs. A busy plasterer like Joseph Rose II (1745–99) also owned, at the time of his death, three sets of 75 boards and 25 poles each, 4 crosses, 2 ladders, 4 tressels (again duplicated), 30 extra poles and 7 dozen cords for fastening the scaffolding poles. There were also 'brass drawing instruments, 5 ft rules, an instrument for drawing ovals, parallel scales, 7 T-squares and a pair of caliper compasses'.[7]

4. Colvin, 1978, *Dictionary*, p. 940.
5. Westminster Reference Library, MS 419/311.
6. Christie's catalogue of Joseph Rose II's sale, 10, 12

April 1799: Beard, 1975, *Plasterwork*, p. 17.
7. *ibid*.

The Stuccoist

Apart from the moulded stucco panels created at Nonsuch by Nicholas Bellin of Modena for King Henry VIII, the use of stucco in England was virtually unknown until the early eighteenth century. However, travellers abroad had ample opportunity to observe it in Italy, Bavaria and elsewhere—it abounded in examples of great beauty and dexterity. Reference to the composition and preparation of stucco is found in the writings of Vitruvius and Pliny, and in those of later Renaissance theorists such as Vasari and Scamozzi.[8] No common formula emerges, but in southern countries marble powder was used mostly, while in those north of the Alps lime, sand and plaster in varying proportions was in use.

Sir Christopher Wren set out his own thoughts on stucco:

If there be use of stucco, I have great hopes, from some experience already had, that there are English materials to be brought by sea at an easy rate, that will afford as good plaister as is anywhere to be found in the world; and that with the mixture of cheaper ingredients than marble-meal, which was the old, and is now the modern way of Italy.[9]

One main ingredient of the stucco mixture was slaked lime. When calcium carbonate (limestone) was burned, a pure calcareous earth (calcium oxide) was obtained. The lime was 'slaked', or caused to heat and crumble, by the addition of water. The slaked lime was then mixed with fine, sharp quartz sand in the proportion of 1:1. Lime-mortar resulted and, prepared in large quantities, was kept fresh under a layer of water, and carried from site to site in tubs.

The gypsum (plaster) was obtained by mining and needed, in the eighteenth century, to be 'cooked' in an iron or copper pan. When almost at red heat, it bubbled in the pan like boiling water. As it subsided, it again resembled powdered earth. When taken from the fire, it was passed through a coarse and then a fine sieve.

The preparation of the stucco mixture was described by P N Sprengel in 1772 as follows:

The ingredients of the stucco, as previously shown are gypsum, lime and sand. The sand must be fine and contain no foreign particles. Usually the stuccoist uses only quick-lime, but in many cases the so-called spar or limestone marl renders better services, for the artist can elaborate better on finer points with this material. In addition gypsum does not bind so fast with a mixture of spar-chalk added as it does mixed with quick-lime. Every stucco-worker mixes the ingredients as he, taught by experience, sees fit. He changes sand, gypsum and lime, blended with water, into a paste. However the quality of the gypsum of binding fast, which hinders the artist from elaborating on his work of art, makes it necessary for the stucco-worker to add glue-water, for the glue-water retards the binding of the gypsum.[10]

To model the finest details it was necessary, even for the most experienced stucco-worker, to

8. Vitruvius, 1511 (Venice), *De Architectura*, VII, 2–4; Pliny, 1947 Loeb Edn., *Natural History*, XXXVI, 53–55; Scamozzi, 1615 (Venice), *Architettura*, II, 224.

9. Stephen Wren, 1750, *Parentalia*, p. 277.

10. P N Sprengel, 1772, *Tabellen, Bearbeitung de Erd-und-Steinarten Neunte Sammlung*, pp. 226–27, Berlin.

add ingredients to the stucco mixture as he prepared it in order to retard the process of setting. Besides the glue-water mentioned by Sprengel, curd, sour milk, fermented grape-juice, beer, alcohol, wine, sugar or marshmallow root powder were used. Curd, glue and almond- or nut-oil gave great pliancy; the duration of the setting was also affected by the purity of the water, the temperature of added liquids, the humidity and temperature at the worksite and by the duration of stirring the paste. To harden the stucco, alum was added, although the final density was decided by the density of the gypsum and how well it was all mixed in the preparation stages.

The stucco which projected was modelled around armatures and reinforcements of various kinds—hair, straw, canvas, wooden and metal supports and nails and iron wire. The metal parts oxidised in the mixture and the spreading rust acted as a stiffening agent.

TOOLS AND TECHNIQUES

For the preparation of the lime-sand mixture, the quenching of gypsum and mixing the main materials, a tub, a gypsum trough and pan, a scoop and gypsum bowl were used. The work was built up by gypsum paste being applied with masons' trowels and various poussir-irons (or double spatulas) and evened out, with all unnecessary material removed. A gypsum knife and scrapers with rough or fine serrated blades were used to take off surplus gypsum.

The ceiling was measured and the centre and axes marked with a charcoal pencil. The basic shape of the decoration was then drawn in roughly and the surface of the ceiling scratched over to form a key for subsequent layers. The various profiled ribs of ovals and circles were made by a template, with the required profile being drawn over the stucco by the worker. Again, Sprengel's description of moulded work is explicit; after indicating that a large store 'of modelled ornaments could be made in the leisurely hours of winter', he described the making of hollow ornaments, which saved gypsum, and how they were fixed:

> In the place where the ornament is to be fixed he puts several bigheaded nails into the wall. He drills a hole for each nail into the ornament of gypsum, and when the moulded gypsum-plaster is solid he puts the ornament on the nails and fixes them with a mixture of one third lime to two thirds gypsum. Since this mixture is made mainly from plaster it binds within a short time.[11]

Another technique used was that of press-stucco. On the site press-models of hardwood were pressed against the still ductile stucco mass. It was the technique originating in the late sixteenth century, and was of great use in creating frequently used motifs such as egg-and-tongue, laurel wreaths and ribands.

From its early use stucco has been white, but was also coloured. Sometimes ground earth-colours were added to the stucco; on other occasions the stucco-work itself was left white against a coloured background. Gilding was also applied sparingly. The use of colour,[12] however, was dependent on the attitude and temperament of both patron and artist and seems to have been practised only in countries beyond England and Ireland. Authentic examples of coloured stucco in the British Isles have still to be satisfactorily proven.

11. Spreugel, *op cit.*, pp. 230–22, *(10)*.
12. The question of colour in stucco will be examined in my forthcoming book (*c* 1982), *Stucco in Europe. See* also A F A Morel, 1973, *Andreas and Peter Anton Moosbrugger*, Bern, p. 27, citing various analyses and early sources.

Decorative and House Painting

One of the last stages in the decoration and finishing of a building was to paint certain sections of it with mythological or other imagined scenes, as well as painting all exposed wood and metal for protection against the effects of weather. The first task was the province of decorative painters, who flourished in England from the sixteenth century, the latter being accomplished by a largely anonymous host of house painters. The more ambitious usually attended an academy or drawing school.[13] A plan for an Academy of Art had been drawn up by John Evelyn as early as 1662, but it was not until 1711 that a school in London for working from life was organised. Its supporters included the German artist Sir Godfrey Kneller, the Swedish portrait painter Michael Dahl, the Venetian Giovanni Antonio Pellegrini, the French decorative artist Laguerre and the Englishmen Jonathan Richardson and Sir James Thornhill. While the school concentrated on life classes and portraiture, it had for a time as one of its members the French artist Peter Berchet, who painted the chapel ceiling at Trinity College, Oxford. Also a row developed when Kneller, the school's director, discovered that Thornhill was using the school's models to assist him in studies for the great ceilings he was painting at Greenwich.

Instruction in the academies was also supported by two influential books, Dryden's translation of Du Fresnoy's *The Art of Painting* (1695) and an English edition of Cesare Ripa's *Iconologia* (1709). They were followed from 1715 onwards by several important books on criticism and what to see abroad by Jonathan Richardson,[14] a portrait painter who taught his son-in-law, Thomas Hudson, and George Knapton. While Kneller's academy was a brave attempt to do what was done much more effectively in France, Richardson's writings and those of the 3rd Earl of Shaftesbury were of greater moment. Shaftesbury had the background of many years of travel and study and a philosophy rooted back directly to Platonism;[15] his concern with the arts and moral aspirations was, however, a great deal removed from the experience of most painters, and especially those concerned in painting the woodwork and other structural parts of a great house or church.

TOOLS

The most obvious items the painters used were various sizes of hog's-bristle and camel-hair brushes, scraping or pallet knives, earthen pots to hold the oil and ground colours, cans for various thinning oils and varnishes, and a grinding stone and muller. The stone, of a hard and close-grained consistency, was about 18 in square and heavy enough to hold steady during the processes of grinding and mixing. The muller was a hand implement (in the nature of a pestle) for working the pigment into the oil; nut-oil was used as it was held to be more durable and withstood the weather better. White lead, the principal basis of all stone colours, was in constant use.

TECHNIQUES

A useful reference to the style and colour of interior decoration in the 1660s occurs in accounts

13. An account of the early eighteenth-century academies is given by W T Whitley, 1928, *Artists and their Friends in England*, I, pp. 1–16.
14. G W Snelgrove, 1936, 'The Work and Theories of Jonathan Richardson', PhD thesis, Univ. of London.
15. J E Sweetman, 1955, 'Shaftesbury and art theory in 18th century England', PhD thesis, Univ. of London.

and instructions in the correspondence of John Cosin, Bishop of Durham, for work in the chapel at Bishop Auckland. The painter, John Baptist van Ersell, was instructed to do more work in 1664 on 'the midle rooffe of the midle Ile of his Lordshipp's Chappell at Auckland'. The groundwork of the whole roof was to be of a blue already painted therein 'bordering the flatt within, every coate with yellow, mixed with black stroakes, to showe like teeth'. The painter was also to colour 'the carved myters, and cherubims' heads, which are fixed to the roof . . . with proper coullours and shall guild with leafe gold the carved work . . . in proper places only'.

He was also to paint in stone colour two sides of a wall by the east window, and to paint the chairs and desks the colour of the new wainscot. The carpenter's work was to be painted in a walnut-tree colour, handsomely veined with fruit down the pilasters: 'the freeze blew with large gold letters'. Regrettably it has all gone, but work by the grander painters such as Verrio and Laguerre survives in reasonable quantity.[16]

One of the commissions for painting given to Antonio Verrio by Sir John Lowther, later 1st Viscount Lonsdale, was for work at Lowther Castle. Verrio's paintings were destroyed with the first Lowther in the fire of 1718; what they depicted, however, was set out by Thomas Tickell in his poem *Oxford* (1707), addressed to Richard, 2nd Viscount Lonsdale. Like all Lowthers, and indeed most Cumbrians, he had gone to Queen's College, Oxford.

> Such art as this adorns your Lowther's hall,
> Where feasting Gods carouse upon the wall,
> The nectar, which creating paint supplies,
> Intoxicates each pleas'd spectator's eyes;
> Who view, amaz'd, the figures heavenly fair,
> And think they breath the true Elysian air,
> With strokes so bold, great Verrio's hand has drawn
> The Gods in dwellings brighter than their own.

It merely restated what Verrio, Laguerre and other painters of decoration were adept at—the depiction of mythological scenes culled from a wide repertory of sources. They were set out, almost without exception, in a medium which resisted the English climate: oil on plaster.[17] Of 29 commissions carried out by Verrio and his team, 15 are known to have been executed in oil on plaster.

Before Verrio could commence work on any surface, it had to be primed with a size or thin paint to prevent absorption. The extensive Verrio archive at Burghley House records that, for the painting of the 2nd George Room (then the Drawing Room), John Collins, on 5 August 1691: 'Rec'd then of Sigr. Verrio three pounds six shillings in full for double priming the Drawing Room att 8*d*. the yard'. It was a simple and necessary technique which was learned by such as Collins in their apprenticeships to painter stainers.

In 1713 Richard Scott, a painter of the parish of St Botolph's, Bishopsgate, contracted to paint at St Alphege, Greenwich, one of the 'Fifty New Churches' designed by Nicholas Hawksmoor:[18]

16. *Surtees Society*, 1872, Vol. 55, pp. 361–62.
17. Croft-Murray, 1962, *Painting*, I, pp. 275–76.

18. Lambeth Palace Library, MS, 2703, p. 10.

> For every yard of painting upon the Ironwork in and
> about the said Church reduced to Superficial of flatt
> Measure to be done in the best manner with Good Red &
> White Lead and Linseed oyl 4 times over One Shilling   o. 1. o.
> For every yard of plain Colour done 4 times over with
> good red & white lead and Linseed Oyl after the best
> manner upon the woodwork in the Inside and Outside of
> the sd Church at Eightpence   o. o. 8.

The tasks of North Stainer and Roger Askew working at St Martin-in-the-Fields Church, London, 1721–24, were as onerous: 1721 'By 490⅔ yards of Painting 3 times in Oyl at 4½d p. yard. £9. 4. o.'[19] Three years later Roger Askew coloured the vane and ball on the spire '5 Times over yellow Colour & Flatt Gilding it. £40.'

The painting of items several times over was occasioned partly by a need for a durable finish but as much by the difficulty of achieving an even colour from the pigment suspended in the oil. We have noted the problems of grinding colours (*see* p. 37): they are given emphasis by payments in the Holkham archives. When the Earl of Leicester's great house was ready for painting in the late 1750s, John Neale was paid for 61 days' work in mixing and grinding colours at 2s. 6d. a day.[20] Some idea of the range of items needed may also be gained by Streatfield and Caldwall's bill for painting in the Strangers' wing at Holkham in 1764:[21]

> To Streatfield and Caldwell for 17Ct. 2Qr. 4lb. of Ground White Lead at 35s. p. Ct.
> Ditto, Ground in Nut Oil at 65s. 1 Ct. of dry White Lead at 27s. 2Ct. 2Qrs. 16 lb. of
> Red Lead at 24s. 8 Ct. 1 Qr. 2 lb. of Spanish Brown at 30s. 1 Ct. 1 Qr. 12 lb. Whiting
> at 3s. 45 lb. of Lamb black at 18d. Turpentine Oil. 14½ lb. of Copperas at 9d. 13 lb. of
> Sugar of Lead at 2s 6d. 12 oz. of Prussian Blue at 2s. 4 lb. of Stone Oker at 6d. 40
> Gallons of Linseed Oil at 3s. 4d. 2½ Quarts of Nut Oil at 3s. a Quart. 11½ dozen
> Brushes. Cases, Package etc. Used for painting in the Strangers' Wing etc. £86. 16s. od.

The use of distemper predated that of oil and varnish. Spanish white, which is frequently mentioned in eighteenth-century archives, or whiting was the common distemper colour, broken into water to which strong size had been added. It was used by plasterers to whiten finished ceilings. The house painter was also adept at graining and marbling in imitation of woods and marbles. Imitation wainscot became popular in the late eighteenth century and was obtained by giving the painted work a coat in oil of a brownish tone, the colour being thicker than usual; this was then scratched over with bone combs of varying degrees of coarseness, leaving the ground visible. It was then varnished.

This final process of varnishing required great care and the use of good material, the best copal varnish, to bring out the colours of the work. Two or three coats were applied, especially to marbling, each coat being well rubbed down to obtain an even surface and a high degree of polish. Wainscoting was prepared for receiving coats of varnish by being first sized to prevent

19. Westminster Reference Library, MS, 419/311.
20. Holkham Archives, Country Accounts (8), 1 March 1758; 13 March 1759.
21. *ibid.*, Building Accounts (27), p. 40, 13 September 1764.

the rise of the grain caused when it came into contact with water. A good painter was also associated with the practice of paper-hanging, and some included gilding in their repertory. Gilding was, however, a task given frequently to specialists, especially those who had close association with leading cabinet-makers.

Wallpaper was fastened to a wooden framework set over the surface of the wall. The worker stretched fine canvas on the frames, and then the wallpaper was applied to the canvas. Chinese papers brought to England by the East India Company established the fashion for wallpaper in the late seventeenth century. They were fixed in this way, and it has been possible in several cases of impending destruction of the setting to remove the lengths to other rooms or museums.

The gilder specialised in the two processes of oil and water gilding. The object to be oil-gilded was sized to present a tacky surface to which the gold leaf adhered. In water gilding, preparation of the surface was accomplished by building up layers of white gesso or plaster; when this had dried it was given a coat of coloured bole—an earth combined with iron oxide—and allowed to dry. At the gilding stage, the bole was wetted with sized water so that the gold leaf could adhere. The finished surface was then varnished several times. The process was best described by Thomas Sheraton, writing in 1803:[22]

> In laying on the gold leaf, no water must be left under the gold, but it must be blown out, as much as the nature of the case will admit of; or otherwise, when the cotton wool is applied to burnish it with, the gold will rub off. After thus burnishing, proceed to a second lay or coat of gold as at the first, which will cover all the defects of the first lay occasioned by burnishing, and having waited till this second coat be dry, burnish as before; and if there be any defects of gold, such places must be repaired. Some recommend to have the work done three times over, but twice will do as well, if carefully done.

'Double Burnished Gold' is encountered frequently in eighteenth-century accounts. Many of the ornaments which were gilded were made in 'Composition', a mixture of whiting, resin and size, poured into, and cast from, moulds.

In Polished Marble

The chimneypiece was an important item in house furnishing and considerable care was lavished on its appearance and position by patrons and statuaries alike.

The materials used most frequently in their construction were Italian marble and carved wood. Genoa was the centre through which most marble was exported; John Evelyn, writing in his *Diary* (19 September 1676), tells how he visited 'Lambeth, to that rare magazine of marble, to take order for chimneypieces, etc., for Mr. Godolphin's house. The owner of the works had built himself a pretty dwelling-house; this Dutchman had contracted with the Genoese for all their marble.' However, there were other sources of a more modest nature in Spain, Egypt,

22. Thomas Sheraton, 1803, *Cabinet Dictionary*, p. 227; a useful summary of the existing literature with critical comments is given by John Fowler and John   Cornforth, 1974, *English Decoration in the 18th Century*, pp. 174–210.

England and Scotland.[23] In 1672 several 'Scotch marble' chimneypieces were installed by John Lampen in the principal rooms of the Duke of Lauderdale's house at Ham in Surrey.[24] It was in Genoa, however, from where two elaborate black and yellow marble chimneypieces were shipped in 1683 for use by the Earl of Rutland, costing £742. 3s.;[25] it was a costly transaction, typical of many, and most marble was fashioned in the statuaries' yards around Hyde Park Corner.[26] John van Nost, the Cheere, Collins and Carter families all had their yards near to each other, absorbing and extending into each other's domains as deaths occurred.

The architectural forms which made up the majority of chimneypieces often gave them their name; *The Chimneypiece Maker's Daily Assistant* (1766) divided the types into: (1) the architrave type, and those with (2) trussed pilasters, or (3) caryatid or terminal supports or columns to support the mantelpiece. Chimneypieces were made up of one or two storeys, or, to adopt the terms used by Isaac Ware in his *A Complete Body of Architecture* (1756), were of 'simple' or 'continued' type. The former defined a chimneypiece terminated at its cornice (*see* pl. 139), or by a pediment or other ornament. The 'continued' chimneypiece had an upper structure of stucco or wood, or, in certain important examples, of marble (*see* pls. 136 and 141). The latter was the more important but needed, for its maximum effect, to be related to the overdoor panels of the room it was in (*see* pl. 18).

Some of the principles which, it was alleged, governed size were also set out by Robert Morris in his *Lectures on Architecture* (1751). His first rule was as follows:

> To find the height of the opening of the chimney from any given magnitude of a room, add the length and height of the room together, and extract the square root of that sum, and half that root will be the height of the chimney.

The breadth was established from adding the length, breadth and height of the room and extracting half the square root of the sum; the depth was one-fourth of the breadth and height of the chimney. Sir William Chambers was, however, more general in his dimensions, and preferred two chimneypieces in large rooms 'regularly placed, at equal distances from the centre of the wall in which they both are placed'. The farther the chimneypieces were from a door the better, and they were rarely placed on front window walls due to weakening of the walls by carrying shafts as well as the windows, and the consequent appearance of the chimney on the dominant elevation.

As the eighteenth century progressed, the 'continued' form of chimneypiece was less used, although there are notable examples by Robert Adam (Harewood and Syon) and by James Stuart (Shugborough). There was less attempt to secure rare marbles than in the earlier 'Palladian years', but the *Builder's Magazine* (1774) noted 'Siena was common, also the green Anglesea kind and green and white Egyptian'. Painting on marble was also noted by George Richardson in his *A New Collection of Chimneypieces* (1781), and Robert Adam had the fine example in the Red Drawing Room at Syon House inset with ormolu. The bill for several of the

23. A list of marbles in use is given by Isaac Ware, 1756, *A Complete Body of Architecture*.

24. John G Dunbar, 1975, 'The Building Activities of the Duke and Duchess of Lauderdale, 1670–82', *The Archaeological Journal*, **132**, p. 274.

25. Historical Manuscripts Commission, *MSS. of the Earl of Rutland at Belvoir*.

26. 'The Man at Hyde Park Corner: Sculpture by John Cheere, 1709–87', Temple Newsam House, Leeds, Exhibition Catalogue (1974), pp. 1–5.

Syon chimneypieces survives, submitted in 1768 by Thomas Carter on behalf of the late Benjamin Carter and himself.[27] It was for work in the period from April 1761, and shows they executed those in the Dining Room and the Red Drawing Room to Adam's design.[28] Citation of the bill for the well-known example in the Drawing Room shows the relationship between costs for the marble and for fashioning it:

	£	s	d
1766 March 1. To a Corinthian Column chimn Piece as Designed for Robert Adam Esqr for the Drawing Room at Sion fully inriched according to order.			
To the Statuary Marble, and Masons Work (Marble, £92.)	118.	4.	3.
To drawing and Modeling the ornaments for the Founder. Carving the Mouldings reverse to receive the Brasswork. Carvers time letting in, fitting and working the said Ornaments together	144.	6.	6.
To Masons time putting up do.	15.	6.	9.
To pollishers time assisting the Masons	3.	19.	4.
Lodging for them all	1.	1.	6.

Figure 13 Designs for chimneypieces. Sir William Chambers, 1768, A Treatise on Civil Architecture.

27. Syon Archives, D/1/8.

28. Beard, 1978, *Adam*, col. pl. 9, pl. 84.

The Dining Room 'continued' chimneypiece cost £240, but was amended subsequently by Carter at the Duke of Northumberland's orders 'on Acct of Depth of the Chim'. It was given a whole Truss, with its enrichments to the front, at an additional cost of £51. 5s. 0d. Many days' work also went into the additional tasks of veneering marble slabs with inlays of other marbles; Carter charged for inlaying in 'Jasper, Sienna and the Deep Grecian Verd'—336 days at 3s. a day. The cement used was one of the Duke's invention. Some further idea of costs may be obtained from John Hinchcliff's bill of 1775 for chimneypieces at another Adam house, 20 St James's Square, London. [29] A Pilaster one was £128, an Architrave one for a small dressing-room £42, a Truss chimneypiece £150, and a column chimneypiece £150.

The lucrative trade in chimneypieces soon attracted the attentions of the manufacturers Matthew Boulton and Josiah Wedgwood.[30] Cast-tin or pewter ornaments stamped in relief were supplied to builders—when painted, they had the appearance of carving. The demand for friezes and tablets of classical subjects suggested to Wedgwood that his moulded ware in plaques and panels designed by Flaxman and others could be used. His enterprise, however, was not welcomed by Chambers, Wyatt and others, and in October 1778 he wrote:

> I know they are much cheaper at that price than marble, and every way better, but people will not compare things which they conceive to be made out of moulds, or perhaps stamped at a blow like the Birmingham articles, with carving in natural stones where they are certain no moulding, casting, or stamping can be done.[31]

Wedgwood also had to compete with the fashion for inlaying chimneypieces with coloured compositions other than marble. Peter Bossi, who worked in Dublin in the last quarter of the eighteenth century, specialised in such work, but the profusion of chimneypieces fashioned in this technique suggests many other workers. Adam also noted in his *Works in Architecture*[32] that two chimneypieces at Old Derby House, Grosvenor Square, were in statuary marble inlaid with scagliola. He had also provided strong competition to many marble workers by those he designed for the Carron Iron Company to be cast in metal; many of the fine moulds still survive in the company's possession.

In the early nineteenth century it was, however, the chimneypiece in cast iron (like those made by the Carron Company) which continued, and increased, in popularity. Coalbrookdale and other centres continued to produce cast examples throughout Queen Victoria's reign, and the Birmingham founders' pattern books abounded in examples and related equipment.[33] Soon the 'continued' type returned with a profusion of carving, inset oil-on-canvas paintings and trappings worthy of belonging to the age of King Charles I.

29. NLW, Williams-Wynn Archives, 17/12.
30. Eliza Meteyard, 1865–6, *The Life of Josiah Wedgwood*, II, p. 372.
31. Ann Finer and George Savage, 1965, *Selected Letters of Josiah Wedgwood*, letter of 6 October 1778.
32. 1773–78, *The Works in Architecture of Robert and James Adam*, II, No. 1, p. 3.
33. Michael Owen, 1977, *Antique Cast Iron*, reproduces many pages from nineteenth-century pattern books.

59 (*below*) SUDBURY HALL, Derbyshire. The Saloon, *c* 1675, painting *c* 1691 (photograph: A F Kersting).

Robert Bradbury and James Pettifer, London plasterers, provided the plasterwork ceiling in 1675, a combination of moulded and *in situ* modelled work. The painting 'The Four Seasons' was done some 15 years later by Louis Laguerre. The wainscoting was by Edward Pearce (1678), and Mr Gervase Jackson-Stops has suggested that its pattern was derived from an early seventeenth-century French design by Jean Barbet copied by Robert Pricke in 1674. The portrait over the door is of the patron, George Vernon (1635–1702), by Michael Wright, painted about 1660.

58 (*above*) RAYNHAM HALL, Norfolk. Ceiling of the Belisarius Room, *c* 1660, paintings *c* 1730 (photograph: A F Kersting).

The central oval built up over a timber core has its soffit encrusted with closely packed fruit. Careful examination of the ceiling shows that the oval was moulded in eight sections, two to each segment. The centre medallion, depicting Fame seated before a bust of Alexander Pope, was painted by William Kent. The greyhound and stag in the adjacent panels are the supporters to the Townshend arms.
Lit: John Harris, 1963, *Archaeological Journal*, CXVIII, p. 281.

60 (*facing page*) SUDBURY HALL, Derbyshire.
Great Staircase, plasterwork, 1675, painting *c* 1691
(photograph: A F Kersting).

This view of the soffit below the landing and of
the higher ceiling shows again a combination of
plasterwork by James Pettifer and painting 15
years later by Louis Laguerre. The soffit painting
depicts 'Leda and the Swan' and the main ceiling
'The Rape of Orithyia'. The staircase balustrade at
the left was carved by Edward Pearce (*see* pl. 27).

61 HAMPSTEAD MARSHALL, Berkshire. Drawing by
Edward Goudge of the Dining Room ceiling,
1686, *dest.* 1718 (collection and photograph:
Bodleian Library, Oxford, MS, Gough Drawings,
a. 2 ff. 21–22).

Captain William Winde wrote on the centre oval
of this drawing 'June 22th: 1686: This Drauft for
the Dineing Roome att Hampstead Marshall
marked. A. allowed of by me Will Winde.' In a
letter to his cousin, Lady Mary Bridgeman, on 12
July 1688 Winde, in indicating Goudge's
capabilities, noted that he had been employed by
him for six or seven years and that he was 'an
excellent drauffteman and mackes all his desines
hime selfe . . .'.

62 BELTON HOUSE, Lincolnshire. Staircase ceiling,
c 1688 (photograph: *C Life*).

A further letter from Captain William Winde to
his cousin (*see* pl. 61 above) of 8 February 1690
noted Goudge's presence at 'Sr. John
Brownlowes', that is, Belton. He provided ceilings
in the Chapel and several other rooms in addition
to that over the staircase (*see* pl. 44).

63 (*above*) DUNSTER CASTLE, Somerset. Detail of Dining Room ceiling dated MDCLXXXI (1681) (photograph: Angelo Hornak).

This elaborate ceiling, which may be by Goudge (there is also a splendid staircase in the house (1683), which again may be by Edward Pearce), was set up by Colonel Francis Luttrell and his wife, Mary. Luttrell fought at the Battle of Sedgmoor in 1685, a conflict in which the architect Captain William Winde was also involved. Through their respective careers they may have known one another and Luttrell been brought into contact with Winde's team. In 1688 Winde indicated that he had employed Goudge six or seven years. The matter must remain speculative in the absence of documentation.
Lit: Geoffrey Beard, 1979, 'Edward Goudge: The Beste Master in England', *National Trust Studies*, p. 24.

64 (*below*) GUBBINS, Hertfordshire. Drawing by James Gibbs, *c* 1728. *Ashmolean Museum, Oxford*, Gibbs Drawings, IV, 40 (photograph: museum).

This drawing, inscribed 'Ceiling for Mr. Sambrooks at Gubbins' shows the part the architect took in directing the stuccoists. The ornamentation is carefully sketched in but enough freedom is left to the artist to make individual expressions and the exact curves of the fronded stucco. The house was destroyed *c* 1836.

65 SUTTON SCARSDALE, Derbyshire. Stucco figure of Diana, *c* 1724—house partly demolished 1920 (photograph: Kerry Downes).

This stucco panel has been exposed to the sky since 1920, when some parts of the house were demolished and other rooms (*see* pl. 16) shipped to America. A lead rising-plate (now lost) recorded that Francesco Vassalli and 'Albert' Artari worked as stuccoists. Examination of the panel *in situ* shows the inserted nails and stippling of the background, which acted as 'keys' to the final stucco coating.

66 STONELEIGH ABBEY, Warwickshire. Saloon, detail of capitals, *c* 1725 (photograph: Courtauld Institute of Art).

The Italian stuccoists gathered at the house 1724–25 following their work at Sutton Scarsdale, and at the time when they were also engaged at Ditchley (*see* pls. 67 and 68). This view of work in the Saloon shows their capacity for skilled execution of detailed decorative requirements in stucco and scagliola.

67 DITCHLEY HOUSE, Oxfordshire. Saloon, detail of ceiling, *c* 1725 (photograph: A F Kersting).

The *stuccatori* Francesco Vassalli, Francesco Serena and the two Artaris worked together as partners at this house under the supervision of James Gibbs and Francis Smith. The accounts show that they charged £105 'for finishing the Saloon entirely'. The medallion head depicts the god Mercury.

68 DITCHLEY HOUSE, Oxfordshire. Saloon, detail of stucco overmantel, *c* 1725 (photograph: A F Kersting).

The portrait medallion depicts Cybele, the goddess representing the fecundity of nature. A similar medallion by Vassalli appears over 30 years later in the White Hall at Hagley, Worcestershire. It indicates the dependence by the stuccoist on engravings, frequently outmoded by continued use.

69 (*above*) St Martin-in-the-Fields Church, London. S. Gallery, support of entablature No. 3 from W. end, *c* 1725 (photograph: National Monuments Record).

Chrysostom Wilkins was the plasterer of all those details in St Martin's which were not executed by the stuccoist Giovanni Bagutti. Wilkins' work included these supports, with *putti*, brackets and moulding. He had submitted a slightly lower estimate than Gibbs' favourite plasterer, Isaac Mansfield, and in consequence was given the commission.

70 (*below*) Barnsley Park, Gloucestershire. Oak Room, detail of stucco overmantel, *c* 1730 (photograph: Courtauld Institute of Art).

This overmantel contains a possible portrait of Mrs Brereton Bourchier, mother-in-law of Barnsley Park's builder, Henry Perrot. His wife was the heiress of Brereton Bourchier, and a niece of the 1st Duke of Chandos. The duke had employed Bagutti and Artari at Canons in about 1720–22, and they seem the most likely stuccoists for this further baroque composition. It is almost identical to one at Hall Place (*see* pl. 71), and has similarities with chimneypieces at Christ Church Mansion, Ipswich.

71 (*below*) Hall Place, Maidenhead, Berkshire. Drawing Room, detail of stucco overmantel, *c* 1734 (photograph: *C Life*).

The differences between this overmantel and that at Barnsley Park (*see* pl. 70) are that the bas-relief bust at Barnsley may represent Mrs Bourchier, while that at Hall Place is not a portrait but a Niobe type. Niobe was, in Greek mythology, turned into a rock, which may be a reason for the scagliola background to the head and swag of foliage.

72 (*below*) Clandon Park, Surrey. Entrance Hall, detail of the ceiling, *c* 1730 (photograph: A F Kersting).

This great composition, attributed to Bagutti and Artari, has its centre based on the representation of Hercules and Iole by the Carracci in The Farnese Gallery. Engravings of this great Roman ceiling had been issued by Carlo Cesio in 1657, by Pietro Aguila in 1674, and by French artists such as Nicolas Mignard. This, together with the ceilings by Pietro da Cortona in the Palazzo Pitti in Florence, were but two of a wide repertory of sources adapted by the stuccoists for later use in England and elsewhere.

The figure (left) feigning to support the moulding would have its right arm and leg built on wooden armatures for support.

73 MOOR PARK, Hertfordshire. Ceiling of the
White Drawing Room, *c* 1730 (photograph: A F
Kersting).

When Sir Edward Gascoigne of Parlington in
Yorkshire made a journey south to London, he
visited Canons and Moor Park and encountered
the stucco-work of Giovanni and Giuseppe Artari.
A drawing in the Gibbs collection at Oxford
(Ashmolean Museum, IV, 24) also has an
endorsement on the back 'For Mr. Baguti att
More Parke near Rikmonsworth in Hertfordshire'.
There seems, therefore, no reason to attribute this
fine ceiling depicting Dionysus and Ceres, and that
surrounding Sleter's paintings (*see* pl. 100), to the
Franchinis, as suggested by Christopher Hussey
(1965, *ECH: Early Georgian*, p. 44).

74 (*left*) TEMPLE NEWSAM HOUSE, Yorkshire.
Long Gallery, centre of the ceiling, *c* 1745–47
(photograph: National Monuments Record).

On 27 June 1746 Thomas Perritt of York was paid
£180. 10*s*. 'upon acct of ye Gallery' at Temple
Newsam. Two years later he received another
£19. 0*s*. 9*d*., and his total bill for work at the house
(1741–47) amounted to £419. 16*s*. 1*d*. He was
assisted by Joseph Rose senior (*c* 1723–80).
   The 13 medallions of the Long Gallery ceiling,
charged for at 10*s*. 6*d*. each, have been identified as
George I, George II, his Queen, children and
children-in-law.
Lit: Jacob Simon, 1974, *Leeds Arts Calendar*,
no. 74.

75 RADCLIFFE CAMERA, Oxford. Ceiling of the
Dome, 1744 (photograph: A F Kersting).

James Gibbs assembled a talented team for the
decoration of the important library he designed for
the trustees of Dr John Radcliffe. From the
detailed accounts we know that John Phillips did
the timberwork, and Giuseppe Artari, Charles
Stanley and Thomas Roberts the plasterwork.

Ironwork was by Robert Bakewell, with carved
woodwork by the Linnells. Gibbs approved the
submission of the estimates, made according to his
specifications of lathing and execution, and the
building was completed by 1748.
Lit: S G Gilliam, ed., 1953–54, 'The Building
Accounts of the Radcliffe Camera, Oxford', *Oxford
Historical Society*, XIII.

76 (*below*) KIRTLINGTON, Oxfordshire. Dining Room, detail of the ceiling plasterwork, *c* 1748 (re-erected *Metropolitan Museum of Art, New York*) (photograph: museum).

Sir Francis Dashwood's account book lists a payment on 12 January 1747 of £119 to Thomas Roberts of Oxford. As he had worked with Charles Stanley (*see* pl. 75) prior to 1746, it was natural that the late Mrs K A Esdaile should detect his hand in the Kirtlington plasterwork (*C Life*, 2, 11 October 1936). As Stanley and Roberts only received £232-odd for eight ceilings at the Radcliffe Camera, the £119 paid to Roberts may represent payment for all the work at Kirtlington. *Lit:* Ingrid Roscoe, January 1980, *Apollo*, pp. 22–9.

77 GREAT WITLEY CHURCH, Worcestershire. Detail of ceiling, *c* 1748 (photograph: Courtauld Institute of Art).

In 1747 the heirs of the 1st Duke of Chandos, unable to maintain the great estate at Canons after his death (1744), auctioned the contents of the house and demolished the buildings. The auction catalogue (Greater London Record Office, 262/13) indicated that the 23 inset paintings were by Antonio Bellucci (1654–1726), completed before 1720. When the 2nd Lord Foley acquired these paintings at the sale, it is assumed that, to set them up at Great Witley, his plasterer took 'squeezes' of the original ceiling at Canons, and papier mâché and plaster impressions were then made. The ceiling in the church does not entirely fit the new setting—two of the small Bellucci panels are almost concealed by the organ case (also from Canons) at the W. end. Dr Richard Pococke saw the church on 22 September 1756 and stated that 'the whole church above and on the sides is richly adorn'd with papier mâché gilt in imitation of the finest carvings'.

When restoration of the ceiling was in progress in 1975, a piece of paper with eighteenth-century German printing was found at the back of one of the ceiling ornaments.
Lit: F J B Watson, 1954, 'A Venetian Settecento Chapel in the English Countryside', *Arte Veneta*, pp. 295–302.

78 HOLKHAM, Norfolk. The Hall ceiling, *c* 1760 (photograph: Courtauld Institute of Art).

This great room (46 × 70 × 43 ft high) was inspired by Palladio's plan of a Roman basilica. The Ionic columns of Derbyshire alabaster are after the Temple of Fortuna Virilis at Rome, the ornaments of the cove from the Pantheon of Agrippa, and the ceiling taken from Inigo Jones. The plasterwork by Thomas Clark of Westminster was completed after 1759.

79 RAGLEY HALL, Warwickshire. Hall ceiling, *c* 1756 (photograph: A F Kersting).

The Hall, one of the least-known works of James Gibbs, was executed some years after his death (1754). When Dr Pococke visited the house on 28 September 1756, he recorded that it was 'just new modelled and embellished with ornaments in stucco'. Three years later, in July and September 1759, the Earl of Hertford wrote to his friend Horace Walpole that 'Snr Artario' was working on a coloured design for the Ragley Saloon. It would suggest that Artari was the author of the ceiling shown in this view, executed four years before he left England finally for Cologne, where he died in 1769.
Lit: Beard, 1975, *Plasterwork*, pp. 68–69.

80 (*bottom left*) CROOME COURT, Worcestershire. Detail of ceiling of the Tapestry Room, 1763 (re-erected *Metropolitan Museum of Art, New York*) (photograph: museum).

The ceiling was executed by Joseph Rose with hardly any change from the Robert Adam drawing (Sir John Soane's Museum, London, vol. 11, No. 37) dated 'Janry 1763'. The Croome Archives contain detailed bills by Rose, who charged £48 for the ceiling. The ceiling was re-erected at the Metropolitan Museum of Art, New York, as the gift of the Kress Foundation (1958–59).

81 (*facing page*) SYON HOUSE, Middlesex, Long Gallery, detail of the centre of the ceiling, *c* 1766 (photograph: A F Kersting).

Robert Adam had made designs for this ceiling as early as August 1761 and (as executed) in August 1763. Space was allowed in Joseph Rose's plasterwork to incorporate paintings, which are probably by Francesco Zuccarelli. The complex patterning of the ceiling was part of the architect's method to treat the long, narrow space of the Jacobean gallery in a balanced and considered way (*see also* col. pl. 14).

Enrichments for a Flat Ceiling.

Frets or Guillochis of Various Sorts.

Profile of the Ceiling above.

Enrichments for Soffits of Arches, or Arcs Doubleaux.

W. Chambers Delin.   C. Grignion Sculp.

82 (*facing page*) ORNAMENTS FOR CIRCULAR COVED
AND OTHER CEILINGS AND ARCHES, from Sir
William Chambers, 1759, *A Treatise on the
Decorative Part of Civil Architecture*
(photographs: Victoria and Albert Museum).

The overtones of Roman decoration are apparent
in the details recommended by Chambers—the
'S.P.Q.R.' abbreviating *Senatus Populusque
Romanus*, and the inset paintings. However,
Chambers himself does not seem to have adopted
the patterns within domed buildings (York House,
or Marylebone parish church). He was displaying
his learning and the fact that he 'measured, with
the utmost accuracy . . . many ancient and most
celebrated buildings, both at Rome, and in other
parts of Europe . . .' (*see also* pl. 10).

83 DRAWING FOR A CEILING, by James Wyatt
(1746–1815). Pen, ink and watercolour, *c* 1775
(collection and photograph: Victoria and Albert
Museum, Inv. No. 7231 (1–42)).

This design bears some resemblance in patterning
to the Boudoir ceiling Wyatt created for Lord
Brownlow at Belton House, Lincolnshire, about
1776. Wyatt, however, had an extensive country
house practice (a number of his commissions have
been demolished across the years). The design is,
therefore, for 'an unknown house'—an indication
of what Wyatt had learned successfully in Italy as
Chambers and Robert Adam had done a few years
before him. The plasterer Joseph Rose worked for
Wyatt at a number of London and country houses
and would have been the ceiling's executant.

84 ARBURY HALL, Warwickshire. Vaulted window bay, *c* 1786 (photograph: A F Kersting).

The Saloon (*see* col. pl. 16) was plastered by William Hanwell for Sir Roger Newdigate (1719–1806) in about 1786. The room owed much to Sir Roger's interest in Gothic architecture, a pursuit assisted over many years by the architect Henry Keene, and by careful observation. Some of the inspiration for this splendid vaulted bay came from the Henry VII Chapel at Westminster Abbey.

PART II

Magnificent Building

'The Three chief Principles of Magnificent
Building, viz. Solidity, Conveniency and
Ornament.'

Sir Balthazar Gerbier, 1662

[1]
For Crown and Court
1660–1710

The King's Works

John Evelyn recorded in his diary for 27 October 1664 a conversation with King Charles II when he had presented him with copies of his translation of Fréart and his *Sylva*: 'I presented him with both, and then laying it on ye window-stool, he with his own hands, design'd to me the plot for the future building of Whitehall, together with the rooms of state and other particulars.' A mass of seventeenth-century drawings for the Palace have survived, for the notion of its creation had been cherished not only by Charles II, but by his father. The drawings,[1] distributed between Worcester College, Oxford, Chatsworth and the British Library, are in the hand of John Webb and fall into two groups. They show that, in the first scheme, the Palace was to be realised in accordance with Inigo Jones's ideas of the 1630s.[2] The second scheme was recast by Webb and moved away from the early pencillings. Charles I had not lived to build it, and when his son took up the idea, as related by Evelyn, only Jones's Banqueting House (1619–22), a fragment of a greater conception, was in existence.

In 1669, when Sir Christopher Wren was first involved, Whitehall was the chief royal palace in London, and a sprawling complex of buildings, partly Tudor and partly Stuart in date. When the rebuilding was contemplated, Wren had informed himself what all the early ideas amounted to. He also had the continuity of the craftsmen, many of whom had worked for Jones and for Sir John Denham, his predecessor from 1660 as Surveyor-General of the King's Works.[3] Of the many drawings made, only two have survived (All Souls College, Oxford), and none of the work they represent was carried out. It was to be 1685–86 before Wren built a long new wing for James II, containing a suite of apartments for the queen, a Roman Catholic chapel for her use and some offices. Meanwhile, Charles II had other work for the craftsmen under Wren's control.

In 1668 the king began to feel that a new King's House at Newmarket was necessary if he was to enjoy the sport of horse-racing there in any style or comfort. One of the first tasks which had faced Inigo Jones when he succeeded Simon Basil as Surveyor-General in 1615 was to enlarge the King's House there by a lodging for Charles, Prince of Wales. It is not certain that Wren himself had anything to do with the New House, which was erected by William Samwell (1628–76) about 1668, but the craftsmen of the Works were employed there, and he must have had exact knowledge of its progress from the monthly meetings held to authorise all accounts.

1. Margaret Whinney, 1946, 'John Webb's Drawings for Whitehall Palace', *Walpole Soc*, XXXI; John Harris, 1972, *Catalogue, RIBA Drawings Collection: Inigo Jones and John Webb*; Colvin, 1976, *King's Works*, V, pp. 263–304 (account by Professor Kerry Downes).
2. Sir John Summerson, 1966, *Inigo Jones*, pp. 128–34.
3. *Wren Soc*, VII, p. 72.

At these meetings, however, the emphasis was on the extensive works the craftsmen were conducting at Windsor Castle.

WINDSOR CASTLE

The antiquity of Windsor appealed to Charles II and, after his accession, he was soon contemplating its possibilities as well as those of Whitehall. The dramatic hilltop site afforded scenic and picturesque possibilities beyond those of any royal palace in England, or in the France of his rival, King Louis XIV. Hugh May rebuilt the block on the north side in brick, with stone dressings, and this contained most of the new staterooms. He was careful not to disturb the general character of the medieval buildings, but it was the interiors which were more important. In the course of about nine years, the king was to spend at least £190 000 on the new works, and, under May's direction, the painter Antonio Verrio and his assistants[4] were to paint some 20 ceilings, 3 staircases, the chapel and the hall. Most of these decorations[5] were swept away in the work Wyatville did for George IV about 1824.

The entrance to the royal apartments was made by two staircases named after the king and his queen. The Queen's Great Staircase was built first and stood in a painted hall; as the first grand painted staircase executed in this country, it must have made a tremendous visual impact on visitors entering from the low, columned vestibules. On its walls in about 1678 Verrio and his team painted the stories of Phaeton's sisters changing into trees and Cygnus being changed into a swan. Eight figures in niches were 'copper gilded' by René Cousin and, in the dome far above, Apollo was depicted granting permission to Phaeton to drive the chariot of the Sun.

The later of the two blocks May built contained the King's Staircase, the Chapel Royal and St George's Hall. The King's Staircase was similar to the present arrangement at Chatsworth where, from a hall, flights rise to left and right and return to meet on an upper landing. Again, the roof was domed. On the walls 'The Four Ages of the World' were painted and the giants battled in the frescoes overhead. In the royal bedchambers Alexander Fort, a well-known London master joiner, provided screens of cedar and brass wire to shield the beds, and elsewhere Grinling Gibbons and Henry Phillips decorated down from cornice to wall with carved-wood flowers, fruits, shells and other ornaments.[6] Their work complemented the theme of Verrio's ceiling paintings and was disposed (particularly in the King's Eating Room) with great flair.

It appears from Wren's examination of Verrio's bills that the queen was not above interfering with the designs chosen. Wren said that 'For the worke of the Queen's Round Closett at Windsor I made noe Contract, Her Majesty haveing changed the first Designe, that which is now done, wch is fuller of Figures, though £300 is demanded I hope I doe not under valew it at £250.0.0.' This was the Queen's Drawing Room, on the ceiling of which an 'Assembly of the Gods' was painted. Verrio and Gibbons also enriched the King's Chapel with Verrio's paintings on ceilings, wall and altar-piece and Gibbons's carvings done in 'white natural wood without varnish'. Cousin did some gilding, and the whole rich effect was completed by unseen organs behind the altar, a 'contrivance' much liked by Evelyn.

4. Colvin, 1976, *King's Works*, V, p. 320.
5. Shown in engravings by W Pyne, 1819, *Royal Residences*, reproduced by W H St John Hope, 1914, *Windsor Castle*, 2 vols.
6. Colvin, 1976, *King's Works*, V, p. 325–26; David Green, 1964, *Grinling Gibbons*, p. 43.

In the King Henry VIII Chapel, Verrio's work amounted to £1000—he had been paid £1050 for the King's Chapel scheme. Wren noted that 'For Henry the 8th Chapell at Windsor the Contract was £1,000, it is not fully finished, for what there is done is entered in Windsor Bookes'.[7] In 1680–82 Gibbons did a considerable amount of carving in the chapel, for which he charged a little over £498; Verrio for his part had to wait for six years for £300 of his £1000 due to the death of Charles II and delay before he could depict in paint the new king, James II, enthroned in allegorical splendour.[8]

In these years Wren was involved with two major preoccupations—heading the Office of Works organisation which dealt with the royal buildings, and supervising the erection of St Paul's Cathedral. The richest work in the interior of St Paul's falls into the three categories of wood and stone-carving, including the organ cases, the metal grilles and gates and the paintings on the inside of the dome.

ST PAUL'S CATHEDRAL

By 1696–97 Grinling Gibbons was at work carving in stone, oak and limewood in the completed choir, including the case and screen of the Great West Organ. Charles Hopson, later Master Joiner to the Office of Works, prepared certain models: for the seats in the choir and one each for the altar, organ-case, choir organ-case and the Dean's seat.[9] Some of Gibbon's carving, skilful as it was, however, did give concern as to its price. In July 1696 John Oliver, Assistant Surveyor at St Paul's, was instructed to compare the measurement Gibbons had set down in his bill with his own specially taken measurement; Gibbons had to put prices to Oliver's measurement and no money was to be paid him until this was agreed. In September 1696, Wren was instructed to adjust certain of the prices with Gibbons, particularly in respect of certain work on the organ-cases.

Gibbons had started by carving flowers in stone high in the four spandrels beneath the dome, and continued with the festoons beneath the windows. His greatest surviving work, however, is in the woodcarving in the choir, which was crowned originally with a great screen supporting the organ-case. Except for the carved angels on the organ-case, there was, in deference to Protestant taste, no interior figure-sculpture; the interior thereby lacked the full appeal to the senses typical of its baroque counterparts on the Continent. It all had to be left to Gibbons's swirling foliage, doves, pelicans and emblems, none of which was allowed to project more than 2 in.

The work consisted in providing two banks of choir-stalls (*see* pls. 114 and 115), a bishop's throne and stall, a lord mayor's stall and the organ-cases. The bishop's throne has a canopy supported by oak pilasters and two columns, which were carved very richly. The canopy is surmounted by four *putti* which bear aloft triumphantly the bishop's mitre. Such figures also appear over the bishop's domestic stall, the lord mayor's stall and the dean's stall, flanking appropriate insignia. While these seats were carved up by Gibbons and his assistants, the actual construction of them was executed by cathedral joiners. The surviving drawings, however, only

7. *Wren Soc*, XVIII, p. 148.
8. Green, *Grinling Gibbons*, p. 45, *op cit. (6)*; Croft-

Murray, 1962, *Painting*, I, p. 241.
9. *Wren Soc*, XV, pp. 11–12.

go part of the way towards the final results, suggesting a close collaboration between Wren, Gibbons and the joiners.[10]

The wainscoting in various parts of the cathedral was done in expensive oak from Germany; this had a straighter grain and was less knotty than English oak. It presented a smooth surface for polishing and was not so tricky to carve.[11] In the execution of the Great Organ-case, however, Gibbons returned to his favourite softwood. The entire case was carved on all four sides with scrolls, cartouches, coats-of-arms, festoons and *putti*. Carved frets held the gilded pipes which soared upward in two stages, flanked and surmounted by winged cherubs blowing long trumpets or holding a carved representation of the royal arms. Above this four more figures appeared to support a heavily carved and console-bracketed cornice topped by a metal grille. Unfortunately the whole arrangement of the organ atop its screen was disturbed in the mid-nineteenth century, and the organ sides were split and crammed opposite each other at the western end of the choir.

Apart from Gibbons, another woodcarver of similar skill working at St Paul's was Jonathan Maine of Oxford, whose work at Burghley House, Northamptonshire, and at (the vanished) Kiveton House, Yorkshire, is noted later (*see* p. 142). Maine seems to have been on friendly terms with the Assistant Surveyor, John Oliver, but his work falls a little short of the sensitive achievements by Gibbons. Maine showed his abilities in the carving of the Morning Prayer Chapel screen. The accounts from the two artists for woodcarving indicate the work they did: in the case of Gibbons, to the value of £2992. 11*s*. 4½*d*., and in that of Maine of £1252. 6*s*. 11*d*. For stone-carving, Gibbons was paid a further £586.[12]

Another talented craftsman at St Paul's was the French smith, Jean Tijou, whose work amounted to close on £15 000. He provided the iron rails for the Morning Prayer Chapel, the east windows for the dome, and various chains and girdles used to strengthen the structure. He was equally active under Wren at Hampton Court, and many of the panels he created for the Fountain Garden there still survive; two are illustrated in the smith's *Nouveau Libre de Desseins*, issued in 1693. The book shows Tijou's remarkable ability at relating ironwork to an architectural framework, or one devised to fill exactly a gap or opening in a screen.

10. *Wren Soc.*, IV, pp. 15–17.
11. Green, *Grinling Gibbons*, p. 97.

12. *Wren Soc*, XV, pp. xxii–xxiii.

Colour plate 9 ROUSHAM, Oxfordshire. The Painted Parlour, *c* 1740 (photograph: A F Kersting).

An inventory of 1742 describes some of the furniture and Italian bronzes which still survive in this room. The wainscot (originally oak grained) was provided by a joiner named Johnson, who despised 'the assistance of a country carpenter', and the ceiling was painted by William Kent, who designed the house for General James Dormer. It is in his 'grotesque' style in oil on canvas with a white ground decorated with arabesques, and at the centre a medallion of Ceres, Venus and Bacchus. The end sections contain miniature landscapes. The overmantel to the chimneypiece in carved and gilded wood resembles, with its crouching eagles, the carving often done by James Richards to Kent's design, but appears on this occasion to be by John Marsden, who also worked at Holkham. On the walls are heavy brackets which were designed to display General Dormer's collection of Italian bronzes; they prompted Kent to remark 'the General has gone bronzo-mad'.

At St Paul's in September 1695, Tijou entered into a contract to provide a choir 'Skreen of curious Iron-worke' and to finish it by the summer of 1696. He was to be paid at the rate of 40s. a foot in the sums of £100 in hand, and £100 each month as the work required. He was also to provide two smaller screens and infill certain carved wood doors by Gibbons and Maine with metal panels. The choir screen is perhaps Tijou's finest work in England, and shows a restraint which may owe something to the setting and to Wren's ideas. It is at variance with the flamboyant *repoussé* work, scrolls and mask faces introduced in his work at Burghley House, Northamptonshire, or even at Hampton Court.[13]

Ordinary painting did not form an important part of the work on the cathedral during the first two-thirds of the time of erection. Windows, bolts, nuts and similar small items were painted as a routine matter, but from 1698 to 1710 nearly £2000 was expended on painting the whole interior. Of this work, 962½ yd were treated as a decorative item and painted to simulate white marble. Gilding was also done about the altar, and the organ pipes were gilded in 1698 at a cost of £66. 10s. Wren also had all the stonework, including carvings, oiled as a preparation for painting; it helped in closing the pores of the stone, but gave trouble in later years by reacting to extremes of heat and cold, so affecting the paint layers over it.

When Wren's son, also named Christopher, compiled his collection of notes, documents and reminiscences about the Wren family entitled *Parentalia, or Memoirs of the family of Wren, but chiefly of Sir Christopher Wren,*[14] it was stated that it had been the architect's intention to cover the inside of the dome with mosaics. This, however, may have been a confused recollection, and the section of the Great Model of 1673, engraved by Hulsbergh, shows a coffered interior of the dome.[15] The Committee, however, meeting on 3 March 1708/9:

> *Ordered That* the inside of the Dome be painted with figures, but confined to the Scripturall History taken from the Acts of the Apostles, and that such Painters as are willing to undertake the same, do bring their Designs & proposalls (both as to sume & time) to the Commissioners . . . on Tuesday the 5th Day of April next.[16]

13. John Harris, 1960, *English Decorative Ironwork, 1610–1836*, plates 9, 22, 24.
14. Published in 1750 by the architect's grandson, Stephen Wren.
15. *Wren Soc*, XV, p. xxxvi (mosaics); XIV, pl. 111 (Hulsbergh engraving).
16. *ibid.*, XVI, p. 107.

Colour Plate 10 STRAWBERRY HILL, Middlesex. The Gallery, *c* 1752 (photograph: A F Kersting).

Horace Walpole, youngest son of Sir Robert Walpole of Houghton, bought Strawberry Hill in 1749 when he was 32 years old. He did not settle on altering it in the Gothic style immediately, but his friends John Chute and Richard Bentley (who, with Walpole, formed what he called 'The Committee') encouraged him to pursue a true interest in older English architecture. The Committee picked, chose and adapted from the originals. As Wilmarth S Lewis has observed:

'They saw no impropriety in merging the tombs of John of Eltham, Earl of Cornwall, in Westminster Abbey, and of Thomas, Duke of Clarence, at Canterbury to produce the chimneypiece in the library at Strawberry Hill.'
  The Gallery has a ceiling based on that from Henry VII's Chapel in Westminster Abbey, gold network over the looking-glass from Chantilly, and crimson Norwich damask.
Lit: Wilmarth S Lewis, 1961, *Horace Walpole*, p. 108.

On 5 April 1709 the Committee met and considered designs submitted by Sir James Thornhill, Giovanni Antonio Pellegrini, Giovanni Battista Catenaro, Pierre Berchet and Louis Chéron; consideration was deferred in the matter until the next meeting. The careers of the various painters have been examined elsewhere,[17] as well as Pellegrini's work at Castle Howard (*see* p. 149). Sir James Thornhill and Pellegrini emerged in the lead from the first round of competition by the superiority of their designs; they were commissioned by the Committee at its resumed meeting of 11 February 1709/10 to paint specimens in model cupolas specially made for the purpose. It was perhaps a foregone conclusion that no Romish decorator would be given the task of painting the dome and, while Wren is said to have preferred Pellegrini's work,[18] he was again overruled. He had been ignored on the question of using copper instead of lead for the dome; now it seemed as if he was to be overruled about the paintings. After protracted negotiation the Committee, meeting on 28 June 1715, ordered that Thornhill should paint the dome in *basso-relievo* and finish it by the middle of 1716 at a cost of £4000.[19]

On 13 September of the same year (1715), Thornhill was paid a first instalment of £200 on account. The following July he was asked to make an estimate to paint and gild the lantern; this he did, but consideration of it was delayed for almost two years. By the middle of 1716, Thornhill, with two or three painters working under him, was ready to start painting the story of St Paul. The Commissioners, after their tardiness and pleased possibly with the progress and nature of the work Thornhill was conducting, agreed on 3 March 1717/18 to have the lantern painted, and by further decisions he also painted a series of monochrome friezes round the Whispering Gallery. In summary, therefore, his work was in three phases and totalled £6575:[20]

1715	Cupola	£4000
1717	Lantern	£450
1718–19	Whispering Gallery	£2125
		£6575

Unfortunately, the ruling by the Commissioners that the work should be in monochrome meant that little life and warmth was added by the paintings to Wren's austere interior. While Wren may have felt that the employment of Pellegrini would have provided a great colourful fresco at the crossing, no one in England, other than Thornhill, was capable of even providing what the Commissioners had decided. It finished the cathedral in an adequate enough way, to their minds at least.

WHITEHALL CHAPEL

The Catholic court of James II, on which painters like Antonio Verrio depended for patronage, was short lived; in 1688 the king had to flee abroad. His reign, however, brought with it his own fearless demands for a splendid Roman Catholic chapel. Begun in 1685, so swift was its building and decoration that it was in use by November 1686. This affords some insight into Wren's efficiency in supervising the often tardy works organisation. Erected with a Privy Gallery and other buildings, including the Chapel, near to Jones's Banqueting House, it all

17. Croft-Murray, 1970, *Painting*, II.
18. *Wren Soc*, XIV, p. 169.
19. *ibid.*, XVI, p. 116.
20. *ibid.*, XV, p. 225; XVI, pp. 108–36.

vanished in the great fires of 1691 and 1698[21] which reduced the Palace to ruins. The Banqueting House, by its massive construction and the special exertions at the time, was saved.

For the Chapel all the principal craftsmen of the Works were engaged. The mason's work was entrusted to Thomas Wise, and the Master Carpenter Matthew Banckes chose his oak and spruce deals from Jacobson & Co to use in the Chapel. The Master Bricklayer Morris Emmett had so many labourers at work that his lists extended to one and a half large pages in the accounts.[22] James Groves came in to assist Banckes with the carpentry, and then the joiners assembled: William Emmett, a very skilled worker in the City churches, and John Gibson hurried work along; William Ireland was ready before time for glazing; and a further skilled joiner, Roger Davis (who was to work at Burghley House and Chatsworth), was engaged. Charles Atherton the plumber, Robert Streeter the Serjeant Painter, John Groves, Master Plasterer—all of them hastened their teams of men and, when the plain work was done, the decorative artists moved in.

The ceilings and walls were to be painted by Verrio for an agreed £1250, but by the time he had completed his 'Assumption of the Blessed Virgin according to their tradition' (that is, Catholic tradition), the Salutation over the altar, and the many hordes of figures on the walls, he received £1700.[23] His gilder, René Cousin, charged £27. 12s. 8d. for 3316 leaves of gold used on the ceilings of the Queen's Bedchamber, Closet and Private Chapel.[24]

In the Chapel there were to be two organs, a throne and many enrichments in wood and marble, for which Grinling Gibbons and his fellow craftsman from Antwerp, Arnold Quellin, charged £1800.[25] For the altar-piece in the Chapel they were to use 50 workmen; with such a large and talented labour force at work, the Chapel was finished in time, although Wren, as son of a dean of Windsor, had tried to plan the Sanctuary on Anglican lines.[26] The first service was held there on Christmas Day, 1685. Evelyn had visited it several times while building was proceeding, and his diary entry of 29 December 1686, when the Chapel was open to public use, gives a vivid picture of the rich decoration and the splendour of the Roman ritual. He concluded with his disbelief that he should ever witness such happenings in a king of England's chapel.

Wren's position at this time was difficult; the Queen's Chapel at St James's Palace had been denuded to furnish the new Romish Chapel in Whitehall and the anti-Catholic feeling came to a head in 1688 when the queen moved to the Palace on the eve of the birth of Prince James Edward. Many of the most influential men in the country decided to invite William, Prince of Orange, to come over and ascend the throne. He landed at Torbay on 5 November 1688 with his Dutch Guards, and moved into Whitehall Palace. James II left hurriedly for Rochester and France, and, while persuaded to return a few days later by his Catholic supporters, finally abandoned his dreams to settle popery in England and set out again for France. He left behind him a scattered army and the bitter memories of his persecution of those involved in the Monmouth Rebellion to murder him in 1685—thwarted, ingloriously enough, by the Duke of Marlborough at Sedgmoor. The Roman Catholic services were discontinued at the Chapel early in 1689.

21. *Wren Soc.*, VII, pp. 80–81.
22. *ibid.*, VII, p. 96, cited PRO, Works, 5/33.
23. Croft-Murray, 1962, *Painting*, I, p. 239.
24. *Wren Soc*, VII, p. 114.

25. PRO, Works, 5/145.
26. It had to be altered to suit the Catholic priest: *Wren Soc*, VII, p. 74.

HAMPTON COURT

Within a few months of William's accession, war was declared against France, but this did not stop the king from ordering Wren to prepare schemes to adapt the old Tudor palace at Hampton Court. The accounts begin in April 1689, and have been printed.[27] By June the foundations were begun, some material to the value of £1188 having been removed from the incomplete Winchester Palace. Wren had made his sketches in haste, but even his pencil sketches give a good idea of the grand effect he was aiming at. A pedimented centre flanked by Corinthian pilasters, or perhaps an alternative design with the ever-favourite presence of a dome, were in his mind.[28] At this time, on 2 May 1689, William Talman, an architect of great capability but uncertain in his dealings with patrons, was appointed Comptroller in the King's Works.

Work proceeded steadily for a short time only. In July 1690 Queen Mary visited Hampton Court, and wrote to the king, engaged in Ireland on the vanquishing of James II at the Battle of the Boyne, that things went on very slowly because of the scarcity of both money and Portland stone. Work was also dragging at Kensington Palace, and at both houses there occurred disastrous building failures. At Hampton Court part of the great trusses of the roof on the Privy Garden front fell, carrying away the floor over certain rooms near the Cartoon Gallery. Wren and Talman were called to a meeting on 21 December 1689 and said they would give a report in writing. When both officers were questioned on their reports, on 13 January 1690, Talman tried to use the opportunity to belittle the Surveyor. Where it was attested that piers showed only slight hair-line cracks, Talman asserted that they were sufficient to put a finger in. He went on to claim that the piers were hollow and cramped with iron to keep them together.

The king, on looking at all the evidence, ordered the works at Hampton Court to proceed, unless his officers found material cause why this would be dangerous or ill-advised; no such cause was found. As the task progressed, Queen Mary, who had a passion for building, decorating, gardens and arrangements of porcelain and flowers, asked Wren to complete Charles II's Fountain Garden. At her deeply mourned death in December 1694, however, the king lost interest, and Bishop Burnet recorded[29] that the king's spirits sank so low that it was feared he too would die. In sharp contrast, the officers of the Works, heavy hearted though they might be at the loss of a queen interested in their affairs, had to do one of their ever-present humdrum jobs. This time it had little precedent: they repaired the stairs at Kensington Palace broken when 'carrying ye Q's body down'.[30]

About Christmas 1693, Wren had estimated that it would take £35 315 to complete the new quadrangle at Hampton Court. By 1697, when at the settlements in the Treaty of Ryswick England found herself no longer at war with France, William, his chief occupation gone, resumed his interest in making improvements to his house and gardens. Wren sent the king a letter on 28 April 1699 giving a revised cost for finishing part of the house; he supposed that the king would finish the rooms as decently as their size and position required. In September Talman also wrote to the king in the belief that he would wish to hear how work progressed—

27. PRO, Works, 5/55; *Wren Soc*, IV, pp. 39–54.
28. *ibid.*, IV, plates XII–XIII.

29. David Green, 1967, *Sarah, Duchess of Marlborough*, p. 73.
30. PRO, Works, 19/48/1; January 1694/95.

that five rooms were almost finished and the great stone stairs with its iron balustrade complete. With this insistence from his officers, the king allowed the work to press ahead. The building programme also appears to have coincided with the king's desire for a small Trianon close to Hampton Court.

For this scheme Talman drew up a set of designs,[31] and the section through the Hall depicts an interior which had points of resemblance to King William's palace at Het Loo, designed by Daniel Marot. The stairs, which Talman referred to in his letter, had a fine metal balustrade provided by Tijou, and the walls were painted by Verrio. This was the King's Staircase (*see* pls. 88–90), and Verrio, reluctantly perhaps returning to work for the Protestant king, painted in a medley of gods, goddesses and heroes of ancient Rome. The allegory was complicated, 'associating the Emperor Julian the Apostate and his satire upon the Caesars with William III as the upholder of Protestantism and freedom'.[32]

The Staircase led through to the Guard Room and to the five south-facing State Rooms. In them is a great variety of woodcarving by Grinling Gibbons (*see* pls. 11 and 116), and his designs included many for chimneypieces with woodcarving as an important feature.[33] In the Chapel Wren designed the reredos which Gibbons carved in superb fashion, flanked by two groups of Corinthian columns. His work in 1699 was entered at £941. 14s. 9d. Tijou, presumably for his King's Staircase work, received £265 for balustrades and rails.

In the gardens, in addition to Tijou's spirited metal panels, John Nost and Richard Osgood provided lead figures under the supervision of the Royal Gardener, Henry Wise. Fine-screened gravel was laid in all the walks at 3s. 6d. per yard. The covered tennis court was also repaired and, as Wren declared that he was unacquainted with 'Tennis Play', Horatio Moore gave advice about laying out the ground with a stone floor and a boarded ceiling.

KENSINGTON PALACE

A work which proceeded concurrently with Hampton Court was Kensington Palace. In June 1689 the king bought the Earl of Nottingham's house in Kensington and the work of adding to it began at once. The king did not like living at Whitehall, and work at Hampton Court had only just begun when the building failure occurred on the Privy Garden front. As if this was not enough for the Works to cope with, anxious as it must have been without knowledge of the new king's moods, the additional buildings at Kensington fell down in November 1689. Fortunately for Wren, the queen intervened; she wrote to the king in December that she had often gone over to Kensington to hasten on the workmen. She wanted to take up residence quickly, and all the pressure on them, she insisted, had brought errors in the work, but the hand of God had also intervened. One can imagine that this statement, with which few could argue satisfactorily, endeared her to the hard-pressed officers of the Works.

In the Kensington Palace Contracts Book, 1689–95,[34] it was stated that the stairs were to be of elm, and the joists and floors of oak or yellow fir. The oak door-cases were to be 7 ft high, and

31. John Harris, 1960, 'The Hampton Court Trianon Designs of William and John Talman', *Journal of the Warburg and Courtauld Institutes*, XXIII, pp. 139–49.

32. Edgar Wind, 1939–40, 'Julian the Apostate at Hampton Court', *Journal of the Warburg and Courtauld Institutes*, III, pp. 127–37.

33. *Wren Soc*, IV, plates 27–40.

34. PRO, Works, 5/146.

the floors in the queen's rooms were to be prepared with extra care. The carpenters' work was to be done so that the joiners and plasterers would not be hindered in following them. In the king's absence in Ireland, the queen was approving designs. It is possible to see the annual expenditure from a separate volume of accounts, 1689–94.[35] The total[36] came to £65 995. 8s. 0d.

The joiners preparing the rooms for wainscoting at Kensington were Henry Lobb and Alexander Fort, and, when this work was completed, the important carvers came on to the site. Nicholas Alcock and William Emmett were old friends of the Works officers, Gibbons was the Master Carver to the Crown, and Robert Osgood and Gabriel Cibber were competent sculptors. The plasterer Henry Margetts was employed by sub-contract to the Master Plasterer, John Grove, who was busy at Hampton Court. The smiths, including William Partridge (who worked for Wren in London and Cambridge), and Jean Tijou did work to the value of £2594. 4s. 8d., and the total contracted work amounted to £44 300. 18s. 0d. from 1689–91, and £36 687. 10s. 7d. from 1691–96. Wren's riding charges show that he attended the building on 384 days. By careful paymaster's work the account was concluded £1606. 4s. 3¾d. in surplus, and each officer and master craftsman signed in the margins of the payment book for money received. Work then ceased for a time until Queen Anne came to the throne, at the age of 37, on 23 April 1702. An added complication to all building arose when, in little less time than a fortnight after the accession, England declared war against France.

At her accession Queen Anne determined to make less use of St James's Palace. At Kensington the plan was to have a State Reception suite, of which the Orangery survives. On 17 June 1704 Wren, Sir John Vanbrugh, the Master Mason Benjamin Jackson and Matthew Banckes, junior, the Master Carpenter, signed a report which presented an estimate for building a 'Greenhouse' at Kensington to a design approved by the queen. To be well performed they considered it would be necessary to spend £2599 for a building 170 ft long by 30 ft wide. The analysis of estimated expenditure gave the bricklayer about a quarter of this money (£697. 12s. 0d.) and the carpenter £361. 1s. 0d. Work was started, but it was soon indicated by the Master Bricklayer Richard Stacey that, like all master craftsmen employed by the Works, he was not in a position to extend credit and had already spent out £800 without any advance. It was slow in coming, and many a lesser craftsman would have been penniless and unable to trade.

The gardens at the Palace also needed specialist attentions. John Barrett, pump-maker, and Isaac Thompson, engine-maker, concerned themselves with the fountain mechanisms, raising water over certain levels, and with forms of irrigation. Within the Orangery, Grinling Gibbons provided decorative limewood swags and drops, but to the value of a meagre £7. 12s. 6d. Taste was changing and moving, inexorably, towards use of the decorative painter. The proportioned alcoves and wainscoting were by Alexander Fort and Charles Hopson.

It was at this time, about 1705, that Vanbrugh, who had been appointed Comptroller of the King's Works in 1702, started the process which got rid of the Master Mason Benjamin Jackson from the commission. For some time Vanbrugh had been troubled at Wren's easy practice of allowing Office of Works tradesmen to accept private contracts when, with a salary from the

35. PRO Works, ibid., 19/48/1.
36. The Pay Book differs from the Declared Accounts

(Wren Soc, VII, p. 174), which continue to 1696 with a final total of £80 988. 8s. 7d.

queen, they should have been diligent at seeing she was not imposed upon by others. Jackson was replaced by Thomas Hill, who worked at Kensington as well as at Hampton Court, Whitehall and other royal residences, and had been one of two principal masons at Greenwich.[37]

GREENWICH

The old Tudor palace at Greenwich had fallen into bad repair during the Commonwealth, but King Charles II liked a residence near the river and the Queen's House there, designed by Inigo Jones, was too small to house the Court. John Webb, nephew of Inigo Jones who had been denied the Surveyor-General's post when Charles II came to the throne, intended that the Palace should consist of two blocks at each side of an open court running down to the river. His drawings survive,[38] and the elevation shows the intended use of great 39 ft high Corinthian columns, set in groups of four at each end and at the pedimented centre. This united the façade, and the remainder of the surface was covered with regularly spaced rustication. The general design of the end pavilions with the great columns bore a resemblance to Palladio's Palazzo Valmarana; this had appeared in 1570 in that architect's *I Quattro Libri* (II, p. 17) a work which Webb and his master Inigo Jones knew well, and the windows were a modification of those at the Palazzo Thiene, or derived from Serlio.[39]

Greenwich was also assured of popularity while London was growing in size and population, and the officers of the Works were engaged constantly in work there. In 1699, 30 years after the completion of Webb's wing for Charles II, Wren addressed King William on the subject of converting the site and buildings of the royal Palace for the use of disabled and superannuated seamen. The idea met with royal approval, and a Commission was appointed — some 108 members in all — which conducted its business through a small executive group. John Evelyn was appointed Treasurer, and a sub-committee consisting of Wren, as Surveyor, the Secretary of the Admiralty, the Secretary of the Treasury and 'other Citizens, Gentlemen and Sea Officers' concerned themselves with proposals, schemes and models for the fabric. Much of our knowledge of these details comes from a pamphlet written by Hawksmoor in 1728.[40] What is clear is that work had started late in 1694, and that five years elapsed before it was suggested that the Palace should be put to its charitable use.

Before her death in 1694, Queen Mary had expressed great interest in a renewal of building at Greenwich and opposed the then current idea of pulling part of the Palace down; being utterly determined not to let this happen, the only alternative seemed to be to build. After her death, the work went on and, between 1696 and 1699, all the foundations were dug. Wren's Great Hall was begun in August 1698, finished in November 1704, and ready for Sir James Thornhill's 19 years of painting, which began in 1708.[41] While Vanbrugh may have been connected with

37. *Wren Soc*, XVIII, pp. 160–61.
38. *ibid.*, VI, p. 97, plates XVIII and XX; VII, p. 72; Colvin, 1976, *King's Works*, V, pp. 147–51.
39. John Harris and Prunella Fraser, 1960, '*The Burlington-Devonshire Collection, part I, The Drawings of Inigo Jones, John Webb and Lord Burlington*', p. 102;

Margaret Whinney and Oliver Millar, 1957, *English Art, 1625–1714*, p. 135.
40. *Wren Soc*, VI, pp. 17–27.
41. J H V Davies, 1957, 'The Dating of the Buildings of the Royal Hospital at Greenwich', *Archaeological Journal*, CXIII, pp. 126–36.

building at Greenwich as early as 1703, he had no official connection with the hospital, other than as a director, and by this time it was too late to influence the Wren design to any significant extent.

In 1695 the mason's contract was given to the capable Edward Strong junior, one of a long line of master masons, whose father, also Edward, had worked for Wren at St Paul's in charge of a large team of men. Strong junior lived at Greenwich, and he was joined in the hospital work by Thomas Hill. Thomas Hues was to do the brickwork and Roger Davis the joinery; Henry Doogood, as John Grove's partner, was entrusted with the plasterwork, which was a method Grove was careful to follow throughout his period as Master Plasterer to the Works—while he might benefit indirectly, his name was not involved in the contract when he was involved in other royal work against his salary. Nicholas Hawksmoor was acting as Clerk of Works, and accounts were to be made up monthly. The abstract of payments, June 1696 to July 1699, has been printed[42] and shows a total expenditure of £36 219. 8s. 9½d., of which almost a third (£11 133. 5s. 4¾d.) was for mason's work. This sum had been raised by gifts from the king, subscriptions and free gifts, levies on seamen and fines on French smugglers. Evelyn had kept his accounts with meticulous care, and from 1695 to 1701 the money flowed in from these sources to the amount of £74 831. 16s. 11d., and had kept pace with the expenditure.

By the end of 1704, accommodation was available for the first pensioners, and 42 arrived in March 1705; by December 1708 there were 350. The hospital was opened officially in January 1705. One of its most interesting parts, the Painted Hall, was started in 1703; originally intended as the Hospital Refectory, the Upper Hall was to contain tables for officers, and the Lower Hall for pensioners. It was decided in 1708 to paint the Hall, and for the next 13 years it was closed to enable this to be done. The work was entrusted to Sir James Thornhill, by then the best-known English painter of murals. On 20 May 1708 he attended the Board of Directors' meeting, which discussed his painting of the Hall. It was resolved that he should proceed with all expedition, and it was left to the board to pay him for the work as they judged it deserved.

John James, later to be Clerk of Works at Greenwich, was ordered to get scaffolding ready as soon as possible. Thornhill was to prime the surfaces himself, or by the use of his men, and to make any alterations in the design, inserting what he could relative to maritime affairs, until the board signified its approval. The Lower Hall was the first to be painted, with the theme for the ceiling depicting 'The Glorification of William and Mary'.[43]

By 23 May 1712 Thornhill had advanced far enough to ask the board to appoint such persons as they thought fit to inspect his work in the Great Hall; he also asked for some money to aid his speedy finishing of the Hall, and £300 was granted to him. By May 1714 he was acquainting his masters that he would be clearing away the scaffolding during that month. He was, however, to wait a long time for any money, and before he was paid Wren had retired and Vanbrugh had been appointed Surveyor at Greenwich, at a salary of £200 a year.

From 1716, the date of Wren's retirement, the building proceeded as steadily as the constant lack of money allowed. The unfortunate master masons were helped from time to time by small imprests, as Thornhill had been. By the end of 1718 13 directors, including Vanbrugh, decided

42. *Wren Soc*, VI, p. 33.

43. Croft-Murray, 1962, *Painting*, I, p. 71; *Wren Soc*, VI, p. 69.

on a memorial to the Admiralty pointing out that the arrears due to the hospital from the government—who, with official exactitude were extracting a levy from the seamen, but not passing it on to Greenwich—amounted to £25 499.7s. 9½d.

On 27 July 1717 Thornhill presented his statement[44] in which he recounted the prices paid to many previous painters for their work elsewhere. He instanced Rubens at the Banqueting House, Whitehall (£4000), Charles de la Fosse working for Lord Montagu (£2000), Verrio at Windsor and Hampton Court, Marco Ricci at Bulstrode, and Pellegrini in work for the Duke of Portland and the Earl of Burlington. He made the mistake of hoping that the board would allow him as good a price as any of these, especially as he had spent six years of the prime of his life at the task. The board thought the memorial unsatisfactory, as it did not demand any specific sum of money for the work; Thornhill was asked to be definite, but when he demanded £5 for each yard of painted ceiling and £1 a yard for the walls, the board countered by suggesting £3 and £1 a yard respectively. Wearily, and with much good grace in the circumstances, Thornhill declared himself satisfied, and attended a meeting on 21 September 1717 to show his sketches for the Upper Hall.

By this time George I had succeeded Queen Anne, and the west wall in the Painted Hall was therefore devoted to a representation of his family, backed by the dome of St Paul's. The other walls depicted William of Orange landing at Torbay, and George I landing on Hawksmoor's grand steps at Greenwich. Before his career was done, Thornhill not only had to struggle further for his money—he received £6685 for the complete work[45]—but needed to argue with the Office of Works in 1720 and 1723 for settlement of six small bills amounting to £8. 19s. 5d. Thornhill finished his work at Greenwich in 1727. The Office of Works, in the meantime, was ignoring him and giving jobs of decorative painting at Kensington Palace to William Kent, who was establishing the 'new and lighter decorative fashions'.[46]

For Private Patrons, 1660–1710

We have seen that this period, commencing with the accession of Charles II and ending almost at the death of Sir Christopher Wren (1723), was remarkable for the way patrons and craftsmen became familiar with new architectural forms. The interiors of houses, in particular, were transformed by following the ideas of Palladio and Inigo Jones. There was a regard for proportion, the relationship of rooms and the views or vistas therefrom.[47] Comfort and convenience were often sacrificed to a rigid regard for observing lines drawn by a foreign theorist. Whatever the result, however, all the material parts were accomplished by close liaison between patron, architect and craftsmen.

Advice to patrons was not lacking, but the communication of new ideas was likely to be subject to mistakes and misunderstanding. In addition, architects such as Captain William Winde could hardly trouble to visit the site; when he was engaged by Lord Craven to supervise building at Combe Abbey, Warwickshire, he neglected his duties. Sir Roger Pratt, an amateur architect and recorder, in his notebooks,[48] of much advice to builders, was concerned that a

44. *Wren Soc*, VI, pp. 77–78.
45. Croft-Murray, 1962, *Painting*, I, p. 268.
46. Kerry Downes, 1966, *English Baroque Architecture*, p. 54.

47. John Harris, 1979, *The Artist and the Country House*.
48. R T Gunther, 1928, *The Architecture of Sir Roger Pratt*.

patron should assess what house the estate could afford, and how it could be maintained. Pratt had written the advice Winde may well have felt Lord Craven had in mind: 'Go on with your building, or change it till it please you'. It was a doctrine which suited the enquiring minds of patrons, many of whom, like Wren, were members of the Royal Society. They were accustomed to the processes of thought, argument and decision. It encouraged a gentleman architect such as Winde, who in any case conducted most of his work through slow, casual correspondence, into yet more dilatory ways. He was anxious to introduce grand ornament into his houses. Dutch and French influences were at work, and important steps in influencing taste had been taken when foreign decorative artists were employed to decorate the State Apartments at Windsor. Good craftsmanship was available, but a more flamboyant interior decoration was what marked out the houses of the Caroline years from those which followed. It was achieved in the main by plasterers, woodcarvers and painters under the direction of architects and talented amateurs, some of whom had allegiance both to the Crown and to private patrons.

HOUSES FOR LORD CRAVEN

One of the first houses to be designed after the Restoration was Hampstead Marshall, Berkshire. The 1st Earl of Craven employed Sir Balthazar Gerbier, whose books on building were important statements of current practice of the 1660s. Unfortunately, within a year or two of commencing work for Lord Craven,[49] Gerbier died, and was buried at Hampstead Marshall Church in 1667. The epitaph on his monument states that he 'built a stately pile of Building in the years 1662 to 1665 for the Rt. Hon. William Earl Craven at Hampstead Marshall'. It has been shown[50] that, even before Gerbier's death, Captain William Winde was journeying to the house, and the surviving drawings[51] include some by Gerbier, Winde and the craftsmen employed over some 20 years. These were the mason Thomas Strong, the carver Edward Pearce, and the plasterer Edward Goudge.

Winde, as the 'Master William Wine' of one of the dedicatory epistles Gerbier prefaced to his *Counsel and Advise to all Builders* (1663), has his career documented further on the flyleaf of a letter-book of his client, Lord Craven. This, together with the 80 letters I traced in 1952, gives an idea of the patronage he attracted and the attentions he gave to buildings under his supervision. The letter-book[52] is dated 1679–84, but the flyleaf inscription is based on the statement which appeared in Horace Walpole's *Anecdotes of Painters*,[53] with the one addition that Winde was 'Gerbier's only Scholar'. He was born at Bergen-op-Zoom in Holland of English parents[54] at an unknown date before 1647; after coming to England from Holland at the Restoration, he married into the Bridgeman family, his wife Magdalen being the daughter of Sir John Bridgeman.

The casual attentions Winde gave to his work might be held to have been solely the province

49. Oliver Hill and John Cornforth, 1966, *English Country Houses: Caroline*, p. 137.
50. Colvin, 1978, *Dictionary*, p. 902.
51. Bodleian Library, Gough Drawings, a.2. Some have been reproduced by Hill and Cornforth, *Caroline*, p. 142–43, and by H M Colvin, 1952, *Architectural Drawings in the Bodleian Library*, pls. 2–6.

52. Bodleian Library, MS, Gough, Warwickshire, I.
53. Horace Walpole, 1798, *Works*, III, p. 345. See further, Colvin, 1978, *Dictionary*, pp. 902–5.
54. His father, Henry, was Gentleman of the Bedchamber to Charles I. M Whinney and O Millar, 1957, *English Art, 1625–1714*, p. 219.

of the amateur architects; they could only allocate part of their time to the task in hand, but Winde did not show much diligence and placed great reliance on the skill and acumen of his master workmen. This can be ascertained from the way he handled men when they worked for his cousin at Castle Bromwich Hall, Warwickshire. However, all designs were 'allowed' by Winde and the fine design (*see* pl. 61) by Goudge for the Dining Room ceiling at Hampstead Marshall is endorsed across the centre 'June 22th 1686. This Drauft for the Dineing Roome att Hampstead Marshall marked A allowed of by me Wll. Winde.'[55]

CASTLE BROMWICH HALL

In 1685 Sir John and Lady Bridgeman decided to improve their home at Castle Bromwich, and it seemed sensible that, in the interest of economy, they should employ their architect son-in-law (then a soldier), William Winde. On 7 December 1685 Lady Bridgeman, who conducted the entire correspondence,[56] wrote her first letter to Winde, who endorsed it 'No 1'. She acknowledged his proffered advice, but regretted he had not been able to visit her, especially as Jonathan Wilcox, the master carpenter, had already surveyed the house and was ready to say what alterations were necessary.

From this time, and over the next 15 years, Winde gave attention to the detail of the alterations. In this he was assisted by the decorative painter Louis Laguerre, the plasterer Edward Goudge, the sculptor John van Nost, and the joiner Robert Aiscough. Furniture was provided by Gerreit Jensen, clocks and watches by Thomas Tompion, and portraits by John Baptist Closterman. The gardens at Castle Bromwich were also designed by Winde on the advice of George London and Captain Charles Hatton.[57] There is evidence that Winde counted formal landscape gardening among his many accomplishments; in an undated letter in the Bradford archives of *c* 1690, he wrote to Lady Bridgeman that, when quartered in Kent and employed in altering the Earl of Winchelsea's house at Eastwell, he transplanted trees of a considerable size, which did very well. The best way to follow Winde's work is to quote from two of his surviving letters for work at Castle Bromwich.

5 July 1686
Madame,

In obedience to yr Ladyships commands I shall by ye first opertunity send downe the Joyners Desines wch I have corrected where it was necessary. . . . I have also sent a letter to Mr Goudge to prepare the Draughts for ye Severall Roomes yr Ladyship intends to have fretted and ye price of Every sealing, that before hande you maye bee informed of ye charge wch is ye beste waye of proceeding.

11 September 1688

I receaved a Leter from Mr Goudge of ye 4 instant where in hee gives mee an account of his proceeding att Cassel Bromige. yt hee will not be Longe, about ye two sealing and if might advise yr Ladysp since hee is on ye place, and yr Lady resolves to have any more Frett worke done it is fare better to have it done this season, then to put

55. Bodleian Library, MS, Gough Drawings, a.2. ff. 21–22.
56. Staffs CRO, Earl of Bradford Archives, 18/4.
57. David Green, 1956, *Henry Wise: Gardener to Queen*

Anne; Miles Hadfield, 1960, *Gardening in Britain*, pp. 134–36.

it of to another yeare for now his hand is in hee may aforde it cheaper then if hee where to come agayne, and ye time of the yeare is proper, as any your Lady can make choice of, and there is no dought if hee follow his worke close, it will all bee finished in a small Tyme.

This mention of Goudge allows us to quote a further comment on his abilities by Winde. Writing to Lady Bridgeman on 8 February 1689/90, he indicated that 'Mr Goudge will undoughtedly have a good deall of worke for hee is now looked on as ye beste maste in England in his profession as his worke att Combe, Hampsted & Sr John Brownlowes will Evidence'.[58] The same letter also mentions Goudge's employment by the Earl of Clarendon at Swallowfield. This Berkshire house was designed by William Talman, but there was little of it left in the refacing of 1820 by William Atkinson—what may survive, however, is Goudge's ceiling in the oval vestibule.[59] A list of Goudge's known work to date is given later in this book, and we may note his presence at Petworth with his assistant David Lance, who at a later date became Master Plasterer to the Office of Works (1708–24). Winde's letter of 'London ye 29 . . . 1691, Mr Goudge is at ye Duke of Somerset' and Goudge's letter to Lady Bridgeman, 27 April 1691: 'Mr Lance is at the Duke of Sumersetts at Pettworth in Sussex' give the evidence.

While Goudge was capable of doing his own designs,[60] the rates for the job and all bills went through Winde's hands. Goudge, however, was capable of writing a fair letter, and told Lady Bridgeman, on 11 October 1690, that he would be pleased to take the lowest rate, that he charged 9d. for whitening each yard of his decorated work, 1½d. per yard for the plain work and £3. 4s. 0d. for the charge, time and expense of his man's coming and going.

As well as being a successful plasterer, Goudge also supplemented his income by acting as a clerk of works for building, especially that undertaken in London about 1698 for Thomas Coke. Coke, an important Derbyshire landowner at Melbourne, became Vice-Chamberlain to Queen Anne and to George I. In 1698, while Coke was away after his marriage to Lady Mary Stanhope, his house in St James's Place was enlarged and he also added the adjoining house to his own. Goudge was in charge of the work and wrote that he did not much approve of the way this was to be done, and that he was drawing up his own thoughts on it. The humdrum catholicity of his duties included the provision of household equipment such as jacks, spits, racks, boilers, stoves and cisterns, and to seeing that the arms of the workmen wielding hammers did not stray over the boundary line of property owned by the irascible Lord Godolphin, who was ready for any excuse to quarrel. Within three years Goudge was asking Coke for some sort of business that could act as a livelihood for him, because his own was prejudicial to his health and had dwindled away due to shortage of money occasioned by wars with the French and in Ireland, and the growing popularity of ceiling painting.[61]

58. Combe Abbey, Warwickshire, (partly demolished, 1925) and Hampstead Marshall, Berkshire, (destroyed by fire, 1718) are 'Winde' houses (Hill and Cornforth, *Caroline*, p. 137). The mention of Sir John Brownlow allows the plasterwork at Belton House, Lincolnshire, *c* 1688 (Hill and Cornforth, *Caroline*, p. 202) to be attributed to Goudge.

59. J Betjeman and J Piper, eds., 1949, *Murray's Berkshire Architectural Guide*, p. 146; N Pevsner, 1966, *The Buildings of England: Berkshire*, p. 238.

60. Staffs CRO, Bradford, MS, 18/4, Winde to Lady Bridgeman, 12 June 1688; 'The bearer is Mr Edward Goudge . . . he dide the frett seallings att Combe and I will assure yr Ladyp no man in Ingland has a better Tallent in ye way (of plastering) than himselfe, hee has bine imployed by mee this 6 or 7 yeares, is an excellent drauffteman and mackes all his desines hime selfe.'

61. Geoffrey Beard, 1979, 'The Beste Master in England' [Edward Goudge], *National Trust Studies*, pp. 20–27.

Winde told Lady Bridgeman on 17 November 1693 that, without his diligent enquiries and viewing of work, most workmen would not finish jobs as neatly as they ought to do. He was anxious that, for Castle Bromwich, the joiner Robert Aiscough should 'doe 3 or 4 inches of a sorte' of moulding and set out the prices, as was common in London. The same care was exercised over the other workers at Castle Bromwich: Edward Pearce provided marble chimneypieces, but Winde was not over anxious to pay more than £20, leaving £14 unpaid as £30 had already been paid over. Laguerre was constantly urged to finish his history paintings for the ceiling of the staircase well, and as overdoors, but he was as busy as Goudge. Winde, for his part, needed to know from his mother-in-law what sun came in, and from what compass point, in order that Laguerre could be instructed to give the proper shadow to his picture, to make it look the more beautiful when seen in the proper light.

COMBE ABBEY

Winde, however, led a busy life and his patrons needed to wait many weeks for answers, even if his advice was urgent as to the nature and manner of plastering the Great Hall at Ampthill to receive Laguerre's frescoes. Several years earlier, in March 1681–82, Lord Craven had invited Winde, his godson, to Combe Abbey to see the foundation of the house laid. However, this apparently necessary visit does not seem to have been undertaken by Winde. By 10 July 1682 he had also still not sent the correct plans to Lord Craven. The workmen were at a standstill for want of direction, and Lord Craven indicated that he would need to discharge them if positive direction was not forthcoming. Combe is a good example of a house which only proceeded by the owner's active intervention in what might properly have been regarded as his architect's business. Fortunately the somewhat one-sided interchange of letters[62] shows that Lord Craven was diligent in pressing on with the work. By 5 February 1682/83, Winde was advised that sufficient timber for the stairs had been sawed, and that some of it was stored in water—a practice commended by John Evelyn in his *Sylva*—to prevent later splitting. Lord Craven had been dissatisfied with some deal boards, and asked that more should be sent by way of Gainsborough and the River Trent to Wilden Ferry; they were then loaded into waggons for the remaining 30-mile journey to the house. The letters also indicate the employment of Goudge, the carver Edward Pearce, and Jonathan Wilcox, the carpenter, who was to work later for Lady Bridgeman. They were capable of working without supervision, although rarely given the chance to do so.

AMPTHILL

One of the last enterprises with which Winde's name has been connected was the advice he gave to John, 1st Lord Ashburnham, when he was building Ampthill Park, Bedfordshire, in 1704–07 with the assistance of the master mason John Lumley (1654–1721). In his letter-book[63] Ashburnham copied letters to his agent Brian Fairfax, and three he had sent to Winde. Fairfax was requested to see Winde about statues and to discuss with him the painting of the Great Hall by Laguerre and the provision of ironwork, particularly gates and staircase balusters, by Jean

---

62. Bodleian Library, MS, Gough, Warwickshire, 1, f. 48.　　63. West Sussex CRO, Ashburnham Archives.

Tijou, the French ironsmith. As some of the work by Laguerre was to be on canvas with other parts painted direct on to the wall surface, Lord Ashburnham sent dimensions to Winde and asked further about statues and Tijou's rates for ironwork.

Four important houses which contain late seventeenth-century interior decoration provide interesting contrasts to each other. Warwick Castle and Ham House contain good work by both country and London craftsmen; Burghley House, Northamptonshire, and Chatsworth House, Derbyshire, equally the repositories of local and London work, have in addition splendid decorations by foreign decorative painters. Many of the same craftsmen worked at the two latter houses, as John Cecil, 5th Earl of Exeter, married the sister of the 1st Duke of Devonshire, the creator of Chatsworth. He was also a cousin of the 1st Duke of Montagu.

WARWICK CASTLE

In 1669 Robert, Lord Brooke, owner of one of the finest medieval castles in England, decided to create a range of State Rooms, including an impressive Cedar Room. He entered into agreement in 1669 with the Warwickshire joiner Roger Hurlbut to wainscot the Great Hall, and Roger's brother, William, was sent to look at Kingston Lacy, the Dorset house which Sir Roger Pratt had designed for Sir Ralph Bankes; at his return in 1670 he received the first payment for altering rooms of the castle. The agreement is presumed to cover the whole range of State Apartments to the south-west of the Great Hall; these are now known as the Cedar Drawing Room, the Red and Green Drawing Rooms, the State or Queen Anne's Bedroom and the Boudoir. The so-called 'Italian Room' was also refitted at the same time.

In 1671 over 57 cwt of cedar boards were brought from London to the castle. The various payments to Hurlbut have been noted,[64] but a further examination of the 1669–71 account book (that for 1672–76 is missing) has isolated three references to the fine plasterwork ceilings. In 1671 the 'Accomptant' was paid for coach hire and gifts on a visit to London to view 'ffrettworkes', or decorated plaster ceilings. A few pages before the account book ends, there is the entry: 'Mr Petiver & Mr Pelton for their draught and Estimate about the Frettworke 001. 05. 00'. A little was known of James Petiver's training—he was apprenticed to the competent London plasterer Arthur Toogood in 1658—but Pelton is otherwise unrecorded. We may assume them to be the authors of the deeply recessed ceilings surviving in the Cedar Drawing Room and the Blue Boudoir. Lord Brooke died in 1677, just as the series of rooms was completing—William Hurlbut received a final payment in 1678. His work had entailed using sawyers to cut 19 628 ft of timber at 2s. 2d. per 100 ft and the bringing of the cedar boards from London. The rooms survived the Warwick Castle fire of 1871.

HAM HOUSE

Ham House, Surrey, was built in 1610 and further additions—notably the Great Staircase—were made by William Murray, 1st Earl of Dysart, between 1637 and 1639. The house as it appears today was largely the creation of his daughter, Elizabeth, and her second husband, the 1st Duke of Lauderdale. During the 1670s they enlarged the house, added new suites of rooms,

64. M W Farr, 1969, 'Warwick Castle', *V.C.H., Warwickshire*, VIII, p. 460.

and furnished it with a lavishness even transcending their position. In 1679 the contents were listed in an important inventory and much of the original furniture survives. Many of the rooms have artificially grained wainscoting, carved swags of fruit and flowers, elaborate doors and fireplaces with simple marble bolection-mould surrounds. That in the Queen's Closet (*see* pl. 129), however, is decorated richly in scagliola, and incorporates the initials 'J E L' (for John and Elizabeth Lauderdale).

The Duke, who became Secretary of Scotland through his friendship with Charles II, used many foreign craftsmen at Ham and at his Scottish houses. Dutch joiners and carvers provided wainscoting, window frames and furniture, and other items were bought in Holland.[65] Earlier wainscoting (1639) by Thomas Carter survives on the Great Staircase and in the Long Gallery; that in the Long Gallery incorporates 25 pilasters with gilded capitals, charged at 11*s*. each. The amalgam of decoration from the two periods justified John Evelyn's observation that the house was 'furnished like a great Prince's'. An analysis of the Duke's financial papers[66] shows that he lived as a great prince should.

BURGHLEY HOUSE

There are few houses in England which rival Chatsworth in decoration, but one of these is Burghley House, Northamptonshire. The south front had been damaged in the Parliamentary assault of the house led by Cromwell in 1643, when the 4th Earl was a minor. The 5th Earl was a traveller and lover of architecture and painting, and it seems probable that he turned to the architect William Talman to supervise the alterations he planned at Burghley. The architect visited the house in August 1688. The documents at Burghley are in part summarised conveniently by the Earl of Exeter's bank account—an unusually detailed one—which survives from 1678 in the ledgers of Child's Bank, London. It indicates that Edward Martin was employed at Burghley House from 1682. The woodcarvers at Burghley, apart from Grinling Gibbons, who was paid £100 in two sums of £50 (6 July 1683 and 21 December 1685), were Jonathan Maine and Thomas Young; Maine was a talented woodcarver from Oxford with a long list of good work to his credit, including woodwork at Trinity College, Oxford, and at St Paul's Cathedral.

The second entry for Gibbons in the bank account says 'Paid Mr Gibbons, Carver in full £50. 0. 0.' The 'in full' contrasts with the £402. 11*s*. 3*d*. paid to Maine and Young from 1682–87, and implies that much of the carved work and wainscoting at Burghley is from their

65. John Dunbar, 1975, 'The building activities of the Duke and Duchess of Lauderdale, 1670–82', *Archaeological Journal*, CXXXII, p. 210.

66. A reasonably complete account of the Duke of Lauderdale's finances can be obtained from the Thirlestane Archives, calendared by the Scottish National Register of Archives.
In the duke's absences in London he appointed eight commissioners to manage his Scottish estates (MS, 62/60). Abbreviats of his accounts (MS, 63/7) show that, for 1663–69, only £102 was spent on repairing houses. The following account for 1670–74 shows an expenditure of £47 527. 14*s*. (Scots money, approximately one-twelfth English value.) This was at a time when expenditure on the duke's Surrey house at Ham was active.
He received money from his estate rent-roll for Edinburgh Castle, a proportion of the total receipts of the Signet (MS, 63/7, 'Money Rec'd By the Signet, 1660–74'), a daily £50 allowance as the King's Commissioner, a 'Pension' (£500), part of the Excise Tax assigned to him by the king (13 July 1674) and various other small sums from sources such as coal mining. His debts remained extensive, with large payments of interest to his death in 1682 (MS, 63/50).

hands. John Vanderbank, the tapestry-weaver, was buying silk and 'stuff', and he may also have had oversight of much of the work done by the fringe-maker 'Monsieur Dufresnoy', the upholsterer Francis La Pierre (who also worked at Chatsworth), and the 'Mr Baker' who was paid £120 for 'hangings' in November 1680.

In 1689 John Vanderbank had taken over the working of the Great Wardrobe looms in Soho. His Soho chinoiserie panels of tapestry became justly celebrated, and a number of tapestries by him survive at Burghley. John Leeson provided 12 iron fire-backs, and the painter was Thomas Streeter, who also worked at Kensington Palace and was a brother of Robert Streeter I, the Sergeant-Painter to Charles II. Three chests of statues were shipped through Leghorn from Rome in 1700 to enhance the earl's great house—busts of himself and his Countess, of his brother and several relief groups by the sculptor Pierre Monnot. When Lord Exeter died in France in the year of the receipt of Monnot's sculptures, 1700, it was with the secure knowledge that his monument by Monnot was already commissioned; it was set up in St Martin's Church, Stamford, in 1704 by William Palmer, who also carved the long Latin inscription. Set before a dark pyramid the earl and countess recline in Imperial Roman style— proud representatives of noble and travelled families.

The greatest glory of Burghley, which the earl saw completed, are the painted decorations by Antonio Verrio and his assistants (see col. pl. 2). The extensive archive which survives documents the commission in great detail—recent research (by Dr Eric Till) suggests a different interpretation to that of constant gracious living, which Verrio and his retinue certainly enjoyed for a time. The documents show that Verrio, with his family and assistants, were almost continuously at Burghley between 1687 and 1697. The account opens on 20 April 1687, with Verrio's debt to John Read for supplying wood and nails and 'a Deale Board to Waste Paint'. Mixed between payments for materials are accounts for clothes, food, wine and spirits, school bills and occasional cryptic notes by Culpepper Tanner, Lord Exeter's steward: 'Sig^r Verrio has had 60^{li} more than the Dineing Roome agreement, his bond not being of any validity'. It must have presented great difficulty to the earl and his steward to bind Verrio to any constant performance or price, but much was accomplished.

The State Bedchamber or First George Room (1690) is representative of the superb work in all the State Rooms—great wainscot panels, carved wood overdoors and a flamboyant painted

---

Colour plate 11 WOBURN ABBEY, Bedfordshire. Queen Victoria's State Bedroom, *c* 1755 (photograph: A F Kersting).

In an earlier form this room was occupied by Charles I and Henrietta Maria, and again by Charles in 1645 and 1647. It takes its present name from its use by Queen Victoria in 1841, but is basically a creation of John, 4th Duke of Bedford, in the mid-1750s. The superb chimneypiece was provided by John Devall in 1756 at a cost of £100. The ceiling design was based on Plate XIX, 'Temple of the Sun', in Robert Wood's 1753, *Ruins of Palmyra*. It was a popular source and there are similar ceilings at Milton Abbey, Dorset, and Drayton House, Northamptonshire. Most of the carving and gilding 'in the best burnished and oil gold' was done by the London carver and cabinet-maker Samuel Norman, who also provided much upholstered furniture. The rebuilding, spread over 16 years (1747–63), cost almost £85 000.
Lit: Gladys Scott Thomson, 1949, *Family Background*, pp. 9–82.

ceiling representing the chasing away of Night by Morning. It was worked on over 19 weeks, and the gilder René Cousin and his 'gold beater' enhanced its decoration. The charge was £200, of which Verrio had received £87. 11s. 7d. by April 1690.

The Drawing Room or Second George Room was also in progress before 1691. Verrio receipted a bill for £5 on 24 April 1691 for the start of his work, and John Collins double primed the ceiling at 8d. a yard in August. It was gilded by René Cousin in September—his bill in French survives—and an analysis shows that Verrio received his £200 in the twenty-third, twenty-eighth, thirty-first, thirty-third, thirty-seventh, forty-third, forty-fourth, forty-seventh, forth-ninth, fifty-first and fifty-second weeks of 1691. On 28 September 1691 work was started on the Dining Room (Fourth George Room), when Verrio received his first £20 of the usual £200 for each room. It was almost complete by January 1692/93 when Cousin received £13 of a submitted bill of £13. 3s. 6d. His bill, in French, is not easy to understand, but he charged for '31 *Cartrons*' and 11 books of gold leaf to decorate the cornice and balustrade, 10 '*Quartrons*' (a variant spelling) and 12 leaves of gold to do the angles and fringes of four simulated cloths, as well as £4. 11s. 8d. for a further 22 '*quartrons d'or*'. There is a long account of the various payments to Verrio, or his brother, for colours, for a painter's craike or basket, in which brushes or paints were presumably carried on the scaffold, and even an overpayment of over £24 so that, for once, 'Sigr Verrio is indebted to my Lord'. Finally, across several years to its conclusion in 1696, was the Fifth George Room, Saloon or 'Heaven Room', one of the finest painted rooms in England.

In June 1693 Verrio had again submitted his proposals for painting the Saloon. As for the Third George Room, he wanted £500 and indicated that he could complete it in 18 months. His estimate was set out by the earl's steward as follows, and amended one in which he said he would finish in a year:

If his Architecture Man [? Ricard] Continues all the time he will receive att 30s. p. weeke	117	00	00
proposes to pay the Guilders	40	00	00
yr L'dshps Debt	104	00	00
	261	00	00

Colour plate 12 THE VYNE, Hampshire. The Staircase, *c* 1765 (photograph: A F Kersting).

The Vyne is basically a Tudor house which underwent radical change in the 1650s, and again by John Chute, Horace Walpole's friend (*see* col. pl. 10 above), in the 1760s. About 1765 Chute did away with the Stone Hall and Staircase, and in their place contrived what *The Topographer* of May 1789 described as the 'Grecian theatric staircase'. The space Chute utilised was narrow (18 ft) and unusually long (44 ft). He formed a single, central flight which, at the first landing, branched into two and returned so as to provide galleries. The screen of fluted columns with Corinthian capitals, together with the stair balusters, are in wood. They evoke successfully a style out of its time—Chute designed a staircase worthy of the Palladians of a previous generation, and one in spirit akin to the early Italian Renaissance.

There will remaine for Signo Verrio to receive to
Live, pay Debts & buy Coulers   239 00 00

wch recd. att 30s. per week will be   117
there will then rest att ye finishing the worke
to receive   122
                            to Sig^r Verrio £500 00 00

The assembly of the Olympians attended by spirited creatures of the Zodiac on the ceiling provided the name of the 'Heaven Room'. The walls, colonnaded with painted Corinthian columns with a pediment strung with garlands of bright flowers, are peopled with a host of aerial and muscular figures. A horse and its red-robed rider gallops down from the cornice, and on the north wall Neptune holds Court, a splendid figure in a spirited baroque stance. Most dramatically, the east wall has a representation of Vulcan's forge, with a self-portrait of Verrio himself seated among the attendant Cyclops. The colours for the artist's palette are sent down on an arching rainbow.

Culpepper Tanner, ever busy with accounts and memoranda, noted the Great Room was about 465 yd and that Lord Devonshire's Room—presumably the State Dining Room at Chatsworth, the ceiling of which Verrio painted in 1691–92—was '433 ft'. He had received £500 there, a house, and stabling for his horses. Lord Exeter only wanted to: 'give proporcionally, att soe much agreed, as Lord Devon, His proviso, nobody paints with him, and as for etc., my Ld will provide, and be paying. my Ld will allow? 100Lⁱ more, he not to Lodge or reside in the house'. Even so, an account of 1 July 1693 gives details of food and drink supplied to Verrio by Wildman, with a request from Verrio to Michael Tanner, brother to Lord Exeter's other steward, Culpepper Tanner, to pay it from what was due to him when he had finished the Saloon.

The many accounts for this great room show that Verrio was paid a weekly sum of £3. 6s. 0d., with many advances and extras for colours, oils, pencils, brushes and board for assistants, or for the services of specialist craftsmen such as René Cousin, the gilder. Cousin's bill for materials included charging £37. 0s. 10d. for 4446 sheets of gold leaf, of which 1030 were used on the cornice alone.

When Verrio went from Burghley to Lowther Castle in 1694, an inventory of several things he had left was compiled: books, colours, various pictures, grinding and rubbing stones, sketches, linseed oil, a close stool, a ship, two brass and eight iron guns and an anchor. Mr Edward Croft-Murray has assumed that the last refer to a model ship owned by Verrio, which he may have used in composing marine subjects. A Burghley account of 21 February 1690 notes: 'Sigr Verrios Shipp Carpenters Account—Mr Vario his bill for seven Months worke at three pound pr Month £21. 00s. 00d.'. Was this for an itinerant carpenter in Verrio's retinue who happened to be versed in marine work, or did he help in composing tableaux of model ships and nautical impedimenta? Verrio painted the Danish fleet in the background of a wall painting in the Queen's Drawing Room at Hampton Court.

The visitor ascended to the Lowther State Rooms by a Great Staircase, the ceiling of which represented Verrio's version of 'Hell'. His colours bill (1696) of fine lake, vermilion and blue verditer was mixed in with payments for caviare and a suggestion that, if the recipient found the anchovies good, he would send more. He was being paid £3 fortnightly in 1697 and received his last payment of £10 on 10 March 1697/98. A month or two before, he wrote in French from Chatsworth to Culpepper Tanner that, by the command of 'Mylord Duc DeVonshire', he was obliged to stay at Chatsworth and that his servant Hannah should be given 3 or 4s. to attend to several small tasks for him. At Chatsworth Verrio's work was not extensive—more was done by Laguerre—and the woodcarvers had also been busy there.

CHATSWORTH

The woodcarving in the State Rooms at Chatsworth is of a high standard. The London craftsmen Thomas Young, William Davis and Joel Lobb came on to the house from Burghley House; as their assistant they had the competent services of Samuel Watson, who was born at Heanor in Derbyshire but trained under the London carver Charles Okey. Watson had arrived at Chatsworth in 1689 at the age of 26. His book of *Designs, Bills and Agreements*, and several drawings by him, have survived among the house archives. He worked at the house on and off at wood- and stone-carving until his death in 1715. A further memorandum book by Watson includes a note, dated 16 February 1691: 'ye 16th begun works for Burly', and again, on 20 April: 'dun for Burly'. It may be that this implies a stronger connection between the Chatsworth and Burghley carvers than hitherto suspected, although no similarity of style or motif can be detected in the carvings.

For the work at Chatsworth wood was imported from the Baltic, and oak acquired for wainscoting the State Rooms. Cedar wood was used in the Chapel (*see* pl. 86), and some of the joinery was worked in London by John Chaplin, who sent it by sea to Hull and then by road to Bawtry, from where it was collected by the duke's men. Chaplin himself did not visit the house, as he presumably did when he worked at Kiveton, Yorkshire.

The decorative work at Chatsworth was completed by the decorative painters and the workers in metal. Louis Laguerre arrived in January 1689 with his French assistant, Ricard, and other unnamed helpers to paint in oil on the Chapel walls and ceiling (*see* pl. 87), and the ceilings of the State Drawing Room, State Dressing Room, State Bedroom and the Music Room; they were tasks which were to occupy them, with work at other houses, until 1694. Three years later, Laguerre returned to paint the walls and ceiling of the Entrance Hall (*see* pl. 17). There are frequent references in the Chatsworth accounts to the erection and moving of scaffolding for the painters by the duke's estate carpenters; it is not easy, however, to allot responsibility for the work which was done from its roped planks set alongside walls or below ceilings. Laguerre's work for the most part is dull and confined to the Chapel ceiling and those of the State Rooms. Ricard painted the elaborate grotesques on the Bathing Room ceiling early in 1694, and a very talented anonymous assistant painted nymphs and youths high in the coves of the Music Room and State Bedroom ceilings, and the Evangelists at the corners of the Chapel ceiling (*see* pl. 87).

In iconographic terms, such ceilings were important throughout the seventeenth century. At Whitehall (Rubens), Windsor (Verrio) and Greenwich (Thornhill) in particular, the paintings represented to the viewer political and religious themes common in Stuart court life and attitudes. The purpose of a room and its painted decoration were linked: Mercury holding a portrait of Charles II, displayed to the four quarters of the earth, looked down from Verrio's ceiling at Windsor, and earthly ambassadors were received by the king, and similar considerations, in work at Whitehall and Greenwich, fused together historical realism and spirited decoration. It all drew the abuse of Horace Walpole, who, in writing of Verrio in his *Anecdotes of Painters*, recorded that he was 'an excellent painter for the sort of subjects on which he was employed: that is, without much invention, and with less taste, his exuberant pencil was ready at pouring out gods, goddesses, kings, emperors and triumphs over those public surfaces on which the eye never rests long enough to criticise, and where one would be sorry to place the works of a better master.'

Verrio had been busy at Burghley House, 1690–98, and could only be spared by Lord Exeter to his brother-in-law for limited periods. He painted the walls of the Great Stairs at Chatsworth with the Triumphs of Ceres, Cybele and Bacchus in monochrome, and depicted Cybele in her chariot, attended by Ceres, on the ceiling. In the Great Chamber or State Dining Room he painted the ceiling, and, amid Laguerre's work in the Chapel, he painted the altar-piece, sculpted and carved by Caius Gabriel Cibber and Samuel Watson. Finally, in the Gallery (now the Library), he provided medallions of Apollo, Mercury and Minerva presiding over the Muses, set into a richly plastered ceiling by Edward Goudge.

Verrio's work on the Great Stairs was set off by Laguerre's father-in-law, Jean Tijou, who provided the metal balustrade for £250 in 1688–89 (*see* pl. 31). He received his first payment at Chatsworth on 9 March 1688; his charges included 4s. for a gallon of linseed oil to prime the iron. He may have been assisted by John Gardom from Bakewell nearby, who had also worked with him at Kiveton. Tijou, his wife and daughters settled in England from about 1687 for over 20 years, and it has been established[67] that, when he was living in 1704 in Portugal Row, near Hyde Park Corner, the sculptors John Nost and Andries Carpentier were his neighbours. The painter Louis Laguerre, who may well have first met Tijou at Chatsworth, married his daughter Eleanor, who receipted a payment to her husband in 1699 for his staircase-well painting at Castle Bromwich Hall. Laguerre married again and left his wife many debts to clear when he died on 20 April 1721—an unworthy end for a painter whose godfather had been Louis XIV. He was buried in the churchyard of St Martin-in-the-Fields, London.

PETWORTH

A French architect in the person of Daniel Marot may well have been involved in the design of another great ducal residence, Petworth House, Sussex, building from 1688 for the 6th Duke of Somerset, the 'Proud Duke'.[68] In this year his wife, Lady Elizabeth Percy, was 21—he was 26. He is said to have insisted on his children always standing in his presence and, while imperious and pompous, was the recipient of visits from William III (1693) and the king of Spain (1703). The accounts of Richard Stiles, the Petworth 'paymaster', have survived

67. Information from Mr Edward Saunders based on the rate books, and the St Martin-in-the-Fields Burial registers, 1700–9.
68. Gervase Jackson-Stops, 28 June 1973, 'Petworth and the Proud Duke', *C Life*, CLIII, pp. 1870–74; G H

Kenyon, 1959, 'Petworth Town and Trades, 1610–1760', *Sussex Archaeological Collections*, XCVI; Gervase Jackson-Stops, May 1977, 'The Building of Petworth', *Apollo*, p. 324.

complete for the years 1689 to 1695 inclusive;[69] they total some 700 foolscap pages and cover all the local labour and materials. Most of what was needed was on the estate, and the house remodelling and estate work provided employment for about 100 local men the year round.

The system of payment for the rebuilding was that the duke himself paid one or two of the leading master craftsmen, such as the carver Grinling Gibbons. John Bowen, Clerk of the Kitchens, paid the remaining outside master craftsmen and for the loads of Portland stone; Stiles paid the local accounts. The stone was shipped to Littlehampton and then transferred to small barges, which came as far as Greatham Bridge; it was then carted over the final 10 miles to the house. The duke's annual income at this time was about £17 000, of which only £2000 came from the Sussex estates within about six miles of the house.

The blending of local with London talent combined the work of men whose usual occupation was domestic building with the achievements of those who enhanced great houses. Grinling Gibbons received £173 for statues in March 1692 and, on 10 December in the same year, 'for Carveing £150'.[70] His woodwork, fashioned with great dexterity (*see* pls. 110 and 111), was only set out in the 'Carved Room' about 1790, having been installed originally in a small 'cabinet'. On hand with work of almost equal standard was the resourceful Petworth carver John Selden, acting in very much the same supporting role as Samuel Watson did at Chatsworth. His annual salary was £40, and he worked in the Chapel and Hall of State; he did *putti*, mouldings, picture frames and general carving. His main achievement is set out in the Marble Hall (one of the few rooms to survive the 1714 fire) where, with Thomas Larkin, George Turner and Edward Goudge, he produced a panelled room (*see* pl. 14) with niches and a handsome fireplace surmounted by a carved coat-of-arms and supporters. Goudge was also paid £26 for the fretwork ceiling in the Chapel in 1691.

A large part of the rebuilding was complete by 1697, and a surviving painting of the west front (at Syon House), done about 1695, shows it to have had a four-sided dome. This is shown again in Laguerre's painting on the staircase walls (*see* pl. 96) depicting 'the triumph of Elizabeth, Duchess of Somerset, surrounded by her family', painted a little after the fire in which the dome was destroyed.[71]

BOUGHTON

Apart from Petworth, the other major English house on which French influences were at work is Boughton, Northamptonshire.

Created for Ralph Montagu, on whom Queen Anne bestowed a dukedom in 1705 to add to his earldom and viscountcy, the house has remained largely unaltered. It also has a fascinating

69. The account rolls form part of the Egremont Archives in West Sussex CRO, and are listed in Volume 2 of the calendar to them.
70. West Sussex CRO, Egremont Archives, 6th Duke of Somerset's Red Disbursement Book.
71. John Harris, 1979, *The Artist and the Country House*, pl. 85. Mr Harris has also pointed out that a rear elevation drawing from the Bute sale (Sotheby's, 22 May 1951, lot 17/2) of Wren's Winchester Palace, 1683–85, shows such a dome, (*repr.* John Summerson,

1959, *Architecture in Britain, 1530–1830*, pl. 90A); the Winchester elevation shows 'marked French influence', and the plan of Winchester 'has affinities with Le Vau's Versailles' (Whinney and Millar, *English Art*, p. 217). All are significant pointers to Petworth's French origins. John Bowen's roll, 1690, records a payment of £42 for 'French' glass (West Sussex CRO), and in 1695 the duke paid 'the Frenchman for gilt sconces and other small things at Petworth' (Red Disbursement Book).

uncompleted north-east pavilion which affords good evidence of building techniques in the 1690s. The architect, as at Petworth, is unknown, but many theories have been advanced, and the most likely solution is that, whoever redesigned Montagu House in London, extended and improved Boughton soon afterwards.[72] We have noted the possibility of Daniel Marot being the designer of Petworth—the source of the north front of Boughton is held to be plate 83 in his father Jean Marot's *Recueil des Plans, Profils* ... (1660–70). Furthermore, the heiress to Petworth was the Duchess of Montagu's daughter, Elizabeth, who married the 'Proud Duke of Somerset'. However, the most likely candidate is the French architect Pierre Boujet.[73]

Ralph, Duke of Montagu, was Ambassador to the French Court between 1669 and 1672, and again between 1676 and 1678. On his first trip he noticed Molière's friend, the painter Antonio Verrio, and invited him back to England into the bright circle of the Caroline Court. The duke also bought back French chairs which were black-japanned with red damask cushions.[74] In the mid-1680s the duke's town house, built in 'the French pavilion way', as Evelyn wrote, was burned down. In the rebuilding a competent team of Frenchmen under the supervision of Charles de la Fosse, and including Jacques Rousseau, Jacques Parmentier and Jean-Baptiste Monnoyer, decorated it.

A few years later, work started at Boughton. A number of accounts of the executors of the 1st Duke survive but, unfortunately, no letters or private accounts of any sort; the executors' accounts,[75] amounting to £20 601. 10s. 8d., include payments to craftsmen (and many of their widows) for work done up to 20 years previously, but not paid for. There is also no means of separating out the money due to work in London and at Boughton. The history painter Louis Chéron (1660–1725), who did oil-on-plaster paintings in several rooms as well as the Great Staircase about 1694, was still owed £115 at the duke's death in 1709; the carver and gilder Thomas Pelletier, as executor of his mother, René, was owed the large sum of £2382. We know that the £115 due to Gideon du Chesne was for carving stone heads at the duke's house at Ditton Park, Buckinghamshire, and for carving the coat-of-arms over the stable pediment at Boughton (£15); yet another widow, Elizabeth Verhuyck, claimed £136 for carving done by her husband. Even Sir James Thornhill was owed £80 for painting a coach and chariot. The joiner Roger Davies, who had worked for Sir Robert Hooke at Ragley Hall, Warwickshire, and who was later employed at Burghley House, was owed the substantial sum of £3606; we can assume he provided wainscoting and staircases, although 'Peter Rimsset, joyner' was also due to £4860. Finally, among many payments to clockmakers, painters, cabinet-makers and plasterers, the upholsterer and fringe-maker Francis La Pierre was owed £1432.

The use of many local craftsmen at houses like Boughton and Petworth gave welcome employment, but a near monopoly over work in their localities was exercised by the Livery Companies in centres such as York, Bristol, Newcastle, Chester and Norwich. They did not take kindly to oversight by, or work given to, craftsmen from London; there is no better example of this than the building of Sudbury Hall, Derbyshire, from 1665 to the early 1690s.

72. James Lees-Milne, 1970, *English Country Houses: Baroque*, p. 41.

73. G Jackson-Stops, May 1977, The Building of Petworth, *Apollo, p. 324;* Colvin, 1978, *Dictionary*, s.v. 'Pouget'.

74. Peter Thornton, February 1975, 'The Parisian Fauteuil

of 1680', *Apollo*, pp. 102–7.

75. Boughton House, Northamptonshire. Parcel 'D11', Pt. 2. I am also indebted for information (supplementary to my own archival searches) to Mr P I King, Sir David Scott and Mr Gervase Jackson-Stops.

Sudbury Hall

Sudbury Hall was built for George Vernon, who inherited the estate in 1658. Soon after the Restoration he started his house in a late Jacobean style, and in diapered brick. There are extensive building accounts,[76] which show that, by the late 1660s, the upper walls were rising fast and work on the porch was in progress. In 1669 Blakely and Dick agreed to provide 'all my neither cornish att 9*d*. per yd', and Sam Adams and Thomas Phillips agreed to do 'the over cornish' at 10*d*. a yard. In 1670 William Wilson (then coming up to 30 years old, and later to become a successful architect, an associate of Wren and to be knighted by Charles II) agreed to finish the 'two frontispieces' of the house for £35 and to provide various stone carvings, as he was to do later at Castle Bromwich Hall. At Sudbury he provided 'boys over ye porch . . . heads & frontage . . . & ye bores heade'; at Castle Bromwich, figures of 'Peace' and 'Plenty', for which he charged 12 guineas in 1697. They are still above the main entrance porch.[77]

There is a delightful oval portrait at Sudbury attributed to William Dobson which has on it the inscription 'George Vernon Esqr by whom Sudbury was built'. His house was splendid but old fashioned, based on the letter 'E' in plan, and may be compared, not too unfavourably, with the great Lauderdale mansion, Ham House. The Entrance Hall runs the full depth of the house and divides the ground floor into two equal portions—if one ignores a Victorian wing to the south which lessens the symmetry of the Stuart house. Inside, the State Dining Room has a broad frieze of stiff plaster acanthus foliage by a local plasterer from Derby, Samuel Mansfield (d. 1697), the father of James Gibbs's favourite English plasterer, Isaac Mansfield. The work bears little comparison to the rich plasterwork elsewhere in the house, but Mansfield did provide the Queen's Room with an elaborate ceiling of swirling naturalistic work to crest William Wilson's alabaster chimneypiece.

In 1675 decoration was continued with a new zeal and extravagance. Robert Bradbury and James Pettifer were engaged from London as plasterers. They agreed to do six ceilings at the rate of 6*s*. a yard, and their principal achievement was the ceiling of the Long Gallery, stretching over some 350 sq yd. Their bill totalled £101. 2*s*., and for this they and their assistants created within seven oval compartments curling flowers and foliage, shells, emperors' heads, horses galloping out of cornucopiae, dragons and wild boars. They put up the staircase and parlour ceilings for £64, and the staircase balustrade was carved in wood by Edward Pearce, whose work for William Winde has been mentioned earlier. Pearce was a leading London craftsman but his work may have come to Vernon's notice by the staircase he did at Wolseley Hall, Staffordshire.[78] His staircase at Sudbury (*see* pl. 27), now painted white (a colour which, despite the 'evidence' of paint scrapes, was considered wrong by some art historians) is superb—baskets of fruit on the newel posts and riotous foliage within the balustrade. Pearce was paid £112. 5*s*. 6*d*. for it and the complexity of his carving harmonises with the plasterwork (*see* pl. 60) far overhead. The painted panels by Laguerre were not added until some 15 years later, in 1691. It is surprising that Grinling Gibbons, to whom Vernon paid £40 in 1676 for the

76. Summarised in *C Life*, 15, 22 and 29 June 1935, and by Hill and Cornforth, *Caroline*, pp. 162–73. *See also* John Cornforth, 10 June 1971, 'Sudbury Hall Revisited', *C Life*, CXLIX, pp. 1428–33.

77. Geoffrey Beard, 18 March 1954, 'Sculpture by Sir William Wilson', *C Life*, p. 780.

78. Noted as by Pearce in Robert Plot, 1686, *Natural History of Staffordshire*, p. 383, and illustrated by H A Tipping, 1929, *English Homes, 1649–1714*, p. xi.

Drawing Room overmantel swags, was not given more woodcarving to do in the house; the carver was at this time, however, little known, but he carved the fish, dead game and fruit in such swags with a skill that was to earn him the poetic praise of Nahum Tate,[79] and lead him finally to be 'Carver in Wood' to the king.

KIVETON

One of the leading politicians of the late seventeenth century, Treasurer of England, Lord President of the Council and an active supporter of the Prince of Orange, was Thomas Osborne, 1st Duke of Leeds (1620–1712). While described by contemporaries as a 'thin ill-natured ghost' and 'a gentleman of admirable natural parts, great knowledge and experience . . . but of no reputation with any party', he amassed a considerable fortune and, in the later years of his career, spent large sums of money on building and decoration. This was at his Yorkshire house, Kiveton, which was built 1694–1704, but pulled down about 1812. A few fragments survive incorporated in outbuildings, and the staircase by John Chaplin, a London joiner, was incorporated in a house at Penistone, elsewhere in Yorkshire, some 20 years after the demolition sale. The architect of Kiveton may again have been William Talman.

Talman's career, including his arguments with patrons, still remains obscure, despite detailed research.[80] An elevation of Kiveton by Talman[81] is endorsed: 'For ye D. of Leeds at Keiton in Yorkshire', but does not represent the house that was built, as a subsequent engraving by Badeslade and Roque establishes.[82] Talman is also nowhere mentioned in the many documents about the house.[83] The contract, which has been noted previously, specified that the house was to be 'of such dimensions and with materials and ornaments and in such form and manner as in designs for the same in draughts of the ground platt, the first and ground storey and of the uprights thereof hereunto affixed'.

A slightly smaller house of 11 bays, less than the 15 of Talman's elevation, was erected, and some £10 344. 4s. 6d. was spent on the structure in eight or nine years, decoration apart. Agreements were made with the master craftsmen—Chaplin's has survived—but for the remainder only their names and what they were paid in total is known with one further exception: Louis Laguerre's contract and drawing (1702) for the ceiling paintings survives and has been published.[84] Laguerre painted scenes from the story of Cupid and Psyche and received £357. 15s. The other craftsmen who gathered—Jean Tijou (ironsmith), Jonathan Maine (woodcarver), Henry Margetts (plasterer) and the joiner John Chaplin—produced a lavish scene which can be re-created partially from various manuscripts found at Kiveton House, Yorkshire and held by the Yorkshire Archaeological Society Library, Leeds.[85] There were 24 chimneypieces, that in the Great Dining Room being composed largely of purple marble.

79. Nahum Tate, 1684, 'To Mr Gibbons On His Incomparable Carved Works', cited by David Green, 1964, *Grinling Gibbons*, p. 180.
80. Colvin, 1978, *Dictionary*, pp. 802–7; Margaret Whinney and John Harris, articles in *Journal of the Warburg and Courtauld Institutes*, XVIII (1955), pp. 123–39; XXIII (1960), pp. 139–49.
81. London, RIBA, Drawings Collection, B4/5.
82. 1739, *Vitruvius Britannicus*, IV, pls. 11 and 12.

83. Yorkshire Archaeological Society Library, Leeds. *See* Geoffrey Beard, 1961, *Leeds Arts Calendar*, No. 46, pp. 4–11, and Beard, 1966, *Craftsmen*, pp. 184–85. A detailed analysis of the building of Kiveton is given by E Y Prins in a Leeds Univ. BA thesis (1976).
84. Yorkshire Archaeological Society Library, Leeds. Box 13, item 20; Norbert Lynton, June 1956, 'Laguerre at Kiveton', *Burl Mag*, LIXVIII, pp. 204–207.
85. *ibid.*, Box 33.

As at Dyrham, Gloucestershire, Honington, Warwickshire, and Ham House, Surrey, gilt-leather panels hung in the lower vestibule. Some 12 ft high and ranging in width from 1 ft to 4 ft 6 in wide, they complemented Jonathan Maine's woodcarvings, which were also to be found over the altar of the private Chapel. There were 56 panels over doors and chimneypieces painted by Louis Hauduroy—Laguerre's work was not added until 1702—and the staircase balustrading was probably by Jean Tijou, as well as the entrance gates, reproduced in Badeslade's engraving of the house. Tijou's follower John Gardom agreed on 11 June 1700 to make and erect in workmanlike manner an iron fence to enclose the courtyard to the house.

THORESBY HOUSE

There is again no sign in the surviving papers of Talman's involvement at Thoresby House, Nottinghamshire, but some strong pointers to his submitting designs have been noticed.[86] Thoresby, twice ravaged by fire and finally destroyed in 1745 (the present house is by Salvin, 1864), was an important example of a new departure in planning and decoration on the scale of palace architecture. While Talman seems never to have travelled abroad (although a visit to Holland may have been undertaken), he had a sound knowledge of foreign pattern-books. The façade at Thoresby bore relationship to those of certain Italian palaces, and the plan incorporated rooms around a courtyard (a feature found in other 'Talman houses' such as Chatsworth), as well as other interesting spatial arrangements which permitted easier movement than hitherto. The patron, William Pierrepoint, 4th Earl of Kingston, agreed to the employment of Edward Goudge (plasterer), John Nost and C G Cibber (carvers), Antonio Verrio and Louis Laguerre (painters) and René Cousin (Verrio's gilder). The interiors they provided may be envisaged from their surviving work at Chatsworth and Burghley.

The problem of authorship is, however, complicated by a sketch (All Souls College, Oxford) which depicts a variation on the Thoresby design; it cannot be ascribed to Talman, Hawksmoor or Wren. Talman's name, as noted, is not in the accounts for 1685–87 but there is a payment of 5 guineas in June 1686 to 'Sr Christopher Wren's man', which presumably means Hawksmoor. The old house seems, therefore, to have been remodelled rather than rebuilt; it was burned out as soon as built, and the 4th Earl died of an apoplexy in 1690.

DYRHAM PARK

In 1698 William Blathwayt, Secretary of State, retained Talman for designs for the east front of his house, Dyrham Park, Gloucestershire. After his work at Thoresby and Chatsworth, Talman introduced a new type of house with a great rectangular block, three storeys high, with the roof concealed by heavy cornice and balustrade. Statues and urns were used to soften the impressive outline and, with this type of house, apart from his appointment in 1689 as Comptroller of the Royal Works, Talman became a much sought after, if somewhat temperamental, architect. He came to William Blathwayt's attention just after the statesman

86. John Harris, 1961, 'Thoresby House, Nottinghamshire', *Architectural History*, IV, pp. 11–20; 1963, VI, pp. 103–5. Documents survive in British Library, Egerton MSS, 3256, 3539, and Nottingham University, Pierrepont Archives, 4205–6, 4210, both noted by Colvin, 1978, *Dictionary*, p. 805. *See also* Clive Aslet, 28 June 1979, 'Thoresby. I.', *C Life*, pp. 2082–85.

had inherited Wynter estates at his wife Mary's death in 1691. The building of the west front was undertaken first to a design by Samuel Hauduroy,[87] one of a Huguenot family working on various decorative tasks in England.

The east front which Talman designed, and which Colen Campbell subsequently engraved in *Vitruvius Britannicus* (II, pls. 91 and 93), was a smaller version of the Thoresby pattern and the new building at Hampton Court, which Wren and Talman supervised for the Office of Works, 1689–94. Campbell stated that Talman made the design in 1698. Blathwayt wrote[88] from the Hague on 19 July 1699 to his cousin to ask him to be sure to be at Dyrham when Talman and his mason Benjamin Jackson (who was also used at Thoresby and Drayton) visited, and to write down what faults they found. By September 1701 deals for the floors were coming in from Stockholm, and J Robinson, a Bristol timber merchant, provided deals for the best floors. Site supervision was put in the hands of Edward Wilcox, a master carpenter who had worked under Talman at Hampton Court and Kensington Palace, and son of Jonathan Wilcox, who had supervised similar jobs for Captain William Winde.

John Povey and Robert Barker, London joiners of the parish of St Martin-in-the-Fields, agreed to do all the joiner's work of the Great Staircase and Balcony Room. Again, as Thomas Carter had done at Ham House in decoration of 50 years or so earlier, Barker divided the pine panels with Ionic pilasters. The contract specified that four master workmen were to be sent down to Dyrham, and Barker was to receive 3s. a day each for their services and 5s. a day for himself; if any local Dyrham workers were used, they were to receive 2s. a day. By 1704, the plasterwork by Thomas Porter of London and the joinery was finished, and 'Monsieur Hauduroy'—either Samuel or the Louis Hauduroy employed at Kiveton—veined the walls of the Staircase and the Ionic pilasters in the Balcony Room over the West Hall. The brass door furniture was provided by Henry Walton. The Staircase was made in cedar and Virginian walnut by the London joiner Alexander Hunter, who also wainscoted the Diogenes Room.

Blathwayt's opinion of his agent and his craftsmen was not a high one. In 1701 he wrote that they all needed stirring into action and were not to be overfed with money. He paid as late and as little as possible, reserving his money to buy books, pictures, gilt-leather hangings, china and, through his colonial contacts, to order timber and garden plants from America. When William III died, Blathwayt lost his appointments and in 1702 he was dismissed as acting Secretary of State. Two years later, in 1704, he was dismissed from his post as Secretary at War, and his income was still further diminished in 1707 when he lost his position as Secretary to the Lords of Trade.[89] Perhaps for these reasons the interior decoration of Dyrham is restrained, with no grand staircase paintings such as Sir James Thornhill had painted for Blathwayt's friend at Stoke Edith, Herefordshire, in 1705.

DRAYTON PARK

Talman's country-house practice, while more extensive than that of Robert Hooke, Wren and Captain Winde put together, was not great and suffered a set-back when Vanburgh replaced him as architect at Castle Howard in 1699. His work at Drayton Park,

87. Mark Girouard, 15 February 1962, 'Dyrham Park', *C Life*, CXXXI, p. 335.

88. Gloucestershire CRO, Blathwayt Archives, B15/5.

89. G A Jacobsen, 1932, *William Blathwayt*, p. 24.

Northamptonshire, is documented by mentions in the contract of 24 August 1702 between Sir John Germaine and Talman's mason, Benjamin Jackson.[90] When Lord Peterborough died at Drayton in 1697, his heir was his daughter Mary, who, while married to the 7th Duke of Norfolk, had been living openly since about 1685 with Sir John Germaine, a soldier and financier said to have been an illegitimate son of William II, Prince of Orange. The duke divorced her finally in 1700, and she married Sir John the following year.

Prior to that event William Winde had written to his cousin, Lady Mary Bridgeman, on 20 December 1697 that he was about to visit the Duchess of Norfolk at Drayton. He was probably responsible for the forecourt gate piers,[91] and one assumes the ironwork to be by Jean Tijou (as he also worked within the house) or by someone influenced by him. Furthermore, the whole style of the house shows Talman (as Mr John Harris has observed) being aided probably by the more spirited imagination of his son, John. The centre of the south façade and its flanking colonnades, while owing some allegiance in detail to Hampton Court, has many interesting overtones which could have been culled from John Talman's large collection of drawings and prints.[92]

As well as Talman's work within, concentrated mostly in the Great Hall, there is much work from the 1670s paid for by Lady Mary's father, the 2nd Earl of Peterborough. The most significant addition was the Walnut Staircase in the east tower; this, despite its name, has oak steps carved from single pieces of wood, with the balusters alone of walnut. Cantilevered out from the wall, it spirals upwards—its carpenter is unknown, as is the joiner responsible for the grained wainscot in the King's Dining Room, to which the staircase leads. It has been noted that the staircase design is based on one by Palladio, which was available in the English translation of his works of 1668.[93] Finally, the decorations at Drayton received the attentions of a painter of decoration, Gerard Lanscroon (fl. 1677–1737), a pupil of Verrio; he painted the Stone Staircase about 1712, based on an allegory on the rule of William III. He had also worked at Powis Castle for another of William III's Dutch supporters, William Henry van Nassau van Zuylesteyn, later 1st Earl of Rochford (signed, 1705), and at Burley-on-the-Hill, Rutland (c 1708), for Daniel Finch, 2nd Earl of Nottingham. At Powis the architect may well have been William Winde, who had told his Bridgeman cousin in 1698 that he was to visit Powis Castle after leaving Drayton.

BURLEY-ON-THE-HILL

Owners of houses looked frequently at those built for their peers or friends when wishing to act as their own architects. Daniel Finch, 2nd Earl of Nottingham, had measurements taken at Lord Berkeley's London house in Piccadilly (1655), designed by Hugh May, and at Montagu House, designed by Robert Hooke and rebuilt by an unknown French architect after the fire of January 1685/86. He had been assembling money and ideas to build at Burley-on-the-Hill,

90. G F Webb, 1953, 'Drayton House' *Archaeological Journal*, CX, p. 189.
91. John Cornforth, 27 May 1965, 'Drayton House, III', *C Life*, CXXXVII p. 1287.
92. John Talman's collection of drawings—in 1725 consisting of 200 volumes—is noted by Colvin, 1978, *Dictionary*, p. 802; Hugh Honour, August 1954, 'John Talman and William Kent in Italy', *The Connoisseur*, CXXXIV pp. 3–7; T F Friedman, December 1975, 'The English Appreciation of Italian Decoration', *Burl Mag*, pp. 841–47.
93. John Cornforth, 20 May 1965, 'Drayton House, II', *C Life*, CXXXVII, p. 1219.

Rutland, an estate he had acquired in 1694 from the executors of the 2nd Duke of Buckingham. A voluminous archive of letters and monthly accounts survives,[94] making it possible to plot progress in detail; regrettably, the house was damaged by fire in 1908, but Lanscroon's painted staircase, referred to above, survived. Lord Nottingham turned first to a supervising mason-architect, Henry Dormer, who practised in Northamptonshire and Leicestershire; however, within three years Dormer was replaced by John Lumley. Whether both were supervised by Robert Hooke, as has been suggested,[95] is not clear. In a letter of 1700, Lord Nottingham refers to a model of Lowther Castle made for his friend John Lowther, 1st Viscount Lonsdale, by the king's joiner, Alexander Fort. Hooke knew Lord Lonsdale and he had built Ragley Hall, Warwickshire, for Lord Nottingham's uncle, Lord Conway. However, there is strong evidence that Lord Lowther turned to many architects for advice besides Hooke. Plans survive for the rebuilding of his castle (which he had pulled down in the 1690s) by Hooke, William Talman, Colen Campbell and James Gibbs.[96]

Daniel Finch created a house with pedimented centre, and quadrants linked it to sweeping colonnades. He had visited Rome in the mid-1660s, when Bernini was engaged on the piazza in front of St Peter's, and seems to have attempted his own version on a Rutland plateau. The bills for ashlar, sawyers, pond cleaning, stone from Clipsham, timber and marble all survive. Edward Chapman sent all the wrong sizes of marble from London; it came by ship to Boston and Spalding, delivered at £10 a ton. On 26 May 1711 Catherine Chapman said her father had supplied chimneypieces too cheaply; she therefore asked Lord Nottingham to send the extra money, as she was obliged to pay out large sums which it was difficult to raise. Lumley also asked his patron for 30s. to save the pond cleaners from starving.[97]

These small routine considerations should not detract from Lord Nottingham's achievement in building his baroque house, even if it lacked a continental bravura and the full, colourful frescoes of a Verrio or Laguerre. Lanscroon was a slighter follower but, as some of his work was destroyed in the 1908 fire, a full assessment of his achievement is not possible. His feigned marble columns and his hordes of unconsidered gods and goddesses provided almost the last major scheme of decoration (1708) in the colonnade style, set out so pre-eminently by Verrio at Burghley House some 15 years before. Daniel Defoe, on his tour through Great Britain in 1724, enthused about the house, however: it excelled the rest of them, and he did not know of one that did this 'in so many particulars, or that goes so near to excelling them all in every thing'.[98]

HANBURY HALL

Finally in this group of late seventeenth-century houses with painted staircases there is Hanbury Hall, Worcestershire, finished by 1701, the date over the centrepiece of the east front. There are mysterious elevations for it by James Withenbury, a Worcester sculptor, and by

94. Leicestershire CRO, Finch Archives (DE.585), especially DG 7/1/127–8; H J Habakkuk, 1955, 'Daniel Finch, 2nd Earl of Nottingham: His House and Estate', *Studies in Social History*, ed. J H Plumb.
95. Kerry Downes, 1966, *English Baroque Architecture*, p. 64.
96. Geoffrey Beard, 1978, *The Greater House in Cumbria*, p. 16, Kendal. The plans are in Carlisle CRO, and

were published, 1981, in *Architectural History*, Monograph 2.
97. Leicestershire CRO, DG 7/1/127(6); Pearl Finch, 1901, *Burley on the Hill*, pp. 64–65.
98. Daniel Defoe, *A Tour Through the Whole Island of Great Britain*, Everyman edition, 1962, ed. G D H Cole and D C Browning, I, p. 104.

William Rudhall of Henley-in-Arden, the latter basing his drawing on that of Talman's Thoresby.[99] Hanbury is an advanced house in style, and it has been suggested[100] that possible architects, if one looks beyond Rudhall, are William and Edward Stanton; Hanbury bears a resemblance to William Stanton's Belton, and the lawyer builder of Hanbury, Thomas Vernon, was a member of the Temple, and Edward Stanton worked there stone-carving and as a master builder. Thomas Vernon's monument in Hanbury Church is by Edward Stanton and Christopher Horsenaile, and similarly at Belton the monument to Sir John and Lady Brownlow is by William Stanton. The work seems to have the refinement of a London mason-builder with all the consequent poise and breeding which provincials emulated, often with great skill, but rarely at this period attained. Whatever the truth—for this is no more than an attractive theory—Hanbury is assured and sophisticated, and, within, the staircase was decorated late in 1710 by Sir James Thornhill with scenes (*see* pl. 32) from the life of Achilles. It is complemented by a staircase balustrade (*see* pl. 33) of competent joiner's work by an unknown craftsman.

EASTON NESTON

Something of the differing levels of attainment can be seen by comparing the east front of Hanbury (1701) with the east front of Easton Neston, Northamptonshire, dated 'MDCCII' (1702). With finely dressed stone from Helmdon, the architect of Easton Neston, Nicholas Hawksmoor, erected a house for Sir William Fermor with elevations of tight and effective classical detailing, partly set out on the surviving wooden model (*see* pl. 7).[101] This differs from the house in many respects, however, and there also seems to be evidence to connect Wren with the scheme, with Hawksmoor then taking over from his master.[102] In 1692 Sir William married the widowed daughter of Thomas Osborne, 1st Duke of Leeds, who was to engage Talman to advise him when building at Kiveton a few years later. This hastened the work, already made difficult by the existence of brick wings to the forecourt, finished in 1682 and some 125 ft apart. The entrance bay with its segmental head has a French look about it, and the church of St Gervais, Paris, by Salomon de Brose (1616) has been cited as a prototype.[103]

Within, the house is dominated by the great staircase with its superb wrought-iron balustrade (*see* pl. 34). The work is worthy of Jean Tijou,[104] and several times incorporates an intertwined 'L' and coronet to commemorate Lord Lempster, as Sir William Fermor had now become. The plasterwork may be by Edward Goudge, but he had turned away from plasterwork increasingly from 1700 and it is more likely to be by Henry Doogood, who had worked on several occasions for the Office of Works. Regrettably, there are no surviving documents and the exact details are therefore lacking. Thornhill, in less exuberant style than normally, complemented the ironwork and plaster ceilings with grisaille paintings of scenes in the life of King Cyrus.

99. John Harris, 1961, 'Thoresby House, Nottinghamshire', *Architectural History*, IV, pp. 19–20.
100. In a letter to me from Edmund Esdaile, May 1970.
101. H M Colvin, 15 October 1970, 'Easton Neston Reconsidered', *C Life*, CXLVIII, p. 968.
102. Kerry Downes, 1979, *Hawksmoor*, pp. 31–34.
103. J Kenworthy-Browne, October 1964, 'Easton Neston I', *The Connoisseur*.
104. Gervase Jackson-Stops, 28 January, 4 February 1971, 'English Baroque Ironwork, I, II', *C Life*, CXLIX, pp. 182–83, 262–66.

CASTLE HOWARD

The most important houses where Hawksmoor gave some realisation to the architectural ideas of Sir John Vanbrugh are Castle Howard, Yorkshire, and Blenheim Palace, Oxfordshire. Building commenced at Castle Howard in 1699, but it was well towards the middle years of the eighteenth century before all was complete. A long series of Building Books, 1700 to 1736, the 3rd Earl of Carlisle's personal account books, and folders of bills, 1700 to 1740, allow us to probe in detail a commission which has been examined often enough in broad terms.[105] The facts, briefly, are that Sir John Vanbrugh, then known as a dramatist and soldier, was invited by the 3rd Earl of Carlisle to succeed William Talman in designing Castle Howard; Talman had demanded a high price for his plans and, in an interesting letter of 1703[106] written to the Duke of Newcastle at Welbeck, a house for which Talman had also submitted plans, Vanbrugh revealed the rivalry existing between them. Subsequent events indicate that Vanbrugh's triumphs at Castle Howard were at Talman's expense. In 1702 Vanbrugh, with Lord Carlisle's support (the earl was then Lord Treasurer), superseded Talman as Comptroller of the Office of Works.

Sixteen drawings for Castle Howard came to light in 1951,[107] and fall into two categories as first and second proposals for the design. A set of five, forming the earliest drawings, show that there was much rearrangement to be done before the full, rich engravings in Colen Campbell's *Vitruvius Britannicus* (1717) reflected a true idea of the scale of the house. In early plans the kitchen and stable courts do not appear. By the time of the second group, big changes had been made, and the area near the Hall was being prepared for the reception of a heavy dome and cupola. With these plans Vanbrugh overcame the attempts of William Talman to be chosen as architect.

The high cupola is still absent from his second proposal—it was not built until 1706, and took its place among the early examples of English baroque which Wren had demonstrated at St Paul's, Greenwich Hospital and some of the City churches. The extensive Castle Howard archives contain only one letter from Vanbrugh, and two from Hawksmoor, within the main years of building activity. Vanbrugh's letter, written in 1700, was concerned with the provision of a suitable labour force, and the hope that the master mason and carpenter would agree to a lower rate of pay than they were accustomed to in London; if not, he feared the quality of work would decline and that they would have a loophole to be dilatory. The names of these two master craftsmen are not recorded: it has been assumed that the leading men employed by Wren (and in consequence known to Hawksmoor)—Edward Strong and John Longland—were used. Lord Carlisle spread the expenses for building the house over some 36 years, and to the midsummer of 1737 he had spent over £78 000 on it. By comparison, Vanbrugh estimated that Blenheim, with the nation's coffers to draw on in its gratitude for the victories of the Duke of Marlborough, had cost £287 000.[108]

When negotiations with London craftsmen to work at Castle Howard fell through, Vanbrugh

105. H A Tipping, June, August, 1927, 'Castle Howard', *C Life*, LXI, p. 884 and LXII; H A Tipping and Christopher Hussey, 1928, *English Houses*, Period IV, 2, pp. 1–62; Laurence Whistler, 1954, *The Imagination of Vanbrugh and his Fellow Artists*; Kerry Downes, 1979, *Hawksmoor*; 1978, *Vanbrugh*.

106. First printed in *C Life*, 30 January 1953; Whistler, *Imagination of Vanbrugh*, pp. 35–38 *op cit. (105)*.

107. Sotheby's, 23 May 1951. Purchased for Victoria and Albert Museum, London.

108. David Green, 1951, *Blenheim Palace*, p. 137.

turned to the capable workers in the nearby city of York, assisted by a number of itinerant foreigners. Work started in the east kitchen wing and there are some memoranda concerning Norwegian deals obtained from Scarborough.[109] By 1703 this was completed with a corridor connecting it to the house, as indicated in the second group of plans. Samuel Carpenter of York and the Huguenot refugee Nadauld, together with 'Mr Sabyn, joiner', worked in wood and stone, and the Clerk of Works was William Etty, member of a distinguished York family of mason-builders. In the drawing-room next to the main pile, Carpenter charged for cartouches (4s.), roses (2s. 6d.), astragal moulding (2s. 6d. per foot) and beading moulds (3d. per ft); in the Grand Cabinet he charged for 72 cartouches, or 'cartozzas' as he listed them, at 3s. 6d. each. Carpenter also embellished the south garden front of the house with 'stone drapery', charging 50s. each for 27 pilaster capitals of the Corinthian order. These include those on the main pile, where, for an additional 50s., he carved a shield and cherubim head on the keystone of the upper central window. For the same sort of work and in the same year (1705), the accounts show payments to 'Mr Nedos' (Nadauld) for carving; he worked in wood in many of the rooms, and also did stone-carving on the south front, including the tritons and lions on the great cornice. The four figures in niches which flank the main entrance on the north front are also his work. He also enriched the cupola (1706) and the keystones of the Great Hall until 1710.

The Hall, an unfamiliar feature in this form in an English country house, and the fine wrought-iron balcony at the first floor are in the grand baroque manner. The balustrade, in the manner of Tijou, is probably by John Gardom, who also provided iron garden gates in 1708. Several chimneypieces came from William Harvey, and the royal locksmith, Josiah Kay, provided brass locks, keys and hinges. John Bagnall of York did plain plasterwork and whitening throughout all the building.

York was an important centre for carpenters and joiners, and deals and wainscot were supplied by William Stephenson. The joiner Sabyn was paid for two days at York choosing out deals for flooring. The York joiner William Thornton (1670–1721) was also employed, and in 1708 he agreed to wainscot the Saloon, Dining Room and Ante-room with a good cornice and coloured according to his plan at the rate of 2s. 6d. per superficial yard; the Dining Room was to be wainscoted with base, surbase, bolection and cornice, as was usual, at the rate of 2s 2d. per yard. All the marble work was entrusted to John Thorp of Bakewell. The marble chimneypiece in the Saloon was costed at a little over £23, and Thorp also provided marble for door casings at 4s. 6d. per ft. The squares to be fitted in the Great Hall floor cost £7. 13s. 3d. The house was now ready to be painted by John Etty and Thomas Horsley's men, and preparations were made to receive the decorative painters, Giovanni Antonio Pellegrini and Marco Ricci. For £852. 5s. 0d. Pellegrini painted the Dome interior in colourful tempera with a scene depicting the fall of the Sun God; his bill shows that he moved to and from the house, and that £40 was given to 'Sign.r Marco'.

Lord Carlisle's friend, the Duke of Manchester, had brought Pellegrini and Ricci to England when he returned from his second embassy to Venice. They were to work for the earl and Sir John Vanbrugh at Kimbolton a few months before coming to Castle Howard. As well as the Hall, Pellegrini also decorated the High Saloon and Garden Hall, which were, alas, destroyed

109. Castle Howard Archives, Folder 1, 'Building Bills, 1700–40'. Further bills are in Folder 2, and 'Decorator's Bills' in Folder 3.

by the fire at Castle Howard in November 1940. This fire also destroyed the staterooms of the eastern range, including all Pellegrini's work except for that on the pendentives to the Dome.

One of the most interesting facts to emerge from the study of the Castle Howard accounts is the first recorded employment in England of the *stuccatori* Giovanni Bagutti and 'Mr Plura'. It seems reasonable to assume they provided the stucco fireplace (*see* col. pl. 4) and the facing scagliola niche in the Great Hall, as well as work (destroyed in 1940) over the doors in the High Saloon. Their account relating to this shows a total payment to them of £156. 7s.; further entries in the Building Book for 1711, however, bring the total received by these two stuccoists to £321. 7s. 0d.

BLENHEIM PALACE

The main work at Castle Howard was far advanced by 1705, and would have been enough for most architects to deal with; Vanbrugh, however, was also to be now involved in the building of Blenheim Palace. Here, Queen Anne proposed to have built a great house to present to the Duke of Marlborough in appreciation of his considerable military victories. The royal manor of Woodstock in Oxfordshire was chosen as the site, but the duke was free to choose his own architect; it is assumed he found it difficult to avoid the officers of the Queen's Works, and the reputations of Wren, Vanbrugh and Hawksmoor were in any case sound. Vanbrugh was chosen and, after due preparations, the foundation stone of the new house was laid on 18 June 1705. Vanbrugh and Hawksmoor were present, but, amid the celebrations and tossing down of golden guineas under the foundation stone, one person was opposed firmly to it all—the duke's wife, Sarah, Duchess of Marlborough.

The early opposition the duchess showed carried right through the long building cycle, starting with the initial designs of 1704. Her husband had chosen to ignore Wren, as the duchess may not have done, though the matter seems to have occasioned no ill will between the two architects. Later in life, in 1719, Vanbrugh declared that he might have also replaced Wren as Surveyor to the Office of Works, but that he refused out of 'tenderness to Sr. Chr. Wren'.[110]

Apart from the grant of the royal manor and a large sum of money to the duke, the Duchess of Marlborough was also involved in considerable expense over the building. Treasury payments were erratic and the building of the house dawdled along and, on occasions, ceased altogether. Many of the craftsmen whose pay was already years in arrear sued the duke. He, just as

110. *Wren Soc*, IV, p. 71.

Colour plate 13 WEST WYCOMBE PARK, Buckinghamshire. The Brown Drawing Room, *c* 1765 (photograph: A F Kersting).

Sir Francis Dashwood created in the middle of the Chiltern Hills 'a villa which might have been transplanted from Italy, and a landscape embellished with Greek and Roman temples'. Most of his building operations took place from about 1745 to 1771. In 1751 the painter Giuseppe

Mattia Borgnis came to the house to do paintings and, after his death in 1761, his son, Giovanni, continued to work there. Giovanni was helped by a Scottish painter, William Hannan, who painted the ceiling of the Brown Drawing Room in the mid-1760s. He copied two antique Roman paintings, a sleeping Cupid in the Barberini Palace and 'Augustus refusing the Crown' from the collection of Dr Richard Mead.

understandably, resented and resisted this—the notion of having to pay for his own reward was not acceptable. Vanbrugh and Hawksmoor had carried the work forward to the best of their ability, had used competent men, and assembled the best craftsmen for the decorative work. Work, however, halted from 1712 to 1716, and when it recommenced, Vanbrugh was not anxious to spend further years arguing with the irascible duchess; she had tried to lower rates of pay he had agreed and had interfered at each turn. The duke, meanwhile, was ill, and had relinquished all control in the matter to his wife.

Sir James Thornhill, who was doing decorative painting, was also soon involved, alongside Vanbrugh, in argument with the duchess. Work was again stopped, and no more was attempted at Blenheim until 1722. At this time Hawksmoor, who had not been involved in Vanbrugh's troubles with a patron who interfered constantly, was asked to return to complete the gardens and park; it was only then that the house could also move forward towards completion. And yet, by the date of Defoe's tour, published in 1724 and in conformity with the delays experienced in mighty schemes, all was not done. Defoe wrote:

> I shall enter no farther into the description, because 'tis yet a house unfurnish'd, and it can only be properly said what it is to be, not what it is: The stair-case of the house is indeed very great, the preparations of statues and paintings, and the ornament both of the building and finishing and furnishing are also great, but as the duke is dead, the duchess old, and the heir abroad, when and how it shall be all perform'd, requires more of the gift of prophecy than I am master of.[111]

The Duchess of Marlborough declined to accept Thornhill's price of 25s. a yard for painting the Saloon (1719), and turned, testily, to Louis Laguerre; while Thornhill had painted a most effective 'Glorification of the Duke of Marlborough' (*see* pl. 91) on the Great Hall ceiling, Laguerre was cheaper. He turned back in style to frescoes set within feigned columns, set around three marble door-cases and a marble dado. The door-cases were carved by Grinling Gibbons with great verve, the sense of grandeur heightened by a surmounting shell supporting a ducal coronet. It was a room worthy of a victor, and rivalled those created in Versailles and Vienna to the equally imperious soldiers Louis XIV and Prince Eugene of Savoy. It was given a

111. Defoe, *Tour*, II, p. 29 *op cit. (98)*.

Colour plate 14 SYON HOUSE, Middlesex. Detail of the Long Gallery, *c* 1763–68 (photograph: A F Kersting).

Adam had been concerned about the decoration of this room as early as 1761. The problem was its Jacobean length contrasted to meagre width and height. The solution was partly linear, with the introduction of 62 painted pilasters executed by Michelangelo Pergolesi in 1768. The gilder (1765) was Thomas Davis, and the plastering (*see* pl. 81) was done by Joseph Rose & Company. The semicircular painting over the overmantel mirror (one of two) was by Francesco Zuccarelli in 1766—he received £126 for the two paintings. On 7 June 1765 the 1st Duke of Northumberland wrote to William Hamilton in Naples to see if he could procure him vases or urns for the circular recesses, and 'Statues, Vases, Tripods or other Pieces of Vertu' for the round-headed niches which now contain books.

Lit: Beard, 1978, *Adam*, col. pls. 12–14, pl. 82.

final touch by Laguerre's ceiling, where he presented a colourful apotheosis of the Duke of Marlborough.

The Saloon windows look out through the south portico. Progressing to the right through Ante-chamber, Drawing Room and Great Bedchamber brings a visitor to the grandest State Room in England, the two-storey Gallery or Long Library running 180 ft along the whole of the west front. Entering through a marble door-case (*see* pl. 48) set within a two-columned tabernacle with its trophied and coroneted frieze, the eye is arrested by the plaster-coffered false dome—one at each end—done by Isaac Mansfield in 1725. Gazing down the long length of the room, with the swell of the two-storey bow at its centre, is Rysbrack's full-length statue of Queen Anne (*see* pl. 135).[112] Its inscription summarises what Blenheim is about—an amalgam of foreign and native talent set out with skill and dedication against considerable odds:

To

The Memory

of

Queen Ann

Under Whose Auspices

John Duke of Marlborough

Conquered

And to Whose Munificence

He and His Posterity

with Gratitude

Owe the Possession

of

Blenheim

A.D. MDCCXXXX. VI:

The duke was laid, grandly, to rest in 1733 (*see* pl. 134), outliving his architect Vanbrugh by eight years. Those who remembered Sir John clung to the past; his first patron, the 3rd Earl of Carlisle, in the many draft wills made at his instruction left legacies to Vanbrugh (after his death to his son), Hawksmoor and William Etty. They were an expression of the earl's faith, and seem to imply a vindication of them against the followers of Lord Burlington, who tried to alter many of the last stages of Castle Howard—the Mausoleum and the west wing. Patrons were now turning to the most important architect and publicist of the Palladian style, Colen Campbell; he, in turn, was trying to keep ahead of his fellow Scot, James Gibbs, who refused to be tied to any style or faction. They had both done a great deal before the reign of George I was over, and had given splendid opportunities to the master craftsmen on whom they relied. Their joint achievements have rarely been surpassed, and Campbell was concerned enough at the standard of competition to exclude later all mention of Gibbs from his three great folios, *Vitruvius Britannicus*.

112. M I Webb, 1954, *Rysbrack*, p. 164. The duchess's original intention had been to place the statue in the Bow Window Room, but it was finally decided to put it in the bow of the Gallery. It has been moved more recently to its present position, looking down the full length of the room.

85 (*above*) ST LAWRENCE JEWRY, London. Vestry ceiling, 1678, *dest* 1940 (photograph: *C Life*).

This ceiling was painted with the apotheosis of St Lawrence by Isaac Fuller II (*fl.* 1678–1709). He received 12 guineas for the painting and £16 for gilding Thomas Meade's plasterwork. Fuller had painted the 'Martyrdom of St Lawrence' in the vestry overmantel. His work was destroyed in an air raid in December 1940.
Lit: Wren Soc, XIX, pp. 24–26; Croft-Murray, 1970, *Painting*, I, p. 221.

DECORATIVE PAINTINGS

86 (*below*) CHATSWORTH, Derbyshire. The Chapel, 1687–92 (photograph: A F Kersting).

The collection of materials for the Chapel was begun in the autumn of 1687. Cedar for the wainscoting was collected from Hull, alabaster was delivered from Tutbury, marble was cut at Gotham, and black marble for the altar steps at Ashford-in-the-Water, five miles from the house. The design for the altar was submitted by Caius Gabriel Cibber (1690–91), but there is no reason to think he executed its carving, other than the two flanking statues of Faith (left) and Justice. The other 'ornaments' were carved by Samuel Watson. The woodcarving was by the group (Young, Davis, Lobb) who had come on from Burghley to join Watson, the resident carver.
   The walls and ceiling were painted by Louis Laguerre with depictions of 'Christ healing the sick' (walls) and 'Christ in glory' on the ceiling (*see* pl. 87). The picture over the altar was by Verrio, *c.* 1689–90.

87 (*below*) CHATSWORTH, Derbyshire. The Chapel, ceiling (photograph: National Monuments Record).

Laguerre, assisted by Ricard, started work in the Chapel in January 1689. Scaffolding was also in position for work on the altar and woodcarving, and the commission forms one of the best examples of the sequence of work—each part done so that its execution did not spoil or hinder other parts of the room. The scaffolding was taken down in August 1691, by which time all was more or less complete. Laguerre's ceiling depicts 'Christ in glory' and was painted in oil on plaster.

88, 89, 90 HAMPTON COURT, Middlesex. The King's Staircase (*above*), a detail of its decoration (*facing page, below*) and of the King's Bedroom ceiling (*facing page, above*) (photographs: National Monuments Record).

Verrio's most important commission in his last years—he died in 1707—was the decoration of Hampton Court. He arrived with his assistants in January 1700–01, and by the summer of 1702 had finished the Great Staircase and the bedchambers. The Staircase, as Mr Edward Croft-Murray has noted, is painted with a complicated allegory 'associating the Emperor Julian the Apostate and his satire on the Caesars with William III as the upholder of Protestantism and freedom'. However, what might have been his masterpiece was rendered by garish colouring and coarse execution as an unpleasant daub. The cove of the King's Bedroom ceiling (pls. 89–90) is painted with gilt scrollwork on a yellow ground with incidents from the story of Diana and roundels of *putti* holding baskets of flowers.

Lit: E Wind, 1939–40, 'Julian the Apostate at Hampton Court', *Journal of the Warburg and Courtauld Institutes*, III, pp. 127–37; Croft-Murray, 1962, *Painting*, I, pp. 59, 237.

91 BLENHEIM PALACE, Oxfordshire. Hall ceiling,
1716 (photograph: A F Kersting).

Sir James Thornhill painted the walls and ceiling
of the Hall, receiving £978 for his work. The
ceiling painting represents 'The Glorification of
the Duke of Marlborough'. The scroll at the right
centre is painted with the disposition of the army
at the Battle of Blenheim. Sarah, Duchess of
Marlborough, wrote to the duke's business
manager, James Craggs: 'I told Mr Thornhill that
I was very sure that there never was a piece of
painting of the size of that in the Hall even of
Rubins or the greatest master that cost so much as
this had don . . . This hee would by no means
agree to.'
Lit: David Green, 1967, *Sarah, Duchess of
Marlborough*, p. 214.

92 GREENWICH HOSPITAL, Kent. Lower Hall, centre of ceiling, *c* 1708–12 (photograph: Department of the Environment).

The Painted Hall at Greenwich may be reckoned as Sir James Thornhill's most important work. This centre oval of the ceiling depicts William III and Queen Mary attended by a host of mythological figures. The king receives an olive branch from 'Peace' (with her doves and lambs), and hands to 'Europe' (on a white horse) the Athenian cap of Liberty. He tramples on 'Tyranny' in the person of Louis XIV, his power lying broken and scattered. Painted, oil on plaster.

93 GREENWICH HOSPITAL, Kent. Detail of the
Lower Hall ceiling, *c* 1708–12 (photograph:
Department of the Environment).

'Architecture' pointing to a drawing of the
hospital, painted in part of the central oval (*see* pl.
92).

94 (*above*) GREENWICH HOSPITAL, Kent. Upper
Hall. Drawing for the ceiling painted *c* 1720.
Victoria and Albert Museum, London, Inv. No. E.
5199–1919 (photograph: museum).

Some six drawings of Thornhill's proposals for the
Upper Hall ceiling survive, depicting, as the
ceiling does, the qualities of Queen Anne and
Prince George of Denmark.

95 (*below*) MOOR PARK, Hertfordshire. Drawing
for Hall decoration, *c* 1725. *Victoria and Albert
Museum, London*, Inv. No. D. 18–1891
(photograph: museum).

This drawing, inscribed 'Demetrius comes to Save
Greed from Tyranny: Plut[arch] vol. 5, p. 24',
represents one of eight inset pictures of Heroic
Virtues. They were painted for Benjamin Styles
but, as noted in Part II, Chapter 2, Styles and
Thornhill quarrelled and the painter's work was
replaced by canvases by Jacopo Amigoni (*see* col.
pl. 8).

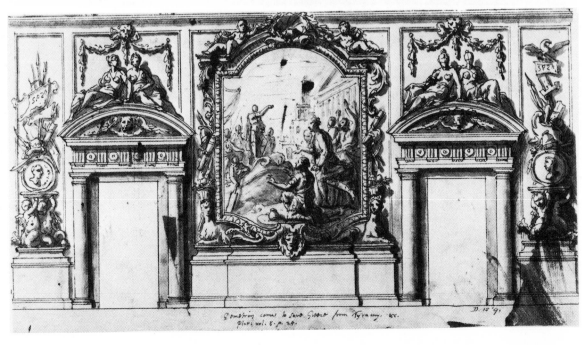

96 PETWORTH HOUSE, Sussex. Staircase Hall, *c* 1719 (photograph: A F Kersting).

A fire in 1714 destroyed the Petworth staircase, as well as much of the W. front. In 1719 Laguerre's man, Mr (William?) Oram, took measurements and Louis Laguerre painted it, presumably at that time. An 'Assembly of the Gods' appears on the ceiling and the walls depict 'The triumph of Elizabeth, Duchess of Somerset, surrounded by her family'. The London joiner John Simmons, who worked for the Commissioners of the Fifty New Churches, provided the original staircase; the one in this photograph shows the treads and balusters as replaced by Sir Charles Barry, *c* 1845.

97 KENSINGTON PALACE, London. The King's
Staircase, *c* 1725–27 (photograph: Department of
the Environment).

Sir James Thornhill, as Sergeant Painter, had a
right to be the artist employed on this work but
William Kent got the better of him. As George
Vertue put it: 'March 1721/22 the beginning of
the month a mighty mortification fell on Sir James
Thornhill, who being Sergeant-Painter and
History Painter to the King, see Mr. Kent
imployed to paint the King's new apartments at
Kinsington.' Kent underbid Thornhill's estimate
of £800 by £500, but was finally paid £500 instead
of £300.
   The decoration in *trompe-l'oeil* style, painted on
canvas, shows an arcaded loggia crowded with
members of George I's court, including a dwarf,
two Turkish grooms, a 'wild boy' and a Quaker.
Lit: Colvin, 1976, *King's Works*, V, p. 200.

98 KENSINGTON PALACE, London. Detail of the
King's Gallery ceiling, *c* 1726 (photograph:
National Monuments Record).

Kent decorated this ceiling with scenes from the
Odyssey and surrounded his oil-on-canvas
painting with sculptural motifs painted on a gold
ground. Kent was not a very competent painter
and the Board of the Office of Works received a
critical report about his work at Kensington in
1722. He did, however, have the powerful support
of Lord Burlington, and his paintings evidently
met with George I's approval. He received £700
for the King's Gallery work, which also included
designing door-cases (executed by James Richards)
and furniture.

99 MOOR PARK, Hertfordshire. Detail of Hall ceiling, *c* 1732 (photograph: A F Kersting).

The feigned cupola and balustrades is attributed to Gaetano Brunetti, a Lombard painter who worked in England from the early 1730s to 1739. Probably repainted by Nicholas Dall about 1769. The surrounding stucco is attributed to Giovanni Bagutti and Giuseppe and Giovanni Artari, who certainly worked at the house (*see* col. pl. 8, pl. 73). *Lit:* Croft-Murray, 1970, *Painting*, II, p. 177.

100 MEREWORTH CASTLE, Kent. Ceiling of the Gallery, *c* 1739–40 (photograph: A F Kersting).

The Gallery fills the entire S. front of the house. The ceiling paintings were at one time attributed to Giacomo Amiconi, but my discovery of Francesco Sleter's bills shows he was paid £300 for the painting, and £304. 13*s.* for gilding (Bodleian Library, Dashwood Archives, C8/1–18, C8/34). *Lit:* Croft-Murray, 1970, *Painting*, II, p. 325; *C Life*, 1966 *Annual*, p. 33 (in colour).

101 MOOR PARK, Hertfordshire. Detail of Long Drawing Room ceiling, *c* 1765 (photograph: A F Kersting).

This ceiling was commissioned by Sir Lawrence Dundas and painted by Giovanni Battista Cipriani. The various compartments are filled with groups of marine deities, and are an early example of painting in oil on paper (*see also* pl. 102). The Dundas archives record that Cipriani was paid £240 for his work in 1767.

Lit: Croft-Murray, 1970, *Painting*, II, p. 189; John Harris, September 1967, 'The Dundas Empire', *Apollo*, p. 176.

102 SYON HOUSE, Middlesex. Detail of Red
Drawing Room Ceiling, 1765–66 (photograph:
A F Kersting).

Giovanni Battista Cipriani came to England in
1756 in the company of the architect William
Chambers and the sculptor Joseph Wilton. Within
four years or so he was painting the panels on
George III's State Coach designed by Chambers.
Robert Adam used him to decorate the Drawing
Room ceiling at Syon. A letter (4 November 1764)
from the architect to his patron, the 1st Duke of
Northumberland, noted:

I am sorry there appeared any mistake between
us about the price fixed for the Paintings which I
am persuaded will be very easy set right but it
proceeded in a great degree from what Cipriani
himself told me when I showed him the two
Paintings, one with a Single, the other with
Double Figures which were done as Specimens
and which I am certain he then offered to paint for
the whole room at Two Guineas each picture and
to finish them in the best manner.

The pictures are probably oil on paper. The
duke's agent and the artist visited the house in
February 1766 to supervise setting up the
roundels.
Lit: Beard, 1966, *Craftsmen*, p. 85.

103 (*below*) 20 ST JAMES'S SQUARE, London. Detail of Great Drawing Room ceiling, 1772–74. *The Distillers' Company* (photograph: A F Kersting).

Robert Adam designed this important house for Sir Watkin Williams-Wynn. It contains a number of fine ceilings, plastered by Joseph Rose junior with inset paintings by Antonio Zucchi. The artist's bill (NLW, Williams-Wynn Archives) amounted to £614. 14s. For this room he charged £25 each for the rectangular panels, £40 for the six circles in the apse (one shown at left), and £3 each for the semi-circles containing two figures and a tripod.
Lit: Beard, 1978, *Adam*, col. pls. 44–46.

104 (*above*) OSTERLEY PARK, Middlesex. Etruscan Dressing Room, detail of painted decoration, *c* 1775. *Victoria and Albert Museum, London* (Photograph: museum).

Robert Adam seems to have taken his inspiration for the decoration of this room at Osterley both from classical urns and vases, as he acknowledged in his 1778, *Works in Architecture*, 2, pt. I, and from the designs for chimneypieces published by his erstwhile friend, Piranesi. A preliminary design for the wall decoration (Victoria and Albert Museum, Inv. No. 3436/41) was varied by the substitution of painted dancing maidens and the omission of ovals surmounting the tripod pedestals. The painter was presumably Pietro Maria Borgnis, who painted the walls, door and ceiling (except for the centre roundel, which is by Antonio Zucchi).

105 (*below*) CRICHEL, Dorset. Drawing Room ceiling, *c* 1773 (photograph: A F Kersting).

The 1770s work at Crichel is attributed to James Wyatt, and includes this good barrel ceiling made up of round, oblong, lunette and rhomboidal panels, probably painted by Biagio Rebecca. The Dining Room walls are also painted with medallions of classical subjects.

[2]
The Spirit of Building
1710–60

Gentlemen Architects

In July 1708 Sir John Vanbrugh wrote to the 1st Duke of Manchester: 'all the world is running Mad after building as far as they can reach'. Twelve or so years later, he was still able to write from Yorkshire on 20 August 1721 to Brigadier Watkins that 'here are several gentlemen in these parts of the world that are possess'd with the Spirit of Building'.[1] For the first years of the eighteenth century it is necessary to think of houses which were the work of 'gentlemen-amateurs' and those which were erected by a competent man, such as Francis Smith of Warwick, but under the supervision of an architect like Colen Campbell or James Gibbs. In the first category, Lord Burlington and his contemporaries Bolingbroke, Leicester, Pembroke, Cobham and Bathurst[2] had considerable knowledge of buildings; their activities implied the triumph and superior taste which belonged to the amateur, and, while Lord Pembroke needed the architect Roger Morris to help along his ideas, he was well able to decide the correctness and suitability of what he proposed.

In these enterprises none was more skilful than Robert Benson, Lord Bingley (1675–1731). In his activities he was as much a 'craftsman' by his knowledge of building style and technique as those men of lesser station whose work he directed. Benson was born at the Red Lodge, Wrenthorpe, near Wakefield, Yorkshire, in 1675. According to Thomas Wentworth, Lord Raby, Benson travelled in Italy where he had the good fortune to strike up a friendship with Lord Dartmouth,[3] his future brother-in-law. Dartmouth and Benson both married daughters of Daniel Finch, 2nd Earl of Nottingham. Benson, who married Elizabeth Finch in 1703, was Deputy Lieutenant for the West Riding of Yorkshire and Member of Parliament for Thetford.

1. Geoffrey Webb, ed., 1928, *The Complete Works of Sir John Vanbrugh, IV, The Letters*, p. 25.
2. James Lees-Milne, 1962, *Earls of Creation*.
3. J J Cartwright, 1883, *The Wentworth Papers, 1705–39*, p. 15.

Colour plate 15 HEVENINGHAM HALL, Suffolk. The Hall, *c* 1778 (photograph: A F Kersting).

When Sir Gerard Vanneck wished to rebuild his Queen Anne house, he turned to the London architect Sir Robert Taylor. After some work, including the centrepiece of the N. front, Taylor was superseded by James Wyatt, who provided some of the best interiors he ever accomplished. The principal was the two-storey hall, with its sienna-coloured scagliola columns and pilasters, and attractive barrel-vaulted ceiling. The floor was made of white stone and red and black marble, reflecting the pattern of the ceiling. In 1784 the house was visited by Francois de la Rochefoucauld, who wrote accounts of what he had seen in England for his father's information and interest. He described this great room as 'extremely dignified and magnificent'. One assumes that Wyatt used the Rose family for the plasterwork and Joseph Alcott for the scagliola work.

Even so, he still found time to help his friends with their buildings and to superintend the progress of his own house at Bramham, near Leeds. Benson's standing may be gauged in part of a letter written to him on 3 September 1719 by the 1st Duke of Chandos:

> Mr Gibbs was very much in the right to apply himself to your Lordship, whose Judgement he knows very well, I have the greatest opinion of & to whose good taste I shall always readily submit my own.[4]

The farther one delves into the confused maze of patronage—the associations Benson had with the architects Thomas Archer and James Gibbs, and his friendship with Gibbs's patrons, the Duke of Argyll and the Earl of Mar—it becomes apparent that there are no tidy groups of those who supported architecture in Baroque or Palladian styles.

The death of Queen Anne prevented Benson from taking up his post as Ambassador to the Court of Spain, and a change of government was in train. The Earl of Mar became an exile at the Jacobite Court in Avignon following the half-hearted rising in 1715, but Gibbs could still rely on the Duke of Argyll and Benson, and may have worked for the latter at Bramham.[5] The experience the owner of Bramham was gaining by his building and decorating made him a useful friend when the building of Wentworth Castle in South Yorkshire was in hand.

WENTWORTH CASTLE

In 1703 Lord Raby was appointed our Ambassador at Berlin. He accumulated capital and bought Stainborough (as Wentworth was then known) when it came on the market in 1708; it had a most remunerative rent-roll. Money was needed by Lord Raby in more than ordinary quantity for he was seeking to regain the Strafford earldom. It was at length given to him in 1711, and every attention was paid to building and altering at Stainborough. There is extensive documentation.[6] In 1709 Peter Wentworth wrote to his brother, then still in Berlin, mentioning that he had showed the plans to their mother and Lady Bathurst; they were amazed by their complexity and implied cost. Strafford had chosen a Prussian architect, Jean von Bodt (1670–1745), and conducting affairs from afar cannot have been easy for patron and architect. Peter Wentworth lamented on building without a surveyor, and he wrote to his brother with the

4. C H and M I Collins-Baker, 1949, *The Life and Circumstances of James Brydges, First Duke of Chandos*, pp. 140–41.

5. There are, however, no payments to Gibbs in Benson's account (Hoare's Bank, London).

6. BL, Add. MSS, 22221–2, 22239–41, 22257–62.

Colour plate 16 ARBURY HALL, Warwickshire. The Saloon, *c* 1786 (photograph: A F Kersting).

Sir Roger Newdigate (1719–1806) spent most of his long life altering and amending his house, as well as his Oxford college (University College), in the Gothic style. He was assisted for many years by the architect Henry Keene, but his own abilities were considerable. Furthermore, as Keene died in 1776, he needed to direct the workmen himself in later years, although he also employed Henry Couchman, a Warwickshire 'surveyor'.

The Saloon, the principal room on the E. front, was plastered by William Hanwell in 1786. The ceiling, as at Strawberry Hill (*see* col. pl 10 above), owed some of its inspiration to the Henry VII Chapel at Westminster Abbey. The room also has a magnificent vaulted bay (*see* pl. 84). Romney's portraits of Sir Roger and his second wife (Hester Mundy) are on the far wall, and were painted in 1791. The most important piece of furniture, *c* 1630, is Archbishop Laud's cabinet (extreme right), bearing his coat-of-arms impaled with that of the See of London.

advice Benson always gave. Strafford went on from Berlin to the Hague, where he negotiated the Treaty of Utrecht (1713). He was allowed to continue there until 1714 but, as an ardent Tory, he was not welcome to the active Whigs who assumed control at the accession of George I. Whilst abroad, it was left to his stewards to provide him with frequent reports and answers to his letters of enquiry.

The most interesting facts which emerge from the Strafford papers are in the letters[7] written by the York joiner William Thornton (1670–1721). He gave details of the thickness of glazing bars and dimensions of sash windows and glass at various houses, which has allowed association of his name with them as craftsman, and in one case (Beningbrough) as architect. Wentworth Castle also provided an early setting (c 1715) for work on a staircase off the Long Gallery by the *stuccatore* Giovanni Bagutti. It was perhaps his earliest association with the architect James Gibbs, who designed the Long Gallery for Lord Strafford. Bagutti and his partner Giuseppe Artari also worked for Gibbs in 1720 at the Octagon House, Twickenham. Gibbs used the same joiner, Charles Griffiths, at both commissions, and Bagutti and Artari also worked for him at St Peter's, Vere Street (1723–24), St Martin-in-the-Fields, London (1724–25) and Ditchley, Oxfordshire (1725).

COLEN CAMPBELL

At about 1715 when Thornton was working for Gibbs, he also came into contact with the most important architect of the early eighteenth century, Colen Campbell (1676–1729). In 1716 Campbell designed a house at Beverley, east Yorkshire, for Sir Charles Hotham;[8] he used Thornton as joiner and the plasterer John Bagnall of York, who had been employed on plain work at Castle Howard. John Thorp of Bakewell provided two marble chimneypieces, equal in dimensions and quality to one he had supplied to the Duke of Newcastle's London house, for £40.[9] Thornton received £1116 for work done prior to his death in September 1721, and, on 23 November, his son Robert (d.1724) received a final payment of £64. 13s. 0d.[10]

A year or so later than the Beverley house, Campbell was busy in 1718 designing Ebberston Hall on the slopes of the Yorkshire moors. This was for Hotham's bachelor relative, William Thompson, MP for Scarborough and something of a dilettante. In Italy Ebberston would have been a casino but, if it was designed as a pleasure house, it was also probably intended for use as a hunting and shooting lodge. Campbell included an elevation of Ebberston in the third volume of *Vitruvius Britannicus* (1725)—'this small rustick Edifice stands in a fine part well planted, with a River, which forms a Cascade and Canal 1200 Feet long, and runs under the Loggio in the back front'.

The year given for the building, 1718, is that in which William Benson[11] managed to get Sir Christopher Wren ousted from the post of Surveyor-General to the Office of Works and himself appointed in his place. Colen Campbell was made his deputy and was also given the office of

7. *BL*, Add. MS, 22238, ff. 145–46, 150, 165, 169; 22239, ff. 88–90, noted by Beard, 1966, *Craftsmen*, pp. 47–50.

8. K A Macmahon, 1956–58, *East Riding, Georgian Society*, IV, Pt. III.

9. East Riding, Yorks, CRO, Hotham Archives, DD/HO/14/5.

10. *ibid.*, DD/HO/15/4.

11. Colvin, 1976, *King's Works*, V, pp. 57–65.

Chief Clerk; the arrangement lasted only a year, when Benson was dismissed, and with him Campbell. Benson may, however, have advised about the water garden at Ebberston. Before George I came to England, Benson, one of the first of those to take an interest in Palladian architecture in the revived form made popular in England by Inigo Jones, had visited Sweden and Germany, particularly Hanover. He designed a machine for pumping water to the big fountain at Herrenhausen, a great possession of George, Elector of Hanover, who became, in 1714, King George I of England. On returning home, Benson inherited property and married a daughter of Lord Hervey of Ickworth. His sister Jane married the banker Henry Hoare, who in 1720 bought Stourhead, Wiltshire, and engaged Benson's friend, Campbell, to build his house there.[12]

The relationship between patron and architect at this time was close, and each relied on a competent and well-tested team of craftsmen. Benson's own house in Wiltshire, Wilbury Park, remarkable as the earliest example of the Jones–Palladio revival and important as a villa,[13] preceded that group of villas which arose from the Palladian revolution and from pattern-books. By 1715 the first volume of Campbell's *Vitruvius Britannicus* had already circulated widely, and Giacomo Leoni, the Venetian architect working in England, started to issue his edition of *Palladio*, translated by Nicholas Dubois.

WANSTEAD

Benson may well have sought out Campbell because of his publications and because of the justified reputation he had acquired with the great house of Wanstead, Essex, for the banker Sir Richard Child, later Viscount Castlemaine. Built in the main between 1714 and 1720, it survived until its demolition in 1824. Its great Ballroom, remodelled from the Library, is known from Hogarth's picture 'An Assembly at Wanstead House' (Philadelphia Museum), painted about 1730. It is depicted with a great two-tier, console-bracketed chimneypiece. The 24 figures gathered before it and beneath the gilded-wood candle-chandelier were representative of those who came to admire Wanstead. Campbell, in his description, noted that the visitor ascended from the court by the double semi-circular curved type of *perron* staircase to the *piano nobile*, or principal floor. He passed through the porticoed entrance into the Hall, 51 ft long, 36 ft wide and 36 ft high, and went forward into the 30-ft single-cube Salon, flanked by four rooms on either side.

Apart from Castle Howard and Blenheim, Wanstead was probably the largest house of its time, and Campbell paid enough attention to its design to ensure it being a prototype of far-reaching influence. When it was finished, the house was much admired and visited. From the two designs in Campbell's volumes to Walpole's letter to Richard Bentley extolling its virtues, from Hogarth's glittering picture to the 32-day sale in 1822, Wanstead was being described. Here, with some grandeur, was a tribute to Rome with a basically Palladian façade, which down the years was to echo again in another, even more extended design at Wentworth Woodhouse, at Nostell Priory, and away in Somerset at Prior Park, high above the classical city of Bath.

12. Kenneth Woodbridge, 1970, *Landscape and Antiquity, Aspects of English Culture at Stourhead*, Ch. 1.

13. Sir John Summerson, July 1959, 'The Classical Country House in Eighteenth-century England', *Journal, Royal Society of Arts*, CVII, pp. 570–87.

The design had started as a purely Palladian one and may have owed some of its detail—the giant portico for example—to a design by John Webb. By the time of the second design (1720), Campbell had added the proposed end towers, possibly derived from a study of the south front of Wilton House, Wiltshire, then regarded as one of Jones's masterpieces. From Vanbrugh's Castle Howard he took the idea of the cupola, showing that, despite his Palladianism, he was willing to take a feature from a baroque architect who was one of the leading country-house architects of the time. The end towers also appeared in Campbell's design of Houghton for Sir Robert Walpole, with its hall imitating that in Jones's Queen's House at Greenwich.

When John Macky visited Wanstead in 1722, it had been completed on the exterior, although the interior was still incomplete at Campbell's death.[14] He did, however, place over doors his favourite reclining *putti*—they recur at Houghton and Mereworth, for example—and his medallion portrait was incorporated in the Hall door-case, as it was (in plaster) in the south Gallery bow at Compton Place, Eastbourne.[15]

During his short time at the Office of Works in 1718–19—a time of considerable upheaval with Benson's public disgrace—Campbell obviously encountered the London carver James Richards. Both Campbell and William Kent used him on many occasions, and Richards, who became Master Carver to the Crown in 1724, became most skilled in their service. He had the unenviable task of succeeding the talented Grinling Gibbons who, as one of his own last tasks, had erected a great monument (*see* pl. 130) to the 1st Duke of Chandos—'princely Chandos'. Richard's first work for Campbell was at Burlington House, Piccadilly, which commission the architect had taken over from James Gibbs in 1717. His patron was the 3rd Earl of Burlington, destined to rival the reputation of Chandos for magnificent building and to outshine him with scholarly application.

BURLINGTON HOUSE

Richard Boyle succeeded his father in 1704, at the age of 10, to become 3rd Earl of Burlington and master of considerable estates in Yorkshire and Ireland. On 20 May 1714, at the age of 20, he set out on his Grand Tour of Italy. It would be wrong to suggest that the course of English architecture was destined to change as a result of his journey; indeed, on his first visit he took little note of buildings by Palladio, and hurried through Vicenza. At his return there were the lavish folios by Campbell and Leoni which stirred his interest and, whereas Campbell certainly benefited, Leoni is not known to have been patronised. In the summer of 1719 Burlington again set out for Italy, this time eager to stay at Vicenza and study Palladio. He acquired on this journey Palladio's drawings of the Roman Baths and was to draw upon himself the comment by Scipio Maffei 'My Lord Conte de Burlington il Palladio e il Jones de nostri temp'. It was on this second trip that Lord Burlington met William Kent, the architect, decorator and landscape gardener with whom his name is so often linked.

Kent, like his patron, had Yorkshire connections, having been born at Bridlington. He was baptised there on 1 January 1686, the son of William and Esther Cant, and is said to have been

14. Descriptions of Wanstead are given by Colen Campbell, 1715, *Vitruvius Britannicus*, I, pls. 21–22; 1717, II, pls. 23–26; 1725, III, pls. 39–40; P Morant, 1768, *History of Essex*, p. 31; D Pinkerton, 1808, *Voyages and Travels*; F Kimball, 2 December 1933 'Wanstead House', *C Life*, LXXIV, p. 605; 28 July 1950, CVIII, p. 294.

15. Beard, 1966, *Craftsmen*, pl. 45.

apprenticed to a coach-painter in Hull, but his name, or its variant, Cant, has not been traced in the apprenticeship rolls there. George Vertue said of him that his:

> Parents or Friends' circumstances being not in a condition to forward his practise and the expence of a profession they had the good fortune to find some Gentlemen of that Country to promote his studyes, raised a contribution and recommended him to propper persons at London to direct him to Italy, where he went with Mr J. Talman and Mr W. Locke aged about 20.

Two manuscript volumes[16] (Bodleian Library, Oxford) have bearing on the subject: the first consists of letters written by John Talman between March 1708 and April 1712, the second is a diary kept by William Kent during an Italian tour he made in 1714. In Rome, Kent painted the ceiling of S Giuliano dei Fiamminghi, the only ceiling by an English artist in a baroque Roman church. In 1713 he was awarded the pope's annual prize for painting. Kent returned from Italy with Lord Burlington, and was to live with him at Burlington House and Chiswick until his death.

Burlington House was much altered in the 1870s but a few interiors of Campbell's design survive. The doorways by Richards, with the familiar reclining *putti*, in the Saloon and an adjacent room allowed access to a small, richly decorated suite fully worthy of the town house of an important nobleman. The coffered ceilings, based on Jonesian patterns of the 1620s, were plastered by John Hughes and Isaac Mansfield. Hughes (and Richards) had worked for Campbell at the Rolls House in Chancery Lane in 1718, and Hughes was to superintend work for the architect 10 years later at Compton Place, Eastbourne.[17]

In the summer of 1720 Campbell left Lord Burlington's service; he had failed to help his patron's agents, Richard Graham and Jabez Collier, in a dispute over the carpenter Robert Baker's bill. Lord Burlington's attention was also now concentrated on his protégé William Kent, and on developing property to the north of his town house.[18] Campbell had also been meeting increasing competition for the attention of suitable patrons from the architects James Gibbs, the Venetian Giacomo Leoni and, to a lesser extent, Thomas Archer.

THOMAS ARCHER

Thomas Archer had considerable experience of official life as Groom Porter to Queen Anne, Comptroller of Customs at Newcastle, and one of the commissioners for building Fifty New Churches under the Act of 1711.[19] While he worked at a dozen houses before 1720, he first came to notice as an important architect with his design in 1704 for the north front of Chatsworth. He had travelled abroad in the 1690s and touches of continental baroque invested his work with style and individuality.

In 1685 Andrew Archer, Thomas Archer's elder brother, succeeded to the Warwickshire estate of Umberslade; 10 years later he started to rebuild the Hall. He seems to have used as his

16. Hugh Honour, August 1954, 'John Talman and William Kent in Italy', *The Connoisseur*, CXXXIV, pp. 3–7.
17. Beard, 1975, *Plasterwork*, pp. 59–60, 225; Colvin, 1976, *King's Works*, V, pp. 357–59.
18. 1963, *Survey of London*, XXXII, pp. 442–45.
19. Marcus Whiffen, 1950, *Thomas Archer*; Colvin, 1950, *Arch Rev*.

builder Francis Smith of Warwick (1672–1738), an architect whose work, both on his own account and for other architects, has become well known in recent years.[20] Smith was involved, *c* 1705–08, in building Heythrop House, Oxfordshire, for the Duke of Shrewsbury to Archer's design. The work, as at Thoresby, was innovative in planning details, and the apsed vestibule at Heythrop was one of the earliest examples of its form in an English country house. Some of its other rooms were equally impressive, with a Hall (32 × 27 ft) rivalling that at Castle Howard in size, and an 81 × 21 ft Gallery on the garden front.[21]

Archer next turned his attention to three important churches: St Philip, Birmingham; St Paul, Deptford; and St John, Smith Square, in Westminster. At Birmingham Archer again used Smith, and the Derby plasterer Richard Huss (partner with Samuel Mansfield) provided rosettes in the coffering of the arches. It was, however, the influence of the Italian architects Borromini and Bernini—the inturned volutes on the capitals, the strange pediments over the doors—which gave St Philip's (and Archer's other work) its greatest significance. Joseph Pedley as mason worked the Rowington stone into a fine complexity of concave and convex surfaces. The stone and most of the timber came from Archer's elder brother Andrew's Warwickshire estate. The architect, in magisterial stance, attended only the August 1709 meeting of the board of local gentry acting as commissioners to present his design.

The most expensive church to be built under the Act of 1711 for Fifty New Churches was St John's, Smith Square; here Archer used competent London masons and carpenters. They were descendants of Wren's master craftsmen families, the Tufnells and Strongs, and were aided by Christopher Cass, John James and Robert Jelfe. All continued with careers of significance in building and the allied trades. The great twin towers flanking the pediment exerted enormous pressures and Archer's craftsmen needed to make certain alterations in the design as work proceeded. At about the same time, 1712, but again, as at St John's, with consecration only possible almost 20 years later, the same masons worked for Archer at St Paul's, Deptford. James Ellis and James Hands (who had worked for Hawksmoor at another of the Fifty New Churches, St Alphege, Greenwich) were the plasterers who provided the great enriched cornice and panelled ribs in the aisle ceilings.

Before he met Archer, Smith's career had settled into supervision of his marble yard at Warwick, building on his own account and working for other architects as the need arose. It was natural that, as a prominent Warwick craftsman—he was mayor of the town twice—Smith should be turned to when St Mary's Church there needed rebuilding after the fire of 1694. Both Wren and Sir William Wilson (1641–1710) submitted designs, and those of the Surveyor-General were passed over in favour of the gentleman carver and architect from Leicester. While Smith was a very capable mason, the tower failed and had to be pulled down and rebuilt. However, it did not discourage patrons from using Smith, and he completed half-a-dozen commissions, in a slightly old-fashioned style, before attempting something more ambitious in 1714 at Stoneleigh, near to his native town of Warwick.

STONELEIGH ABBEY

In 1714 the 3rd Lord Leigh, who had succeeded to Stoneleigh in 1711, returned from his

20. Colvin, 1978, *Dictionary*, pp. 747–53.   21. Whiffen, *Archer*, p. 22.

Grand Tour and turned to Francis Smith for a design for a great house. The estimate[22] survives at the house and shows that Lord Leigh was to find all materials, including new stone, bring them conveniently to the site, and provide scaffolding, ladders, trestles, tackle and ropes. The old house was to be pulled down by Lord Leigh's men, who were also to dig the new foundations and clear the rubbish. Stone from the old house was to be used only on the inside of the new one, and, for his services, Smith, ever an inexpensive architect, was to receive £545. This was for completing the exterior—on the interior, his joiners and Italian stuccoists (*see* pls. 35 and 66) assembled to lavish their considerable skills. The parish registers at Cubbington, two miles from Stoneleigh, record that the house was finished in May 1726.[23]

SUTTON SCARSDALE

During the early 1720s Francis Smith was also working on a rebuilding of his own design at Sutton Scarsdale, Derbyshire. A lead rising-plate, formerly at the house (but since the demolition of Sutton Scarsdale in 1920, now lost), recorded that 'Francis Smith of Warwick, gentleman architect' was in charge in 1724, and that, in addition to the carpenter (Francis Butcher), joiner (Thomas Eboral), stone-carver (Edward Poynton) and plumbers, upholsterers and a locksmith, 'Albert Artari and Francis Vessali, gentlemen, Italians who did stuke work' were there.[24] The stucco-work at Stoneleigh, dating presumably from 1724–25, may be compared with the Sutton Scarsdale work, at least by means of photographs. The Derbyshire house, a poignant ruin with stucco still clinging to its shell, was visited by the late Margaret Jourdain in 1918, and her illustrated account appeared in *Country Life* in February 1919, a few months before the sale of fittings (*see* pl. 16). It would be rash to insist that the work at Stoneleigh was by Artari and Vassalli, but it comes into the category of their known style, with its lavish use of panels depicting mythological events. The Birmingham locksmith John Wilkes worked at both houses—the rising-plate records his name at Sutton Scarsdale and he signed a lock at Stoneleigh. It may be assumed that most of the craftsmen went on to Stoneleigh from the Derbyshire house. Support to the close connections of the 'team' is found in the stone-carver Edward Poynton's will of 1737; money or mourning rings were left to Francis and William Smith, George and Thomas Eboral and to 'William Watts, carver of London'.

HOUGHTON HALL

Smith's work was of a high standard, if slightly archaic, and he used many motifs taken from works by Bernini and Borromini. It could not compare, however, with Campbell's major achievements in these same years of the early 1720s—at Houghton and Mereworth. On 24 May 1722 the foundation stone of Sir Robert Walpole's imposing Norfolk mansion, Houghton Hall, was laid. At its conclusion, Horace Walpole presented his father with a catalogue *raisonné* of the splendid collections, concluding the dedication of *Aedes Walpolianae* thus: 'Could those virtuous men your father and grandfather, arise from yonder church, how would they be

22. The text is given by Canon G H Parks, 1964, *Transactions of the Birmingham Archaeological Society*, LXXXIX, pp. 76–84, and repeated, with one small variant reading, by Andor Gomme, 1971, *Archaeological Journal*, CXXVIII, p. 247.

23. *VCH, Warwickshire*, VI, p. 232.

24. The text of the plate is given in *C Life*, 15 February 1919, p. 171, and by Colvin, 1978, *Dictionary*, p. 751. 'Thomas Broral' should be read as 'Thomas Eboral'. Most of the craftsmen are listed in Part III of this book.

amazed to see this noble edifice and spacious plantations where once stood their plain, homely dwelling.' As Smith worked in many houses to Gibbs's instructions, so Houghton was supervised, after Campbell had submitted his plans, by Thomas Ripley, a senior officer of the Board of Works.

Ripley was born in Yorkshire in 1683 and this may have accounted for the connections and local knowledge which led him to suggest the use of stone from Aislaby, near Whitby, rather than from nearer quarries. It was a decision that might have found support with another talented Yorkshireman who lavished time and attention on Houghton, William Kent. He had been occupied at this time with the important paintings at Kensington Palace, in which he used Italian-style *grotteschi*; they were a prelude to his very important and varied contribution to English interior decoration. Campbell's name is nowhere mentioned in the surviving documentation,[25] which is sparse for the building period. Ripley made all payments and, while the record is far from complete, he disbursed over £22 000 between 1726 and 1733. The story commences in 1721 when John Glover supplied 100 trees, delivered sawn, in 227 loads. Other timber came into King's Lynn from the merchant Samuel Browne—80 Frederickstadt Deals, a barrel of tar, 6 bunches of fir laths, deals and sawn deals. The ship *Benjamin Susan* held '100 Large Spars, short and half deals' which Ripley paid for on 4 November 1721. Stone[26] was being delivered by Nicholas Hindrey and Richard Nichols for the use of the London masons Christopher Cass and Andrew Jelfe, a significant partnership, who also erected the stables and other new buildings at Houghton in the early 1730s. At the same time, local men were not forgotten, and a list of 20 masons and 10 carpenters—all freemen of King's Lynn—is among the 1722 vouchers.

The vast quantities of nails, bricks, timber, hinges, poles, sand and lime—all the impedimenta of building—came to the site from various sources. Samuel Thurlow supplied Dutch and other pantiles, and, as time advanced, more exotic supplies were obtained. In 1725 'Lateward, Butlin and Partners' supplied 305 mahogany planks from Jamaica, and Capt Hannar's *Dolphin* and *The Rose* brought in a further 26 and 88 planks respectively. John Griffiths was busy sawing it, and the 1725 vouchers also indicate the presence of Isaac Mansfield, the York plasterer. More significantly in respect of the fine stairs, with its $9\frac{1}{2}$-in wide handrail, and superb doors at Houghton, the joiner and carver James Richards was there by 1728–29. The plumber George Devall was given £300 on account in 1725—his estimate of work in lead and plumbing for 1730–36 also survives—and a most significant entry occurs on a scrap of paper among the 1727–28 vouchers: 'To Mr Altery for Saloon ceiling, £131. 14s. 5d.', part of three payments to the stuccoist (totalling £560. 10s.) made between February and May 1728. The 'Saloon' ceiling, in this case, was the one in the Stone Hall, as only a painted ceiling (*see* col. pl. 6) was erected in the Saloon itself.

On 16 June 1726 Sir Robert Walpole was made a Knight of the Garter—the expenditure on

25. CUL(CH). Various account books (Nos. 23/1, 25, 26, 27, 28, 39/1, and vouchers (1721–34), cover the building period but many of them are obviously not a prime source. Scraps of information are found mingled with deliveries of food, household items, oats, etc., and, regrettably, 'Goods Rec'd for Houghton' (39/1), does

not commence until 1729.

26. Stone was delivered by sea to King's Lynn, and 130 tons were carted to Houghton (vouchers, 1722–24). This may only represent a proportion of the whole. Cass and Jelfe were also using Portland stone at a later date (vouchers 1730–34, 'Masons work, 1732–3').

the celebrations (1726 vouchers) was extraordinary, even by early eighteenth-century standards—and the Garter Star is found at the centre of Giuseppe Artari's Stone Hall ceiling. The humdrum catholicity of the duties of one member of the Houghton household staff included recording the consumption of wine, and by whom: 'To ye Italians, 2 Red Port' (occasionally white, Lisbon or Mountaine) was noted down daily between 10 July and 10 October 1726; if one accepts the reliability of this record of drinking habits, Artari and his team were at the house in these four months from July to October. There are other gifts of wine to 'Mr Ripley' and 'Mr Cass', and occasional and incomplete records of whose horses were stabled ('Mr Deval's horse')—minute clues which build towards a total picture, and also including the sombre record of the price paid in suffering: of William Morris scalded by lead (1725), of workmen falling from scaffolding, and of the expenses of doctors attending them.

Apart from 184 yd of fine Dutch canvas to line tapestries at Houghton, charged in 1726 (vouchers) at 9*d*. a yard and 62 squares of crown glass 'for the Chamber Windows over the 2 Arcades to West front' (1729) among the various records of goods received, specific mention of important goods for Houghton is rare. A date can be obtained, however, when John Cleaves, the London smith, provided '3 Brass window Barrs with Catches & Screws for the Salloon' in February 1729, and marble was obtained for the Marble Parlour in October 1730. The record (1730 vouchers) of the cubic capacity of Plymouth, Black and Gold, Purple and White, and Veined marbles was all placed to Mr Cass's account after being obtained from Henry Bowman. There is, unfortunately, no record of work on the Marble Parlour chimneypiece by the finest of the eighteenth-century sculptors, John Michael Rysbrack, but 'Swan the Carver' was paid 'for travelling to Houghton & return on Acct of the Dining Room chimneypiece' on 24 November 1733; this was presumably Abraham Swan of London, whose important treatise on staircases was used by many joiners in later years. Finally Cass and Jelfe, who were now (1733) busy on the stables, cleaned the Great Stairs and Great Hall and 'painted the Cornice of Main House'. It was all included in their November–December 1733 account, along with the expenses of masons travelling from London to Houghton and back again (57 days), battering axes, shuting saws, extra charges on Portland stone, carriage of tools, freight of plaster and 'Mr Jelfe's travelling'.

The record of furnishings provided for Sir Robert's new house is similarly sparse, although the upholsterer Thomas Roberts was in almost constant attendance in 1726 and later. There is also the important bill of 1723 from Richard Hill, Walter Turner and Robert Pitter in the Strand for gold vellum, lace, fringes and velvet for the State Bed, amounting to £1219. 3*s*. 11*d*.[27] There is a payment of £113. 16*s*. 5*d*. to Christopher Cock in 1734 for a 'filigree cabinet', and the cabinet-maker George Nix received money from time to time. But of Walpole's own involvement there is little trace, a deliberate erasing of record; it has been noted that 'after 1718 the personal letters almost disappear and they are replaced by the typical correspondence of a successful statesman',[28] and one in which the whole system of eighteenth-century patronage and office-seeking is reflected. His great house, built in Yorkshire stone, gave him a status but, at his fall from power in 1742, it was time to hide expenditure on it from prying eyes.

27. CUL(CH), vouchers 1732.

28. Introduction by Professor J H Plumb to the *Calendar of the Cholmondeley (Houghton) Manuscripts*, CUL.

This cautious approach has certainly effaced any record of William Kent's paintings and involvement with the design of various parts; some of the aspects of his attention may be gained in the volume which Isaac Ware published in 1735, *The Plans, Elevations and Sections of Houghton in Norfolk.*

MEREWORTH CASTLE

While Campbell's and Kent's designs for Houghton were put into effect under the supervision of Thomas Ripley, the Scottish architect seems to have been in charge of the overall effect at Mereworth, Kent. Regrettably, documentation about its building years, 1720–23, has not survived, although there is some about the painter Francesco Sleter working at the house in the late 1730s.[29] We are, therefore, dependent on the facts that Sleter signed one of his ceilings in 1729, and that Campbell, in *Vitruvius Britannicus* (III, p. 3), noted that the stucco ornaments 'are executed by Signor Bagutti, a most ingenious artist'. These are the glory of the circular domed Hall, but Sleter's paintings dominate the Gallery (*see* pl. 100), running 82 ft along the south side of the house. We know a little about this decoration again from a distant source—the gardener's accounts to his master about progress at another late Campbell house, Compton Place, Eastbourne. Writing to his master Lord Wilmington in June 1728, William Stuart reported 'the German plasterers are gon from Bourn today, to coll fains'.[30] Campbell was working at Mereworth for Colonel John Fane, later 7th Earl of Westmorland.

The 'Germans', although they may have included the Anglo-Danish stuccoist Charles Stanley, were responsible presumably for the gilded compartments framing Sleter's paintings and for some of the wreathing stucco set in the frieze and amid Sleter's *trompe l'oeil* reliefs in the deep cove. Horace Walpole visited the house in 1752 and described the walls as hung with green velvet; this survived until the 1930s, throwing into relief the two marble chimneypieces and fire doors (*see* pl. 50). To the east and west of the dome, Campbell set bedrooms and dressing-rooms; the east and west suites have compartmented ceilings, again painted by Sleter, and corner chimneypieces (introduced to England in the late seventeenth century) with surmounting pyramids of carved and painted wood. When Walpole visited Mereworth he found it 'so perfect in the Palladian taste that it has recovered me a little from the Gothic . . . though it has cost £10000 it is still only a fine villa, the finishing of in and outside has been exceedingly expensive.'[31]

DITCHLEY PARK

Within six years of the roofing of Mereworth in 1723, Campbell was dead. His last years had, in any case, to take note of the dominance of James Gibbs at Ditchley Park and elsewhere. The stuccoists were all anxious to find work and assembled at Ditchley in 1725; the receipts are often signed by Giuseppe Artari and Francesco Vassalli for 'worke done by me & my partners'. They were working for a Catholic architect and a Catholic patron, George Lee, 2nd Earl of Lichfield.[32] The house has a great Hall with a huge oval canvas on the ceiling painted by

29. Bodleian Library, Oxford, Dashwood Archives (DD, C.8). Mereworth passed in 1762 to Sir Francis Dashwood, as son of the childless Lord Westmorland's sister.

30. Beard, 1975, *Plasterwork*, p. 59.

31. Horace Walpole, 1798, *Works . .*, p. 201.

32. Beard, 1975, *Plasterwork*, p. 54.

William Kent depicting the Olympians. Below are assured great door-cases (*see* col. pl. 5) topped with reclining figures by the stuccoists, and a niche and two-tier chimneypiece carved by the London statuaries, Christopher Horsenaile and Edward Stanton III. The scale of work is well suited to a room which is a little over a 30 ft cube—a blend of local, London and Italian workmanship, overlooked by an architect well versed in the Roman baroque and supervised on the spot by Francis Smith of Warwick.

Gibbs carried out the single cube Great Hall earlier and more effectively, however, at Sudbrooke Park, Surrey, for the Duke of Argyll. The assurance of its twin Corinthian pilasters, the scrolled pedimented door-heads, and chimneypiece surmounted by the duke's arms show Gibbs at his best and some seven or eight years[33] before the work at Ditchley.

St Martin-in-the-Fields, London

One of the best documented of Gibb's early commissions is the erection of the London church of St Martin-in-the-Fields. The survival of the accounts and the minute book of the commissioners appointed to control its rebuilding allow every small aspect of the work to be allocated.[34] The team worked under the control of the architect but, in addition, individual craftsmen appeared before the board at its committee meetings from time to time to show models and drawings, or to answer questions. The commissioners included the architect Nicholas Dubois, and the master mason, on whom much depended, as at Houghton, was Christopher Cass.

The board started its deliberations on 23 June 1720, and in the following weeks a sub-committee considered plans and estimates submitted by Sir James Thornhill, James Gibbs, John James and George Sampson. The sub-committee in due time recommended Gibbs as the 'properest Person to be employed as Surveyor', and, by a majority vote over James, he was so elected by the board on 24 November 1720. One of the first tasks was to supervise the erection of a temporary tabernacle for worship to continue in—a task entrusted to the carpentry firm of Benjamin Timbrell and Thomas Phillips. There was also the morbid task of moving many corpses and gravestones and of fencing the churchyard. Cass was appointed as Mason on 4 August 1721, having given 'Sufficient Security', and the plumber's and bricklayer's men were set to work alongside the large team of masons.

Gibbs had prepared contracts and specifications, and various craftsmen were asked to submit prices. Advertisements in the *Daily Courant* solicited offers for surplus materials from the old church. Through their existing work Timbrell and Phillips had been appointed carpenters, and submitted their proposals and a plan of the roof structure in August 1721. With the rates set out for each contractor, work proceeded smoothly, apart from an admonishment to Cass for taking certain materials from the old church without permission, and a stopping of the brickwork programme through faulty work and bad bricks. By April 1722 Gibbs estimated £22 497 had been spent or committed; Timbrell and Phillips were, however, allowed to change the formation of a truss for the roof which would cost £50 more than that intended originally.

33. The earlier date of 1717–18 from that of *c* 1725 (Hussey, 1965, *ECH, Early Georgian*, p. 17) was proposed by Miss Mary Cosh, 13 July 1972, 'Two Dukes and their houses', *C Life*, CLII, p. 78.

34. Westminster Reference Library, MSS, 419/309 (Minutes 1720–24); 419/311 (Accounts, 1721–27). I am indebted to Dr Terry F Friedman for loaning me microfilm and photocopies of these items.

The joiner appointed was Charles Griffith who, as a St Martin's parishioner, was given preference over John Lane; he was also well known to Gibbs for work at Wentworth Castle and the Octagon at Twickenham. He provided all the wainscoting to walls and Gallery, patterns for the altar-rail, the pulpit, altar-piece and organ loft, the pews and 181 locks for the pew doors. What emerges from the records is the play and counterplay of each craftsman to the other—the carpenter erecting scaffolding for the plasterer, the mason's team clearing up after the plasterer. The joiner made moulds for the plasterer and smith and also helped the clockmaker as he fitted the clock dials; he fashioned a Virginia walnut rail to which the smith set the altar-rails. The bricklayer carried away rubbish out of the Gallery for the plasterers and joiners to go to work. The architect allowed all accounts, after measurement, and the Scottish banker Andrew Drummond, as Treasurer, paid out the money.

In April 1724 the church was ready for plastering. Isaac Mansfield and Chrysostom Wilkins presented proposals for the plain work (excluding the 'Fretwork') at £471. 12s. and £415. 9s. 6d. respectively; the cheaper estimate by Wilkins was accepted, and Giovanni Bagutti agreed to do the ornamented work as set out in a design marked 'B' for £250. With other work including gilding, Bagutti estimated £320; his final bill, including additional ornamentation, came to £419. 6s., which he received in seven payments between December 1724 and July 1727. James and William Price set in the painted east window (£130), and Thomas Bridgewater finished carving about the pulpit, the brackets between each gallery pew, Doric capitals and cherubims' heads. Roger Askew gilded the vane and ball on the steeple, coloured the stucco royal arms three times over, and varnished them with best white-spirit varnish to prevent their discolouration.

The many drawings by Gibbs in the Ashmolean Museum, Oxford, show his ability to indicate exact detailing to craftsmen, particularly stuccoists. The drawings for work at Fairlawne, Gubbins (see pl. 64) and St Martin's show how the stuccoists Bagutti and Artari were instructed as to the overall disposition of the design. The stuccoists had started work in earnest for Gibbs at the Octagon House, Twickenham (see pl. 18); working through the two London church commissions, St Peter's, Vere Street, and St Martin-in-the-Fields, Artari alone went on in 1725 to Ditchley, where he was joined by his friends Vassalli and Serena. They were to remain in demand by Gibbs, Francis Smith and Giacomo Leoni in the late 1720s and 1730s. Their work for Leoni at Moulsham, Essex—a house demolished in 1809—shows that the owner's main agreement was with Bagutti, and that Artari 'who did the Bustos & Figures' assisted him.[35]

MOULSHAM HALL

Benjamin Mildmay, Earl Fitzwalter (d. 1756), bought the Tudor Moulsham Hall from his sister-in-law, the Dowager Lady Fitzwalter, in May 1728. He visited the hall within three weeks and, almost certainly, Leoni accompanied him. He visited again in July, when on the 15th he paid Leoni £21 for his plan and tipped the bricklayers 2 guineas when he and Lady Fitzwalter laid a nominal first brick. This section of the house, the south front, was up and roofed by the

35. The Fitzwalter account books are at Essex CRO (D/DMA5–7), with one at Hampshire CRO (15 M 50/31). I am indebted to Arthur C Edwards for details of Leoni's Moulsham commission.

end of October 1729, and work was well in progress on the next section. On 26 September 1729 Fitzwalter drove a nominal first pin into the carpenter's work on the east front, and on 11 November he paid William Mantle the final instalment of a bill of £74. 15s., presumably for interior work on the south range.

There is nothing to suggest that Mantle was anything more than an ordinary skilled plasterer; moreover, the east front (as in the old building) was the main front. It seems reasonable to assume that the Italian stuccoists were not called in before 1730, and probably arrived in the early autumn. They had been working for Leoni at Clandon a year or so before. In May 1730 a sufficient amount of the building was finished for Fitzwalter to visit it 'in order to settle my family here for the summer'; he did not return to London until late November. The stucco-work was therefore probably done in the late autumn and before February 1731—a terminal date fixed by an entry in the account book:

> 1731   Feb 13. having [paid] Mr Bagutti the Italian stuccatori for his work done in my
> Hall and dining room at Moulsham £115. 15–0 I have this day also paid him
> 45–13–0 wch in the whole amts to 161–8–0, wch in full for all the work Mr
> Altari and he have done for me to this day, my agreamt. was only with Mr
> Bagutti & Mr Altari who did the Bustos & Figures assisted him. £45–13–0.

This is useful confirmation of the respective roles of these two talented stuccoists and there seem enough reasons to think that they worked together at Clandon and at Moor Park. In addition to stucco, Lord Fitzwalter also paid Giacomo Amiconi for 'a Picture of Architecture and little figures' and for an overmantel. Picture frames and a table frame were obtained from Isaac Gosset, and, significantly, in view of his work at Moor Park and Mereworth, 'Mr Slater' (or Francesco Sleter) was paid for doing the ornaments about Andrea Soldi's oval pictures of the Earl of Holderness (Fitzwalter's stepson) and the Earl of Ancram, his son-in-law, which were set in over the dining-room doors. Amiconi, Sleter and Leoni were all friends, and all three acted as witnesses to the marriage in 1734 of the music master Adamo Scola.[36] The architect, Leoni, worked for Lord Fitzwalter from 1728 almost until his death (1746); he received 27 payments in that period for plans, marking out of the site of new buildings, and for various incidentals such as £3 to replace that when he was robbed on the coach to Moulsham, and one guinea for a sundial.

MOOR PARK

The combination of artists—Amiconi, Sleter and the stuccoists—suggests that they worked under Leoni's supervision at Moor Park. Two lawsuits brought by the owner, Benjamin Styles, in 1728 and 1730 have established that work, including painted decorations (*see* pl. 95), was carried out by Sir James Thornhill as 'Cheife Architect'. The disagreement which had arisen through Styles being dissatisfied with the nature and cost of the work led to Thornhill, who denied the charges, being dismissed from the work. It has been suggested[37] that, at this point in 1728, Leoni was probably called in. Styles replaced Thornhill's paintings in the hall with those

---

36. Croft-Murray, 1970, *Painting*, II, p. 164.

37. T P Hudson, November 1971, 'Moor Park, Leoni and Sir James Thornhill', *Burl Mag*, CXIII, pp. 657–59.

by Amiconi (*see* col. pl. 8), and introduced the stuccoists and Francesco Sleter. We know of Bagutti's presence by the addressing to him at Moor Park of a Gibbs drawing for work elsewhere, and of the two Artaris being noted there by Sir Edward Gascoigne, the Yorkshire patron who used them at his own house (*see* 'Artari', Select Dictionary, p. 243).

MAWLEY HALL

Unfortunately, there is no documentation at all for Mawley, the house which Sir Edward Blount built near Cleobury Mortimer about 1730. He may well have provided his own design[38] and then had it realised by Francis Smith. There is splendid stucco and joinery in the house (*see* pls. 38 and 39). When the Nottingham carver Edward Poynton died in 1737, he left money or mourning rings, as noted previously, to Francis and William Smith, George and Thomas Eboral, the Warwick joiners, a London carver, William Watts, and a mourning ring to 'George Cromp of Morley Forge in Shropshire'. May it be assumed, therefore, that this slight link between Poynton, a craftsman who is known to have worked for Smith, and Cromp may imply his presence at Mawley Hall? Poynton was for the most part a stone-carver, but he or William Watts could have done the elaborate woodcarving in the house (*see* pl. 39). The intricate inlaid wood, some with the addition of brass inlays, remains without an author—Christopher Hussey suggesting that the 'application of inlay to mural decoration in these remote houses may be that the desuetude of marquetry for furniture, subsequent to the Palladian vogue, induced some unemployed expert to develop this fresh field'.[39] It has not yet proved possible to trace the wills of the other craftsmen Poynton mentioned to see if they remembered one another by small bequests; certainly William Smith used some of them at Kirtlington in the early 1740s. This fidelity to early friendships was nowhere more evident in the 1730s, however, than in the great house Lord Leicester planned at Holkham. As surveyor, receiving a salary of £100 a year, was Matthew Brettingham (who claimed the design in 1761 *The Plans and Elevations of the late Earl of Leicester's House at Holkham*); he worked for the owner and for William Kent.

HOLKHAM HALL

Recent research on the architectural evolution of Holkham[40] has revealed only one small payment (£50) to William Kent. Despite assertions as to Lord Burlington's share in the design,[41] it has been established that some of the important decisions were taken by the owner, Thomas Coke, Earl of Leicester. He had lost a great deal of money in the South Sea Bubble (1720), and it was a courageous act to start upon a great house in 1734 on what he himself called 'an open barren estate'. Work was started in the south-west 'Family Wing' (complete by 1741), and was continued after Coke's death (1759) by his widow. The family continued to use the old house while building was in progress, and it was not demolished until 1757, when it was in the way of erection of the last wing—the north-west 'Stranger's Wing'—staked out in 1755.

The extensive archives at Holkham list all the building materials used—every brick, nail, hod

38. To be published in a forthcoming volume of the Yale edition, *The Correspondence of Horace Walpole*.
39. Hussey, 1965, *ECH, Early Georgian*, p. 111.
40. By Leo Schmidt for a doctoral thesis, Freiburg University (in progress), and by John Cornforth (and

Leo Schmidt) for four articles on the house, *C Life*, January/February 1980.
41. Rudolf Wittkower, 1945, 'Lord Burlington and William Kent', *The Archaeological Journal*, CII, p. 128.

of lime, bushel of hair and leaf of gold which went to make up the house. It has been established that the money Lord Leicester laid out was not spent evenly: until 1753, the annual expense varied between £500 and £2500, with the average at about £1500; it reached £6500 in 1755 and fell again slowly to £1200 by 1759. Some of this extravagance was occasioned by Coke being determined to complete a worthy house, but the more so in the death of his only son and heir in 1753. What matter the debts to his nephew, Wenman Roberts Coke; when the nephew inherited the house and its debts in 1759 neither he nor, later, his son Thomas William (called 'Coke of Norfolk') had the means to change much. It has ensured the survival of Holkham in the form its first owner and builder intended. The long story set out in the archives is best noted here firstly in tabular and annotated form.[42]

4 May 1734. Foundation stone of S.W. 'Family Wing' laid.

1738–41. Family wing finished: decorated and furnished by collaboration between the owner and William Kent (d.1748). Some carving to door friezes by 'Mr Marsden'. Furniture from William Bradshaw and Benjamin Goodison.

October 1740. Foundations dug for Main House.

December 1740. Joseph Pickford of Derby and London paid for certain chimneypieces.

1741. Gilding and Painting, S.W. wing. Chimneypieces in 'My Lady's Closet' obtained from Benjamin Carter.

1742. Statues (acquired in 1732) set up in Gallery.

1743. Foundations, and stone acquired, for Main House.

1744. Timber for Main House. A mason (Joseph Howell) looked for stone in Yorkshire. Bricklayers and carpenters assembled. Thomas Coke, Lord Lovel, created Earl of Leicester.

1747–54. Matthew Brettingham purchased art treasures in Rome on the earl's behalf. Landed in 1752. Bath and Portland stone acquired.

1753. Gallery and Dining Room glazed. The talented joiner and carver James Lillie at work on the house. Various rooms plastered by Thomas Clark.

1754. Purbeck marble and paving stones arrived. The walls for steps in the Chapel Wing set. Statues received. Pictures hung.

1755. Alabaster from Castlehey arrived. Thomas Carter and Joseph Pickford fashion chimneypieces. Clark plastering.

1756. Mrs Lybbe Powys visited the house and admired the staterooms. More alabaster arrived. Niches for statues cut in Great Hall. Marble columns and statues unloaded.

1757. John Neale gilding in various rooms and on four bookcases in the Gallery. The Old Hall demolished. James Lillie made models for sofas and chairs. More plastering by Clark.

1758–59. Floor behind columns in Hall prepared. More carving by Lillie. Death of Lord Leicester.

42. I am indebted to Dr W O Hassall for the loan of his extensive notes, gathered over many years as archivist to the earls of Leicester.

1760.   Timber acquired for Chapel ceiling.

1761.   Matthew Brettingham issued his book on Holkham. Balustrade in Hall fashioned.

1764.   Chapel plastered.

1765.   Workmen dismissed.

The details of construction of various parts of Holkham, noted briefly above from house archives,[43] reveal a vast amount of information about materials and their cost—perhaps the fullest of those available for any eighteenth-century private house. As early as 1730 the obelisk had been erected, and by 1733 Sir Andrew Fountaine was providing gold leaf (18d. a book) and sending his man to gild Kent's Temple. It is, however, inevitable that attention should be concentrated on details about certain important parts of the house, and in particular the Marble Hall (see pls. 78 and 143). The original design of the Hall consisted of two cubes, one inside the other, obviously in the tradition of the cube hall and, perhaps, a play on Inigo Jones's 'Double-Cube Room' at Wilton House. A detailed drawing by Kent of the plan, section, two elevations and the ceiling survives in the house archives; it is annotated, with the precise dimensions its classical origins determined, with phrases such as: 'the whole Basement is ½ the Hight of Collumia', and 'Cove 1/3 of Whole order'. The ceiling (see pl. 78) was intended to contain a painting by Kent, which was not executed; indeed, most of what he designed was altered.

In 1755 the great room was half finished, and Kent had been dead almost 10 years. It was decided to amend the staircase to one unbroken flight (the original had been divided and was intended to feature a great statue of Jupiter in the centre), to replace the chimneypiece with a heated floor, alter the main floor and ceiling, and replace the stone balustrade with one in block tin. The order was changed from Corinthian to Ionic, and an interior wall (which allowed support for access to all four sides of the hall) was removed. All these changes were made by the patron—Kent, as noted, had been dead for nearly 10 years and his mentor, Lord Burlington, for almost 4. It made a fitting ascent to the Saloon, and a bust of the builder gazes down on all who now ascend.

In 1758 the great columns in the Marble Hall (see pl. 143) were in position and William Aram provided '100 Garden Mats to Cover the Columns' (£4. 3s. 4d.), and to protect them. By August 1760 Thomas Clark had done the remainder of the plasterer's work (£307. 10s.) in the Hall, and 2 guineas was given on 21 November to the marble masons to entertain themselves 'on finishing the Hall'. William Townson started work on the mahogany doors (£83. 2s. 8d.), which were set into marble surrounds fashioned by William Atkinson.

In April 1760 Joseph Spackman provided over 3 cwt of 'Block Tin for the Banisters in the Hall' (£10. 12s. 2d.). It is not known who fashioned them into shape—a wooden pattern was provided 'for the Smith to work from' by two of James Miller's men working on the pattern rail for four and a half days each—but they are remarkably like those which Benjamin Holmes provided in 1744 to Kent's design at 44 Berkeley Square, London (see pl. 40). Holmes was paid for a 'Copper Ball and neck' at Holkham in 1748, but there is no evidence to associate him with the fashioning of the Marble Hall balusters. There was also a resident master smith, Thomas

43. I have used in particular Holkham Archives, Building Accounts 26, 27, and Country Accounts, 8.

Hall, who was paid £40 a year, and work was also being done in 1758 at the house by the talented London smith Thomas Tilston, who was later to provide metal balustrades to several staircases in houses designed by Robert Adam. Whatever the exact truth, the accounts do record the varnishing of the balusters with $14\frac{1}{4}$ lb of 'tin Glass' supplied by Tapenden and Hartley (£1. 4s. 11d.), and the provision of 70 ft of straight mahogany handrail and 20 ft of circular (at 2s. 6d. and 3s. 6d. per ft respectively) by the joiner William Townson (£12. 5s. 0d.).

Much of the credit for the overwhelming appearance of this great room must, however, go, in terms of workmanship rather than conception, to William Atkinson and his team of marble- and stonemasons, and to the plasterer Thomas Clark. Atkinson, who was in partnership in the earlier years of Holkham's erection with Joseph Pickford (d.1755), died in 1766, two years after the completion of the house. Included in the sale of his effects (2 April 1767) at his Piccadilly yard was 'a large and magnificent vase in Bath stone, designed by Mr Kent'. Atkinson supplied to Holkham not only chimneypieces, but veined, Plymouth, black and yellow, and statuary marble, firestone hearths and coverings and Portland and Bremen paving. He also fixed the statues in the niches he had cut out in the Hall. He worked throughout to a careful programme, collaborating with the joiners, Robert May and Peter Moor, who provided the mahogany door linings, as well as working in the Chapel on the cedar screen and altar-rails.

One of the precise (and still functioning) minor arts required at Holkham was the provision and installation of intricate locks. These were from the Birmingham locksmith Thomas Blockley (1705–89), called by *Aris's Birmingham Gazette* (5 January 1789) at his death: 'One of the first locksmiths in the kingdom'. Blockley's locks, provided along with bolts, hinges, screws and brass handles in 1761 (£110. 5s. 0d.), are just a little early to be affected by the full neoclassical style; he later adopted it (*see* pl. 56) and worked extensively at several Adam houses.

The plasterer Thomas Clark also needed the collaboration of other craftsmen apart from his own team of men. We have noted in the work done by Bagutti at St Martin-in-the-Fields Church, London, in the 1720s that it was the carpenter who moved the plasterer's scaffolding; at Holkham James Lillie was paid in 1760 for 'raising a Scaffold for the Plaisterers to colour the Hall ceeling and Striking it'. To fix the eight-petalled stylised flowers, *putti* and other ornaments on the ceiling (*see* pl. 78), Clark used lead bonds obtained from John Bullin (12s. 9d.). The flails and thongs he used to thrash the plaster with were supplied by John Parker (6s. 6d.), and the hair came from Robert Drosier. One of James Miller's men had spent two days carving 'a reverse moulding for the Hall ceiling, and one for the chapel ceiling at 3s. 6d. a day'. In 1760 alone, 35 st of Spanish white, 4 barrels of 'Lamp black' and 5 qt of Florence oil were used by the plasterers, and much money was subsequently spent on gilding by John and Thomas Neale, and on furnishings.

It is not entirely to our purpose to chronicle the extensive provision of furniture which accompanied the various stages of completing parts of Holkham. The Holkham archives do, however, indicate[44] that, to 1759, Lord Leicester spent £5465. 17s. 9d., and after his death, and to 1771, Lady Leicester paid a further £3096. 5s. 8d., a total of £8562. 3s. 5d. This included the surprising entry for Brettingham 'carving 35 chairs, 4 Sophas, 4 Settees, 4 Picture Frames'

---

44. Holkham Estate Office, Family Deeds, 66, 'Furniture for Holkham'.

(£86. 12s. 10d.). Materials in damask and velvet came from a London mercer (Carr), totalling £3166. 13s. 0d., and were used to embellish rooms such as the Saloon and Drawing Room. In all, therefore, Lord Leicester spent almost £90 000 on the structure of his house, and a further £5500 on furnishings before his death in 1759. It contrasts sharply with the more modest expenditure of £32 541 which Sir James Dashwood spent on Kirtlington, his Oxfordshire house, between 1741 and 1762.

KIRTLINGTON PARK

Sir James Dashwood, at the commencement of the outworks of his new house begun on 12 September 1741, started a 'Generall Account of Money Expended. . .'.[45] It records in precise detail that the foundations were started on 5 April 1742 and the first stone laid on 22 April. Four years later Sir James recorded proudly that, on 30 August 1746, he 'went into my New house, my Son Henry Watkin, being on that Day A year old'. Having received plans in 1741 from both Daniel Garrett and James Gibbs, Sir James advanced to the builder William Hiorns 'on Account with Mr Wm Smith' £210; he paid later sums to Smith through his London bankers, Hoare's. A competent local team of men provided timber and other minor supplies, but most of the money was laid out through Smith.

The plasterwork at Kirtlington (and that from the house in rooms re-erected at the Metropolitan Museum, New York, see pl. 76), was by the competent Oxford plasterer Thomas Roberts (£119), and chimneypieces came from Henry Cheere (see pl. 139). At William Smith's death in 1747, the supervision of the final stages of the house was entrusted to the architect John Sanderson—he received £65 on 7 April 1748. One of Francis and William Smith's craftsmen, the Warwick joiner George Eborall, received money in November 1748 (£64), October 1751 (£50) and July 1757 (£3. 15s.); a small notebook kept by Francis Smith[46] shows that this payment to Eborall was only a part one. He created deal wainscoting, oak sashes, deal and mahogany doors, Norway oak flooring and moulded decorations. The staircase was one of the more important items in his bill—for £90 he did the 'Oak work to rail and balluster (8d. a ft), working and laying of steps & 2 pieces of the best Staircases & the architrave, frize & cornice, the oak up the flights & round up 1st landing, and the molded ramp rail & Ballusters with turning'. Locks and hinges came, as at Holkham, from Thomas Blockley.

Sir Francis completed his house with furniture from William Hallett and 15 busts provided in two lots by Richard Dalton, later Librarian to King George III. In 1752 he turned his eager attention to the grounds: Lancelot 'Capability' Brown received the first £100 of an agreement in January 1752, and further payments totalling a little over £1220 up to 1757. Sir Francis, on the fly-leaf of his book, noted what is at slight variance with his accounts, that 'Mr Brown, the Landscape Gardener began 3 March 1755. Sept 16. 1762, last settlement with Mr Brown £152. 12s. 0d. Say Mansion and Stables cost 30 Thousand Pounds.' At a little over, he was near enough to the truth. Here Brown had been a gardener, albeit one talented with landscape, but architecture was among his considerable accomplishments, and we encounter him again at the

45. Bodleian Library, Oxford, MS, F.552. I am indebted to Dr Andor Gomme for loaning me a photocopy of this item.

46. ibid., MS, F.556. I am indebted to Mrs Ingrid Roscoe for drawing my attention to this item, noted in research for her article on Kirtlington (*Apollo*, January 1980).

threshold of the neoclassical years—at Croome Court, Worcestershire, the house decorated for the 6th Earl of Coventry by Robert Adam on a scale as though his patron was the undisputed Maecenas of his age.

ROCOCO WORK FOR JAMES PAINE

As the great exponents of the Palladian style went their way, a new feeling was coming to interior decoration. The rococo style was making itself very evident in the 1740s; it had been introduced from France and the swirling asymmetry, which is its main characteristic, found ready acceptance, not only with the Italian *stuccatori*, but with their English counterparts working in plaster and wood.

In 1740 the 7th Viscount Irwin commissioned Thomas Perritt of York to provide the plaster ceilings at Temple Newsam House, Leeds. Perritt had been apprenticed to his father Jonathan, a York bricklayer. By 1737–38 he had been made a freeman of the city, and, with his father, was employed at the York Assembly Rooms in 1741 (and for several years after) cleaning various rooms and colouring the stucco-work. At Temple Newsam, Perritt, with the apprentice he had taken in 1738. Joseph Rose senior (*c* 1723–80), provided the plasterwork and received in all £419. 16s. 1d., of which sum £190. 10s. 9d. was for the execution of the Long Gallery ceiling. This fine piece of work presents an iconographical problem in that its design incorporates what the account[47] calls '13 Medals at 10s. 6d. each. £6. 16s. 6d.' (*see* pl. 74); these plasterers were to use similar 'medals' at other houses.[48]

Perritt's principal commissions, however, were given to him by the architect James Paine: these were at Cusworth Hall, Nostell Priory and the Doncaster Mansion House. Like Colen Campbell 20 years before, James Paine found ready encouragement for his talents from Yorkshire gentlemen. He put it neatly in the Preface to his book of 1751, *Plans, Elevations, Sections and other ornaments of the Mansion House Belonging to the Corporation of Doncaster*: 'Having at that Time the Honour to be engaged in several Gentlemen's Buildings in that Country, I was made Choice of for their Architect. . .'. He noted that the foundation stone of this splendid Doncaster town house was laid in the spring of 1745, but the Jacobite rebellion stopped the work for a time. It was finished by 1748 'with the Approbation of the Gentlemen who engaged to inspect into it, on behalf of the Corporation. . .'.

The manuscript *Courtiers' Book* and other documents[49] give evidence for some theories about the decoration. But, firstly, the entry for 8 December 1744 shows that the committee appointed to 'get plans . . . drawn by such persons as they think fit' accepted 'Dr Stead's plan for a Mansion House', and that 'such variations in ye sd. Plan as shall be advised and thought necessary' were to be by 'Mr Pain of Wragby'. Then, as Paine noted, came the Jacobite troubles, the first committee's powers were revoked and a new one appointed. 'Deals and Polls bought by

47. Leeds Archives Dept, Temple Newsam Archives, E.A.12/10.
48. N and S Staircase, Nostell Priory; 'Whistle-jacket Room', Wentworth Woodhouse. They are also shown in Paine's book on the Doncaster Mansion House (1751, pl. XXI), but were not executed. Medallions are also depicted in William Jones, 1739, *Gentleman's or Builder's Companion . . .*, pl. 57.

49. Doncaster Corporation Archives, *Courtiers Book*, III, and Parcel 26. The mason was George Gibson; interior mason's work by John Beal, *ibid.*, 14 December 1744. The carpenter was William Rickard, who married in 1727 Elizabeth Platt, daughter of the Rotherham architect George Platt (1700–43); he (with Rickard) was employed at Cusworth Hall, Doncaster.

the former Comee at Hull at ye same prices they gave for them there & Charges of bringing ye same from thence' were allowed. Paine inspected the accounts in November 1745 and, on 26 February 1745/46, it was agreed 'that Mr James Paine of Pontefract is to finish the Mansion House according to the Designs he has this day given in, the Estimate of the whole amounting to four thousand five Hundred, twenty three pounds four shillings and sixpence'. He was to receive £700 before Lady Day, a second payment of £500 in 12 months, and a third payment 'when the House is finished which shall be against Michaelmas 1747'; this remaining sum was to be paid at £500 a year, with interest added at 4 per cent. John Stead was appointed one of the 'Inspectors' and is presumably the 'Dr Stead' who provided a first plan; Paine noted him as 'John Stead. M.D.' in the dedicatory epistle of the 1751 volume.

When the house was finished in 1748—there is a note in the 'Money disbursed for the Corporation, 15 April 1749': 'Paid ye Musick at opening the Mansion House, 5s. 0d.'[50] —it was not exactly as Paine had planned it. In the note to plate XXI of the descriptive volume of 1751, he first observed that 'the ornaments in it [the Banqueting Room], and on the Sides of the Room, are of stucco (executed by Mr Rose, and Mr Thomas Perritt), inferior to none of the Performances of the best *Italians* that ever work'd in this Kingdom'. These various designs and sections show elaborate ceiling paintings within the stucco framework, and, in the Dedication, Paine noted that 'stucco work forming Compartments for Painting' is 'much more elegant than Cieling and Sides finish'd entirely with either painting, or stucco. I have therefore design'd, and with my own Hands drawn, suitable compartments of Ornament, and that nothing should be wanting to render the Work compleat, have been at the Expence to have them filled with proper Subjects for Paintings.'

The surviving documents do not mention any paintings and I am sure they were not executed.[51] Paine had left a generous cove to the ceiling for them and, three years after completion, was still trying to indicate to the city fathers, in the book devoted to their Mansion house, that paintings would 'render the Work compleat'.

A few clues are available to suggest the painter Paine had in mind: the title-page of the book shows a portrait of the architect drawn by Francis Hayman and engraved by Grignion; Hayman also did decorative paintings and it is significant that Paine employed him at Cusworth Hall, some two miles north-west of Doncaster. The spaces in Paine's book, filled 'with proper subjects for Paintings', are an indication of what Hayman intended, and were presumably drawn by him. But, apart from considering a chandelier from Ranelagh which, eventually, Paine could not obtain 'at the price proposed', no 'outside' touches were allowed; Perritt and Rose's swirling rococo plasterwork alone captivated the dour Yorkshire committee as they danced at their assemblies to the 'town musick' and sipped the wines provided by Mr Jaques.

The many gentlemen who visited Paine's work here—he was also using Perritt and Rose at nearby Nostell about this time—may have included William Wrightson of Cusworth Hall, Doncaster. He had started to build his house[52] in 1740 to his own design, with the help of the

50. Doncaster corporation archives, *Courtier's Book*, III, Parcel 26.
51. The entry in *Courtiers Book*, III, 26 September 1747–48, about 'Mr Paine giving security to ye Corporation to finish ye painting yet to be done in the

sd. house at such times as the Corporacon shall direct' relates, it seems, to ordinary painting, and not decorative treatments.
52. Leeds Archives Dept, Battie-Wrightson Archives, A22–32.

Rotherham architect George Platt. The central hall was completed by 1745 but, his second wife having died, building was temporarily abandoned. The work went on in due course, but Wrightson's son-in-law complained that he considered the south front 'too tall for its length', and Paine was asked to design two wings which would help to correct this impression. The west wing was to contain a Chapel and that on the east and south side, a Library. Eleven letters from Paine, and estimates and bills for materials, document the work in considerable detail. Wrightson tried to arrange for economies in the original estimate of £894. 8s. 11½d., and Paine suggested that he could lessen it 'by finishing plainer', and that the owner might find his 'own timber, Bricks, Lime, Sand & Common Wall Stones, and as the Laths and Nails will be but a trifle I would Advise you Also to Provide them. . .'. Paine's attention to detail is indicated in his statement of 18 January 1749/50: 'I made three different Designs for y^r intended Additions 'ere I cou'd Please my Self.' His busy life within these years is hinted at when he tells Wrightson in a letter of 3 July 1750: 'I have got the Drawing of the Front very Forward (Altho I never was so hurried in Business in me life).'

The work at Cusworth was in the hands of a team of Yorkshire workers[53] with the addition of two accomplished craftsmen, Joseph Rose senior for plasterwork and Francis Hayman for the paintings in the Chapel. Rose's detailed bill shows his rates for work, per foot:

| Running of enrichment | 2d. | Laurel leaf | 1/0d. |
| Enriched Astragal | 4d. | Festoon of Leaves | 1/6d. |

Hayman provided a fresco, *The Ascension*, for the Chapel ceiling, and a painting, *The Good Samaritan*, for the altar-piece. He was paid £26. 5s. 'in full' on 19 March 1752. Rose then surrounded it with four 'flowers' at 23s. each, and added cherubims, festoons and carved trusses elsewhere; he framed Hayman's altar painting with a stucco border for £4, and received £266. 8s. 2d. for all his work. His man Luke Green assisted.

Paine, meanwhile, was still busy.[54] He sent instructions through his clerk, Joseph Rumball, to the carpenter, John Wilson, who was working at Cowick some 20 miles from Doncaster; Paine was reconstructing the house for Viscount Downe, and needed to know 'whether Ld. Downe gave Orders for a New Chimney Piece for his Bed Chamber or not', and 'how forward all the works are at Cowick'. As well as being busy with buildings, a letter to Wrightson of 8 February 1749 indicated that Paine had married again (his first wife was Sarah Jennings of Wragby, near Nostell Priory, in March 1740/41) to a Charlotte Beaumont.[55]

Cusworth Hall was, however, a much less significant commission for Paine than Serlby Hall, near Bawtry, for Viscount Galway,[56] or Felbrigg, Norfolk, for William Windham.[57] For

53. The workers under George Platt, c 1740, included, as carpenters, his son-in-law William Rickard, John Morton and John Bower; plasterer Richard Wilkinson of Wakefield; Samuel Brookesbank; slater Thomas Aldom; lead, William Harwood. Paine used John Mosley as mason (stone from nearby Brodsworth); carver in wood and stone, Christopher Richardson; painter William Cave; decorative painting, Francis Hayman; plasterer Joseph Rose; and carpenters James Norris, Lionel Garlick and John Wilson. Doors and windows were by Richard Middlebrook. Bricks (163 000) were supplied at 6s. 6d. a thousand.

54. Apart from the list of works by Paine given in Colvin, 1978, *Dictionary*, reference should be made to an Oxford D Phil thesis on the architect by Peter Leach (1973).

55. Charlotte Beaumont (1722–66) of Whitley Beaumont, Yorks., Joseph Foster, 1874, *Pedigrees of the County Families of Yorkshire*.

56. Nottingham University Library, Galway Archives, 12415, is headed: 'Prices of different kinds of work allow'd at Serlby p. Jno. Carr & Jas Paine, Esq^{rs}.'. As the book is dated 1774, it does not seem that Paine and Carr were working together at Serlby.

57. R W Ketton-Cremer, 1962, *Felbrigg*, pp. 131–43.

Felbrigg, Paine again used Joseph Rose as plasterer, assisted by George Green, who may have been a relative of Luke Green, Rose's man at Cusworth. In February 1752 an incompetent plasterer (unnamed) had been sent down, and Hull (Paine's foreman at Felbrigg) 'must write to Mr Rose for another'. In April Rose was there himself, working on the staircase and again, in June, executing to Paine's designs the reliefs of the four seasons on the dining-room ceiling Green did the Library ceiling, that of the Cabinet and further work on the staircase; there is a letter to Green from Joseph Rumball, written from Paine's office in Holles Street, enclosing a drawing of this ceiling. By 1753 the work was completed, but, even with the money paid to him, Paine was writing from London to Wrightson on 19 March 1754: 'I need not tell you that Building is expensive, As you have been so large a Benefactor but permitt me to Acquaint you its more so here than in the Country which ocasions a Scarcity of Money with me. . .'. It was April 1761 before he opened his bank account at Coutts, preparatory to work at Sandbeck, Alnwick, Gopsal, Thorndon and a variety of the kind of commissions which, in exterior style, remained Palladian. The interior work was composed of an individual variation of Adamesque which showed, as Hardwicke said, 'the superiority of his taste in the nicer and more delicate parts of decoration'.

NORFOLK HOUSE, LONDON

While Paine designed excellent rococo-style ceilings and superb room settings for Perritt and Rose to execute (and more can be attributed to them as research proceeds), they did not quite match in skill of execution the work at Norfolk House, London. In 1960 Norfolk House was described and illustrated in detail in the *Survey of London* volumes (XXIX–XXX); it need only be said here that the house was designed for the 9th Duke of Norfolk by Matthew Brettingham senior. The house was demolished in 1938 and the collections dispersed, but, fortunately, the Music Room was saved and re-erected at the Victoria and Albert Museum, London (*see* pls. 124 and 140). Careful descriptions of this room have been published. The absence of all but one account book led firstly to the reasonable speculation that the plasterwork was probably by William Collins, who worked later for the Duchess of Norfolk at Worksop, a house she was having built to James Paine's designs.

The prototype of the Music Room ceiling at Norfolk House was that of the Banqueting Hall in Whitehall by Inigo Jones; the eight compartments which surround the central oval, however, are filled with very accomplished rococo plasterwork, richly gilded. The names of the persons who carried out this work remained unknown until December 1968, when the Duke of Norfolk's archivist, Francis Steer, made a special search of the Arundel Castle archives on my behalf; the plasterer's and carver's accounts were found and proved that the plasterwork was done in 1755 by Thomas Clark, who later became Master Plasterer to the Office of Works, and that the richly gilded woodcarving, as noted elsewhere in this book, was by John Cuneot. Clark's bill for work on the 'Principal Floor' amounted to £225. 7s. 8d., and included 'Scaffolding, Colouring and adding to Ornaments—according to Mr Bora's Directions'. An 'Ornament Plaisterer' was employed for 45 days, assisted by seven plasterers, two labourers and two boys. Fine lime and hair and nine hods of stucco were used, as well as 'prepared Plaister of Paris'; a sum of £3. 15s. 6d. was also paid 'for different degrees of Colour'. The Entablature in the Great Room was also decorated by Clark 'according to **Mr Bora's Design**'. In summary, therefore, everything in carved wood on the walls seems to be the work of Cuneot, and, as one would expect, everything in plaster and stucco on the ceiling is by Thomas Clark, guided by Borra.

Not a great deal is yet known about Borra's connection with the work at Norfolk House, his previously recorded English activities having been associated with Stowe House, Buckinghamshire.[58] He was the Giovanni Battista Borra who accompanied Robert Wood and his friends Dawkins and Bouverie on their journeys to Asia Minor; here he helped to make the surveys and the drawings which were finally engraved by Fourdrinier, and produced by Wood in his books *The Ruins of Palmyra* (1753) and *The Ruins of Balbec* (1757).

Horace Walpole was at the opening of Norfolk House in 1756 and, like everyone else, spent much time 'gazing in the air' as he looked at the 'delightful' ceilings, many of which, in view of Borra's connection, were an early attempt at emulating those at Palmyra. Isaac Ware, however, in his book *A Complete Body of Architecture,* was to deprecate the representation of wind instruments, flowers and books of music on ceilings straggled over with meaningless C's and O's and tangled semi-circles. Such decoration was, nevertheless, to appear on many more occasions and it has been shown[59] that Ware himself designed rococo interiors in Woodcote Park, Hertfordshire, and Belvedere, Kent, as well as those in Chesterfield House, London. Drawings made by Vardy, Lightoler and the Hiornes at this time also show enriched coves in stucco or chiaroscuro, and delicate swags of flowers or fruit carved in wood or plaster. It was all contrived with a sense of balance and tension—the 'wanton kind of chace' which Ware mentioned. The ceiling of the Court Room of the Foundling Hospital in London and that in the library of Christ Church, Oxford, are good examples which show how William Wilton and Thomas Roberts, respectively, handled the sensuous mood in plaster.

It was, however, preoccupation with ornament of this nature which caused the 'milords' returning from the Grand Tour to concern themselves, not only with the rococo style, but with the Gothic and Chinese rages. In Worcestershire George Lyttelton and his architect, Sanderson Miller, were busy erecting at Hagley a ruined castle, and bringing Gothic into the church. The Bateman family were doing the same at Shobdon in Herefordshire, and Horace Walpole and his 'Committee of Taste' were working hard to remain the leaders of the strange style of the moment which owed so much to medieval precedent. At Strawberry Hill, Walpole used William Robinson, the Clerk of Works at Greenwich Hospital, to supervise his workmen. There was a need to create atmosphere—it was left to Robinson to see that the effect was structurally sound, for, as 'Gilly' Williams[60] said, 'Mr Walpole had already outlived three sets of his battlements', and noted, on another occasion, that 'Horry is now as much a curiosity to all foreigners as the tombs and lions.' Bewildered Frenchmen, accustomed to the niceties of rococo, struggled to understand the Gothic of Strawberry Hill, to which they were welcomed with music playing in the cloister and complimentary verses for the ladies set up in type at the

58. Laurence Whistler, 29 August 1957, 'Signor Borra at Stowe', *C Life,* CXXII, pp. 390–93.

59. John Harris, May 1961, 'Clues to the Frenchness of Woodcote Park', *The Connoisseur,* CXLVII,

pp. 241–50; *see also Apollo,* August 1969.

60. George James Williams—'Gilly'—was a friend and correspondent of Walpole and his circle.

printing house. It was built, as Walpole said, 'to please my own taste, and in some degree to realise my own visions'.[61]

The Gothic style, the origins and details of which have often been discussed,[62] had strongly entrenched itself by the late 1750s. In 1757 James Adam was writing to the portrait painter Allan Ramsay 'with respect to the treatise of Gothic architecture', and in the Soane Museum and elsewhere are a number of sketches which show the study the Adam brothers gave to this vogue.[63] Gradually, all obstacles were being cleared by Robert Adam for his début in London. He returned from his Italian tour in the winter of 1758. Within a year or two a new, young monarch who was a patron of the arts was to come to the throne. By 1762, when Walpole wrote 'if there are any talents among us, this seems the crisis for their appearance', the 'Adam style' had taken hold; the long years of apprenticeship in Scotland and study in Italy had brought success within Robert Adam's grasp.

The 60 years of an age which had involved itself so fully with the architectural orders and had bred patrons, architects and craftsmen dedicated to following them strictly, although there had been divergences and frivolities, was over. It was to be no longer easy to choose rococo, Gothic or Chinese. True to the pattern of his muddled life, Sir George Lyttelton was one of the last to decorate his house at Hagley in 1759 with rococo plasterwork by the Italians.[64] By 1761 they had gone abroad, and everyone was ready to turn to William Chambers and Robert Adam. Each had visions of what might be, and assumed that the revivals of ancient style were now solely in their hands.

61. Horace Walpole, 1798, Preface to 'A Description of the Villa . . . at Strawberry Hill', *Works*, II, p. 398.
62. R W Ketton-Cremer, 1940, *Horace Walpole*, p. 226. For Walpole and the Gothic Revival, *see* Kenneth Clark, 1950, *The Gothic Revival* and W S Lewis, 1961, *Horace Walpole*.
63. John Fleming, 1962, *Robert Adam and his Circle in Edinburgh and Rome*, p. 85.
64. Late commissions were Hagley (Vassalli, 1759); Ragley (Artari, 1759); and Croome Court (Vassalli, 1758–59).

WOODCARVING

106 (*right*) COSIMO PANEL, carved in lime wood by Grinling Gibbons, 1648–1721. Detail, 1682. *Bargello Museum, Florence* (photograph courtesy of David Green).

While this is a crowded composition, Gibbons did no finer work, and it included (as if he were proud to claim it) his name. The panel, measuring overall some 5 ft × 3 ft 6 in, was sent by Charles II to Cosimo III, Grand Duke of Tuscany. The duke had visited England in 1669 and had become very friendly with the king; this commission had to delight both king and duke, and by its dazzling technique and clever allusions to matters interesting to its intended recipient, succeeded in establishing Gibbons, in John Evelyn's words (1693), as 'the most excellent of his profession not onely in England but in the whole world . . .'. *Lit*: David Green, 1964, *Grinling Gibbons*, pp. 51–52, pls. 45–49.

107 (*below*) BADMINTON, Gloucestershire. Detail of Dining Room overmantel, *c* 1683–84 (photograph courtesy of David Green).

In the Child's bank account of the 1st Duke of Beaufort, I discovered two payments to 'Mr. Grymlin Gibbons, Carver': 6 July 1683, £50, and 4 June 1684, £98 (for 'Pictures'). These include presumably the cost of the Dining Room overmantel carved in pear wood. Headed by a ducal coronet with a crest incorporating the Garter and the name of 'Beaufort', the sides are flanked (as in this view) by assemblages of dead game, fruit and flowers. *Lit*: David Green, 1964, *Grinling Gibbons*, pls. 153–54.

108 (*below*) BURGHLEY HOUSE, Northamptonshire. Detail of carved overmantel in the Jewel Closet, *c* 1685 (photograph courtesy of David Green).

In researches in the Child's bank ledgers, I discovered the account of the 5th Earl of Exeter. It contained two payments (6 July 1683, 21 December 1685) of £50 each to Gibbons. This is little more than a quarter of the money paid to Jonathan Maine and Thomas Young. The standard of all the carved work at Burghley is good, with these doves very much in Gibbons's manner.

109 TRINITY COLLEGE, Cambridge. Sir Henry
Newton Puckering's cypher, library, *c* 1691
(photograph: A F Kersting).

When Charles Seymour, 6th Duke of Somerset,
and a Trinity man, was made Chancellor of the
University in 1689, activity on Wren's library was
hastened. On the eastern side of the long room the
benefactors were commemorated with their coats
of arms carved in lime wood by Gibbons. That for
Sir Henry Newton Puckering shows a cypher set
in oak leaves, forget-me-nots and crocuses.
Lit: M D Whinney, 1948, *Grinling Gibbons in
Cambridge.*

110 and 111 PETWORTH, Sussex. The Carved Room, details, *c* 1692 (photographs: A F Kersting).

The present Carved Room was originally two separate rooms which were made into one about 1794–95. Carvings by Gibbons, John Selden, the Petworth carver, and nineteenth-century ones by Jonathan Ritson were gathered together from various parts of the house. Payments to Gibbons occur in the house archives, and he seems responsible for these great pendants.
Lit: David Green, 1964, *Grinling Gibbons*, pp. 105–06.

112 and 113 TRINITY COLLEGE, Oxford. The Chapel Reredos, details, *c* 1693 (photographs: A F Kersting (*below*), courtesy of David Green (*left*)).

On her second visit in 1694, the indefatigable traveller and recorder Celia Fiennes observed 'the very fine carving of thin white wood just like that at Windsor, it being the same hand'. The reredos frame, with an acanthus frieze typical of work by Gibbons, is flanked by fine Corinthian columns and a riot of carving—a chalice of grapes and frowning cherubim. While Jonathan Maine and the local joiner Arthur Frogley worked elsewhere in the Chapel, this noble reredos surely belongs to Gibbons—it may have been the gift of his friend, John Evelyn (*see also* col. pl. 3).

114 and 115 ST PAUL'S CATHEDRAL, London.
Details of the Choir Stalls, N. side, *c* 1696–97
(photographs: A F Kersting).

In oak and lime wood, Gibbons carved the Choir
of St Paul's—organ case and screen, thrones,
columns, panels, friezes—'the most magnificent
woodcarving in England'.
Lit: David Green, 1964, *Grinling Gibbons*, pp.
91–92; *Wren Soc*, XV, p. 32.

116 (*left*) HAMPTON COURT, Middlesex. King William III's State Bedroom, detail of carved door-frame (photograph: National Monuments Record).

When Queen Mary died in 1694, King William lost interest in Hampton Court Palace and work was halted for five years. While Gibbons had prepared drawings for carving in the state apartments, much of the work does not correspond to them—the result of the delays, and of finishing work begun some years earlier. His bills included charges for all the carving over doors and windows.

Lit: Colvin, 1976, *King's Works*, V, p. 164.

117 (*below*) QUEEN'S COLLEGE, Oxford. Carved panel in the library, *c* 1695 (photograph: A F Kersting).

Celia Fiennes observed 'good carvings' at Queen's College in 1694. They included the pierced door panels in Norway oak by the Oxford joiner Thomas Minn. Tighter in execution than work by Gibbons, the sharpness and control of the carving is nevertheless of a high order.

118 (*facing page*) CHATSWORTH, Derbyshire. The State Drawing Room, 1689–94. Detail of overmantel (photograph: National Monuments Record).

The Chatsworth archives do not often differentiate the respective contributions of the carvers Joel Lobb, Roger Davis and Samuel Watson. They never quite reached the standard of Grinling Gibbons, but their work, as in this room, was of a high order. The Mortlake tapestries (*c* 1630) have been 'cruelly cut about with the object of making them fit into the space available' (*see also* col. pl. 1).

120 and 121 BENINGBROUGH HALL, Yorkshire. Details of capital in Saloon (*above*) and overdoor in Green Silk Bedroom (*below*), *c* 1716 (photographs: National Monuments Record).

In the Metropolitan Museum, New York, is a *Builders' Dictionary* of 1730 with annotations noting the architects of certain houses. Beningbrough is given to the York joiner William Thornton (1670–1721). The staircase at the house has a parquetry insert on a quarter-landing which incorporates the date '1716'. Certain parts of the panelling have similarities with that at Wentworth Castle, where Thornton also worked. The woodcarving may well have been influenced by the good provincial masons' and joiners' abiding interest in foreign pattern-books—Beningbrough has some capitals with in-turned volutes (not in pl. 120), a feature used by Borromini and in England by Thomas Archer and Francis Smith.
Lit: Beard, 1966, *Craftsmen*, p. 24; D Linstrum, 1978, *West Yorkshire: Architects and Architecture*, p. 385.

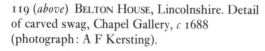

119 (*above*) BELTON HOUSE, Lincolnshire. Detail of carved swag, Chapel Gallery, *c* 1688 (photograph: A F Kersting).

The carved overmantels in the Marble Hall at Belton are attributed to Edmund Carpenter and Grinling Gibbons. The legend of the latter's involvement should not be discounted, because Carpenter's bill (1688) does not cover all the carved work in the house, including that in the Chapel. The work here, while competent, does not have any of the assurance which Gibbons brought to his work.
Lit: C Life, 10 September 1964, pp. 622–23.

122 CHISWICK HOUSE, Middlesex. Circular Room, detail of carving above fireplace, S. side, *c* 1728 (photograph: Department of the Environment).

The illustrations in this book (*see* pls. 50–52), include fine carved work by James Richards, who succeeded Grinling Gibbons in 1721 as Master Carver to the Crown. He was much employed by Colen Campbell, Lord Burlington and William Kent, apart from his work for the Office of Works. At Chiswick his spirited work is found in many doors (*see* pl. 52), and asserts him as the leading mid-century carver. He died in 1759.

123 STATE BARGE for Frederick, Prince of Wales, 1732. Detail of the carving of the 'State House'. *National Maritime Museum, Greenwich* (photograph: museum).

The 'State House' was constructed on the barge by the joiner Hercules Taylor, and it was carved by James Richards. Taylor frequently had to take off trusses and shelves 'to be Curved Hollow', fitted the coving, provided some timber for coving, prepared the 18 windows and sashes, framed and fixed the seats, provided lockers, steps and gang boards and made moulds for hinges and locks. He received £102. 2s. 2d.

Richards's bill was itemised in 31 main categories of carving foliage, festoons, mask faces, dolphins, sea lions, beading, mouldings, etc. He received £150. 16s. 6d.

Lit: Geoffrey Beard, August 1970, 'William Kent and the Royal Barge', *Burl Mag*, pp. 488–95.

124 NORFOLK HOUSE, London. Music Room, detail of mirror above chimneypiece, c 1755. *Victoria and Albert Museum, London*, Inv. No. W70–1938 (photograph: museum).

When Norfolk House was demolished in 1938, much of great decorative beauty was lost. The Music Room, the finest interior, was fortunately saved and re-erected in the Victoria and Albert Museum. In 1972 I managed to locate the bills for its original decoration, and these were edited with great skill by Desmond Fitz-Gerald. The woodcarving and gilding was all done by John Cuenot: he received £647. 7s. 3d. for this room alone. The fine scrolls centring on an Aurora mask, illustrated here, were probably based on engravings by Jean Bérain (*see also* pl. 140). *Lit:* Desmond Fitz-Gerald, ed., 1973. *The Norfolk House Music Room*, Victoria and Albert Museum.

125 CROOME D'ABITOT CHURCH, Worcestershire.
Detail of pulpit and sounding-board, 1762
(photograph: National Monuments Record).

The Croome Archives show that the octagonal
framing for the pulpit was provided by the joiner
John Hobcraft, and that all the carving in oak,
particularly on the sounding-board, was by
Sefferin Alken.
Lit: Croome Archives, Building Bills, Nos. 22, 25.

126 CLAYDON, Buckinghamshire. Detail of
wooden ceiling of Staircase Hall, *c* 1768
(photograph: National Monuments Record).

With such decoration normally in plasterwork, it is
surprising to find carved wood applied to the
ceiling. Carried out by the erratic joiner and carver
Luke Lightfoot, and incorporating the cypher of
his patron, Ralph, 2nd Earl Verney, the ceiling is
set above a staircase with plastered walls by Joseph
Rose junior (*see also* pl. 42).

127 CLAYDON, Buckinghamshire. The North Hall, S. wall, detail of one of the niches, *c* 1768 (photograph: A F Kersting).

The carved wood niche, of which this is a detail, is shown in pl. 53.

128 OSTERLEY PARK, Middlesex. State Bedroom, detail of carved sphinx on pier mirror, *c* 1776. *Victoria and Albert Museum, London*, Inv. No. OPH 34/1949 (photograph: museum).

While there is no documentary evidence as to the authorship of this gilded and painted pine pier mirror, a considerable amount of furniture was provided for Osterley by the London cabinet-maker John Linnell. The Adam designs for it (Soane Museum, 20, Nos. 46–47) are dated 1775.

[3]
Visions and Revivals
1760–1820

Robert Adam

The measure of the first stage of this important period was given in a letter from Robert Adam to his brother James, written at Naples on 18 April 1755. Concerned with the considerable abilities of William Chambers, he concluded:

> Time alone can determine whether I am meet to cope with such a rival. And if I find that I make the improvement I require then I can with more certainty trust to English employment and can advise you from time to time if I think I have any prospect of arriving at a taste superior to what I ever thought of . . . as it will require a very considerable interest to succeed Chambers who has tolerable friends and real merit.

Adam was still worrying about Chambers six months later. In a letter of 13 September to his sister Elizabeth, he wrote: 'Chambers is a more formidable foe [than Roger Morris], and being already sometime in England is no doubt establishing himself well in business.'[1] Adam also wanted to cut out the younger Brettingham, who had been two or three years in Italy and who, on return to England, 'has £15 000 or £20 000 from his father'. He considered, however, that he could draw comfort and hope from Brettingham 'not being invincible . . . from his genius being much inferior to his fortune'.

It was in Rome in the 1740s and 1750s that the heady doctrines were being expounded that imparted an urgent driving force to the development of classicism. Chambers had mixed with the groups of young artists, living in Rome at their king's expense, studying at the French Academy and concentrating on the famed examples of classical antiquity.[2] These lay almost undiscovered and in weed-covered splendour; they excited all impressionable minds by their scale and precise decoration. In addition, a considerable amount of new building was in progress—the Spanish Steps, the façade of San Giovanni in Laterano, the Fontana di Trevi. They vied with the established masterpieces by the Renaissance architects, and all received engraved treatment at the skilled hands of the Bibiena family and Giovanni Battista Piranesi. Neoclassicism soon replaced the spirited delights of the rococo, and everyone in England who cared wanted to be rid of a style which lacked symmetry and was uncontrollable in format; soon, patrons were to be as involved in promoting neoclassicism. The *goût grec*, or the *style antique*, were terms which set out meaning one thing and ended as those labelling antique exaggerations.

1. Fleming, 1962, *Adam*, p. 160; Scottish Record Office, Clerk of Penicuik Archives, GD. 4787 (September 1755, letter).

2. John Harris, 1967, 'Le Geay, Piranesi and International Neo-classicism in Rome, 1740–1750', *Essays in the History of Architecture presented to Rudolf Wittkower*.

They represented the Baron de Grimm's comment of 1 May 1763: 'If one cannot avoid exaggeration, then it is better to exaggerate something good than something bad.'[3]

Unfortunately, it cannot be said that English workmen were too successful at translating these ideas of architects and patrons into effective decoration. The Abbé Le Blanc, in his *Letters on the English and French Nations* (1747), mentioned the great skill of English workmen, 'but notwithstanding all their endeavours, they have not been able to attain it [gracefulness in the shape of things]. As much as I admire their invention in mechanical arts, I am equally offended at all their productions in the arts of taste.' He thought that, guided as our craftsmen were by the rule and compass, they were unhappy in their inventions, unacquainted with the exactness of proportions, and that they succeeded no better in the taste of their furniture 'than in that of the ornaments of their houses'. He judged the English harshly because they had not adhered to the 'simplicity'[4] of the ancients. The rococo, and the exotic Gothic and Chinese derivatives, had affected the appearance of almost everything, and violated simplicity. There was a reluctance to design anything to be contained within a regular pattern: Hogarth's line of beauty was the 'S' curve, and it accompanied all over-ornamentation. In seeking to establish principles by which taste could be defined, the very nature of taste itself was neglected and overlooked.[5] It was this situation which Chambers and Adam sought to correct; both realised that part of the solution lay in the education of their craftsmen.

In May 1757, a year or so before Adam returned from Italy, William Chambers (who had returned to England in the spring of 1755) wrote:

An architect from the nature of his employment must have many dependants among Artificers. His Bussiness is to penetrate into the Capacities of all and to Employ each according to his talents. Justice, Humanity and Reason require that all as far as in his power lyes should partake of his favour but his Judgement should guide him to Employ each in the branch he is most capable, by which means he will serve his dependants without suffering in his reputation or doing prejudice to his patrons.[6]

Extensive quotation of similar extracts[7] has allowed the conclusion to be drawn that, in the correspondence between Chambers and his patrons, the emerging situation was that of client and reliable agent; the emergence of the architect to his position of professional dignity had finally come. As for the craftsmen, apart from a favoured few we have noted at the outset of this study, they lived dependent on payments for work which always came late, and sometimes too late. Chambers summarised it neatly in 1774 when informing the Surveyor-General to the Office of Works, Thomas Worsley, of the plight of the widow of the Kew carpenter George Warren:

I cannot help wishing her success, more especially as her family distresses arise from a loss sustained by the death of the late Prince of Wales, the father of our Gracious

3. Svend Eriksen, 1974, *Early Neoclassicism in France.* pp. 51, 264–65.

4. R D Havens, 1953, 'Simplicity, A changing Concept', *Journal of the History of Ideas*, XIV, pp. 3–32.

5. E N Hooker, 1934, 'The Discussion of Taste, from 1750 to 1770 . . .', *Publications, Modern Language Association*, XLIX, p. 578.

6. RIBA Library, letter of 5 May 1757. I am indebted for this reference to Mr John Harris.

7. H M Martienssen, April 1964, 'Chambers as a professional man', *Arch Rev*, CXXXV, pp. 277–83.

Master, whose debts were never paid. Those rogues, the Roman Emperors, generally paid their predecessors' debts, but our gracious princes always let theirs die insolvent.[8]

But, despite unpaid accounts, there was an autocratic insistence on quality of work. The bank accounts of both William Chambers and Robert Adam (Drummond Bank) give precise testimony to their success, and to many of the craftsmen they employed. Much of their respective reputations rested on their abilities. Talented groups of masons, bricklayers, carpenters, joiners, carvers and plasterers worked alongside those more skilled in fashioning marble, locks, ormolu and silver. They followed the 'drawings at large' from each office, and their masters computed the time employed by their clerks, the high wages paid them, and the particular attentions which work at a variety of country sites demanded. James Paine's bank account (Coutts) from 1761 to 1782 also shows the steady rise attributed to his success: from £1192 in 1761 to £13 890 in 1771, and a slow decline to £4000 by 1785. It may not have been his main account, but payments appear to a similar group of craftsmen to those used by Adam: Thomas Blockley, the Birmingham locksmith, Henry Cheere and Joseph Wilton, sculptors, William Kinsman, the coppersmith, Joseph Rose and Francis Engleheart, plasterers, and William Atkinson, mason. The opportunities to both architects and their men were considerable. Adam's main chance to establish his position came with work at Croome, Kedleston and Syon. Chambers, who had started a little earlier, enjoyed at first the patronage of the Earl of Pembroke and the Duke of Richmond, and tried to erase from his mind having his plans for Harewood rejected by its wealthy owner, Edwin Lascelles.

CROOME COURT

One of the patrons most ready to recognise the skill and talent of Robert Adam was the 6th Earl of Coventry, who was engaged on building at Croome Court, Worcestershire. He used 'Capability' Brown as his architect and landscape gardener, and probably accepted much advice—some unlooked for—from his friend, the gentleman architect Sanderson Miller. In December 1752, Lord Deerhurst (as he then was) wrote to Miller and said: 'What ever merits it [Croome] may in future time boast it will be ungrateful not to acknowledge you the Primary Author.' This was interpreted many years ago as conclusive support to the theory that, because Croome resembled Hagley (which in turn, according to Horace Walpole, resembled, and was 'stolen' from, Holkham), Miller must have designed both houses. Examination of the family papers in 1951 indicated Brown's share in the design of the house and the nearby church, and the close resemblance to Claremont and Redgrave (houses indisputably by Brown) was pointed out.[9] The Sanderson Miller letters (at the Warwickshire CRO) show that, as the busy squire of Radway, he took only a spasmodic interest in an advisory capacity. Lord Guernsey wrote to Miller: 'I am glad of your surprise at what Deerhurst has done at Cromb, as I wish him success in his undertakings.' Soon these undertakings merited more skilled attention.

The Adam accounts for Croome, beginning in August 1760 and tabulated neatly on folio sheets, are augmented by a full series of bills and vouchers. The accounts open with the charges for an elevation and plan of the Greenhouse or Orangery (£15. 15s.), and the first 'Design of a

---

8. Martienssen, p. 278 citing BL Add MS, 41135, p. 34.   9. Dorothy Stroud, 1975, *Capability Brown*, pp. 47–49.

Ceiling for the Gallery', submitted in September at £12. 12s. This was rejected and, in March 1761, 'A new design (as executed) for the Ceiling of the Gallery' was listed at £9. 9s. It was intended to fit the Gallery up as a Library, and the ceiling design, of the early Syon type, depicted elongated octagons and lozenges which harmonised well with the rest of the lavish decoration. In May 1761 an 'Elevation and Plan of a Bridge' (£15. 15s.)—possibly the bridge in Richard Wilson's painting of the house—preceded the 'Sections of the Inside Finishings of the Gothic Church'. The 'new' church at Croome, in which material from the old church appears to have been incorporated, was designed, as Repton has said, by Brown, but we know that his work was 'confined to the carcase while the internal treatment, as in the case of the principal rooms of the house, was handed over to Adam'.

As in most architectural accounts, a certain number of items listed were never executed or failed to satisfy Lord Coventry. Some were repeated at full size for the craftsmen, and others slightly adapted. The design in the Soane Museum for the Library ceiling of January 1763 was used for the Tapestry Room ceiling; this is now in the Metropolitan Museum of Art, New York[10] (see pl. 80). In June 1763 Adam sent a section of the Gallery 'finished in the Antique Taste with Statues, Bas Reliefes etc' and all the 'mouldings at large for Messrs Cobb and Vyle', the cabinet-makers, and 'the ornaments for Mr Alken for the Bookcases of the Library'. This is Sefferin Alken, who worked at Shardeloes for Adam and was at Croome over many years; he carved friezes, architraves to doors, windows, the fine guilloche mouldings around the windows, the dentils of the chair rail and the fascia and leaf moulding around the base-board of the Tapestry Room, as well as working in the Church (see pl. 125) and Park.

Adam visited the site in October 1763 and, a month later, sections of the 'Tapestry Room, Staircase and Dairy Offices' were sent for Lord Coventry's approval. His Lordship had visited the Gobelins tapestry manufactory in August 1763, and had ordered a set of Boucher-Neilson tapestries; these were finally ready by 1771. The Tapestry Room ceiling, on fir laths, was by now painted bluish-white, and the chimneypiece was given a red Veronese marble background and trims in white and lapis lazuli. Joseph Wilton, the state coach carver and sculptor to his majesty, carved this and the caryatid chimneypiece for the Gallery.

The master carpenter was John Hobcraft, who worked in the house and Church carrying out Adam's Gothic designs. The family firm of Joseph Rose and Co. were the plasterers, and John Gilbert provided the brass furniture, such as doorknobs and lock plates. Lord Coventry also fully patronised the cabinet-makers of the time: 128 bills survive for the period 1757 to 1800. All the leading names are represented: Cobb, Vile, Ince and Mayhew, statues and tables from the two Thomas Carters and, from John Cheere, furniture from France provided by Poirier and in England by Peter Langlois; Chippendale and Rannie provided boxes, fire-screens and a shaving table. Ince and Mayhew put up the Gobelins tapestries when they reached Croome in 1772. The whole house and its contents reflected the best that Adam could create, and Lord Coventry could afford.

10. The history of the room and its tapestries is given by James Parker and Elizabeth Standen, November 1959, Metropolitan Museum of New York *Bulletin* and 1965, *Decorative Art from the S. H. Kress Collection at the Metropolitan Museum of Art*. Dr Eileen Harris dealt with Lord Coventry's visit to the Gobelins factory, *Apollo*, April 1962, and in her book *The Furniture of Robert Adam*, 1963, pp. 10–12. Microfilm copies of the bills are at the Victoria and Albert Museum (Department of Furniture and Woodwork) and the Metropolitan Museum, New York.

KEDLESTON

Similar details to those for Croome can be established for several Adam houses. Kedleston in Derbyshire has been researched carefully in recent years, and only a brief summary of it is necessary here. In 1768 Horace Walpole paid a visit to the house: 'The front is heavy,' he wrote, 'there being no windows, but niches behind the columns.' This north front (1761) was the work of James Paine, who had taken over from Matthew Brettingham, and is illustrated in his *Plans and Elevations of Noblemen's Houses* (1783). They were supplanted, however, by Robert Adam, with Samuel Wyatt, a competent architect in his own right, acting as clerk of works; he supervised taking down the old house and, in an account book (3R) at Kedleston, the 'state of Samuel Wyatt's Account ... ending 1st December 1764' was entered at £4701. 16s., and allowed by Robert Adam. The craftsmen[11] included the usual blend of leading London artificers—Joseph Rose, William Kinman, William Cobbett and William Chapman—and many local men, such as the sculptor and carver James Gravenor.

Advice had been given to Lord Scarsdale on the interior decorations by James 'Athenian' Stuart, but this was rejected on receipt of Adam's plans; they included those for the great Saloon or Rotunda (*see* pl. 23). The niches contained originally sculptured figures on handsome pedestals, but these were supplanted by heating stoves, disguised as classical vases and set atop equally grand pedestals. Most of the furniture was provided by the London firm of cabinet-makers William and John Linnell, although local workmen also took their share at repairing and altering London pieces; James Gravenor, for example, designed and carved gilt pier glasses and a pair of eagle support console tables, as well as working on the magnificent palm-tree bed, mirrors and candlestands made *en suite* and completed in 1768. He also carved the ornaments on the organ case and one assumes, in view of Lord Scarsdale's statement in his notebook about his 'Country House of Pleasure' of 'rooms of fair extent enriched with decent ornament, choice friends, rare books [and] sweet musick's strain . . .', that it was much used. Kedleston and its park took some 30 years to create, with many a precarious and expensive step in achieving what the family motto states, 'Let Curzon Holde What Curzon Helde'.

SYON HOUSE

It has been said[12] that 'the gallery at Syon may, I think, possibly be the place where the Adam style was actually initiated. This room presented to its designer a rather special challenge and elicited a correspondingly original response.' King James I had granted the old nunnery at Syon to the 9th Earl of Northumberland and a Jacobean mansion was erected round the quadrangle.

11. Helena Hayward and John Hardy, 2 and 9 February 1978, 'Kedleston Hall, Derbyshire', *C Life*, CLVIII, give a useful summary of the building cycle. The craftsmen were: *masons* Joseph Hall, John Chambers, James Denston (new Bridge, 1770), £6596. 1s.; *bricklayers* £2685. 12s.; *carpenters/joiners* William Johnston, assisted by Richard Clark, Charles Sowter, Thomas Dedson, £5104. 8s.; *glaziers* Joseph Taylor, William Cobbett, £477. 10s.; *slaters* Pratt and Co., £344. 8s.; *plumber* Joseph Taylor £27. 15s. 6d.; *leadwork* William Chapman, £1079. 9s.; *painter* Thomas Smith, £113. 17s.; *ironmonger* and *smiths* £478. 12s.; *coppersmith* William Kinman, £307; *carvers* George Moneypenny and Joshua Hall,

£2501. 3s.; *plasterers* (plain) Abraham Denston £412. 15s. 9d., (decorative) Joseph Rose £1107. 16s. 8d.; *chimneypieces* to four rooms, J M Spang, £990. Some stone came from the Horsley Castle Quarry (John Whilton) 5 miles away. The furnishing of the house is discussed by John Hardy, July 1978, 'Robert Adam and the furnishing of Kedleston Hall', *The Connoisseur*, CXCVIII, pp. 196–207, and by Helena Hayward and Pat Kirkham, 1980, *The Linnell Family: 18th Century London Cabinet Makers*.

12. Sir John Summerson, 27 August 1953, 'The Adam Style', *The Listener*, L, p. 335.

The whole length of the east front was devoted to a corridor-like Long Gallery, and it is this room (*see* col. pl. 14) which provided a special challenge in bringing it to a classical pattern. In ceiling and carpet a certain amount was done to give breadth, but it was in the treatment of the walls that the architect's ingenuity held full sway. A series of thin pilasters of the Corinthian order divided the walls into bays; the whole was finished, as Adam said, 'in a style to afford great variety and amusement', with plenty of delicate arabesque ornamentation.

At Alnwick Castle and at Syon, among a rich collection of documents, are a few[13] which enable us to learn a little more of the decoration of Syon at this time. Mr Butler's two volumes of 'Receipts and Disbursements' for 1760–77, together with the Duke of Northumberland's bank account, 1757–67, at Hoare's, show that Michele Angelo Pergolesi was paid in all £160. 14*s*. between 1765 and 1768 for ornamenting the 62 pilasters in the Long Gallery, of which £20 was 'a present from His Grace'.[14] Pergolesi was also paid £24. 5*s*. for 'his Designs for the Carpet & Tapestry at Syon House'; this was presumably the design sent to Thomas Moore for the Long Gallery carpet. Zucchi did a similar drawing to send to Moore for the carpet for 20 St James's Square. The agent, Mr Butler, visited 'Mr Moors to see his Tapestry' on 13 September 1765, two months before the payment to Pergolesi. The carpet is signed 'by thomas moore 1769' and measures 34 ft 8 in by 14 ft 2 in. The Drawing Room doors at Syon (*see* pl. 57) have always excited admiration for their metal ornamentation. Payments indicate the authors, one of whom, Diederich Nicolaus Anderson, was a bronze-founder also employed by Sir William Chambers.

1766. Jan. 7.	Paid Mr Brimingham on Acc^ot of the Gilt ornaments for the Drawing Room Doors at Syon.	£2. 2. 0.
1767. Jan. 7.	Paid Mr Bermingham on Account for the Gilt Metal Ornaments for the Drawing Room Window Shutters at Syon House.	£30. 0. 0.
1767. Jan. 24.	Paid Mr Anderson on Accot of his Bill for Brass Edgings gilt to the Mosaic Tables & Medals for the Drawing Room Doors at Syon.	£10. 0. 0.

In the Dictionary entry for Bermingham (Part III), I advance the view that 'Bermingham' may be identified with Nathaniel Bermingham, a herald painter who had invented 'a curious art of cutting out . . . in vellum with the point of a pen-knife . . .'. The metal enrichment on the Red Drawing Room door could well have been designed by such a skilled practitioner of a delicate art.

The archives at Syon have yielded a detailed account[15] for chimneypieces, provided by Benjamin and Thomas Carter from 1761 onwards. Included in their bill is an item (22 June 1766), 'To Modelling two Models in Wax for Doorcase, £6. 6*s*. 0*d*.'. These can still be seen, along with the door enrichments, on the door jambs of the Red Drawing Room door (*see* pl. 57)

13. Alnwick Castle Archives, 94, UI. 41/44/46.
14. This is at variance with the first duchess's Syon House

Book '62 Pilasters by Pergolesi at 3.3*s*.0*d*. each'.
15. Syon Archives, D/1/8.

which allows access through to the Long Gallery. In addition, Carter also drew out 'many Moddels' for Thomas Smith, a house painter (who later worked at Kedleston), 'in order to have the same cast in papier mâché, and Modeling in Wax'. These ornaments were used on the ceiling and doorcase of the Dining Room, and were charged at £49. 8s. 0d., including the expenses of visiting the house, making moulds 'and altering the same according to your Lordship's pleasure'.

The superb decorations in the Adam style at Syon[16] are among the richest in any Adam house—a considerable interest was taken during the alterations by the architect's patron, the 1st Duke of Northumberland. There is a draft of a letter dated 4 November [1764] from the duke to Robert Adam; he wanted the Gallery to be proceeded with, and for Joseph Rose to do the plastering before the frosts so that it would be dry:

> Fit to be gilt early in the Spring by which Time I hope the Paintings will be ready
> to be fixed up. I must desire you will order those Carved Mouldings which have
> been so ill executed by Mr [John] Adair to be returned him & amended in such a
> manner as you shall approve of for I would not, upon any account, suffer any work
> to be fixed up at Sion that is not compleatly finished to your satisfaction.[17]

A further letter from the duke (7 June 1765) was addressed to Sir William Hamilton, the British envoy in Naples;[18] he was asked to 'purchase any Statues, Vases, Tripods or other Pieces of Vertu' fit to stand in the Long Gallery niches. The circular niches (*see* col. pl. 14) were fit 'for placing any flat Vases or Sepulchral Urns'. The duke also wanted coloured drawings of any paintings, mosaic pavements or stucco ornaments found at Cumae, or elsewhere near to Naples. This spirit of enquiry and willingness to spare time and money to the acquisition of classical fragments—either for their own sake or to be reinterpreted—depicts the owner of Syon as being typical of Adam's leading patrons.

One of the most notable features in the Adam Ante-Room at Syon was the use of 12 disengaged columns in verd-antique said to have come from the bed of the River Tiber. James Adam, in a letter to the duke dated 22 April 1765:

> Has the pleasure to inform his Lod^s that by last Mail he receiv'd from Rome the
> Bills of Lading for the Columns & Pilasters &c. The ship sail'd from Civita Vecchia
> the 27th of last month with a fair wind & in a few hours was out of sight. Mr Adam
> has insur'd his own things & those of Lord Shelburne, but has not insur'd My Lord
> Northumberland's as his Lop^s seemed rather against it.

His Lordship's agent, Mr Thomas Butler, on 3 July 1765 paid £56. 8s. in 'fees & dutys at Custom House on Landing the Colums & Pilasters for Syon House', and on 9 September Mr Hillier was paid £12. 6s. 6d. for 'Lighterage & carrying columns &c to Syon & 2 Statues from Milbank'. We do not know the cost of the columns, but in 1762 on 2 August Mr Butler, on behalf of his master, 'Paid Mr Adams for a Bill of Exchange drawn on My Lord by his brother at Rome which he had paid £125.0.0.'; this may have some connection with these famous

16. Beard, 1978, *Adam*, col. pls. 9–15.
17. Alnwick Castle Archives, UI. 46.   18. Syon Archives, 9/1/4.

columns. Adam added gilt Ionic capitals and bases in white and gold, and on 15 November 1763 a porter was paid 1s. for 'carrying the capital of a column sent from Syon to Mr Adam's'. A further search in the Alnwick and Syon archives has yielded no further details about the life-size plaster figures, fully gilded, in the Ante-Room other than the fact that Joseph Rose was assisted by the gilder Thomas Davis. They are the only example of Rose's involvement with casting large figures, a speciality which had been hitherto monopolised by the sculptor William Collins.

KENWOOD

In 1764, William Murray, 1st Earl of Mansfield, commissioned Robert Adam to remodel his Hampstead house of Kenwood. As a fellow Scot, the choice was natural, and Lord Mansfield remained a staunch supporter of the architect and his brothers, particularly in the Liardet patent stucco case, heard before him. Adam added a storey to the main block of the house and, observing symmetry, added a library on the east side to balance the Orangery.

The Library, one of Adam's most important interiors, was also intended by him to act as a room for receiving company. It was given circular recesses for the books, and the body of the room was 'made suitable for the latter'. With gilded plaster decorations by Joseph Rose junior, paintings by Antonio Zucchi and furniture from William France and Thomas Chippendale,[19] Lord Mansfield had every reason to be satisfied with the outcome.

Apart from the mentions of the house in Adam's *Works in Architecture* (1774, Vol I, No 2), two groups of documents and Lord Mansfield's bank account (Hoare's) survive to document the commission.[20] As yet Adam's own accounts have not appeared, but the builder was John Phillips and timber was supplied in 1768–69 by William Adam & Co. For the interior Adam employed the carver John Minshull, the smith William Yates, the mason and statuary John Devall and another carver, Saffron Nelson. Wallpaper was supplied presumably by Thomas Bromwich, but only an early bill of his (1757) survives.

In the Library Minshull enriched the window shutters, the soffits of the windows, the doors, bookcases, pilasters and the frame of David Martin's portrait of Lord Mansfield above the chimneypiece. For his work in the Library, Great Staircase and various other rooms he received £249 on 9 August 1769, and his bill was, as usual, 'Examined by Robt Adam'. The smith William Yates provided 'Iron Work on the Best Stairs Maid According to The Honney Suckel Pattarn Containing Fifty Eight Feet Nine Inches Running a Long. The Top Rail, Making of pattarns for Works. . .at 36 Shillings p. Foot – £105.15s.0d.' Yates also worked the ironwork for the Back Stairs (£18. 6s. 0d.), and received in all £124. 1s. 0d. in February 1770. Finally in 1771, in a bill not oversigned by Adam, statues were provided by Hoskings and Oliver.

During the late eighteenth century, two flanking wings to Adam's south front were built by

19. Christopher, Gilbert, 1978, *The Life and Work of Thomas Chippendale*, I, pp. 256–57.

20. I am indebted to the Earl of Mansfield for allowing me to quote from the Scone Palace Archives (Bundles 1400 and 2365), and to Mrs Joan Auld, Dundee University Archivist, for her particular help. *Bundle 1400* contains bills from Thomas Chippendale, William France, Antonio Zucchi, John Arpin, John Tean and Thomas Bromwich. *Bundle 2365* contains further bills from Chippendale (plate glass, 1769), Zucchi (furniture,

1769), William France (furniture for Library, 1770–71), and various bills for furniture, hangings, cornices, glass, etc. (1769–70) from France and William Twaddell. The bills from John Minshull (carver), William Yates (smith) and Hoskings and Oliver (statues) are quoted in my account of Kenwood. The bank account (Hoare's) is the evidence for payments to Devall, Nelson and to unidentified craftsmen John York and George Burns.

George Sanders, and the mirrored recesses were converted into bookshelves. Bills of 1779 survive for carpenter's work by John(?) Jean, and for painting balustrades by John Arpin; each bill was allowed by Robert and James Adam.

20 ST JAMES'S SQUARE, LONDON

At 20 St James's Square,[21] Rose, whose bill amounted to £2684, collaborated with the mural painter Antonio Zucchi. The Great Drawing Room (*see* pl. 103), the Music Room, Sir Watkin Williams Wynn's Dressing Room, the Drawing Room—all were decorated by Zucchi. He also provided the drawings of a 'Bas relief representing Aurora going before the Sun and the different Hours to be executed in marble in first drawing room', as well as the 'two figures for the jambs of the said chimney', £8 in all. Zucchi's complete bill amounted to £614. 14s., but he promised to 'retouch the 2 bookcases & finish them to the satisfaction of Mr Adam'. Eight chimneypieces were provided by John Hinchcliff for £360. 10s., and Thomas Moore (who provided the carpets at Syon and Osterley) charged £232. 10s. 6d. for a 'Persia carpet' to match the ceiling; Zucchi provided a small pattern of the ceiling for Moore to work from. 'For Two Bookcases Extraordinary to a design of Messrs Robt. and James Adam', Richard Collins charged £15. 18s. 7¼d.—there are many payments to Collins in Adam's bank account. They were of 'rich mahogany' with '12 Ovall Patterae let into the Legs' and '130 Small [Patterae] let into the Pannels of the Doors'. Hopkins and Co provided the steel fenders, grates and various items in copper (£70. 19s. 6d.), and Robert Jones, the 'Hinges Tacks & Pins and various fittings for Lady Williams Wynn's Bird Cage' (13s.). Thomas Tilston, Thomas Blockley of Birmingham and Mr Thomas Gascoigne supplied the intricate locks and door furniture (£500), and Tilston did all the 'smith's work'; his complete bill was for £1261.

The Grand Staircase at the St James's house was Tilston's work, again working in company with William Kinman. They provided the '3 Balconies, the Copper Railing of the Best Stair Case & sundry other work in the brass & cast iron way'. 'Sir William's New House', as it was frequently called in the accounts, was erected by the mason and sculptor John Devall, the younger (1728–94); his bill amounted to £4064. 14s. 10d., and he was paid in instalments over six years, 1771–77. And so one could go on, but accounts are not the easiest of reading. The payments to Robert and James Adam bring us to a conclusion. They charged £1388. 15s. for 'Surveying, Plans, Measuring &c' and, as late as 25 July 1783, Robert Adam was writing to advise certain repairs in the laundry and kitchen areas. Here, if anywhere, 'something like truth' of the quality of his work was bound to be spoken.

Neoclassical Painted Interiors

No Adam interior after the early years was complete without painted decoration, and it is convenient to discuss here the more important artists.[22] They did on occasion work for architects such as Chambers and Wyatt, but to the casual mind their achievements are related solely to those of Robert Adam and the development of his neoclassical style. In addition to the

21. NLW, Wynnstay Archives; 1960, *Survey of London*, XXIX–XXX.

22. Full biographical details and a catalogue of their works are given in Croft-Murray, 1970, *Decorative Painting in England, 1537–1837*, II.

foreigners, there were many native decorators—the architect James 'Athenian' Stuart (1713–88), for instance, who had a vast knowledge of ancient art and antiquities, and decorated some of the interiors he designed, such as the Painted Room at Spencer House, St James's.

It is, however, with such painters as Angelica Kauffmann, her second husband Antonio Zucchi, Giovanni Battista Cipriani, Michele Angelo Pergolesi and Biagio Rebecca that we must concern ourselves. Many decorations have been attributed to Angelica Kauffmann, probably because documented ceiling paintings by her are very rare.[23] Born in Switzerland, she trained in Italy and came to England in the early years of Adam's important building activities. As a foundation member of the Royal Academy—there are authenticated ceiling paintings by her at Burlington House, for which she received £100—Angelica showed regularly at the annual exhibitions; her engravings were also used as the basis of decorative work on furniture, and for Matthew Boulton's decorative paintings 'process'. She finally left England for Italy in 1781, the year in which she married for the second time.

Antonio Zucchi (1726–95), Angelica's second husband, was probably employed by Robert Adam in 1757 to engrave plates for the *Spalatro* book,[24] and at the architect's invitation he later came to England. He appears many times as a payee in Robert Adam's bank account, on one occasion in 1770 for £1000.

In England Zucchi centred himself in London and was much visited by prospective patrons. Therese Parker, *née* Robinson, wrote to her brother Frederick in London on 17 September 1769,[25] asking that he call about the pictures ordered from Zucchi by her husband, John Parker, for the Library of their Devon house at Saltram; they are still to be seen there and form one of the chief attractions of this interesting house. Occasionally Zucchi's detailed bills survive, as for 20 St James's Square, or the one, in broken French, headed '*Mémoire de Mr Zucchi pour des Tableaux peints pour Son Excellence My Lord Mansfield*' for Kenwood; they show that, as with most artisans, he was subjected to supervision by Robert Adam, and is perhaps the painter most closely identified with the architect's work.

Giovanni Battista Cipriani came to England with the architect Sir William Chambers, and within a year or two had the honour to decorate King George III's State Coach,[26] designed by his new-found architect friend. Adam gave him the important commission of decorating in the Drawing Room at Syon. In the draft of the letter of 4 November 1764 from the Duke of Northumberland to Robert Adam, the duke mentioned a price disagreement:

> I am sorry there appeared any mistake between us about the price fixed for the Paintings which I am persuaded will be very easy set right but it proceeded in a great degree from what Cipriani himself told me when I showed him the two Paintings, one with a Single, the other with Double Figures which were done as Specimens and which I am certain he then offered to paint for the whole room at Two Guineas each picture & to finish them in the best manner.

23. *Angelica Kauffmann*, Exhibition of Paintings, The Iveagh Bequest, Kenwood, 1955. The catalogue cites the relevant literature about her life and work.
24. John Fleming, February 1958, 'The Journey to Spalatro', *Arch Rev*, CXXIII, pp. 103–7.
25. Leeds Archives Dept, Studley Royal Archives, Robinson letters, 14476.
26. Edward Croft-Murray, 1953, 'Three Famous State Coaches', *C Life*, Coronation number, CXIII, pp. 80–87; Harris, 1970, *Chambers*, pp. 80–82.

The roundels in the Drawing Room have been repeatedly ascribed to Kauffmann rather than Cipriani, yet further support of the latter's authorship is again provided by Mr Butler's Receipt and Disbursement Books (at Alnwick):

1765. July 5.	Paid for Post Chaises for Mr Cipriani & myself going to Eaton to examine the Antique Paintings there.	58s.
1766. Feb. 24.	Coach hire to Syon with Mr Cipriani, whole day.	16s. 10d.
Feb. 27.	Paid for a Post Chaise to Syon with Mr Cipriani when he went to alter the Ground of his picture.	18s. 6d.

In Sir William Chambers's letter book,[27] there are letters of 1773 to Lord Melbourne telling him that 'Cipriani has finished all the paintings for the Great Room' at Melbourne House.[28] The letter book gives an interesting idea of the care needed to prepare a room for the reception of such paintings. In 1770 Chambers was retained by the Duke of Bedford to fit up the Library and Dining Room at Woburn;[29] Cipriani with Biagio Rebecca provided the paintings, and three extracts from Chambers's letters speak for themselves of the progress made:

19 May, 1770 . . . I believe one of the painters that is about the Library Ceiling will go downe next week to make his remarks upon the light & to verify some measures & as he cannot speak a word of English I should be obliged to you if you would desire anyone in the family that understands Italian to ask for any thing he may want of the workmen. . . .

1 June, 1770 . . . as I shal want to fix up some paper Patterns in the Library Ceiling at Wooburn Abbey be pleased to have 2 or 3 Plaisterers trusses in the room to form a Moving Scaffold high enough to reach to the top of the Cove.

22 November, 1770 . . . the painters have nearly finished the Ceiling for the Library at Wooburn Abbey & will be down soon to put it up. I hope therefore that all your things in the room are nearly done, as when they come the room must be cleared for them & they must have moving Trussels to stand upon.

By 1771 Cipriani had finished his part of the Library ceiling and Chambers wrote to ask for the remainder of the money due to the artist 'which is £217.10 his Agreement being 350 Guineas or £367. 10 Mr Biagios part not being yet finished he is not entitled to the Remainder of his Mony.' Biagio Rebecca was to be paid £220. 1s. 'for Painting the Ornaments' and £10 travelling expenses. Rebecca's chief skill lay in the imitation of antique bas-reliefs, and his monochrome *trompe l'oeil* style was much in evidence in late Georgian interiors. He worked for Adam, Sir William Chambers and James Wyatt in particular, and his best-known work is for the latter at Heveningham. At Audley End Rebecca, using Vertue engravings, created an

27. BL Add MS 41133.
28. Harris, 1970, *Chambers*, p. 226.
29. *ibid.*, p. 253.

interesting series of portraits after the sixteenth-century picture *The Visit of Queen Elizabeth to Blackfriars*, attributed to Marcus Gheeraerts the younger and now at Sherborne Castle.[30]

Michele Angelo Pergolesi is known only for his work at Syon. It is probable that he was sent to London by James Adam when on his Italian tour. Between 1777 and 1785, he issued several books on ornament and design.

Theodore de Bruyn, a Swiss artist, had a good practice. The Duchess of Queensberry wrote to Sir William Chambers on 23 November 1772 to advise him:[31]

> That she can now acquaint him of the name and abode of that Artice sent from abroad by the Dutchesse of Norfolke, his name is de Bruyn, his dwelling place little Castle street, Cavendish Square, being near Sr William he will easily & soon judge by what he will shew and explain having done for Lord Radnor from designs of Montfaucon.

She wondered 'whether or not such will answer well for the Chinese house'; this was a temple which Chambers designed for her at Amesbury, Wiltshire, in that year. His principal work in this country was in the Dining Room at Farnley Hall, Yorkshire.[32] He painted some 18 pictures, charging in all £59. 9s. 8d. The medallions in the Dining Room, painted in sepia on canvas, are sculptural in effect and, surrounded by Joseph Rose junior's plasterwork, stand out boldly from the background. One of the overdoor panels is signed and dated 1789.

It was inevitable that this demand for ceiling paintings should make Matthew Boulton of Birmingham turn his attention to cheaper but good quality versions. Although his part in eighteenth-century industrial development is well known, less attention has been paid to his many artistic achievements. Something is known about the manufacture of silver and Sheffield plate which went on at Boulton's factory at Soho near Birmingham, and his work in ormolu has been described carefully, but little has been written about the buttons, cut-steel trinkets and watch-chains, and there is no really satisfactory account of all his activities. His work on coinage, for example, is an important field for research which still remains largely unexplored. Nevertheless, some valuable work has been published, especially where the significance of one group of surviving manuscripts[33] has been recognised. These record in considerable detail Boulton's work on 'mechanical paintings'.

The method used was a form of aquatint in which the engraver employed a brush and a mixture of resin and nitric acid upon a copper plate. The colour was applied in the inking-in stage and frequently only one plate seems to have been used to receive all the colours. The canvas which took the impression was covered with gum to receive the print more easily. Finally, the impression, now transferred to the canvas, was touched up by hand and varnished to give the appearance of an oil painting. The touching-up process was highly skilled, and the painter employed most frequently by Boulton was Joseph Barney of Wolverhampton, who had connections with Angelica Kauffmann; he is described by Boulton and Fothergill as 'superior to

30. R J B Walker, 'Biagio Rebecca at Audley End', *The Connoisseur*, April 1957, CXXXIX, p. 164.
31. BL Add MS 41133.
32. Illustrated in *C Life*, 3 June 1954, p. 1809.
33. Birmingham Assay Office MSS. *See Apollo*, January, March 1950, September 1951; *C Life Annual*, 1950;

Annals of Science, IX, December 1953; *Econ. Hist. Rev.*, XVI, No. 1 (1963); Robert Rowe, 1965, *Adam Silver*, and Nicholas Goodison, 1974, *Ormolu: The Work of Matthew Boulton* include studies of the Assay Office MSS.

any of his brother Artists in or about Birmingham'. He worked on the mechanical paintings for the ceilings of Montagu House. Other painters were Richard Wilson of Birmingham and a Mr Simmons, also of Birmingham. On some occasions the impression was taken up to London so that it could be corrected from the original; on others, the picture was brought up to the Midlands, and Boulton wrote to many owners of important paintings for permission to copy them. A very high standard of craftsmanship was demanded throughout all stages.

Elizabeth Montagu, a distant cousin by marriage to Matthew Boulton, was the first to use mechanical paintings on a large scale. John Wyatt was asked to call upon Mrs Montagu in 1776. From 10 June in that year to 5 November, several letters between Matthew Boulton and John Wyatt in London concerned themselves with the pictures for Mrs Montagu's dressing-room; these were to be inserted at Montagu (afterwards Portman) House in Portman Square, designed by James Stuart and erected from 1775 to 1782. It was regrettably destroyed by bombing in 1940. The paintings were designed by Biagio Rebecca and Cipriani.

It was in November 1778 that Boulton made a real effort to enlist the architect James Wyatt's attentions in the promotion of mechanical paintings. It was obvious that architects would be the best persons to introduce commissions of this kind to Soho. Boulton therefore wrote to John Wyatt on 23 November asking him to make the following enquiries from his cousin James:

> 1st. Would Mr James Wyatt like to introduce Soho paintings supposing it to be done well and upon such terms as he would be satisfyd with if so—2nd will Mr Jam^s Wyatt favour Soho with two or three of the figures he was so kind to offer Eginton when hear [*sic*]. 3rd—Can he oblige Soho with the sight of any other specimens of such kind of Painting which he thinks most likely to be useful. 4th Can he send a Design either in Painting, Drawing or writing for either Compartments in Cielings, Pannels or Ornaments for Soho to execute and thereby give an Idea of their work and price. 5th He should be inform'd that although such subjects that will bear repetition are the most proper for our purpose yet if he wants any Single subject Painted it can be done at Soho as cheap or cheaper than he can have it done in London of the same Quality.

It may have been the mechanical painting which led Mrs Montagu to renew her acquaintance with James Wyatt, whose genius, she wrote, 'is so universal that he cd. design the most beautiful temple or Superb palace or prettiest cottage'. She had long been tiring of James Stuart's delays, and she considered him 'idle and inattentive'. As for Stuart's assistant, Gandon, she declared, 'I believe Mr Stuart made choice of him as men do of their Wives for their passive qualities rather than Serviceable talents.' Gradually she turned more and more to Wyatt for the completion of her great designs, though, in view of Wyatt's later characteristics, the change was perhaps ill-advised.

James Stuart and James Wyatt were not the only architects to be approached by Boulton on the subject of mechanical paintings. In 1777 Boulton and Fothergill sent samples to Robert Mylne, who was then architect for Lord Arundell.

Despite the display at Montagu House of ceiling paintings and door panels, and the attention which they undoubtedly attracted, the mechanical painting business was not a financial success. Boulton, busy with steam engines, was ready by 1781 to try to bring the trade to an end. Some paintings were commissioned for export by Messrs Clark and Green in this year, but, by the time Isaac Hawkins Browne, MP, inquired about such paintings for his Shropshire house, Badger Hall, which James Wyatt was building for him, it was too expensive to revive the process. Browne was referred to Joseph Barney, but for Boulton a remarkable enterprise was ended.[34]

There were rivals and claimants to Adam's position but, while he worked with many whom he replaced in the patrons' esteem, few spoke ill of him. John Carr and Capability Brown wrote favourably of him, and James Paine, James Stuart and Robert Mylne remained on friendly terms. Sir William Chambers, James Wyatt and Horace Walpole were less tolerant of the brothers—the 'brace of self-puffing Scotch coxcombs', as the Reverend William Mason called them.

Sir William Chambers

It is not difficult to establish which craftsmen Chambers used to support and extend his business.[35] An early liaison, titled 'William Chambers and Thomas Collins', to the extent of a joint bank account at Drummonds (continued in later years in Chambers's name only), is a useful starting-point. It explains Chambers's long association, until the Somerset House days, with this plasterer;[36] they also worked together in the 1760s at Milton House, Northamptonshire, for Lord Fitzwilliam. Chambers was an 'official' architect in the sense that he became in 1761 (as did Robert Adam) one of the two 'Architects of the Works' to King George III, to whom, when Prince of Wales, he had been architectural tutor.

Sir William's four letter books give some of his views on interior decoration. The Duchess of Queensberry, writing to him on 23 November 1772 about colours, said: 'Sir William knows that the assemblage & blending of couleurs are Great Principals of his own masterfull supream taste.' Chambers was decorating Lord Melbourne's house in Piccadilly using, as we have seen, the decorative painter Cipriani; Thomas Chippendale was providing furniture.[37] On 14 August 1773 Chambers wrote to Lord Melbourne: 'Chippendale called upon me yesterday with some Designs for furnishing the rooms wch upon the whole seem very well but I wish to be a little consulted about these as I am really a very pretty Conoisseur in furniture. . . .'

He wanted 'fewer sophas & more chairs' in the great room, thinking this better 'than as Chippendale has designed'. Lord Melbourne wrote on 13 October 1774 to indicate that he 'is averse to admitt any gilding whatever in the furniture, in my opinion the Elegance of that room is from the lightness of well disposed, well executed ornaments. . . .' Chambers replied that the 'Glasses and Soffas in the Niches should be gilt, for glasses without gilding are large black spots that kill the effect of everything about them, and the dead coloured silk with which the Soffas are to be covered must have gold to relieve it . . .'.

34. A list of subjects with dimensions appears in the Boulton and Fothergill out-going Letter Book, 23 December 1780 (pp. 667–68), and in the 22 June portion of the 1782 *Inventory of the Contents of Soho* (Assay Office, Birmingham) I am indebted to Mr Eric Robinson for much information on this subject.

35. The architect's career and works are fully discussed by Harris, 1970, *Chambers*.

36. The active partnership seems to have concluded in 1773. Chambers to Henry Errington (BL Add MS 41133, 12 May 1773).

37. Christopher Gilbert, 1978, *Thomas Chippendale: His Life and Work*, 1, pp. 260–64.

In May 1770 he told Gilbert Mason, 'merchant at Leith', that 'with regard to the painting Your Parlours, if they are for Common use Stone Colour will last best & is cheapest but if you mean them to be very neat pea green and white, Buff Colour & white, or pearl or what is called Paris Gray and White is the Handsomest'. Good advice still. This period gave attention to minute detail—'Would your Lordship have brass rising hinges to the doors', 'I think from his small Drawings that some parts may be improved a little', and so on.

During the early years of the 1770s, Chambers reconstructed Milton Abbas, Dorset, for Joseph Damer, Lord Milton. In October 1771: 'The painting is going on as fast as possible. Ansell has not yet been able to make out his Estimate for the Gilding . . . I find it is to be like some Gilding done by Norman at the Queens House. I hope it will not be so dear for the Cornice of one room there was charged at near £200.' Ansell also provided mirror frames and consoles at Blenheim to Chambers' design, and the reference to 'Norman' is to the cabinet-maker, Samuel Norman.

In the late 1760s Chambers moved into a dominant social position. He had grand town and country houses to live in, was Comptroller to the Office of Works and Treasurer of the new Royal Academy. In 1770 he was knighted by George III and his career moved forward grandly—to the great commission of Somerset House and, in 1783, to the position of Surveyor-General to the Office of Works. Adam, who had waited impatiently to issue his book on the ruins of Diocletian's Palace (1764) while James Stuart and Nicholas Revett issued the first volume of their *Antiquities of Athens* (1762), so anticipating him in being first with an important neoclassical statement, could only retaliate by issuing, with his brother James, the grand folio parts of their *Works in Architecture . . .* (1773–78).

Chambers, of course, claimed that he interpreted the classical style in more chaste form than Adam. He had referred to Adam's filigrane toy work and had presumably supported Walpole's invectives about the Scottish architect. By the time the *Works* were published, the adoption of the 'ancient style' was held paramount in interior decorations by followers and opponents of the brothers or of Robert Mylne. A principal rival was the architect James Wyatt, the sixth son of a Staffordshire builder and timber merchant.

James Wyatt

In 1762 James Wyatt travelled to Italy with Lord Northampton and his secretary, Richard Bagot, of the Staffordshire Bagots seated at Blithfield, for whom Wyatt's family worked. He is said to have stayed in Italy for four years. Bagot's brother, Sir William Bagot, was an amateur architect and employed James 'Athenian' Stuart (who was also working for Bagot's friend Thomas Anson at nearby Shugborough) and James's brother, Samuel.

Shortly after his return, London society was excited about the important building he designed—the Pantheon in Oxford Street, in which the interior plasterwork was by Joseph Rose. Walpole thought it 'the most beautiful edifice in England' and recorded in the 27 January 1772 issue of *The Gentleman's Magazine* that 'imagination cannot well surpass the elegance and magnificence of the apartments, the boldness of the paintings, or the disposition of the lights . . .

Besides the splendid ornaments which decorate the rotundo, or great room, there are a number of statues, in niches, below the dome.'[38]

Wyatt's career has been tangled with the large and complex family from which he sprang;[39] his relationship in a working capacity with his brother Samuel, for example, has been underestimated. The problems surrounding them both are complicated and we are not always ready to admit that, on many occasions, their work (*see* col. pl. 15) surpassed that in the 'Adam style'. In addition, as at Fonthill, James created an essentially picturesque, if structurally unsound, Gothic pile which William Beckford and the age clamoured for. The effects of overwhelming splendour for which he strove at Salisbury he achieved here. He was full of ideas but, in the execution of his schemes, he would often lose his first ardour—many of his clients grumbled at his dilatory and unbusinesslike ways—and he lacked the ability to conceive and appreciate mass, as Vanbrugh did so well at Blenheim. Perhaps a capable 'Hawksmoor' to Wyatt would have enabled firm realisation as it did on the earlier occasion with Vanbrugh's restless pencillings. His character was weak, his mind untidy and he chose, according to Lord Liverpool, 'to engage in a great deal more business than he was capable of'.

In his mausolea at Cobham and Brocklesby, Wyatt revealed his debt to Sir William Chambers, but we need to turn to one of his late classical houses, Dodington, Gloucestershire, built for Christopher Codrington, to appreciate the expenditure and effort involved in a Wyatt house. There are detailed accounts and over 700 drawings and plans, but only a small number are signed or dated. Wyatt received £4026. 17s., but this amount also included reimbursement for sundry outlays. Some £3000 a year was spent between 1797 and 1817. Bartoli and Alcott were used for the scagliola work,[40] and Edward Wyatt (1757–1833) did woodcarving. The arrangement of the staircase was designed to incorporate wrought ironwork from old Fonthill House, which was demolished in about 1808.

In the Drawing Room there is splendid joinery, and the original chimneypiece with Wedgwood medallions was supplied in 1810 by Richard Westmacott at a cost of £98. 15s. James Wyatt had little chance to dine in the splendid scagliola dining-room, with its black and gold marble chimneypiece, for on 14 September 1813, travelling from Dodington to London in his patron's coach, there was an accident in which the coach overturned. Codrington escaped unhurt (and indeed lived until 1843), but Wyatt received a blow on the head which killed him instantly.

John Carr

I have left to the end one of the most accomplished provincial architects, John Carr

38. 1964, *Survey of London*, XXXI.
39. Anthony Dale, 1956, *James Wyatt*, 2nd edn.; J Martin Robinson, 1979, *The Wyatts: An Architectural Dynasty*, and October 1979, 'The Country Houses of Samuel Wyatt', *Arch Rev*, CLXVI, pp. 219–24.
40. Sir William Chambers writing to William Key, 13 October 1773, said: 'Messrs Ritter Bartoli, Newport Street, near Newport Market, London, imitate almost any sort of marble. . . .' John Richter took out a patent (1770, No. 978) for 'my invention of "an Art or Method of inlaying Scagliola or Plaister in and upon Marble and Metals to imitate flowers, trees, fruits, birds . . . and all sorts of ornaments".' He was living at this time at Berwick-upon-Tweed.

(1723–1807).[41] In his early years he was following the Palladianism of Lord Burlington—he had been clerk of works at Kirby Hall, Yorkshire, designed by Burlington and Roger Morris—but soon saw that he must adopt, adapt, and in many cases exceed, in interior decoration at least, the new ideas of Adam. He did not look back to other styles, except for the odd essay in revived Gothic, and when he added a south wing to the Elizabethan Farnley Hall for the Fawkes family, it was not in imitation Elizabethan but in the best style of which he was capable. At Harewood, Carr, a distant relative of the Lascelles family, did most of the supervisory work and the State Rooms were decorated under Adam's care; it is evident that Carr did not often use the fashionable talent of the day. No work by Zucchi or Rebecca was done under his supervision, and at Cannon Hall, Barnsley, he used in 1766 the York plasterer James Henderson rather than the Rose family. It seems that Carr, as well as Henderson, did use the services of the Italian stuccoist Guiseppe Cortese, for Henderson acted as executor (together with the Wakefield upholsterer Edward Elwick) at Cortese's death in 1778. The two were obviously in some form of partnership.

One of Carr's most interesting houses is Everingham Park in the East Riding of Yorkshire, near Market Weighton. The documents[42] show that work was started in 1757 and finished about 1764. The brickwork was by Richard Swale, the carpenter's work by Richard Bainton and James Cade, and Bainton then joined William Taylor for the joinery work. The skilled carver was Daniel Shillito, who also worked at Harewood, Fairfax House in York and Tabley Hall in Cheshire. At Tabley, where Carr's model of the house and stables is preserved, the building accounts give Thomas Oliver as plasterer, and a carver, Matthew Bertram, assisted Shillito. The timber was bought in Liverpool and, as at Cannon Hall, most of the chimneypieces were obtained at York, probably from John Fisher, with some coming from William Atkinson, whose work we have noted at Holkham Hall, Norfolk.

Carr's early work had been improved on by his contact with Robert Adam, but he was often still hindered by the absence of good craftsmen to carry out his wishes and by his insistence, for instance, that York men, like the gilder Blakesley, could do the gilding for the drawing-room at Wentworth Woodhouse 'as well as any man in this county, and he certainly will do it as well as anybody out of London'. The supremacy of York and Bristol had declined during the years when the foreign painters were at work under Adam and in which the cabinet-makers of London were competent at doing everything from debugging the bed—as William Vile did for Lord Coventry—to carving the mirror frames and hanging the tapestries.

Carr, of course, retained at least the sense to try to make his patrons go on London buying expeditions. Walter Spencer Stanhope recorded in his diary[43] for 29 April 1768: 'Mr Carr went with me to Mr Tyler the Notary and paid him his bill, from there he went with me to Cobbs, Chippendales and several other of the most eminent Cabinet makers for the order of proper furniture for my Drawing Room.' Amusingly enough, some of the costs were probably too high

41. The early researches of Mr R B Wragg did much to establish Carr's activities (*York Georgian Society, Report*, 1955–56, pp. 55–65). Since that date the extensive researches of Dr Ivan Hall (University of Hull) have further charted the details of Carr's career. *See* Ivan Hall, 1972, 'John Carr: A New Approach',

York Georgian Society, 1973, *ibid.*; *The Works in Architecture of John Carr*; Exhibition Catalogue, Ferens Art Gallery, Hull, 1973.

42. East Riding, Yorks., CRO, Beverley.

43. Sheffield Reference Library, Spencer-Stanhope Archives.

and, on 18 May, 'Mr Carr called upon me, discoursed him about furniture of my drawing room. Said he would speak to Ellick & write to me.' Edward Elwick[44] lived at Wakefield, nine miles away, and the provincial man won part of the day, as the diary records for 21 May. Some furniture did, however, arrive from London on 9 November and 'Ellick's man' put it up and cleaned and measured it. Stanhope must have been satisfied and Carr often dined at Cannon Hall, attending to alterations on three more occasions, and as late as 1804.

By this time Adam had been dead 12 years and Chambers for 8, and George Dance (the Younger, 1741–1825), Holland and Soane were the successors. The latter, in his Royal Academy lectures, spoke kindly of 'Messrs Adam' to whom 'we are more particularly indebted for breaking the talismanic charm which the fashion of the day had imposed, and for the introduction from Ancient works of a light and fanciful style of Decoration . . .'. But within a few years Joseph Gwilt was comparing James Stuart with 'the opposite and vile taste of Robert Adam'. The new men for the moment were raised triumphant until the great nineteenth-century exhibitions of Adam-style furniture and a resurgence of books again focussed attention on the superb realisations of a man and a style. He had given craftsmen the chance for their finest achievements, and many strove beyond competence to near virtuosity.

During the years Adam, Chambers, Wyatt and Carr had been at their most active, the arts had been adapting slowly to the powerful workings of the Industrial Revolution. As Adam was working on many of his London town-houses, Thomas Farnolls Pritchard was designing the cast-iron bridge (1779) over the River Severn at Coalbrookdale. The way of life was industrial, and too complex for the settled world which had been created under the leadership of William Pitt. Retarded by a lack of adequate transport and banking facilities, the way was open for vast improvements in these directions. The number of country banks rose in number from less than 300 to over 700 between 1780 and 1815.[45] Cheap money and cheap credit enabled industrialists to take risks, and the craftsmen surrounding Matthew Boulton and Josiah Wedgwood profited from the waves of prosperity. In 1793, however, the outbreak of war with France applied a stay to many activities, building among them.

The violent events which soon came about in France destroyed complacency and encouraged some English landed proprietors to even extend the scope of their charitable aid; it was still possible, however, to find those who ignored the poverty at their lodge gates, and who emerged on peace with more land under cultivation, even if the new age was one of turbulence and great social change. It was, however, also one of release from classicism and of fervent enthusiasm for things medieval and Gothic. Sir Uvedale Price added to his *Essay on the Picturesque* (1794) one on *Architecture and Buildings* (1798), and his neighbour Richard Payne Knight joined in asserting that 'whatever its style, a house should bear the character of its own age and nation, not be slavishly imitated from either a pagan temple, medieval church, or feudal castle; and comfort should be given precedence . . .'.[46] But appreciation of architecture of all periods proceeded apace, even if concern for its exact condition was not always apparent.

44. Christopher Gilbert, 1976, 'Wright and Elwick of Wakefield, 1748–1824', *Furniture History*, XII, pp. 34–50.

45. L Pressnell, 1956, *Country Banking in the Industrial Revolution*, p. 49.

46. Richard Payne Knight, 1805, *Analytical Inquiry into the Principles of Taste*, p. 157.

In earlier years, when there were conflicts between the rococo and Gothic styles, an interest in the revival of medievalism was mooted, but was in conflict with much that was building. In particular, the ideas of John Nash and Humphry Repton (in partnership from 1797 to 1802) embraced all aspects of the Picturesque, and were set out in Italian villas, rural cottages and in several country houses. In addition, there were two architects who had the ear of George, Prince of Wales, as Regent or when he became king: these were Henry Holland (1745–1806) and Sir Jeffry Wyatville (1766–1840).

Henry Holland

Henry Holland started work in his father's building firm, became assistant to 'Capability' Brown in 1771 and married Brown's daughter Bridget in 1773.[47] The liaison with Brown introduced him to a wide and influential circle of patrons, who in turn brought him to the notice of George, Prince of Wales. Estranged from his father (George III), and with a complicated personal life which led him into severe debt, the prince nevertheless built lavishly in London and at Brighton. He commenced the process in 1783 on coming of age. At Carlton House, a new wing, hall, staircase, lodges and stables were costed by Holland at over £30 000. He intended much of it to be in a French style, characterised by a blend of work, to exacting standards, from French and English craftsmen.[48] The Frenchmen included Jean Dominique, who was related to the skilled *ébéniste* Peter Langlois, and some of Adam's former men, such as the plasterer Joseph Rose and mason John Deval. They produced decorations of which Horace Walpole could tell Lady Ossory in 1785: 'Madam: I forget to tell you how admirably all the carving, stucco and ornaments are executed.'

Walpole's remark was probably occasioned by witnessing the revival of marbling, graining and painting at Carlton House. As well as the Frenchmen working for Holland, some had been introduced into England by Sheringham of Great Marlborough Street.[49] They were also skilled at painting in metallic colours, and the younger Crace, whose family firm was to work at the Brighton Marine Pavilion, stated that his father remembered the introduction of such arts 'by French workmen at Carlton House'.[50] In Robert Pyne's invaluable description and illustrations of Carlton House, bronzed and silvered ornaments are depicted; the ornaments of the cornice and architrave in the Rotunda were silvered and set against a ground colour of lavender, and the *putti* supporting festoons of fruit and foliage were painted in imitation of bronze.[51] The Entrance Hall was marbled—walls of green, blended in with actual marble and porphyry. But these lavish decorations were to be eclipsed by the splendour of those created in the remodelling of Thomas Kemp's Brighton house into the prince's Marine Pavilion.

Even as the sale was in its final stages early in 1787, Holland was already at work. The Prince Regent's taste for Chinese-inspired decorations—the Chinese Drawing Room at Carlton House was also illustrated by Thomas Sheraton in his *Cabinet-Makers' and Upholsterers' Drawing*

47. Dorothy Stroud, 1966, *Henry Holland, His Life and Architecture*, p. 12.
48. Crook and Port, 1974, *King's Works*, VI, pp. 307–12; Stroud, *Holland*, pp. 61–85; *George IV and the Arts of France*, Exhibition Catalogue, The Queen's Gallery, Buckingham Palace, London, 1966, pp. 3–5.
49. Wyatt Papworth, 1879, *John B. Papworth*, p. 11.
50. *Papers read at the RIBA Session, 1857–8*, 1858, p. 12.
51. Robert Pyne, 1819, *Royal Residences*, III, p. 24.

Book (1791–94)—again came to the fore. The decoration was entrusted to the firm of John Crace & Sons, whose principal designer was John's son, Frederick. In 1817 his team was joined by Robert Jones, who designed most of the furniture for the Banqueting Room. The room itself was painted with its ceiling representing an Eastern sky. By the time Crace came to paint the Music Room, he had 34 assistants to help him and samples of the designs had to be placed in position for approval.[52]

As well as his royal patron, Holland was much employed by Francis, 5th Duke of Bedford, by George, 2nd Earl Spencer, and by the Whitbread family of brewers.

WOBURN ABBEY

Francis Russell succeeded to the Bedford estates in 1771 at the death of his father John, the 4th Duke of Bedford, who had spent some 25 years remodelling Woburn Abbey from 1747 to 1761.[53] The heir used Holland to extend and reface parts of the house, improve the entrances and build several groups of outbuildings, including the attractive Chinese Dairy. This work began in November 1787 with the delivery of great quantities of Roche Abbey stone, and the employment for carpentry, bricklaying and slating of Holland's cousin, Richard Holland.

Inside the house, Holland's main task was to create a new library, set out precisely with pairs of Corinthian columns as he was to do a year or so later (but with Ionic columns) at Althrop and Southill. The sculptor George Garrard worked in the adjoining 'Eating Room' setting sculptured reliefs over the doors, and the French cabinet-makers, painters and founders provided chairs, bookcases, cupboards and painted panels.

ALTHORP

When George, 2nd Earl Spencer, succeeded to his Northamptonshire estates at the death of his father, he soon turned to Holland to work on the family house. The brick kilns on Thomas Coke's Norfolk estate at Holkham had been used over many years to produce white 'mathematical tiles'—a thin veneer of moulded clay; they succeed admirably on dressing the Holkham stable buildings, and in the autumn of 1787 Holland told Lord Spencer that 'the white brick tyles are at Lynn in their way to Althorp . . .'. It is, however, as at Woburn, the triple library that is the greatest example of Holland's skill. That it was achieved at all says much for the architect's persistence, with a client reluctant to produce money to pay the craftsmen. Much of what Lord Spencer had went on adding books to his extensive library, and in supporting Fox and opposing Pitt.

The new rooms were papered by Robson Hale & Co, 'Paper Hanging Manufacturers to the Prince of Wales', and in 1790 T H Pernotin was paid £25 for '4 panels over doors and glass', and £126 for '6 Pilasters in My Lady's Room'. While the earl's librarian, Dibdin (author of the valuable treatise on the house, (1822) *Aedes Althorpianae*), was ever preoccupied finding more and more space for books, the countess judged that Holland had given them a house 'the image of comfort, so convenient, so cheerful, so neat, so roomy, yet so compact'. Holland had supervised many firms and individuals, had expended some £20 257 and earned himself but a 5

52. Clifford Musgrave, 1959, *Royal Pavilion*, p. 160.
53. Gladys Scott Thomson, 1949, *Family Background*,

pp. 9–82, based on archives now reassembled at the Bedford Estate Office, London.

per cent commission (£1012). While he had been willing to lend money at interest to his patron, the matter was finally solved by Lord Spencer selling his rotten borough of Okehampton for £20 000.[54]

SOUTHILL

Samuel Whitbread acquired Southill, Bedfordshire, in 1795 from the 4th Lord Torrington for £85 500. It was, however, left to his son, Samuel II, to improve the estate with Henry Holland's advice. Work was in progress from 1796 to 1803, but Holland's plans are dated 1800. The architect also acted as contractor, receiving £54 188. 16s. 10d. between these years, with over half the cost (£38 293. 14s. 11d.) expended in the years 1798–1800. Four groups of documents record the building progress at the house, and include drawings by Holland's office and a set of accounts, 1796–1813.[55] In addition the owner, who was MP for Bedford from 1790 until his death in 1815, knew the type of house he would get from Holland's work at Carlton House for the Prince Regent (1783) and for Earl Spencer at Althorp, Northamptonshire (1787–91).

The interior is characterised by light, delicate mouldings with decorations either gilded or painted, as at Althorp, by T H Pernotin, but in a more restrained style than would have been acceptable in Adam's lifetime (he died four years before Southill was commenced). The plaster overdoors in the Entrance Hall, rectangles with representations of various animals, are by George Garrard, who also painted an interesting picture of the house under construction.

Sir John Soane

One of Holland's most distinguished pupils was John Soane (1783–1837), the son of a Berkshire bricklayer. Trained in the Royal Academy Schools, some 10 years after their foundation, he submitted a splendid design for a triumphal bridge and won the Gold Medal (1776).[56] He worked firstly for George Dance, and then for Holland; through the intervention of Sir William Chambers, however, he received 'King George III's Travelling Scholarship' from the Academy in 1778, and set out to study for two years in Italy. At his return in 1780 he tried to build up a modest country-house building practice, but after a few years was diverted and supported materially when William Pitt appointed him, in 1788, as Architect to the Bank of England at the death of Sir Robert Taylor. He was soon in demand, however, as an architect well able to put together Gothic and Greek elements, and created at least 15 fine houses before 1800.[57] His office grew large and, over Soane's lifetime some 30 pupils worked in it, 12 hours a day, for an average of five years.[58] That Soane continued to work at such a pace says much for

54. I am indebted to the late Earl Spencer for showing me all the relevant Althorp archives; a part of Holland's correspondence with the 2nd Earl is given by H Avray Tipping, 1937, *English Homes, Period VI, Late Georgian, 1760–1820*, p. 306; Stroud, *Holland*, pp. 97–102, and *C Life*, 19 and 26 May 1960, are further useful accounts.

55. A E Richardson *et al.*, 1951, *Southill: A Regency House*; Hussey, 1958, *ECH: Late Georgian*, p. 33.

56. Dorothy Stroud, 1961, *The Architecture of Sir John Soane*, and April 1957, 'Soane's Designs for a Triumphal Bridge', *Arch Rev*, CXXI, pp. 261–62.

57. P De La R Du Prey, 1972, 'Soane and Hardwick in Rome: A Neo-classical partnership', *Architectural History*, 15, pp. 51–67.

58. J Mordaunt Crook, 1969, 'The pre-Victorian architect: professionalism and patronage', *Architectural History*, 12, p. 64.

his character: he had been left a fortune in 1788 by his wife's uncle, George Wyatt, and need have done little more thereafter but dream visions—of triumphal bridges and Piranesian spaces.

One interesting aspect of Soane's work was indicated by the architect in his lecture on construction. Delivered to Royal Academy students among a long series of lectures in the first 30 years of the nineteenth century, he set out much of acceptable technique, including his views on models:

> Many of the most serious disappointments, that attend those who build would be avoided if Models were previously made of the Edifices proposed to be raised . . . In my own practice I have seldom failed to have a Model of the Work proposed . . . I must add that wherever the Model has been dispensed with, I am afraid the building has suffered in consequence thereof, either in solidity or convenience, or perhaps in both.[59]

What the models did for Soane and his patrons was to enable discussion to take place about the spatial arrangements within the house—the best ways of lighting staircases and reception rooms, with a consequent avoidance of dark corridors and corners. To provide a clearly lit space over the staircase was a prerequisite in most houses. Soane and his craftsmen produced some elegant solutions—for example, at Chillington Hall, Staffordshire, where the oval dome (1788), carried on pendentives, soars upwards to a small oval clerestory. It was a prototype for the Stock Office in the Bank of England, designed four years later, a room which also incorporated fire-resistant vaulting made of hollow earthenware cones.

While Soane's work attracted criticism by its ingenious innovations and austere detail, the nature of it was intellectually ahead of all the competition. But his work went unheeded by the king, and he was almost at the end of his life before he was knighted in 1831. At Wimpole in Cambridgeshire he made additions to the library (*see* pl. 25) and added the dome saloon—it is one small example of his unerring instinct for the control of an internal space. If he had a deficiency, it was the inability to strike out grand external silhouettes. The consequences were, as G Wightwick put it: 'If any one shall ask "In what style is such, or such, of his buildings?", the answer would be "It is . . . Soanean".'[60]

In the late eighteenth century Soane, in common with a number of architects, used Coade stone[61] to achieve decorative effects, such as caryatid figures; it was used at his houses in Lincoln's Inn Fields and at Pitzhanger. He also turned back to an earlier device and, alone among the important architects of his time, issued his *Plans, Elevations and Sections of Buildings erected in the Counties of Norfolk, Suffolk . . .* (1788), dedicated to George III.[62] In it he stated that his main objects were to 'unite convenience and comfort in the interior distributions, and simplicity and uniformity in the exterior . . .'.

In 1793 one of Soane's most important private commissions was given to him by the banker

59. J Wilton-Ely, 1969, 'Soane and the Architectural Model', *Architectural History*, 11, p. 6.
60. J Mordaunt Crook, 1972, *The Greek Revival*, p. 115.
61. John E Ruch, 1968, 'Regency Coade: a study of the Coade record books, 1813–21', *Architectural History*, 11, p. 38; a full study of Coade stone is in progress by Miss Alison Kelly, who has contributed the Coade and Croggon entries to the Dictionary (Part III).
62. Sandra Blutman, 1968, 'Country House Design Books, 1780–1815', *Architectural History*, 11, p. 27.

William Praed. It involved rebuilding Tyringham, Buckinghamshire, and was a work of which Soane was especially proud. In his unpublished *Memoirs* he indicated that:

> This villa, with its numerous offices, greenhouses, hot-houses, and extensive stabling, the great bridge and the lodge . . . engaged a large portion of six of the most happy years of my life. The greater part of the mansion-house and offices was most effectively warmed with steam.[63]

In his 1815 lecture to the Royal Academy students, Soane advocated central heating for private houses by methods then available from Boulton and Watt, or through a high-pressure system by Perkins.

When Soane was near the end of his career in 1834, 350 subscribers contributed to the striking of a gold medal bearing the inscription 'A Tribute of Respect from the British Architects'. The presentation of it to Soane was made in the library of his Lincoln's Inn Fields house by Sir Jeffry Wyatville.[64]

Sir Jeffry Wyatville

A pedigree chart of the Wyatt family, full of precise lines and sub-lines, records the complexity of the family genealogy, said to comprise 25 architects, 11 surveyors, 8 builders, 5 sculptors, 3 painters and 2 engineers. It was 'to distinguish himself from the numerous branches of his family of the same profession', spiced with a desire to record the especial marks of royal favour, that brought about the 'Wyatville' and the knighthood which elevated it to notice.

Of almost 150 major commissions executed by Wyatville, most of them were started in the first 20 years of the nineteenth century. It is possible from their careful listing[65] to establish some of the craftsmen used frequently: the London plasterer of Italian descent, Francesco Bernasconi, worked at Ashridge, Badminton, Chatsworth and Longleat, as well as at Kensington Palace and Windsor Castle, Wyatville's most prestigious commissions; chimneypieces came from Richard Westmacott (*see* pl. 145) and Charles Rossi. A number of firms such as the London Marble and Stone Working Co., the Birmingham locksmiths Standley's, the London painters and gilders Hutchinson & Co., the joiners Armstrong and Siddon were representative of a group of larger contractors.

Greater comfort was now required in large houses. A steam engine was installed at Lilleshall Hall, Shropshire, to pump water to the top of the house, central heating was put into most large houses, and conservatories, orangeries and sculpture galleries were attached. Furniture came from the Lancaster firm of Gillow and from Morel and Seddon, who were to work extensively for King George IV, Wyatville's most important patron. While he often copied Elizabethan details, as at Longleat, Wyatville did not attempt to 'fake antiquity'. A younger architect who seemed to have the ability to satisfy those patrons with a passion for the medieval, as well as building up a more general practice, was Robert Smirke (1780–1867). He was knighted in 1832.

63. Dorothy Stroud, 10 September 1953, 'The Country Houses of Sir John Soane', *C Life*, CXIV, p. 784.

64. Derek Linstrum, 1972, *Sir Jeffry Wyatville: Architect to the King*, p. 1.

65. *ibid.*, pp. 228–58.

Sir Robert Smirke

Smirke emerged after the period of the French wars as an outstandingly successful architect. His control of craftsmen working on the great castles at Lowther in northernmost Cumberland and Eastnor in Herefordshire was exemplary; he intervened on their behalf to ask for money due to them, explained fluently his own charges, and generally conducted his business in a way that soon put him at the top of his profession. In the Memoir[66] which Edward Smirke read at Robert's funeral, we are told that on the Grand Tour the architect was:

> Everywhere forcibly impressed with the simplicity and dignity of the Great Works which 2000 years of decay and destruction had left behind, and the memory of those grand architectural features was ever after present in his mind, counteracting the more popular inclination to superficial decoration, in which I think he was always disposed to indulge but sparingly in the exterior of his buildings.

At Lowther, the Earl of Lonsdale inherited a site on which at least two previous houses had stood, and at which work had been in progress since 1802, three years before Smirke's involvement; he owed the commission to the united recommendation of Sir George Beaumont and the architect George Dance. The surviving archives[67] show that the architect visited the house under construction on 13 occasions between December 1805 and November 1813. On 21 May 1814 'An Account of sums paid for Lowther Castle' from 24 May 1802 was rendered in the amount of £73 591. 19s. 10½d.; the masons and labourers took almost half of the whole amount (£30 050. 15s. 11d.). Some of the mason's work was contracted to Websters, the Kendal firm of architects and builders; they were in the earl's employment prior to Smirke's first visits, and payments were made to John Webster as clerk of works and to 'Webster' for chimneypieces (£1293. 4s. 4d.).

Bernasconi, the London plasterer who specialised in rendering Gothic ornament in 'composition'—a mixture of gypsum, water, glue and size poured into moulds—was employed at both Lowther and Eastnor. His detailed bill for Lowther shows the progress of work:

1808–9 (January to December)
    East wing; Dining Room; Drawing and
    Ante-Room; Rooms over them   £1919. 7s. 3½d.

31 December 1809–31 December 1810
    All the Rooms above the Principal Floor;
    N. and S. of the Great Staircase   £795. 7s. 3¾d.

31 December 1810–31 December 1811
    The Great Staircase; The Hall   £2579. 15s. 11½d.

31 December 1811–31 December 1812
    Saloon; Bedchambers over Drawing Room
    and Library   [No price recorded]

66. Printed in 1867, *The Builder*, pp. 604–6.   67. Cumbria CRO, Carlisle, D/Lons/L., Accounts 629.

31 December 1812–31 December 1813
 Library; West Ante-Room   £427. 6s. 6¾d.
The Prices in these Accounts are subject to
a reduction of 2½ per cent.
£6348. 18s. Deduct 2½% £158. 18s.
  Total £6190 [received in nine payments]

The earl had a stock of various building materials from which Bernasconi took items to the value of £756. These included 736 bundles of laths, 66 loads of sand and 264 bushels of hair. His equipment on the site included a heating oven for preparing the plaster, and £125 was expended on the carriage of wood, oil, clay and wax and for ready-made plaster models.

When Smirke rendered the final account in June 1814, he wrote to Lord Lonsdale that, as some expenses, including the superintendence of the clerks of works, had been agreed prior to his being employed, he would deduct £5000. With several other sums this reduced the overall bill by over £9300 to £64 243. 2s. 4d.

Eastnor was commissioned by John, 2nd Baron Somers, representative of a family that had been long seated in Herefordshire; the 1st Baron was Lord High Chancellor to William III and the friend of Addison and Steele. To document the building we have 17 detailed account books (and a number of letters) recording every penny spent on the vast project and preserving each tradesman's receipt.[68] Work on the castle commenced in 1812—Smirke noted 'The first stone of the Foundations was paid on April 24th', and Lord Somers wrote in his notebook for 23 June 1812: 'I laid this day the first ashlar ornamental stone . . . and placed under it a piece of money of Queen Elizabeth I (I believe half a crown), my family having settled in Eastnor in that reign; and also a three-shilling bank token of the year 1811 when the foundations of Eastnor Castle were marked out and begun.'

Smirke estimated the expense of building thus:

	£
Masonry, including the expenses of the carriage of stone from the Forest of Dean, quarrying, lime, sand, etc.	13 000
Carpenter, Plumber, Slater and Smith	18 500
Joiners, Plasterers, Painters and Glaziers	27 500
Value of old materials in the present house included	
	59 000
Terraces and Walls of Embankment round the House, excavating to form the Water, Building the Outer Court, Lodge and approach	6000
Kitchen and Stable Offices with embankments; Fence Walls	17 000
	£82 000

68. I am indebted to the Hon Mrs Elizabeth Hervey-
 Bathurst for loaning the Eastnor account books to me
 over an extended period.

Lord Somers annotated the memorandum: 'Mr Smirke repeatedly assured me (although he could not be precise as to a small sum) the Above he was quite convinced and thoroughly satisfied is a very full estimate.' A summary is given below of the yearly expenditure. While the accounts conclude in 1819, it is significant to note that the Great Entrance Arch is carved with a Latin legend which indicates final completion in 1824.

In the early stages Smirke was hurried constantly by a family anxious to leave their ancient nearby home of Castleditch. The architect defended his work at Eastnor, which had received adverse comment from the Duke of Norfolk in a long letter of 20 August 1813. Part of it referring to constructional techniques reads:

His Grace has mistaken entirely the use of the long pieces or plates of Timber alluded to; In a work raised with great expedition they are indispensable; they connect and keep steady the masses of wall between the high openings of windows or Doors which, until the cement or mortar becomes hardened, are extremely liable to be removed from their perpindicular position; They serve also, while the walls are raising, to distribute the incumbent weight equally along their whole extent in the inside of the wall as the closely jointed ashlaring does on the outside. . . .

These arguments your Lordship will observe do not at all apply if the walls of a Building are raised slowly; if we had occupied two years instead of one, in raising those of Eastnor Castle, the plates wd. have been unnecessary; their expence however will not have exceeded about one hundred pounds.

Lord Somers was presented by his Architect with a number of alternatives for cheaper finishings as the work progressed. Some of these were occasioned by the death of the eldest son, Edward Charles Cocks, in action against the French at Burgos in 1812, and also because of the rapid and unexpected alteration in the prevailing prosperity and the difficulties which arose from the Peninsular War.

In 1814 marble chimneypieces were provided by Messrs Shell and Milton, and notes appeared about 'unbarring rock on Malvern Hills in search of Marble for Chimneypieces'; Thomas Milton was paid a little over £208 for his work on the chimneypieces. The Great Staircase, the finishing of which was estimated in 1817 at £2800, or in a more temporary manner with only one coat of plaster and no enrichments at about £1500, was entrusted, with all the other plasterwork, to Bernasconi. The painters, as at Lowther, were the experienced London firm of Cornelius Dixon & Son, who had also worked for James Wyatt at 15 St James's Square and for Wyatville at Wollaton. Hundreds of elm flooring boards were prepared and laid, the kitchen offices were covered with 'anti-corrosion composition', and heating supplies came from Boulton and Watt. The sums of money expended annually were painstakingly recorded by the clerks of works Thomas Carpenter and, after 1817, John Fortune:

1812	£16 334.	1816	£10 132. 18s. 9d.
1813	£25 893. 19s. 10d.	1817	£8311. 9s. 10d.
1814	£8326. 2s. 8¼d.	1818	£5078. 19s. 10½d.
1815	£11 040. 5s. 3½d.	1819	£5659. 0s. 4¼d.

This totalled £90 776. 15s. 7½d., and other incidental work in 1820 brought the total to over £100 000, excluding furnishing. Smirke visited the site three times a year, receiving his expenses for attendance and a 5 per cent commission.

The decade in which Eastnor was erected was one when the British people seem to have been involved in trade, commerce and agriculture to a very active degree. Prosperity seemed as inevitable in the future as in the present.

Anyone who gazes from the far side of the lake at Eastnor may be forgiven for indulging in day-dreams. The lofty towers and windy terraces, with the British Camp in the background, are representative of an age which built lavishly. After Smirke's work had been concluded, the 2nd Earl, who lived on until 1841, had rooms decorated to designs by Pugin and G E Fox. The immediate past had encompassed much in a similar romantic style—the Royal Pavilion on its lawns by the sea at Brighton, or the creation of Sezincote and the castellated wonders designed by Anthony Salvin. In the future lay effects to be created by mechanical carving machines or Mr Prosser's mosaic tesserae, and in the lofty halls of the Crystal Palace. The careers of William Morris and Norman Shaw, to say nothing of Owen Jones, followed on from the creation of Shrubland Park, Trentham or Scarisbrick and heralded 'High Victorian Design'. Brooding over all were those black frock-coated members of the aristocracy, painted with plans for further improvements on the table at their side. They garnered money, attended to their estates, coalmines and factories, and forced architects and craftsmen to be competent to survive and to improve their skills. At the point at which design and invention were set to the greatest advantage, it was inevitable that convenience also had come to reign.

No more the Cedar Parlour's formal gloom
With dullness chills: 'tis now the Living Room,
Where guests, to whim or taste or fancy true,
Scattered in groups their different plans pursue . . .
Here politicians eagerly relate
The last day's news or the last night's debate;
And there a lover's conquered by checkmate.[69]

---

69. By Humphrey Repton, cited by Hussey, 1958, *ECH: Late Georgian*, p. 19.

129 HAM HOUSE, Surrey. Chimneypiece in the Queen's Closet, *c* 1675. *Victoria and Albert Museum, London* (photograph: museum).

The panels surrounding the fireplace are in scagliola. The initials 'J.E.L.' (for John and Elizabeth Lauderdale), together with a ducal coronet, are incorporated in the design. The same initials can be seen in the marquetry floor, which originally continued without a break from the raised area in the adjoining Queen's Bedchamber (so named following its preparation for a visit by Charles II's queen, Catherine of Braganza).

130 WHITCHURCH, Middlesex. Church of St
Lawrence, monument to 1st Duke of Chandos and
his two wives, 1717 (photograph: A F Kersting).

In 1717 the duke ordered a tomb from Grinling
Gibbons for himself and his two wives, Mary Lake
and Cassandra Willoughby. Yet a third duchess,
Lydia, was to have shared it but she outlived him
(he died in August 1744). The duke argued with
Gibbons over the cost of the monument, which
depicted him in Roman costume. Its fashioning
may have been contributed to by John van Nost,
who was later employed at the duke's great house
of Canons (*dest* 1747). The painted decoration over
the monument, a feigned cupola pierced to show
glimpses of the sky, was an enrichment, *c* 1736, by
Gaetano Brunetti.
Lit: C H and M I Collins-Baker, 1949, *The Life
and Circumstances of James Brydges, 1st Duke of
Chandos*.

FIDE ET CONSTANTIA

131 VARIOUS CHIMNEYPIECES by James Gibbs, from 1728, *A Book of Architecture*, pl. 91 (photograph: Manchester University, John Rylands Library).

The period when Gibbs was doing most of his best work, in the 1720s and 1730s, was one in which the architecturally styled overmantel enjoyed great favour with patrons. With broken pediment (left), scrolled open pediment centring on a cartouche (centre) or pedimented (right), they provided ample opportunity for carver and statuary to embellish them.

132 DITCHLEY, Oxfordshire. Detail of Hall overmantel, *c* 1725 (photograph: A F Kersting).

The decoration of Ditchley was supervised by Francis Smith on behalf of the architect James Gibbs. The overmantel bears a resemblance to that shown (right) in pl. 131 above. The type, however, was a usual one. It was provided by the Holborn statuaries Edward Stanton III and Christopher Horsenaile; the portrait by William Aikman is of the patron, George Lee, 2nd Earl of Lichfield.

133 CLANDON, Surrey. Detail of overmantel, Hall chimneypiece, *c* 1729 (photograph: A F Kersting).

Clandon was built by Thomas, 2nd Baron Onslow, *c* 1728–30, and includes splendid work by the Italian *stuccatori* (*see* pl. 72). The great double-cube Entrance Hall also contains two marble chimneypieces, facing each other, sculpted (and signed) by John Michael Rysbrack. The reliefs in them are free copies of antiques, the small model for one of them being at Stourhead. As Frederick, Prince of Wales, was entertained at the house in 1729, it may be assumed that they were in position by that year.
Lit: M I Webb, 1954, *Michael Rysbrack: Sculptor*, p. 130.

134 BLENHEIM, Oxfordshire. Chapel, monument to John, 1st Duke of Marlborough, 1733 (photograph: A F Kersting).

Hawksmoor prepared a design for the duke's monument which Sarah, his duchess, did not accept. She turned for a design to William Kent, and Rysbrack was chosen to sculpt it in marble. The chapel was consecrated in 1728—the tomb bears a shield held by 'Fame' and 'Envy' inscribed: 'To the Memory/of/John/Duke of/Marlborough/And his Two Sons/Sarah/His Duchess/Has Erected This Monument/In the Year of Christ/MDCCXXXIII.'

Sarah's daughter, Mary (who married the 2nd Duke of Montagu), visited Rysbrack's studio while the 'Tomb for Blenheim' was in preparation. Her mother was displeased, writing: 'they always make a Model in Clay to make that in stone by and what is done first in Clay is often more like than that in marble'. Mary begged for one of the maquettes of Marlborough's son, Lord Blandford—the duke is shown in Roman costume with his wife and two sons; she did not get it, but Sarah did. Her wrath was further incurred, however, as Rysbrack let Mary have that of the duke instead.
Lit: David Green, 1967, *Sarah, Duchess of Marlborough*, p. 257.

135 QUEEN ANNE. Marble statue by J M
Rysbrack, 1738, Long Library, Blenheim Palace,
Oxfordshire (photograph: A F Kersting).

The decoration of Blenheim, a great achievement
and torment to its creators, Queen Anne, Sarah,
Duchess of Marlborough, Sir John Vanbrugh and
Nicholas Hawksmoor, was conducted well into the
1740s. One of Sarah's acts was to commission a
statue of Queen Anne from Rysbrack. The plinth
bears the date 1746 (in Roman numerals)—it was
completed by 1738. It cost about £300, a sum
which Sarah fixed in advance and which she was
unwilling, presumably, to exceed.
Lit: M I Webb, 1954, *Michael Rysbrack: Sculptor*,
p. 163.

136 and 137 DITCHLEY, Oxfordshire. Drawing Room, chimneypiece (*right*) and detail (*above*), *c* 1738 (photographs: A F Kersting).

The architect Henry Flitcroft charged from 1736 to 1741 for 'designs, with all the mouldings at large' for various ceilings, and for chimneypieces—'a Chimney Top with ornaments and three rich Frizes for the Plasterer', and 'Lower Part of Chimneypieces and mouldings for Mr. Cheere'. This chimneypiece may therefore be given to Flitcroft for its design, and Henry (later Sir Henry) Cheere for its execution. Its Corinthian columns, open pediment and rich carving in wood and marble demonstrate Cheere's considerable abilities.

138 DRAWING FOR A CHIMNEYPIECE by Sir Henry Cheere (1703–81). Pen, ink, wash and watercolour, *c* 1750. *Victoria and Albert Museum, London,* Inv. No. D 715(3)–1887 (photograph: museum).

Cheere developed a good rococo style with delicate naturalistic motifs—flowers, animals and figures. He used rich varied marbles, particularly yellow 'sienna', and his work was in considerable demand by patrons and architects. His surviving bank account (Drummonds) also reflects his great success.

139 KIRTLINGTON, Oxfordshire. Dining Room chimneypiece, *c* 1745 (re-erected *Metropolitan Museum of Art, New York*) (photograph: museum).

Sir Francis Dashwood's account book for the building of his house, 1741–47 (Bodleian Library), includes payments to Henry Cheere in June 1745 (£186) and February 1748 (£9. 18s. 6d.), and one to John Cheere in July 1748 (£47. 14s.). Henry Cheere seems, therefore, to have provided most of the chimneypieces at Kirtlington. This one is in the style of the drawing (*see* pl. 138) with carved trusses and terms.

140 (*left*) NORFOLK HOUSE, London. Music Room chimneypiece, *c* 1755. Music Room re-erected *Victoria and Albert Museum, London* (photograph: museum).

This fine chimneypiece was probably designed by Giovanni Battista Borra, a Piedmontese architect who spent several years in England. He had accompanied Robert Wood, James Dawkins and John Bouverie (who died) on their expedition to Baalbec and Palmyra. He returned to England with the two surviving members in 1751. The actual making of the chimneypiece is attributed to James Lovell, who worked with Borra at Stowe and who was accomplished at fashioning in plaster and papier-mâché as well as in marble (*see also* pl. 124).

141 (*below*) WOBURN ABBEY, Bedfordshire. Hall chimneypiece, *c* 1755 (photograph: A F Kersting).

In about 1750 Rysbrack sculpted a marble relief of Diana for the Stone Hall of Robert Walpole's house at Houghton. Twenty-five years later he repeated the relief in Portland stone for the 4th Duke of Bedford at Woburn. By this time, as he was getting older, he collaborated with the sculptor-mason John Devall to provide the chimneypiece itself. Both Rysbrack and Devall's bills survive. For the 'Sacrifice to Diana' illustrated here (and a companion 'Sacrifice to Apollo'), Rysbrack charged £105 for the two, and Devall a further £94 (£47 each).
Lit: M I Webb, 1954, *Michael Rysbrack: Sculptor*, pp. 129–30.

142 (*below*) WOBURN ABBEY, Bedfordshire, Saloon, detail of chimneypiece plaque, 1756 (photograph: A F Kersting).

In April 1756 Rysbrack was paid for a small plaque; the bill reads 'Drawing, modelling and carving and polishing a tablet for a chimneypiece representing a nymph laying on the ground, and a boy running to her, being frightened by a sea monster, £25. 0. 0.' The 4th Duke of Bedford's wife was a grand-daughter of Sarah, Duchess of Marlborough, who had long patronised Rysbrack (*see* pl. 135). This may therefore have been remembered when a sculptor was needed; Sarah herself had died 12 years earlier than the commission, in 1744.

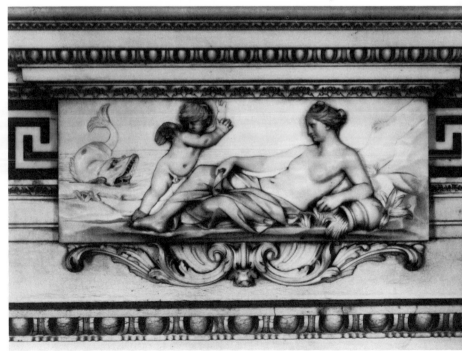

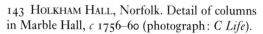

143 HOLKHAM HALL, Norfolk. Detail of columns in Marble Hall, *c* 1756–60 (photograph: *C Life*).

The building activities at Holkham from 1730 onwards continued for 34 years, with a group of craftsmen involved in the execution of the Marble Hall from 1756–64. Two guineas was paid to William Pickford's marble masons on 21 November 1760 'to Entertain themselves on finishing the Hall'. The white-on-black fret beneath the base of the columns was fastened to the marble by brass wire supplied by Anthony Hingham. The block tin balusters were fashioned in 1760, and the joiner William Townson provided the mahogany hand-rail.

144 (*right*) HULNE PRIORY, Alnwick, Northumberland. Chimneypiece in the Lord's Tower, *c* 1778 (photograph: A F Kersting).

Two miles north-east of Alnwick Castle are the ruins of Hulne Priory, a Carmelite house. The interior was Gothicised in the 1770s by Robert Adam at the time he was working at Alnwick for the 1st Duke of Northumberland. Much of his work in the castle was swept away in Sir Anthony Salvin's remodelling in 1854, but the Hulne Priory interiors and Brislee Tower survive. The chimneypiece shown here, in a saloon on the 1st floor of the fifteenth-century tower, has a frieze bearing heraldic devices of the Percy family.

145 POWDERHAM CASTLE, Devon. Music Room, detail of chimneypiece frieze, *c* 1794 (photograph: A F Kersting).

In the early 1790s the architect James Wyatt, the sculptor of this chimneypiece, Richard Westmacott the elder, and the cabinet-makers Marsh and Tatham were at work for the 3rd Viscount Courtenay. He had 13 sisters, and for their musical education it must have seemed a good idea to build a large music-room. The marble chimneypiece frieze is flanked by two figures playing the flute and tambourine.
Lit: *C Life*, 18 July 1963, p. 141.

PART III

Select Dictionary
of
Craftsmen

DICTIONARY

ABBOTT, John (*fl.* 1639/40–1727). Plasterer. Son of Richard Abbott, baptised at Frithelstock, N. Devon on 20 February 1639/40. Worked extensively in Devon and many decorations have been credited to him through the patterns in his sketch-book. Had an apprentice Lawrence Mabyn. Abbott died on 28 April 1727.
1676 FRITHELSTOCK CHURCH, DEVON
Royal coat-of-arms, etc. Received £13. 6s. 8d.
Lit: Churchwardens' Accounts, cited in *C Life*, 2 March 1940, p. 222.
1680 CUSTOM HOUSE, EXETER, DEVON
Ceilings. Received £35.
Lit: Accounts, Exeter City Record Office, cited by Kathleen and Cecil French, 1957, 'Devonshire Plasterwork', *Devonshire Association, Transactions*, 89, pp. 124–44. Abbott's sketch-book and four of his plastering tools are in the Devon County Record Office. *See also* Margaret Jourdain, 2 March 1940, 'A Seventeenth Century Plasterer, John Abbott of Barnstaple and his Sketch Book', *C Life*, pp. 222–25.

ABBOTT, Thomas (*fl.* 1750–60). Painter.
1750–60 HORSE GUARDS, WHITEHALL, LONDON
Lit: RIBA Library, MSS, HOR.

ADAIR, John (*fl.* 1763–71). Carver/Gilder.
Wardour Street, Soho (Mortimer, 1763).
1763/69 SHUGBOROUGH, STAFFORDSHIRE
Lit: *C Life*, 4 March 1954, p. 593.
1764 SYON, MIDDLESEX
Criticised for 'ill-executed' mouldings in a letter from 1st Duke of Northumberland to RA.
Lit: Letter, 4 November 1764. Alnwick Castle Archives, 94, ff. 44–45.

ADAIR, William (*fl.* 1798–1805).
Carver/Gilder.
Of 26 Wardour St, Soho.
1778/79 NEW BURLINGTON STREET, LONDON (Sir John Griffin-Griffin).
Ante-room chimneypiece.
Lit: Stillman, 1966, *Adam*, p. 49.
1799–1805. Acted as Carver and Gilder to George IV.
Lit: H Clifford Smith, 1931, *Buckingham Palace*, p. 277.

ADAMSON, David (*fl.* 1768–76). House painter.
1768 MOOR PARK, HERTFORDSHIRE
Received £79. 14s. 9¼d.
Lit: North Riding CRO, Dundas Archives.
1776 20 ST JAMES'S SQUARE, LONDON
Received £415.
Lit: NLW Wynnstay MS, 115/17/19.

ADDINAL, – (*fl.* 1772). Plasterer.
Only recorded in connection with the following commission:

1772 KILNWICK HALL, YORKSHIRE
Worked under Joseph Cortese (q.v.).
Lit: Edward Ingram, 1952, *Leaves from a Family Tree*.
1729 A William Addinell did painting and gilding at Wentworth Castle, Yorkshire, some to surround painted decorative work by Amigoni.
Lit: BL Add. MS, 22, 241, ff. 225, 233.

AFFLETT, W (*fl.* 1693–1710). Plasterer.
Apprenticed to Henry Doogood (q.v.). Made free of The Worshipful Company of Plaisterers, 21 October 1700.
1708–10 ST PAUL'S CATHEDRAL, LONDON
Worked under Chrysostom Wilkins (q.v.).
Lit: Guildhall Library MS 6122/3; *Wren Soc*, XV, pp. 169, 196.

ALBORN, Thomas (*fl.* 1667–78). Plasterer.
Lived in Glasgow. Took W Lindores as apprentice in 1667.
1671–74 THIRLESTANE CASTLE, BERWICKSHIRE
Architect: Sir William Bruce.
Received £1324. 14s. 4d.
Lit: Scottish Record Office, Thirlestane Castle Archives.
Worked under George Dunsterfield and John Houlbert (q.v.), but received £1100 on 25 August 1675 and £659. 10s. on 9 August 1676 'for several sorts of Plaister work'.
1675–76 STIRLING (PALACE AND CASTLE)
Received £823. 6s. 6d.
Lit: R S Mylne, 1893, *The Master Masons to the Crown of Scotland and their Works*, pp. 195, 201.
1675–77 HAMILTON PLACE, LANARKSHIRE
Architect: James Smith.
Lit: Rosalind K Marshall, 1973, *The Days of Duchess Anne*, p. 265.
Presumably the same as the 'Thomas Aliborne' who worked at the Palace in the 1660s.
1699 CRAIGHALL, FIFE
Lit: Scottish Record Office, Bruce of Arnot Archives. I am indebted to Mr John Dunbar for this information.
Attributed work:
1673 KINROSS HOUSE, KINROSS-SHIRE
Architect: Sir William Bruce.
Great Staircase.
Lit: *Sir William Bruce, 1630–1710* (Scottish Arts Council, Exhibition Catalogue 1970, No. 128).

ALCOCK(E), Nicholas (*fl.* late 17th cent.)
Carver.
1695 KENSINGTON PALACE, LONDON
With William Emmett and Grinling Gibbons provided '1405 feet of Ionicke modillion and hollow cornish for the wainscoting, 942 feet of picture frame over ye doores and chimneyes and 89 feet of astrigall molding about ye glasses in ye chimneyes, carving the Kinges armes, supporters, Crowne and Garter, the

rules and ballisters in ye chappell and several other services for Kensington Palace'.
Lit: R W Symonds, 1955, *C Life Annual*; *Wren Soc*, VII, pp. 153, 157, 175, 166, 178, 181.

ALCOTT, Joseph (*fl.* 1786–1815).
Carpenter, Scagliola worker.
Began life as a carpenter but learned the Italian process of scagliola and set up on his own account. Worked at: Stoke Park; Arbury Hall; Coventry House, Piccadilly; and Goodwood (Gunnis, 1953, *Dictionary*.) Subscribed to George Richardson's *Vitruvius Britannicus*, 1802, and was living at 81 Queen Anne Street, London, in 1795.
1795 SHUGBOROUGH, STAFFORDSHIRE
Eight scagliola pillars for Hall, 'in imitation of yellow-antique'.
Received £112. 9s.
Lit: Staffs CRO, 1240/1; 11 March 1954, *C Life*, p. 678.

ALEXANDER and SHRIMPTON. Brass Founders and Ironmongers.
Wood Street, Cheapside (Mortimer, 1763, p. 37).
1758 MANSION HOUSE, LONDON
Supplied stoves, chandeliers and railings.
Lit: Hussey, 1965, *ECH: Early Georgian*, p. 233.
1760–62 CORSHAM COURT, WILTSHIRE
Gallery, Steel grate.
Lit: ibid., p. 233.
1765 MERSHAM-LE-HATCH, KENT
Wrought-iron staircases, entrance and stair-hall.
Received £275.
Lit: Hussey, 1956, *ECH: Mid-Georgian*, p. 100.

ALKEN, Oliver (?–1769). Carver.
Little Titchfield Street, London. Brother of Sefferin Alken (q.v.), but also had a son named Sefferin, who was under 21 years of age at his father's death in 1769. He entrusted the care of his son and his daughter, Ann, to James Thorne of Westminster, carver, and to Richard Lawrence (q.v.), who had been apprenticed in 1746 to Sefferin Alken, senior.
1760 GERMAN LUTHERAN CHAPEL, THE SAVOY, LONDON
Lit: Harris, 1970, *Chambers*, p. 229, fn. 94; PRO, Prob 11/979, f. 119.

ALKEN, Sefferin (*fl.* 1744–82). Carver.

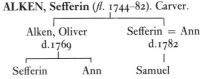

Alken, Oliver
d.1769

Sefferin = Ann
d.1782

Sefferin   Ann   Samuel

Resident in 1763 at Dufours Court in Golden Square, London. Of St James's, Westminster, at the time of his death (1782). Worked for

RA, and at several houses, including Somerset House, for Sir William Chambers. These included Shardeloes; Blenheim Palace; Charlemont House, Dublin; Duddingston; The Hoo; Kew Gardens; 45 Berkeley Square, London; Fought's shop in St Martin's Lane, London; Peper Harow, Surrey; Stanmore Park, Middlesex; and Walcot House, Salop. Their range indicates the high regard in which he was held by architects of great ability and connection. Chambers, in a letter of 12 March 1772, referred to him (with others) as one of 'her late Royal Highnesses workmen'. He is noted as 'Sefferin Alkin' in Henry Flitcroft's bank account in 1747 (Drummonds). Took Richard Lawrence (q.v.) as apprentice in 1746. Subscribed in 1764 to RA's book on Diocletian's Palace, and assisted John Cobb carving chairs for 6th Earl of Coventry, apart from other carving (1763–82) at Croome Court and Croome Church, Worcestershire, in wood and stone. At Shardeloes he was working with his partner as 'Alken and Lawrence' under the direction of Stiff Leadbetter, who in turn was answerable to RA.
Lit: RABA; Croome Court Archives, Nos. 35, 38, 52, 54, 62 (microfilm, Victoria and Albert Museum, Dept of Furniture and Woodwork); Beard, 1966, *Craftsmen*, p. 172; Harris, 1970, *Chambers*, p. 39; Bucks. CRO, MS D/DR5/10 (Shardeloes).

ALLEN, Antony (*fl.* 1683). Plasterer.
1683 ST PAUL'S CATHEDRAL, LONDON
Made a model.
Lit: *Wren Soc*, XIII, p. 168.

ALLISON, John (*fl.* 1660). Plasterer.
1660 THE TOWER, LONDON
Worked under John Grove I.
Lit: PRO Works, 5/1, November 1660.

ALLNUTT, — (*fl.* 1664). Joiner.
1664 CLARENDON HOUSE
Worked with Thomas Kinward and did the wainscoting in several rooms.
Received about £420.
Lit: R T Gunther, 1928, *The Architecture of Sir Roger Pratt*, p. 42.

ANDERSON, Diederich Nicolaus (d.1767). Modeller and Chaser.
Worked for Sir William Chambers and James Stuart, and for RA at Kedleston and Syon.
Resident: Garrard Street, Soho.
Lit: Harris, 1970, *Chambers*, p. 204.
1767 SYON, MIDDLESEX
Drawing Room doors; metal enrichments on architraves (modelled by Thomas Carter (q.v.)).
Lit: Goodison, 1974, *Ormolu*, p. 22.

ANDREWES, Ambrose (*fl.* 1664). Carver.
1664 Worked on the London buildings of the Carpenters' Company: 'Item pd to Ambrose Andrewes Carver for carveing worke about the new great roome in the Garden . . . xxv[li] vs.'
Lit: E B Jupp, 1887, *Historical Account of the Carpenters' Company*, 2nd edn., p. 230.

ANSELL, Robert (*fl.* 1767). Carver/Gilder.
Subscribed to James Paine, 1767, *Plans . . . of Gentlemen's Houses*.

1770–71 MILTON HOUSE, LONDON
Architect: Sir William Chambers.
Gilding.
Lit: Harris, 1970, *Chambers*, p. 225.
1771–73 20 ST JAMES'S SQUARE, LONDON
Architect: RA.
Provided two figures on the Organ.
Lit: NLW, Wynnstay MS, 115/9, pp. 33–36.
c 1773 BLENHEIM PALACE, OXFORDSHIRE
Architect: Sir William Chambers.
One of Sir William's team for extensive amendments to Vanbrugh's house for the 2nd Duke of Marlborough.
Lit: Harris, 1970, *Chambers*, p. 199.

APPLEBY, Gabriel (*fl.* 1723–29). Joiner.
1716–27 ST MARY WOOLNOTH, LONDON
Lit: Colvin, 1950, *Arch Rev*, p. 196.
1723–29 CHRISTCHURCH, SPITALFIELDS, LONDON
Lit: *ibid.*, p. 195.

ARROW, James (*fl.* 1750–95). Joiner.
Mentioned in Henry Flitcroft's bank account in 1750 (Drummonds Bank).
1768 OBSERVATORY, RICHMOND GARDENS, SURREY
'James Arrow's interior joinery is a noteworthy example of the best of Georgian craftsmanship.'
Lit: Harris, 1970, *Chambers*, p. 244.
1776–95 SOMERSET HOUSE, LONDON
Received £2878. 17s. 10d.
Lit: Colvin, 1976, *King's Works*, V, p. 466.
1781–89 CHAPEL, GREENWICH HOSPITAL
Supervised by William Newton.
Arrow was assisted by George Seddon.
Lit: RIBA, Library, New/1.

ARTARI
The history of this family, settled at Arogno towards the end of the sixteenth century, is very complex. An extensive literature (summarised in *Dizionario Biografico Degli Italian*, 1962, IV, pp. 351–52) assumes that Giovanni Battista Artari was born at Arogno, near Lugano, in 1660 and that his son Giuseppe, who worked in England with Bagutti (q.v.), was born there in 1697. Searches in the 'Liber Baptizato' and 'Liber Matrimoni' at Arogno made in 1966–67 in the company of Professor Giuseppe Martinola (Cantonal Historical Commission, Lugano) revealed how the errors arose, but have not provided a satisfactory solution. The alternatives are:
1. Giovanni Battista Artari, son of Joseph and Jecomina, was baptised at Arogno on 19 October 1664 (not 1660). He married 'Catherina de Maini' in the same church on 1 March 1688.
2. Giovanni and Catherina had at least two children: Carlo Giuseppe, born 5 September 1692, and Adalbertus, born 7 October 1693. There is no entry for the birth of an Artari in 1697. A problem arises in assuming this Carlo Giuseppe to be the stuccoist who worked in England since his death is recorded at Arogno on 27 May 1757, 'in the sixty-fifth year of his age', although most sources suggest that Artari died in Cologne in 1769. The entire problem is further complicated by the birth of another Giuseppe Artari, son of Domenico Artari and

Bartolomea, *née* Pianca, at Arogno on 20 September 1700. There was also an Artari family settled at Bissone nearby.
It is therefore clear that the statements about the lives of these two stuccoists in existing literature, my own 1966, *Georgian Craftsmen and their Work* included, need to be viewed in relation to the Arogno registers. In the seeming absence of a solution, they must be listed here under names of convenience.

ARTARI, Adalbertus (1693–1751). Stuccoist.
Born at Arogno. Presumed to be the 'Albert Artari' who assisted Giuseppe Artari at Sutton Scarsdale. Either he or his father, Giovanni Battista (see below), could have been one of the 'two Mr. Artares' mentioned in the Ditchley archives. He is presumably the Albert Artari who died at Arogno on 22 October 1751.
1724 SUTTON SCARSDALE, DERBYSHIRE
Architect: Francis Smith.
Lit: Text of lead rising-plate formerly at house. House destroyed *c* 1920 (fragments of stucco remain adhering to ruin). Sale catalogue dated 6 November 1919; text of rising-plate, *C Life*, 15 February 1919, p. 171.
1725 DITCHLEY, OXFORDSHIRE
Architect: James Gibbs.
Worked with Giuseppe Artari, Francesco Serena (q.v.) and Francesco Vassalli (q.v.). The accounts record: 'Ap. 9. 1725 pd the two Mr Artare's in part by my Lord. 10. 10. 0.' 'Joseph' Artari is mentioned elsewhere in the account.
Lit: Oxford CRO, Dillon Archives, Dil I/33 p, h.

ARTARI, Giovanni Battista (1664–?). Stuccoist.
Born at Arogno. Worked in England. As some sources (e.g. Benezit, 1948, *Dictionnaire . . . des peintres . . .*) give a third Christian name of 'Alberti' to him, he has been confused with his son Adalbertus (see above). In 1707 he was working with Gian Battista Genone at Fulda Cathedral and they were also employed at Rastatt Cathedral, Brühl and Aquisgrana. The stuccoist Alfonso Oldelli (1696–*c* 1770), writing to Giovanni Oldelli at Meride on 2 July 1721, mentions the 'Signori Artari' working in England and states that they were doing well and that he had a mind to join them.
Lit: 1962, *Dizionario Biografico Degli Italiani*, IV, p. 351; F Hermanin, 1935, *Gli artisti in Germania*, II, pp. 35, 44, 64; Nicolas Powell, 1959, *From Baroque to Rococo*, p. 38; Giuseppe Martinola, 1963, *Lettere dai paesi Transalpini degli Artisti di Meride*, p. 117.
1735 PARLINGTON HALL, YORKSHIRE
dest: *c* 1950.
Lit: see 1737 entry under Giuseppe Artari (below).

ARTARI, Giuseppe (late 17th cent.–1769). Stuccoist.
Born at Arogno in 1692 or 1700 (see introduction above). Stated to have trained with his father and to have worked in Rome, Germany and Holland before coming to England. He is known to have associated with Giovanni Bagutti. His first recorded

employment in England was in 1720. He married and his wife 'Mary Gertrude' Artari occasionally received payment on his behalf for his work, such as that at the Radcliffe Camera, Oxford (1744–45). He left for Germany some time after 1760, having been called to work for the Elector of Cologne, and died there in 1769.

c 1715 DUNCOMBE PARK, YORKSHIRE
Lit: Horace Walpole, MS, 'Book of Materials', p. 158, recorded 'William Wakefield Esq., built Helmsley Mr. Duncomb's about 1713. The Stucco work there by one Vassalli and some better by Attari.' Cited from the original in Wilmarth S Lewis Library, Farmington, Connecticut, USA by Michael McCarthy, April 1976, 'The Building of Hagley Hall', *Burl Mag*, p. 224, fn. 69.
I am indebted to Mr Lewis for permission to quote the extract.
1720 OCTAGON HOUSE, TWICKENHAM, MIDDLESEX
Architect: James Gibbs.
Artari assisted by Giovanni Bagutti.
Lit: Gibbs, 1728, *B of A*, p. xix; *C Life*, 15 September 1944; Hussey, 1965, *ECH: Early Georgian*, pp. 40–42.
1720–30 AACHEN CATHEDRAL
Octagon of Nave (removed 1870–73).
Lit: Dehio and Gall, *Handbuch der Deutschen Kunstdrukmäler, Wordlichen Hessen*, pp. 276, 279; *Die Rheinlande*, p. 108.
1722–26 ST MARTIN-IN-THE-FIELDS, LONDON
Architect: James Gibbs.
Artari assisted by Giovanni Bagutti.
Lit: Gibbs, 1728, *B of A*, p. v.: 'the ceiling enrich'd with Fretwork by Signori Artari and Bagutti, the best Fretworkers that ever came into England'; John McMaster, 1916, *A Short History of the Royal Parish of St. Martin-in-the-Fields*; K A Esdaile, 1944, *St. Martin-in-the-Fields*; Little, 1955, *Gibbs*, p. 91.
1722–30 SENATE HOUSE, CAMBRIDGE
Architect: James Gibbs.
Artari assisted by Giovanni Bagutti.
Lit: Willis and Clarke, 1886, *Cambridge*, III, p. 47; Little, 1955, *Gibbs*, p. 61. The ceiling was replaced by a replica 1898–1900; I am indebted to Mr Robert Taylor (RCHM, Cambridge) for this information.
1723–24 ST PETER'S, VERE STREET, LONDON (Formerly known as the Oxford or Marylebone Chapel)
Architect: James Gibbs.
Artari assisted by Giovanni Bagutti.
Lit: Gibbs, 1728, *B of A*, p. vii: 'the ceiling is handsomely adorned with Fret-work by Signori Artari and Bagutti'.
1725 DITCHLEY, OXFORDSHIRE
Architect: James Gibbs.
Artari assisted by Giovanni Artari, Francesco Serena and Francesco Vassalli.
Lit: Oxford CRO, Dillon MSS, 1/3/p/h.
1726 HOUGHTON HALL, NORFOLK
Architect: Colen Campbell; interior: William Kent; 'the ceiling and the Frieze of Boys are by Artari' (Horace Walpole, 1819, *Anecdotes of Painters*, II, p. 34).
Received £131. 14s. 5d. for the Saloon ceiling, and £560. 10s. overall.
Lit: Isaac Ware, 1735, *Plan, Elevations and Sections of Houghton in Norfolk*, p. 7; Margaret Jourdain, 1948, *William Kent*, p. 63;

Hussey, 1965, *ECH: Early Georgian*, p. 80; CUL (CH), Vouchers, 1727, 1730.
1729–32 FALKENLUST, BRÜHL (HUNTING LODGE)
Architect: François de Cuvilliés.
Lit: 1962, *Dizionario Biografico Degli Italiani*, IV, pp. 351–52.
1729 CAVENDISH SQUARE, LONDON
Worked with Francesco Serena (q.v.).
Lit: Baker, 1949, *Brydges*, pp. 199, 277.
1730–31 MOULSHAM HALL, ESSEX
Architect: Giacomo Leoni.
Artari assisted by Giovanni Bagutti.
Dest 1809. Artari did 'Bustos and Figures'. He continued to work at Moulsham in later years; he was engaged on the ceiling of the Great Room in 1746. 24 March 1746: 'Pd Mrs. Artari in part of £27 due to her husband, £5. 5.'
Lit: Mildmay Account Books, Hampshire CRO (15M50/31) and Essex CRO (D/DMA5–7).
c 1732 MOOR PARK, HERTFORDSHIRE
Work by Giovanni and Giuseppe Artari noted there by Sir Edward Gascoigne (*see* Parlington, below, *also* entry under Bagutti).
1735 PARLINGTON HALL, YORKSHIRE
dest c 1950.
Assisted Giovanni Artari.
Drawing Room, Hall, Staircase, etc.
Lit: Elizabeth Done, 1975, 'Sir Edward Gascoigne, Grand Tourist', *Leeds Arts Calendar*, no. 77, p. 11.
1736 CASTLE HOWARD, YORKSHIRE
Submitted a drawing to the 3rd Earl of Carlisle for finishing the Temple of the Four Winds in stucco. The task was, however, given to Vassalli (q.v.) and Artari was paid £2. 2s. for his drawing.
Lit: Castle Howard MSS, 3rd Earl of Carlisle's Disbursement Book.
1737 UPTON HOUSE, NORTHAMPTONSHIRE
Ceiling is signed and dated 1737.
Medallion ceiling; statue of *Apollo* s. & d. 1737.
Lit: N Pevsner, *Buildings of England: Northamptonshire*, 2nd edn. I am indebted to Mr Bruce Bailey for this reference.
1737–38 TRENTHAM, STAFFORDSHIRE
Architect: Francis Smith.
New Library. The accounts also note, 22 March 1737/38 'Paid for Pipe-Clay for Moulds for Mr. Artari'. I am indebted to Mr John Cornforth for this reference.
Lit: Staffordshire CRO, Trentham Archives, D593/F/3/2/12.
1742 CASTLE HILL, DEVON
Stucco-work; *basso-relievos* in Best Hall. Received £32 plus travelling expenses. I am indebted to Dr H M Colvin for this reference.
Lit: Castle Hill Archives, Box C.1.
1743–44 PALACE, POPPELSDORF
Worked with Carlo Pietro Morsegno and the brothers Castelli.
Lit: 1962, *Dizionario Biografico degli Italiani*, IV; pp. 351–52.
1743–44 WIMPOLE HALL, CAMBRIDGESHIRE
Received £76. 9s.
Lit: BL Add. MS, 36228.
1744–45 RADCLIFFE CAMERA, OXFORD
Architect: James Gibbs.
Received £98. 16s. 8d. (Artari's wife, Mary Gertrude, received this amount on his behalf).
Lit: 1958, 'The Building Accounts of the Radcliffe Camera, Oxford', *ed.* S G Gillam,

Oxford Historical Society, XIII, 1953–54; S Lang, April 1949, *Arch Rev*, pp. 183–90; Little, 1955, *Gibbs*, pp. 134–35.
1748–61 SCHLOSS BRÜHL, COLOGNE
Stucco-work started in 1748 in a building erected to the designs of J S Schlaun and, later, François de Cuvilliés. It continued in 1756–57 in the first-floor State Room, south wing. All work was completed by 1761, the date of the death of Clemens August, the Archbishop and Elector of Cologne.
Lit: Letter from Artari in Düsseldorf Stadtarchiv, reproduced in *Berliner Jahrbuch*, 100, pp. 101 ff.; E Renard and F G W Metternich, 1934, *Schloss Brühl*; Nicolas Powell, 1959, *From Baroque to Rococo*, pp. 102, 148.
1756–60 RAGLEY HALL, WARWICKSHIRE
Lit: BL Add. MS, 29218: letters of Horace Walpole to 1st Earl of Hertford, 14 July and 3 August 1759, 1 September and 13 December 1760; Dr Richard Pococke's record of his visit to the house in 1756.
Attributed works
A considerable amount of careless attribution has taken place respecting Artari's work. James Gibbs used his services consistently, in company with Giovanni Bagutti, and possibly they worked at such houses as Sudbrook, Kelmarsh and Fairlawne. A comparison of details of the ceilings at Moor Park, Hertfordshire, and Clandon Park, Surrey, allows reasonably that they worked at Clandon (Beard, 1966, *Craftsmen*, pls. 37, 38, 50–53). Comparison of the Hall at Houghton, Norfolk, with the work at Bedale Hall, Yorkshire (*Craftsmen*, pls. 57–58) reveals close connections, but the Bedale ceiling is too coarse in execution to be by Artari, and may be by Giuseppe Cortese. Artari may also have provided the ceiling at 11 Henrietta Place, St Marylebone (now in the Victoria and Albert Museum, W5–1960). It is close to Gibbs (1728, *B of A*, plates) in style and the stucco surrounds paintings by Bellucci.
It is certain that Artari slipped abroad to work from time to time. In addition to the work cited, he is credited with stucco decoration in Bonn and Munster (1962, *Dizionario Biografico degli Italiani*, IV, pp. 351–52).

ARTIMA, Baldassare (*fl.* 1680–86).
Plasterer.
Ordered from Court as a Papist in January 1680/81, when a servant of Lady Williams of 14 St James's Square. Presumably re-employed in the short reign of King James II.
1686 WHITEHALL PALACE, LONDON
'Allowed for one Chimney piece with a frame wrought out of stuccoe. . . .'
Lit: *Wren Soc*, VII, p. 116; PRO Works, 5/54; 1960, *Survey of London*, XXIX, pp. 140, 562 fn. 289.

ASHLEY, William (*fl.* mid-17th cent.).
Joiner.
Worked at Peterhouse, Cambridge.
Lit: *C Life*, 23 November 1935.

ASKEW, Thomas (*fl.* late 17th cent.).
Carver.
Carved Royal Arms at St Peter, Cornhill; worked with Thomas Pulteney.

Lit: H Avray Tipping, 1914, *Grinling Gibbons and the Woodwork of his Age*, p. 164.

ATHERTON, Charles (*fl.* mid-17th cent.). Plasterer.
Although he worked for Sir Robert Hooke, Atherton is presumably to be identified with the Serjeant Plumber, who did extensive work for the Office of Works.
Lit: Sir Robert Hooke, *Diary*, 1935 edn., p. 311; *Wren Soc*, XX (references cited).

AUDSLEY, David (*fl.* 1726–28). Plasterer.
Subscriber to Leoni, 1726, *Alberti*.
1728 WHITEHALL, PRIVY GARDEN, HOUSE OF THE COUNTESS OF MAR, LONDON
Received £14. 15s. 0d.
Lit: Scottish Record Office, GD124/16.No.47(1).

AUSTEN (AUSTIN), Cornelius (*fl.* late 17th cent.). Joiner, Carver.
Responsible for much fine work in Cambridge, Pembroke College Chapel, Emmanuel College, and Trinity College Library.
Lit: *Wren Soc*, V, pp. 28–29, 37–38, 41–44.

AUSTIN, John (*fl.* 1700–03). Joiner.
c 1700 ST CATHERINE'S COLLEGE, CAMBRIDGE
Carpentry in Chapel, which was dedicated 1 September 1704.
Lit: W H Aymer Vallance, 1947, *Greater English Church Screens*, p. 135.
1701–03 CHRIST'S COLLEGE, CAMBRIDGE
Received £639. 13s. 5d.
Lit: *C Life*, 2 May 1936.

AYLMER, Charles (*fl.* 1768). Painter.
1768 CROOME COURT, WORCESTERSHIRE
Lit: Croome Court Archives, Nos. 45–46 (microfilm, Victoria and Albert Museum, Dept of Furniture and Woodwork).

BACON, George (*fl.* 1779–89). Plasterer.
1779–89 OSTERLEY, MIDDLESEX
Retouching and general plastering.
Lit: Victoria and Albert Museum, Osterley Archives. (I am indebted to Dr Damie Stillman for this information.)

BAGNALL, John (*fl.* 1710–46). Plasterer.
Resident at York and Richmond (1746).
1712 (and after) CASTLE HOWARD, YORKSHIRE
Architect: Sir John Vanbrugh.
Plain plastering.
Lit: Castle Howard Archives, Building Books.
1726 TEMPLE NEWSAM HOUSE, LEEDS
Plain plastering £3. 4s. 0d.
Lit: Leeds Reference Library, EA 12/10, September 1726.
1731–34 ASSEMBLY ROOMS, YORK
Architect: Lord Burlington.
Entablature capitals and 'all the plaister work of the Great Room'. Paid £400, an extra £20 at the recommendation of Lord Burlington, and 4 guineas for doing festoons in the Great Room.
Lit: Minute Book, York Reference Library. Entries dated as follows: 22 January 1731; 18 January, 13 April, 23 June 1732; 22 January, 22 August 1733; 22 August, 29 August 1734. In 1746 Bagnall submitted an estimate for work at Minto House, Scotland.

Lit: National Library of Scotland, Minto Papers, Box 2. (I am indebted to Dr H M Colvin for this information.)

BAGUTTI, Giovanni (1681–after 1730). Stuccoist.
Born on 14 October 1681 at Rovio, near Lugano, Switzerland. Son of Bernard Bagutti and Angela Maria (*née* Falconi). He married Caterina Bagutti, presumably his cousin, on 22 March 1713. He was in England by 1709, but it is doubtful if he came from Italy with James Gibbs as sometimes suggested. He must be regarded as the senior partner to Giuseppe Artari, and Daniel Defoe called him 'the finest artist in those particular works now in England'. Subscribed to Leoni, 1726, *Alberti*, and to Gibbs, 1728, *B of A*.
His name occurs in a list of the family and other people assembled in the house of the Duke of Chandos at Canons, Middlesex, on New Year's Day 1722—'Mr Bagutti, his partner Mr Artree [Artari]'. Lord Chandos's 'smith', Walter Husbands, was also there to help and was probably employed on the metal frameworks for the stucco figures which are a feature of his work. Bagutti should not be confused with a painter Abbondio Bagutti, nor with Pietro Martire Bagutti of Bologna.
1710 CASTLE HOWARD, YORKSHIRE
Architect: Sir John Vanbrugh'
Bagutti did the stucco chimneypiece and facing scagliola niche in the Great Hall, assisted by Plura:
1710. Feb. 10 Mr. Bargotee, Italian, given him

Upon Acct. of work	25	0	0
June Pd Mr. Bargotee	20	0	0
Given Mr. Bargotee	10	15	0
Given Mr. Bargotee	10	15	0
Given Mr. Bargotee	10	0	0

Lit: Castle Howard MSS, Building Books.
Before 1720 CANONS, MIDDLESEX
Architects: John James and James Gibbs.
Chapel ceiling (surrounding Antonio Bellucci's paintings, some of which are now at Great Witley Church, Worcestershire (*see* pl. 77). Received £210. The chapel was dedicated in August 1720. In 1722 Bagutti was assisted at Canons by Artari.
Lit: Canons Inventory—'fretwork ceiling by Mr. Burgooty'; J Macky, 1722, *Journey through England*—'gilded by Pargotti'; Daniel Defoe, 1725, *Tour Through the Whole Island of Great Britain . . .*—'by Pargotti'; Baker, 1949, *Brydges*, p. 149; F J B Watson, 1954, *Arte Veneta*, p. 209.
1720 OCTAGON HOUSE, TWICKENHAM, MIDDLESEX
Architect: James Gibbs.
Bagutti assisted by Giuseppe Artari.
Lit: Gibbs, 1728, *B of A*, p. xix; *C Life*, XCVI, 15 September 1944.
1722–25 MEREWORTH CASTLE, KENT
Architect: Colen Campbell.
Lit: Colen Campbell, 1725, *Vitruvius Britannicus*, III, p. 3—'the ornaments are executed by Signor Bagutti, a most ingenious artist'; Hussey, 1965, *ECH: Early Georgian*, p. 58.
1722–26 ST MARTIN-IN-THE-FIELDS, LONDON
Architect: James Gibbs.
Received £419. 6s. Bagutti presumably divided the money with Artari, who is not mentioned in the accounts.

Lit: Gibbs, 1728, *B of A*, p. v—'the ceiling enrich'd with Fretwork by Signor Artari and Bagutti, the best Fretworkers that ever came into England'; John McMaster, 1916, *A Short History of the Royal Parish of St. Martin-in-the-Fields*; K A Esdaile, 1944, *St. Martin-in-the-Fields*.
1723–24 ST PETER'S, VERE STREET, LONDON
Formerly known as the Oxford or Marylebone Chapel.
Architect: James Gibbs.
Lit: Gibbs, 1728, *B of A*, p. vii—'the ceiling is handsomely adorned with Fret-work by Signori Artari and Bagutti'.
1725–26 SENATE HOUSE, CAMBRIDGE
Architect: James Gibbs.
Bagutti assisted by Giuseppe Artari.
Plain plasterwork by Isaac Mansfield (q.v.). Bagutti received £310. The ceiling fell in 1898–1900 and was replaced with a replica (information from Mr Robert Taylor, RCHM, Cambridge).
Lit: University Registry, XLVI, 5 October 1725; Vice-Chancellor's Receipts, 31 March 1726: 'Receiv'd then of the Reverend Dr Davies Vice-chancellr of the University of Cambridge one hundred and fifty pounds in part for the ornaments of the ceiling of the New Senate House by me John Bagutti'. Similar receipt on 8 September 1726 for the balance of £160. Willis and Clark, 1887, *Cambridge*, III, p. 47; Little, 1955, *Gibbs*, p. 61. An alternative design by Bagutti is in the Ashmolean Museum, Oxford, Gibbs Collection, II, 63–64.
1730–31 MOULSHAM HALL, ESSEX
Architect: Giacomo Leoni.
Lit: Mildmay Account Books, Hampshire CRO (15M50/31); Mildmay Account Books, Essex CRO (D/DMA5–7). The Hampshire entries read:
'1730. Decr. 7. Pd. Mr. Bagutti, the Italian stuccatori for work by agreemt. he and Mr. Altari did at Moulsham Hall for wch. [he] is to have £150 having pd. him before. £10.10.0. Pd. this day £100.0.0. . . . £100.0.0.
1731. Febry. 13th, having [paid] Mr. Bagutti the Italian stuccatori for his work done in my Hall and dining room at Moulsham—

	£115	15	0
I have this day also pd. him	45	13	0
Wch in the whole amts to	£161	8	0

in full for all the work Mr. Altari and he have done for me to this day, my agreemt. was only with Mr. Bagutti & Mr. Altari who did the Bustos & Figures assisted him.'
c 1732 MOOR PARK, HERTFORDSHIRE
Lit: Drawing in the Ashmolean Museum, Oxford, Gibbs Collection, IV, 24; *Burl Mag*, November 1971, p. 659. This drawing for the four walls and cove of a minor room at Down Hall or Stowe is inscribed 'For Mr. Baguti att More Parke near Rikmonsworth in Hertfordshire'. This suggests that Bagutti did work at Moor Park and was responsible for the plasterwork surrounding the paintings by Francesco Sleter. Sir Edward Gascoigne visited the house in the early 1730s and noted work there by Giovanni and Giuseppe Artari (q.v.).
Date uncertain
CASSIOBURY PARK, HERTFORDSHIRE
Horace Walpole, 1797, *Anecdotes of Painting*, III, p. 397; Vertue, IV, p. 7 (*The Walpole*

Society, XXIV, 1935)—'a ceiling for Lord Essex representing Flora and other figures and boys in alto-relievo by Bagotti'.
Attributed works
1724 THE MYNDE, NEAR HEREFORD
The 1st Duke of Chandos acquired this house in 1715. He did some building there in 1724, hoping to go into residence the following year. However, by 1726 he was negotiating its sale. There is good plasterwork attributable to Bagutti and Artari.
Lit: Baker, 1949, *Brydges*, p. 272, fn.
1731–35 CLANDON PARK, SURREY
Architect: Giacomo Leoni.
The architect of Clandon, Leoni, engaged Bagutti and Artari to work at Moulsham Hall, Essex, in 1730–31, and it seems very likely that the Clandon work is due to them, the figurework being by Artari. A comparison of the Moor Park ceilings, which are thought to be Bagutti's work, with those at Clandon supports this attribution.
Lit: Geoffrey Beard, October 1956, *Connoisseur*, CXXXVIII, No. 556.

BAKER, Thomas (*fl.* 1775). Plasterer.
Mentioned in Sketchley's 1775 Bristol Directory as a 'tiler and plasterer'.

BALSHAW, John (*fl.* 1712–33). Joiner.
1712–24 ST ANNE, LIMEHOUSE, LONDON
Architect: Nicholas Hawksmoor.
Lit: Colvin, 1950, *Arch Rev*, p. 196; Lambeth Palace Library, MS, 2703.
1727–33 ST LUKE, OLD STREET, LONDON
Lit: ibid., p. 196; MS, 2703.
1728–33 ST JOHN, HORSLEYDOWN, LONDON
Lit: ibid., p. 196; MS, 2703.

BANCKES (BANKES, BANKS), Matthew (*fl.* 1683–1706). Master Carpenter.
Master Carpenter to the Crown 1683 until his death in 1706. Master of the Carpenters' Company in 1698. Worked at six Wren City churches and in 1700 at Winslow Hall, Bucks. His estimate for making a 130-ft promenade for the Duke of Beaufort at his Chelsea house (BL, Sloane MS, 4066 f. 260) supports the entries in the Beaufort bank account (Child's Bank) for his work at Badminton.
Lit: *Wren Soc*, XVII, pp. 67–80; Colvin, 1976, *King's Works*, V, pp. 315, 478.

BARKER, Robert (*fl.* 1694–1719). Master Carpenter.
Master Carpenter, Office of Works, 9 September 1718 until his dismissal, November 1719.
1694 UNIVERSITY COLLEGE, OXFORD
Constructed the screen in oak in the Corinthian order. Finished by 1694.
Lit: Colvin, 1954, *Dictionary*, citing College Records, Box JJ fasc. No. 2a; Aymer Vallance, 1947, *Greater English Church Screens*, p. 166, fig. 136; *C Life*, 6 February 1937; *Wren Soc*, VII, pp. 190–91, 204, 220, XIX, p. 36; Colvin, 1976, *King's Works*, V, pp. 59, 392–96, 72.

BARLOW, William (*fl.* 1740–54). Carver.
1745–46 44 BERKELEY SQUARE, LONDON
Architect: William Kent.
Received £53. 14s. 0d.
Lit: Accounts, Sir John Soane's Museum,

London; M Jourdain, 1948, *The Work of William Kent*, pp. 88–89.
1749 ARLINGTON STREET, LONDON
Architect: William Kent.
Mr Pelham's house. Received £109 for carving in the Great Room in 1749. Worked with James Richards. Received £27. 16s. 6d., and also worked for Pelham at his 'new buildings next the Park'. His detailed bill includes:
Egg and tongue to Door Cornices at 6d. p. ft.
3 leaved grass at 2d., 5 leaves at 1d.
5 leaved grass on doors, shutters at 5d.
Friezes with Foliages, Festoons, Shells & Flowers at 48s. ea.
Flowers between modillions, 2½ in. dia. 1/10 ea.
Corinthian modillions 5 inch long at 2/6 ea.
Semi octagon pannels on Shutts with foliages, shells, etc. at 6s.
Sofitt Panells with Festoons, Foliages &c., at 20s.
Long pannels on Shuttes with vases, foliages, festoons, flowers &c. at 34s. ea.
Lit: RIBA Library, MS, 728.3 (42.13A).

BARNES, James (*fl.* 1775). Plasterer.
Mentioned in Sketchley's 1775 Bristol Directory as a 'tiler and plasterer'.

BARTOLI, Domenico and **Giuseppe** (*fl. c* 1765–94). Scagliola workers.
Worked for RA at 20 St James's Square, London (received £33), and for James Wyatt at Castlecoole, Ireland. Combined as 'Bartoli and Richter' at Kedleston. In 1783 Domenico wrote to Sir William Chambers to thank him for help while in London. However, a bill for work, 1791–94, at 15 St James's Square implies he returned to England.
Lit: NLW, Wynnstay MS, 115/7; Beard, 1966, *Craftsmen*, p. 173; Beard, 1975, *Adam*, p. 77; *C Life*, 26 January 1978, p. 197; RIBA Library MS, Cha 2/105; 1960, *Survey of London*, XXIX, p. 148; Packington Hall, Warwicks., Account Book, 1785–91.

BATES, W (*fl.* 1710). Plasterer.
1710 ST PAUL'S CATHEDRAL, LONDON
Worked under Chrysostom Wilkins.
Lit: *Wren Soc*, XV, p. 196.

BATTERSBY, Francis, and Company.
Masons.
1775/76 KEDLESTON HALL, DERBYSHIRE
Hall. Fluted and polished columns under supervision of Joseph Pickford, *c* 1736–1782, the Derby architect.
Received £180.
Lit: Beard, 1966, *Craftsmen*, p. 80; *C Life*, 9 November 1972, p. 206.

BAXTER, Francis (*fl.* 1721). Joiner.
1721 CHICHELEY HALL, BUCKINGHAMSHIRE
Architect: Francis Smith.
Staircase (oak inlaid with walnut).
Lit: Joan D Tanner, 1961, 'The Building of Chicheley Hall', *Records of Bucks*, XVII, Part I; James Lees-Milne, 1970, *English Country Houses, Baroque*, pl. 368.

BAXTER, John (*fl.* 1689). Plasterer.
1689 HAMPTON COURT, MIDDLESEX
Worked under John Grove (q.v.).
Lit: PRO, Works, 5/55, May 1689.

A John Bayley worked on plain plastering at Ditchley, Oxfordshire, in 1769 (Oxford CRO, MS, Dil/I/p/3r). With Joseph Bayley, John acted as principal plasterer to Sir John Soane. His bust is in the Soane Museum together with some of his models of Soane buildings. He worked for Soane at Wotton House, Aylesbury, Bucks. (1821–23) and in 1818–19 at 3 St James's Square, London.
Lit: *C Life*, 15 July 1949; 1969, *Architectural History*, 12, p. 25; 1960, *Survey of London*, XXIX, p. 96 fn.

BAYLY, Abraham (*fl.* 1775). Plasterer.
Mentioned in Sketchley's 1775 Bristol Directory as a 'tiler and plasterer'.

BAYLY, William (1817–20). Carver.
1817–20 PAVILION, BRIGHTON
Lit: RIBA, Library, MS, NAS/1.f.29.

BEALE, – (*fl.* 1721). Joiner.
1721 CHICHELEY HALL, BUCKINGHAMSHIRE
Staircase: assisted Thomas Baxter and Mr Illison.
Lit: Joan D Tanner, 1961, 'The Building of Chicheley Hall', *Record of Bucks.*, XVIII, Part I.

BEALE, Henry (*fl.* 1716–17). Plasterer.
Official of the Worshipful Company of Plaisterers.
1716 Upper Warden.
1717 Master.
Lit: London, Guildhall Library, MS, 6122/3.

BEDDINGTON, Edward (*fl.* 1775). Plasterer.
Mentioned in Sketchley's 1775 Bristol Directory as a 'tiler and plasterer'.

BEDSON, Thomas (*fl.* 1765–66). Carpenter.
1765/66 KEDLESTON, DERBYSHIRE
Music Room. Organ case.
Worked for 71¼ days.
Lit: Kedleston Archives, Vouchers No. 14.

BEDWELL, Charles (*fl.* 1690). Plasterer.
1690 KENSINGTON PALACE, LONDON
Worked under Henry Margetts (q.v.).
Lit: PRO, Works, 19, 48/I.f.108.

BEDWELL, Francis (*fl.* 1731–38).
Locksmith.
1731–32 ROYAL BARGE (for Frederick Prince of Wales)
Provided springs, gilt wood screws, hinges, locks, keys, knobs, etc.
Worked also at Kew in 1738.
Lit: Duchy of Cornwall, Vouchers 11, 1731–32, p. 264, XX, 1738; (cited by Geoffrey Beard, August 1970, *Burl Mag*, CXII, No. 809, p. 495).

BENNETT, Richard (*fl.* 1660). Plasterer.
1660 THE TOWER, LONDON
Worked under John Grove I.
Lit: PRO, Works, 5/1, 16 November 1660.

BENT, William (*fl.* 1767–*c* 1806).
Ironmonger.
Of St Martin's Lane, London.

1767 NOSTELL PRIORY, YORKSHIRE
Door furniture.
Lit: Goodison, 1974, *Ormolu*, p. 188, fn. 16.
1773 20 ST JAMES'S SQUARE, LONDON
Lit: NLW, Wynnstay MS, 115/17/1.
1781 GREENWICH HOSPITAL, CHAPEL
Lit: RIBA Library, MS, New/1.

BERMINGHAM, Nathaniel (*fl.* 1763–66).
Herald Painter, (?) Worker in Metal.
It is tempting to associate Bermingham with
the craftsman who provided gilt enrichments
at Syon House. In 1763 Bermingham is noted
in Mortimer's 'London Directory' as:
'Herald Painter, and improver of a curious art
of cutting out Portraits and Coats of Arms in
vellum with the point of a penknife: several
specimens of this, his peculiar talent, may be
seen at his house, the corner of Great Queen
Street, opposite Long Acre.'
The metal enrichment on the Red Drawing
Room door at Syon (*see* pl. 57) could well have
been designed by such a skilled artist. One
noted as 'Mr. Briming[e]ham' and 'Mr.
Bermeingham' was paid for the gilt ornament
on doors, and for window shutter knobs, etc.
He was also paid £10 by Mr Butler, the Duke
of Northumberland's agent, when arrested in
September 1766.
Lit: Mortimer, 1763, p. 5; Beard, 1966,
Craftsmen, p. 81, citing Alnwick Castle MSS,
U.I.44 and U.I.46; Beard, 1978, *Adam*, col.
pl. 10.

BERNASCONI, Bernato (*fl.* 1770–1820?).
Plasterer.
Presumably of the family of stuccoists of this
name who settled at Riva St Vitale, birthplace
of Vassalli (q.v.) near Lugano. C R Cockerell
told the *Select Committee on Arts and their
connection with Manufactures* (27 July 1835–
13 August 1836) on 28 August 1835, that 'a
few artists still survived in Ireland and there
remained in England a Mr. Bernasconi till
1820 . . .' (I am indebted to Mr Edward
Croft-Murray for this reference). There is a
will (1786) of a Bartholomew Bernasconi filed
in PCC (Public Record Office).
1770–84 CLAYDON, BUCKINGHAMSHIRE
Plasterwork in Hall and Ballroom. Money
became short, and in 1782 Bernasconi
complained of the accommodation provided
for him—a cottage in East Claydon—and
noted he was 'a poor man with a large fameley
in the town of Buckingham'.
Lit: *C Life*, 7 November 1952, pp. 1483–84;
Gunnis, 1953, *Dictionary*, p. 51.
c 1790 NEW COLLEGE CHAPEL, OXFORD
Vault, Organ Screen and Stalls.
Lit: *C Life*, 19 April 1979, p. 1189.

BERNASCONI, Francis (1762–1841).
Plasterer.
Said to have been the son of Bartholomew
Bernasconi (d.1786). As well as being 'the
most fashionable purveyor of Regency Gothic
stucco', Francis was largely employed on
scagliola work, and there is no doubt that the
following list only represents a fraction of his
work. He was admitted a Freeman of the
Worshipful Company of Plaisterers on 9
November 1805.
Lit: Hussey, 1958, *ECH: Late Georgian*,
p. 25; London, Guildhall Library, MS, 6125.

1800–9 COBHAM HALL, KENT
Received £1556 for plasterwork, Gothic
mouldings, etc.
Lit: Earl of Darnley's Archives; Gunnis,
1953, *Dictionary*, p. 51.
1803 WESTMINSTER ABBEY, LONDON
Received £826 for plasterwork in the Great
Tower.
Lit: Westminster Abbey Archives; Gunnis,
1953, *Dictionary*, p. 51.
1803 SHUGBOROUGH, STAFFORDSHIRE
Work in Saloon.
Lit: Hussey, 1956, *ECH: Mid Georgian*,
p. 85.
1803–05 YORK MINSTER
Work in south transept: stucco birds, finial on
canopy of Archbishop de Grey monument.
Lit: York Minster Library, Fabric Rolls and
Bills, E3, E4a.
1804 CARLTON HOUSE, LONDON
Lit: PRO, Works, 5/94, cited in Crook and
Port, 1974, *King's Works*, VI, p. 313.
1805 WINDSOR CASTLE
Architect: Sir Jeffry Wyatville.
Gothic compo mouldings, enriched spandrels,
etc.
Lit: PRO, Works, 5/93; Gunnis, 1953,
Dictionary, p. 51; W St John Hope, 1913,
Windsor Castle, pp. 350, 352, 366–67, 369,
557.
He also worked there in 1824.
1805 SHUGBOROUGH, STAFFORDSHIRE
Supplied 12 capitals to scagliola columns
worked by Joseph Alcott (q.v.).
Lit: *C Life*, 11 March 1954, p. 678.
1806 COMPTON PLACE, EASTBOURNE, SUSSEX
Outside compo, stucco, colouring and inside
works.
Received £1754 18s. 5¾d.
Lit: Compton Place Archives, Box Q.
1807 GROSVENOR HOUSE, LONDON
Received £2097 for plasterwork.
Lit: Grosvenor Archives, Eaton Hall,
Cheshire. (I am indebted to the late Mr
Rupert Gunnis for this reference.)
c 1810 DODINGTON PARK, GLOUCESTERSHIRE
Architect: James Wyatt.
Lit: *C Life*, 29 November 1956, p. 1232.
1810–11 LOWTHER CASTLE, CUMBERLAND
Architect: Sir Robert Smirke; house survives
as a ruin.
Received £6190.
Lit: Cumbria CRO, Lowther Archives,
D/Lons/L, Accounts, 629.
c 1810 LONGLEAT, WILTSHIRE
Architect: Sir Jeffry Wyatville. Bernasconi
was then resident at Alfred Place, Bedford
Square, London.
Lit: D Linstrum, 1972, *Sir Jeffry Wyatville*,
p. 245.
1811 BADMINTON, GLOUCESTERSHIRE
Library.
I am indebted to Dr H M Colvin for this
reference.
c 1812 EATON HALL, CHESHIRE
Architect: William Porden.
Lit: *C Life*, 18 February 1971, p. 361.
1813–15 ASHRIDGE PARK, HERTFORDSHIRE
Received £879.
Lit: Brownlow Archives, Belton; Gunnis,
1953, *Dictionary*, p. 51.
1813–19 ASHBURNHAM PLACE, SUSSEX
Worked under George Dance and S W
Reynolds, and refaced the house in stucco.

Bernasconi was still living at Alfred Place,
Bedford Square, London.
Lit: East Sussex CRO, Ashburnham
Archives, 2809, 2847–48; *C Life*, 30 April
1953, p. 1336.
1814–15 CAXTON HALL, NORTHAMPTONSHIRE
Cornices, etc.
Lit: Information from Mr Robert Taylor,
RCHM, Cambridge.
1816 EASTNOR CASTLE, HEREFORDSHIRE
Architect: Sir Robert Smirke.
Received £961. 16s. 8d.
Lit: Eastnor Castle Archives, Building Books,
1812–20.
1816 CHICKSANDS PRIORY, BEDFORDSHIRE
Lit: Hussey, 1958, *ECH: Late Georgian*,
p. 25.
1819–21 GARNONS, HEREFORDSHIRE
Lit: Herefordshire CRO, Cotterell Archives.
1820– CHATSWORTH, DERBYSHIRE
Extensive work, including Cabinet Library as
late as 1830.
Lit: Linstrum, *Wyatville*, pp. 141–62.
1822 BLITHFIELD, STAFFORDSHIRE
The Great Hall in Gothic style, of which the
patron Lord Bagot said that it was 'as perfect
a specimen . . . as has ever been executed in
modern times'. Bernasconi was at work at
Blithfield for most of the first quarter of the
nineteenth century.
Lit: *C Life*, 4 November 1954, p. 1577;
Staffordshire CRO, Dyott Archives.
c 1824 LILLESHALL HALL, SHROPSHIRE
Received £1456. 5s. 10d.
Lit: Linstrum, *Wyatville*, p. 240.
1827 69–70 ST JAMES'S STREET, LONDON
Architect: Thomas Hopper.
Lit: 1960, *Survey of London*, XXIX, p. 477.
1827–28 STAFFORD HOUSE, LONDON
Received £6696.
Lit: 1967, *Architectural History*, X; *C Life*, 14
November 1968.
1833 KENSINGTON PALACE
As 'Bernasconi & Son'.
Lit: Linstrum, *Wyatville*, p. 242.
1833 ST JAMES'S SQUARE, LONDON
House for Earl de Grey.
Lit: *C Life*, 2 July 1970, p. 20.
1839 CADLAND HOUSE, HAMPSHIRE
dest. 1950.
Architects: Henry Holland, 1775; enlarged,
Sir Jeffry Wyatville, 1837.
Drawing Room.
Lit: Plan dated 15 April 1839, endorsed 'The
ornaments for this ceiling are now being
modelled in London by Mr. Bernasconi' in
Drummond Archives, Cadland Manor. (I am
indebted to Mrs C M Ellis for this reference.)
Other work
A design by Thomas Stothard (1755–1834) for
Bernasconi's work at Buckingham Palace is
reproduced by A P Oppé, 1950, *English
Drawings at Windsor*, p. 93. He is also known
to have worked in Wales, and in Scotland,
c 1810, at Taymouth Castle, Perthshire. He
probably did the work at Penrhyn Castle,
Caernarvonshire.
Lit: Hussey, 1958, *ECH: Late Georgian*,
p. 191.
He may also have done the French-style work
at Wrest Park, Bedfordshire.
Lit: *C Life*, 2 July 1970, p. 20.

BERRILL, Jeremiah (*fl.* 1668–69). Plasterer.

1668 WHITEHALL PALACE, LONDON
Worked under John Grove I.
Lit: PRO, Works 5/12.

BEST, George (*fl.* 1715). Carpenter.
c 1715 SIR CHARLES HOTHAM'S HOUSE,
BEVERLEY
Architect: Colen Campbell.
Lit: East Riding of Yorkshire, 1956–58,
Georgian Society, Transactions, p. 42.

BETLEY, Arthur (*fl.* 1745). Plasterer.
c 1745 COPPED HALL, ESSEX
Dest 1917.
Lit: Essex CRO, Copped Hall Archives, 'An
Estimate of Plaisters Work proposed to be
done for Esqr Conyers by Order of Mr
Sanderson Encluding Labour only by Arthur
Betley', no date.

BETSON, Thomas (*fl.* 1730–51). Plasterer.
Mentioned in Henry Flitcroft's bank account
(Drummonds) from 1744. His will (23 April
1751) describes him as of Cambridge St, St
James's, Westminster (PRO, Prob 11/787,
f. 255). His brother, John, was left the
'Utensils belonging to my Business', so may
have been a builder or plasterer.
1730–33 COMPTON PLACE, EASTBOURNE,
SUSSEX
Various works other than the decorative
plasterwork.
Lit: Compton Place Estate Office (Box P,
File 2, 6 July 1730; Lord Wilmington's
account book, 1 August 1733).
1745 WIMPOLE HALL, CAMBRIDGESHIRE
Received £56. 11s. 6d. Decorative plasterwork
by Giuseppe Artari.
Lit: BL Add. MS, 36228, f. 190.
1749 WIMPOLE CHURCH
Architect: Henry Flitcroft.
Received £4. 13s. 7d.
Lit: BL Add. MS, 35679, f. 54.

BETTINGTON, Joseph (*fl.* 1775). Plasterer.
Mentioned in Sketchley's 1775 Bristol
Directory as a 'tiler and plasterer'.

BEVAN, Richard (*fl.* 1789). Painter.
1789 WARWICK CASTLE
King's Room ceiling, '4 times over pickt in
French Grey, dead white ornaments'.
Received £10. 5s. 0d.
Also '9 Thousand of Gold for the ceilings
used at £8 per thou'.
Received £72.
Lit: Warwicks. CRO, Warwick Castle
Vouchers, 1789, No. 147.

BEVER, – (*fl.* 1770–83). Plasterer.
1770 THE REPOSITORY, ST MARTIN'S LANE,
LONDON
Various works. His clerk was Charles Clarke
(q.v.).
Lit: Charles Clarke, 1783, *The Plaisterer's Bill
for Works done at the New Building, Somerset
House . . .*

BIRCH, John (*fl.* 1720). Plasterer.
1720 PURLEY HALL, BERKSHIRE
Received £1. 6s. 0d. for plain work at the
house of Francis Hawes.

Lit: 1721, *The Particulars and Inventories of
the Late Directors of the South Sea Company,* 2.

BLACKLEY, S (*fl.* 1708–10). Plasterer.
1708–10 ST PAUL'S CATHEDRAL, LONDON
Worked under Chrysostom Wilkins (q.v.).
Lit: Wren Soc, XV, pp. 169 and 196.

BLAKESLEY, Robert (*fl.* 1772–84). Carver.
Of Micklegate, York. In 1772 he dissolved his
partnership with James Officer. In 1776 he
took up his Freedom.
1784 WENTWORTH WOODHOUSE, YORKSHIRE
Gilding. Worked under John Carr, who said
that Blakesley would do the gilding 'as well as
any man in this County'.
Lit: R B Wragg, 1955–56, *York Georgian
Society, Report,* p. 61.

BLINCOE, Christopher (*fl.* 1719–20).
Plasterer.
1719–20 CARSHALTON, SURREY
Received £39 for work at the house of Sir
John Fellowes.
Lit: 1721, *The Particulars and Inventories of
the Late Directors of the South Sea Company,*
I, p. 10.

BLINCOE, John (*fl.* 1719–20). Plasterer.
1719–20 CARSHALTON, SURREY
Assisted Christopher Blincoe (q.v.).
1720 WIMBLEDON, SURREY
Received £40 for work at the house of Sir
Theodore Janssen, Bt.
Lit: 1721, *The Particulars and Inventories of
the Late Directors of the South Sea Company,*
I, p. 10.

BLOCKLEY, Thomas (1705–89).
Locksmith.
Of Birmingham. Appears in the Birmingham
Directories as follows:
1767 Locksmith and Grate-maker, Bull Street.
1770 Locksmith and Grate-maker, 61 Bull
Street.
1775 Locksmith and engine turner, 65 Bull
Street (this entry for Richard Blockley.
Thomas listed at 61 Bull St.)
1777 Blockley, Richard, Locksmith, 65 Bull
Street.
1777 Blockley, Thomas, Locksmith, 61 Bull
Street.
1780–88 Blockley, Thomas, Locksmith, 61
Bull Street.
Aris's Birmingham Gazette, 5 January 1789,
recorded his death: 'Last week in the 84th
year of his age Mr. Blockley of this town and
one of the first locksmiths in the Kingdom.
Till within a few days of his death he followed
his occupation with all the vigour & spirit of a
young man.'
1734–39 LAMPORT, NORTHAMPTONSHIRE
Lit: Northants. CRO, I.L. 3966, 4208, 4212.
1746 KIRTLINGTON, OXFORDSHIRE
Architect: William Smith.
Received £40 (22 December 1746).
Lit: Hoare's Bank, Dashwood account.
1750 RADCLIFFE CAMERA, OXFORD
Architect: James Gibbs.
Locks, hinges, etc. Received £49. 9s. 6d.
Lit: S G Gillam, 1958, *Building Accounts of
the Radcliffe Camera* (Oxford Hist. Soc.),
pp. 86–87.
1753–60 PRESTON-ON-STOUR, WARWICKSHIRE

Lit: Warwicks. CRO, West Archives, Box 34. **247**
1760 CROOME COURT, WORCESTERSHIRE
Door furniture, etc.
Lit: Croome Court Archives, Nos. 20, 47
(microfilm, Victoria and Albert Museum,
Dept of Furniture and Woodwork).
1761 HOLKHAM HALL, NORFOLK
Locks, bolts, hinges, screws. Received
£110. 5s. 0d.
Lit: Holkham Archives, Building Accounts,
27.
c 1763 SHARDELOES, BUCKINGHAMSHIRE
Architect: RA
Brass Bolts, 10s. ea; door furniture.
Lit: Bucks. CRO, Shardeloes Archives,
TD 17/2.
1763 EGREMONT HOUSE, LONDON
Lit: West Sussex CRO, Petworth II. 6614.
c 1766 20 ST JAMES'S SQUARE, LONDON
Architect: RA
Locks, door furniture, etc.
Lit: NLW, Wynnstay MSS, 115/17/5: 1721.
1773 HAREWOOD HOUSE, YORKSHIRE
Door furniture. Installed by his man 'Mr
Walls', who attended about 90 days to fit
locks, clean and lacquer door-plates, etc.
Lit: Mary Mauchline, 1974, *Harewood House,*
pp. 92, 107.

BLOUNT, – (*fl.* 1688–89). Plasterer.
1688–89 ST SEPULCHRE'S, HOLBORN, LONDON
'To be employed for performing the
Plasterer's work for the Church and Vestry.'
Lit: Wren Soc, XIX, p. 51, citing the Vestry
Minutes (London, Guildhall Library), 2
March 1689.

BODETT, Mr – (*fl.* 1673). Carver.
1673 BADMINTON, GLOUCESTERSHIRE
Received £15 on 19 August.
Lit: Child's Bank, 1st Marquess of
Worcester's account.

BOSON, John (*fl.* 1727–43). Carver.
With his partner John How, he did all the
carved woodwork on the façade of East India
House, Leadenhall Street, London, and
provided chimneypieces. Boson is, however,
better known for the work he did at Kew for
William Kent on behalf of Frederick, Prince
of Wales, and for carving in wood and stone at
several London churches. He also worked
(1725) at 4 St James's Square, London. Boson
subscribed to Leoni's edition of *Alberti* (1726)
and died at Savile Street, Westminster, April
1743.
Lit: Duchy of Cornwall, Vouchers LX(1),
p. 121, IV, p. 238; 1960, *Survey of London,*
XXIX, p. 90; Will in PCC.

BOYLE, James (*fl.* 1763). Carver and Gilder.
At the Golden Eagle in Great Pulteney Street.
Carved in the Italian, French, Gothic and
Chinese tastes.
Lit: A Heal, 1953, *The London Furniture
Makers, 1660–1840,* plate, p. 11; Mortimer,
1763.

BOYSE, William (*fl.* 1723–24). Plasterer.
1723–24 NEWBY PARK, YORKSHIRE
Architect: Colen Campbell.
Lit: Leeds Reference Library, Vyner letters,
13595. (I am indebted to Dr L O J Boynton
for this reference.)

BRADBURY, Robert (*fl.* 1675–76).
Plasterer.
1675–76 SUDBURY HALL, DERBYSHIRE
Worked with James Pettifer (q.v.) and charged
at the rate of 6s. a yard. Six ceilings: Drawing
Room, Parlour, Staircase Hall, Staircase
Landing, Queen's Bedroom, Long Gallery.
Payments of £64 (Staircase and Parlour) in
1675 and £101 in 1676; all payments were
made to Bradbury.
Lit: Vernon Archives, cited in *C Life*, 22–29
June 1935, 10 June 1971; *The Connoisseur
Yearbook*, 1953.

BRAMAH, Joseph (1748–1814). Inventor.
The inventor of many devices, including a
flushing lavatory (patented 1778) and a
hydraulic press (1795).
Wrote 1787, *A Dissertation on the Construction
of Locks*. His own lock had the reputation of
being unpickable, but this was accomplished
at the Great Exhibition, 1851, and Bramah
lost the £200 he had offered to anyone who
could do so.
Lit: Dictionary of National Biography, II,
p. 110; Mark Girouard, 1978, *Life in the
English Country House*, p. 265.

BRANDIS, John (*fl.* 1680). Glazier.
1680 14 ST JAMES'S SQUARE, LONDON
Lit: 1960, *Survey of London*, XXIX, p. 139.

BRASSE, John (*fl* 1663). Joiner.
Of Durham.
1663 BISHOP AUCKLAND, DURHAM
Chapel, Screen. Paid 40s. for each linear yard
of work, 11 ft high.
Assisted by Abraham Smith, carpenter.
Lit: 1872, 'Correspondence of John Cosin,
Bishop of Durham', *Surtees Soc.*, 55,
pp. 369–70.

BRETON, Luc-François (1731–1800).
Sculptor.
1762 SYON, MIDDLESEX
Dining Room. Relief of the Three Graces.
Lit: Scottish Record Office, Clerk of Penicuik
MS, No. 4929, letter from James Adam to his
sister Helen, 7 March 1762.

BRICE, Robert (*fl.* 1660). Plasterer.
1660 THE TOWER, LONDON
Worked under John Grove I.
Lit: PRO, Works, 5/1 November 1660.

BROCKWAY, R (*fl.* 1639–47). Plasterer.
c 1639 EAST KNOYLE CHURCH, WILTSHIRE
He deposed in 1647 that in the chancel of East
Knoyle Church he had put up for the Rev
Christopher Wren pictures 'in frett work' of
Evangelists, the Ascension, the Trinity and
Jacob's Ladder.
Lit: A G Matthews, 1948, *Walker Revised*, p.
382. (I am indebted to Dr H M Colvin for
this reference.)

BROMFIELD, Joseph (*fl.* 1771–95).
Plasterer.
Of Shrewsbury. Subscribed to George
Richardson, 1776, *A Book of Ceilings composed
in the Style of the Antique Grotesque*. He also
worked as a builder and architect.
1771 WYNNSTAY, DENBIGHSHIRE
Theatre in grounds.

Lit: C Life, 6 April 1972, p. 851.
1782 HARTLEBURY CASTLE, WORCESTERSHIRE
Library ceiling, and the ceiling and walls of
the Saloon.
Lit: E H Pearce, 1926, *Hartlebury Castle*,
p. 287.
1784 OAKLY PARK, SHROPSHIRE
Lit: Hussey, 1958, *ECH: Late Georgian*,
p. 153.
1794 ST ALKMUND'S CHURCH, SHREWSBURY
Lit: D H S Cranage, 1901, . . . *Churches of
Shropshire*, 2, p. 895, citing *The Shrewsbury
Chronicle*, 7 November 1794 and 30 October
1795.
Attributed work
c 1790 LION INN, SHREWSBURY
Assembly Room at rear.
Lit: Sacheverell Sitwell, 1945, *British
Architects and Craftsmen*, pp. 172–73, pl. 177.

BROMWICH, Thomas (*fl.* 1740–87). Paper-
stainer/Paper-hanger.
Flourished as a linen draper and upholsterer,
1740–48, 'At the Golden Lyon', Ludgate Hill,
London. From *c* 1758–76 as 'Thomas
Bromwich & Leonard Leigh, Paper-Stainers',
and 1777–84 as 'Bromwich, Isherwood &
Bradley, Paper-hangers, 35 Ludgate Hill'. In
1763 appointed 'Paper Hanging Maker to the
Royal Wardrobe'. Bromwich's name is that
most often encountered as supplying and
hanging wallpaper to the order of many
patrons and architects, particularly Horace
Walpole.
Lit: E A Entwisle, October 1952, *The
Connoisseur*; Beard, 1966, *Craftsmen*, p. 174;
Mortimer, 1763, p. 54; West Sussex CRO,
Petworth MS II, 6615; Paget Toynbee ed.,
1927, *Strawberry Hill Accounts*, pp. 66–68. He
is also mentioned in Henry Flitcroft's bank
account for 1744 (Drummonds).
1765 ALSCOT PARK, WARWICKSHIRE
Dining Room ceiling. Ornamenting with 'rich
Gothick Papier-Mâché'. Received £54. 12s.
Similar work in Dining Room, £21.
Lit: Warwicks. CRO, West MSS, Box 42(7).
1773 CORSHAM COURT, WILTSHIRE
Gallery. Crimson flock paper. Received £144.
Lit: Hussey, 1965, *ECH: Early Georgian*,
p. 233.
1781 CROOME COURT, WORCESTERSHIRE
Lit: Croome Court Archives, No. 59
(microfilm, Victoria and Albert Museum,
Dept of Furniture and Woodwork).

BROWN, John (*fl.* 1774). Gilder.
1774 HAREWOOD HOUSE, YORKSHIRE
Window-shutter ornaments and handles.
Possibly the carver of the organ case at
Kedleston, Derbyshire, 1766.
Lit: Kedleston MS, Vouchers No. 14; Mary
Mauchline, 1974, *Harewood House*, p. 93.

BROWN, William (*fl.* 1755). Plasterer.
c 1755 POWDERHAM CASTLE, DEVON
Staircase (assisted John Jenkins). His
signature on a mould used at the Castle. The
moulds were sold several years ago by B T
Batsford Ltd, the London publishers—
present whereabouts unknown.

BROWNE, Joseph (*fl.* 1814–20). Scagliola-
and Marble-worker.
Worked for John Nash from his works in

Carmarthen Street, London.
Lit: RIBA, Library, MS, NAS/1, f. 209.

BROWNE, Thomas (*fl.* 1562–70). Plasterer.
Attributed work
1562–70 LOSELEY, SURREY
The Loseley Archives contain a petition from
Browne (NRA list 9475) which might indicate
he was employed at the house.
Lit: C Life, 9 October 1969, p. 894.

BROWNRIG, G (*fl.* 1710). Plasterer.
1710 ST PAUL'S CATHEDRAL, LONDON
Worked under Chrysostom Wilkins (q.v.).
Lit: Wren Soc, XV, p. 196.

BRUNIAS, Agostino (*fl.* 1754–85).
Draughtsman.
Employed by RA in Italy and encouraged to
come to England. There are five paintings by
him in distemper at Kedleston.
Lit: Fleming, 1962, *Adam*, p. 360; Stillman,
1966, *Adam*, p. 54; *C Life*, 26 January 1978.

BUCHAN, Robert (*fl.* 1795). Plasterer.
1795 INVERARAY CASTLE, ARGYLLSHIRE
Received £18. 1s. 11½d.
Lit: Inveraray Archives, Chamberlain's
Accounts, 1795. (I am indebted to Miss Mary
Cosh for this information.)

BUCK and SWAN (*fl.* 1768). Mercers.
1768 LANSDOWNE HOUSE, LONDON
Provided furniture upholstery silk for Lord
Shelburne's house.
Lit: Bolton, 1922, *Adam*, p. 8.

BUMPSTEAD, John (*fl.* late 17th cent.).
Carver.
Worked at the Mathematical School, Christ's
Hospital, and valued carving at St Stephen,
Walbrook, London.
Lit: Wren Soc, X, p. 121, XI, p. 69.

BUNCE, John (*fl.* 1717–78). Plasterer.
Official of the Worshipful Company of
Plaisterers.
1717 Upper Warden.
1718 Master.
Lit: London, Guildhall Library MS, 6122/3.

BURGES, Robert (*fl.* 1671). Joiner.
1671 THE APOTHECARIES' HALL, LONDON
Great Hall, Panelling and Screen.
Assisted Roger Davies (q.v.).
Lit: G W Whiteman, 1970, *Halls and
Treasures of the City Companies*, p. 156.

BURNETT, John (*fl.* 1726). Plasterer.
Assistant to John Hughes (q.v.).
1726–27 COMPTON PLACE, EASTBOURNE,
SUSSEX
Architect: Colen Campbell.
19 November 1727:
John Burnett, Hewes's man.   8.14.8
When he came with Mr. Campbell.   1. 1.0
Lit: Compton Place Archives, Box P, File 5.

BURNOP, William (*fl.* 1799). Plasterer.
1799 HESLEYSIDE, BELLINGHAM,
NORTHUMBERLAND
Plastering, and supplying eight capitals of the
Corinthian order.
Lit: 1940, *History of Northumberland*, XV,
p. 253.

BURRIDGE, John (*fl. c* 1620). Plasterer.
c 1620 SHERRIFF HUTTON HALL, YORKSHIRE
Bird and Baby Room ceiling; ceiling and fireplace in the Oak Parlour.
Lit: Christopher Gilbert, 1965, guidebook to house quoting archives.
c 1620 SIR ARTHUR INGRAM'S HOUSE, YORK
Lit: 1972, *Leeds Arts Calendar*, No. 71, p. 62.

BURTON, Thomas (*fl.* 1676–89). Plasterer.
A 'Thomas Burton', possibly a son, was one of five contestants for the job of Plaisterer to Christ's Hospital, London, in 1698, 10 years after Burton's death. Burton's will is PCC, 1689, fol. 1.
1678–79 ST STEPHEN, COLEMAN STREET, LONDON
Worked with Robert Horton (q.v.).
'Plastered Vestry, walls, Ceiling and Cornice in the Vestry Room and Stairs. Rendering the Brickwork in the Upper Room for £15. 14 August 1676.' The total bill submitted by Burton and Horton was £136.
Lit: Wren Soc, X, pp. 53, 124, XII, p. 53, XIX, p. 53.

BUTCHER, Francis (*fl.* 1724). Carpenter.
Of Duckmanton.
1724 SUTTON SCARSDALE, DERBYSHIRE
Name on lead rising-plate (now lost).
Lit: C Life, 15 February 1919, p. 171.

BUTLER, Matthew (*fl.* 1753). Joiner.
Of York.
1753 ST MARTIN-CUM-GREGORY, YORK
Communion rails. Received £8.
Lit: RCHM, 1972, *City of York*, III, p. 24, pl. 127.

BUTTON, John (*fl.* 1761–77).
Bricklayer/Mason.
1761–63 BOWOOD, WILTSHIRE, MAUSOLEUM, *and*
1769–77 'DIOCLETIAN' WING
Lit: Bolton, 1922, *Adam*, I, pp. 210, 215.

CAESAR, Anthony (*fl.* 1727–28). Carver.
1727–28 HARCOURT HOUSE, CAVENDISH SQUARE, LONDON
All carving in Lord Bingley's house.
Lit: Bramham Park Archives, Bingley letter-book, 1727–28. This letter-book has been retained at Bramham; the remainder of the Lane-Fox Archives are in Leeds Reference Library.

CALDERWOOD, Samuel (*c* 1687–after 1734). Plasterer.
Born in London and apprenticed to Robert Dyer in 1701.
1726–27 MAVISBANK HOUSE, MIDLOTHIAN
Architect: William Adam.
Lit: Fleming, 1962, *Adam*, p. 42; Edinburgh Register House, GD 18/1765–1774 (accounts), 18/4719–4736 (letters).
1727 DRUM HOUSE, MIDLOTHIAN
Lit: Fleming, 1962, *Adam*, p. 43, pl. 14.
1734 WHIM, PEEBLESSHIRE
Lit: National Library of Scotland, Saltoun MSS, Box 423; RCHM, 1967, *Peebleshire*, II, p. 327. (I am indebted to Mr John G Dunbar for this reference.) Calderwood's work is to be suspected at many William Adam houses, and

certainly at New Hailes (Fleming, 1962, *Adam*, p. 43). Calderwood may also have worked for the Scottish architect James Smith (*c* 1646–1731).

CALDWALL, James (*fl.* 1774). Engraver.
1774 THE OAKS, EPSOM, SURREY
Engraved view of the Supper Room erected by RA for a Fete Châmpetre given by the Earl of Derby.
Lit: Bolton, 1922, *Adam*, II, p. 75.

CAMPBELL, Archibald (*fl.* 1770). Builders' Supplier.
Mentioned in RABA 1770, f. 320.
William Adam and Company held 5/6th share to 1/6th held by Archibald Campbell in builders' suppliers, Adams, Campbell and Company.
Lit: Blair Adam Archives, 4/12.

CAMPELMAN, Ralph (*fl.* 1735–36). Plasterer.
1735–36 CASTLE HOWARD, YORKSHIRE
Plain plastering.
Lit: Castle Howard Archives. (I am indebted to Miss Mary Lawson-Tancred for this reference.)

CAMPION, Giles (*fl.* 1685). Gilder.
c 1685 WHITEHALL PALACE, CHAPEL, LONDON
Gilded the Organ. Received £100.
Lit: 1940, *Survey of London*, XIII, pt. 2, pp. 106–07.

CARABELLAS, – (*fl.* 1798). Plasterer.
c 1798 ICKWORTH HOUSE, SUFFOLK
In 1813 the architect Fulcher stated in his *Hints to Noblemen and Gentlemen of Landed Property . . .*, that he had invented a stucco, 'it being the same as that used by the Signor Carabellas, two Italian Artists, at the Right Honourable the Earl of Bristol's Palace at Ickworth . . . which has stood fifteen years, in ornamental Pannels, at a height of eighty feet from the Ground.'
Lit: Colvin, 1954, *Dictionary*, p. 182.

CARLILE, Charles (*fl.* 1713). Plasterer.
Apprenticed to Isaac Mansfield (q.v.) of York.
Lit: London, Guildhall Library, *Boyd's Index to Apprenticeship Registers.*

CARPENTER, Edmund (*fl.* 1688). Carver.
1688 BELTON, LINCOLNSHIRE
Received £26 for 'a very rich chimneypiece in the withdrawinge roome to the great parlor, done with a varietie of fish and shells wit birds, fouliage, fruit and flowers', £25 for 'one rich chimney-piece with birds, fruits and flowers in the withdrawinge roome in ye little parlor' and £18 for one 'chimneypiece in the great parlor with fruit and flowers'.
Lit: Gunnis, 1953, *Dictionary*, citing Belton Archives (now lost).

CARRON IRON COMPANY, Scotland
In 1760 Samuel Garbett, John Roebuck and William Cadell set up the Carron Iron Company, near Falkirk in Stirlingshire. John Adam invested money in the company, which was set up as a chartered company with £150 000 capital in 600 shares. Thomas Pennant visited the works in 1769 (1790, *Tour*

in Scotland in 1769) and noted them as 'the greatest of the kind in *Europe* . . . Above twelve hundred men are employed. Cannon and all kinds of castings produced.' Firebacks and grates, stoves, etc., were fashioned in neo-classical form to RA's designs. They tried to interest Catherine the Great in buying guns, and it has been suggested (by Dr A A Tait) that RA's design of such decorative niceties as harpsichords (Soane Museum drawing, **25**, no. 9; Beard, 1978, *Adam*, pl. 162) for the empress were intended to interest her in commissioning work which could be made at the Carron Works.
Lit: Bolton, 1922, *Adam*, II, pp. 196, 200; Blair Adam Archives; R H Campbell, 1961, *Carron Company*.

CARTER, Benjamin (*fl.* 1755–66). Sculptor.
Subscribed to RA's book on Diocletian's Palace, 1764.
Brother of Thomas Carter, Senior (q.v.).
1755–64 EGREMONT HOUSE, LONDON
With Thomas Carter.
Lit: West Sussex CRO, Petworth II, 6624.
1764 BOWOOD, WILTSHIRE
Provided four chimneypieces.
Received £750.
Lit: Bolton, 1922, *Adam*, I, p. 214; Gunnis, 1953, *Dictionary*, p. 84; Stillman, 1966, *Adam*, p. 47; Colvin, 1978, *Dictionary*, p. 482, fn. 3.

CARTER, Thomas, senior (?–1795).
Sculptor.
First employer of the eminent French sculptor Roubiliac. He and his son, also Thomas, supplied many chimneypieces in Adam houses—at Shardeloes, Bowood, Syon, Croome and Lansdowne House, for example. In 1759, together with his assistant John Eckstein, he sculpted the monument to the memory of Lieutenant Colonel Roger Townshend (Westminster Abbey), designed by RA.
Lit: Bolton, 1922, *Adam*, I, p. 213, II, p. 9; Gunnis, 1953, *Dictionary*, p. 84.

CASELL, R (*fl.* 1710). Plasterer.
1710 ST PAUL'S CATHEDRAL, LONDON
Worked under Chrysostom Wilkins (q.v.).
Lit: Wren Soc, XV, p. 196.

CATTON, Charles (*fl.* 1770–81). Painter.
c 1770 BUCKINGHAM PALACE, LONDON
Architect: Sir William Chambers.
Second Drawing Room, painting ornaments in gold and colour.
Received £120.
Lit: Harris, 1970, *Chambers*, pp. 217–18.
1781 GREENWICH HOSPITAL, CHAPEL
Supervised by William Newton.
Lit: RIBA, Library, MS, New/1.

CERACCHI, Giuseppe (*c* 1751–1801). Sculptor.
An Italian who came to England in 1773.
Exhibitor at the Royal Academy, 1776–79.
Involved in a plot in France against Napoleon and executed.
Provided bas-reliefs, and worked also for Chambers at Somerset House (received £203. 3s. 0d.).

Lit: Bolton, 1922, *Adam*, II, p. 339; Gunnis, 1953, *Dictionary*, p. 89; J T Smith, 1828, *Nollekens and his Times*, II, p. 56; RIBA, Library, Somerset House accounts.

CHAMPION, Charles (*fl.* late 17th cent.). Gilder.
Paid for gilding the organ in the Chapel, Whitehall.
Lit: *Wren Soc*, VII, p. 131.

CHANARDEN, Lewis (*fl.* 1675–76). Carver.
1675–76 BADMINTON, GLOUCESTERSHIRE
1675, 11 May Received £15.
1676, 9 June Received £10.
Lit: Child's Bank, London, Account of the 1st Marquess of Worcester.

CHANT, John (*fl.* 1761–62). Carpenter.
1761–62 THE PAGODA, KEW GARDENS, LONDON
Architect: Sir William Chambers.
Received £27. 19s. 8d.
Lit: Harris, 1970, *Chambers*, pp. 213–14.

CHAPMAN, William (*fl.* 1763–72). Plumber.
At St Martin's Lane (Mortimer, 1763, p. 58). Mentioned in RABA.
1764 CROOME COURT, WORCESTERSHIRE
Lit: Croome Archives No. 30 (microfilm, Victoria & Albert Museum, Dept of Furniture and Woodwork).
1767 HANOVER SQUARE, LONDON
(Lord Le Despencer.)
Lit: RIBA, MS, Box 14, cited by Stillman, 1966, *Adam*, p. 56.
1770 KEDLESTON, DERBYSHIRE
Did the leadwork and used over 55 tons on the Dome (£245. 2s. 6d.).
Received in all £1354. 4s. 6d.
Lit: Kedleston Archives, Accts. 3R.
1772 20 ST JAMES'S SQUARE, LONDON
Lit: NLW, Wynnstay MS 115/17/25.
Worked also for Chambers at 45 Berkeley Square, London.
Lit: Harris, 1970, *Chambers*, p. 216, no. 58.

CHEEK, Thomas (*fl.* 1760–80). Plasterer.
Official of the Worshipful Company of Plaisterers.
c 1760–80 Mentioned in the Minutes of the Company. Acted as Master in 1760.
Lit: London, Guildhall Library, MS, 6122/4, 6126.

CHEERE, Sir Henry (1703–81) and **John** (1709–87). Sculptors/Plasterers.
Among the most successful of eighteenth-century sculptors, providers of chimneypieces, statues and plaster busts. Sir Henry Cheere (knighted 1760, baronet 1766) had a yard at Old Palace Yard in succession to that used by John van Nost and, secondly, Andrew Carpenter. His younger brother John had a yard at Hyde Park Corner.
Lit: Gunnis, 1953, *Dictionary*; Victoria and Albert Museum, Henry Cheere sketchbook; Temple Newsam House, Leeds, Exhibition Catalogue, May–June 1974; Drummonds Bank, London, Henry Cheere's bank account.

CHESNE, Gideon du (*fl.* 1703–09). Carver.
Principally a stone-carver but may have worked in wood. Owed £120 by the executors of Ralph, 1st Duke of Montagu. Carved heads at Ditton, 1703–05, and cut coat-of-arms over the stables at Boughton for £15.
Lit: Boughton House Archives. Parcel D11, Part 2. (I am indebted to Mr P I King for this reference.)

CHICHELEY, Richard (*fl.* early 18th cent.). Carver.
ST PAUL, DEPTFORD, LONDON
Architect: Thomas Archer.
Lit: Colvin, 1950, *Arch Rev*, p. 196; Gunnis, 1953, *Dictionary*, p. 100.

CHILLINGWORTH, William (*fl.* *c* 1803). Plasterer.
c 1803 AYNHOE PARK, NORTHAMPTONSHIRE
Worked under the architect Sir John Soane.
Lit: *C Life*, 16 July 1953, p. 205.
A Thomas Chillingworth acted as a witness to the will (1751) of the plasterer Thomas Betson (q.v.).

CHIPPINE, Henry (*fl.* 1652). Plasterer.
Official of the Worshipful Company of Plaisterers.
1652 Master.
Lit: London, Guildhall Library, MS, 6122/2.

CHISLO, – (*fl.* 1730). Plasterer.
1730 SHAW HALL, BERKSHIRE
Received £20 for work for James Brydges, 1st Duke of Chandos, presumably at this house.
Lit: Baker, 1949, *Brydges*, p. 370, fn. 2.

CHUKE, Michael (1679–1742). Carver.
Apprenticed to Grinling Gibbons. Worked at Stowe, where he carved a pulpit and cedar wainscoting in the Chapel.
Lit: Gunnis, 1953, *Dictionary*, p. 101.

CHURCHILL, John (*fl.* 1706–15). Master Carpenter.
Master Carpenter, Office of Works, 1706–15. Succeeded his father-in-law, Matthew Banckes (q.v.) in 1706, until his own death in 1715. His mother-in-law, Patience Banckes, was the daughter of the Master Plasterer to the Office of Works, John Grove I (d.1676).
Lit: Colvin, 1976, *King's works*, V, pp. 27, 54, 238, 402, 414, 455, 472, 478.

CLAIFIELD, George (*fl.* 1720–30). Painter.
1720–30 ST GEORGE, BLOOMSBURY, LONDON
Lit: Colvin, 1950, *Arch Rev*, p. 196; Lambeth Palace Library, MS, 2703.

CLARK, Richard (*fl.* 1765–66). Carpenter.
1765–66 KEDLESTON, DERBYSHIRE
Worked for 21½ days (at 18d. a day) on the Music Room Organ case.
Lit: Kedleston Archives, Accts. 3R, No. 14.

CLARK, Thomas (*fl.* 1742–82). Plasterer.
Clark was one of the most successful plasterers of the late eighteenth century. Based at Westminster, he was Master Plasterer to the Office of Works from 1752 until his death in 1782. From about 1770 he had Charles Clarke (q.v.) as his partner. Despite his eminence, he was fined in 1742 by the Worshipful Company of Plaisterers for bad work at St James's Palace. He subscribed in 1767 to the first volume of *James Paine's Plans . . . of Noblemen and Gentlemen's Houses.* His will does not seem to survive in PCC.
1745–60 HOLKHAM HALL, NORFOLK
Various rooms; Clark was working on the Saloon in 1753 and the Hall after 1759.
Lit: Holkham Archives, Building Accounts 8, 26. (I am indebted to Dr W O Hassall and Mr Leo Schmidt for information about the building sequence at Holkham.)
1750 MILTON HOUSE, NORTHAMPTONSHIRE
Received £542. 11s. od.
Lit: Northants CRO, Fitzwilliam Archives, Misc., Vol. 156.
1753 HORSE GUARDS, WHITEHALL, LONDON
Designed by William Kent, executed after his death.
Lit: RIBA, Library, Building Accounts; Jourdain, 1926, *Plasterwork*, p. ix, fn.
1755 NORFOLK HOUSE, LONDON
Received £225. 7s. 8d.
Lit: West Sussex CRO, Duke of Norfolk's Archives; Victoria and Albert Museum, January 1966, *Bulletin*, pp. 1–11; D Fitz-Gerald, 1973, *The Norfolk House Music Room*, Victoria and Albert Museum publication, pp. 9–10.
1755–59 EGREMONT HOUSE, LONDON
Architect: Matthew Brettingham.
Lit: West Sussex CRO, Petworth II, 6609, 6624 (work at various dates).
1758 OLD UNIVERSITY LIBRARY, CAMBRIDGE
Received £532. 15s. od.
Lit: University Registry Audit Book, 1759, Vice Chancellor's Vouchers, 16 May 1759.
1760 ASHBURNHAM PLACE, SUSSEX
Lit: *C Life*, 23 April 1953.
c 1765 BURLINGTON STREET, LONDON
House for Sir Richard Lyttelton, rebuilt 1761–67 by Matthew Brettingham, senior and junior.
Lit: Herts CRO, Ashridge Deeds.
c 1782 SOMERSET HOUSE, LONDON
Architect: Sir William Chambers.
Received £1176. 8s. 6d. (*see* Charles Clarke, below).
Lit: Somerset House Accounts, RIBA, Library; PRO AO3/1244.

CLARKE, Charles (*fl.* 1770–83). Plasterer.
1783 SOMERSET HOUSE, LONDON
Architect: Sir William Chambers.
Worked with Thomas Clark (*see* above). Charged £1352. 11s. 3d., but his bill was disputed and the architect James Paine suggested a reduction in the cost. In reply Clarke, indignant at the treatment of the matter by Sir William Chambers, published in 1783 *The Plaisterers' Bill for works done at the New Building Somerset House in the Strand By the late Mr. Thomas Clark and his surviving partner Charles Clarke, Plaisterer.* In this he indicates that he started his career with Thomas Clark, left him for a time to go to a Mr Bever, and returned in about 1770, at Thomas Clark's suggestion, as his partner. Clarke finally received £1170. 19s. 6¾d.
Lit: Pamphlet cited (copy in RIBA, Library).

CLARKE, Robert (*fl.* 1685). Plasterer.
1685 WHITEHALL PALACE, LONDON
Worked under John Grove I.
Lit: PRO, Works, 5/39, January 1685.

CLARKE, Samuel (*fl.* 1683). Plasterer.
1683 St Paul's Cathedral, London
Made a model.
Lit: Wren Soc, XIII, p. 168.

CLARKE, William (*fl.* 1776–94). Joiner.
1776–94 Somerset House, London
Received £5500. 10s. 10d.
With George Warren from 1794.
Lit: Colvin, 1976, *King's Works*, V, p. 466.

CLAY, Henry (*fl.* 1765–78). Papier mâché
maker.
Of Birmingham, and Bedford Street, Strand,
London.
Achieved notice when his manufactory was
visited by Dr Samuel Johnson. Became
Japanner in Ordinary to His Majesty (George
III) and to the Prince of Wales. J T Smith in
Nollekens and his Times, 1828, noted that:
'Clay died worth £80 000 made entirely out of
his papier-mâché enterprise.'
c 1765 Kedleston, Derbyshire
Hall doors faced with papier-mâché panels.
Lit: Hussey, 1956, *ECH: Mid-Georgian*,
p. 77.

CLAYTON, Thomas (and **Thomas
Clayton junior**). Plasterers.
Clayton's birthplace is unrecorded, but it was
probably in London. No record of his
apprenticeship there has, however, been
traced. As far as is known, he worked entirely
in Scotland from about 1740 for at least 20
years. His son, Thomas Varsallis Clayton,
born in 1743, seems to have been responsible
for work at Inveraray Castle, the Edinburgh
Register House in the 1780s, and possibly at
Mellerstain. It has not yet proved possible to
establish the exact connection of this Thomas
Clayton, but it seems useful to give a
conjectural pedigree. This owes much to the
researches of Miss C H Cruft, who has
recorded the evidence in files at The Scottish
National Monuments Record, Edinburgh.

Thomas Clayton, senior = Elizabeth Wilson
(*fl.* 1710–60; married
c 1735; lived mostly
at Hamilton)

Thomas   Archibald   James (?)
Varsallis =?   (b. at   (b. at
(b. at   Hamilton,   Hamilton,
Hamilton,   25 December   April 1747)
8 March   1745)
1743; d.
October
1793)

Isabella =   Rev John Reston (ordained
(married   1783; sometime minister at
3 September   Alnwick, Biggar, Kilsyth and
1778)   Bridgeton, Glasgow. *See*
                 William Hunter, 1867, *Biggar
                 and the House of Fleming*)

If Thomas Varsallis Clayton is the same
person as the 'Thomas Clayton, plasterer,
Edinburgh', father of Isabella Clayton, then
account needs to be taken of Thomas's
brother, Francis, a merchant in North and
South Carolina. Research may eventually
prove that, as with the Rose family, there were
several relatives, all plasterers, and all bearing

the same Christian name.
1740 The Drum, Edinburgh
Architect: William Adam.
Probably the Drawing Room.
Lit: Lennoxlove, Duke of Hamilton's
Archives (Hamilton section, Box 127).
1740 Holyroodhouse, Edinburgh
Decoration of the Hamilton apartments under
the supervision of William Adam.
Lit: Lennoxlove, Duke of Hamilton's
Archives (Hamilton section, Box 127).
c 1742–46 Hamilton Palace, Lanarkshire
Plasterwork in various rooms, and in 1743 at
Châtelhêrault, the garden pavilion at
Hamilton Palace.
Lit: Letter of 7 April 1742, and bill for
materials. Lennoxlove, Duke of Hamilton's
Archives (Hamilton section, Box 127);
Hamilton Baptismal Registers, April 1743.
1747–57 Blair Castle, Perthshire
Received £140. 12s. 8d.
Lit: Blair Castle Archives, 40 II D(4) 31–39,
40 III, 39–40 (letters).
1753–54 St Andrew's Church, Glasgow
To be finished by January 1754. Clayton to
'find stucco, lime, sand, hair, carriages and all
other materialls necessary' for £487.
Lit: Glasgow, City Minute Book, 9 March
1753; James Thomson, 1905, *History of St.
Andrew's Parish Church, Glasgow.*
Attributed works
c 1750 Glendoick, Perthshire
Drawing Room ceiling; staircase.
Lit: David Walker, 30 March 1967,
'Glendoick', *C Life*, pp. 706–12.
c 1752 130 Clyde Street, Glasgow
(Information from Mr David Walker.)
c 1754 Hopetoun House, West Lothian
Architect: William Adam and his sons.
Yellow and Red Drawing Rooms.
Lit: John Fleming, 1962, *Adam*, p. 332;
C Life, 12 January 1956.
Note should also be taken of the stuccoist
John Dawson (q.v.), who was working at
Hopetoun House in 1757.
Lit: Hopetoun House, Building accounts,
1757. (I am indebted to Mr John Dunbar for
this reference.)
c 1756 Dumfries House, Ayrshire
Architects: John and Robert Adam.
Lit: Sir John Stirling Maxwell, 1938, *Shrines
and Homes of Scotland*, pp. 193–94.
c 1760 Yester House, East Lothian
Architect: Robert Adam.
Saloon. Noted by Dr Richard Pococke in 1760
as having unfinished ornamentation. The
painted panels by William Delacour are dated
1761.
Lit: Pococke, cited by John Swarbrick, 1915,
Robert Adam and his Brothers, p. 220.
1771–72 36 St Andrew Square, Edinburgh
Architect: Sir William Chambers.
House for Sir Lawrence Dundas.
Worked with Coney (q.v.).
Lit: BL Add. MS, 41133, f. 53; George
Richardson, 1776, *Book of Ceilings . . .*, p. 4.
Clayton or his descendants probably worked
also at Pollok House, Glasgow, Touch,
Stirlingshire, and Oxenford (Fleming, 1962,
Adam, p. 333). In 1745–46 he submitted an
estimate for work at Minto House (National
Library of Scotland, Minto Papers, Box 2);
this gives the prices charged for various kinds
of work.

CLAYTON, Thomas, junior? (1743–?93).
Plasterer.
Worked at the Register House in Edinburgh,
1785–91 (charged at 1s. a yard), and seemingly
at Inveraray Castle and Mellerstain. Was the
son of Thomas Clayton senior, flourished
1710–60, who worked in accomplished rococo
style for both William Adam (d.1748) and RA.
Lit: Bolton, 1922, *Adam*, II, pp. 230, 232;
Beard, 1975, *Plasterwork*, p. 210.

CLEARE (CLEERE), Richard (*fl.* 1662–82).
Carver.
1662 Coleshill, Berkshire
dest 1952.
'The bill of Carvers work done for the Right
worthy Sr George Pratt for his house at
Cowsell by Richard Cleare.' The work was
done in London for certain 'festoons' which
were sent down in a basket, with a man who
was paid 26s. 'ffor his goeing down to set up
the ffestoons on the stayres'.
Lit: H Avray Tipping, 29 July 1919, *C Life*,
p. 116. This document was not among the
Pratt papers when R T Gunther wrote in 1928
The Architecture of Sir Roger Pratt, p. 97.
Cleare also worked in the 'Master of the
Roabe's lodging over the library' (Clarendon
House) and his work was certified by Hugh
May:
ffor 2 strings of fflowers & a
piece of Ribbon on the Chimney
peice   £7. 10. 0.
ffor 6½ ft of great Leaves at
18d. per foote   9. 9.
small leaves at
4d. per foot
ffor 22½ ft Bunches of Leaves
and berryes at 4s. per foot
ffor a double palme branch   1. 0. 0.
He received finally, in all £28. 13. 2.
Lit: Gunther, *Pratt*, p. 157.
In 1674 Cleare worked on the Great Model of
St Paul's (*Wren Soc*, XVI, p. 205); at the
Sheldonian Theatre, Oxford (*Wren Soc*, XIX,
pp. 94, 96–98); the City churches of St Olave,
Jewry; St Stephen, Walbrook; St Swithin,
Cannon Street; and St Bartholomew,
Exchange (*Wren Soc*, X, pp. 56, 121, XIX,
pp. 10, 55–56).

CLEERE, William, senior (*fl.* 1668–d.1690).
Carver and Joiner.
1668 Badminton, Gloucestershire
20 November, 'Mr Cleare, joyner.' £50.
Lit: London, Child's Bank, Account of 1st
Marquess of Worcester.
Cleare also worked at the Sheldonian Theatre,
Oxford; Chelsea Hospital; Whitehall; many
City churches including St Mary,
Aldermanbury, St Michael, Cornhill, and on
the first Model for St Paul's, and the Great
Model.
Lit: Wren Soc, VII, p. 106, X, pp. 23, 50,
124, XVI, pp. 193–95, XIX, pp. 7, 77–78,
94–95, 112, 117. For full references see Index
(Vol. XX) of the *Wren Soc* volumes.
1683 East Hattley, Cambridgeshire
Wainscoting at Sir George Downing's house
at 8/6d. a yard. His wife Anne received
£366. 17s. 5¾d. after her husband's death in
1690.
Lit: Castle Howard, Yorks., Executor's
Accounts, Sir George Downing.

CLEERE, William, junior (*fl.* 1695–96).
Joiner.
1695–96 ST PAUL'S CATHEDRAL, LONDON
Various payments for work.
Lit: Wren Soc, XV, pp. 3, 6, 7.

CLERICI, Charles (*fl.* late 18th cent.).
Scagliola worker.
Worked at Wentworth Woodhouse, Yorks.,
where he did the scagliola floor in the Saloon,
and at Thoresby where he was employed by
John Carr and assisted by the York plasterer
Ely Crabtree (q.v.).
Lit: C Life, 10 October 1957.

CLOUGH, Robert (1736–1800). Plasterer.
Son of Robert Clough, 1708–91, master-
builder of York; Clough junior was admitted
to the York Freedom in 1758.
1769 28 GILLYGATE, YORK
Saloon ceiling.
Lit: RCHM, 1975, *City of York*, IV, p. 74.

COADE, Eleanor (1742–1821). Artificial
Stone Maker.
Daughter of George Coade and Eleanor
Enchmarch, of Lyme Regis and Exeter, one of
whom discovered the formula for a ceramic
body, technically a stoneware, which is almost
impervious to weathering, and so closely
resembles natural limestone that it is regularly
mistaken for it. Eleanor II (described by
George Roberts, 1823, *History of Lyme Regis*,
as 'the daughter of the person that discovered
the "composition"') began manufacture at
Narrow Wall, Lambeth, in 1769. By 1784 she
was able to issue a catalogue of more than 700
items, including all kinds of architectural
features—capitals, plaques, friezes, etc.—
statues, portrait busts, vases, funerary
monuments, and details, including chimneypieces and tripods, for interior decoration. Her
designs are mainly neoclassical, but there is a
substantial body of Gothic work, mainly in
churches, i.e. St George's Chapel, Windsor
(architect Henry Emlyn), but also domestic,
i.e. Dalmeny House (architect: William
Wilkins). She employed the best designers,
particularly John Bacon the elder. She issued
engravings of her designs (collections in
London—Sir John Soane's Museum,
Guildhall Library, etc.) and established such
good relations with the architectural
profession that there is hardly a Georgian
architect of note who did not employ her,
from Robert Adam to John Yenn. In 1799,
joined in partnership by her cousin John
Sealy, she opened a showroom at Pedlar's
Acre, Lambeth, for which an elaborate
guidebook survives (British Library). The
firm remained 'Coade and Sealy' until his
death in 1813, and then reverted to 'Coade'.
Eleanor then took on as manager a distant
cousin, William Croggon (q.v.), who ran the
firm until her death in 1821, when he took it
over. He went bankrupt in 1833 (Croggon
family records), but his son Thomas John re-
established the firm (as Croggon and Co.) on
his father's death in 1835 and it survives
today. He ceased to manufacture Coade stone
c 1840. M H Blanchard, a former employee,

advertised himself as the successor to Coade
and user of the Coade formula (*The Builder*,
29 December 1855), but, with the Victorian
taste for red terracotta, Coade stone went out
of use and its composition was forgotten.
A few of the many hundreds of Coade stone
commissions are: 20 Portman Square, London
(Robert Adam); Croome Court, Worcs.
('Capability' Brown and Adam); Tsarskoe
Selo, Russia (Charles Cameron?); Somerset
House, London (Sir William Chambers); the
Royal Pavilion, Brighton (Henry Holland);
Hammerwood Park, Sussex (Benjamin
Latrobe); the Royal Naval Hospital,
Greenwich (Chapel, 'Athenian' Stuart;
pediment sculpture in memory of Nelson,
Benjamin West; Trafalgar block, John Yenn);
Buckingham Palace (John Nash); the Bank of
England (Sir John Soane); Heaton Hall,
Lancs. (James Wyatt); and Belmont, Kent
(Samuel Wyatt). Notable Coade monuments
can be seen at Rochester Cathedral, Beverley
Minster and Westminster Abbey. Four
commemorative monuments (Bristol,
Weymouth, Southampton and Lincolnshire)
were put up for George III's jubilee, and
there were numerous pieces in memory of
Nelson, including a striking bust (private
collection).
Gunnis, 1953, *Dictionary* gives a partial list of
Coade work, and numerous other examples
are mentioned in the various volumes of N
Pevsner's *The Buildings of England*.
(This entry provided by Alison Kelly.)

COBB, Samuel (*fl.* 1750–60). Painter.
Worked for Frederick, Prince of Wales, and
the Dowager Princess, and in 1757 came
under the supervision, for work at Kew, of Sir
William Chambers.
Lit: Harris, 1970, *Chambers*, p. 214.

COBBE, John (*fl.* 1601). Plasterer.
1601 ST JOHN'S COLLEGE, CAMBRIDGE
Cobbe was responsible for the 'frettishing of
the ceiling of the great chamber and long
gallery'.
Lit: Jourdain, 1926, *Plasterwork*, pp. 22–23.

COBBETT, Richard, William and **John**
(*fl.* 1724–95). Glaziers.
Richard Cobbett is first noted working under
Thomas Ripley at Houghton Hall, Norfolk,
1724, and at Sir Robert Walpole's London
house in Chelsea. He later worked under
William Kent at Henry Pelham's house,
Arlington Street, London, 1742, and for
Frederick, Prince of Wales, at Leicester
House, 1750.
Richard and John worked for Sir William
Chambers at Somerset House and
Buckingham House.
William Cobbett is mentioned in RABA, and
received over £477 for his work at Kedleston,
Derbyshire, 1770.
Lit: CUL (CH) Acct. Bk. 22, 18 December
1724, 28 February 1729; Beard, 1966,
Craftsmen, pp. 79, 86; Duchy of Cornwall
VI(1), p. 257; Royal Archives, Windsor,
55135; Harris, 1970, *Chambers*, pp. 218, 231;
Colvin, 1978, *Dictionary*, p. 482, fn. 3; Colvin,
1976, *King's Works*, V, p. 465.

COLE, Charles (*fl.* 1776–84). Carpenter.
1776 Worked at Somerset House; from 1784
as Charles Cole & Martin.
Also did miscellaneous work for the Office of
Works.
Lit: Colvin, 1976, *King's Works*, V, p. 465;
London, RIBA, Library, Somerset House
Accounts.

COLE, J (*fl.* 1708–10). Plasterer.
1708–10 ST PAUL'S CATHEDRAL, LONDON
Worked under Chrysostom Wilkins (q.v.).
Lit: Wren Soc, XV, pp. 169, 196.

COLLEDGE, Stephen (*fl.* 1670–81). Joiner.
1670 STATIONERS' HALL, LONDON
Livery Hall, wainscoting. Received £300.
Colledge was called 'the Protestant joiner'. He
was hanged at Oxford in 1681.
Lit: G W Whiteman, 1970, *Halls and
Treasures of the City Companies*, p. 147.

COLLETT, Nicholas (*fl.* 1760–65). Carver.
A friend of Thomas Gainsborough and of the
actor Waldron. Did decorative woodcarving
on the State Coach designed for George III
by Sir William Chambers.
Lit: Gunnis, 1953, *Dictionary*, p. 111.

COLLINS, Richard (*fl.* 1774). Joiner.
1774 20 ST JAMES'S SQUARE, LONDON
Provided bookcases and carved figures on the
organ case.
Lit: NLW, Wynnstay MS, 115/17/10.

COLLINS, Thomas (1735–1830). Plasterer.
Apprenticed in 1750 to William Wilton (q.v.).
Married, 17 November 1761, Henrietta
Patterson at St Mary le Bone, Middlesex. Had
a bank account (Drummonds) with Sir
William Chambers, and also developed
various properties with his partner. In 1796 he
was appointed an executor and trustee at the
death of Sir William Chambers. Portraits of
Collins by von Breda, the Swedish artist, and
Beechey exist in the Dr J Gurney Salter
Collection, and at Marylebone Town Hall. He
died on 3 May 1830.
Lit: A detailed account of Collins's long
career was prepared, 1965–66, by Colonel J H
Busby (copy RIBA, Library).
1764 DUDDINGSTON, EDINBURGH
Hall ceiling.
Lit: Harris, 1970, *Chambers*, p. 207.
1765 WALCOT, SHROPSHIRE
Worked with William Wilton.
Lit: Bills at house.
1765–66 45 BERKELEY SQUARE, LONDON
Lit: India Office Library, Clive Papers.
1771 MILTON HOUSE, NORTHAMPTONSHIRE
Work under Sir William Chambers for Lord
Fitzwilliam.
Received £301. 18s. 6d.
Lit: BL Add. MS, 41133, 9 November 1771.
1773 MELBOURNE HOUSE, PICCADILLY,
LONDON
Architect: Sir William Chambers.
Lit: BL Add. MS, 41133, 14 August 1773.
1773 STRATTON STREET, LONDON
Received £764. 1s. 2¾d. for work at Lord
Fitzwilliam's house.
Lit: Northants CRO, Milton Archives,
Vouchers, 114, and letter from Collins.

1774 Drapers' Company Hall, London
Worked with Joseph Rose. Cost of work
£1384. 6s. 7d.
Lit: Bill preserved at the Worshipful
Company of Drapers.
1777 Peper Harow, Surrey
Architect: Sir William Chambers.
Lit: Bill of June 1777; *C Life*, 26 December
1925.
1780 Somerset House, London
Architect: Sir William Chambers.
Work divided between Collins and Thomas
Clark (q.v.), with Collins doing the modelling
'under the pretence of his being more used to
Sir William's manner'. Collins was paid
£1990. 2s. 0d. and, from 1784, in company
with John Papworth (q.v.), £7915. 2s. 8d.
Lit: RIBA, Library Accounts; PRO,
A.O.3/1244.
Other work
Collins was listed in the Somerset House
accounts for ceilings at the Royal Academy
(1780), the Royal Society Meeting Rooms
(1783), and for other work jointly with
Papworth. A full list of work by Sir William
Chambers is given in Harris, 1970, *Chambers*.

COLLINS, William (1721–93). Plasterer.
For details of Collins's career as a sculptor, *see*
Gunnis, 1953, *Dictionary*, p. 111.
A pupil of Sir Henry Cheere, he was much
employed in providing classical statues and
bas-reliefs. There is little doubt that many of
the features in houses designed by Robert
Adam were from his hand, and are
documented as such at Kedleston. Collins,
who lived in Channel Row, Westminster
(Mortimer, 1763), died on 24 May 1793, and
was buried in the old cemetery at King's
Road, Chelsea. Subscribed to James Paine's,
1767, *Plans . . . of Noblemen and Gentlemen's
Houses*, I.
1756 Magdalene College, Cambridge
Chapel: altar-piece in plaster of Paris, now in
the College Library.
Subject: 'The Three Marys by the Holy
Sepulchre'.
Lit: 1764, *Cambridge Depicta*, p. 77; Gunnis,
1953, *Dictionary*, p. 111; N B Pevsner, 1954,
Cambridgeshire, p. 96, pl. 40.
1760 Harewood House, Yorkshire
Architect: RA.
Various medallions, including figures of Mars
and Neptune for the Great Hall.
Lit: E Hargrove, 1798, *History of
Knaresborough*, p. 157; Richard Buckle, 1959,
Guidebook to Harewood House; Mary
Mauchline, 1974, *Harewood House*.
1763 Kedleston, Derbyshire
Architect: RA.
Statues in the Great Hall and medallions.
Lit: Curzon Archives, Kedleston; James
Lees-Milne, 1947, *The Age of Adam*, p. 122;
Geoffrey Beard, 1958, *The Connoisseur
Yearbook*, p. 26.
1769 Burton Constable, Yorkshire
Medallions in the Dining Room, one depicting
Pan and the Graces. The stucco frame is the
work of Giuseppe Cortese (q.v.).
Lit: *Georgian Soc., East Yorkshire*, IV, pt. I
(1953–55), p. 45; *C Life*, 3 September 1932,
10 September 1959, ill. p. 256; Collins's bill of
10 September 1769 (£21 plus half the cost of

travelling from London: £3. 3s. 0d.) is cited
by Dr Ivan Hall, 1970, *William Constable as
Patron*, Hull Art Gallery, Exhibition
Catalogue, No. 46. *See also* T F Friedman,
Sculpture by John Cheere, Temple Newsam
House, Leeds, Exhibition Catalogue, Summer
1974.

COLOMBANI, Placido (*fl.* 1744–80).
Plasterer.
1775 Downhill, Co Antrim, N Ireland
Lit: *C Life*, 6 January 1950.
c 1780 Mount Clare, Surrey
Lit: Hussey, 1956, *ECH: Mid-Georgian*,
p. 240.
c 1797 Ickworth, Suffolk
Lit: *C Life*, 7 November 1925; Hussey *ECH:
Mid-Georgian*, p. 240.

COMBES, John (*fl.* 1681–1711). Plasterer.
Official of the Worshipful Company of
Plaisterers.
1701 Master (succeeded Henry Doogood).
1709 One of the Company Auditors.
He died 17 September 1711 and, together
with his wife Damaris (d.1707), was buried at
St James's, Piccadilly (memorial tablet,
Gallery S. side).
Lit: London, Guildhall, Library, MS, 6122/3
(29 September 1711).
1681–87 St Augustine, Watling Street,
London
Worked with Henry Doogood (q.v.).
He received £98.
Lit: *Wren Soc*, XII, p. 44.
1688 St James's, Piccadilly, London
Offered to plaster the outside walls 'with lime
and sand and other materialls like Stone work
call'd finishing'.
Lit: 1960, *Survey of London*, XXIX, p. 36.
1707–08 Petitioned for post of Master
Plasterer to the Office of Works vacant on the
death of John Grove II (given to David
Lance, q.v.). Stated he had been plasterer at
Berkeley House and St James's, but was set
aside at Queen Anne's accession.
Lit: 1708 (1905), *Cal., Treasury Books*, XXII,
p. 133.

COMBES, Thomas (*fl.* 1695–1719).
Plasterer.
Apprentice of John Combes (q.v.). Free of the
Worshipful Company of Plaisterers by 25 July
1702. In 1718 he was Upper Warden and in
1719 Master of the Company. In 1709 some
£50 was still owed to him for unspecified
work for the Duke of Montagu. In 1712 he
worked at 5 St James's Square, London.
Lit: London, Guildhall Library, MS, 6122/3;
Boughton House (Northants), Executors'
Accounts, of the estate of Ralph, Duke of
Montagu; 1960, *Survey of London*, XXIX,
p. 100.

CONEY, – (*fl.* 1771–83). Plasterer.
A Stephen Coney worked at Powderham,
Devon, *c* 1765.
Lit: *C Life*, 11 July 1963, p. 83.
1771–72 36 St Andrew Square, Edinburgh
Architect: Sir William Chambers.
House for Sir Lawrence Dundas.
Worked with Thomas Varsallis Clayton (q.v.).
Lit: BL Add. MS, 41133, f. 53; George

Richardson, 1776, *Book of Ceilings . . .*, p. 4.
1783 Somerset House, London
Architect: Sir William Chambers.
Worked under Charles Clarke (q.v.).
Lit: Charles Clarke, 1783, *The Plaisterers' Bill
for Works done at . . . Somerset House . . .*

CONEY, Stephen (*fl.* 1770–90). Plasterer.
1790 Archerfield, Berwick
His name is on an Adam drawing (Soane
Museum, XXVII, 11).
A 'Mr Coney' worked as a plasterer for Sir
William Chambers at Sir Lawrence Dundas's
house in St Andrew Square, Edinburgh, and
at Somerset House, London.
Lit: Boltong, 1922, *Adam*, II, p. 359; *Beard*,
1975, *Plasterwork*, p. 212.

CONSIGLIO, Francesco (*fl.* 1734–39).
Plasterer.
1734 Lyme Park, Cheshire
Architect: Giacomo Leoni.
Staircase Hall.
Lit: *C Life*, 26 December 1974.
1739 Euxton Hall, Lancashire
Lit: *C Life*, 6 February 1975.

COOK, John (*fl.* 1748–63). Plasterer.
In 1763 Cook was apprenticed, presumably at
the age of 14 years, to George Fewkes (q.v.).
Lit: London, Guildhall Library, MS, 6122/4.

COOMBS, – (*fl.* early 18th cent.). Plasterer.
Paid £13 by James Brydges, 1st Duke of
Chandos, for unspecified work, presumably at
Canons. Possibly 'Coombs' was John or
Thomas Combes (q.v.).
Lit: Baker, 1949, *Brydges*, p. 199.

COOPER, Charles (*fl.* 1683). Plasterer.
In 1683 Cooper signed a receipt on behalf of
John Grove (q.v.).
Lit: *Wren Soc*, XIII, p. 176.

COOPER, George (*fl.* 1824). Painter.
1824 Windsor Castle, Berkshire
Lit: D Linstrum, 1972, *Sir Jeffry Wyatville*,
p. 253.

CORDEY, John (*fl.* 1710–11). Plasterer.
Official of the Worshipful Company of
Plaisterers.
1710 Upper Warden.
1711 Master.
Lit: London, Guildhall Library, MS, 6122/3.

CORLETT, Richard (*fl.* 1804–13). Plasterer.
Worked on two recorded occasions for Lord
Grosvenor:
1804–12 Eaton Hall, Cheshire
Architect: William Porden.
1809–13 Eccleston Church, Cheshire
Lit: Grosvenor Archives, Eaton Hall,
Cheshire. (I am indebted to Dr H M Colvin
for this reference.)

CORTESE, Giuseppe (*fl.* 1725–78).
Presumably of the family of stuccoists long
settled at Mendrisio, near Lugano. The first
mention of his name seems to be 'For Mr
Cortesy' on a plan in the Colen Campbell
collection, RIBA, Library, perhaps by
William Wakefield and intended for Gilling

Castle, Yorkshire, c 1725. Cortese lived for a time at Whitby, had an assistant named Taddei (possibly the Michel Angelo or Francesco Taddei who worked later at Augustenborg in Denmark), and had an extensive practice in the north, working mainly for the architect John Carr. He died at York in 1778, his executors being the Wakefield cabinet-maker Edward Elwick and the York plasterer James Henderson (q.v.).
Lit: *York Courant*, cited in York Georgian Society, 1955–56, *Report*, p. 58.
1739 NEWBURGH PRIORY, YORKSHIRE
Cortese's name first appears in the accounts in July 1739. He did other work in 1743, 1744, 1745, and later in 1764–67.
Lit: Archives at house; Beard, 1966, *Craftsmen*, pl. 109; *C Life*, 7 March 1974, p. 484.
1745–52 STUDLEY ROYAL, RIPON, YORKSHIRE
Dest by fire in 1945.
Main rooms of the house for William Aislabie. Received, in all, £409. His measurement of 28 December 1751, and several bills, survive. His work in the Temple also survives.
Lit: Leeds Archives Dept, Studley Royal Archives, Parcel 286; *C Life*, 25 July, 1 and 8 August 1931, 10 September 1959.
1747–49 BRANDSBY HALL, YORKSHIRE
Worked for Francis Cholmely. House attributed to John Carr.
Received £328.
Lit: Archives at house, cited by John Cornforth in *C Life*, 2–9 January 1969.
c 1750 GILLING CASTLE, YORKSHIRE
Plasterwork of the Great Hall, etc. Cortese also worked for the Fairfax family at Newburgh Priory, Coxwold (below), as early as December 1744, when he was paid for drawing paper, and in 1765.
Lit: Leeds, Yorkshire Archaeological Society, Library, Newburgh Archives; J E Thorold Rogers, 1902, Agriculture and Prices in England, VII, p. 452 – 'Dec. 1744, Coxwold. 2 sheets of drawing paper for Mr. Cortese, 1s.'
1752 and 1757 ELEMORE HALL, DURHAM
Various ceilings; one uses the same Neptune motif as the ceiling at Lytham Hall, Lancs.
Lit: Durham CRO, Baker–Baker papers. (I am indebted to Mr Neville Whittaker for this reference.)
1757 HARDWICK PARK, DURHAM
Architect: James Paine.
Garden Temple.
Lit: As for Elemore Hall, above. Cortese's 1757 letters to George Baker of Elemore were written while working at Hardwick. This work under Paine's supervision may imply that Cortese also worked at St Helen's Hall, St Helen Auckland, Durham, although Thomas Perritt (q.v.) and Joseph Rose senior (q.v.) are other possible contenders. The work is, however, not close to the style of either, and it is necessary to remember work by the Franchini family of *stuccatori* for the architect Daniel Garrett (*cf. C Life*, 12 March 1970, 19 September 1974).
1762 GUILDHALL, BEVERLEY
Cortese's work in the Court Room is recorded:
15 November 1762: 'Ordered the sum of Forty Quineas be laid out in Ornamenting the Town's Hall, lately Rebuilt, by Erecting on The Inside thereof the King's Arms in

Plaister or Stukoe for which the Corporation have this day agreed with Mr. Courtezie to be by him finished for the above sum.'
24 October 1763: 'Ordered that Mr. Cortese's bill of twenty-five pounds and five shillings as a present be paid by the Town's Receiver.'
Lit: *Beverley Corporation Minute Books* (Yorks. Arch. Soc. Record Series, 1958, CXXII, *ed.* K A Macmahon, pp. 42–43, extracts quoted above); R H Whiteing, 1950, *Trans., East Yorks., Georgian Soc.*, II, pt. 4, p. 62; *C Life*, 19 April 1956, p. 808.
1769 BURTON CONSTABLE, YORKSHIRE
The stucco frame to the panel of the Three Graces by William Collins (q.v.) in the Dining Room.
Lit: *William Constable as Patron*, Hull Art Gallery, Exhibition Catalogue, 1970, No. 46.
1772 KILNWICK HALL, YORKSHIRE
Architect: John Carr.
Worked with Addinal, and for Colonel Condon.
Lit: Edward Ingram, 1952, *Leaves from a Family Tree*.
Attributed work
Arncliffe Hall, Yorkshire, c 1753–54; Escrick, Yorkshire; Bedale Hall, Yorkshire; Rievaulx Temple, Duncombe Park, Yorkshire; Somerset House, George Street, Halifax; Lytham Hall, Lancashire, same motif as Elemore; and The Old Hall, Ripon, Staircase Hall.

COUSIN, Peter (*fl.* 1702). Gilder.
Possibly a relative of Verrio's gilder, René Cousin. Worked at Hampton Court.
Lit: *Wren Soc*, XVIII, pp. 160–61.

CRABTREE, Ely (*fl.* 1760–1803). Plasterer.
Of York, where he lived for a time in Lendal. Worked in liaison with John Carr for many years. In 1803 he did the apsidal staircase at Wentworth Woodhouse to Carr's design. He had already worked there in 1783 at the Mansoleum with Thomas Henderson (q.v.).
Lit: R B Wragg, York Georgian Society, 1955–56, *Report*, p. 60; *C Life*, 19 October 1957, p. 719.
The York firm of Crabtree worked at Everingham Roman Catholic Church, Yorkshire.
Lit: *Arch Rev*, September 1957, pp. 198–200.

CRESSWELL, Joseph (*fl.* 1777). Merchant.
1777 20 ST JAMES'S SQUARE, LONDON
Provided candlesticks and glass cases.
Received £168. 8s.
Lit: 1960, *Survey of London*, XXIX, p. 165 fn.

CRISP, William (*fl.* 1719–20). Plasterer.
1719–20 PURLEY HALL, BERKSHIRE
Received £4. 9s. 0d. from Francis Hawes for work at this house.
Lit: 1721, *Particulars and Inventories of the Late Directors of the South Sea Company*, 2.

CROGGON, William (1787–1835).
Artificial Stone and Scagliola Manufacturer.
A distant cousin of Eleanor Coade (q.v.) through one of her Enchmarch aunts, and came from Grampound, Cornwall, where the family still survives. His Cornish relations probably supplied the china clay, difficult to

obtain in the 1760s and 1770s, which was used in the Coade formula. On the death of Eleanor Coade's cousin John Sealy in 1813, Groggon was appointed manager of the Coade works in Lambeth. On Eleanor's death in 1821 he bought the works and ran it until his bankruptcy in 1833. His main work during this period was at Buckingham Palace, for which he was paid many £1000's (Crook and Port, 1974, *King's Works*, VI)). Though his work books for the 1813–21 period are in the PRO, none has come to light for 1821–33. A letter among the Croggon family archives attributes his bankruptcy to speculation, but says that he did £20 000 worth of work for the Duke of York. As the duke almost never paid tradesmen (H M Colvin, 1958, 'The Architects of Stafford House', *Architectural History*), this involvement no doubt contributed to the disaster. As well as Coade stone, Croggon manufactured scagliola successfully, notable surviving examples being at: Ickworth, Suffolk; Downing College, Cambridge; and Willey Hall, Salop. William's second son Thomas John refounded the firm on his father's death in 1835, and it survives today (information from the directors), but Coade stone ceased to be manufactured c 1840.
(This entry provided by Alison Kelly.)

CROMPTON & Son (*fl.* 1761–75).
Wallpaper suppliers.
As Crompton & Spinnage, 1762–66 (Cockspur St, Charing Cross), and as Benjamin Crompton & Son, 1771 (same address).
Supplied to George IV.
Lit: H Clifford Smith, 1931, *Buckingham Palace*, p. 277.
1761 CROOME COURT, WORCESTERSHIRE
Lit: Croome Court Archives, No. 28 (microfilm, Victoria and Albert Museum, Dept of Furniture and Woodwork).
1775 20 ST JAMES'S SQUARE, LONDON
Paper for Nursery and Attic. Received £6.
Lit: NLW, Wynnstay MS, 115/7.

CROMWELL, Henry (*fl.* 1698). Plasterer.
Official of the Worshipful Company of Plaisterers.
1698 Master.
Lit: London, Gildhall Library, MS, 6122/3.

CROUCH, John (*fl.* late 17th cent.–1715).
Plasterer.
Official of the Worshipful Company of Plaisterers.
1714 Upper Warden.
1715 Master.
Lit: London, Guildhall Library, MS, 6122/3.
1714 ST STEPHEN, WALBROOK, LONDON
Unspecified work.
Lit: *Wren Soc*, X, pp. 115 and 124.

CROUCH, Mr (*fl.* 1767). Joiner.
Subscribed to James Paine, 1767, *Plans . . . of Noblemen and Gentlemen's Houses*.

CROUCHER, John (*fl.* 1775). Trade unknown.
1775 20 PORTMAN SQUARE, LONDON
Received £257. 4s. 0d. for unspecified work.
Lit: M D Whinney, 1969, *Home House*, p. 20.

CRYER, Clement (*fl. c* 1769–1800).
Plasterer.
The Christie's sale catalogue of Joseph Rose junior's effects, 1st day, 10 April 1799, states: 'Clement Cryer, Plasterer Humbly solicits the Favours of the Employers of Mr Joseph Rose of Queen Anne Street East . . . as he has permission of the Executor to make this Application and flatters himself that a servitude of near thirty years as Apprentice and Assistant, under the inspection of his late Ingenious Master . . . He has engaged part of the premises in which the trade was carried on. Orders for present to 18 Edward St, Queen Anne Street East.' He presumably worked on most Rose junior's commissions and is mentioned specifically at Packington Hall, Warwickshire, 1785–86.
Lit: *C Life*, 16 July 1970, p. 229.

CUNEGO, Domenico (*c* 1727–94).
Engraver.
Worked on many engravings for James and Robert Adam.
Lit: Fleming, 1962, *Adam*, pp. 371, 373.

CUNEOT, John (*fl.* 1744–62). Carver.
Seemingly the son of a French sculptor. He worked for the Duke of Northumberland (1752) and the Duke of Montagu (1759), but is best known for his work for the Duke of Norfolk. At Norfolk House he received over £2643 for carving and gilding, 1752–56. He lived at Warwick Street, Golden Square, London.
Lit: D Fitz-Gerald, 1973, *The Norfolk House Music Room*, Victoria and Albert Museum, cites relevant MSS; Gunnis, 1953, *Dictionary*, p. 90, under 'Ceunot'.

CURRYER, Thomas (*fl.* 1730–32).
Plasterer.
1730–32 ST BARTHOLOMEW'S HOSPITAL, LONDON
Lit: Hospital Archives, Ha 19/5/2–3.

DANIEL, John (*fl.* 1732–35). Joiner.
Of Northampton
1732–33 LAMPORT HALL, NORTHAMPTONSHIRE
Architect: Francis Smith.
Wainscoting; Staircase (oak).
Lit: Northants CRO, Isham Archives, 4014; *C Life*, 3 October 1952, p. 1025, 10 October 1952, p. 1106.
1732–35 LAMPORT RECTORY, NORTHAMPTONSHIRE
Staircase.
Lit: Northants CRO, Isham Archives, 5279, 14 August 1732: 12 September 1735, Payment of £50 on account. Some work in oak, although Daniel purchased a walnut tree in 1732; information from the late Sir Gyles Isham.

DARBY, John (*fl.* 1723–33). Carver.
1723–29 CHRISTCHURCH, SPITALFIELDS, LONDON
Architect: Nicholas Hawksmoor.
1727–33 ST LUKE, OLD STREET, LONDON
Architects: Wren, Hawksmoor.
Lit: Colvin, 1950, *Arch Rev*.

DAVENPORT, John (*c* 1593–1668). Master Carpenter.

Master Carpenter, Office of Works, July 1660–68. He appears to have held the same office before the Restoration.
Lit: Colvin, 1954, *Dictionary*, p. 168.

DAVIES, Charles (*fl.* 1653). Plasterer.
Official of the Worshipful Company of Plaisterers.
1653 Master.
Lit: London, Guildhall Library, MS, 6122/2.

DAVIES, Roger (*fl.* 1671–1709). Joiner.
1671 THE APOTHECARIES' HALL, LONDON
Great Hall, Wainscoting and Screen (assisted by Robert Burges).
Received £117. 12s. for panelling and £75 for screen.
Lit: G W Whiteman, 1970, *Halls and Treasures of the City Companies*, p. 156.
c 1680 RAGLEY, WARWICKSHIRE
Architect: Sir Robert Hooke.
Lit: Hooke's *Diary*, 1935 edn. 26 March, 11 July 1676, 27 March 1670; M'Espinasse, 1956, *Robert Hooke*, pp. 101–02, 137.
1682–83 BURGHLEY HOUSE, NORTHAMPTONSHIRE
23 June, received £50, being presumably the 'Mr Davies' referred to.
Lit: Glyn Mills, Child's Branch Bank, Exeter account.
The other alternative is William Davis, seemingly a relative, who worked at Chatsworth (Francis Thompson, 1949, *A History of Chatsworth*, p. 449).
1687–92 BOUGHTON HOUSE, NORTHAMPTONSHIRE and MONTAGU HOUSE, LONDON
The executors of Ralph, 1st Duke of Montagu, declared in 1709 that, for work between 1687–92, some £3606 was due to Davies—£1546 of this was for work due to 4 October 1690 at Boughton and £2560 at Montagu House to 1692. For 223 yd of wainscoting and the provision of a communion table at Weekly Church, *c* 1700, he was paid £45.
Lit: Boughton Archives, Parcel D11, Part 2.
Davies also worked at Whitehall in the Chapel (1686) with John Smallwell, on the choir stalls of Canterbury Cathedral, at Chelsea Hospital, St Paul's (in partnership with Hugh Webb), Greenwich Hospital and several City churches.

DAVIS, Thomas (*fl.* 1765). Gilder.
1765 LONG GALLERY, SYON
Gilded by Davis at 2s. 6d. per sq ft.
Lit: Alnwick Castle Archives, U.I.46, 16 July 1765.

DAVIS, William (*fl.* late 17th cent). Carver.
Of London. Worked with Thomas Young, Joel Lobb and Samuel Watson at Chatsworth, 1692–94.
Lit: Francis Thompson, 1949, *A History of Chatsworth*, pp. 149–50.

DAWSON, John (*fl.* 1750–65). Plasterer.
Apprenticed in 1738 to Charles Stanley (q.v.), but most of the recorded mentions of him depict him as a woodcarver. However, when John Adam was preparing designs at Yester House, East Lothian, in 1751, he told Lord Tweeddale that he was proposing to employ as

stuccoist 'the person who did the two glass frames for my Lady Marchioness, who works also in stucco. He is a Scotch lad, but served his time in London.' He has been identified fairly positively as the 'Mr Dawson' who was employed as a carver by the Adam brothers at Lord Tweeddale's Edinburgh home in the early 1750s. He also worked at Inveraray Castle, Argyll, and in 1757 at Hopetoun House. In September–October 1752 a 'Dawson, Plasterer' worked at Stanmer Park, Sussex. A 'John Dawson, plasterer' was also married in Edinburgh in 1773.
Lit: Information from Mr John Dunbar; Beard, 1966, *Craftsmen*, p. 175: Mary Cosh, 1973, *Inveraray*; John Dunbar, 1972, 'The Building of Yester House', *Transactions, East Lothian Antiquarian Society*, XIII, p. 41, fn. 72; BL Add MS, 33163 (Stanmer).

DAWSON, John (*fl.* 1764). Carver.
Of Horseferry, Westminster.
1764 OKEOVER, STAFFORDSHIRE
Asked to make a mahogany chimney surround at a cost of £115, he complained the payment was insufficient 'because the stuff is excessive dear':
To complete the chimneypiece in mahogany £45
4 large pilasters, trusses, lions heads, etc., in the pilasters in mahogany £33
4 trusses and two friezes in mahogany £7. 10
Two doors at £11. 10s. each £23
Lit: Derbyshire CRO, Okeover Archives, 'Building file: Leak Okeover'.

DAWSON, Robert (*fl.* 1742–51). Plasterer.
1742–51 17 ARLINGTON STREET, LONDON
Architect: William Kent.
Received £779. 13s. 4½d. for work at the house of the Rt Hon Henry Pelham. Also worked on the 'New Building next the Park att Mr. Pelham's House in Arlington Street', received £253. 16s. 7d.
Lit: London, RIBA, Library, MSS, 728.3 (42.13) A.
It was presumably Robert Dawson who was foreman to Isaac Mansfield (q.v.). He was described as such, and made 'Master Plaisterer to his Majesty's Palaces in the room of his said deceas'd Master'.
Lit: *London Daily Post and General Advertiser*, Monday, 21 January 1739–40, No. 1635.
1743 44 BERKELEY SQUARE, LONDON
Architect: William Kent.
Lit: London, Sir John Soane's Museum, accounts; Margaret Jourdain, 1948, *The Work of William Kent*, p. 55.

DAY, John (*fl.* 1680). Carpenter.
1680 14 ST JAMES'S SQUARE, LONDON
Day's work and his claim that he had paid workmen on the owner's behalf (Sir John Williams) led to a Chancery dispute between Day and Lady Williams.
Lit: 1960, *Survey of London*, XXIX, p.139.

DAYON, John (*fl.* 1766). Ironmonger.
1766 SYON, MIDDLESEX
'Locks, Latches and Bolts for the Doors at Syon House—£20.'
Lit: Alnwick Castle Archives, U.1.41., 30 December 1766.

DENNIS, Thomas (*fl.* late 18th cent.). Plasterer.
Son of John Dennis of Bristol, tiler.
c 1780 Made apprentice to Thomas Stocking, senior (q.v.).
Lit: Bristol City Archives, *Apprentices' Book, 1777–1786*, p. 369.

DENSTON (DENSTONE), family of (*fl.* 18th cent.). Plasterers.
Joseph Denston, a plasterer of Derby, was buried at All Saints' Church there in 1728. His son Abraham was a plasterer, and his grandson, also named Abraham, worked extensively at Kedleston for Robert Adam. This Abraham had a son, James, and at least two brothers: Thomas, a plasterer like himself, and James, a masonry contractor who sometimes styled himself architect. Thomas tendered for the plasterwork at Yoxall Lodge, Derbyshire, but little else. Abraham died at his home in St Mary's Gate, Derby, on 24 March 1779. He was buried on 27 March in All Saints' Churchyard. W Millar, 1897, *Plastering Plain and Decorative*, p. 20, stated that Denston, 'a Derbyshire plasterer', assisted Artari and Bagutti. This must have been in 1725–26 on The Senate House, Cambridge (architect: James Gibbs).
1759–64 KEDLESTON, DERBYSHIRE
Plain plastering, the main decorative work being by Joseph Rose (q.v.).
Received £412. 5s. 9½d.
Lit: Kedleston Archives, Book 3R, pp. 60–63, Bills, 1759.
1773–74 THE ASSEMBLY ROOMS, DERBY (demolished)
Lit: Kedleston Archives, letters from James Adam to Lord Scarsdale; photographs, Derby Borough Library; will of Abraham Denston, 1779 (filed at Lichfield). (I am indebted to Mr Edward Saunders for information about the Denston family.)

DERINGER, – (*fl.* 1688). Carver.
1688 Recommended for employment at St Paul's Cathedral.
Lit: Wren Soc, XVI, p. 62.

DEVALL, George (*fl.* 1725–36). Plumber.
1725 HOUGHTON, NORFOLK
Received £300 on account for work on main house. Submitted 1733 estimate for lead and plumbing work on stables and various other buildings.
Lit: CUL(CH), Vouchers 1725, Account Book 42 (1730–36).

DEVALL, Jeremiah (*fl.* 1776–83). Plumber.
1776–83 SOMERSET HOUSE, LONDON
Received £5022. 13s. 10d.
Joined by George Holroyd in 1783, and continued by John Holroyd from 1789. Possibly connected with the Devall family of masons (q.v.).
Lit: Colvin, 1976, *King's Works*, V, p. 466.
1782–90 CHAPEL, GREENWICH HOSPITAL
Lit: RIBA, Library, MS, New/1.

DEVALL, John, senior (1701–74), **junior** (1728–94). Masons/Plumbers.
Both members of the family were talented masons and statuaries. They were both Master

of the Masons' Company (1760 and 1784 respectively). They worked extensively for Robert Adam (20 St James's Square, Nostell Priory, Kedleston), Samuel Wyatt (Shugborough) and Chambers (Somerset House). A Sergeant Plumber, John Devall held that post in the Office of Works, 1742 until his death in 1769. He also worked at Egremont House, Piccadilly.
Lit: Gunnis, 1953, *Dictionary*, p. 128; Bolton, 1922, *Adam*, II, p. 102; *C Life*, 20 June, 1, 15, 22 August 1947, 9 February 1978; N L W Wynnstay MS, 115/17/22, 24, 26; Colvin, 1976, *King's Works*, V, p. 466; PRO, LC/5/105, p. 85; Staffs. CRO, MS, D1240/1.

DEW, John (*fl.* 1664–80). Plasterer.
1664 SHELDONIAN THEATRE, OXFORD
Lit: VCH, *Oxfordshire*, III, p. 51.
1680 OLD ASHMOLEAN MUSEUM, OXFORD
Lit: ibid., p. 48.

DEWEZ, Laurent-Benoit (1731–1812). Draughtsman.
He worked with RA in Italy on the revision of Desgodetz's book on the antiquities of Rome (1682), assisted by Agostino Brunias (q.v.).
Lit: Fleming, 1962, *Adam*, pp. 216, 255, 359–60; Stillman, 1966, *Adam*, p. 54.

DEWICK, Petty (*fl.* 1697). Plasterer.
1697 SIR JOHN MOORE'S SCHOOL, APPLEBY, LEICESTERSHIRE
Architects: Sir Christopher Wren, Sir William Wilson.
Received £23. 15s. 6d.
Lit: Wren Soc, XI, p. 100.

DIBBINS, Edward (*fl.* 1775). Plasterer.
Listed in Sketchley's 1775 Bristol Directory as living at 14 Tower Street, Bristol.

DIRWICK, James (*fl.* 1774–79). Pavior.
1774–79 EGREMONT HOUSE, LONDON
Lit: West Sussex CRO, Petworth II, 6609.

DIXON, Cornelius (*fl.* 1791–94). Painter.
1791–94 15 ST JAMES'S SQUARE, LONDON
Painted friezes and panels.
Lit: 1960, *Survey of London*, XXIX, p. 148.

DIXON, Richard (?) (*fl.* 1767–75). Carpenter.
Presumably Richard Dixon of St George's, Hanover Square, who was in partnership for a time with John Phillips (q.v.).
1767–75 KENWOOD, MIDDLESEX
Lit: Bolton, 1922, *Adam*, I, p. 316; 1960, *Survey of London*, XXIX, p. 328.

DODGSON, John (*fl.* 1762–69). Plasterer.
1762–67 HAREWOOD HOUSE, YORKSHIRE
Bricklaying and plain plastering.
Lit: Mary Mauchline, 1974, *Harewood House*, p. 48.

DOEGOOD, Joseph (*fl.* 1692). Plasterer.
1692 His will is PCC, 1692, fol. 165.

DOOGOOD, Henry (*fl.* 1663–1707). Plasterer.
Doogood, with John Grove II, was employed very extensively by Sir Christopher Wren and

worked at 32 City churches. In 1700 he was made Master of the Worshipful Company of Plaisterers (London, Guildhall Library, MS, 6122/3). He died in 1707.
1663 PEMBROKE COLLEGE CHAPEL, CAMBRIDGE
Lit: Willis and Clark, 1887, *Cambridge*, I, p. 147; *Wren Soc*, VI, pp. 27–29, pl. XI; N B Pevsner, 1954, *Cambridgeshire*, p. 27, pl. 58.
c 1681 ST MARY ALDERMARY, LONDON
Architect: Sir Christopher Wren.
Lit: Wren Soc, X, p. 13; A E Daniell, 1896, *London City Churches*, p. 233.
1670–94 CITY CHURCHES, LONDON
Architect: Sir Christopher Wren.
The following alphabetical list is based on *Wren Soc.*, XII. A useful summary, with further information, is given by Colvin, 1978, *Dictionary*, pp. 922–31.
ST ALBAN, WOOD STREET, 1682–85
With John Grove. Dest 1940.
ALL HALLOWS, LOMBARD STREET, 1686–94
Demolished 1939.
ALL HALLOWS THE GREAT, UPPER THAMES STREET, 1677–83
With John Grove and Thos. Sherwood. Demolished 1893–94.
ALL HALLOWS, WATLING STREET, 1677–84
With John Grove. Demolished 1876–77.
ST ANDREW BY THE WARDROBE, 1685–93
Destroyed 1940.
ST ANTHOLIN, WATLING STREET, 1678–82
Demolished 1875.
ST AUGUSTINE, WATLING STREET, 1680–83
With John Combes. Partly destroyed 1941.
ST BARTHOLOMEW EXCHANGE, 1674–79
With John Grove. Demolished 1840–41
ST BENET, GRACECHURCH STREET, 1681–86
With John Grove. Demolished 1867–68.
ST BENET, PAUL'S WHARF (now the Welsh Church), 1677–83
CHRIST CHURCH, NEWGATE STREET, 1677–87
Destroyed 1940.
ST CLEMENT, EASTCHEAP, 1683–87
With John Grove.
ST DIONIS BACKCHURCH, FENCHURCH STREET, 1670–74
With John Grove. Demolished 1878–79.
ST GEORGE, BOTOLPH LANE, 1671–74
With John Grove. Demolished 1903–04.
ST JAMES, GARLICK HILL, 1676–83
With John Grove.
ST MAGNUS, MARTYR, LOWER CHURCH STREET, 1671–76
With John Grove.
ST MARGARET, LOTHBURY, 1686–90
ST MARGARET, PATTENS, 1684–87
With John Grove.
ST MARTIN, LUDGATE, 1677–84
With John Grove.
ST MARY ABCHURCH, 1681–86
With John Grove. Damaged 1940.
ST MARY AT HILL, 1670–76
Doogood whitewashed the church for £18, *Wren Soc*, XII, p. 32.
ST MARY MAGDALEN, OLD FISH STREET, 1683–85
Demolished 1887.
ST MARY SOMERSET, THAMES STREET, 1686–95
ST MARY LE BOW, CHEAPSIDE, 1670–73
With John Grove. Damaged 1941.
ST MATTHEW, FRIDAY STREET, 1681–85
With John Grove. Demolished 1881.
ST MICHAEL, CROOKED LANE, 1684–88
With John Grove. Demolished 1831.

ST MICHAEL, PATERNOSTER ROYAL, COLLEGE HILL, 1686–94.
ST MICHAEL, QUEENHITHE, 1676–87
With John Grove. Demolished 1876.
ST MILDRED, BREAD STREET, 1677–83
With John Grove. *Dest* 1941.
ST MILDRED, POULTRY, 1670–76
With John Grove. Demolished 1872.
ST PETER, CORNHILL, 1677–81
With John Grove.
ST STEPHEN, WALBROOK, 1672–79
With John Grove.
ST SWITHIN, CANNON STREET, 1677–85
Dest 1941.
1681 WESTMINSTER ABBEY CLOISTERS, LONDON
House of Dr Richard Busby. Received £43. 15s. 0d. for 'fretwork, plastering, etc.'.
Lit: *Wren Soc*, X, p. 22.
1682 and 1690 ST CHARLES THE MARTYR, TUNBRIDGE WELLS, KENT
Dated ceilings by Doogood. Received £190.
Lit: Marcus Whiffen, 1947, *Stuart and Georgian Churches*, p. 97.
1686–87 TRINITY COLLEGE, CAMBRIDGE
See entry for John Grove.
1689 BISHOP'S PALACE, LICHFIELD, STAFFORDSHIRE
Architect: Edward Pearce.
Doogood's work no longer survives.
Lit: H M Colvin and Arthur Oswald, 30 December 1954, *C Life*, citing Church Commissioners' MS, 123828.
1689 MONTAGU HOUSE, LONDON
Received £826 in 1689–90.
Doogood also worked on the New Chapel in Whitehall, at Boughton House, Northants (1694–96 and 1701), Geddington, Weekley Church and Ditton Park. The total of his bills submitted to the executors of the Duke of Montagu was £2027.
Lit: Boughton House, Duke of Montagu's Executors' Accounts, 2, ff. 609–24. (I am indebted for information to Mr Patrick King, Mr John Cornforth and Sir David Scott.)
1695 CHRIST'S HOSPITAL, LONDON
Received £33. 18s. 6d.
Lit: *Wren Soc*, XI, p. 75. In 1698 Dogood was one of five contestants for the job of Plaisterer to Christ's Hospital (*Wren Soc*, XI, p. 70); the others were Thomas Burton, John Eales, Jerome Hall and William Smith.
Attributed work
1688 5 MARKET HILL, CAMBRIDGE
Ceiling dated 1688.
Lit: Sir Arthur Clapham, 1943–47, *Cambridge Antiquarian Society*, XLI, pp. 56–59.

DOOGOOD, Ralph (*fl.* 1708–10). Plasterer.
1708–10 ST PAUL'S CATHEDRAL, LONDON
Worked under Chrysostom Wilkins (q.v.).
Lit: *Wren Soc*, XV, pp. 169, 196.

DRAKE, Nathan (*fl.* 1760). Colourman.
'Nathan Drake. Colourman. Successor to Mr. Robert Keating at the White Hart in Long Acre, London. Sells all sorts of fine colors and oils for painting. Prym'd Cloths, Pencils, fine Tools and Palletts. . . all sorts of Colours and Oils for House Painting at the Lowest Rates. . . .'
Lit: Trade Card *repr.* by A Heal, 1968, *London Tradesmen's Cards of the Eighteenth Century*, p. 33.

DRAPER, – (*fl.* 1690). Locksmith.
1690 PETWORTH, SUSSEX
Provided locks.
Lit: West Sussex CRO, Egremont Archives, John Bower's account roll.

DRYHURST, James (*fl.* 1727–62). Carver.
1727–28 Employed by James Brydges, 1st Duke of Chandos, on his London house in Cavendish Square. He took an apprentice, George Davidson, in 1733. He is presumably the James Dryhurst who was working in 1761–62 on Lord Northampton's house in Grosvenor Square.
Lit: Baker, 1949, *Brydges*, p. 277; Compton Place, Eastbourne, Box Q; London, Guildhall Library, Boyd's Index to Apprenticeship Registers, VIII, p. 1522.
A Thomas Dryhurst (carver) is one of 13 figures in a picture by Robert Pyle painted in 1760 destroyed in a fire at Buxted Park, Sussex, 1940. He worked for the architect, Henry Keene.
Lit: *C Life*, 30 March 1945, *ill.* p. 556; Colvin, 1978, *Dictionary*, p. 482.

DUBOIS, Nicholas (*c* 1665–1735). Architect and Carver.
For his architectural career *see* Colvin, 1978, *Dictionary*. He erected the unusual staircase at Chevening House, Kent, in 1721.
Lit: H Avray Tipping, *English Homes*, Period V, I, p. 23; Kent CRO, U1590, E26/2, E26/4.

DUFFOUR, – (*fl. c* 1760). Carver/Gilder.
'Carver, gilder and original maker of papier-mâché at the *Golden Head* in Berwick Street, Soho.' Succeeded by René Stone, *c* 1765, at the same address.
Lit: Trade Card, *repr.* by A Heal, 1953, *The London Furniture Makers*, pp. 50, 51, 176.

DUGDALE, James (*fl.* 1675). Plasterer.
c 1675 CLIFTON HALL, NOTTINGHAMSHIRE
Lit: *C Life*, 25 August 1923.

DUGDALE, Thomas (*fl.* 1678–1714). Carver.
Of Liverpool.
1678–79 CHIRK CASTLE, DENBIGHSHIRE
Long Gallery, panelling.
Lit: N L W, Myddleton MS, cited by W M Myddleton, *Chirk Castle Accounts, 1666–1753*. Dugdale also worked for Lady Wilbraham at Weston Hall, Staffordshire: Oliver Hill and John Cornforth, 1966, *English Country Houses: Caroline*, p. 227; Gunnis, 1953, *Dictionary*, p. 133.

DUKING, Francis (*fl.* 1697). Plasterer.
1697 SIR JOHN MOORE'S SCHOOL, APPLEBY, LEICESTERSHIRE
Architects: Sir Christopher Wren, Sir William Wilson.
Supplied plaster.
Lit: *Wren Soc*, XI, p. 99.

DUNGAN, Richard (*fl.* 1606–9). Plasterer.
1606–09 WHITEHALL PALACE, LONDON
Received £303. 6s. 0d. for plastering the ceiling of the old Banqueting House.
Lit: 1953, *Archaeological Journal*, CX, p. 151.

DUNN, Richard (*fl.* 1775). Plasterer.
Mentioned as a tiler and plasterer in Sketchley's 1775 Bristol Directory.

DUNSTERFIELD, George (*fl.* 1660–75). Plasterer.
Possibly to be identified with 'George Dunstervile' who worked at Whitehall in November 1660.
Lit: PRO, Works, 5/1, September 1660: 'George Dunstervile, xxii dayes, 1s.'.
In 1674 he was sent north with John Houlbert by the Earl of Lauderdale to work for Sir William Bruce at Balcaskie, Thirlestane, and Holyroodhouse.
1673–74 BALCASKIE HOUSE, FIFE
Architect: Sir William Bruce.
Worked in most of the rooms of the house. He was paid at the daily rate of 3s. 6d. Probably assisted by William Lindores (q.v.).
Lit: Scottish Record Office, Kinross House Archives, cited in *Sir William Bruce, 1630–1710*, Scottish Arts Council, Exhibition Catalogue, 1970, No. 77.
1674–76 THIRLESTANE CASTLE, BERWICKSHIRE
Signed receipts 10 July 1674 and 6 March 1676 for plastering.
Lit: Scottish Record Office, Thirlestane Castle Archives.
1674–79 HOLYROODHOUSE, EDINBURGH
Assisted John Houlbert (q.v.).
Lit: R S Mylne, 1893, *The Master Masons to the Crown of Scotland*, p. 197.

DURAND, Jonas (*fl.* 1709). Plasterer.
1709 Due for almost £50 for unspecified work done for Ralph, 1st Duke of Montagu.
Lit: Boughton Archives, Parcel D.11, Part 2.

DUXON, Joseph (*fl.* 1710–16). Carpenter.
Partner of Edward Johnson.
1710–16 3 ST JAMES'S SQUARE, LONDON
Repairs, timber shoring.
Lit: 1960, *Survey of London*, XXIX, p. 84.

EALES, John (*fl.* 1698). Plasterer.
1698 One of five contestants for the job of Plaisterer to Christ's Hospital, London.
Lit: *Wren Soc*, XI, p. 70.

EARL, James (*fl.* 1791–92). Plasterer.
A 'James Earle', plasterer, appears in 1789 in the York Freeman's Roll.
1791 Living at Trinity House Lane, Kingston-upon-Hull. There is a counterpart of a lease in the Civic Records of a messuage in High Street, at the south end of the town.
1792 Living at 'Southend', Kingston-upon-Hull.
Lit: Kingston-upon-Hull, Civic Records M843, 1791 Directory.

EBORAL, George (*fl.* 1737–60). Joiner.
Mentioned in the will of Edward Poynton (q.v.), and known as one of Francis and William Smith's craftsmen. Worked at Kirtlington, Oxon., and in his native Warwick. A William Eborall did mason's work at Warwick Castle, 1777.
Lit: Information from Mrs Ingrid Roscoe; Warwicks. CRO, Warwick Castle Vouchers, 1777.

EBORALL, Thomas (*fl.* 1721–37). Joiner.
Of Warwick.
Mentioned in the will (1737) of a fellow craftsman, Edward Poynton (q.v.).
Presumably son or brother of George Eborall (q.v.).
1721 CHICHELEY HALL, BUCKINGHAMSHIRE
Architect: Francis Smith.
Lit: Joan D Tanner, 1961, 'The Building of Chicheley Hall', *Records of Bucks.*, xvii, pt. 1.
1724 SUTTON SCARSDALE, DERBYSHIRE
Architect: Francis Smith.
Lit: C *Life*, 15 February 1919, p. 171; as 'Thomas Broral of Warwick, Gentleman joiner' on a lead rising-plate (now lost). The house survives as a ruin; three rooms were re-erected (1928) at Philadelphia Museum of Art, USA.

EDISBURY, Kenridge (*fl.* 1685). Plasterer.
1685 ST PAUL'S CATHEDRAL, LONDON
Glacis paving.
Lit: Wren Soc, XIII, p. 201, XVI, pp. 20–21.

EDMONSON, John (*fl.* 1694–1704).
Plasterer.
Master of Worshipful Company of Plaisterers, 1704.
1694–95 ST SWITHIN, CANNON STREET, LONDON
Received £20.
Lit: Wren Soc, XIX, p. 56, citing the churchwardens' accounts at the Guildhall Library.

EDWIN, Francis (*fl.* 1760). Plasterer.
1760 Fined 40s. for bad materials used in a 'new house in New London Street, Crutched Fryers, London'.
Lit: London, Guildhall Library, MS, 6126, 7 August 1760.

ELLIOTT, Charles (*fl.* 1689). Plasterer.
1689 HAMPTON COURT, MIDDLESEX
Worked under John Grove (q.v.).
Lit: PRO Works, 5/55, April 1689.

ELLIS, James (*fl.* 1703–58). Plasterer.
Of 'Watling Street in Parish of St Antholin, London'. In partnership with James Hands (q.v.). Dismissed from the 'Livery' of the Plaisterers' Company in 1711 for 'disturbing the good order and government of the said Company'. He did, however, get readmitted to office in 1715 and 1719 and, at his death in 1758, left a gift of money to the Company to distribute '40 Bushells of Coal at the discretion of the Company's Renter-Warden'. He took an apprentice, John Wright of Southwark, in 1703.
Lit: London, Guildhall Library, MS, 6122/3.
1712–14 ST ALPHEGE, GREENWICH, LONDON
Architect: Nicholas Hawksmoor.
Lit: Colvin, 1950, *Arch Rev*, p. 196.
c 1715 ST PAUL, DEPTFORD, LONDON
Architect: Thomas Archer.
Worked with his partner James Hands (q.v.). The church was under construction from 1712 to 1730.
Lit: Colvin, 1950, *Arch Rev*, p. 196.

ELSEY, Richard (*fl.* 1707–88). Plasterer.
Official of the Worshipful Company of Plaisterers.

1707 Upper Warden.
1708 Master.
Lit: London, Guildhall Library, MS, 6122/3.

ELSON, James (*fl. c* 1765). Plasterer.
c 1765 POWDERHAM, DEVON
Lit: C Life, 11 July 1963, p. 83.

ELWELL, John (*fl.* 1779). Locksmith.
1779 EGREMONT HOUSE, LONDON
Lit: West Sussex CRO, Petworth II, 6609, 6611.

EMMETT, William (*fl.* 1641–1700). Carver.
Probably born in 1641. Sculptor to the Crown before Gibbons, succeeding his uncle Henry Phillips. Liveryman of the Joiners' Company in 1666, Warden in 1698.
1690 KENSINGTON PALACE, LONDON
62 Ballisters in ye railes before ye Communion Table,
2 Large Imperial Crowns over ye door,
4 Spandrells of foliage and cyphers of their Majesties.
Lit: 1951, *Jnl., British Arch. Assoc.*, p. 4.
He worked also at Whitehall, Hampton Court, several City churches, Chelsea Hospital (received £212. 4s. 4d.) and the Temple Church. Two carved capitals by Emmett from this church are at the Bowes Museum, Barnard Castle, Durham.
Lit: Wren Soc, IV, pp. 22, 25, 44, 52, VII, pp. 98, 99. 104, 114–15, 121, 124, 126, 153, 157, 164, 171, 178, 181, X, pp. 19, 27, 41, 54, XIX, p. xxiii, XIX, pp. 10, 14, 31; 1872, *Papers illustrative of the History of Chelsea Hospital*, pp. 169–70; London, Guildhall Library, MS, 8046, 3.

ENGLEHEART, Francis (1713–73).
Plasterer.
Born in Germany in 1713 and is traditionally supposed to have come to England about 1721–22. He settled in Kew and married Ann, the daughter of the parish clerk of Kew, in 1734. Either he or his wife was a nephew or niece of John Dillman, also a German, who worked at Kew Gardens for Frederick, Prince of Wales. He had 10 sons, 5 of whom survived infancy. The two elder, John Dillman Engleheart (1735–1810) and Paul Engleheart (d.1774), were also plasterers. In his will of 1772 he left his 'moulds and scaffolding' to these two eldest sons. Francis Engleheart is mentioned from time to time in Sir William Chambers's letters and in James Paine's bank account. He worked consistently at Kew in the employment of the Princess Dowager, and was said by his grandson, Nathaniel, writing about 1850, to have 'with his own hands fabricated some of the admirably ornamental ceilings at Hampton Court, and some other Royal Palaces. . .'.
John Dillman Engleheart seems to have been the plasterer at 356 and 358 Kew Road, houses he built and owned in 1776. 21 Kew Green and 352 Kew Road also have good ceilings.
Lit: Letter-books of Sir William Chambers, BL Add MS, 41133 (13 May 1770, 12 March 1772); Paine's Bank Account (Coutts); Duchy of Cornwall Office, Vouchers XLI, 1757, p. 63; information kindly communicated by

Mrs J Wilners, and particularly by his descendant H F A Engleheart of Stoke by Nayland, Suffolk; Harris, 1970, *Chambers*, pp. 39, 214, 242.

ENZER (ENZIER), Joseph (*fl. c* 1725–43). Plasterer.
Known for his work at Arniston and Yester, Enzer is said to have been Dutch. He married 'Helen Arskin' (Erskine) on 22 July 1738 at Edinburgh, and on 18 May 1739 a daughter Susan was born. Enzer was then described as 'plaisterer at Yester', and 'John Adams son to Wm Adams architect' was one of the two witnesses. William, John and Robert Adam had known Enzer, and William, in a letter of 5 July 1743, informed the Marquess of Tweeddale, their patron at Yester House, East Lothian, that 'poor Joseph Enzer died last week'. The testaments made at the time of Enzer's death were not proved until 1745.
Lit: Edinburgh, Register of Marriages, Canongate (Scottish Record Society, 1915); Commissariat of Edinburgh, printed lists, 30 April 1745 (copy Scottish Record Office); information from Miss C H Cruft (National Monuments Record of Scotland).
c 1730 ARNISTON HOUSE, MIDLOTHIAN
Architect: William Adam.
Lit: Jourdain, 1926, *Plasterwork*, p. x; *C Life*, 9 October 1915; *Burl Mag*, March 1969, pp. 132–140.
1736–39 YESTER HOUSE, EAST LOTHIAN
Architect: William Adam.
Great Staircase and Dining Room. Assisted by Philip Robertson, Francis Nicols, Daniel Ross and Abraham Lester.
Lit: National Library of Scotland, Enzer's account book, Yester House archives; John Dunbar, 1972, *Transactions, East Lothian Antiquarian Society*, XIII, p. 28; *C Life*, 16 August 1973, p. 432.
c 1740 ROYAL INFIRMARY EDINBURGH
Architect: William Adam.
In the Testament made at the time of Enzer's death in 1743, a sum of £230 was due 'as part of a greater sum for work done by the defunct upon the sd. Infirmary'.
Other work
There is little doubt that, with Samuel Calderwood (q.v.), Enzer shared the task of providing plasterwork at William Adam houses. These are discussed by Fleming, 1962, *Adam*, and may have included Dun House, Montrose; Duff House, Banffshire; Lawers, Perthshire, *c* 1725; and Fullarton House, Troon. The emblematic heads in the cove of the Old Library ceiling at Touch, Stirlingshire (*C Life*, 2 September 1965, figs. 2, 3) are similar in treatment to work at Dun House. His work at Yester House, East Lothian, being documented provides a reliable point for future comparisons. The Yester accounts show that Enzer's apprentices, Philip Robertson and Daniel Ross, went 'on to Leslie', which may imply work at Leslie Castle, Aberdeenshire, or elsewhere.

ESSEX, James (d. 1749). Carpenter.
Of Cambridge. Did much woodwork in university buildings, such as the interior joinery, sashes, etc., at the Senate House (received over £2300). His son James Essex (1722–1784) became an architect.

Lit: Willis and Clark, 1887, *Cambridge*, III, pp. 540–41; Little, 1955, *Gibbs*, p. 58; Colvin, 1978, *Dictionary*, p. 297.

ETTY, John (*c* 1634–1708). Carpenter/Joiner
Of the well-known York family of architects and carpenters. It was to John Etty that Grinling Gibbons went at York. He died on 28 January 1707/08, aged 75, and was buried 30 January. His epitaph in All Saints, North Street, York reads:
'By the strength of his own genius and application had acquired great knowledge of Mathematicks, especially Geometry and Architecture in all its parts, far beyond any of his Contemporaries in this City.'
In 1674 Etty rebuilt most of the roof of the West Wing of Temple Newsam House, Leeds. His major piece of woodcarving is the reredos in St Michael-le-Belfrey, York, for which he was paid £68. There is little doubt that, while little of Etty's activities have yet been established, he was one of the most important York artisans of the late seventeenth century.
Lit: York Reference Library, Skaife MSS; J B Morrell, 1950, *Woodwork in York*; Beard, 1966, *Craftsmen* (pedigree); RCHM, 1972, *City of York*, III, p. 9.

ETTY, William (*c* 1675–1734).
Joiner/Builder.
Etty was an important member of a prominent family of York master builders and joiners. He acted as clerk of works to Colen Campbell for the building of Baldersby, Yorkshire (1720), and for Sir John Vanbrugh at Seaton Delaval (1719) and Castle Howard (1721).
c 1712 ST MICHAEL LE BELFRY, YORK
Altar-piece.
Lit: Beard, 1966, *Craftsmen*, p. 3.

EYKYN, Roger (*c* 1725–95).
Architect/Builder/Joiner.
A man of several skills, Eykyn trained as a joiner, first appearing at Wolverhampton in 1760. The 'fine doorcases' at Styche Hall, Salop, for the 1st Baron Clive may be his work if he is the 'Me Eykyn' of the accounts.
Lit: Harris, 1970, *Chambers*, p. 248; Colvin, 1978, *Dictionary*, p. 304.

FERRAND, Thomas (*fl.* 1823). Carver.
Of Stonegate, York.
Lit: Baines, 1823, *York Directory*, II, p. 119. (I am indebted to Dr Eric Gee for this reference.)

FEWKES, George (*fl. c.* 1750–63). Plasterer.
1760 Appointed by Worshipful Company of Plaisterers as one of the assessors for bad work.
1763 Takes an apprentice, John Cook.
Lit: London, Guildhall Library, MS, 6122/4, 6126.
c 1750 MANSION HOUSE, LONDON
Architect: George Dance, senior.
Worked with Humphrey Wilmott.
First floor, received £905; second floor and attic, received (with Wilmot) £750; Egyptian Hall, Wilmot received £600; total of £2255.
Lit: N B Pevsner, 1957, *Buildings of England, London*, Pt. 1, p. 176, pl. 68b.

FIFIELD, David (*fl.* 1690). Plasterer.
1690 Makes oath that Henry Margetts (q.v.) was to do work for Sir George Downing, then deceased, at East Hattley, Cambridgeshire, 1684.
Lit: Castle Howard Archives, Executors' accounts, Sir George Downing.
1712 CLARENDON BUILDING, OXFORD
Lit: VCH, *Oxfordshire*, III, p. 55n, 140.

FILEWOOD, Richard and **James** (*fl.* 1748–95). Carpenters.
1748–50 (Richard Filewood) 14 ST JAMES'S SQUARE, LONDON
Lit: 1960, *Survey of London*, XXIX, p. 140.
1776–95 (James Filewood) SOMERSET HOUSE, LONDON
Received £14 426. 19s. 4d.
Lit: Colvin, 1976, *King's Works*, V, p. 465.

FLOODMAN, Daniel (*fl.* 1769–81).
Plumber.
Sergeant Plumber to the Office of Works, 1769, until his death in 1781. The post was then abolished.
Lit: Colvin, 1976, *King's Works*, V, p. 473.

FLUDYER, William (*fl.* 1691). Plasterer.
1691 His will is PCC, 1691, fol. 5.

FLY, J (*fl.* 1710). Plasterer.
1710 ST PAUL'S CATHEDRAL, LONDON
Worked under Chrysostom Wilkins (q.v.).
Lit: Wren Soc, XV, p. 196.

FOOTE, Edmond (*fl.* 1660). Plasterer.
1660 THE TOWER, LONDON
Worked under John Grove I (q.v.).
Lit: PRO, Works, 5/1.

FORT, Alexander (*c* 1645–1706). Joiner.
Apprenticed to Henry Phillips, 1659. In 1678 obtained the reversion of post of Master Joiner in the Office of Works, which he claimed on Thomas Kinward's death in 1682. Charles II refused to allow the patent to be taken up, and James II declined to help because, Fort alleged, he had been working on the Duke of Monmouth's house at the time of his Rebellion. He took up the post fully at the accession of William III. Worked on royal commissions, and at Salisbury Cathedral, Fawley, measuring at Chatsworth, etc. Had a son Thomas (q.v.).
Lit: Colvin, 1976, *King's Works*, V, pp. 28, 46, 453; Colvin, 1978, *Dictionary*, p. 314.

FORT, Thomas (?–1745). Joiner.
Son of Alexander Fort (q.v.), he applied unsuccessfully for his father's post as Master Joiner in the Office of Works in 1706. Worked as clerk of works at Hampton Court, having gained experience as Master Joiner to the future William III at Het Loo in Holland. Worked at Sunbury, Chevening, Canons, etc.
Lit: Colvin, 1976, *King's Works*, V, pp. 53, 60, 335; Colvin, 1978, *Dictionary*, p. 314.

FOSTER, – (*fl* 1737). Plasterer.
1737 CAVENDISH SQUARE, LONDON
Architect: Edward Shepherd.
End house, north side, Staircase for James Brydges, 1st Duke of Chandos. Received £70.

Lit: Baker, 1949, *Brydges*, pp. 199 and 285; Colvin, 1978, *Dictionary*, p. 732.

FOSTER, James (*fl.* 1824). Plasterer.
1824 WINDSOR CASTLE, BERKSHIRE
His contract of 9 August 1824 is PRO, Works, 1/13.
Lit: D Linstrum, 1972, *Sir Jeffry Wyatville*, p. 252.

FRANCEYS, Samuel (*fl.* 1760). Plasterer.
Possibly of Liverpool and connected with the statuaries of this name.
1760 MELBOURNE HALL, DERBYSHIRE
Decorative work.
Lit: Melbourne Archives, cited by Gunnis, 1953, *Dictionary*, p. 156.

FRANCHINI (FRANCINI) Paul and **Philip** (*fl.* 1730–60). Stuccoists.
As with all the Italian-speaking *stuccatori* working in England, exact identification is not possible. It has been suggested that they came from Modena, but in view of the births of those *stuccatori* working in England being recorded in the vicinity of Lake Lugano, the village of Mendrisio near there appears most likely. The parish archives there record the baptism on 3 May 1694 of 'Jacobus Philipus', son of Filippo Franchini and Anna Maria. One of the godparents was the well-known *stuccatore* Giovanni Battista Clerici. No trace has been found of Paul Franchini's birth. There may well have been two, or even three, of the family at work in England and particularly Ireland.
Their work in both these countries is obscure, with little documentation. Two payments in James Gibbs's bank account (Drummonds) show he had some association with one of them:
1731 December 20 Paid la Franchino £10. 10. —.
1736 August 4 To ditto paid Mr. La Franchino £95.
While their work in Ireland is beyond the scope of this book, I have had the opportunity of discussing their activities with Dr C P Curran (*see* his *Dublin Decorative Plasterwork of the 17th and 18th Centuries*, 1967) and with Mr Edward Murphy. Dr Peter Leach has also noted their connections with the northern architect Daniel Garrett, and Professor Giuseppe Martinola of Lugano has discussed their origins with me, and in his various publications on Mendrisio and the *stuccatori* of the Ticino. It should be noted that he refers to the births of four members of the family: Cosimo, Pietro Antonio, Giovanni Battista and Guiseppe, in addition to Paul and Philip (*see* G Martinola, 1964, *Le Maestranze d'Arte del Mendrisiotto in Italia nei Secoli XVI–XVIII*, p. 62).
1740–41 WALLINGTON, NORTHUMBERLAND
Dining Room. Received £23. 19s. 6d.
Saloon. Received £44. 19s. 6d.
The Dining Room chimneypiece has affinities with that in the Garter Room, Lumley Castle, Durham (below).
Lit: Wallington House Archives; Alnwick Castle Archives, Countess of Northumberland's Diary, cited in *C Life*, 12 March, 23 April 1970, 19 September 1974.

1748 FENHAM HALL, NORTHUMBERLAND
Received £60.
Lit: C Life, 19 September 1974, p. 767.
1750 HOUSE FOR DUKE OF CLEVELAND,
LONDON
Received £31 10s.
Lit: C Life, ibid.
1750–54 NORTHUMBERLAND HOUSE, LONDON
Demolished 1874.
Received £830 in several payments.
Lit: C Life, 12 March 1970, p. 635.
Attributed work
Work in Bath (15 Queen Square) and at St
Mary's Chapel, Queen Square (demolished
c 1875) has, in my opinion, been attributed
erroneously to the Franchinis by G N Wright,
who did guides to both Bath and Dublin in
the 1820s. In the Dublin one, he makes
attributions to them which are very doubtful.
The Franchinis obviously became his
favourite citation. John Wood, in his 1743,
Description of Bath, makes no reference to
them. A panel at Fairfax House, Castlegate,
York, is identical with one in the President's
House, Phoenix Park, Dublin, taken as a cast
from one formerly at Riverstown House where
the brothers worked. There is, however, no
need to credit the York panel to them.
The most likely further attribution is work in
the Garter Room, Lumley Castle, Durham. It
compares well with their work in Ireland
(particularly Castletown, Co Kildare). There
is use of an identical medallion at Lumley and
the Music, or Muses, Room, Lancaster. As
noted above, they had association with the
architects James Gibbs and Daniel Garrett. As
knowledge of the work of both, and
particularly the latter, emerges, it seems likely
more commissions will be recorded for these
talented *stuccatori*.

FREEMAN, Edward (*fl.* late 17th cent.).
Carver.
Worked at St Peter, Cornhill, London.
Lit: Wren Soc, X, pp. 52, 54.

FRIME, Charles (*fl.* 1750–60). Carver.
Worked at Kew under the supervision of Sir
William Chambers.
Lit: Harris, 1970, Chambers, p. 214.

FIRTH, Robert (*fl.* 1719–21). Plasterer.
1719–21 LEICESTER HOUSE, LONDON
Lit: Windsor, Royal Household Accounts,
Establishment Book, 1719–21, p. 5.

FRITH, William (*fl.* 1731). Carpenter.
1731 6 ST JAMES'S SQUARE, LONDON
Received £355.
Lit: 1960, Survey of London, XXIX, p. 104.

FROGLEY, Arthur (*fl.* 1660–1700). Master
Carpenter.
Master Carpenter for Sir Christopher Wren,
with Richard Frogley, at the Sheldonian
Theatre, Oxford. Worked also in the colleges
of Brasenose, Corpus Christi, Lincoln,
Merton and St Edmund Hall.
Lit: RCHM, Oxford; Wren Soc, XIX, p. 92.

FROGLEY, Richard (*fl.* late 17th cent.).
Master Carpenter.
Carpenter, 1679–83, at the Old

Ashmolean, Oxford. Worked as a contractor
for the Bishop of Oxford at Cuddesdon. In
1681 he was engaged in a lawsuit with the
Oxford mason Thomas Wood. Worked with
Arthur Frogley at the Sheldonian Theatre,
Oxford.
Lit: Gunnis, 1953, Dictionary, p. 440.

FRY, Alexander (*fl.* 1775). Plasterer.
Mentioned as a 'tiler and plasterer' in
Sketchley's 1775 Bristol Directory.

GAMBLE, – (*fl.* 1770). Carver and Gilder.
1770 KEDLESTON, DERBYSHIRE
Received £6. 16s. for gilding the organ case.
Lit: Kedleston Archives, 3R; 1958, The
Connoisseur Yearbook, p. 26.

GARD, Philip (*fl.* 1730–32). Plasterer.
1730–32 CHILSTON HOUSE, DEVON
Lit: Exeter City Library, Mallock Archives,
2085–90.

GARRARD, George (1760–1826). Sculptor.
Born 31 May 1750. Studied as a boy under
Sawrey Gilpin. After attending the Royal
Academy Schools c 1778–85, he deserted
painting for sculpture. 'He became well
known for his reliefs and accurate small-scale
models of animals in plaster and bronze.'
Lit: Gunnis, 1953, Dictionary, pp. 163–64, for
a full biography; Dorothy Stroud, 1950,
Henry Holland, pp. 37, 49 and *frontis*.

GASCOIGNE, Edward (*fl.* 1772–74).
Brazier.
Mentioned in RABA.
1772–74 20 ST JAMES'S SQUARE, LONDON
Lit: NLW, Wynnstay MS, 115/17/4.

GIBBONS, Grinling (1648–1721). Master
Carver.
Born 4 April 1648 of English parents at
Rotterdam. His father, James, who was
admitted to the freedom of the Drapers'
Company on 12 September 1638, lived at
Rotterdam until 1659. He married Elizabeth
Gorlings (Gurlings) c 1638/39.
Gibbons came to England c 1667 and early on
went to York where he was with (but not
apprenticed to) John Etty (q.v.). Finally, he
left for London and settled with his family at
Deptford and did ship-carving. He was
probably trained in the Quellins' workshop,
and the influence of Dutch still-life and
flower-painters made a profound impression
on him.
He was 'discovered' on 18 January 1671 by
John Evelyn. There is a portrait group at
Audley End by Lely showing the painter with
the architect Hugh May and a bust of
Gibbons in the background.
Gibbons was appointed Master Carver in
Wood to the Crown by Charles II, a position
he held until the reign of George I. He
worked extensively also in stone, as well as
wood (*see* pls. 106–116). He died on 3 August
1721 at his house in Bow Street, Covent
Garden, and in November of the following
year his collection was sold.
Lit: Gunnis, 1953, Dictionary; H Avray
Tipping, 1914, *Grinling Gibbons and the
Woodwork of his age*; Connoisseur, April and

August 1941; *Notes and Queries*, 4th series, 3,
4; David Green, 1964, *Grinling Gibbons*.
c 1669 Wooden carving 6 × 4 in representing
the history of Elijah under the Juniper tree,
supported by an angel (I Kings, 19). Done by
Gibbons at York and in the collection of the
early eighteenth-century diarist and historian,
Ralph Thoresby.
Lit: Thoresby's *Museum* in T R Whitaker,
1816, *Ducatus Leodiensis*, p. 49.
c 1671 Wood relief, 'The Stoning of St
Stephen'. Said to be the work Gibbons was
doing when discovered by Evelyn. Now in the
Victoria and Albert Museum, London.
Gibbons's wood reliefs are a difficult subject—
another is at Dunham Massey Hall, Cheshire.
1676 SUDBURY, DERBYSHIRE
'Mr. Gibbons had for ye carved work on ye
drawing room chimney, £40.'
Lit: C Life, 22 June 1935, p. 655, fig. 13;
Sudbury, Vernon Archives.
Gibbons worked at Windsor in the apartments
decorated by Antonio Verrio, and at
Kensington Palace (£839), Trinity College,
Cambridge, and St Paul's. His name occurs in
the bank account of the 1st Duke of Beaufort
(Child's Bank) for Badminton,
Gloucestershire:
1683 July 6. Paid Mr. Gibbons, Carver. £50
1684 June 4. Paid Mr. Grymlin Gibbons for
Pictures £98
And that of the Earl of Exeter (Child's Bank)
for Burghley House, Northants:
1683 July 6. Paid Mr. Gibbons, Carver, £50
1685 Dec. 21. Paid Mr. Gibbons, Carver in
full
In 1683 he completed the altar-piece at St
James's, Piccadilly, mentioned by Evelyn in
December 1684. Walpole (1798, *Anecdotes of
Painting*, III, p. 86) attributed the font to him
also. He did the reredos at St Mary,
Abchurch, but it is perhaps his work at
Cambridge and St Paul's which should claim
our attention.
M D Whinney in *Grinling Gibbons in
Cambridge*, 1948, attributes two wooden busts
of Ben Jonson and 'Anacreon' in the Library
of Trinity College to him. There is also a
marble statue of the 6th Duke of Somerset by
Gibbons, who worked at Petworth for him.
The coats-of-arms in the Library are in light-
coloured lime-wood, fashioned out of built-up
blocks of planks about 2½ in thick glued
together, cut in the round and then applied to
the panelling. The carvings relate to Somerset
on the west side; those on the east are coats of
masters or benefactors of the college:
1 John Hacket, Bishop of Coventry and
Lichfield, 1661–70.
2 John Pearson, Master, 1662–73. Bishop of
Chester, 1672–86.
3 Isaac Burrow, DD, Master, 1673–77.
4 Hon John Montagu, Master, 1683–1700.
5 Sir Thomas Sclater, Bt.
6 Sir Robert Hildyard, Bt.
7 Sir George Chamberlaine.
8 Humphrey Babington, DD, Senior Bursar.
9 William Lynett, DD.
10–12 Sir Henry Newton Puckering (*see*
pl. 109), who in 1691 presented his Library to
the college. The coats cost £5 each, Schlater,
Chamberlaine, Babington, Lynett and Bishop
Pearson paying for their own, the college for
the remainder.

13 Robert Drake. This was carved by
Cornelius Austin.
On the north and south walls of the Library,
Gibbons carved pediments over the doors,
drapery, cherubs' heads, flowers and fruit. He
received £245 for the statue of the duke, a
number of 'bustos' (unspecified), nine named
and other unnamed coats-of-arms, and an
additional £160 for unspecified work.
At St Paul's Cathedral (*see* pls. 114 and 115),
on the other hand, his bills in 1696–97
amounted to £2894. 11s. 6d. but, as St Paul's
was largely erected on credit, he only received
in cash £1683, and had his bills finally cleared
about 1700.
Lit: Wren Soc, IV, p. 16, V, pp. 22, 34, 40,
VII, pp. 157, 160, 178, 181, X, pp. 7, 93, XI,
p. 118, XIII, p. 5.
After 1700 Gibbons worked for the Earl of
Carlisle and was paid £35 'for carving' 1705–
06, and a further £5 on 9 April 1706 by Nevil
Ridley, the agent. This was probably for some
work in connection with Castle Howard or
Carlisle House, Soho Square (Castle Howard
Archives, Nevil Ridley's Accounts, 1704–12).
He was paid £156. 9s. 4d. for unspecified
carving at Hawksmoor's church, St Alphege,
Greenwich, erected 1712–24 (Colvin, 1950,
Arch Rev., p. 196).

GIBBONS, Simon (*fl.* mid-17th cent.).
Master Carpenter.
A Master Carpenter who worked for Inigo
Jones.
Lit: H Avray Tipping, 1914, *Grinling Gibbons
and the Woodwork of his Age*, p. 47.

GILBERT, John (*fl.* mid-18th cent.). Carver
and Furniture Maker.
Of London. Lived in Great Queen Street and
was Upholder to His Majesty George III.
Mentioned in Mortimer, 1763, p. 11, and in
RABA, 1764.
1752 MANSION HOUSE, LONDON
All carved woodwork: in the Venetian Parlour
he achieved some superb effects.
Lit: H Clifford Smith, December 1952, *The
Connoisseur*, p. 181, and 1957, *The Mansion
House*, pp. 13, 19.
1767 CROOME COURT, WORCESTERSHIRE
Architect RA
'Carving a Scutchin to Cast for Doors. This
Pattern for casting the Brass Furniture was
done to our order, James Adam.'
Lit: Geoffrey Beard, 1960, *Trans., Worcs.
Arch. Soc.*; Metropolitan Museum (New
York) *Bulletin*, November 1959.
1768 MERSHAM-LE-HATCH, KENT
Architect RA
Door-cases, over-mantels. Received
£469. 14s. 0d.
Lit: Hussey, 1956, *ECH: Mid-Georgian*,
p. 100.
Gilbert also worked for RA at Shardeloes and
the Dining Room of Lansdowne House (now
Metropolitan Museum, New York).
1768 LANSDOWNE HOUSE, LONDON
Lit: Bolton, 1922, *Adam*, II, p. 344.
Probably also provided the bookcases in the
Library at Osterley Park.

GILL, E (*fl.* 1697). Plasterer.
1696–97 PETWORTH, SUSSEX
Received £10 in 1696, £89. 15s. 0d. in 1697.

Lit: West Sussex CRO, Egremont Archives,
William Miller's Account Rolls, 1696–97.
See also Edward Goudge *and* David Lance.

GILL, Robert (*fl.* 1718–29). Plasterer.
Presumably of Liverpool.
1718–29 KNOWSLEY, LANCASHIRE
Lit: Lancs. CRO, Derby (Knowsley)
Archives. (I am indebted to Mr S A Harris for
this reference.)

GILL, Westby (*fl.* 1719–46). Carpenter.
Master Carpenter to the Office of Works,
1735 until his death in 1746. Previously
Deputy Surveyor.
Lit: Colvin, 1954, *Dictionary*, p. 237; Colvin,
1976, *King's Works*, V, pp. 87–88.

GILLIAM, John (*fl.* 1712–30). Joiner.
1712–30 ST PAUL, DEPTFORD, LONDON
Altar-piece, Pulpit, reader's and clerk's desks.
Received £200.
Lit: Colvin, 1950, *Arch Rev.*, p. 196.

GINKS, C (*fl.* 1708). Plasterer.
1708 ST PAUL'S CATHEDRAL, LONDON
Worked under Chrysostom Wilkins (q.v.).
Lit: Wren Soc, XV, p. 169.

GINKS, T (*fl.* 1710). Plasterer.
1710 ST PAUL'S CATHEDRAL, LONDON
Worked with C Ginks under Chrysostom
Wilkins (q.v.).
Lit: Wren Soc, XV, p. 169.

GLYNN, – (*fl.* 1707). Plasterer.
1707 ST JAMES, GARLICK HILL, LONDON
Small payment made to Glynn.
Lit: Wren Soc, X, p. 124; XIX, p. 22.

GODFREY, T (*fl.* 1710). Plasterer.
1710 ST PAUL'S CATHEDRAL, LONDON
Worked under Chrysostom Wilkins (q.v.).
Lit: Wren Soc, XV, p. 196.

GODIER, Jonathan (*fl.* early 18th
cent.–1732). Carver.
'June 1732. Jonathan Godier the joiner died
about a fortnight ago at Doncaster. He killed
himself with drinking. He did most of the
Joiner's work at Stainborough Hall
(Wentworth Castle) being then servant to Mr.
Thornton [William Thornton, q.v.]'
Lit: H Avray Tipping, 25 October 1924, *C
Life*, quoting from a MS, diary kept by John
Hobson of Dodsworth Green, 1726–35.
Godier (or Goodyear) is mentioned frequently
in the Strafford archive relating to Wentworth
Castle, Yorkshire (BL Add MSS, 22, 241,
ff. 102, 114, 129).

GODWIN, James (*fl.* 1775). Plasterer.
Mentioned as a 'tiler and plasterer' in
Sketchley's 1775 Bristol Directory.

GOLDSMITH, Nathaniel (*fl.* 1776–95).
Joiner.
1776–95 SOMERSET HOUSE, LONDON
Received £145. 10s. 6d.
Lit: London, RIBA, Library, Somerset
House Accounts.

GOOD, William (*fl.* 1720–21). Plasterer.
1720–21 PURLEY HALL, BERWICKSHIRE

Received £1. 4s. 10d.
Lit: Typewritten sheet of Building Accounts
of 1720–21 (source unspecified) preserved at
Purley Hall. (I am indebted to Dr Peter Willis
for this reference). The source may be 1721,
*The Particulars and Inventories of the . . . Late
Directors of the South Sea Company.*

GOODENOUGH, Edward (*fl.* 1656).
Plasterer.
Official of the Worshipful Company of
Plaisterers.
1656 Master.
Lit: London, Guildhall Library, MS, 6122/2.

GOSSET family (*fl.* 18th cent.). Carvers.
Isaac Gosset (1713–99) did some woodcarving
(at Moulsham Hall, Essex, for example) but is
better known as a wax-modeller (Gunnis,
1953, *Dictionary*). Jacob Gosset of St Martin-
in-the-Fields Parish was a carver and picture-
frame maker. He subscribed in 1726 to
Leoni's edition of *Alberti*, and also took an
apprentice from Jersey, John Le Fousey.
In 1760 charged £202. 12s. 4d. for frames,
lining and stretching pictures for the Earl of
Northampton.
Lit: Compton Place, Eastbourne, Earl of
Northampton's Archives, Box Q; London,
Guildhall Library, *Boyd's Index to
Apprenticeship Registers*, 18, p. 3531; West
Sussex CRO, Petworth II, 6613.

GOUDGE (GOUGE), Edward (*fl.* late 17th
and early 18th cents.). Plasterer.
One of the most talented of 'late Renaissance'
plasterers, Goudge seems to have had an early
connection with Hawksmoor. Vertue says that
Goudge did 'some fretwork ceilings' at Justice
Mellust's house in Yorkshire. This was
probably Samuel Mellish of Doncaster,
Deputy Lieutenant for Yorkshire, who died in
1707. Vertue says that Hawksmoor was 'Clerk
to Justice Mellust', and it seems probable that
Goudge introduced him to London circles.
It is, however, with the architect Captain
William Winde that Goudge's name is
generally connected, and we owe it to Winde's
letters on occasion to indicate works by
Goudge. Writing on 8 February 1690 to Lady
Mary Bridgeman, Winde said that 'Mr.
Goudge will undoughtedly have a goode deall
of worke for hee is now looked on as ye bests
master in England in his profession as his
worke att Combe, Hampstead, & Sr John
Brownlowe's will Evidence'. It is this
statement which not only suggests that
Goudge was the plasterer at Belton, but that
Winde may have been the architect. The
mason contractor was William Stanton.
Goudge also worked for Thomas Coke at his
London house and was also engaged to work
at Hampton Court. It is not known whether
he was the 'Mr. Edward Goudge' granted a
pass to go to Harwich and Holland in 1693
(*Calendar, State Papers, Domestic*, 1693, p. 37).
Lit: Geoffrey Beard, 1979, 'The Beste Master
in England', *National Trust Studies*,
pp. 20–27.
1682–83 COMBE ABBEY, WARWICKSHIRE
Architect: William Winde.
Lit: Bodleian Library, MS, Gough,
Warwickshire, 1, 5 February 1682–83, 1
October 1683.

1684–88 Sessions House, Northampton
Received £150 and £5 as a gratuity.
Lit: 1953, *Arch Jnl.*, CX, p. 181.
1686 Thoresby House, Nottinghamshire
Architect: William Talman.
Lit: Nottingham University Library,
Pierrepont Archives, 4206.
c 1688 Hampstead Marshall, Berkshire
Architect: William Winde.
House completed for Lord Craven by Winde.
Goudge was also said by Winde (18 August
1688) to have worked 'in a late building att
Drury House'. This Drury House was owned,
as was Combe Abbey (below), by Lord
Craven.
Lit: Staffs CRO, Earl of Bradford's Archives,
Winde letters, Box 18/4; Geoffrey Beard, 9
May 1952, *C Life.*
1688 Belton, Lincolnshire
Architect: William Winde.
Goudge's work at Belton is referred to in
Winde's words: 'as his worke at . . . Sr John
Brownlowe's will Evidence'.
Lit: See notes above, and letters of William
Winde to Lady Bridgeman, Earl of Bradford's
Archives; Geoffrey Beard, 12 October 1951, *C
Life*, p. 1157.
1688–90 Castle Bromwich, Warwickshire
Architect: William Winde.
Lit: Geoffrey Beard, 9 May 1952, *C Life*,
citing Winde and Goudge letters in Earl of
Bradford's Archives.
1690–91 Swallowfield, Berkshire
Architect: William Talman.
Winde's letter to Lady Bridgeman, 8 February
1690, states: 'Mr. Goudge is employed by ye
Earle of Clarendone att his house at
Swallowfield where I believe hee will have
above a 12 monthes worke.'
Lit: Earl of Bradford's Archives, as above.
1691–92 Petworth, Sussex
Chapel Ceiling and Hall of State. Received
£49. His assistant David Lance was also there.
Lit: West Sussex CRO, Egremont Archives,
Richard Stiles's Account Rolls, 1691–92. (I
am indebted to Miss G M A Beck and the late
Mr G H Kenyon for much assistance at
Petworth.)
1696–97 Chatsworth, Derbyshire
Gallery ceiling. Received £155 in four
payments.
Lit: Chatsworth, Devonshire Archives, James
Whildon's Account, 1685–99, pp. 121, 123,
125, 135; Francis Thompson, 1949, *A History
of Chatsworth*, pp. 56, 166–68.

GRAINGER, Ambrose (*fl.* 1688). Plasterer.
1688 His will is PCC, 1688, f. 15.

GRAVENOR, James (*fl.* 1760–70). Carver.
1766 Kedleston, Derbyshire
Did both stone-carving and woodcarving on
the organ case, the Drawing Room 'glass
frames', mirrors, etc.
Lit: Gunnis, 1953, *Dictionary*, p. 178;
Kedleston Archives., Accts. 3R; *C Life*, 2,
9 February 1978.

GRAY, Edward (*fl.* 1772–74). Bricklayer.
Mentioned in RABA.
Seems to have acted as principal bricklayer to
RA, and to Sir William Chambers at Somerset
House (1776–95, received £39 19s. 9s. 0d.).

1772–74 20 St James's Square, London
Received £3310. 17s. 1d.
Lit: NLW, Wynnstay MS, 115/17/3; Harris,
1970, *Chambers*, pp. 75, 175, 216, 229.

GREEN, Charles (*fl.* 1723). Plasterer.
1723 Guildhall, Worcester
Architect: Thomas White.
'Agreed with Charles Green and Samuel
Robinson to plaster all Worcester Guildhall
including all the mouldings with the
ornaments belonging to the same and to find
all materials for £180 allowing them the thirty
barrells of lime, eighty strikes of haire, six
cords of sand and 3000 of lath nails and the
white hare already used. And they doe hereby
promise to doe all the said work with the best
sand, lime, lath nails, haire and white haire for
the second coate, and to be done in the best
workmanship like manner.'
Lit: Worcester City Archives, Guildhall
Building Accounts, 29 April 1723.

GREEN, D (*fl.* 1775). Trade unknown.
1775 20 Portman Square, London
Received £147 for unspecified work.
Lit: M D Whinney, 1969, *Home House*, p. 20.

GREENELL, William (*fl.* 1750–82). Joiner.
Worked at Kew and Somerset House under
the supervision of Sir William Chambers.
Appointed Master Joiner in the Office of
Works, 1761–82.
Lit: Harris, 1970, *Chambers*, p. 214; Colvin,
1976, *King's Works*, V, pp. 466, 472; London,
RIBA, Library, Somerset House Accounts.

GREENHOUGH, James (*fl.* 1791).
Plasterer.
Living in 1791 at Eastgate, Beverley,
Yorkshire.
Lit: Battle, Hull and Beverley *Directory*, 1791.

GREENHOUGH, William (*fl.* 1768–70).
Plasterer.
1768–70 Boynton Church, Yorkshire
Architect: attributed to John Carr.
Lit: *C Life*, 22 July 1954, p. 283.

GREENWAY, Robert (*fl.* late 17th cent.).
Locksmith.
Provided locks for Winslow Hall, Bucks.,
c 1700. As the Royal Locksmith he was
criticised by the architect William Talman.
Lit: *Wren Soc*, IV, p. 60, XVII, pp. 73, 86.

GREW, John (*fl.* late 17th cent.). Carver.
Assistant to Edward Pearce (q.v.). Worked
with him in the 1670s at Sudbury Hall,
Derbys.
Lit: *C Life*, 22 June 1935.

GRIFFIN, John (*fl.* 1742). Plasterer.
1742 Exchange, Bristol
Architect: John Wood the elder.
Lit: Bristol City Archives, Exchange Building
Book; John Wood, 1743, *A Description of the
Exchange of Bristol*, list of subscribers.

GRIFFIN, William (*fl.* 1690). Plasterer.
1690 Kensington Palace, London
Worked under Henry Margetts (q.v.).
Lit: PRO, Works, 19, 48/1, f. 108.

GRIFFITHS, Charles (*fl.* 1722–24). Joiner.
1722 St Martin-in-the-Fields, London
Architect: James Gibbs.
Received over £2012.
Lit: John McMaster, 1916, *A Short History:
Royal Parish of St. Martin-in-the-Fields*,
p. 79; Westminster Reference Library, MS,
419/311, Accounts, 1721–27.
1724 Wentworth Castle, Yorkshire
Long Gallery (architect: James Gibbs).
Agreed to wainscot for £255, including
carriage.
Griffiths wrote to Lord Strafford on 3
September 1724 to indicate that he was
proceeding with the Gallery and the 'picture
of ye 3 Kings is ye same size as ye Chimney
piece att Secretrey Johnsons att Twickenham',
that is the Octagon at Twickenham designed
by Gibbs in 1720 for James Johnston,
Secretary for Scotland. Presumably Griffiths
did the joinery.
Lit: BL Add MSS, 22, 241, ff. 128, 154.

GRILTEN, R (*fl.* 1710). Plasterer.
1710 St Paul's Cathedral, London
Worked under Chrysostom Wilkins (q.v.).
Lit: *Wren Soc*, XV, p. 196.

GRINSELL, John (*fl.* 1712–13). Plasterer.
Official of the Worshipful Company of
Plaisterers.
1712 Upper Warden.
1713 Master.
Lit: London, Guildhall Library, MS,
6122/3.

GRIVENS, R (*fl.* 1708). Plasterer.
1708 St Paul's Cathedral, London
Worked under Chrysostom Wilkins (q.v.).
Lit: *Wren Soc*, XV, pp. 169, 196.

GROOME, Richard (*fl.* 1780). Plasterer.
1780–, Somerset House, London
Architect: Sir William Chambers.
Ornamental plasterer working under Charles
Clarke (q.v.).
Lit: Charles Clarke, 1783, *The Plaisterers' Bill
for Works done . . . Somerset House.*

GROVE, John (?–1676), **John II** (?–1708).
Plasterers.
During their careers both John Grove and his
son became Master Plasterers to the Office of
Works. John II succeeded his father in 1676.
John I's will, proved PCC, 29 March 1676,
shows that his mother had remarried, her
second husband being a member of the Tucke
family of plasterers, possibly Anthony. His
daughter Patience was married to the master
carpenter Matthew Bankes. John I left to
Bankes his 'modell or Draught of St. Paul's
Church together with all the drawings and
draughts hereunto belonging'. He left to his
sons John II and James (another master
carpenter) his library of books and, in
addition, to John II his 'Scaffolding Boards &
poles'.
In 1657 Grove senior was Renter Warden of
the Worshipful Company of Plaisterers. His
son John II frequently worked with Henry
Doogood, and a list of their joint work on the
City churches is given in the entry on
Doogood. The work prior to 1676 in the

following list is by Grove senior, possibly assisted by his son John.
Accounts of Carpenters' work by James and John Grove, 1686–1718, survive (BL Add MSS, 30,092). James Grove was also employed on many Office of Works Commissions (K Downes, 1977, *Vanbrugh*, p. 201) and London churches (Colvin, 1950, *Arch Rev*, pp. 195–96).
John Grove II's will is PCC, Barrett, 39. He left property to his wife and his brother James. The overseers were James and the 'Queen's Carpenter', John Churchill.
1661 QUEEN'S HOUSE, GREENWICH
Ceiling, East Bridge Room, under the superintendence of John Webb.
Lit: 1937, *Survey of London*, XIV, pp. 72, 74, pls. 65–67.
1662 Worked in 'the Queen's Privy Chamber, Secretary Bennett's Lodgings, etc.'.
Received £67. 18s. 0d.
Lit: PRO, E351/3276.
1664–67 CLARENDON HOUSE, PICCADILLY, LONDON (demolished 1683)
Architect: Sir Roger Pratt.
Received £2082. 14s. 0d. 'Whereof the fret ceilings came to about £820 besides "bracketting" which I conceive came almost to as much more.'
Lit: R T Gunther, 1928, *The Architecture of Sir Roger Pratt*, p. 164.
1675 EMMANUEL COLLEGE CHAPEL, CAMBRIDGE
Architect: Sir Christopher Wren.
Lit: Willis and Clark, 1887, *Cambridge*, II, pp. 703–09; *Wren Soc*, V, pp. 29–31; N B Pevsner, 1943, *Cambridgeshire*, p. 27.
c 1678 ROYAL COLLEGE OF PHYSICIANS, LONDON (demolished 1879)
Architect: Sir Robert Hooke.
Dining Room.
Lit: H W Robinson and W Adams, eds., 1935, *The Diary of Robert Hooke*.
c 1681 and 1687 WINDSOR CASTLE
Minor works. Paid £18. 11s. 4d. in 1681 and £31. 9s. 6d. in 1687.
Lit: W St John Hope, 1914, *Windsor Castle*, pp. 321 and 329.
1682–83 BADMINTON HOUSE, GLOUCESTERSHIRE
7 March: 'Paid Mr. Groves, Plasterer, £115.'
Lit: Child's Bank, Account of the 1st Marquess of Worcester.
1685–87 WHITEHALL PALACE, LONDON
Chapel, Privy Gallery, etc.
Lit: PRO, Works, 5/54.
1686–87 TRINITY COLLEGE, CAMBRIDGE
Staircase to Library.
Lit: Willis and Clark, 1887, *Cambridge*, II, pp. 533–51, esp. p. 540; *Wren Soc*, V, pp. 32–44.
Attributed work
c 1660 COLESHILL, BERKSHIRE
1664 CORNBURY PARK, OXFORDSHIRE
Architect: Hugh May.
Chapel for the Earl of Clarendon.
c 1690 EASTON NESTON, NORTHAMPTONSHIRE
Grove's relative, the Master Carpenter James Grove, worked at the house. It may be assumed, therefore, that work was kept in the family.
Lit: BL Add MSS, 30092 (I am indebted to Dr H M Colvin for this reference); *C Life*, 15 October 1970, p. 969.

GUILLOT, James Lewis (*fl.* 1754). Carver.
1754 Lived in the parish of St Ann, Westminster. Had an apprentice, John Lemaitre.
Lit: London, Guildhall Library, *Boyd's Index to Apprenticeship Registers*, 18, p. 3540.

GUM, Richard (*fl.* 1670–71). Plasterer.
1670–71 WHITEHALL PALACE, LONDON
Worked under John Grove.
Lit: PRO, Works, 5/15, June 1670.

GUY, – (*fl.* 1719). Carver.
1719 ALL SOULS COLLEGE, OXFORD
Chapel Screen. Received £127.
Lit: *C Life*, 23 June 1928.

HAINES, John (*fl.* 1680–90). Carpenter.
Haines, apart from designing the second vestry room at the church of St James's, Piccadilly, held office as Governor of Bridewell and Bethlem, was High Constable of Westminster, and first churchwarden of the parish of St. James's. He was buried in that church (with his wife May, d. 1719) on 10 January 1690/91.
Lit: 1960, *Survey of London*, XXIX, p. 48.

HALE, Joseph (*fl.* 1775). Plasterer.
Mentioned as a 'tiler and plasterer' in Sketchley's 1775 Bristol Directory.

HALL, Jerome (*fl.* 1698). Plasterer.
1698 One of five contestants for the job of Plaisterer to Christ's Hospital, London.
Lit: *Wren Soc*, XI, p. 70.

HALL, Joseph (*fl.* 1745–63). Mason/Carver.
Lived at Derby.
1760–65 KEDLESTON, DERBYSHIRE
Received £6596 for mason's work and certain of the main construction of the house.
Received £993. 12s. 5d. for the columns in the Hall, fluted 10 years later by Francis Battersby (q.v.).
Also did some framing of mahogany doors.
Lit: Kedleston Archives, Accts. 3R; Gunnis, 1953, *Dictionary*, p. 185.

HALLAM, John (*fl.* late 17th cent.). Joiner.
Worked as Master Joiner at Chatsworth.
Lit: Francis Thompson, 1949, *A History of Chatsworth*, pp. 37, 67.

HANDLEY, Francis (*fl.* 1708–09). Plasterer.
Official of the Worshipful Company of Plaisterers.
1708 Upper Warden.
1709 Master.
Lit: London, Guildhall Library, MS, 6122/3.

HANDS, James (*fl.* 1712–18). Plasterer.
Of 'Wild Street'. Partner to James Ellis (q.v.). Was described as 'late' in the minutes of the Worshipful Company of Plaisterers, 25 July 1718 (London, Guildhall Library, MS, 6122/3).
1694 QUEEN'S COLLEGE, OXFORD
Library ceiling. Altered in 1756 by Thomas Roberts (q.v.)
Lit: VCH, *Oxfordshire*, III, p. 138.
1712–14 ST ALPHEGE, GREENWICH, LONDON
Architect: Nicholas Hawksmoor.

Lit: Colvin, 1950, *Arch Rev*, p. 196.
c 1715 ST PAUL, DEPTFORD, LONDON
Architect: Thomas Archer.
The church was under reconstruction from 1712 to 1730.
Lit: Colvin, 1950, *Arch Rev*, p. 196.

HANDS, William (*fl.* 1764–65). Joiner.
1764–65 WARWICK CASTLE
Received £117. 15s. 10½d., probably for work in the Library. Bill examined by Timothy Lightoler (cf. Colvin, 1978, *Dictionary*, p. 520) and William Taylor.
Lit: Warwicks. CRO, Warwick Castle Vouchers, 1764–65.

HANSOM, Richard (*fl.* 1766–68). Carpenter.
1766–68 THE BAR CONVENT, YORK
Architect: Thomas Atkinson.
Roof and other woodwork.
Lit: RCHM, *City of York*, III, p. 40.
A joiner, Henry Hansom, worked at Middleton's Hospital, Skeldergate, York, in 1827–29 (*ibid.*, p. 51) and in Blossom Street, 1837 (*ibid.*, p. 63).

HANWELL, William (*fl.* 1780–90). Plasterer.
1786–89 ARBURY HALL, WARWICKSHIRE
Saloon. Received £36. Assisted by G Higham and Robert Hodgson.
1785–89 WARWICK CASTLE
New Library, Cornice (1785). King's Room, ceiling, charged for 68 ft of circular moulding, leaves, fruit, etc. Received £60. 1s. 9d.
Lit: Warwicks. CRO, Warwick Castle Vouchers, 1785, 1788–89 (no. 151).

HARDY, Robert (*fl.* 1750–60). Joiner.
1750–60 HORSE GUARDS, WHITEHALL, LONDON
Lit: RIBA, MSS, HOR.

HARROD, Robert (*fl.* 1670–80). Plasterer.
1670–80 WIMBLEDON, SURREY
Worked for the Marquis of Carmarthen.
Lit: BL Add. MSS, 28094, f. 139.

HARVEY (HERVÉ), Daniel (1683–1733). Sculptor/Carver.
Born in 1683 in France. Worked mainly in stone at Castle Howard and Wentworth Castle, but also carved four capitals in wood for the latter house in 1725. Died 11 December 1733. Buried at St Olave's, York.
Lit: BL Add. MSS, 22241, ff. 11, 20, 29: 29 August 1720 'Carving 4 Capitals of wood in the Ionick order at 0. 12s. 0d. each. £2. 8. 0.'; Francis Drake, 1736, *Eboracum*, p. 29.

HAUDUROY (HODUROY), Louis and Mark Anthony (*fl.* late 17th cent.). Painters.
These two painters, who were relatives, did mural painting and imitation marbling, veining, etc. Louis worked at Culverthorpe Hall, Lincs., for Sir John Newton (*C Life*, 15 September 1923, p. 355). Mark Anthony (or Louis ?) worked in 1694 at Dyrham Park, Gloucs.: 'To Monsieur Hauduroy in part for painting of ye house. Aug. 22, 1694. £10.' Painted rooms, staircase, veining in imitation of marble, etc.
Received in all £229. 4s. 7d.

Lit: Gloucestershire CRO, Blathwayt Archives, B/3/2, B 15/5.
c 1735 CAVENDISH SQUARE, LONDON
Worked in the Dressing Room of the Duke of Chandos's house. Engaged by Brunetti, the decorative painter, to gild and colour the ceiling. His bill of December 1735 for £41. 4s. 1d. survives; £27. 15s. 0d. of this was for the ceiling. He also made frames and was something of a dealer.
Lit: Baker, 1949, *Brydges*, pp. 285–86.

HAWKINS, James (*fl.* 1775). Plasterer.
Mentioned as a 'tiler and plasterer' in Sketchley's 1775 Bristol Directory.

HAWKINS, John (*fl.* 1750). Carver.
1750 5 ST JAMES'S SQUARE, LONDON
Received £200.
Lit: 1960, *Survey of London*, XXIX, p. 101.

HAWORTH, Samuel (*fl.* 1763). Carver.
1763 EGREMONT HOUSE, LONDON
Lit: West Sussex CRO, Petworth II, 6615.

HAYES, William (*fl.* 1713–14). Plasterer.
Official of the Worshipful Company of Plaisterers.
1713 Upper Warden.
1714 Master.
Lit: London, Guildhall Library, MS, 6122/3.

HAYWARD, Richard (1728–1800). Sculptor.
Born at Bulkington in Warwickshire, his important career is summarised in Gunnis, 1953, *Dictionary*. Note also:
1763 ARBURY HALL, WARWICKSHIRE
Parlour chimneypiece.
Lit: Warwicks. CRO, CR 136/B24/2420.

HEBBERD, – (*fl. c* 1780). Plasterer.
1780– SOMERSET HOUSE, LONDON
Architect: Sir William Chambers.
Worked under Charles Clarke (q.v.).
Lit: Charles Clarke, 1783, *The Plaisterers' Bill for Works done . . . Somerset House.*

HEFFORD (HEAFFORD), Thomas (*fl.* 1748–64). Plasterer.
Presumably the plasterer 'Heafford' who was paid for work at Northumberland House, London, in 1752–53 (Alnwick Castle MS, U-1-25). He worked elsewhere in London, at 14 St James's Square (1748) and the church of St James's, Piccadilly (1764). He was one of 13 figures in a picture of 1760 by Robert Pyle, which was destroyed by fire in 1940.
Lit: C Life, 30 March 1945; 1960, *Survey of London*, XXIX, pp. 37, 140 fn.; Colvin, 1978, *Dictionary*, p. 482.

HENDERSON, James (*fl. c* 1755–87). Plasterer.
This York plasterer is best known for his association with the architect John Carr. Mr R B Wragg has suggested that he probably did not come of a York family because, when taking up the Freedom of York in 1764, Henderson paid the levy of £25 rather than claiming free entry by patrimony. He was established near Bootham Bar in York, and in 1744 advertised in the *York Courant* for an apprentice.

In 1765 he took William Holliday of Byland as an apprentice 'to be taught, learned and informed in the five orders of the Inrichment of Architecture & whatever mouldings may occur'. A year later he took Thomas Nicholson of Richmond 'to learn the art, trade or mystery of a Plaisterer as to Mouldings in general'. His own son, Thomas, was apprenticed to him in 1764. Henderson was then living at Gillygate, York. It can be assumed that Henderson was the plasterer at most of Carr's ventures, and the liaison may be compared to that between Robert Adam and Joseph Rose (q.v.). There was a strong connection between Henderson and Cortese, and Henderson was executor at Cortese's death in 1778. The list of his activities will extend when Dr Ivan Hall's study of John Carr is published.
Lit: R B Wragg, 1955–56, *York Georgian Society Report*; York Reference Library, *Register of Apprentice Indentures*, D 14, 1766, f. 93.
1762 FAIRFAX HOUSE, CASTLEGATE, YORK
Lit: Leeds, Yorkshire Archaeological Society Library, Newburgh Archives.
1765 HAREWOOD HOUSE, YORKSHIRE
Plastering other than State Rooms (Joseph Rose, q.v.) with a partner, Rothwell (q.v.).
1766 SWINTON, YORKSHIRE
Architect: John Carr.
Submitted bill, 7 April 1766.
Lit: Cartwright Hall, Bradford, Danby Archives, Account Book II, p. 6; *C Life*, 7 April 1966, p. 791.
1766–67 CANNON HALL, BARNSLEY, YORKSHIRE
John Carr wrote to his client Spencer Stanhope: 'I am at a loss how to advise you as to the Execution of it [the Dining Room ceiling], as I assure you we have no person in the country that can execute it but Henderson and if you do not chuse to have Imploy'd some person must be sent from London.' Henderson did the Library ceiling in 1766 and the Drawing Room ceiling in 1767. The latter was destroyed *c* 1956.
Lit: R B Wragg, 1955–56, *York Georgian Society Report*, p. 59; Geoffrey Beard, 1966, Cannon Hall *Guidebook*.
1767 KIRKLEATHAM HALL, NEAR REDCAR, YORKSHIRE
Lit: Wragg, Report.
1771 TEMPLE NEWSAM HOUSE, LEEDS, YORKSHIRE
Minor alterations.
Lit: Wragg, Report.
1771 GILLING CASTLE, YORKSHIRE
Minor alterations to the 'Gothic Temple'.
Lit: Wragg, Report.
1773 THIRSK HALL, YORKSHIRE
Architect: John Carr.
Lit: North Riding, Yorks., CRO, Bills.

HENDERSON, Thomas (*fl. c* 1749–90). Plasterer.
Son of James Henderson above. Apprenticed to his father for seven years on 13 June 1764. He took over the business in Blake Street, York, in about 1785, and 'continued the relationship with Carr at Wentworth Woodhouse, particularly on the Mausoleum, in company with Ely Crabtree' (q.v.). Submitted a specification for a mathematical

instrument in January 1787, when he was described as a 'Stucco Plaisterer'.
Lit: R B Wragg, 1955–56, *York Georgian Society Report*, p. 60; York Reference Library, *Register of Apprentice Indentures*, D14, 1764, f. 73; Deputy Keeper of the Public Records, 6th Report, Appendix II, p. 177.

HERRING, Richard (*fl.* 1663). Carver.
1663 BISHOP AUCKLAND, DURHAM
Chapel. Carved eagles, mitres, cherubim heads.
Lit: 1872, 'Correspondence of John Cosin, Bishop of Durham', *Surtees Society*, 55, p. 361.

HEWORTH, Robert (*fl. c* 1730–54). Carpenter.
Of York. Apprenticed on 1 May 1745 for seven years to John Heworth to learn the trade of carpenter and cabinet-maker. There were perhaps two Heworths of this name, for in the 1740s Robert Heworth was working as a joiner at Temple Newsam House, Leeds, where it is possible he was responsible for much of the fine woodwork.
On 5 March 1754 he inserted in the *York Courant* the following advertisement:
'This is to inform the PUBLICK,
That Robert Heworth, Joiner and Carpenter in the City of York, has got a Patent and Toleration from John Baynes of the City of London, who, by Application and Study, invented and brought to Perfection a new Method of making Sash Frames, which, by concealing the Line and Pully, will be a great Ornament to the better Sort of Buildings: That the Sashes will not be so liable to be out of Repair as those now in Use, but will be confined, so that the most prevailing Winds will not occasion their making any Noise. And will have this particular Property; no naucious Fogs or penetrating Winds, so pernicious to Health, can anywise affect the Room: and upon representing the same to his present Majesty King GEORGE, he did grant his special Licence for the space of fourteen Years, to make, use, and vend the same; With a Prohibition of all Persons whatsoever, other than him the said John Baynes, his Agent, or Deputy, to make, use or vend the same. Any Person that has a Curiosity, may, by calling upon the said Robert Heworth, see upon what Principle the said Sashes are erected; as it is allowed, by everyone that has seen it, to be a great improvement upon the same.'
He may have been the wood-merchant who went bankrupt in 1761 (*York Courant*, 21 April 1761, 25 December 1764, 10 April 1770). He was certainly the Robert Heworth who was Chamberlain of York, 1753.

HIGGINSON, – (*fl.* 1771–72). Plasterer.
1771–72 SOHO WAREHOUSE, BIRMINGHAM
Work for Matthew Boulton.
Lit: Birmingham Assay Office, John Scale Archives, Box 9. (I am indebted to Mr Nicholas Goodison for this reference.)

HIGHAM, G (*fl.* 1779). Plasterer.
ARBURY HALL, WARWICKSHIRE
Dining Room. Worked with Robert Hodgson.
Lit: Hussey, 1956, *ECH: Mid-Georgian*, p. 44.

HILL, Richard (*fl.* 1775). Plasterer.
Mentioned as a 'tiler and plasterer' in
Sketchley's 1775 Bristol Directory.

HILLAM, James and **John** (*fl. c* 1780).
Plasterer.
1780– SOMERSET HOUSE, LONDON
Architect: Sir William Chambers.
Ornamental plasterers working under Charles
Clarke (q.v.).
Lit: Charles Clarke, 1783, *The Plaisterer's Bill
for Works done . . . Somerset House.*

HINCHCLIFF, John (?–1796). Sculptor.
Master of the Masons' Company, 1790.
Worked for RA at 20 St James's Square,
where he provided chimneypieces to the value
of £360. 10s. In 1768 he exhibited at the
Society of Artists 'a specimen of a new
manner of ornamenting chimneypieces, tables,
etc., with scagliola inlaid with marble', which
found favour with many of RA's patrons.
Lit: Gunnis, 1953, *Dictionary*, p. 202; NLW,
Wynnstay MS, 115/17/12.

HOBCRAFT, John (*fl.* 1730–79).
Carpenter/Builder.
Of Titchfield St, London.
Subscribed to RA's book on Diocletian's
Palace, 1764.
His architectural career summarised in Colvin,
1978, *Dictionary*, pp. 422–23.
1758–64 CROOME COURT, WORCESTERSHIRE
Carpentry and joinery.
Lit: Croome Court Archives, cited by J
Parker, 1964, 'The Croome Court Tapestry
Room' in *Decorative Art from the Samuel H.
Kress Collection*, p. 31.
Worked also at Coventry House, 29 Piccadilly,
London, for the same patron (6th Earl of
Coventry).
1766 CORSHAM COURT, WILTSHIRE
Gallery, mahogany doors.
Lit: Hussey, 1965, *ECH: Early Georgian*,
p. 233.

HOBSON, Samuel (1720–90). Carver.
Monumental inscription in St Martin-in-the-
Fields, London: died 1 January 1790, 'late of
this Parish'.

HODGSON, Robert (*fl.* 1780–90). Plasterer.
1780–90 ARBURY HALL, WARWICKSHIRE
Worked with G Higham and W Hanwell (*see*
col. pl. 16).
Lit: *C Life*, 29 October 1953, p. 1415.

HOLDEN, Thomas (*fl.* 1712–24). Joiner.
1712–24 ST ANNE, LIMEHOUSE, LONDON
Lit: Colvin, 1950, *Arch Rev*, p. 196.

HOLLIDAY, William (*fl.* 1750–78).
Plasterer.
Of Byland, Yorks. Apprenticed for seven years
in 1765 to James Henderson of York (q.v.).
Admitted as a Freeman of York in 1778.
Lit: York Reference Library, *Register of
Apprentice Indentures*, D14, f. 93.

HOLLINGSHEAD, William (*fl.* 1683).
Plasterer.
His will is PCC, 1687, f. 49.

HOLLINS, William (*fl.* 1660). Plasterer.
Official of the Worshipful Company of
Plaisterers.
1660 Master.
Lit: London, Guildhall Library, MS, 6122/2.

HOLMES, Benjamin (*fl.* 1742–60). Smith.
One of Henry Flitcroft's most trusted
craftsmen, mentioned frequently in the
architect's bank account from its opening in
1741 (Drummonds Bank). Probably present
at most of the architect's commissions.
1742–44 44 BERKELEY SQUARE, LONDON
Staircase, iron balustrade (*see* pl. 40).
Lit: London, Sir John Soane's Museum,
Accounts.
1749 WIMPOLE CHURCH, CAMBRIDGESHIRE
Architect: Henry Flitcroft.
Received £1. 6s. od.
Lit: BL Add, MSS, 35679, f. 54.
1759–60 HORSE GUARDS, WHITEHALL,
LONDON
Lit: RIBA, Library, MSS, HOR.
1758 UNIVERSITY LIBRARY, CAMBRIDGE (Old
Schools)
Great Staircase. Received £60. Not executed
as 'from a Gothic drawing'.
Lit: CUL Vice-Chancellor's Vouchers, 10 (I
am indebted to Mr Edward Saunders for this
reference).

HOLMES, Robert (*fl.* 1760).
Carpenter/Builder.
Of Twickenham.
c 1760 STRAWBERRY HILL, MIDDLESEX
Lit: Paget Toynbee, ed., 1927, *Strawberry
Hill Accounts*, pp. 46, 186.

HOOKE, Jonathan (1677–78). Joiner.
1677–78 CHIRK CASTLE, DENBIGHSHIRE
Long Gallery. 403 yd of wainscot. Received
£100. 15s.
Lit: W M Myddleton, 1908, *Chirk Castle
Accounts, 1666–1753*, p. 32.

HOOPER, William (*fl.* 1775). Plasterer.
Mentioned as a 'tiler and plasterer' in
Sketchley's 1775 Bristol Directory.

HOPKINS, William and Company (*fl.*
1772–95). Stove Grate Maker and
Ironmongers.
Of Greek Street, Soho.
1772/74 20 ST JAMES'S SQUARE, LONDON
Provided iron and steel grates and various
copper items.
Received £70. 19s. 6d. as part of an overall bill
of £270. 10s. 2d.
Lit: NLW, Wynnstay MS, 115/17/13.
1789 CARLTON HOUSE, LONDON
Estimated for work at £2000.
Lit: H Clifford Smith, 1931, *Buckingham
Palace*, p. 104.
1795 SHUGBOROUGH HALL, STAFFORDSHIRE
Worked under Samuel Wyatt.
Provided stoves, fenders, etc. Received
£259. 13s. 6d.
Lit: Staffs. CRO, D 1240/1.

HOPSON, Sir Charles (?–1710). Master
Joiner.
1708 Master of the Joiners' Company. In
1706 he was appointed Master Joiner to the
Office of Works. He supervised the execution
of important joinery work at St Paul's, Eton
College, Hampton Court, St James's Palace,
Somerset House, Whitehall Palace, etc. His
son John (d. 9 June 1718) was also Master
Joiner to the Office of Works, 1710–18.
Lit: Wren Soc, XV, p. xxi, XX, pp. 104–05;
London, Guildhall Library, MS, 8046, 4;
Colvin, 1976, *King's Works*, V, pp. 44, 54,
472.

HORTON, Robert (*fl.* 1672–79). Plasterer.
1672–79 ST STEPHEN, COLEMAN STREET,
LONDON
Architect: Sir Christopher Wren.
Worked with Thomas Burton (q.v.). Their bill
totalled £136.
Lit: Wren Soc, X, pp. 53, 124, XII, p. 53,
XIX, p. 53.

HOULBERT (HULBERT), John
(*fl.* 1674–79). Plasterer.
A London plasterer, known for his work for
the Earl of Lauderdale and for the Crown in
Scotland.
1674–77 THIRLESTANE CASTLE, BERWICKSHIRE
Signed receipts on 15 November 1674 and 31
August 1677.
Lit: Scottish Record Office, Thirlestane
Castle Archives.
1675–78 HOLYROODHOUSE, EDINBURGH
Worked with George Dunsterfield (q.v.).
Received £1564. 2s. 6d. (1675); £2406. 9s. 9d.
(1677); £1996. 2s. od. (1679).
Lit: R S Mylne, 1893, *The Master Masons to
the Crown of Scotland*, p. 197.

HOW, John (*fl.* 1712–30). Carver.
Subscribed to James Gibbs, 1728, *A Book of
Architecture.*
1712–24 ST GEORGE, HANOVER SQUARE,
LONDON
1720–30 ST GEORGE, BLOOMSBURY, LONDON
Lit: Colvin, 1950, *Arch Rev*, pp. 195–96.

HOWES, Richard (*fl.* late 17th cent.).
Carver.
Worked in London at St Peter, Cornhill.
Lit: Wren Soc, X, pp. 52, 54.

HOWGILL, John (*fl.* 1727). Carver.
Of York. Provided a 'Cartouch for the
Chimney in your Lordsps Bed Chamber
below Stairs' at Robert Benson, Lord
Bingley's London house in Cavendish Square.
Lit: Bramham Park Archives, Letter-book,
1727–28, 28 November 1727.

HUGHES, John (*fl.* 1718–29). Plasterer.
1718 THE ROLLS HOUSE, CHANCERY LANE,
LONDON
Architect: Colen Campbell.
Lit: PRO, A.O. 1/2494/407.
1719–21 BURLINGTON HOUSE, PICCADILLY,
LONDON
Architect: Lord Burlington.
Worked with Isaac Mansfield (q.v.).
Received £230 in six instalments between 24
September 1719 and 26 January 1721.
Lit: Chatsworth, Burlington account book.
1725 GOODWOOD, SUSSEX
Lit: West Sussex CRO, Goodwood Archives,
G.121/1/107; information from Mr
T P Connor.

1729 COMPTON PLACE, EASTBOURNE, SUSSEX
Presumably the 'Mr Hewes/Hughes' who died
in November 1729, and who employed three
'German' plasterers to do decorative work.
Lit: Compton Place Archives, Box P.

HUISH, John (*fl.* 1775). Plasterer.
Mentioned as a 'tiler and plasterer' in
Sketchley's 1775 Bristol Directory.

HURLBUT, Roger and **William**
(*fl.* 1669–83). Joiners.
Of Starton, near Coventry.
1669 WARWICK CASTLE
State Rooms.
Agreed to wainscot the Great Hall.
William Hurlbut, Roger's brother, was sent to
look at Sir Ralph Bankes' house (Kingston
Lacy, Dorset, designed by Sir Roger Pratt,
completed 1665) as a pattern. The first
payment was made in 1670. In 1671 57 cwt of
cedar boards were sent down from London. A
final payment was made in 1678.
Lit: Warwicks. CRO, Account Book 1669–71
(1672–76 missing), entries 24 January, 20
February 1669; 1670–71, State of Account
entries, cited by M W Farr, 1969, VCH,
Warwickshire, VIII, p. 460. (I am indebted to
Mr Farr for the use of his notes.)
1679–83 RAGLEY HALL, WARWICKSHIRE
Architect: Sir Robert Hooke.
Lit: Walpole Soc, XXV, p. 98.

HURST, – (*fl.* early 18th cent.). Plasterer.
Worked at Greenwich Hospital, and
corresponded with Sir James Thornhill.
Provided Derbyshire lime for plasterwork.
Lit: Wren Soc, VI, pp. 67–68.

HUSS family (*fl.* 17th and 18th cents.).
Plasterers.
This Derbyshire family numbered Richard,
Henry (probably Richard's brother) and
Samuel (Henry's grandson) as plasterers in the
period from the 1680s to Samuel's death on 19
January 1786 (St Alkmund's, Derby). Henry
was married in 1686 and Richard in 1714.
Henry died in 1716; Richard's death has not
been traced.
1694 CHATSWORTH, DERBYSHIRE
Worked with Samuel Mansfield (q.v.).
Received £162. 8s. 6d.
Lit: Chatsworth, Building Accounts, Lady
Day to September 1694; letter in Chatsworth
MSS, 21 April 1694, to James Whildon, the
steward, indicating they will not continue with
work 'unless the money already promised is
paid'.
1700–10 ST WERBURGH'S CHURCH, DERBY
Henry Huss received £43. 16s. 7d., including
£32. 12s. 7d. for the Queen's Arms, altar-
piece, etc., finished in 1710.
1710 ST PHILIP'S CHURCH, BIRMINGHAM
Architect: Thomas Archer (Richard Huss).
Lit: Marcus Whiffen, 1950, *Thomas Archer*,
p. 15.
1720 WENTWORTH CASTLE, YORKSHIRE
(Richard Huss)
Unspecified work.
Lit: BL Add. MSS, 22241.
(I am indebted to Mr Edward Saunders for
details of the Chatsworth and Derby
commissions.)

HUTCHINSON, James (*fl.* 1782). Plasterer.
1782 INVERARAY CASTLE, ARGYLLSHIRE
Unspecified work. Received £7. 10s. 0d.
Lit: Inveraray Archives, Chamberlain's
Accounts, 1781–82.

ILLISON, – (*fl.* 1721). Joiner.
1721 CHICHELEY HALL, BUCKINGHAMSHIRE
Staircase. Assisted Thomas Baxter and Mr
Beale.
Lit: Joan D Tanner, 1961, 'The Building of
Chicheley Hall', *Records of Bucks.*, XVII,
pt. I.

IVES, Edward (*fl.* 1750). Plumber.
1750 5 ST JAMES'S SQUARE, LONDON
Received £46.
Lit: 1960, *Survey of London*, XXIX, p. 101.

JACKSON, Amos (*fl.* 1660). Plasterer.
1660 THE TOWER, LONDON
Worked under John Grove I.
Lit: PRO, Works, 5/1, November 1660.

JACKSON, George (1756–1840). Plasterer.
When George Jackson & Sons, Ltd., the firm
of plasterers and modellers, advertised in the
RIBA Exhibition Catalogue 'One Hundred
Years of British Architecture 1851–1951', they
stated that 'When Robert Adam bought the
famous recipe for composition from John
Liardet, George Jackson made reverse moulds
in boxwood and pressed out the ornament in
this material. This laid the foundation in 1780
at 49 Rathbone Place, London, of the present
firm of G. Jackson & Sons, Ltd. Their
collection of moulds is now unrivalled and
numbers many thousands.'
George Jackson's son, John, brought the
Carton-Pierre process from France, and his
son introduced 'fibrous plaster'.

JAMES, John (*c* 1672–1746). Carpenter and
Architect.
Trained under Matthew Banckes (q.v.).
As partner to Robert Jelfe, he worked as a
carpenter at several London churches, but
turned to surveying and architecture at
Greenwich and elsewhere.
Lit: Colvin, 1950, *Arch Rev*, pp. 195–96;
Colvin, 1978, *Dictionary*, p. 451.

JEAN, Peter Dominique (*fl.* 1764–95).
Brassfounder/Gilder.
Married Marie Francoise Langlois, daughter
of the cabinet-maker Pierre Langlois, in 1764.
Seemingly involved in the London cabinet-
making and ormolu trade of his father-in-law
and of Matthew Boulton of Birmingham.
Took an apprentice Daniel Langlois (Pierre's
son) in 1771.
1783–86 CARLTON HOUSE, LONDON
Received £1409. 16s. 0d.
Lit: H Clifford Smith, 1931, *Buckingham
Palace*, p. 103; Margaret Jourdain, 1934,
Regency Furniture, 1965 edn., p. 107;
Goodison, 1974, *Ormolu*, p. 173.

JEFFREY, William (*fl.* 1724). Plumber.
Of Chesterfield.
1724 SUTTON SCARSDALE, DERBYSHIRE
Name on lead rising-plate (now lost), formerly
at house.
Lit: C Life, 15 February 1919, p. 171.

JELFE, Robert (*fl.* 1712–30). Carpenter.
Of the well-known family of London master
masons. In partnership with John James of
Greenwich, he worked at several London
churches for Thomas Archer, Nicholas
Hawksmoor and James Gibbs.
Lit: Colvin, 1950, *Arch Rev*, pp. 195–96;
Colvin, 1978, *Dictionary*, p. 457.

JEMMETT, Thomas (*fl.* 1689–1710).
Plasterer.
1689 HAMPTON COURT, MIDDLESEX
Worked under John Grove (q.v.).
Lit: PRO, Works, 5/55, May 1689.
1710 ST PAUL'S CATHEDRAL, LONDON
Worked under Chrysostom Wilkins (q.v.).
Lit: Wren Soc, XV, p. 196.

JENKIN, – (*fl.* 1767). Locksmith.
1767 SYON HOUSE
Provided locks.
See also John Dayon.
Lit: Alnwick Castle Archives, U.1.44, 27
September 1767.

JENKINS, John (*fl.* 1755). Plasterer.
c 1755 POWDERHAM CASTLE, DEVON
Staircase (assisted by William Brown).
Lit: C Life, 11 July 1963, p. 80.

JENNER, Thomas (*fl.* 1824). Joiner.
1824 WINDSOR CASTLE, BERKSHIRE
Lit: D Linstrum, 1972, *Sir Jeffry Wyatville*,
p. 253.

JENNINGS, David and **Judith** (*fl.* 1830s).
Plasterers.
1834–35 THE BAR CONVENT, YORK
Refectory (David Jennings).
1837 19 BLOSSOM STREET, YORK
(Judith Jennings).
Lit: RCHM, 1972, *City of York*, III, pp. 46,
63.

JENSET, T (*fl.* 1708). Plasterer.
1708 ST PAUL'S CATHDERAL, LONDON
Worked under Chrysostom Wilkins (q.v.).
Lit: Wren Soc, XV, p. 169.

JERMAN (JARMAN), Roger (*fl.* 1662–78).
Carpenter.
Younger brother of the City Carpenter (until
1657), Edward Jerman (d.1668), who rebuilt
several Livery Company Halls after the Great
Fire, 1666. Roger Jerman was City Carpenter
1662–78. He also acted as Carpenter to the
Vintners' Company.
1671 ROYAL EXCHANGE, LONDON
Carpenter's work.
Lit: Colvin, 1954, *Dictionary*, p. 297.
1671–76 VINTNERS' HALL, LONDON
Hall, Courtroom, Staircase.
Lit: G W Whiteman, 1970, *Halls and
Treasures of the City Companies*, p. 94.

JOHNSON, Edward (*fl.* 1710–16).
Carpenter.
Partner of Joseph Duxon.
1710–16 3 ST JAMES'S SQUARE, LONDON
Repairs, timber shoring.
Lit: 1960, *Survey of London*, XXIX, p. 84.

JOHNSON, John (*fl.* 1755). Plasterer.
Foreman to Francesco Vassalli (q.v.).

1755 EGREMONT HOUSE, LONDON
Received £20 on behalf of his master.
Lit: West Sussex CRO, Petworth MS, 6266.
A carpenter, John Johnson, worked at the German Lutheran Chapel, The Savoy, London, in 1766.
Lit: Harris, 1970, *Chambers*, p. 229.

JOHNSON, Joseph (*fl.* 1767–75). Sawyer.
1767 KENWOOD, MIDDLESEX
1775 Worked under a carpenter named Dixon.
Lit: Bolton, 1922, *Adam*, I, p. 316.

JOHNSON, William (*fl.* 1765–66).
Carpenter.
1765–66 KEDLESTON, DERBYSHIRE
Worked on the organ case (158 days): carved mouldings, pedestals, altered picture-frames, bookcases, etc.
Lit: Kedleston Archives, Accts. 3R, No. 12.

JONES, Aaron (*fl.* 1757–75). Carver and Gilder.
In Sketchley's 1775 Bristol Directory, he was living at 10 Clare Street and was described as 'Carver, Gilder, and Looking glass Manufacturer'.
1757 MORAVIAN CHAPEL, BRISTOL
Made a wooden chandelier.
Lit: Bryan Little, 1954, *City and County of Bristol*, p. 221.
A 'Mr Jones' did house painting at Houghton Hall, Norfolk, in 1732.
Lit: CUL (CH) Account Book 39/1, entries dated 22 March, 22 May 1732.

JONES, Henry (1649–1721). Joiner.
Of Walgrave. Settled later at Lamport, where he died.
1686 LAMPORT HALL, NORTHAMPTONSHIRE
Music Room, wainscoting; measured by Henry Dormer.
Jones seems to have undertaken the rebuilding of All Saints Church, Northampton, and the construction of the Sessions House there after the fire of 1675.
Lit: Colvin, 1954, *Dictionary*, p. 271; Sir Gyles Isham, 1951, 'Lamport Hall, *Northants. Architectural and Arch. Soc.*, p. 19; *C Life*, 30 October 1952, p. 1023, 10 October 1952, p. 1108; information from the late Sir Gyles Isham.

JONES, Richard (*fl.* 1712–24). Carver.
Of Wapping.
1712–24 ST ALPHEGE, GREENWICH, LONDON
Lit: Colvin, 1950, *Arch Rev*, p. 196.

JONES, Robert (*fl.* late 17th cent.). Carver.
Submitted proposals at Greenwich Hospital.
Lit: *Wren Soc*, VI, pp. 31, 35, 52, 54, 57, 69, 70.

JONES, Robert (*fl.* 1777). Brass-founder?
1777 20 ST JAMES'S SQUARE, LONDON
Provided tacks and pins, hinges and various fittings for Lady Williams-Wynn's Bird Cage (13s.).
Lit: NLW, Wynnstay MS, 115/7.

KAY (KEY), Josiah (*fl.* late 17th–early 18th cents.). Locksmith.

King's Blacksmith, 1699. Worked at the Cottonian Library, Kensington Palace and Hampton Court. In 1709–10 he supplied brass locks, keys and hinges for Castle Howard, Yorks.
Lit: *Wren Soc*, IV, pp. 60, 72, VII, pp. 188, 213, XI, p. 53, XVIII, pp. 152–53, 160–61; Castle Howard Archives, Building Bills, 1700–40, Folder 2, Bill, 12 January 1709–10.

KELSEY, William (*fl.* 1791–96). Joiner.
1791–96 SOMERSET HOUSE, LONDON
Received £736. 0s. 4d.
Lit: London, RIBA, Library, Somerset House Accounts.

KENDALL, Robert (*fl.* 1660). Plasterer.
Possibly a grandson of William Kendall, who worked at Nonsuch Palace, Surrey, in 1541.
1660 THE TOWER, LONDON
Worked under John Grove I in November.
Lit: PRO, Works, 5/1.

KERROD, Samuel (*fl.* 1795–98). Plasterer.
Of Reading.
1795–98 MAPLEDURHAM HOUSE, OXFORDSHIRE
Several ceilings, including Gothic one in Chapel.
Lit: Bills at house. (I am indebted to Dr H M Colvin for this reference.)

KIBBLEWHITE, – (*fl.* 1774–77). Plasterer.
1774–77 REDBOURNE HALL, LINCOLNSHIRE

1774, 14 June.	To the Plaisterers 5s.	
20 Oct.	Kibblewhite, Plaisterer in full of £39. 3. 0.	
	£19. 3. 0.	
1775 Nov.	Kibblewhite, Plaisterer.	
	£15. 16. 0.	
1776 Dec.	Kibblewhite, Plaisterer.	
	£44. 1. 0.	
1777 16 July	Kibblewhite, Stuccoing chancel aisles. £14. 3. 0.	

Lit: Lincolnshire CRO, Red. 3/1/4/6/2, pp. 34, 36, 44, 51. (I am indebted to Mrs Joan Varley for this reference.)

KIDGELL, Henry (*fl.* 1628–86). Plasterer.
Apprenticed in May 1642 to Arthur Toogood (q.v.) of London. No commissions are known by him. His will is PCC 1686, f. 32.

KILMINSTER, – (*fl.* 1772). Plasterer.
1772 CHIRK CASTLE, DENBIGHSHIRE
Saloon ceiling.
Lit: *C Life*, 12 October 1951.

KING, Benjamin (*fl.* mid-18th cent.).
Carver.
Of Warwick. Worked in wood and stone at Radway Grange, Arbury Hall, Packington Hall, Newnham Paddox, Stivichall, Warwick Castle and Kyre Park, Worcs.
Lit: G C Tyack, 1970, 'Country House Building in Warwickshire, 1500–1914', BA thesis, Univ. of Oxford, p. 143; Warwicks. CRO, Warwick Castle Vouchers, 1766–67; Gunnis, 1953, *Dictionary*, p. 228; Hussey, 1965, *ECH: Early Georgian*, p. 218.

KING, Thomas and **William** with **PADGET, Joseph** (*fl.* 1776–77). Mercers.
'Mercers to His Majesty' of King Street, Covent Garden, London.

1776–77 20 ST JAMES'S SQUARE, LONDON
Provided 141½ yd of striped furniture satin (£45. 19s. 9d.) and 1000 yd of Pea Green Damask 'to hang the Principal Rooms — Curtains, Cushions, etc.'
Lit: NLW, Wynnstay MS, 115/7.

KINMAN, William & Company (*fl.* 1774).
Brass-Founders.
Mentioned in RABA.
c 1774 20 ST JAMES'S SQUARE, LONDON
Provided '3 Balconies, the Copper Railings of the Best Stair Case and sundry other work in the brass and cast iron way'. Kinman also worked at Kedleston, where his two men fixed the skylight (received £268. 19s. 0d.).
Lit: Beard, 1966, *Craftsmen*, pp. 40, 69, 80, 83; NLW, Wynnstay MS, 115/17/8.

KINSMAN, Joseph (*fl.* 1637–55). Plasterer.
Official of the Worshipful Company of Plaisterers.
Fined for bad work 9 October 1655, the year he was appointed Master of the Company. He was also arrested in the same year for disagreements with Bartholomew Clarke.
Lit: London, Guildhall Library, MS, 6122/2, 6126.
1637–38 HAM HOUSE, SURREY
Staircase (£38. 17s. 0d.), North Drawing Room (£35. 4s. 0d.), Hall.
Lit: Ralph Edwards, 1950, *Guide to Ham House*, Victoria and Albert Museum, p. 36.

KINWARD, Thomas (?–1682). Joiner.
Master Joiner to the Office of Works from 1660 until his death in 1682. He worked at Whitehall, Hampton Court and St James's Palace, as well as other Crown estates. In 1663 he carved the staircase at Hinchingbrooke, Huntingdonshire, for the 1st Earl of Sandwich, part of which survives. In 1664 he was joiner at Clarendon House.
Lit: Colvin, 1976, *King's Works*, V, references cited; Oliver Hill and John Cornforth, 1966, *English Country Houses: Caroline*, p. 232; Walpole, 1798, 'Anecdotes of Painting', *Works*, 2, p. 280: noted 'Mr Kingwood' walking in the procession at Cromwell's funeral; R T Gunther, 1928, *The Architecture of Sir Roger Pratt*, pp. 135–66; PRO, E 351/3276.

KIPLING, John (*fl.* 1761). Plasterer.
1761 Freeman of York.
Lit: Surtees Society, 102.

LAGUERRE, Louis (1663–1721). Decorative Painter.
Godson of Louis XIV. Came to England about 1684 and worked on the following major commissions:
1689–94 CHATSWORTH, DERBYSHIRE
Chapel, Hall, Music Room, State Bedroom, etc.
c 1692 SUDBURY HALL, DERBYSHIRE
1698 BURGHLEY, NORTHAMPTONSHIRE
Ballroom walls.
c 1699 HAMPTON COURT, MIDDLESEX
Fountain Court: roundels.
c 1699 WOLLATON HALL, NOTTINGHAMSHIRE
Great Hall, Staircase.
after 1702–03 KIVETON, YORKSHIRE
Great Hall, Staircase, *dest*.

before 1706 AMPTHILL PARK, BEDFORDSHIRE
after 1705 BUCKINGHAM HOUSE, LONDON
Dest after 1825.
c 1710 PETERSHAM HOUSE, SURREY
before 1715 CANONS, MIDDLESEX
Staircase ceiling.
after 1714 PETWORTH HOUSE, SUSSEX
Staircase.
1715 ST PAUL'S CATHEDRAL, LONDON
Preliminary work for Dome decoration.
Commission given to Sir James Thornhill.
1715 ST LAWRENCE'S CHURCH, WHITCHURCH
c 1720 BLENHEIM PALACE, OXFORDSHIRE
Saloon.
Lit: Croft-Murray, 1962, *Painting*, I, pp.
250–54.

LAMB, William (*fl.* 1775). Plasterer.
Mentioned as a 'tiler and plasterer' in
Sketchley's 1775 Bristol Directory.

LANCE, David (*fl.* 1691–1724). Plasterer.
Lance may have been a son of Nicholas
Lance, a plasterer who worked under John
Grove at Whitehall in June 1670 (PRO,
Works, 5/15). In the late seventeenth century,
he worked for Edward Goudge. Captain
William Winde, writing to his cousin Lady
Mary Bridgeman on 27 April 1691, indicated
that 'Mr. Lance is at the Duke of
Summersetts at Pettworth in Sussex'. Lance
was presumably present on most of the
commissions in which Edward Goudge was
involved.
He was appointed Master Plasterer to the
Office of Works in succession to John Grove
II (q.v.) on 27 May 1708 (PRO, Works, 6/14,
f. 171). His appointment was reconfirmed by
George I, 27 May 1715 (Works, 6/11, f. 41).
In his capacity as Master Plasterer Lance
submitted many proposals for work. With
Robert Wetherill, he shared certain work at
Hampton Court in 1716 (PRO, Works, 4/1, 6
March 1716).
He was owed £655. 16*s*. in 1714 by Lord
Ashburnham, probably for work in St James's
Square, London. He also engaged in 1713 in
building activities in St James's Square for
Lord Berkeley.
Lit: PRO, Works, as cited; *Post Boy*, 27
December 1712, cited by David Green, 1951,
Blenheim, p. 305; *Wren Soc*, VI, pp. 58, 62,
63, VII, pp. 201–02, 214, 222–24, 228;
Calendar of Treasury Papers, XXIX, pt. 2,
p. 102; *Survey of London*, XXIX, 1960, pp.
84 fn., 100, XXVII, 1956, p. 33.

LANE, John (*fl.* 1731–37). Joiner.
1731–32 KEW PALACE, SURREY
Received £250 for unspecified work.
1735–37 ST JAMES'S PALACE, LONDON
Supervised by William Kent and Thomas
Ripley.
Received £165. 5*s*. 11*d*.
Lit: Duchy of Cornwall, Vouchers II,
1731–32, p. 288, VI(1), 1735–37, p. 257.

LANE, W (*fl.* 1818–19). Carpenter.
1818–19 3 ST JAMES'S SQUARE, LONDON
Architect: Sir John Soane.
Lit: 1960, *Survey of London*, XXIX, p. 86 fn.

LANGDALE, Edward (*fl.* 1668). Carver.
Foreman to the Carver at Wren's Sheldonian
Theatre, Oxford.
Lit: *Wren Soc*, XIX, p. 92.

LANGLEY, John (*fl.* 1714–28). Joiner.
1714–28 ST JOHN, WESTMINSTER, LONDON
Architect: Thomas Archer.
'Framing Timber and Pewing Gallery'.
Lit: Colvin, 1950, *Arch Rev*, p. 196.
A relative(?) William Langley made a model
of the spire of St Mary Woolnoth *c* 1716.
Lit: *ibid.*

LANGLEY, Thomas (*fl.* 1660). Plasterer.
1660 THE TOWER, LONDON
Worked under John Grove.
Lit: PRO, Works, 5/1, November 1660.

LANSCROON, – (*fl.* 1695–96). Carver.
Not to be confused with the decorative
painter.
1695 Appears in the Chatsworth accounts. He
was paid £10 'in part for carving of sixteen
Festoones of Limetree wood for the Gallery'
in the first quarter of 1696. He received £42
in September 1696.
Lit: Chatsworth, Building Accounts.

LARKIN, Thomas (*fl.* 1686). Joiner.
Of St Martin-in-the-Fields, London.
1686 PETWORTH, SUSSEX
Wainscoting, window shutters, door
pediments.
Lit: Gervase Jackson-Stops, May 1977, 'The
Building of Petworth', *Apollo*, p. 326.

LAWRENCE, Richard (*fl.* 1732–83). Carver.
Apprenticed, 1746, to Sefferin Alken (q.v.).
1760–61 Surveyor and Repairer of Carved
Work, Windsor Castle.
c 1764–73 MANOR HOUSE, MILTON,
BERKSHIRE
Carving, including panelling and overmantel
in Dining Room.
He worked in wood and stone at Somerset
House in the 1780s, and on Greenwich
Hospital Chapel. He is presumably the
Richard Lawrence who worked in the New
Room at Strawberry Hill for Horace Walpole.
Lit: London, Guildhall Library, *Boyd's Index
to Apprenticeship Registers*, XVIII, 1st ser.,
p. 3484; Gunnis, 1953, *Dictionary*, p. 236;
RIBA, Library, Somerset House accounts;
ibid., MS, New 25–26; Paget Toynbee ed.,
1927, *Strawberry Hill Accounts*, p. 157;
Colvin, 1976, *King's Works*, V, p. 479 (an
earlier Richard Lawrence, carver, worked with
James Richards (q.v.) in 1737, *ibid.*, p. 243).

LAY, Eleanor (*fl.* 1789). Frame Maker.
1789 SOMERSET HOUSE, LONDON
'To carving and Gilding 5 Circular Frames for
the Navy Board Room at ea. £2. 5. 0. Total
£11. 5. 0.'
Lit: London, RIBA, Library, Somerset
House Accounts, 3.

LE SAGE, John (*fl.* late 17th cent.). Carver
and Gilder.
His name appears on a bill made out in 1690
to the Earl of Bristol. Worked also at
Hampton Court.
Lit: *Wren Soc.*, IV, p. 60.

LIGHTFOOT, Luke (*c* 1722–89). Carver.
Son of Theophilus Lightfoot of St Giles-in-
the-Fields, London. Admitted to the Freedom
of the Drapers' Company, 1743. Took seven
apprentices between 1749 and 1767. After a
stormy career, he ended his life as a victualler
at Denmark Hall, Dulwich.
1757–69 CLAYDON HOUSE, BUCKINGHAMSHIRE
Provision of fittings and items in wood, stone
and marble; the carving in particular is of
considerable virtuosity (*see* pls. 41, 53, 127).
Engaged in litigation with the 2nd Earl
Verney due to his overcharging.
Lit: L O J Boynton, 1966, 'Luke Lightfoot
(?1722–89)', *Furniture History*, II, pp. 7–17;
Hussey, 1965, *ECH: Early Georgian*, pp.
244–52.

LINDORES, William (*fl.* 1667–72).
Plasterer.
Apprenticed to Thomas Alborn of Glasgow
(q.v.).
1672 WEMYSS CASTLE, FIFE
Worked with John Nicoll (q.v.).
Lit: *C Life*, 6 January 1966, p. 23.

LINE, John (*fl.* 1734). Carpenter.
1734 LONGLEAT, WILTSHIRE
Lit: Accounts, house archives.

LINNELL, William (*fl. c* 1730–63). Carver
and Cabinet-maker.
Supplied furniture to Sir Richard Hoare and
to William Drake for Shardeloes, from his
premises at 28 Berkeley Square, London. He
did carver's work at the Radcliffe Library,
Oxford. He estimated that his work would
amount to £329. 3*s*. 6*d*., and the final bill was
£348. 1*s*. 4*d*. In 1746–47 he received
£507. 15*s*. 8½*d*., a total of £855. 17*s*. 0½*d*.
Lit: S G Gillam, 1958, 'Building Accounts of
the Radcliffe Camera', Oxford Hist. Soc., pp.
53, 64; *Wren Soc*, XVII, p. 82; information
from Helena Hayward and Pat Kirkham from
their study of William and John Linnell
(1980).

LIPSHAM, Joseph (*fl.* 1712). Glazier.
1712 5 ST JAMES'S SQUARE, LONDON
Lit: 1960, *Survey of London*, XXIX, p. 100.

LLOYD, James (*fl.* 1777). Glazier.
1777 20 ST JAMES'S SQUARE, LONDON
Lit: NLW, Wynnstay MS, 115/17/7,
115/17/20.

LOBB, Joel (*fl.* late 17th cent.) and **Henry**
(*fl.* 1700–21). Joiners and Carvers.
Of St Giles-in-the-Fields, Middlesex.
The Lobbs had an extensive practice in
London and the provinces (working at
Chatsworth and Castle Howard). In London,
Joel Lobb was one of a competent team who
worked on the Wren church, St James's,
Piccadilly. His son, Henry, was apprenticed to
William Hickman, carver, in 1714 for seven
years.
Lit: Francis Thompson, 1949, *A History of
Chatsworth*, pp. 36–37, 43, 59, 67, 114, 136,
148–49, 167, 170; London, Guildhall Library,
MS, 8052, 4, p. 41; 1960, *Survey of London*,
XXIX, p. 36.

LOCATELLI, John Baptiste (*c* 1735–1805). Sculptor.
Of Verona. Came to London in the mid-1770s and was there until *c* 1796.
Some of his pieces were designed for RA for the embellishment of chimneypieces, and he also worked for Mrs Coade at her artificial stone manufactory.
Lit: Gunnis, 1953, *Dictionary*, p. 240; Bolton, 1922, *Adam*, II, p. 339.

LOCK, – (*fl. c* 1770–80). Plasterer.
Worked for Sir William Chambers.
Lit: Laurence Turner, 1927, *Decorative Plasterwork in Great Britain*, p. 249.

LOCK, Matthias (*fl. c* 1710–65). Carver.
A talented carver with a large trade in carved mirrors and table frames.
His father, also Matthias, took his various sons as apprentices—Edward (1701), James (1722), John (1729) but Matthias was apprenticed to Richard Goldsaddle (1724).
Lit: London, Guildhall Library MS, 8052, 3, p. 41, 4, p. 141, 5, p. 87; Furniture History Society, 1979, *Journal*, XV, pp. 1–23.

LOERHUICK, Anthony (*fl.* late 17th cent.). Carver.
Carving in the Chapel Royal, Whitehall.
Lit: Wren Soc, VII, p. 131.

LONGUEVILLE, – (*fl.* 1733–34). Gilder.
1733–34 PARLINGTON HALL, YORKSHIRE
Dest c 1950.
Chapel and other rooms, gilding.
Lit: Elizabeth Done, 1975, 'Sir Edward Gascoigne, Grand Tourist', *Leeds Arts Calendar*, No. 77, p. 11.

LOUDER, James (*fl.* 1715). Plasterer.
Worked at Whitehall Palace, London.
Lit: PRO, Works, 4/1, f. 60.

LOVELL, James (*fl.* 1750–80). Plasterer.
Worked at Norfolk House, London, in the 1750s, and at Waldershare, Kent, Wroxton Abbey, Oxfordshire and Stowe, Buckinghamshire, 1754–77, in plaster and papier-mâché. Worked in wood and stone, 1758–61, at Croome Court, Worcestershire. He was also a sculptor and worked extensively for the Lyttelton circle at Hagley and elsewhere.
Lit: D Fitz-Gerald, 1973, *The Norfolk House Music Room*, Victoria and Albert Museum, pp. 25–26; *Burl Mag*, April 1973, pp. 220–32; Croome Court Archives, Nos. 6a, 19 (microfilm, Victoria and Albert Museum, Dept of Furniture and Woodwork).

LOWE, Thomas (*fl.* late 17th cent.). Carver.
Worked at Christ Church, Newgate Street, and the Temple Church.
Lit: Wren Soc, X, p. 124, pls. 58, 60.

LUDBEY, John (*fl.* 1751). Carpenter.
1751 ST JAMES'S, PICCADILLY, LONDON
Lit: 1960, *Survey of London*, XXIX, p. 37.

LUNDY, William (*fl.* 1731). Plasterer.
Brought up by Lord and Lady Lundy and recommended by Lady Lundy and William Adam to Sir John Clerk.

1731 MAVISBANK, MIDLOTHIAN
Dining Room and Summer House; other work by Samuel Calderwood (q.v.).
Lit: John Fleming, 1962, *Adam*, p. 332; Roxburghe Club, 1895, *Memoirs of Sir John Clerk*.

LYCENSE, Thomas (*fl.* 1612–59). Plasterer.
Apprenticed in 1626 to Thomas Widmore, then transferred to Clement Kelley. Master of the Worshipful Company of Plaisterers in 1659.
Lit: London, Guildhall Library MS, 6122/2.

MABBS, Robert (*fl.* 1715–16). Plasterer.
Official of the Worshipful Company of Plaisterers.
1715 Upper Warden.
1716 Master.
Lit: London, Guildhall Library, MS, 6122/3.

MABYN, Lawrence (*fl.* late 17th cent.). Plasterer.
Apprentice to John Abbott (q.v.).
Lit: C Life, 2 March 1950, p. 222.

MacGLASHAN, – (*fl.* 1770–80). Plasterer.
c 1770–80 worked for Sir William Chambers.
Lit: Charles Clarke, 1783, *The Plaisterers' Bill for Work done . . . Somerset House*.

MACKELEAN, Herman (*fl.* 1731–32). Glassman.
'At the Golding Key in Leadinghall Street'.
1731–32 ROYAL BARGE FOR FREDERICK, PRINCE OF WALES
Provided glass and putty.
Lit: Duchy of Cornwall, Vouchers 11, 1731–32, p. 263. Cited Geoffrey Beard, August 1970, *Burl Mag*, CXII, no. 809, p. 495.

MADDEN, John (*fl.* 1745). Carver and Gilder.
Of Bath. Subscribed to John Wood the elder's 1745, *A Description of the Exchange of Bristol*.

MAGNIAC, Charles (*fl. c* 1740–69). Chaser/Modeller.
Matthew Boulton regarded Magniac as a 'fine designer, modeller and chaser'. He designed much for the jeweller and automata maker, James Cox.
Lit: Goodison, 1974, *Ormolu*, p. 21.

MAHATLOE, Richard (*fl.* 1669). Plasterer.
1669 CONVOCATION HOUSE YARD, LONDON
Work in one room.
Lit: Wren Soc., XIII, p. 58.

MAINE (MAYNE), Jonathan (*fl. c* 1680–1709). Carver.
Maine (with Grinling Gibbons, Edward Pearce, Thomas Young and Roger Davies) was one of the most important woodcarvers of the late seventeenth century. He was a liveryman of the Joiners' Company in 1694.
Lit: C Life, 31 December 1948.
1682 ST ANTHOLIN, WATLING STREET, LONDON
Lit: Wren Soc, XIX, p. 7.
1682–85 BURGHLEY HOUSE, NORTHAMPTONSHIRE

1682/3	Feb. 2	Paid Tho Young & Jona Mayne for work at Burgh.	£100. 0. 0.
1683	Sept. 17	Paid Mr. Young & Mayne	£100. 0. 0.
1684	Dec. 19	Paid Young & Mayne	£100. 0. 0.
1684/5	March 5	Paid Mr. Young & Mayne in full	£102. 11. 3.

Maine was also paid £50 on 29 December 1687, and Young £50 on 31 December.
Lit: Child's Bank, Exeter Bank Account.
1687 ST CLEMENT, EASTCHEAP, LONDON
Lit: Wren Soc, X, pl. 47 (font), XIX, p. 16.
1688 ST MARY MAGDALENE, ST ANDREW'S, WARDROBE, ST AUGUSTIN, OLD CHANGE, ST STEPHEN, WALBROOK, LONDON
Lit: Wren Soc, X, pp. 46, 54, 93, 113, 115, 118, 124–25.
1689 ETON COLLEGE, NEW SCHOOL
Lit: Wren Soc, XIX, pp. 109–10.
1695 CHRIST'S HOSPITAL
Lit: Wren Soc, XI, p. 76.
1695 TRINITY COLLEGE, CHAPEL, OXFORD
W G Hiscock in *C Life*, 31 December 1948, printed the text of two letters (one in the Bodleian Library, the other at Corpus Christi) which established that most of the carving at Trinity, other than the reredos (*see* col. pl. 3, pls. 112–13), said to be by Grinling Gibbons, was by Maine. He worked in conjunction there with Arthur Frogley (as well as in the Chapel of Corpus Christi, where he did the screen). For the latter, Frogley prepared some of the wood, glueing it together before sending it up to London for Maine to finish.
1696–1709 ST PAUL'S CATHEDRAL, LONDON
Carved in the vestries, screen to the Morning Prayer Chapel, Model for the Dome windows, Cornice above the Whispering Gallery, in the Consistory Court, and Library. Worked also in stone.
Lit: Wren Soc, XV, pp. xxiii, 26 (pl. 89), 40–41 (pl. 44), 62, 72 (pl. 31), 99, 129, 137–38, 175–76 (pls. 45, 80, 88); Gunnis, 1953, *Dictionary*, p. 250.
1703–04 KIVETON, YORKSHIRE
Received £27. 16s. (1703) and £76 (1704), a total of £103. 16s.
Lit: Leeds, Yorkshire Arch. Soc., Library, Duke of Leeds Archives, Box 33.
1704 ST MICHAEL, QUEENHYTHE, LONDON
Lit: Wren Soc, XIX, p. 43, presumably the 'John Mayne' referred to. As Maine worked with Roger Davies at Burghley House, he, Gibbons or one of this late seventeenth-century talented group of carvers, may have worked at Holme Lacy, Herefs. James Scudamore, the owner, married a daughter of the Earl of Exeter. The carvings formerly there are very fine, and H Avray Tipping, 1914, *Grinling Gibbons and the Woodwork of his Age*, illustrated them *in situ* (pls. 199–203).

MANEFIELD, – (*fl. c* 1750). Wallpaper Manufacturer.
His Trade Card reads: 'Original Mock India Paper Hanging, and Papier Machie Manufactory in the Strand, London. The

Nobility etc. may be supplied on the best Terms, with all sorts of Paper Hangings, Paintings of Landscapes, Festoons and Trophies, India paper, Papier Machie, Ornaments etc. and a Mock India Paper, made after a method peculiar to himself, which surpasses every thing of the kind yet attempted and for Variety, Beauty and Duration, equal to the Real India Paper.'
Lit: Trade Card, *repr.* A Heal, 1968, *London Tradesmens' Cards of the Eighteenth Century*, p. 33.

MANLEY, Thomas (*fl.* 1766). Plasterer.
Of Bristol.
Built Cumberland Street, St Paul's, Bristol, with Isaac Manley, mason.
Lit: Andor Gomme, Michael Jenner and Bryan Little, 1979, *Bristol: An Architectural History*, p. 206.

MANOCCHI, Giuseppe (1731–82). Painter.
Mentioned in RABA (1766, ff. 319–20).
Drawings of scagliola floors signed by Manocchi are in the Soane Museum, London.
Lit: Thieme-Becker; Bolton, 1922, *Adam*, II, p. 358.

MANSFIELD, Isaac (*fl.* before 1697–1739).
Plasterer.
Isaac Mansfield may have been born at Derby. His father Samuel (q.v.) was a plasterer and was living at Derby at the time of his death. He left Isaac only one shilling in his will. We hear further of Isaac when, on 4 October 1704, 'Isaac Mansfield of London' was admitted a Freeman of York on payment of £25. He seems to have alternated between York and London, being described as 'of York' in 1713 when he took an apprentice Charles Carlile, and of 'St. James, Westminster' in 1724, when he took Samuel Smith. When working at Houghton in 1729 he had an assistant, John Moxion (Gibbs, 1728, *B of A*). Mr Derek Sherborn points out that Mansfield had a house in Henrietta Street, a few doors away from Gibbs.
Mansfield was Sheriff of York in 1728–29. He subscribed to the third volume of *Vitruvius Britannicus*, 1725, and, together with Isaac Mansfield, junior, to Gibbs's *B of A*. He did unspecified work (£68) for James Brydges, 1st Duke of Chandos. At the end of his life he became bankrupt.
Lit: Surtees Society, 102, p. 186; York Reference Library, Sessions Book, 1728–44; Baker, 1949, *Brydges*, p. 199. His death is recorded in *The Daily Post* 4 January 1740, No. 6341, and *The London Daily Post and General Advertiser*, 5 January 1739–40, No. 1621—'Yesterday Morning died at his Lodgings at Charing Cross, Isaac Mansfield, Joint-Plaisterer with Geo. Worrall to his Majesties Palaces, and likewise Plaisterer to his Royal Highness the Prince of Wales'.
1710 CASTLE HOWARD, YORKSHIRE
Architect: Sir John Vanbrugh.
Assisted Bagutti and Plura and did the following: '1710 June. Pd. 1s. Mansfield for whª he did & pd upon Acct £2. 13. 0d.'
He worked in 'the Library (£3. 1s. 11d.); My Lady's Closett (£1. 5s. 3d.); My Lady's Dressing Room (£1. 4s. 5d.); in the Bedchamber (£3. 1s. 10d. and £2. 16s. 6d.);

Withdrawing roome (two payments of £1. 11s. 6d.); lath work (£9. 10s. 0d.)', in all received £105. 2s. 6d.
Lit: Castle Howard Archives, Building Books.
1712–24 ST GEORGE'S CHURCH, HANOVER SQUARE, LONDON
Architect: John James.
Lit: Colvin, 1950, *Arch Rev*, p. 196.
1714–28 ST JOHN'S CHURCH, WESTMINSTER, LONDON
Architect: Thomas Archer.
Lit: ibid.
1718 January, paid £10 by Robert Benson, Lord Bingley.
Lit: Hoare's Bank, Benson account.
1720–30 ST GEORGE'S CHURCH, BLOOMSBURY, LONDON
Architect: Nicholas Hawksmoor.
Lit: Colvin, 1950, *Arch Rev*, p. 196.
1720–21 BURLINGTON HOUSE
Architect: Lord Burlington.
Worked with John Hughes (q.v.)
Received £220 in seven instalments between 4 July 1720 and 23 January 1721.
Lit: Chatsworth, Burlington account book.
1721 CHICHELEY HALL, BUCKINGHAMSHIRE
Hall and Staircase. Received £108.
Assisted by Joshua Needham (q.v.).
Lit: Joan D Tanner, 1961, 'The Building of Chicheley Hall', *Records of Bucks.*, XVII, pt. I; *C Life*, 20 February 1975, p. 437.
1721 LANGLEYS, ESSEX
Received £85 on 14 June 1721 for plastering the Hall.
Lit: Essex CRO, Samuel Tufnell's accounts; *Connoisseur*, December 1957, p. 211.
1723–29 CHRISTCHURCH, SPITALFIELDS, LONDON
Architect: Nicholas Hawksmoor.
Lit: Colvin, 1950, *Arch Rev*, p. 196; Lambeth Palace Library, MS, 2703.
1725–29 HOUGHTON HALL, NORFOLK
Work other than that by Giuseppe Artari (q.v.).
Lit: CUL (CH) Vouchers, 1725, Account Book 40/1 (entry dated 19 July 1729).
1725 GOODWOOD, SUSSEX
Lit: West Sussex CRO, Goodwood Archives, G.121/1/107; information from Mr T P Connor.
1725 BLENHEIM PALACE, OXFORDSHIRE
Architect: Nicholas Hawksmoor.
Long Library; Chapel.
'I presume Mr. Mansfield has near upon finnished great part of the Gallery by this time and I hope to your satisfaction . . . I suppose the Chapel will not be taken in hand till the Gallery is quite done. . . .'
Lit: Blenheim MS, E47, Hawksmoor to Sarah, Duchess of Marlborough, 23 December 1725, cited by David Green, 1951, *Blenheim Palace*, pp. 310–11.
1725 SENATE HOUSE, CAMBRIDGE
Architect: James Gibbs.
Plain plasterwork (decorative work by Bagutti and Artari). Received £315.
Lit: Little, 1955, *Gibbs*, pp. 60–61.
1727–33 ST LUKE'S CHURCH, OLD STREET, LONDON
Architects: Wren and Hawksmoor.
1730 CLAREMONT, SURREY
Altering Drawing Room. Received £22. 12s. 0d.
Lit: BL Add. MS, 33161, 27 February 1730.

1730 KEW PALACE, SURREY
Architect: William Kent.
Work for Frederick, Prince of Wales.
Received £625. 8s. 9¼d.
Lit: Duchy of Cornwall Office, Vouchers, IV, p. 229.
Attributed work
c 1730 RAYNHAM HALL, NORFOLK
Lit: M Jourdain, 1948, *The Work of William Kent*, p. 65.

MANSFIELD, Samuel (*fl.* 1672–97).
Plasterer.
Father of Isaac Mansfield (q.v.). Samuel lived at Derby. His will (at Lichfield) is dated 20 April 1697, and was proved on 8 October 1697. In it he left to his wife Hannah his cottages 'near to St. Mary's Gate in Derby for life and then the same to my six daughters, Elizabeth, Anne, Mary, Sarah, Hannah and Rebecca' and to his son 'Isaac Mansfield, one shilling'. He left the residue to his wife, who was appointed as executrix.
1672–75 SUDBURY HALL, DERBYSHIRE
Mansfield agreed with George Vernon in 1672 to 'fretworke my roome wᵗʰ archa: frieze & cornishe', and did the plain plastering throughout the house.
In 1675 he agreed to 'frettworke the greate staire heade chamber, £20'. This refers to the Queen's Room.
Lit: *C Life*, 22–29 June 1935.

MANTLE, William (*fl.* 1726–29). Plasterer.
Subscribed to Leoni's edition of *Alberti*, 1726.
1729 MOULSHAM HALL, ESSEX
Architect: Giacomo Leoni.
Interior work on south range. Received £74. 15s. 0d.
Decorative plasterwork by Artari and Bagutti.
Lit: Essex CRO, D/DM A5. (I am indebted to Mr Arthur C Edwards for this reference.)

MARGETTS, Henry (*fl.* 1684–1704).
Plasterer.
Worked on Office of Works contracts under John Grove II.
1684 EAST HATTLEY, CAMBRIDGESHIRE
Work with two labourers at Sir George Downing's.
Received £12. 14s. 7d., paid in 1690 by Sir George's executor, the 2nd Earl of Carlisle.
Lit: Castle Howard Archives, Executor's Accounts, Sir George Downing.
1690 KENSINGTON PALACE, LONDON
Outworks, stables, etc., received about £40. Also worked in Palace.
Lit: PRO, Works, 19/48/1, f. 108.
?–1695 CHATSWORTH, DERBYSHIRE
As Master Plasterer.
Lit: Francis Thompson, 1949, *A History of Chatsworth*, pp. 36, 59, 67.
c 1700 KIVETON, YORKSHIRE
Architect: William Talman.
Received £372. 16s. 0d.
The house was under construction 1694–1704.
Lit: Leeds, Yorkshire Archaeological Society, Duke of Leeds MSS, Box 33.

MARSDEN, James (*fl.* 1740–50). Carver.
Resident carver in the service of the Earl of Leicester at Holkham Hall, Norfolk.
Succeeded by J Miller.
Lit: Holkham Archives, Account Books, 8, 26.

MARTIN, (MARTYN), Edward
(*fl.* 1648–99). Plasterer.
Son of John Martin (see below). Made free of
the Worshipful Company of Plaisterers, 21
September 1655. Fined for arrears, 25 January
1657. Beadle of the Company 1660, and
Master, 1699. Fined for bad work in 1671 and
1685. His name appears in the 1668–1724
Contracts Book of the Office of Works (PRO,
Works, 5/145, f. 13) for work at 'The great
foott Guard in Scotland Yard'. Both Edward
and John worked at The Tower, November
1660.
Lit: London Guildhall Library, MSS, 6122/2,
6126 (12 May 1671; 27 April 1685); PRO,
Works 5/1.
1671 31 ST JAMES'S SQUARE, LONDON
This work has since been destroyed. Martin
was fined for bad work at the house.
Lit: London Guildhall Library, MS, 6126 (2
May 1671); 1960, *Survey of London*, XXIX,
p. 198, for description of house in 1671 when
owned by Thomas Belasyse (Lord
Fauconberg).
1671–81 ST NICHOLAS COLE ABBEY,
QUEENHITHE, LONDON
Worked with John Sherwood (q.v.).
Lit: Wren Soc, X, p. 73.
1678 ARBURY, WARWICKSHIRE
Chapel ceiling. The agreement also mentions
doing 'my wife's closet fretworke, hee is to
have £48 besides comeing and going and
goate's haire'.
Lit: Warwicks. CRO, MS, CR 136/B24/2451;
Wren Soc, X, p. 22; L Turner, 1927,
Decorative Plasterwork in Great Britain,
p. 142.
1682 BURGHLEY HOUSE, NORTHAMPTONSHIRE
Received £150, but this probably represents
only a portion of his full bill.
Lit: Child's Bank, Exeter Bank Account,
entries dated 1 July 1682, 14 February 1682/3.
1682 NORTHUMBERLAND HOUSE, LONDON
Received £21. 10s. 0d. for 'whiteing'.
Lit: Alnwick Castle Archives, UI, 17, 18
December 1682.

MARTIN, John (*fl.* 1660–82). Plasterer.
1660 WHITEHALL and THE TOWER, LONDON
Worked under John Grove I.
Lit: PRO, Works, 5/1, September, November
1660.
1676–82 WINDSOR CASTLE, BERKSHIRE
Lit: W H St John Hope, 1911, *Windsor
Castle*, I, pp. 314, 321, 485.

MARTYR, Thomas (*fl.* 1818–19).
Carpenter.
1818–19 3 ST JAMES'S SQUARE, LONDON
Architect: Sir John Soane.
Lit: 1960, *Survey of London*, XXIX, p. 86 fn.

MASTERS, John (*fl.* late 17th cent.).
Plasterer.
1680 ST CLEMENT DANES, OLD CHURCH,
LONDON
Lit: Wren Soc, X, p. 109.

MATHEWS, John (*fl.* 1689–1710). Plasterer.
1689 HAMPTON COURT, MIDDLESEX
One of the plasterers working under John
Grove II (q.v.).
Lit: PRO, Works, 5/55, April 1689.

1710 ST PAUL'S CATHEDRAL, LONDON
Worked under Chrysostom Wilkins (q.v.).
Lit: Wren Soc, XV, p. 196.

MATTHEWS, Robert (*fl.* 1717). Joiner.
1717 CHEVENING, KENT
Estimated for boards, nails, panelling, etc.
Lit: Kent CRO, Stanhope Archives, U. 1590,
60B.

MAY, Robert (*fl.* 1760). Joiner.
Partner with Peter Moor.
1760 HOLKHAM HALL, NORFOLK
Great Hall, door-case linings; Chapel, Cedar
Screen and Altar-rails.
Lit: Holkham Archives, Building Accounts,
27.

MEADE, Thomas (*fl.* late 17th cent.).
Plasterer.
Mentioned in Robert Hooke's *Diary*,
1935 edn., p. 60.
1678 ST LAWRENCE JEWRY, LONDON
Architect: Sir Christopher Wren.
Meade agreed to do the ceiling for the Vestry
Room to Wren's design.
Received £26 on 1 October 1678.
Lit: Wren Soc, XIX, pp. 24–26.
1685 ST MARY ABCHURCH, LONDON
Lit: Wren Soc, X, p. 124.

MEARD, John (*fl.* 1712–24). Carpenter.
1712–24 ST GEORGE, HANOVER SQUARE,
LONDON
Architect: John James.
Lit: Colvin, 1950, *Arch Rev*, p. 195.
1712–24 ST ANNE, LIMEHOUSE, LONDON
Architect: Nicholas Hawksmoor.
Lit: ibid., p. 195.
1714–17 ST MARY LE STRAND, LONDON
Architect: James Gibbs.
Lit: ibid., p. 196.
1715–23 ST GEORGE, WAPPING, LONDON
Architect: Nicholas Hawksmoor.
Lit: ibid., p. 195.

MEW, – (*fl.* 1668). Locksmith.
1668 BADMINTON, GLOUCESTERSHIRE
22 June. Received £13.
Lit: Child's Bank, Account of 1st Marquess of
Worcester.

MILLER, James (*fl.* 1761–63). Carver.
1761–63 HOLKHAM HALL, NORFOLK
Carving in various rooms.
Lit: Holkham Archives, Building Accounts,
26, 27.

MILLER, John (*fl.* 1686). Carver.
1686 ST MICHAEL, QUEENHYTHE, and ALL
HALLOWS, LOMBARD STREET, LONDON
Lit: Wren Soc, X, pp. 46, 54, 124, XIX, p. 43.

MINES, John (*fl.* 1726–30). Plasterer.
1726 WESTMINSTER SCHOOL, LONDON
New Dormitory. Charged £220. 13s. 0d.
Received £186 in November 1726.
Lit: Westminster Abbey Archives, MS,
35394; *Wren Soc*, XI, p. 45.
1730 WOLTERTON, NORFOLK
Worked for Sir Robert Walpole.
Lit: C Life, 25 July 1957, p. 168.

MINN, — (*fl.* 1712–24). Joiner.
1712 CLARENDON BUILDINGS, OXFORD
Received £294. 10s. 0d.
Lit: C Life, 2 June 1928.
1719 ALL SOULS COLLEGE, OXFORD
Chapel Screen. Received £8 as Joiner.
Lit: C Life, 23 June 1928.

MINNS, Richard (?) (*fl.* 1712–50). Glazier.
1712–14 3 ST JAMES'S SQUARE, LONDON
Lit: 1960, *Survey of London*, XXIX, p. 84 fn.
1730–31 HOUGHTON HALL, NORFOLK
Provided 62 squares of Crown Glass, W.
front.
Lit: CUL (CH), Account Book 39/1, entry
dated 29 January 1730/31.
1749 WIMPOLE CHURCH, CAMBRIDGESHIRE
Lit: BL Add. MS, 35679, f. 54.

MINSHULL, John (*fl.* 1767–68). Carver.
1767/68 KENWOOD, MIDDLESEX
Carved work in Library and certain other
rooms.
Lit: Bolton, 1922, *Adam*, II, p. 348; Stillman,
1966, *Adam*, p. 48.

MIST, Edward (?–1745). Pavior.
When he died, the administration of his estate
was granted to his executor, John Devall
(q.v.). A John Mist, 'earthtaker', also worked
on commissions supervised by William Kent
for the Prince of Wales.
Lit: Duchy of Cornwall, VI(1), 1735–37,
p. 257, LX(1), 1738–50, p. 115.

MITCHELL, John (*fl.* 1697). Carpenter.
Of London.
1697 ST PETER'S, BRISTOL
Reredos and reseating.
Lit: C F W Dening, 1923, *The XVIIIth
Century Architecture of Bristol*, p. 47.

MITLEY, Charles (1705–58). Carver.
His sculpture is listed by Gunnis, 1953,
Dictionary. He worked at Castle Howard
(1736), and did monuments in Yorkshire with
his partners, Harvey and Raper. In 1741 he
carved the Gothic pulpit in York Minster
made by Leonard Terry to the designs of
William Kent. His daughter married William
Peckitt, the glass painter. He is buried at St
Cuthbert's, York, and the cartouche tablet is
inscribed:
'Near this place lies the Body of Charles
Mitley, of this City, Carver, who Departed
this life, the 26th of August, 1758, Aged 53
years.'
Lit: J B Morrell, 1951, *York Monuments*, pp.
41, 59, 60, 122.
I have been able to add the following details
to his career.
Mitley was apprenticed in 1720 to 'Daniel
Harvey carver of York' (q.v.); this explains
the high order of his workmanship. He was
described as 'Charles George Mitley Carver,
of Featherstone, Co. Yorks'.
Lit: London, Guildhall Library, *Boyd's Index
to Apprenticeship Registers*.
In 1748 he worked for William Aislabie at
Studley Royal, Yorks. He carved the
chimneypiece in the Chinese Bedchamber
(*C Life*, 1 August 1931, pl. 13, p. 133):
for 6 ft. 6 of Egg Mould in the high Cornice at
6d. 00. 03. 3.

for 13 ft of twist rope in the pannell.
egg & tongue
4 roses at 1/- ea.
Side scrowls.
2 flooroams down the side of the pannell.
To a Shield in the pediment.
3 Jan. 1748 in all £4. 4. o.
Lit: Leeds Archives Dept, Studley Royal
Archives, Parcel 286.

MONEYPENNY, George (*fl.* 1776). Carver.
1776 KEDLESTON, DERBYSHIRE
Saloon Door, North Door, Side Doors to
Hall.
Frames to paintings in Hall. Received
£250. 7s 10d., October 1776.
Lit: Kedleston Archives, Accts. 3R.

MOOR, Peter (*fl.* 1760). Joiner.
Partner with Robert May.
1760 HOLKHAM HALL, NORFOLK
Great Hall, Door-case linings. Chapel, Cedar
Screen and Altar-rails.
Lit: Holkham Archives, Building Accounts,
27.

MOORE, Edward (*fl.* 1660). Plasterer.
1660 THE TOWER, LONDON
Worked under John Grove.
Lit: PRO, Works, 5/1, November 1660.

MOORE, John (?–1809). Carver (stone).
1763–64 AUDLEY END, ESSEX
Chimneypieces.
Lit: Stillman, 1966, *Adam*, p. 56, fn. 102.

MOORE (MOOR), Robert (*fl.* 1745–74).
Plasterer.
Lived at Warwick and worked extensively in
the county. Took an apprentice John Leure
in 1761.
Lit: London, Guildhall Library, *Boyd's Index
to Apprenticeship Registers*, 18, p. 3554.
c 1745 RADWAY, WARWICKSHIRE
Architect: Sanderson Miller.
In Sanderson Miller's account books
(Warwicks. CRO), there are occasional
payments to 'Mr Moor', which may indicate
the employment of Robert Moor at the Gothic
castle built at Radway. It is just possible that
Moor came from Banbury, as Miller refers on
occasion to 'the Banbury plasterer and his
man'.
1750–52 ALSCOT, WARWICKSHIRE
Staircase (1750–52); Great Hall ceiling
(*c* 1763).
'I have not seen Mr. Moore for some time but
his man has finished the first coat on the
Great Hall ceiling.'
Lit: *C Life*, 22 May 1958, p. 1126, citing a
letter at Alscot from the steward Mr Allen to
his master James West, MP.
1755 ARBURY, WARWICKSHIRE
Library.
Lit: Warwicks. CRO, Newdigate Archives,
cited in Hussey, 1956, *ECH: Mid-Georgian*,
p. 43.
1760–65 WARWICK CASTLE
Lit: Warwicks. CRO, Warwick Castle
Vouchers, 1760–61, 1768, 1773.
c 1760 STONELEIGH, WARWICKSHIRE
Received £75.
Lit: Stratford-upon-Avon, Shakespeare's
Birthplace Trust, Leigh Archives.

Moore also worked at Packington Hall,
Compton Verney, Charlecote, Barrells and
Stivichall.
Lit: G C Tyack, 1970, 'Country House
Building in Warwickshire, 1500–1914', BA
thesis, Univ. of Oxford, p. 143.

MOORE, Thomas (*fl.* 1756–78). Carpet-
maker.
1756. The Society of Arts of London offered a
premium for making carpets in England in
imitation of those made in Turkey and Persia.
The name of Thomas Moore of Chiswell
Street, Moorfields, is the first on the list of
recipients. A carpet he produced was considered to be 'in many respects
equal, and in some respects superior to those
imported from Persia and Turkey'. He
received a premium of £25 in 1757.
Lit: A F Kendrick and C E E Tattersall,
1922, *Hand-woven Carpets*, I, pp. 80–81.
1768. Lady Mary Coke in her *Journal* notes a
visit she paid on 18 April to Moore's
manufactory and noticed a carpet in hand for
Lord Coventry 'that he had agreed to give a
hundred & forty guineas for'.
Lit: 1889, *The Letters and Journals of Lady
Mary Coke*, ed. J A Home, 2, p. 242.
1769. Provided the carpet (which survives) to
Robert Adam's design for Syon House,
Middx. Measures 34 ft 9 in × 14 ft 2 in.
Signed and dated 'by thomas moore 1769'.
Also provided a carpet to Adam's design for
Osterley.
c 1774. Provided the carpet to Robert Adam's
design for 20 St James's Square, London.
Received £232. 10s. 6d.
Lit: NLW, Wynnstay MSS; 1958,
Connoisseur Yearbook.
Horace Walpole also had a fine carpet by
Moore.
Lit: Paget Toynbee, ed., 1927, *Strawberry
Hill Accounts*, pl. 126; 1842 Sale Catalogue of
Strawberry Hill, 24th day, lot 16.
Moore's trade card is illustrated by A Heal,
1968, *London Tradesmen's Cards of the
Eighteenth Century*, pp. 119–20; Beard, 1966,
Craftsmen, pp. 81, 83, 179. Wendy Hefford,
December 1977, 'Thomas Moore of
Moorfields', *Burl Mag*, pp. 840–48 (notes
knotting technique which enables
identification).

MORE, T (*fl.* 1708). Plasterer.
1708 ST PAUL'S CATHEDRAL, LONDON
Worked under Chrysostom Wilkins (q.v.).
Lit: *Wren Soc*, XV, p. 169.

MORGAN, William (*fl.* late 17th cent.).
Carver.
c 1685 CHELSEA HOSPITAL, LONDON
Received £175. 3s. 7d.
Lit: *Wren Soc*, XIX, pp. 61–86; 1872, *Papers
illustrative of the History of Chelsea Hospital*,
pp. 169–70.
1688 ABBEY CHURCH, HOLYROODHOUSE,
EDINBURGH
Lit: SRO, E28/477/2, cited Colvin, 1978,
Dictionary, p. 757.
c 1695 HAMILTON PALACE, LANARKSHIRE
All panelling, some carving, especially Dining
Room overmantel (some now at Boston
Museum of Fine Arts, USA).
Lit: Rosalind K Marshall, 1973, *The Days of
Duchess Anne*, pp. 206–07, pl.f. p. 161.

MORRIS, Daniel (d.1697/98). Plasterer.
Plasterer to Christ's Hospital, Newgate Street.
Succeeded by James Pettifer after his death on
10 December 1697/98.
Lit: *Wren Soc*, XI, p. 70.
1675 ST EDMUND THE KING, LOMBARD
STREET, LONDON
Worked with John Sherwood. Received £85.
Lit: *Wren Soc*, XII, p. 44.
ST MICHAEL, WOOD STREET, LONDON
Worked with John Sherwood. Received £81.
Lit: *Wren Soc*, XII, p. 44.

MORRIS, Thomas (*fl.* 1775). Engraver.
1775 Exhibited at the Society of Artists, and
worked for RA on 1773–, '*The Works in
Architecture . . .*', issued in parts.

MOSS, James (*fl.* 1762–76). Joiner.
c 1762–76 BUCKINGHAM PALACE, LONDON
Architect: Sir William Chambers.
Lit: Harris, 1970, *Chambers*, p. 218.

MOSS, T (*fl.* 1710). Plasterer.
1710 ST PAUL'S CATHEDRAL, LONDON
Worked under Chrysostom Wilkins (q.v.).
Lit: *Wren Soc*, XV, p. 196.

MOTT, Richard (*fl.* 1752–99). Plasterer.
Came from Martin, Lincolnshire. Apprenticed
in 1752 to Joseph Rose senior. He worked for
the Rose firm and is mentioned in Rose's will
in 1780. In 1799 he bought items at Joseph
Rose junior's sale (Christie's, 10, 12 April
1799). He must have worked at most of Rose's
commissions and certainly at Kedleston in
1775, where he did the Hall frieze.
Lit: Harewood Archives, Rose sketchbook;
London, Guildhall Library, *Boyd's Index to
Apprenticeship Registers*.

MOUNTAIN, Charles (*fl.* 1780). Plasterer.
1780 CHARTERHOUSE HOSPITAL, HULL,
YORKSHIRE
Architect: Joseph Hargrave.
Lit: Ivan and Elisabeth Hall, 1978, *Georgian
Hull*, p. 65.

MOXION, John (*fl.* 1729). Plasterer.
1729 HOUGHTON HALL, NORFOLK
Received money on behalf of his master Isaac
Mansfield (q.v.), who had worked at the house
from 1725.
Lit: CUL (CH), Account Book 40/1, entries
of 19 July, 15 August 1729.

MURRAY, George (*fl.* 1750–61). Carver.
Assistant to James Richards (q.v.). At the
latter's adjudged 'infirmity' in 1754, Murray
carried on his master's duties as 'Master
Sculptor and Carver to the Crown'. He
assisted Richards on work in 1752 at Henry
Pelham's house in Arlington Street, and
1750–60 at the Horse Guards, Whitehall. He
died in 1761, having formally occupied his
Office of Works post for only one year.
Lit: RIBA, Library MSS, 728.3 (42.13A);
MS, HOR; Colvin, 1976, *King's Works*, V,
p. 473.

NADAULD, – (*fl.* early 18th cent.). Carver.
Worked at Castle Howard (1703) and
Chatsworth on various carving jobs in wood
and stone. Assisted by a man 'Robinson'.

Lit: Castle Howard Archives, Building Bills, 1700–20.

NADUE, – (*fl.* late 17th cent.). Plasterer.
1698 HAMPTON COURT, MIDDLESEX
Lit: *Wren Soc*, IV, p. 25, where Nadue is erroneously listed under the name 'Medoe'. He appears as 'Nadue' in the account books of the Office of Works.

NEALE, George (*fl.* 1776–95). Joiner.
1776–95 SOMERSET HOUSE, LONDON
Received £11 278. 18s. 4d.
Lit: London, RIBA, Library, Somerset House Accounts.

NEALE, John (*fl.* 1750). Gilder/Painter.
1750 HENRY PELHAM'S HOUSE, ARLINGTON STREET, LONDON
Gilded frames and mirrors. The work was done well and £2. 2s. 0d. was allowed 'to the gilders men'.

To John Neale for 65 Days Work at 4/6 p.d.	£14. 12. 6
To his men 373 Days work at 3/6 a day	£65. 5. 6.
To preparations for Table and glass frames & doors	11. 0.
To 24 Pound of Gold Size at 3.6. p. lb.	4. 4. 0.
Brushes & pencils	2. 0. 0.
Received £86. 13. 0.	

Lit: London, RIBA, Library, MS, 728.3 (42.13)A.
1756–60 HOLKHAM HALL, NORFOLK
State Rooms, gilding and painting.
Lit: Holkham Archives, Country Accounts, 8.

NEALE, Thomas (*fl.* 1764). Gilder/Painter.
Presumably a son of John Neale above.
1764 HOLKHAM HALL, NORFOLK
Strangers' Wing, gilding and painting.
Lit: Holkham Archives, Building Accounts, 26.

NEEDHAM, Joshua (*fl.* 1721–25). Plasterer.
1721 CHICHELEY HALL, BUCKINGHAMSHIRE
Lit: *C Life*, 27 February 1975, p. 499; Joan D Tanner, 1961, 'The Building of Chicheley Hall', *Records of Bucks.*, XVII, pt. 1
1724 SUTTON SCARSDALE, DERBYSHIRE
Architect: Francis Smith.
Name appears on lead rising-plate (now lost), formerly at house.
Lit: *C Life*, 15 February 1919, p. 171.
1724 DITCHLEY, OXFORDSHIRE
Architect: Francis Smith; built by James Gibbs.
Plain work.
Lit: Oxford CRO, Dillon Archives.
1725 GUILDHALL, WORCESTER
Architect: Thomas White.
Received £77. 2s. 0d.; 'Needham the Plasterer at several times as pr. Receipts'.
Lit: Worcester Guildhall, Building Accounts, 20 April 1725.

NELSON, Saffron or **Sefferin** (*fl.* 1775–89). Carver/Gilder.
Lived in Marshall Street, Golden Square, London.
Mentioned in RABA.
1775 20 PORTMAN SQUARE, LONDON

Lit: M D Whinney, 1969, *Home House*, pp. 19–20.
1781 CROOME COURT, WORCESTERSHIRE
Capitals to columns and two pilasters.
Lit: Croome Court Archives, No. 62 (microfilm, Victoria & Albert Museum, Dept of Furniture and Woodwork).
1782 CHATSWORTH, DERBYSHIRE
Carving, gilding.
Lit: Ivan Hall, June 1980, 'A neoclassical episode at Chatsworth', *Burl Mag*, pp. 400–414.
1789 CARLTON HOUSE, LONDON
Estimated for work at £6500.
Lit: H Clifford Smith, 1931, *Buckingham Palace*, p. 104.

NELTHORPE, Richard (*fl.* 1724–31). Plasterer.
1724 NEWBY PARK, YORKSHIRE
Architect: Colen Campbell.
Lit: Leeds Reference Library, Vyner letters, 13595.
1731 SALOON, YORK MANSION HOUSE
Lit: York City Archives, Chamberlains' Rolls.

NEWMAN, Richard (*fl.* 1752). Sculptor.
c 1752 EDGECOTE, OXFORDSHIRE
Marble and other chimneys. Received £178.
Lit: Hussey, 1965, *ECH: Early Georgian*, p. 210.

NEWMAN, William (*fl.* 1676–94). Carver.
1676 ST STEPHEN, COLEMAN STREET, LONDON
Altar Table and Rails; Altar-piece.
Lit: *Wren Soc*, X, pls. 28, 31, 32, XIX, p. 53.
ST MARTIN, LUDGATE, LONDON
Lit: *Wren Soc*, XIX, p. 30.
1683 ST JAMES, GARLICK HILL, LONDON
Lit: *Wren Soc*, XIX, p. 14.
1686 ST MARY ABCHURCH, LONDON
Lit: *Wren Soc*, X, pls. 19, 27, 31, 41, 43, 51, XIX, pl. 31.
1686 ST MICHAEL, QUEENHITHE, LONDON
Lit: *Wren Soc*, XIX, p. 43.
1688–89 ST MICHAEL, CROOKED LANE, LONDON
Lit: *Wren Soc*, XIX, p. 44.
1694 ALL HALLOWS, LOMBARD STREET, LONDON
Lit: *Wren Soc*, XIX, p. 3.
ST STEPHEN, WALBROOK, LONDON
Lit: *Wren Soc*, X, pp. 115, 119–21.

NICHOLLS, Anthony (*fl.* 1748–50). Painter.
1748–50 14 ST JAMES'S SQUARE, LONDON
Lit: Essex CRO, D/DD c.A.

NICHOLLS, Thomas (*fl.* 1748). Carver.
With Charles Ross (q.v.) measured the carver's work at 5 St James's Square, London, by John Gilbert and John Hawkins.
Lit: 1960, *Survey of London*, XXIX, p. 101.

NICHOLSON, Thomas (*fl.* 1754–74). Plasterer.
Of Richmond, Yorkshire. Apprenticed on 24 February 1766 at York to James Henderson (q.v.) for seven years 'to learn the art, trade or Mystery of a Plaisterer as to Mouldings in general'. In 1774 became a Freeman of York.
Lit: York Reference Library, *Apprenticeship Register, 1756–86*; Surtees Society, 102.

NIND, Philip (*fl.* 1762–76). Ironmonger.
c 1762–76 BUCKINGHAM PALACE, LONDON
Architect: Sir William Chambers.
Nind also provided a hot stove, fender poker and shovel for King George III's State Coach (1761–62).
Lit: Harris, 1970, *Chambers*, pp. 218, 220.

NOBLE, Henry (*fl.* 1668–69). Plasterer.
Worked under John Grove II at Whitehall.
Lit: PRO, Works, 5/12.

NOLLEKENS, Joseph (1737–1823). Sculptor.
Well-known sculptor. George Richardson in his *Book of Ceilings*, 1776, p. 3, records that the bas-reliefs of the two ceilings in the Drapers' Company, London, are said to have been 'excellently modelled by the ingenious Joseph Nollekens'. Work for this Company was also done by Joseph Rose junior and Thomas Collins (q.v.).

NORMAN, Samuel (*fl.* 1732–82). Cabinet-maker, Carver and Gilder.
Apprenticed to Thomas Wooding of St James, Westminster, Carver and Gilder, in 1746. Mentioned in RABA, 1764. In 1761 Norman was appointed 'Master Sculptor and Carver in Wood' for the Office of Works, a post he held until 1782. He worked for many patrons, especially Sir Lawrence Dundas and the 2nd Earl of Egremont. Norman also acted as a gilder, e.g. for RA at Moor Park. He went bankrupt in 1768.
Lit: London, Guildhall Library, *Boyd's Index to Apprenticeship Registers*, XXII, p. 4248; Pat Kirkham, August 1969, 'Samuel Norman', *Burl Mag*, pp. 501–03; Bolton, 1922, *Adam*, II, p. 346; West Sussex CRO, Petworth II, 6624; *London Gazette*, 29 October 1768; PRO, LC5/105, p. 74.

NORRIS, Richard (*fl.* 1756–75). Coppersmith/Brazier.
Lived at 105 Jermyn Street, London.
1756 ST JAMES'S, PICCADILLY, LONDON
Repairs.
Lit: 1960, *Survey of London*, XXIX, p. 37.
1763 EGREMONT HOUSE, PICCADILLY, LONDON
Supplied stoves.
Lit: West Sussex CRO, Petworth II, 6615.
1775 20 PORTMAN SQUARE, LONDON
Lit: M D Whinney, 1969, *Home House*, p. 19.

OAKEY (OAKY), Charles (*fl.* 1683). Carver.
Samuel Watson (q.v.) was apprenticed to him. (Gunnis, 1953, *Dictionary*; Daniel Lyson, 1800, *Magna Britannia*, V, *Derbyshire*, p. 153.)
1683 BADMINTON, GLOUCESTERSHIRE
July 9 'Paid Mr. Charles Okey, Carver. £18.'
Lit: Child's Bank, Account of the Duke of Beaufort.

OLIVER, Thomas (?–1776). Plasterer.
Of Warrington. His will, of 1776, is filed at Chester.
1762–67 TABLEY HOUSE, CHESHIRE
Dining Room and other rooms.
Lit: Hussey, 1956, *ECH: Mid-Georgian*, p. 58.
1763 CHIRK CASTLE, DENBIGHSHIRE
New Drawing Room.
Lit: *C Life*, 12 October 1951.

ORAM, William (*fl.* 1713–d.1777). Master Carpenter and Painter.
Worked at Royal Palaces (1713) and was later Master Carpenter to the Office of Works, 1748–77. Designed the Triumphal Arch erected in Westminster Hall for the coronation of George III, 1761. As a painter worked under Sir William Chambers at Buckingham Palace in the late 1760s.
Lit: *Wren Soc*, XVIII, p. 164; Harris, 1970, *Chambers*, p. 218; Croft-Murray, 1970, *Painting*, II, pp. 251–52; Colvin, 1978, *Dictionary*, p. 602.

ORSON, John (*fl.* 1760). Carver.
1760 KYRE PARK, WORCESTERSHIRE
Enriched doorways, chimneypieces, etc. Received £70.
Lit: Hussey, 1965, *ECH: Early Georgian*, p. 219.

OWEN, Robert (*fl.* late 17th cent.). Joiner.
Of London. Worked with Henry Lobb at Chatsworth.
Lit: Francis Thompson, 1949, *A History of Chatsworth*, pp. 37, 67, 114, 148, 167.

PAGE, Joseph (?–1775). Plasterer.
Born in Lincolnshire, Page completed his apprenticeship at Hull in 1740 and worked extensively with the bricklayer-plasterers Aaron Pycock, Thomas Scott and Charles Mountain the elder (*c* 1743–1805). In 1743 he was designing the Maister's House in Hull. His proposals were scrutinised by Lord Burlington. The gallery was plastered in 1744. In about 1750 Henry Maister the younger wrote to John Grimston: 'Page the Man who was employed to do the stucco in my house will be with you today'—presumably a reference to work for Grimston at Kilnwick. He may have done the work *c* 1760 at 6 High Street, Hull.
Lit: Edward Ingram, 1952, *Leaves from a Family Tree*, p. 177; Georgian Soc., E. Yorks, 1952–53, *Trans.*, 3, pt. 3, pp. 56–57; *VCH*, East Riding, 1969, pp. 445–46; Ivan and Elisabeth Hall, 1978, *Georgian Hull*, p. 53.

PALMER, James (*fl.* 1766).
Smith/Brassfounder.
Smith/Brassfounder to George III. Lived at Air Street, Piccadilly.
Worked for both RA and Sir William Chambers.
1766 CORSHAM COURT, WILTSHIRE
Provided gilt-metal door furniture. Received £65.
The house was designed by 'Capability' Brown, but Palmer worked also for RA. He provided some steel razors for a Chippendale dressing-table at Nostell, which are stamped 'PALMER/CAST'.
Lit: Baldwin's London Directory, 1768, p. 147; Hussey, 1965, *ECH: Early Georgian*, p. 233; Harris, 1970, *Chambers*, pp. 175, 216, 218, 229; Christopher Gilbert, 1978, *Thomas Chippendale*, 1, pp. 34, 170.

PAPWORTH, John (1750–99). Plasterer.
Of Italian origin. Apprenticed to Joseph Rose & Co and became a leading stuccoist in the second half of the eighteenth century.

Employed many times by Sir William Chambers. He married Catherine Searle, daughter of the potter Robert Searle, and had at least two sons, Thomas (below) and John Buonarotti (1775–1847), an architect and friend of James and Matthew Cotes Wyatt. He worked at Greenwich Hospital Chapel, the Royal Academy of Arts and Somerset House. Here he collaborated (1784) with Thomas Collins (q.v.), whose business he may have carried on. They received jointly £7915. 2s. 8d. At Inveraray Castle, Argyllshire, he worked under the architect Robert Mylne (1781–82). His account reads: 'Plaster work in casts, models and moulds for ornamented ceilings and walls of hall and the dining-room by Mr Papworth £150. 0s. 6d.' Papworth was rated for a house in Wells Street, Marylebone, 1778–91. At his death his business was carried on by his eldest son, Thomas.
Lit: R S Mylne, 1893, *The Master Masons to the Crown of Scotland*, p. 277; Wyatt Papworth, 1879, *John B. Papworth*, pp. 4–5; RIBA, Library, Somerset House Accounts; *ibid.*, MS, New/1; *C Life*, 25 June 1953, p. 2061; Jourdain, 1926, *Plasterwork*, p. xii; information from Colonel J H Busby and Miss Mary Cosh.

PAPWORTH, Thomas (1773–1814). Plasterer.
Son of John Papworth (above). Owner of the last stucco and plastering business (G Jackson & Sons, apart) carried on in London on a large scale. Plasterer to the Office of Works. Subscribed to George Richardson's *Vitruvius Britannicus*, 1802. A Thomas Papworth was admitted a freeman of the Worshipful Company of Plaisterers, 7 April 1812.
Lit: Wyatt Papworth, 1893, *John B. Papworth*, p. 3; Crook and Port, 1974, *King's Works*, VI, p. 217; London, Guildhall Library, MS, 6125.

PARKER, William (*fl.* 1677–96). Plasterer.
Mentioned in the records of the Worshipful Company of Plaisterers (London, Guildhall Library).
1691–95 DENHAM PLACE, BUCKINGHAMSHIRE
Chapel (1692), Tapestry Room (1693), etc. Received £274. 11s. 0d.
Lit: Archives at house; John Harris, 1957–58, 'The Building of Denham Place', *Records of Bucks.*, XVI, pt. 3, pp. 193ff.
A William Parker worked in 1764–67 at Shardeloes, Buckinghamshire, and in the 1770s at West Wycombe Park, Buckingham.
Lit: Bucks. CRO, Tyrwhitt-Drake MSS; Hussey, 1965, *ECH: Early Georgian*, p. 239.

PARKIN, Robert (*fl.* 1791). Plasterer.
In 1791 Parkin was living at Kelgate, Beverley, Yorks.
Lit: Battle, 1791, *Hull and Beverley Directory*.

PARTRIDGE, William (*fl.* 1683).
Locksmith.
1683 EAST HATTLEY, CAMBRIDGESHIRE
Locks, hinges, shutter bars, latches, etc., for Sir George Downing's house. Received £111. 3s. 9d.
Lit: Castle Howard Archives, Executors' Accounts of Sir George Downing.

PASTORINI, Benedict (1746–1839). Engraver.
Came to London about 1775 and stayed there until his death. Mentioned frequently in RABA. He engraved many views which appeared subsequently in 1773–78, '*The Works in Architecture of Robert and James Adam*'.
Lit: Thieme–Becker.

PATROLI (*fl.* late 18th cent.). Plasterer.
'An Italian artist of great ingenuity' long employed at Claydon, Buckinghamshire, late eighteenth century. He would work here to the supervision of the Rose firm, and is perhaps to be identified with the 'Signor Pedrola' who worked with Joseph Rose senior at Ormsby Hall, Lincolnshire, *c* 1755. Certain stucco waste material recovered at Audley End, Essex, in 1978–79 (a Rose commission) suggests an Italian stuccoist in the Rose team.
Lit: George Lipscombe, 1847, *... County of Buckingham*, I, p. 186; N Pevsner and John Harris, 1964, *Buildings of England: Lincolnshire*, p. 370; information from Paul J Drury (Chelmsford Excavation Committee).

PATY, family (*fl.* 18th cent.). Carvers.
In the main, woodcarving was done by Thomas Paty (1712/13–89). He worked as an 'ornament carver' (in stone) during the building of John Wood the elder's Royal Exchange at Bristol, 1744. Between 1741 and 1743 he executed the wood and stone carving at Redlands Court, near Bristol. The archives for this rebuilding contain a contemporary note which observes that Paty 'is generally esteemed one of the best carvers in England, either in wood or stone', and that 'all the ornaments in the Chapel were designed and carved by him'. He subscribed for seven copies of John Wood the elder's 1743, *A Description of the Exchange of Bristol*. His assistants were Michael Sidnell (who subscribed to Gibbs, 1728, *B of A* and William Halfpenny.
Lit: Colvin, 1978, *Dictionary*, p. 626; Andor Gomme, Michael Jenner and Bryan Little, 1979, *Bristol: An Architectural History*, pp. 439–40.

PEARCE (PIERCE), Edward (*c* 1635–95). Carver.
Talented carver in wood and stone. It is suggested in *Wren Soc*, X, p. 93, that 'he may also have been a modeller in plaster, if the profuse ornamentation of St. Clement Danes is due to his large share in that work'. Pearce's father, also named Edward (*fl.* 1630–58), issued a *Book of Freeze work* in 1640 (reissued in a second edition), which may have been used by plasterers.
Lit: *Wren Soc*, as cited; Croft-Murray, 1962, *Painting*, I, p. 206; 1952, *Guildhall Miscellany*, I, pp. 10–18 (article on Pearce by June Seymour).
1675 PAINTER-STAINERS' HALL, LONDON
Carved door.
Lit: W A D Englefield, 1923, *History of the Painter-Stainers' Company of London*, p. 138.
1676 EMMANUEL COLLEGE, CAMBRIDGE
Designed woodwork with John Oliver; executed by Cornelius Austin.

Lit: Willis and Clark, 1887, *Cambridge*, II, p. 707.
1676–77 SUDBURY, DERBYSHIRE
Staircase, carving. Received £112. 15s. 5d.
Hall, carving. Received £20. 9s.
Great Stairs. Two door-cases at top; panel at 'stairs head chamber'.
Received £20.
Lit: Sudbury Hall, Vernon account book; 22 June 1935, *C Life*.
Pearce had an extensive patronage in the late seventeenth century and worked at most of the London City churches (*Wren Soc*, XX, references cited), and for Sir Robert Hooke at the Royal College of Physicians. He also provided the staircase at Wolseley Hall, Staffordshire (R Plot, 1686, *Natural History of Staffordshire*).

PEARCE, William (*fl*. 1762–72). Plasterer.
In Sir John Soane's Museum is a quarto notebook with the name 'R. Pearce' on the first page. It contains accounts for plasterwork by William Pearce, many of the projects being for the architect Henry Holland.
1762–76 BOWOOD, WILTSHIRE
Architect: RA.
Pearce worked with Joseph Rose and William Snow (q.v.).
Lit: Bowood, Lansdowne Archives. (I am indebted to Mr J R Hickish for this reference.)
1772 CLAREMONT, SURREY
Lit: Hussey, 1956, *ECH: Mid-Georgian*, p. 135.
Attributed work
BERRINGTON HALL, HEREFORDSHIRE
May have worked here under Henry Holland.

PEART, Charles (1759–98). Plasterer.
1790 STOWE, BUCKINGHAMSHIRE
Queen's Temple.
Three panels, signed and dated 1790.
Lit: Gunnis, 1953, *Dictionary*, p. 298; *C Life*, 9 January 1969, p. 79.

PELLETIER, René and Thomas (*fl*. late 17th–early 18th cent.). Gilders.
Presumably the mother and brother of John Pelletier who worked at Boughton for the Duke of Montagu and at Hampton Court. René and Thomas received £2382. 13s. 6d. for gilding at Boughton and Montagu House, 1692–1708, and Thomas claimed it in 1709 as executor of his mother.
Lit: Boughton, Lord Charles Scott's Notebooks, 19, pp. 63–64, Boughton Archives, Parcel D11, Part 2.

PELTON, – (*fl*. 1671). Plasterer.
Of London. Only recorded in respect of the following commission:
1671 WARWICK CASTLE
Submitted an estimate with James Petiver (q.v.) for ceilings of the State Rooms.
Lit: Warwicks. CRO, Warwick Castle Accounts, 1669–71, entries in 1671, 'State of Account'.

PERFETTI, Joseph (*fl*. 1771–75).
Carver/Gilder.
Took an apprentice, Thomas Ledieu, in 1760.
Lit: London, Guildhall Library, *Boyd's Index*

to Apprenticeship Registers, 4, 2nd series, p. 692.
1771 Provided a pair of side tables and pier glasses to an Adam design for John Parker of Saltram.
Lit: Harris, 1962, *Furniture*, p. 69.
1775 LANSDOWNE HOUSE, LONDON
Gilding, painting, carving.
Received £145. 12s. 10d.
Lit: Bolton, 1922, *Adam*, II, p. 12.

PERRITT, Thomas (1710–59). Plasterer.
When Perritt's father, Jonathan, a well-known York bricklayer, died in 1741, he left three sons, William, John and Thomas, the subject of this entry. Trained by his father, Thomas Perritt dominated plastering in Yorkshire until his death in 1759. He was made a Freeman of York (1737/38) and took his first apprentice, Joseph Rose senior, in 1738. He married twice: firstly Ann Etty (presumably a daughter of William Etty, the York joiner) at the Minster on 8 December 1739, and secondly Grace Perritt of York at Hampsthwaite on 8 July 1749. In 1742 he took another apprentice, William Whatson. Perritt lived in York in the Mint Yard and, at his death, was stated to be of 'Bederns in the City of York'. He died intestate and the letters of administration were granted to the guardians of Anne and Dorothy Perritt, minors. Anne had been baptised at St Michael-le-Belfry, York, on 3 March 1741/42. Perritt was made Chamberlain of York in 1753.
Lit: York Reference Library, Skaife MSS; Yorks., Parish Register Society, II, p. 196; Surtees Society, 102, p. 246; York, Borthwick Institute, Wills and Administrations, 13 December 1759.
1738–53 RABY CASTLE, DURHAM
Architect: James Paine.
Various work, some in company with Joseph Rose senior (q.v.).
Lit: *C Life*, 1 January 1970, pp. 20–21.
1741–47 TEMPLE NEWSAM HOUSE, LEEDS
Long Gallery (£190. 10s. 9d.), Library (£130) and other principal rooms.
Received a total sum of £419. 16s. 1d.
Lit: Leeds Archives Dept, Temple Newsam Archives, EA 12/10. Jacob Simon in *Leeds Arts Calendar*, No. 74, 1974, identified the 13 medallions as George I, George II, his queen, children and children-in-law (*see* pl. 74).
1744 ASSEMBLY ROOMS, YORK
'June 16, 1744. Ordered that Mr Thos Perritt do clean the weekly Assembly Room, the Cube Room and the Circular Room, and Colour the Stucco with a good Stone Colour sized, and white wash the Ceilings before the next Assizes. . . .
October 17, 1744. To Mr Thos Perritt. £8. 5. 0.
Lit: York Reference Library, York Assembly Room Minute Book, entries as above, and similar ones for 5 June 1751, 12 July 1753.
1745 MANSION HOUSE, DONCASTER
Architect: James Paine.
Lit: J Paine, 1751, *Plans, Elevations, Sections and other Ornaments of the Mansion House at Doncaster*.
1749 KILNWICK HALL, YORKSHIRE
Received £53. 18s. 11¾d.
Lit: Edward Ingram, 1952, *Leaves from a Family Tree*.

Attributed work
c 1740 NOSTELL PRIORY, YORKSHIRE
Architect: James Paine.
Dining Room, Music Room, North and South Staircase, medallions similar to those at Temple Newsam (see above).
Lit: *C Life*, 23 May 1952, pp. 1573–74.

PERRITT, William (*fl. c* 1724–70). Plasterer.
Presumably William was a son of Jonathan Perritt of York, and elder brother of Thomas Perritt (see above).
1724–28 BALDERSBY, NEWBY PARK, YORKSHIRE
Lit: Leeds Reference Library, Newby Archives; L O J Boynton, 1970, 'Newby Park, the first Palladian Villa in England', *The Country Seat: Studies presented to Sir John Summerson*, pp. 97–105, where Perritt is referred to in the archives, quoted as 'Jon Perrott and young Perrott'.
1728 STUDLEY ROYAL, YORKSHIRE
'Oct ye 15, 1728. A Mesurement of ye Plastering Woork don for John Aislabie by Wm Perritt.'
Received £22. 5s. 8d. John Aislabie of Studley Royal was related to Sir William Robinson, who employed Perritt at Baldersby.
Lit: Leeds Archives Dept, Studley Royal Archives, Parcel 286.
1741–42 RANELAGH AMPHITHEATRE, CHELSEA, LONDON
Lit: PRO, C/105/37/32.
1748–49 5 ST JAMES'S SQUARE, LONDON
Received £630. 2s. 2d.
Lit: BL Add. MS, 22254, f. 24.
1750 FARNBOROUGH, WARWICKSHIRE
Received £434. 4s. 4d. Work measured by James Morris.
Lit: *C Life*, 18 February 1954; bill at house.
1755 BLAIR CASTLE, PERTHSHIRE
Estimate for work done in various rooms—'to be done like that at the Duke of Argyle's at Whitton', presumably work by Perritt.
Lit: Blair Castle Archives, Box 40 (iv), 91.
1761–63 GROSVENOR SQUARE, LONDON
Received £98. 0s. 8¼d.
Lit: Eastbourne, Compton Place, Earl of Northampton Archives, Box Q.
1761–68 GLYNDE CHURCH, SUSSEX
Architect: Sir Thomas Robinson.
Coved ceiling. Joseph Rose senior (?) was paid 4 guineas 'for fruitless designs'.
Lit: Sussex Arch. Soc., *Collections*, 20; *C Life*, 28 April 1955.

PERWICK, Edmund (*fl*. 1661–62). Plasterer.
1661–62 Master, Worshipful Company of Plaisterers.
Lit: London, Guildhall Library, MS, 6122/2.

PETIT, Paul (*fl*. 1731–32). Gilder, Frame-maker.
1731 Provided picture frames to various households of Frederick, Prince of Wales.
Lit: Duchy of Cornwall, Vouchers VI(1), 1735–37, p. 320, LXIV, 'Analysis of Expenditure, 1731–46.'
1731–32 ROYAL BARGE FOR FREDERICK, PRINCE OF WALES
Double gilding and painting. Received £252 and a further £7. 10s. for alterations and mending and gilding the oars.

Lit: Duchy of Cornwall Vouchers 1731–32, 11, p. 254, cited by Geoffrey Beard, August 1970, *Burl Mag*, CXII, No. 809, p. 492.
1733 NEWCASTLE HOUSE, LONDON
Carving in the 'Best Parlour'.
Lit: BL Add. MS, 33161, 10/20 April 1733.

PETIVER, James (*fl.* 1658–89). Plasterer.
Son of William Petiver, a Northamptonshire yeoman. Apprenticed to Arthur Toogood (q.v.) on 23 April 1658 for seven years. His will is filed in PCC (1689, folio 85).
Lit: London, Guildhall Library, MS, 6122/2.
1671–72 WARWICK CASTLE
State Room ceilings. Estimated for them in July 1671.
Lit: Warwicks. CRO, Warwick Castle Accounts, 1669–71 (1672–76 missing), entries in 1671 'State of Account'. Worked with— Pelton.

PETTIFER, James (*fl.* 1675–1702). Plasterer.
Fined in 1685 for bad work at two houses in Red Lion Fields, London.
He succeeded Daniel Morris as Plasterer to Christ's Hospital, Newgate Street, London, in 1698.
Lit: London, Guildhall Library, MS, 6216, 27 April 1685; *Wren Soc*, XI, p. 70.
1675–76 SUDBURY, DERBYSHIRE
Worked with Robert Bradbury (q.v.).
Lit: *C Life*, 22–29 June 1935.
1702 ST BRIDE'S, FLEET STREET, LONDON
Received £2. 18s. 6d.
Lit: *Wren Soc*, XIX, p. 14.
1702 ST JAMES'S PICCADILLY, LONDON
Lit: *Wren Soc*, X, p. 124.

PHILIPSON, Thomas (*fl.* 1775). Carver/Gilder.
Lived at 28 Great Castle Street, Oxford Street, London.
1775 20 PORTMAN SQUARE, LONDON
Received £100.
Lit: M D Whinney, 1969, *Home House*, p. 19.

PHILLIPS, – (*fl.* 1763). Carver.
1763 CHIRK CASTLE, DENBIGHSHIRE
New Drawing Room.
Lit: *C Life*, 12 October 1951, p. 1150.

PHILLIPS, Henry (*fl.* 1662–93). Carver.
Master Sculptor and Carver in wood to the Crown.
Mentioned firstly in 1662 for sundry carved work in royal residences, and worked there until his death in 1693.
Lit: PRO, E351/3276; *Wren Soc*, IV, p. 71, XIV, p. XV; Colvin, 1976, *King's Works*, V, pp. 155, 233–34, 274–75.

PHILLIPS, John (*fl. c* 1709–75). Master Carpenter.
Of Brook Street, Grosvenor Square, London. Nephew of Thomas Phillips (*c* 1689–1736). In partnership with George Shakespear. A list of his considerable work appears in Colvin, 1978, *Dictionary*. His father, Matthew (d.1771), and his brother, William (d.1782), outlived him. He was one of Gibbs's favourite craftsmen and appears consistently in the architect's bank account.

There was also a joiner John Phillips apprenticed to William Phillips, joiner, in 1700.
Lit: Colvin, 1978, *Dictionary*, p. 633; 1960, *Survey of London*, XXIX, p. 328; Gibb's bank account (Drummonds); BL, Add. MSS, 36228, f. 190, 23281, 3 August 1759; London, Guildhall Library, MS, 8052, 111, pp. 33, 49; Bolton, 1922, *Adam*, II, p. 42–43; Mortimer, 1763, p. 47.

PHILLIPS, Thomas (*c* 1689–1736). Carpenter.
Partner of Benjamin Timbrell (q.v.). This firm was an important one and they worked at several London churches (St Martin-in-the-Fields, St Peter's, Vere Street, St George, Bloomsbury); the Tower of London; Senate House, Cambridge; the Treasury Buildings, Whitehall, etc. Thomas's son, John Phillips (q.v.), was a Master Carpenter in a considerable way. Both father and son were much patronised by James Gibbs.
Lit: Colvin, 1950, *Arch Rev*, p. 196; Lambeth Palace Library, 50 New Churches Archives; Colvin, 1978, *Dictionary*, pp. 633, 828.

PICKERING, William (*fl.* 1756–64). Painter.
1756 and 1764 ST JAMES'S, PICCADILLY, LONDON
Assisted in repair programmes.
Lit: 1960, *Survey of London*, XXIX, p. 37.

PIGGOTT, – (*fl.* 1665). Plasterer.
1665 COBHAM HALL, KENT
Architect: Peter Mills.
Several ceilings.
Lit: PRO, *c* 108/53, cited by H M Colvin, 1970, 'Peter Mills and Cobham Hall, Kent', *The Country Seat: Studies presented to Sir John Summerson*, p. 45.

PITSALA, Francis (?–1769). Painter.
Mentioned in RABA (1768, f. 320).
1770 LANSDOWNE HOUSE, LONDON
Mrs Sarah Pitsala received £260. 5s. as balance of a bill for paintings done by her late husband.
Lit: Horace Walpole, 1798, '*Anecdotes of Painters*', IV, Addenda.

PLESTED, Nicholas (*fl.* late 17th cent.). Carver.
Employed in London and at Winslow, Bucks.
Lit: *Wren Soc*, XVII, p. 74.

PLURA (*fl.* 1711–12). Stuccoist.
Possibly connected with J Plura, who died in 1756 (Gunnis, 1953, *Dictionary*). See also John Fleming, November 1956, *The Connoisseur*, writing of the Plura family of Turin and Bath.
1710–12 CASTLE HOWARD, YORKSHIRE
Assisted Giovanni Bagutti (q.v.) with the stucco fireplace and scagliola niche in the Great Hall.

1710 June	Given Mr. Plewra	34. 8. 0
March 1711	Given Mr. Plewra when went to London	10. 15. 0
	Given Mr. Plura	34. 11. 6
Aug. 1712	Pd Mr Plura & Bargote in full of all work done to this day	156. 0. 0

With Bagutti's work, the full bill came to ....£321.17s. 0d.
Lit: Castle Howard Archives, Building Books.

POPE, William (d.1678). Master Carpenter.
Warden of the Carpenters' Company, 1670–2.
Lit: Colvin, 1954, *Dictionary*, p. 472.

POPE, William (*fl.* 1719–20). Plasterer.
1719–20 Upper Warden and Master, Worshipful Company of Plaisterers.
Lit: London, Guildhall Library, MS, 6122/3.

PORTER, Thomas (*fl.* 1683–1703). Plasterer, in London.
1683 ST PAUL'S CATHEDRAL, LONDON
Paid for a model.
Lit: *Wren Soc*, XIII, p. 168.
1694 DYRHAM, GLOUCESTERSHIRE
Architects: William Talman and Samuel (?) Hauduroy.
Great Hall, Staircase, etc.
Lit: Gloucestershire CRO, Dyrham Archives, B/13/2, B/15/5; *C Life*, 15 February 1962, p. 338.

POULTENEY, Thomas (*fl.* late 17th cent.). Carver.
Carved Royal Arms at St Peter Cornhill, with Thomas Askew.
Lit: H Avray Tipping, 1914, *Grinling Gibbons and the Woodwork of his Age*, p. 164.

POWELL, Robert (*fl.* 1680–1706). Plasterer.
Master of the Worshipful Company of Plaisterers, 1706.
1680–88 ST CLEMENT DANES, LONDON
Received £450.
Lit: *Wren Soc*, X, p. 111; London, Guildhall Library, MS, 6122/3.

POWELL, Thomas (*fl.* 1668–69). Plasterer.
Worked under John Grove II at Whitehall.
Lit: PRO, Works, 5/12.

POYNTON, Edward (?–1737). Carver.
Of Nottingham. Carved mostly in stone. In his will (Nottingham CRO), he left bequests to Francis and William Smith, the joiner Thomas Eboral of Warwick, and 'William Watts of London, carver'.
1719–21 CHICHELEY HALL, BUCKINGHAMSHIRE
Architect: Francis Smith.
Lit: Joan D Tanner, 1961, 'The Building of Chicheley Hall', *Records of Bucks.*, XVII, pt. I.
1724 SUTTON SCARSDALE, DERBYSHIRE
Architect: Francis Smith.
Lit: *C Life*, 15 February 1919, text of lead rising-plate at house, (now lost) listed Poynton's name.

PRATT, John and Company (*fl.* 1760–74). Slaters.
Brook Street, Hanover Square, London.
Mentioned in RABA (1768, f. 358).
1760–65 KEDLESTON, DERBYSHIRE
Received £344. 18s. 5½d.

Lit: Kedleston Archives, Accts. 3R.
1772–74 20 ST JAMES'S SQUARE, LONDON
Lit: NLW, Wynnstay MS, 115/17/2.

PREEDY, James (*fl.* 1714–27). Painter.
1714–17 ST MARY-LE-STRAND, LONDON
Architect: James Gibbs.
Painted carving over Altar.
Lit: Colvin, 1950, *Arch Rev*, p. 196.
1716–27 ST MARY WOOLNOTH, LONDON
Architect: Nicholas Hawksmoor.
Lit: ibid., p. 196.

PRESCOTT, Richard (?–1747). Carver.
Of Lord Street, Liverpool. Said to have
been patronised by William, 4th Viscount
Molyneux. The administration of his will in
1747 is filed at Lancs. CRO.
1700–04 ST PETER'S CHURCH, LIVERPOOL
Dem. 1922 (carvings moved to N. Meols
Church).
1702 CROXTETH HALL, LANCASHIRE
Wainscoting.
c 1709 WOOLTON HALL, LANCASHIRE
Wainscoting.
1724 ST GEORGE'S CHURCH, LIVERPOOL
Lit: Sir James Picton, 1875, *Memorials of
Liverpool*, p. 46; information from Mr S A
Harris; Peter Fleetwood-Hesketh, 1955,
Lancashire, Architectural Guide, pls. 84–85.

PRICE, John (*fl.* 1714–21). Carpenter.
Of Bristol. Built several houses in Orchard St,
Bristol. His apprentice, George Tully, who
became a surveyor, also designed houses
(Hotwell Rd and Dowry Square, Bristol, 1725,
1749–50).
Lit: Andor Gomme, Michael Jenner and
Bryan Little, 1979, *Bristol: An Architectural
History*, p. 103.

PRIDE, Henry (*fl.* 1803). Plasterer.
1803 ST JAMES'S, PICCADILLY, LONDON
Repairs to ceiling.
Lit: Westminster Reference Library, D. 1767,
7 April 1803.

PRITCHARD, William (*fl. c* 1780).
c 1780 NORTHUMBERLAND HOUSE, LONDON
Architect: RA.
Worked with Joseph Rose junior. Received
£62. 14s. 7¾d.
Lit: Alnwick Castle Archives, U.III.7.

PUJOLAS, Henry (*fl.* 1760–62).
Painter/Gilder.
c 1761 STATE COACH FOR KING GEORGE III
Painting, varnishing and gilding. Received
£933. 14s.
Lit: Harris, 1970, *Chambers*, p. 220.

PUTTENHAM, Richard (*fl.* 1749).
Plasterer.
1749 BURLINGTON GARDENS, LONDON
'Plaisterers work done for Mr. Robinson att
his House in Burlington Gardens. By order of
Mr Bradshaw [William Bradshaw].' Received
£4. 5s. 9d. on 26 September 1749.
Lit: Leeds Archives Dept, Newby Hall
Archives, 2277/20/4.

RAMSAY, – (*fl.* late 18th cent.). Carver and
Gilder.
Of Sheffield.

Sir Francis Chantrey was apprenticed to
Ramsay, *c* 1796. Chantrey started life as a
woodcarver, as well as portrait painting,
before turning to sculpture.
Lit: Gunnis, 1953, *Dictionary*, p. 91.

RANDAL, J (*fl.* 1710). Plasterer.
1710 ST PAUL'S CATHEDRAL, LONDON
Worked under Chrysostom Wilkins (q.v.).
Lit: Wren Soc, XV, p. 196.

RATHBONE, Richard (*fl.* 1784–85). Carver.
1784–85 Worked at Somerset House,
London. Received £87 (1784) and
£83. 12s. 0d. (1785).
Lit: London, RIBA, Library, Somerset
House Accounts, 2.

RAWSTORNE, Thomas (*fl. c* 1773).
Decorative Smith.
c 1773 CLAREMONT, SURREY
Best Staircase balustrade. Received £880.
Lit: Hussey, 1956, *ECH: Mid-Georgian*,
p. 136.

READING, Joshua (*fl.* 1724). Painter.
1724 SUTTON SCARSDALE, DERBYSHIRE
Name on lead rising-plate (now lost).
Lit: C Life, 15 February 1919, p. 171.

REYNOLDS, John (*fl.* 1712–24). Painter.
1712–24 ST ANNE, LIMEHOUSE, LONDON
Lit: Colvin, 1950, *Arch Rev*, p. 196.

RHODES, William (*fl.* 1771–76). Plasterer.
Subscribed to George Richardson's *Book of
Ceilings* (1776).
1771–72 DRAYTON HOUSE,
NORTHAMPTONSHIRE
Dining Room. Charged £304. 7s. 6d.
Drawing Room £125. 13s. 10d.
Lit: N V Stopford Sackville, 1939, *Drayton*,
pp. 33–35; G W Whiteman, 1951, *Some
Famous English Country Homes*, p. 100.

RICHARDS, James (*fl.* 1718–59). Master
Carpenter/Carver.
Succeeded to the post of Master Sculptor and
Carver in Wood in the Office of Works in
1721 at the death of Grinling Gibbons.
Richards was one of the most accomplished
carvers of his age, and worked for Colen
Campbell and William Kent in particular.
Subscribed to Leoni's edition of *Alberti*, 1726.
By 1754 he was judged 'infirm' and was
succeeded by his assistant, George Murray.
When he was working at Houghton in 1729,
his assistant was Ralph Kite.
1718 THE ROLLS HOUSE, LONDON
Lit: Colvin, 1976, *King's Works*, V, p. 358.
1718–19 BURLINGTON HOUSE, PICCADILLY,
LONDON
Lit: 1960, *Survey of London*, XXIX, p. 29.
1722 KENSINGTON PALACE, LONDON
Lit: Colvin, 1976, *King's Works*, V, pp. 200–1.
1722 CHICHELEY HALL, BUCKINGHAMSHIRE
Garden front rooms: overdoors.
Lit: Joan D Tanner, 1961, 'The Building of
Chicheley Hall, *Records of Bucks.*, XVII,
pt. I.
c 1725 GOODWOOD, SUSSEX
Lit: West Sussex CRO, G.126; information
from Mr T P Connor.

1728–31 COMPTON PLACE, EASTBOURNE,
SURREY
Staircase Doors.
Lit: Compton Place Archives, Box P.
c 1729 HOUGHTON, NORFOLK
His presence at the house (*see* col. pl. 6,
pl. 51), perhaps responsible for the staircase
and most of the carving, door-cases, etc., is
based on the entry of 15 August 1729, 'Ralph
Kite for Mr Richards, Carver, £3'.
Lit: CUL(CH), Account book 40/1.
1730–33 WESTMINSTER SCHOOL, LONDON
New Dormitory.
Lit: Wren Soc, XI, pp. 36, 44.
1731–32 ROYAL BARGE
Commissioned Frederick, Prince of Wales.
Lit: Duchy of Cornwall, Vouchers II,
1731–32, cited Geoffrey Beard, August 1970,
Burl Mag, pp. 488–95.
1737 ST JAMES'S PALACE, LONDON
Queen Caroline's Library.
Lit: Colvin, 1976, *King's Works*, V, pp. 220,
243, 358, 432, 438.
1742 ARLINGTON STREET, LONDON
House for Henry Pelham. Received
£211. 18s. 8d.
Lit: London, RIBA, Library, MS,
728.3(42.13.A).
1748 HORSE GUARDS, LONDON
Received £41. 4s. 5¼d.
Lit: London RIBA, Library, MS,HOR.

RICHARDSON, Christopher (*fl.* 1767).
Carver.
Of Doncaster.
Subscribed to James Paine's 1767, *Plans . . . of
Noblemen and Gentlemen's Houses*.

RICHARDSON, George (*c* 1740–*c* 1813).
Designer/Plasterer.
Accompanied James Adam on the Grand
Tour and was employed as a draughtsman and
designer by the Adam brothers. Lived in
Great Titchfield Street, London. Important
mainly for his published works (Colvin gives a
list in his biography of Richardson), which
included 1776, 1781, 1793, *A Book of
Ornamental Ceilings, in the style of the Antique
Grotesque*, and 1779–80, *Iconology, or a
collection of Emblematical Figures*, 2 vols.
These circulated widely among plasterers
(both, for example, were in the possession of
Joseph Rose junior).
Lit: Fleming, 1962, *Adam*, pp. 368–69.
1775 KEDLESTON, DERBYSHIRE
Architect: RA.
The Hall ceiling appears in Richardson's *Book
of Ceilings*, which is dedicated to Lord
Scarsdale. The other decorative plasterwork at
Kedleston is by Joseph Rose, but he only
charged £29. 0s. 6d. for work in the Hall,
which strengthens the theory that the ceiling
is by Richardson.
Lit: Kedleston Archives, bills and account
book, 3R; *C Life*, 26 January 1978, p. 197;
Colvin, 1978, *Dictionary*, p. 687.

RICHTER, John Augustus (*fl.* late 18th
cent.). Scagliola worker.
Richter and Bartoli were the leading scagliola
workers in the late eighteenth century. Mr
R B Wragg has confirmed that Richter had
premises in Great Newport Street, London,
1767–96. He married Mary Haig and was the

father of the portrait painter Henry Richter. He worked for RA at Nostell Priory, where he provided scagliola tables. Horace Walpole employed him at Strawberry Hill in the Round Room and Chapel (1768–74). He charged Lord Harrowby 16 guineas for two 'Marble Scariole' tables, and did the scagliola columns for the Saloon at Holland House, Kent.

Sir William Chambers wrote to William Key, 13 October 1773, to say that 'Messrs. Ritter Bartoli, Newport Street, near Newport Market, London, imitate almost any sort of marble.' John Richter took out a patent (1770, No. 978) for 'my invention of "an Art or Method of inlaying Scagliola or Plaister in and upon Marble and Metals to imitate flowers, trees, fruits, birds . . . and all sorts of ornaments"'. He was then living at Berwick-upon-Tweed. In 1781 he estimated for scagliola columns and pilasters at Greenwich Hospital Chapel.

Lit: R B Wragg, 10 October 1957, *C Life*, p. 719; P Toynbee, ed., 1927, *Strawberry Hill Accounts*, pp. 154, 159; Harrowby Archives, 337, 1st Lord Harrowby's Account Book (I am indebted to the Harrowby Manuscripts Trust for permission to quote this reference); Stillman, 1966, *Adam*, p. 50; Beard, 1966, *Craftsmen*, p. 93; *C Life*, 10 October 1957, pp. 718–21; RIBA, Library, MS Newton 3 (Greenwich).

RIDLEY, William (*fl.* 1661). Plasterer.
Of Elvett, near Durham.
1661 DURHAM CASTLE
20 November 1661. Agreement with Bishop John Cosins 'to lath, plaister and seale all and every the roomes and chambers in the Castle of Durham, and the several walles thereof. Sealing of the said severall upper rooms, eleaven shillings the roode, the walls playstring after the rate of seaven shillings the roode.'
Lit: Surtees Society, 1872, 55, p. 356.

RIMSSET, Peter (*fl.* 1709). Joiner.
1709 Due to £4860 for unspecified work for Ralph, 1st Duke of Montagu.
Lit: Boughton Archives, Parcel D11, Part 2.

RITSON, Jonathan (?–1846). Carver.
Son of a Whitehaven carpenter. He worked at Greystoke, where his skill was noted by the Duke of Norfolk, who employed him at Arundel. After the duke's death in 1815, he went on to Petworth, but his obvious skill in carving was not admired by W G Rogers (q.v.) on a visit there in 1833.
Lit: H Avray Tipping, 1914, *Grinling Gibbons and the Woodwork of his Age*, pp. 195–96; Gervase Jackson-Stops, May 1977, 'The Building of Petworth', *Apollo*, p. 329.

ROANE, Thomas (d.1690). Plasterer.
Of Southwark.
His will is PCC, 1690, fol. 61.

ROBERTS, James (*fl.* 1745–79). Plasterer.
Roberts came of an Oxford family and was nephew of Thomas Roberts (q.v.). Advertised in *Jackson's Oxford Journal*, 14 January 1776, 'James Roberts, stucco-plasterer, instructed by the late Thos. Roberts over 30 years in

Oxford has dissolved partnership with his cousin, William Roberts. Each continues on his own account.' Roberts centred his business 'near Carfax Church', and in the *Journal* for 27 April 1776, he denied responsibility for confusion among patrons between the two businesses.

ROBERTS, Nicholas (*fl.* 1711–12).
Plasterer.
No known connection with the Roberts family of Oxford.
Upper Warden and Master, Worshipful Company of Plaisterers, 1711–12.
Lit: London, Guildhall Library, MS, 6122/3.

ROBERTS, Thomas (1711–71). Plasterer.
Of Oxford.
Roberts was the uncle of James Roberts (q.v.) and had an extensive practice in the Oxford area. He may well have been in active collaboration with the Danish stuccoist Charles Stanley (q.v.). A fire broke out in his workshop in 1761 (*Jackson's Oxford Journal*, 16 February 1761). For a time, his son William and his nephew James assisted him; they then set up on their own at Thomas's death but, finally, in 1775, dissolved the partnership. Thomas's death on 21 February 1771 is recorded in *Jackson's Oxford Journal*, 22 February 1771 — 'Thomas Roberts, fretwork plasterer died. Some striking work of his in a room at Lord Shrewsbury's, Heythrop. Succeeded in business by only son William.'
1738 MAGDALEN COLLEGE, OXFORD
Decorated colonnade of New Buildings.
Lit: W G Hiscock, 1946, *A Christ Church Miscellany*, pp. 68–71.
1742 ST JOHN'S COLLEGE, OXFORD
Ceiling of the Senior Common Room.
Lit: RCHM, 1939, *Survey of City of Oxford*, p. 106.
1744 RADCLIFFE CAMERA, OXFORD
Architect: James Gibbs.
Assisted Charles Stanley (q.v.) to do eight ceilings.
Witnessed the receipt by Stanley of £232. 18s. 10d. on 18 February 1744/45.
Lit: Oxford Historical Society, 1958, XIII (1953–54).
c 1745 KIRTLINGTON, OXFORDSHIRE
May have worked here with Charles Stanley. The Aesop's *Fables* medallions are a prominent feature. The archives contain payments to Roberts.
1749, 1760 DITCHLEY, OXFORDSHIRE
Dining Room 'at 17d. per yard for plain floating and 2/6d. per yard for modillion cornice fully enriched'. Received £33. 12s. 3d. Roberts also worked at Ditchley in 1760 in the Library, Temple in park, etc.
Received £24. 18s. 6d.
Lit: Oxford CRO, Dillon Archives, 1/p/3 ab, am.
1750 ALL SOULS, OXFORD
Codrington Library.
Lit: Hiscock, *Christ Church*, p. 71.
1752–62 CHRIST CHURCH LIBRARY, OXFORD
In 1752 the work in the Library was entrusted to Roberts and he worked on the ceiling of the Upper Library for 15 months. He received £663. His name appears in the Building Account in 1759, when he was paid £260 for

carving. From 1759 to 1762 he was constantly employed, receiving £537 'for stucco work and carving'.
Lit: Hiscock, *Christ Church*, p. 70.
1753 BODLEIAN LIBRARY, OXFORD
Ceiling in the Tower Room. This ceiling is now transferred to the Upper Archive Room.
Lit: *Bodleian Library Record*, October 1956.
1756 QUEEN'S COLLEGE, OXFORD
Library ceiling. He added 'new ornaments in the Oval Space in the Middle and the Compartments at the Ends'.
Lit: J R Magrath, 1914, *Queen's College*, p. 20.
1760 DITCHLEY, OXFORDSHIRE
(See entry for 1749.)
1764 HARTWELL, BUCKINGHAMSHIRE
Lit: Hussey, 1965, *ECH: Early Georgian*, p. 201.
1764 ROUSHAM, OXFORDSHIRE
Great Parlour (£170) and other work.
Received in all £266. 1s. 6d.
Lit: *C Life*, 24 May 1946, p. 949; Hussey, 1965, *ECH: Early Georgian*, p. 160.
HEYTHROP HALL, OXFORDSHIRE
Interior, destroyed by fire 1831.
Credited with work here on the authority of Mrs Lybbe Powys, writing in 1778. 'In the arches over the doorways', she adds, are 'Fables of Aesop, finely executed in stucco, with wreathes of vine leaves.'
Lit: 1899, *Passages from the Diary of Mrs. Lybbe Powys*, p. 200; from *Jackson's Oxford Journal*, cited at head of these notes.
Attributed work
c 1750 GREY'S COURT, HENLEY, OXFORDSHIRE
Lit: *C Life*, 30 June 1944. This is not a convincing attribution. The work is mechanical and does not compare in quality with that in Christ Church Library. It does compare with work at Watlington Park nearby by Swan (q.v.). (I am indebted to Mr J A Kenworthy-Browne for information.)
Thomas Hearne junior, writing in *Jackson's Oxford Journal*, 29 November 1766, mentions the 'stuccoed ceiling by the hand of the ingenious Mr Roberts' for the Divinity School, Oxford.
c 1748 PUSEY HOUSE, BERKSHIRE
Architect: John Sanderson.
Staircase and Sitting Room, friezes.
Lit: *C Life*, 23 December 1976, p. 1905.
c 1749 THE MENAGERIE, HORTON, NORTHAMPTONSHIRE
Includes Aesop's *Fables* medallions.
c 1753–58 HONINGTON HALL, WARWICKSHIRE
Hiscock, *Christ Church*, notes that the entrance hall contains a symbolic design of sunlight which appears to be a replica of the design used by Roberts underneath the gallery of the Upper Library at Christ Church, Oxford. Furthermore, his radiating centre ornament of Queen's College Library ceiling is a variation of the same idea.
Roberts and Charles Stanley (q.v.) collaborated at the Radcliffe Camera and possibly at Kirtlington, and the work at Honington has long been credited, somewhat casually in view of the lack of documentation, to Charles Stanley.
1769 NUTHALL TEMPLE, NOTTINGHAMSHIRE
Rococo plasterwork with Aesop's *Fables* motifs to his own designs.
Dest 1929.

Lit: Bucks. CRO, D/LE/11/2, cited in Colvin, 1978, *Dictionary*, p. 934; *C Life*, 18 April, 5 May 1923.

ROBERTS, William (*fl.* 1760–84). Plasterer. Son of Thomas Roberts (see above). A series of advertisements in *Jackson's Oxford Journal* is all that is known of him. He presumably helped his father from his teens, and, at Thomas's death in 1771, it was announced he had succeeded to the business. On 8 April 1772, he announced in the *Journal* that he continued to do carving and gilding. By 1775 he had dissolved partnership with his cousin James (q.v.) and, on 27 April 1776, he inserted an advertisement advising customers to be sure of his address (nr. Worcester College) to avoid confusion with James. By 23 October 1779, he was advertising as a 'stucco plasterer and slater of High Street' and denying a malicious rumour of his quitting the business. He did, however, leave Oxford soon after. His goods were sold on 7 December 1779, and he took over the licence of the Red Lion, Hounslow. On 22 May 1784, the *Journal* inserted his advertisement announcing his return to Oxford.

ROBINSON, – (*fl.* 1703). Carpenter. 'Man' to Nadauld at Castle Howard, 1703. Lit: Castle Howard Archives, Building Book, 1700–20. This 'Robinson' may be Thomas or Edward Robinson, both of whom worked with George Best as carpenters at Sir Charles Hotham's house at Beverley, Yorks. This was designed by Colen Campbell, *c* 1715. Lit: E. Yorks. Georgian Society, 1956–58, *Trans.*, IV, pt. 3, p. 43.

ROBINSON, John (*fl.* 1724). Plasterer. Of Malton, Yorkshire. 1724 CASTLE HOWARD, YORKSHIRE Plain plastering. Lit: Castle Howard Archives, Building Books.

ROBINSON, Peter (*fl.* 1768). Plasterer. 1768 THORNDON HALL, ESSEX Architect: James Paine. Received £931. 3s. 0d. by 1768. Lit: Essex CRO, Petre MSS, (D/DPA58). (I am indebted to Miss Nancy Briggs for this reference.)

ROBINSON, Thomas (*fl.* 1689). Plasterer. 1689 HAMPTON COURT, MIDDLESEX One of the plasterers working under the supervision of John Grove II. Lit: PRO, Works, 5/55, April 1689.

ROBSON & CO. (*fl.* 1789). Paper-hangers. Of Piccadilly, London. 1789 CARLTON HOUSE, LONDON Estimated for work at £500. Lit: H Clifford Smith, 1931, *Buckingham Palace*, p. 104.

ROGERS, W G (1792–after 1867). Carver/Restorer. Born at Dover in 1792. Is said to have been associated with an old craftsman named Birkbeck who was in direct touch with the Gibbons tradition, for he had been employed

in 1754 to restore carved work at Burghley. Rogers, through this influence, became a devotee and a clever restorer of delicate carvings. He exhibited at the Great Exhibition of 1851, and restored the carvings at Belton. There are two swags signed by him at Temple Newsam House, Leeds. Lit: RIBA, 1867, *Proceedings*, p. 180; H Avray Tipping, 1914, *Grinling Gibbons and the Woodwork of his Age*, pp. 197–98.

ROSE, Jacob (alive in 1738). Plasterer. Of Norton, near Sheffield. Stated by Lord Mansfield to have been a plasterer. Father of Joseph Rose senior. Living at Norton, near Sheffield, in 1738 when his son was apprenticed to Thomas Perritt. Lit: Liardet v. Johnson, 1778, law-suit text, cited by Beard, 1966, *Craftsmen*, p. 73.

ROSE, Jonathan (*c* 1772–after 1780). Plasterer. Father of Joseph Rose junior and brother of Joseph Rose senior. Worked with his brother at Wentworth Woodhouse, 1751–63.

ROSE, Jonathan (alive in 1799). Plasterer. Brother of Joseph Rose junior. Worked with his father, brother and uncle in the family firm.

ROSE, Joseph (*c* 1723–80). Plasterer. Son of Jacob Rose. Born probably in Yorkshire; living at Norton, near Sheffield, in 1738. Apprenticed on 16 October 1738 for seven years to Thomas Perritt of York (1710–59), with whom he worked on several commissions. Perritt died intestate, and Rose does not seem to have inherited his business. At Doncaster in 1752–53, where he took two apprentices, Richard Mott and John Wright. At this time he collaborated with his brother Jonathan and, after about 1760, with his nephews Joseph and Jonathan. Together they monopolised all important commissions, particularly those from RA (these for convenience are listed under Joseph Rose junior). Rose was buried at Carshalton, Surrey, on 11 September 1780. He had presumably been living in retirement with his son William Rose, who was Rector of Carshalton for 52 years. His will is PCC 449 Collins, and from a codicil (not executed) we surmise that he was in a position to leave £6000 to each of his nephews. He left his business to Joseph Rose junior. There is no positive evidence that Rose visited Italy, but in the sale of his son William's collection of pictures at Christie's on 30 May 1829, there was a view by Richard Wilson of the *Ruins of the Temple of Venus*, 'Painted for William Rose's father by Wilson', and it is stated that Joseph Rose was there at the occasion of its painting (W G Constable, 1953, *Richard Wilson*, pp. 196–97). In 1768 the architect Sir Thomas Robinson (*c* 1700–77), of Rokeby, Yorkshire, described Rose as 'the first man in the Kingdom as a plasterer'. Robinson was presumably referring to Rose senior, as the latter's nephew would have been only 22 at this time, and Robinson, as a Yorkshireman, presumably knew the firm of Perritt and Rose very well.

1741–47 TEMPLE NEWSAM HOUSE, LEEDS Worked with his master, Thomas Perritt. Receipted bill on 27 June 1745. Lit: Leeds Archives Dept, Temple Newsam Archives, EA 12/10. 1745 MANSION HOUSE, DONCASTER Architect: James Paine. Lit: J Paine, 1751, *Plans, Elevations, Sections and other Ornaments of the Mansion House at Doncaster*. 1752 CUSWORTH HALL, YORKSHIRE Architect: James Paine. Received £226. 8s. 2d. Lit: Leeds Archives Dept, Battie-Wrightson Archives, A/30; Beard, 1966, *Craftsmen*, p. 62. 1751–63 WENTWORTH WOODHOUSE, YORKSHIRE The following entries are from the Wentworth Woodhouse Accounts books and Estate Accounts at Sheffield Reference Library (I am indebted for the information to Mr R B Wragg).

Account Books:
1751 Mr. Jos Rose plaistering & whitewashing
Dec. 22. 1753 Mr. Joseph Rose upon Accot Plaistering — 60. 0. 0.
Mar. 12. 1754 Mr. Joseph Rose Great Hall — 30. 0. 0.
Jan. 1755 Mr. Joseph Rose upon Acct. Ceiling of Grand Hall
July 17 1758 By Mr. Rose in full for Stucco work done in the Great Hall — 76. 11. 3½.
and another payment of — 12. 12. 0.
Jan. 3 1761 To Rose the Plaisterer a Bill.

Estate Accounts:
1760 Aug. 14.
By Mr Jo Rose on Accot for Stucco Work etc. — 50. 2. 11½.
— 10. 0. 0.
1762 Jan. 24. By Mr Jo Rose in full for plaisterers work done in the Dining Room at Wentworth & in the Drawing, Supping & Writing Rooms — 24. 1. 7.
1763 March 28. By Mr Rose of Accot for Stucco work in the Cliffords Lodgings & Mr. Green. — 31. 10. 0.
1763 Dec. 26. By Mr. Rose on Acct & his bror. Mr. Jonathon Rose — 7. 7. 0.

c 1752 FELBRIGG HALL, NORFOLK Architect of eighteenth-century work: James Paine. Lit: Letters and accounts at house cited by R W Ketton-Cremer, 1962, *Felbrigg: The Story of a House*. 1755 ORMESBY HALL, LINCOLNSHIRE Architect: James Paine. Worked with an Italian, Pedrola (Patroli, q.v.). Lit: N Pevsner and John Harris, 1964, *Buildings of England: Lincolnshire*, p. 370. 1760–61 GLENTWORTH HOUSE, LINCOLNSHIRE Architect: James Paine. Lit: Letter from Rose at Sandbeck Park, Yorkshire (see below). *Attributed work* *c* 1740 NOSTELL PRIORY, YORKSHIRE

North and South Staircase, Dining Room, Music Room. The medallions are very similar to those at Temple Newsam House (see above), and, as James Paine had a share in the design of the house, he presumably used his favourite stuccoists.

1758 HEATH HALL, WAKEFIELD, YORKSHIRE
Architect: John Carr.
Drawing Room.
Lit: *C Life*, 3 October 1968, p. 817.
c 1766 SANDBECK PARK, YORKSHIRE
Architect: James Paine.
Lit: *C Life*, 14 October 1965, p. 966.

ROSE, Joseph (1745–99). Plasterer.
Son of Jonathan Rose (see above). Born at Norton, Derbyshire, on 5 April 1745. His father and brother (both named Jonathan) and his uncle, Joseph, were all plasterers and they formed the firm of Joseph Rose & Co., which monopolised the most important plasterwork commissions of the Adam period. The archives of the Worshipful Company of Plaisterers yield the following information:
1765 November 9. Admitted Joseph Rose by Redemption.
Company   £1. 6. 6.
Fine   £2. 2. 0.   £3. 8. 6.
As the means of admission was neither servitude nor patrimony, this reduced the chance of finding details of his forbears in the Plaisterers' records, and only details of uncle Joseph's apprenticeship are recorded at York. Joseph junior was admitted 'into the same livery' in 1766, in which year two apprentices, Bartholomew Bullivant and James Price, were bound to him for seven years. Rose was admitted into the Court of Assistants. In 1767 he took another apprentice, William Smith, and, at the meeting of 5 July 1774, was elected Upper Warden. A year later on 4 July 1775, he was appointed Master of the Worshipful Company of Plaisterers.
To some extent it may be true that this information relates to uncle Joseph, who was more likely, at the age of 51, to be elected Master than his nephew, who at this time was only 28. Indeed, their careers can hardly be separated, and at uncle Joseph's death in 1780, Joseph junior succeeded to the business.
I have assumed that Joseph junior married Mary Richmond on 15 December 1774 at St Mary-le-Bone, Middlesex. The witnesses were Edward Webster and Joseph Rose. The family were to be long associated with Middlesex; their premises were in Queen Anne Street East, Middlesex (now London).
It has been shown (Walpole Society, XXXVI, p. 58, fn. 16, confirming Richard Hayward's MS, list, Department of Prints and Drawings, British Museum) that Rose was in Rome in 1768. He gained a classical education which was to stand him in good stead when he worked in the Neoclassical style for Robert Adam. He subscribed, with his uncle and father, to George Richardson's 1776, *Ceilings in the Antique and Grotesque Tastes*.
Rose's will instructs that £500, a life interest in the residue of his estate and a choice of furniture should go to his wife, and the rest of the furniture should be sold with all 'Books, Moulds, Models, Casts, Scaffolding and every implement which belongs to my business'.

The remaining bequests were to his mother, sister, nieces and nephews. This will was proved on 16 February 1799, five days after his death. I have not traced where he was buried: there is no entry regarding him in the Carshalton, Surrey, parish register, but his uncle and wife were buried there.
Sketch-books
(a) Book, 26 × 16.5 cm (10¼ × 6½ in), in the possession of the Earl of Harewood. Described in an appendix to Jourdain, 1926, *Plasterwork*, pp. 251–53, although some details are omitted. I have re-examined the book and refer to it, where relevant, as 'Rose, sketch-book'.
(b) Book of 331 friezes, London, RIBA, Library, MS, 729–56, presented anonymously in 1836. The title page reads: Sketches of Ornamental Friezes from Original Models in the Possession of Joseph Rose. Many of the Models were made from the designs of the most eminent Architects and the whole executed in stucco work by Joseph and Joseph Rose, London. Sketched by Joseph Rose, MDCCLXXXII.' The book is indexed and designs are noted as the work of Robert Adam, Rose senior, Rose junior, James Wyatt, James Stuart, Sir William Chambers, Henry Keene and 'Yeman', possibly John Yemens or Yeomans, but more likely John Yenn (1750–1821), a pupil of Sir William Chambers.
(c) Two volumes of sketches, 78.7 × 60.9 cm (31 × 24 in), for his decoration of Sledmere, Yorkshire, are at the house. I am indebted to Sir Richard Sykes for letting me examine them. No. 1 contains 37 plans and elevations which do not appear to be by Rose, followed by 10, nearly all of which are signed by him. No. 2 contains 20 plans which are not identifiable, and 24 by Rose.
Portrait
Self-portrait in crayons, 60.9 × 45.7 cm, at Sledmere House, Yorkshire. It was engraved by Bartolozzi, and the engraving is inscribed: *Joseph Rose, Esq*ʳ*. Ob. Feb. 11, 1799. A Etatis Suae 53. From a Drawing in Crayons by himself.*
Letters
Preserved at Nostell, Sledmere, Sandbeck and Castlecoole (N Ireland).
Sale of his collections
Christie's, 10, 12 April 1799.
Lit: London, Guildhall Library, Worshipful Company of Plaisterers, MS, 6122/3; 1908, *Parish Registers of Norton, Co Derby*, ed. L L Simpson, Derby: Harleian Society, *Parish Registers of St Mary le Bone, Middlesex*; Rose's will, PCC 138 Howe; British Museum, Department of Prints and Drawings, Richard Hayward, A 59 S.C. MS, containing list of English visitors to Italy.
In view of the many overlapping dates, the following list of work is arranged alphabetically.
ALNWICK CASTLE, NORTHUMBERLAND
In a letter of 1763(?) to RA, the Duke of Northumberland writes: 'I propose Mr. Rose should do the plaistering'.
Lit: Alnwick Castle Library, 94 (Shelf 22/1), fol. 31; Muniment Room U.I.46 (letter referred to above).
In a 'list of bills and receipts found on the death and in the possession of the late Duke', Joseph Rose is noted as due for £145. 10s. 1d.

(23 January 1779) and £56. 11s. 4d. (6 April 1780).
On 29 May 1779, Rose received £3. 4s. 4d. for two half-capitals in the Briesley Tower at Alnwick, but also mentioned an earlier bill of £53. 7s. 0d. Also received £3. 18s. 0d. from the duke's agent, Mr. Butler, for work at the 'House of Messrs Hill and Pitter' (29 September 1761).
Lit: John Fleming, October 1958, 'Robert Adam's Gothick', *The Connoisseur*, CXLII, pp. 75–79; Alnwick Castle Muniment Room, U.I.41, U.I.46.
1769 AMPTHILL, BEDFORDSHIRE
Architect: Sir William Chambers.
Drawing Room ceiling 'by Mr Rose' (from a letter of Sir William Chambers referred to below).
Lit: 5 December 1769, BL Add MS, 41, 133.
AUDLEY END, ESSEX
From 19 July 1763 to 2 February 1765, Rose received some £450, and payments to him continued until 1786. Payments were also made in 1769–73 to William Rose (q.v.). Rose also worked for Sir John Griffin Griffin in London, at 10 New Burlington Street.
Lit: Essex CRO, Braybrooke Archives D/DBy A 27; J D Williams, 1968, *Audley End, Restoration of 1762–97*, Essex CRO, Publication 45.
BEAUDESERT, STAFFORDSHIRE
The Rose sketch-book contains:
1. An entablature entitled 'Ld. Pagets'.
2. 'Dineing-room and cove att Ld. Pagets. Mr. Wyatt's desine Aug. 18 1771.'
3. 'Staircase. Beaudesert. Mr. Wyatt's design 1771.'
4. 'Suffeat under the Gallery and string of Great Stairs Beaudesert.'
c 1763–64 BOWOOD, WILTSHIRE
Architect: RA.
Several of the Adam rooms and fittings were sold by auction on 30 June 1955. The details of Rose's work given below include the lot numbers of this sale. The auction preceded the demolition of the Big House at Bowood (architect: Henry Keene). Rose received £498 and worked here with William Snow and William Pearce.
Staircase well, ceiling of room 31 (Lot 42, unsold), *dest*, 6.25 × 5.33 m (20 ft 6 in × 17 ft 6 in).
West Bow Corridor. Ceiling of Room 41 (Lot 75, unsold), 2.69 × 1.52 m (8 ft 10 in × 5 ft).
Corridor ceiling (Lot 82, unsold), 10.36 × 1.83 m (34 × 6 ft).
Entrance Hall ceiling (Lot 128, unsold), 9.91 × 6.4 m (32 ft 6 in × 21 ft).
Gallery Lobby (Lot 148, unsold), 2.56 × 1.47 m (8 ft 5 in × 4 ft 10 in).
Dining Room ceiling (Lot 183), 12.19 × 9.14 m (40 × 30 ft) and wall panels (lots 184–89), bought for Lloyd's of London.
The Cube Room ceiling (Lot 198), 5.08 × 5.03 m (16 ft 8 in × 16 ft 6 in).
The King's Room ceiling (Lot 204, unsold), 8.99 × 6.09 m (29 ft 6 in × 20 ft).
Staircase Hall, spandrels (Lot 207), 3.35 × 1.52 m (11 × 5 ft).
Corridor, Room 73, ceiling (Lot 284, unsold), 8.31 × 3.35 m (27 ft 3 in × 11 ft).
Lit: Bowood archives.
1792–97 CASTLECOOLE, N IRELAND

Seven letters from Rose to the 1st Viscount Belmore are preserved at Castlecoole, together with his 'Estimate of Ornamented Ceilings . . . made from Mr. J. Wyatt's designs'. (The plain ceilings are not included in the estimate.)

In all, Rose received £2249. 6s. 4½d. for his work between 1794 and 1797. He sent plasterers to Ireland (Robert Shires, Robert Peterson, William Hartley, Thomas Fitzgerald and Thomas Spence were employed), together with eight packing-cases of casts and moulds for the capitals and frieze in the Saloon. Rose visited Castlecoole twice, in 1792 and 1794.

Lit: R Charles Lines, 1956, 'Castlecoole, Co. Fermanagh', *Connoisseur Year Book*, p. 17, where one of Rose's bills is illustrated.

CHATSWORTH, DERBYSHIRE
Received £44. 3s. 3d.
Lit: Building Account, 22 January 1763.

CLAPTON, MIDDLESEX
The Rose sketch-book contains 'Cornices at Mr. Hollis, Solly House, Clapton, Middx. Nov. 22 1813'. This was presumably drawn by a son of Joseph or of Jonathan Rose junior.

1767–68 CLAYDON HOUSE, BUCKINGHAMSHIRE
Architect: Sir Thomas Robinson
Sir Thomas Robinson's statement about Rose being 'the first man in the Kingdom as a plasterer' has been mentioned. In July 1768, Rose is reported as saying that he 'can finish the staircase and two ceilings by Xmas'. The walls of the staircase are decorated in Neoclassical style.

Robinson, who was working at Claydon for the 2nd Earl Verney, wrote in July that Rose was 'better suited to Mr. Lightfoot's work' in the ceiling. Lightfoot is also said to have 'retarded the staircase by not sending (to Rose) the instructions wanting'. 'The staircase', he continues, 'will be very noble and great, Mr. Rose's part very beautiful indeed, and will be one of the great works of Claydon.'

Lit: Robinson's letters were published in *Arch Rev* June–September 1926, quoted by Christopher Hussey, 1965, *ECH: Early Georgian*, p. 244.

1762 CROOME COURT, WORCESTERSHIRE
The Adam accounts preserved at the Coventry Estate Office, Earl's Croome, list Rose's work with 'Hopcraft' at Croome Court and Church. This is John Hobcraft, the carpenter and builder.

Lit: Colvin, 1978, *Dictionary*, p. 422.

'May 1762 — To mouldings at full size for the different cornices and mouldings of the ceiling for Messrs. Hopcraft & Rose.'

Lit: Geoffrey Beard, October 1953, 'Robert Adam at Croome Court', *The Connoisseur*, CXXXII, pp. 73–76; November 1959, 'The Croome Court Tapestry Room', The Metropolitan Museum of Art, New York, *Bulletin*, XVIII, No. 3, pp. 79–93.

1770–71 FISHERWICK, STAFFORDSHIRE
Architect: Lancelot 'Capability' Brown.
Dest in 1814.
The Rose sketch-book contains:
'North tower room at Lord Donegalls at Fisherwick 1770.'
'Lord Donegall's.'
'Anty Room, Fisherwick, Staffs. Mr. Rose's desine.'
'South Tower Room, Fisherwick.' (coloured)

'Dressing Room, 1771.'
'Staircase ceiling, Mr. Rose's desine.'
Lit: Rose's sketch-book. For Fisherwick, *see* D Stroud, 1959, *Capability Brown*; copy of 1814 Sale Catalogue, Birmingham Reference Library.

1765–70 HAREWOOD HOUSE, YORKSHIRE
The Rose sketch-book contains:
'April 16 1769 — Sketch of part of ceiling and cover in the second drawing room att Harewood house.'
'Best room ceiling, east end of Harewood House.'
'Dining room ceiling, Harewood House, 1766.'
'Room next dressing room, Harewood House.'
'Dressing Room at East end of Harewood House.'
'French couch room, Harewood House.'
'A stone landing in the staircase at Harewood House, with plaister ornaments.'
'1770. Part of Gallery Ceiling at Harwood.'
'Room long 77′ by 24′.' (There is an Adam drawing of 1769 in the Soane Museum for this last ceiling.)

Rose's detailed account survives. He received a total sum of £2829. 17s. 0d. The account (examined by RA) is signed by Joseph Rose junior (for the use of my uncle Joseph Rose) on 7 August 1770. It reads: 'Stucco work done for Edward Lascelles Esq. p. Jos Rose. Jan/24th 1766 to March 10 1770 vizt.

Dining Room	224. 8.	224. 8.
Musick room	130. 3.	
Add to ditto extra work not in the first Estimate viz ornament panels over two doors & two ditto next Picture Frames	35. 5.	165. 8.
Library	221. 9.	
Great Hall	333	
Great staircase	206	
Mr. Lascelles Dressing Room 49 Mr. Lascelles Bedchamber 34 Lady's dressing room 42 Occasional Dressing or Lodging Room	163	
Study	53	
Portico ceiling	20. 10.	
Circular room exclusive of glass frames	125. 0.	
State bedchamber	128	
Principal Dressing room	152	
Ceiling & Cove of Salon 158 Entablature & sides of ditto 167	325	
Drawing room next salon	171. 10.	
Second or great drawing room	235	
Great Gallery	335	
	2858. 5.	

Deduct from Honeysuckles in the Great Drawing Room 8. 8. from the Gallery the finishing over the Chimney not done 20. 0.
28. 8.
2829. 17.

By cash on acct recd of Mr. Popplewell 2085. 13.
1770. July 13. By Mr. Lascelles Draught 300
2385. 13.
Balance 444. 4.
2829. 17.

KEDLESTON, DERBYSHIRE
Architect: RA.
Rose received £1107. 16s. 8¾d. as follows:

Music room	192. 19. 8.
Drawing room	345. 6. 5¼.
Library	212. 7. 1¼.
Portico	22. 12. 5½.
Hall	29. 0. 6.
Saloon	35. 7. 3¼.
Dining Room	270. 3. 3½.

Lit: Kedleston Archives, Book 3 R, fol. 64; the Rose sketch-book contains 'Executed att Lord Scarsdales att Kedleston in the Hall, Decr 1775 by R. Mott' (q.v.), Rose's apprentice, 'Hall frieze, Kedleston'; 1958, *Connoisseur Yearbook*.

KENWOOD, MIDDLESEX
Payments of £200 (4 August 1769) and £276. 8s. 0d. (14 August 1772) are recorded in the 1st Earl of Mansfield's account at Hoare's Bank. It is, however, likely that Rose's work at Kenwood amounted to much more than this, but no plasterwork accounts survive.

KNIGHT HOUSE, WOLVERLEY, WORCESTERSHIRE
17 Jan., 1782. Jos Rose on Stucco work £50.
22 October, 1782. Rose plastering in full £308. 11s. 6d.
6 Sept., 1786. Jos. Rose on acct of Stuccoing £150.
Lit: Kidderminster Public Library, Knight Archives, Edward Knight notebooks, Nos. 289–90.

LONDON HOUSES
Arranged alphabetically within this entry
AUDLEY SQUARE
The Rose sketch-book contains:
'Done at Lord Darnley's and Lord Delaware Audley Square'.
House for Lord Percy. Bill from Joseph Rose & Co. to Duke of Northumberland, detailed room by room. Received £145. 10s. 1¾d. Receipted 23 July 1779.
Lit: Alnwick Castle, Muniment Room, U.I.46.
BERKELEY SQUARE
The Rose sketch-book contains:
'1781. Mr. Thornhills in Berkley Square.'
'Lord Darnley in Berkley Square.'
1786–87 BURLINGTON GARDENS
Rose replaced a plasterer called Pritchard.
1769: Receipt signed John Bullivant, presumably a relative of Bartholomew Bullivant (q.v.) who was apprenticed to Rose in 1766. 11 July 1778–13 February 1779:

Received £239. 14s. 2½d. for work done under RA. Receipts signed by Joseph Rose junior on 27 March and 24 April 1779.
Lit: Essex CRO, Braybrooke Archives, D/DBy.
CHANDOS STREET
The Rose sketch-book contains:
'In Chandos Street, Cavendish Square, Mr. Rose's design.'
1771–72 30 CURZON STREET
Architect: RA for Hon H F Thynne.
The Rose sketch-book contains:
'Domed ceiling at Mr. Thyn's in Curzon Street, Octob. 26 1772.'
DRAPERS' COMPANY HALL
Five drawings for ceilings were among Rose's effects at his death and were sold at Christie's on 12 April 1799, Lot 67.
19 (now 30) DOVER STREET
Architect: RA.
The Rose sketch-book contains:
'Lord Ashburnham's, Hay Hill.' The house was altered for Lord Ashburnham, 1773–76.
GRAFTON STREET
The Rose sketch-book contains:
'Sir George Warens in Grafton Street, Rose's design.'
GROSVENOR SQUARE
The Rose sketch-book contains:
'Lord Grimstons in Grosvenor Square, Mr. Rose's design.'
'Groynd Ceiling. Ld. Stanleys.'
'Two ceilings at Ld. Stanleys, Grosvenor Square. July 1774. Adam's design.'
In 1773–74 Adam built 23 (later 26) Grosvenor Square (Derby House) for Lord Stanley, later Earl of Derby; the house was destroyed in 1862. One of the six drawings in the Sir John Soane Museum for ceilings in this house has a note on it: 'this is drawn at large and ready for Mr. Rose'.
c 1773–75 GROSVENOR SQUARE
Architect: James Wyatt.
Work for William Drake. Rose's charge of £224. 16s. 7d. is included in Wyatt's 'Abstract of Sundry Bills for Alteration and Repair done to a House in Grosvenor Square for Wm. Drake Esq.'
Lit: Buckinghamshire CRO; G Eland, ed. 1937, *Shardeloes Papers*, p. 135.
MANSFIELD STREET
Architect: RA.
The Rose sketch-book contains:
'Sir Edward Deerings, Mansfield Street.'
'at Lord Scarsdale, Mansfield Street.'
'Mr. Hobcraft's desine done in Mansfield Street.'
10 NEW BURLINGTON STREET
20 October 1764–68 March 1766: general repairs and plastering. Received £3. 18s. 4d. 9 July–20 August 1768; received £3. 18s. 4d. 26 August–2 September. For work at the town house of Sir Watkin Williams Wynn in 1776–77 Rose received £2684. The Rose sketch-book contains:
'Groynd Ceiling at Sir Watkin William Wynn in St. James's Square.'
'For Drawing Room, Sir W.W. Wynn's.'
'Back Drawing Room at Sir W. Wynn.'
'Library, Sir W. Wynn.'
Lit: NLW, Wynnstay MSS; 1959, *Connoisseur Yearbook*.
NORTHUMBERLAND HOUSE
Architect: RA.

The Rose sketch-book contains:
(i) 'Dining Room at Northumberland House.'
(ii) The house was decorated for the Duke of Northumberlan in 1770; it was destroyed in 1874.
(iii) Payments to Rose occur in the archives at Alnwick Castle (MSS, U–I–25).
THE PANTHEON
Architect: James Wyatt.
The Rose sketch-book contains coloured sketches described as: 'Ornament above ye Pannells in ye Pantheon, att London, June 1770. Burnt in 1792.'
'Cottillion-Room in ye Pantheon 1770.'
PORTLAND PLACE
The Rose sketch-book contains:
'Black Drg Room 16 Portland Place, Mr. R's design. Done 1780.'
'No. 4 Portland Place, Rose's design.'
'No. 10.'
'At Ld Stormont's Portd Place 1776.'
'Done in several houses in Portland Place.'
1776 20 PORTMAN SQUARE
Lit: Countess of Home's account, Hoare's Bank. (I am indebted to the late Dr Margaret Whinney for this information.)
3 ST JAMES'S SQUARE
House for the Marquess of Donegall.
The Rose sketch-book contains:
'At Lord Donegall in St. James Square. Mr. Rose's desine.'
'Ld Donegall's dineing room, St. James's Square, Mr. Rose's desine.'
'Pannell in drawing room ceiling, Ld Donegalls, St. James Square.'
'Mr. Hobert's Front Drawing room, St. James Square.'
15 ST JAMES'S SQUARE
Architect: James Stuart.
Rose worked here for Thomas Anson, for whom Stuart was working at his Staffordshire house, Shugborough.
Lit: 1963, *Survey of London*, XXIX, p. 143.
20 ST JAMES'S SQUARE
Architect: RA.
Lit: 1963, *Survey of London*, XXXII, pp. 463–66.
ST MARTIN'S LANE
The Rose sketch-book contains:
'Groynd ceiling and alcove head of window done for Mr. Hamilton, St. Martin's Lane.'
SOMERSET HOUSE
1786–91 Received £1188. 4s 8d. Jobs as various as plastering apartments belonging to the Stamp Office '& Plaistering to the East Water Gate'.
Lit: London, RIBA, Library, MS, 725.3; PRO, A.O.3/1244.
SOUTHAMPTON ROW
The Rose sketch-book contains:
'Duke of Bolton's Southampton Row, London.'
OTHER WORK IN LONDON
The Rose sketch-book contains:
'Done at Chelsea by W. end of Battersea Bridge for Mr. Hatchet.'
1766 MERSHAM LE HATCH, KENT
Architect: RA.
Adam paid Rose direct for work at this house and then charged the sum in his own account to Sir Edward Knatchbull. In January 1766, Rose prepared an estimate 'for the Stucco, work of the Ceiling & sides of rooms on the

Principal Story at Hatch House . . . made from Mr. Adam's designs'. The estimate is detailed, and in reference to the Hall is as follows:
'To finish the Plain work ornaments & Mouldings in the Ceiling after the Design except within the small circle in the centre where instead of the Rose drawn is to be Sir Edwards Arms & instead of the roses in the small circles in the end panels is to be Sr Edwards crest—for the sum of £77. 18. 9.'
The Adam design (*English Houses*, VI, fig. 192) shows the roses which were changed finally for the Knatchbull heraldry. Below the ceiling, the 'full enrich'd Dorick Entablature as drawn at Large' was to cost £49. 14s. 8d., and those parts of door-cases and the upper part of chimneypieces not of wood but of composition were to be done for £54. 15s. 6d. The Great Drawing Room ceiling (*English Homes*, VI, Fig. 198) was to cost £111. 4s. 8d. The frieze below it and the floating of the walls 'for hangings or Paper' came to £68. 13s. 6d. The work of the Great Dining Room (so called in the original plan, but 'eating room' in that of 1763) was estimated at £141. 7s. 3d. At the end of the estimate Sir Edward added the note 'sent by Mr. Adam'. The first payment to Rose was £50 on account in the following December.
Lit: Kent CRO, Sir Edward Knatchbull's account book, 1762–84 makes note of five payments to 'Mr. Rose. Plaisterer'. One is listed as 'The Remnant', the other four total £351. 7s. 0d. The dates are 11 December 1766, 2 and 9 November 1770, 15 November 1771, 1 April 1773.
MILTON ABBEY, DORSET
Lit: C Life, 28 July 1966, p. 209.
1771 NEWBY, YORKSHIRE
The Rose sketch-book contains:
'Dining Room at Wm Weddles Esq., at Newby.'
'Hall ceiling Mr. Weddle at Newby.'
The date 1771 is incorporated in the plasterwork on the west wall of the Entrance Hall.
Lit: Hugh Honour, December 1954, 'Newby Hall, Yorkshire', *Connoisseur*, CXXXII, pp. 246–51.
1766–77 NOSTELL PRIORY, YORKSHIRE
Architect: RA.
The statement of accounts which Rose sent to Sir Rowland Winn covers 49 pages. He received £1822. 3s. 0d. On 25 March 1777, he was paid a first instalment of £1013. 12s. 6d., and after much argument about an allowance to be made by Rose for the 'outside Stucco on Riding House etc. which gave way' he received a further £679. 6s. 9¾d.
Lit: For an analysis of Rose's accounts and letters *see* M Brockwell, 1915, *The Nostell Collections . . .*, pp. 24–30, based on the Nostell Archives, C3/1/5, 4/2 and 4/9.
PACKINGTON HALL, WARWICKSHIRE
Architect: Joseph Bonomi.
Received £107
Lit: C Life, 16 July 1970, p. 229.
PADWORTH HOUSE, BERKSHIRE
This house was rebuilt in 1769 for Christopher Griffith by John Hobcroft (or Hobcraft). Hobcroft and Rose have been mentioned in connection with Croome Court, and in Rose's sketch-book some of the designs

are stated to be after Hobcroft. Sir William Mount and Mr Robin Mount have kindly provided information about Padworth and Wasing Place (three miles away) built for John Mount in 1760. This latter house was badly destroyed by fire in the Second World War. Sir William remembers that the bills were destroyed in the fire. We may reasonably assume that Rose did the plasterwork at these two houses.

RIDGELEY, STAFFORDSHIRE
Architect: James Wyatt.
The Rose sketch-book contains:
'Done at Ashton Curzon (Asheton Curzon) Esq., Ridgley, Staffs. Mr. Wyatt's desinge in 1771.'
1792 SAFFRON WALDEN CHURCH, ESSEX
Between 31 May 1792 and December of the same year, Rose was paid £96. 12s. 6d. for work in the chancel.
Lit: Essex CRO, Braybrooke Archives
SHARDELOES, BUCKINGHAMSHIRE
Architect: RA.
Between 10 October 1761 and 19 February 1763, Rose received £1139. 18s. 0d., receipted 10 August 1764. The account is detailed room by room and includes references to 'An Ornamd. Ceiling as p. Estimate delivered to Mr. Adam'.
Lit: Bucks. CRO, Shardeloes Archives; G Eland, ed., 1937, Shardeloes Papers.
SHUGBOROUGH, STAFFORDSHIRE
In a letter of 1766 at Shugborough, James Stuart says 'Rose thanks you for the money'. Hussey ascribes work in the Drawing Room and Library to Rose, and notes that the coved ceiling of the Great Drawing Room was done under Samuel Wyatt c 1795 by Rose for £800. It has now been established from documentation that some of the work here was done by Francesco Vassali (q.v.), as attributed in July 1964, 'Italian Stuccoists in England', Apollo, LXXX, p. 56.
Lit: Christopher Hussey, 1965, ECH: Early Georgian, p. 81.
SLEDMERE, YORKSHIRE
As a result of Rose's friendship with the Sykes family—his self-portrait is still at the house—he assisted in designing the decorative work for Sir Christopher Sykes at Sledmere (1788–90) and carried out the plasterwork. The volumes of his sketches are preserved at Sledmere. The plasterwork was destroyed by fire in 1911 and was subsequently restored by G Jackson & Sons to Rose's original designs.
1762 and after SYON HOUSE, MIDDLESEX
Architect: RA.
No bill has been traced, but the Earl of Northumberland (as he then was) wrote to Adam on 4 November 1763: 'I am glad you have altered some of the Brass mouldings for the Drawing Room chimney piece which I expect will not be finished in a short time and that Mr. Rose will get the ceiling of that room complete before the Frost comes on, so that it may have Time to dry fit to be gilt early in the spring, by which Time I hope the Paintings will be ready to be fixed up.'
Lit: Alnwick Castle, Archives, Library, XCIV, pp. 44–45, rough draft of the letter.
Work unexecuted
The Rose sketch-book contains:
'1779 Mr. Rose's design for Judge Wills but not executed.'

Work unspecified
9 March 1777: 'To Rose, Plaisterer £114.'

Work attributed
c 1770 ROKEBY, YORKSHIRE
Dining Room for Sir Thomas Robinson, who employed the Rose firm at Claydon.
FARNLEY HALL, YORKSHIRE
Family tradition ascribes the plasterwork here to Rose. John Carr added a new wing to the house for Walter Fawkes in 1786, and by this time both Carr's favourite plasterers, Giuseppe Cortese and James Henderson, were dead.
Lit: Hussey, 1956, ECH: Mid-Georgian, p. 217
c 1790 WOOLLEY PARK, YORKSHIRE
Lit: 1971, Leeds Arts Calendar, No. 68, p. 12.

ROSE, William (d. 10 April 1829). Plasterer.
Submitted bills at Audley End, Essex (see list above). If this is William, the son of Joseph Rose senior, he entered the Church and was for 52 years Rector of Carshalton, Surrey. There is a monumental tablet in the church.

ROSS, – (fl. 1788). Joiner, Carver.
Noted as:
'Joiner, Carver, Gilder & Picture Frame maker
At his Composition Ornament Manufactory No. 113 Great Portland Street
Portland Chapel.'
Lit: Trade card (1788), engraved by Pergolesi, repr. by A Heal, 1968, London Tradesmen's Cards of the Eighteenth Century, pl. XXXII.

ROSS, Charles (fl. 1748–65).
Carpenter/Joiner.
Mentioned in RABA. A leading London joiner with a large workforce. Ross worked for several architects besides Adam. He worked for the Earl of Strafford at 5 St James's Square, London, estimating his work at £2682 but reducing the amount drastically to £1480. He often measured work (including that of the carvers at No. 5), and he acted as joiner under Matthew Brettingham at Egremont House, Piccadilly, London, and for Lord Strafford at his Yorkshire house, Wentworth Castle, 1759.
Lit: Colvin, 1978, Dictionary, p. 706; 1960, Survey of London, XXIX, pp. 37, 100–101; West Sussex CRO, Egremont Archives 6615; Norwich Public Library, Hobart MS, 8862.

ROSS, Joshua (fl. 1745). Gilder, Frame-maker.
Of Bath.
Subscribed to John Wood the elder, 1745, A Description of the Exchange of Bristol.

ROTHWELL, James (fl. 1765–87). Plasterer.
1787 MARINE PAVILION, BRIGHTON
Received £272.
Lit: Henry Roberts, 1939, Royal Pavilion, Brighton, p. 28.

ROTHWELL, Thomas (fl. 1765–69). Plasterer.
1765–69 HAREWOOD HOUSE, YORKSHIRE
Assisted by his son James. They were in partnership with James Henderson (q.v.).
Lit: R B Wragg, 1955–56, York Georgian

Society Report, p. 59; Mary Mauchline, 1974, Harewood House, pp. 68–69.

ROWE (Widow) (fl. 1681–82). Plasterer.
1681–82 ST BRIDE'S, FLEET STREET, LONDON
Vestry Minutes:
7 March 1681/2. 'Churchwardens to employ a Plasterer for the plasterwork of the New Gallery and to let Widow Rowe who is an inhabitant of the Parish with her assistants and servants to have the doing of the same.'
Lit: Wren Soc, XIX, p. 13.

RULE, John (fl. 1830–99). Plasterer.
Of a firm established in Sunderland in 1830. Worked in fibrous plaster, and also did granolithic and fireproof floors and scagliola. A Mr Rule of Durham mastered the method of Gothic plasterwork at Ravensworth Castle, Durham, designed in 1808 by John Nash.
Lit: W Millar, 1899, Plastering, plain and decorative, p. 141 and adverts. p. vi.

RUSSELL, John and Thomas (fl. 1776–95). Joiners.
1776–95 SOMERSET HOUSE, LONDON
Received £138. 14s. 5d.
Lit: London, RIBA, Library, Somerset House accounts.

RYDER, Richard (fl. 1668–d.1683). Master Carpenter.
Master Carpenter to the Office of Works, 1668–83.
Lit: Colvin, 1976, King's Works, V, pp. 132, 205, 300, 315, 472, 478.

SABYN, – (fl. 1705–06). Carpenter.
1706 CASTLE HOWARD, YORKSHIRE
'Joyner worke done by Mr. Sabyn. Cornices, friezes etc. Bolectian work. Mr Sabyn 2 days at Yorke choosing out deales for floore.'
Lit: Castle Howard Archives, Masons and Carpenters Book, 1702–08, Building Bills, 1700–40, Folder 2. His work was measured by Nicholas Hawksmoor and William Etty.

SAINT, Gideon (fl. 1760s). Carver.
Mentioned in RABA, 1 April 1768.
Lit: M Heckscher, February 1969, 'Gideon Saint: An 18th Century Carver and his Scrapbook', Metropolitan Museum, New York, Bulletin, pp. 299–311.

ST MICHELE, John Baptist (fl. 1734). Plasterer.
1734 ST BARTHOLOMEW'S HOSPITAL, LONDON
Architect: James Gibbs.
St Michele received £160 for the Great Hall, and a further £32. 16s. 0d.
Lit: Hospital Archives, Ha, 19/5/1.

SANDERS, Francis (fl. 1731). Plasterer.
1731 6 ST JAMES'S SQUARE, LONDON
Received £50
Lit: 1960, Survey of London, XXIX, p. 104.

SAUNDERS, – (fl. 1694). Carver.
1694 Chosen to do work at All Hallows, Lombard Street, London.
Lit: Wren Soc, X, pls. 38, 43, 45, XIX, p. 3.

SEFTON, Thomas (*fl.* mid-18th cent.).
Plasterer.
'Thomas Sefton, plasterer at Newcastle, the
same man who did Mr. Mill's house lately and
is recommended by him as a very honest
careful man.'
Lit: Harrowby Archives (Sandon), Nathaniel
Ryder's notebooks, No. 67. (I am indebted to
the Harowby Manuscripts Trust for
permission to publish this reference.)

SELDEN, John (*fl.* 1688–1715). Carver.
1688–97 PETWORTH, SUSSEX
Carving in Chapel and Hall of State. Seldens'
appear in the Petworth registers in the early
seventeenth century, and a John Selden,
presumably the carver, was buried there on 12
January 1715. Selden was paid at times a
lump sum of £40, which may well have been
his year's wages. He also carved in stone, and
did such diverse jobs in wood as mouldings,
festoons and a periwig stand.
Lit: West Sussex CRO, Egremont Archives,
Account Rolls of John Bowen and Richard
Stiles. *See* especially Stiles 1692, and Bowen
1696; G H Kenyon, 1959, 'Petworth Town
and Trades, 1610–1760, Part I', *Sussex Arch.
Collns.*, XCVI; information from Miss G M A
Beck and the late Mr G H Kenyon.

SELLAR, – (*fl.* 1710). Plasterer.
1710 CASTLE HOWARD, YORKSHIRE
Acted as labourer to Bagutti and Plura (q.v.).
Lit: Castle Howard Archives, Building Book,
1702–20.

SEPPINGTON, John (*fl.* 1709–24).
Carpenter.
Of York. Son of Thomas Seppington. Put
apprentice to William Etty (q.v.) by
indenture, 11 November 1724, for seven years.
Lit: York Reference Library, *Register Book of
Apprentices*.

SERENA, Carlo Ferdinando (*fl.* 1727–28).
Stuccoist.
Worked in England with his brother
Francesco (see below).
Lit: A Leinhard-Riva, 1945, *Armoriale
Ticinese*, Lausanne, pp. 441–42.
1727–28 BRAMHAM PARK, YORKSHIRE
Mentioned in the owner Robert Benson's
bank account (Hoare's Bank) as 'Carlo
Sereney'.
Lit: *C Life*, 27 February 1958, p. 401; bank
account cited.

SERENA, Francesco Leone (1700–after
1729). Stuccoist.
Born at Arogno, near Lugano, Switzerland, on
5 November 1700, and baptised there on 6
November. One of three sons of Domenico
Serena and Giulia Cozzi. There is no record
of his death. His son (?), Giovanni Battista
Serena, died at Arogno on 28 October 1774
aged 47, and is described as 'son of the late
Francesco Serena'.
Lit: A Leinhard-Riva, 1945, *Armoriale
Ticinese*; registers at Arogno, 6 November
1700 and 28 October 1774.
Serena is said to have worked at the Abbey of
Ottobeuren, presumably under the stuccoist
Joseph Anton Feuchtmayer (1696–1770), and
at the Landhaus, Innsbruck.

Lit: Thieme–Becker; Hugo Schnell, 1950,
Ottobeuren, Munich, p. 22.
1725 DITCHLEY, OXFORDSHIRE
Worked with Giuseppe Artari and Francesco
Vassalli.
Lit: Oxford CRO, Dillon Archives, I/p/3h.
1729 CAVENDISH SQUARE, LONDON
Received £30 for a knot-work ceiling done for
James Brydges, 1st Duke of Chandos.
Lit: Baker, 1949, *Brydges*, pp. 199, 277fn.

SHANN, Robert (*fl.* 1709–10). Plasterer.
Official of the Worshipful Company of
Plaisterers.
1709 Upper Warden.
1710 Master.
Lit: London, Guildhall Library, MS, 6122/3.

SHAW, Thomas (*fl.* 1772–74).
Joiner/Bricklayer.
Mentioned in RABA.
Used by Sir William Chambers at Woburn
and Ampthill.
Lit: BL Add MS, 41, 133, 24 March 1770.
1772/4 A Thomas Shaw was Adam's foreman
bricklayer at the building of the Society of
Arts in the Adelphi.
Lit: Bolton, 1922, *Adam*, II, p. 43; RABA
1768, f. 320.

SHEPHERD, Edward (?–1747).
Plasterer/Architect.
According to Vertue (III, p. 51), Shepherd
began his working life as a plasterer. Better
known as an architect.
Lit: Colvin, 1978, *Dictionary*, p. 731.

SHEPHERD, John (*fl.* 1720–30). Plasterer.
Brother of Edward, above. Subscribed to 2nd
edition of Leoni's *Palladio*.
1720 HANOVER SQUARE, LONDON
Sir Theodore Janssen's house.
Received £26. 7s. 0d.
Lit: 1721, *Inventories of the Directors of the
South Sea Company*, 2.
1728 Employed by James Brydges, 1st Duke
of Chandos, in London. Lord Chandos caused
him in 1730 of being 'drunk from morning to
night' and said that he had 'never minded the
workmen' at Shaw Hall, Berkshire.
Lit: Baker, 1949, *Brydges*, p. 370.
A John Shepheard worked under John Grove
II during the Office of Works preparation for
William III's coronation.
Lit: PRO, Works, 5/43.

SHERWOOD, John (*fl.* late 17th cent.).
Plasterer.
Worked extensively in the Wren City
churches.
See the list in *Wren Soc*, X.
Mentioned in Robert Hooke's *Diary*, 1935
edn., pp. 14–15, 180, 229, 320, 338, 401.

SHERWOOD, Thomas (*fl.* late 17th cent.).
Plasterer.
ALL HALLOWS THE GREAT, LONDON
Lit: *Wren Soc*, X, p. 47.

SHILLITO, Daniel (*fl.* 1755–72). Carver.
Of York. John Carr's favourite carver and
employed by him frequently in Yorkshire—at
Everingham (1757), Harewood (1766), etc.
Lit: York Georgian Society, 1955–56, *Report*,

p. 55; Beard, 1966, *Craftsmen*, p. 94; Mary
Mauchline, 1974, *Harewood House*, pp. 87,
101; information from Mr Francis Johnson,
Mr Edward Ingram, Mr Dick Reid and Dr
Ivan Hall.

SHORT, Thomas (*fl.* 1782). Carpenter.
The architect John Yenn recommended Short
as a carpenter who had worked (with Edward
Wepshed) at Somerset House.
Lit: London, RIBA, MSS, Cha., 2/93.

SIMMONS, John (*fl.* 1714–22). Joiner.
1714–17 ST MARY-LE-STRAND, LONDON
Architect: James Gibbs.
Lit: Colvin, 1950, *Arch Rev*, p. 196.
1722 PETWORTH, SUSSEX
Staircase: joinery of 29 steps, 2 balusters to
each step; replaced *c* 1845.
Lit: Gervase Jackson-Stops, May 1977, 'The
Building of Petworth', *Apollo*, p. 329.

SIMMONS, Robert (*fl.* 1660). Plasterer.
1660 THE TOWER, LONDON
Worked under John Grove.
Lit: PRO, Works, 5/1, November 1660.

SMALLWELL, John (*fl.* 1712–61). Joiner.
Employed at St Paul's in 1700, Canterbury
Cathedral in 1704, and in 1705 was appointed
Master of the Joiners' Company. John
Smallwell junior, probably his son, was
Master Joiner to the Office of Works,
1718–61. Smallwell, or his son, worked for the
Duke of Newcastle at several properties under
the direction of Sir John Vanbrugh.
Lit: BL Add MS, 33442; *Wren Soc*, XX,
p. 209; London, Guildhall Library, MS 8046,
3; Colvin, 1950, *Arch Rev*, p. 196; Colvin,
1976, *King's Works*, V, pp. 27, 198, 289, 432.

SMITH, – (*fl.* 1693–94). Locksmith.
Of Lambeth. Provided locks and 'H' hinges
for Dyrham, Gloucs., the house designed by
William Talman.
Lit: Gloucestershire CRO, Blathwayt
Archives, B 15/5.

SMITH, Abraham (*fl.* 1663). Carpenter.
Of Durham.
1663 BISHOP AUCKLAND, DURHAM
Chapel. Screen (with John Brasse, joiner);
architrave, frieze and cornice, pilasters,
wainscot, mouldings about altar table, etc.
Lit: 1872, 'Correspondence of John Cosin,
Bishop of Durham', *Surtees Soc.*, 55,
pp. 369–70.

SMITH, Gervase (*fl.* 1723–29). Carver.
1723–29 Worked at Christchurch,
Spitalfields.
Lit: Colvin, 1950, *Arch Rev*, p. 195.

SMITH, Samuel (*fl.* 1710–24). Plasterer.
In 1724, at the age of 14, Smith was
apprenticed to Isaac Mansfield (q.v.) 'of St
James, Westminster, Plasterer' in the sum of
£10.
Lit: London, Guildhall Library, *Boyd's Index
to Apprenticeship Registers*. Another plasterer
named Samuel Smith was working in 1720–21
at Purley Hall, Berkshire, and was paid 10
guineas.

Lit : Typewritten sheet of *Building Accounts*, 1720–21 (source unspecified) preserved at Purley Hall. (I am indebted to Dr Peter Willis for this information.)

SMITH, Thomas (*fl.* 1770). House-painter.
1770 KEDLESTON, DERBYSHIRE
Received £113. 17s. 5¼d.
Lit : Kedleston Archives, Accts. 3R.

SMITH, William (*fl.* 1698). Plasterer.
One of the contestants for the job of Plaisterer to Christ's Hospital, Newgate Street, London, 1698.
Lit : Wren Soc, XI, p. 70.

SMITH, William (*fl.* 1776–95). Joiner.
1776–95 SOMERSET HOUSE, LONDON
Received £919. 1s. 5d.
Lit : London, RIBA, Library, Somerset House Accounts.

SNARE, Quintin (*fl. c* 1730). Plasterer.
A York bricklayer and plasterer mentioned in the 1730s in the Ordinance Book of the Bricklayers' Tilers and Plasterers, 1721–52 (York Minster Library, BB5).
1732–33 ASSEMBLY ROOMS, YORK
Received £8. 11s. 0d. for stucco modillions flowered with roses for the entablature of the Circular Room (June 1732). Plain-stuccoed the front of the building, and under the portico at 8d. a yard (23 June 1733).
Lit : York Reference Library, Assembly Room Minute Book, 1729–58, pp. 58–59.

SNETZLER, Leonard (1714–72). Stuccoist.
Connected with the Snetzler family of Schaffhausen. Worked in London, and then spent about 20 years (1752–72) working in Oxford for William Roberts (q.v.). He died at Oxford in April 1772. There is a drawing of an overmantel by him in the Victoria and Albert Museum, London (Inv. No. 1042-1935). It depicts an Aesop's fable subject, popular with the Roberts workshop.
Lit : Jackson's Oxford Journal, 11 April 1772; information from Mrs M F Hewitt.

SNOW, William (*fl.* 1762–66). Plasterer.
1762–66 BOWOOD, WILTSHIRE
Architect: RA.
Received £294. Some work in Cube Room; sub-contractor for Henry Holland.
Lit : Bowood Archives. (I am indebted to Mr J R Hickish for this information.)

SOWTER, Charles (*fl.* 1765–66). Carpenter.
1765–66 KEDLESTON, DERBYSHIRE
Worked for two days on the organ case at 10d. a day.
Lit : Kedleston Archives, Accts. 3R.

SPANG, Michael Henry (?–1762). Sculptor.
1759–60 Is said to have worked for RA on the decoration of the Admiralty Screen, on the monument to James Thomson (Westminster Abbey), and in providing chimneypieces at Kedleston.
He took an apprentice, William Chaplin, in 1756.
Lit : Gunnis, 1953, Dictionary, p. 361; Stillman, 1966, Adam, p. 47; London, Guildhall Library, Boyd's Index to Apprenticeship Registers, VI, p. 1017.

SPARROW, William (*fl.* 1752–74). Wire-worker, Birdcage Maker.
At 414 Strand, London, as successor to Isaac Smith. Wire-worker to King George II. Supplied a birdcage to Duke of Bedford, 1752, and to Lady Watkin Williams-Wynn at 20 St James's Square, London, 1772–74.
His trade card is at Westminster Reference Library and indicates he did all forms of wire-work articles.
Lit : Hugh Phillips, 1964, *Mid-Georgian London*, p. 129; NLW, Wynnstay MS, 115/17/6.

SPENCER, John (*fl.* 1750). Carpenter.
Of St George's, Hanover Square, London. Partner of Benjamin Timbrell, carpenter and master builder. He was involved in the development of various buildings on the Berkeley and Grosvenor estates.
Lit : 1960, *Survey of London*, XXIX, pp. 81, 104.

STANLEY, Charles (Simon Carl) (1703–61). Plasterer.
Born in Copenhagen of English parents on 12 December 1703. In 1718 he joined the sculptor-stuccoist J C Sturmberg, and worked at Fredensborg Castle. In 1727, after study in Amsterdam under Jan van Logteren, he left for England and joined the sculptors Peter Scheemakers and Laurent Delvaux. He signed monuments to Thomas Maynard at Hoxne, Suffolk (1742), and the Maynard family at Little Easton, Essex (1746). He married, firstly, Mrs Anne Allen on 21 May 1730 at Eastbourne Parish Church, and, secondly, Magdalene Margrethe Lindemann on 2 August 1737. He worked until the summer of 1746 in England and then left hastily for Denmark, where he had been invited by Frederick V to become Court Sculptor, a post he held until his death on 17 February 1761. His second wife outlived him (d.1763), and his son by this marriage, Carl Frederick Stanley, a sculptor by profession, died at Copenhagen in 1813.
His plasterwork in England presents a confused story.
Lit : A F Büsching, 1757, *Nachrichten von den Künsten*, III, pp. 193–200; Ogveke Helsted, 1952, *Wellbachs Kunstlerlexikon*, III, pp. 262–64, and entries cited therein; Gunnis, 1953, *Dictionary*, pp. 363–66; K A Esdaile, 2 October and 11 December 1937, *C Life*; *Times Literary Supplement*, 3 April 1937.
c 1740 LANGLEY PARK, NORFOLK
'Saloon, Alto Relievo in Stucco, Stanley.'
Lit : Neale, 1823, *Seats . . .*, III.
1744 RADCLIFFE CAMERA, OXFORD
Architect: James Gibbs.
On 5 March 1744, Stanley received £232. 18s. 10d. The bill was witnessed by Thomas Roberts (q.v.) and is headed 'Plaisterers work done for the Honble Trustees at Dr Radcliffes Library, Per Charles Stanley & Thos Roberts'.
Lit : 1958, 'The Building Accounts of the Radcliffe Camera, Oxford', ed. S G Gillam, Oxford Historical Society, XIII, 1953–54.
c 1745 OKEOVER, STAFFORDSHIRE
'One thing we must allow of him [Stanley], is your ceiling is well done and cheap.'
Lit : Letter from Joseph Sanderson to Leak Okeover, 9 December 1746 (Derbyshire CRO).

Attributed work
1728–29 COMPTON PLACE, EASTBOURNE, SUSSEX
Architect: Colen Campbell. *See* pls. 68 and 70.
Stanley was presumably one of four plasterers working under the supervision of John Hughes (q.v.).
Lit : Beard, 1966, *Craftsmen*, pp. 32–33.
c 1745 KIRTLINGTON, OXFORDSHIRE
Lit : Beard, 1966, *Craftsmen*, p. 34; Metropolitan Museum of Art, New York, *Bulletin*, March 1956; K A Esdaile, 2 October and 11 December 1937, *C Life*.
Stanley is also said to have worked at: Barnsley Park, Gloucestershire; Hall Place, Maidenhead; Honington Hall, Warwickshire; Easton Neston, Northamptonshire; and Stratton Park, Hampshire. There is no exact evidence to connect him with any of these houses. The panels at Honington are admittedly similar to those at Langley Park, and Stratton was originally designed by John Sanderson, a possible relative of the Joseph Sanderson who wrote to Leak Okeover (see above).

STANLEY, John (*fl.* 1745). Joiner.
1745 WELBECK ABBEY, NOTTINGHAMSHIRE
Estimate and contract for work.
Lit : Notts. CRO, Portland Archives, 70/55/13.

STANTON, Edward (*fl.* 1709). Joiner.
1709 Due to almost £50 for unspecified work for Ralph, 1st Duke of Montagu.
Lit : Boughton Archives, Parcel D 11, Part 2.

STANYON, Abraham (*fl.* 1657–58). Plasterer.
Fined for taking the work of a carpenter, 13 October 1657.
Master of the Worshipful Company of Plaisterers, 1657–58.
Lit : London, Guildhall Library, MSS, 6122/2, 6126.

STAVEACRE, J (*fl.* 1708–10). Plasterer.
1707–10 ST PAUL'S CATHEDRAL, LONDON
Worked under Chrysostom Wilkins (q.v.).
Lit : Wren Soc, XV, pp. 169, 196.

STEEDE, Miles (*fl.* 1612–54). Plasterer.
Apprenticed in 1626 to William Bennett. Master of the Worshipful Company of Plaisterers in 1654.
Lit : London, Guildhall Library, MS, 6122/2.

STEVENSON, John (d.1692). Plasterer.
His will is PCC 1692, fol. 118.

STOCKING, Thomas, senior (1722–1808). Plasterer.
Practised in Bristol and the south-west, where his reputation was equal to that of the Rose family. He applied for permission as a free burgess at Bristol on 29 September 1762, and became one on 20 July 1763, by vote of the Common Council and the payment of 8 guineas. He may have been influenced by Joseph Thomas (q.v.).
It has perhaps not been noted previously that his son Thomas was apprenticed to him.
'Thomas Stocking, son of Thomas Stocking of Bristol, Tyler & Plaister put to his said father

and Mary his wife for 7 years. 21 Janry 1765' (Bristol Apprentices Book, 1764–77, p. 23). He was joined in about 1790 by Robert Harding, who carried on the business when Stocking retired. He died on 10 September 1808. *Felix Farley's Bristol Journal*, 17 September 1808, records in its obituaries: 'Same day [10 September] having borne with fortitude a lingering and painful illness, Mr. Thomas Stocking of this city, aged 86; a man greatly esteemed and respected by all who knew him.'

Apart from his son, Stocking had another apprentice, Thomas Dennis, who was put to him for the usual seven years on 31 May 1786. Stocking did the plasterwork at The Royal Fort, Arno's Court and St Nicholas's Church. His most important commission was, however, at Corsham Court, Wiltshire. Mr Methuen's Day Book shows that, between 1763 and 1766, Stocking was paid £570. It is possible that £390 of this was for the very fine Long Gallery ceiling, completed in about 1765. Stocking must have been responsible for much work in the south-west, and work at Midford Castle, Somerset (*C Life*, 3–10 March 1944), is attributed to him.
Lit: W Ison, 1952, *Georgian Buildings of Bristol*, pp. 44–45; Bristol City Archives, *Apprentices Book, 1764–77*.

STOREY, (*fl.* 1710). Plasterer.
1710 CASTLE HOWARD, YORKSHIRE
Labourer to Bagutti and Plura (q.v.).
Lit: Castle Howard Archives, Building Books.

SUMMERS, – (*fl.* 1670). Plasterer.
1670 ST MICHAEL, CORNHILL, LONDON
Lit: Wren Soc, XIX, p. 46, X, p. 124.

SWAN, (*fl. c* 1755). Plasterer.
c 1755 WATLINGTON PARK, OXFORDSHIRE
Lit: Information from Mr J A Kenworthy-Browne.

SWAN, Abraham (*fl.* 1733–59). Carpenter and Joiner.
He issued many books of architectural designs (Colvin, 1978, *Dictionary*, p. 799).
1733 HOUGHTON, NORFOLK
Presumably 'Swan, the Carver' who travelled to Houghton 'on account of Dining Room chimneypiece' in November 1733.
Lit: CUL (CH), Vouchers 1730–34.
c 1750 EDGCOTE HOUSE, NORTHAMPTONSHIRE
Received £1990. 10s. 0d.
Lit: *C Life*, 10 January 1920.
1757 BLAIR CASTLE, PERTHSHIRE
Designed front staircase.
Lit: *C Life*, 11 November 1949; Swan, 1757, *Collection of Designs in Architecture*.
c 1759 KEDLESTON, DERBYSHIRE
Clerk of Works, replaced by Samuel Wyatt.
Lit: *C Life*, 26 January 1978, p. 195.

SYMONDS, Richard (*fl.* 1705). Plasterer.
1705 HILL COURT, HEREFORDSHIRE
Lit: *C Life*, 27 January 1966; bills at house.

SYMPSON, – (*fl.* 1662–68). Joiner.
Employed by Pepys. Made the bookcases still to be seen in the Bibliotheca Pepysiana at Magdalene College, Cambridge.
Lit: *C Life*, 3 March 1928, p. 306; Pepys, *Diary*, 16, 24 August 1666, 14 August 1668.

TAYLOR, Hercules (*fl.* 1731–32). Joiner.
1731–32 ROYAL BARGE FOR FREDERICK, PRINCE OF WALES
Some carving, windows, sashes, seats, lockers, etc. Assisted James Richards (q.v.).
Lit: Duchy of Cornwall, Vouchers 11, 1731–32, p. 253, cited by Geoffrey Beard, August 1970, *Burl Mag*, CXII, No. 809, p. 492.

TAYLOR, Joseph (*fl.* 1770).
Glazier/Plumber.
1770 KEDLESTON, DERBYSHIRE
Worked with William Cobbett (q.v.). They received £477. 10s. 11½d.
Taylor also assisted William Chapman (q.v.).
Lit: Kedleston Archives, Accts. 3R.

TENTON, Henry (*fl.* 1670–71). Plasterer.
1670 WHITEHALL PALACE, LONDON
Worked under John Grove II.
Lit: PRO, Works, 5/15, June 1670.

TERRY, Leonard (*fl.* 1741–76). Carpenter.
Of York.
1741 YORK MINSTER
Gothic Pulpit, designed by William Kent, carved by Charles Mitley.
1776 YORK MINSTER
South transept roof.
A John Terry, carpenter, worked at Wandesford House, York, *c* 1740.
Lit: J B Morell, 1950, *York Monuments*, p. 41; RCHM, 1975, *City of York*, IV, N.E., p. 51.

THACKER, Benjamin (*fl.* 1763–1771).
Joiner.
Thacker was a competent London joiner who worked extensively for Sir William Chambers. He assisted at the architect's commissions at The Hoo, Hertfordshire (*c* 1763), 45 Berkeley Square, London (1763–67), Walcot House, Salop, Skelton Castle, Yorkshire (*c* 1771), and Blenheim Palace, Oxfordshire (*c* 1771). He appears to have died in 1771, as Chambers refers to Thacker's executors in a letter of 2 April 1771.
Lit: Harris, 1970, *Chambers*, pp. 199, 210, 216, 246, 250.

THACKHAM, James (*fl.* 1689). Plasterer.
1689 HAMPTON COURT, MIDDLESEX
One of the plasterers working under John Grove II.
Lit: PRO, Works, 5/55, April–May 1689.

THOMAS, Joseph (before 1730–77).
Plasterer/Tiler.
Of Bristol.
Admitted a free burgess on 21 September 1730, being the son of a freeman. In September 1740, was living at 5 Guinea Street, Bristol. The ceiling of 15 Orchard Street may be by Thomas. He died on 6 May 1777. His name does not appear in the Bristol Apprenticeship Books.
1748–50 CLIFTON HILL HOUSE, BRISTOL
Architect: Isaac Ware.
Received £406.

Lit: W Ison, 1952, *Georgian Buildings of Bristol*, p. 198.
Attributed work
1752 UPTON HALL, TETBURY, GLOUCESTERSHIRE

THOMPSON, J (*fl.* 1708–10). Plasterer.
1708–10 ST PAUL'S CATHEDRAL, LONDON
Worked under Chrysostom Wilkins (q.v.).
Lit: Wren Soc, XV, pp. 169, 196.

THORNHILL, Sir James (1676–1734).
Decorative Painter.
Thornhill worked on the following major commissions:
after 1701 CHATHAM DOCKYARD, KENT
Admiral Superintendent's House. Staircase.
after 1702 ADDISCOMBE HOUSE, SURREY
Staircase, Hall and Saloon. *Dest c* 1861.
c 1702–08 CHATSWORTH, DERBYSHIRE
West Entrance Hall, Library Ante-Roome, Sabine Room, West Front Staircase, Yellow Silk Drawing Room.
1702–13 EASTON NESTON, NORTHAMPTONSHIRE
Hall and Staircase.
1705 STOKE EDITH, HEREFORDSHIRE
Façade, Hall, Staircase, Upper Landing, Green Velvet Bedroom. Mr Foley's Bedroom. All *dest* 1927 except bedroom decorations. House demolished 1959.
c 1710 HANBURY HALL, WORCESTERSHIRE
Hall, Drawing Room, Staircase and Bedchamber.
Staircase and Hall restored 1954–55.
c 1710 HEWELL GRANGE, WORCESTERSHIRE
Hall. *Dest c* 1884–92.
1711–14 ST ALPHEGE'S CHURCH, GREENWICH, LONDON
Apse and flanking pilasters. Restored 1954.
before 1712 MONTAGU HOUSE, LONDON
Unspecified decoration. *Dest.*
1713 EDWARD PAUNCEFORD'S HOUSE, PALL MALL, LONDON
Staircase or room. *Dest.*
1714–21 ST PAUL'S CATHEDRAL, LONDON
Dome-Cupola, Lantern and Whispering Gallery.
Whispering Gallery decorations *dest.*
before 1715 HAMPTON COURT, MIDDLESEX
The Queen's Drawing Room, Chapel, Queen's Closet, Queen's Bedchamber and Staircase.
before 1715 MR LOADER'S HOUSE, DEPTFORD
Bagnio and Garden Houses. *Dest.*
1715–25 CANONS, MIDDLESEX
Staircase. Restored 1840.
after 1715 GOSFIELD HALL, ESSEX
Saloon.
c 1715–20 SHERBORNE HOUSE (LORD DIGBY'S SCHOOL), DORSET
Staircase Hall and Staircase. Restored 1950.
before 1716 WOTTON HOUSE, BUCKINGHAMSHIRE
Staircase and Saloon. *Dest* 1820.
1716 BLENHEIM PALACE, OXFORDSHIRE
Hall and Saloon.
c 1716 QUEEN'S COLLEGE, OXFORD
Chapel.
1718–27 GREENWICH HOSPITAL, LONDON
The Painted Hall. Restored 1726, 1742–43, 1776, 1797, 1807–08, 1939 and 1958–60.
before 1719 ALL SOULS COLLEGE, OXFORD
Chapel. *Dest* 1871.

after 1719 EASTBURY PARK, DORSET
Chapel and Dining Room. *Dest.*
1720–28 MOOR PARK, HERTFORDSHIRE
Hall and Gallery. Dismantled *c* 1732.
1721 ST MARY'S CHURCH, WEYMOUTH,
DORSET
Altar-piece.
1721–24 WIMPOLE HALL, NOTTINGHAMSHIRE
after 1722 GRIMSTHORPE CASTLE,
LINCOLNSHIRE
Hall and Staircase.
c 1723 DUNSTER CASTLE, SOMERSET
Chapel altar-piece, *c* 1723, removed to parish
church on destruction of the chapel in
1867–69.
c 1723 LUXBOROUGH HOUSE, SOMERSET
Staircase and Little Hall. *Dest.*
c 1727 ALDERMAN'S COURT ROOM,
GUILDHALL, LONDON
Overmantel, overdoors and ceiling.
Overmantel and overdoors destroyed.
1730–32 BENJAMIN STYLES' HOUSE, LONDON
Unspecified decorations. *Dest.*
c 1731–32 THE QUEEN'S HOUSE, GREENWICH,
LONDON
The Queen's Bedroom.
AMESBURY HOUSE, WILTSHIRE
Either destroyed or not carried out.
BOWYER HOUSE, CAMBERWELL, LONDON
Room in North Wing. *Dest* 1861.
HOUSE ON CAMBERWELL GREEN, LONDON
Hall. *Dest.*
EASTWELL PARK, KENT
Great Hall and Staircase. *Dest.*
HEADLEY PARK, HAMPSHIRE
One room. *Dest* after 1808.
KIVETON HOUSE, YORKSHIRE
Hall. *Dest.*
JOSEPH HATCHETT'S HOUSE, LONG ACRE,
LONDON
Saloon.
LORD BATEMAN'S HOUSE, SOHO SQUARE,
LONDON
Staircase. *Dest.*
INNER TEMPLE, LONDON
Hall. *Dest.*
KENSINGTON PALACE, LONDON
Cupola Room. Design by Thornhill, carried
out by William Kent.
THOMAS HIGHMORE'S HOUSE, LONDON
Staircase. Not located.
THORNHILL HOUSE, DORSET
Drawing Room and Gallery.
WOLLATON HALL, NOTTINGHAMSHIRE
Grand Staircase and Secondary Staircase.
Last restored 1953.
Lit: Croft-Murray, 1962, *Painting*, I, pp.
265–74.

THORNTON, William (*c* 1670–1721).
Joiner.
One of the most skilled of the York joiners.
Buried at St Olave's, York.
Lit: J B Morrell, 1944, *York Monuments*,
pl. 46; Colvin, 1978, *Dictionary*, p. 826.
c 1706–11 CASTLE HOWARD, YORKSHIRE
'To wainscott the Rooms called Saloon,
Dining Roome & Anty Roome.
Saloon with a Good Cornish & Collours
according to ye draft at the Price of 2*s*. 6*d*.
Superficial Yards being girt measure.
1708. Nov ye 26.
Dining room to be thoroughly wainscoted

with Good Cornich, Base, Surbase and
bolectian after the best and usual way at the
price of 2*s*. 2*d*. per yard.'
In 1711 he received £286. 2*s*. 2*d*. for 'Joyner's
worke'.
Lit: Castle Howard Archives,
Masons'/Carpenters' Book, 1702–08.
c 1714 WENTWORTH CASTLE, YORKSHIRE
Wainscoting, flooring, etc.
Lit: Beard, 1966, *Craftsmen*, pp. 48–49.
1716 BENINGBROUGH HALL, YORKSHIRE
Held by a marginal note in a *Builders'
Dictionary*, 1730 (Metropolitan Museum, New
York) to be architect of the house.
Responsible also for joinery. The balusters of
the staircase are identical to those at the
Treasurer's House, York.
Lit: Beard, 1966, *Craftsmen*, p. 51.
1716–20 BEVERLEY MINSTER, YORKSHIRE
Under the direction of Nicholas Hawksmoor
he restored the north front to the
perpendicular by means of an elaborate timber
framing.
Lit: John Loveday, 1890, 'The Diary of a
Tour in 1732', *Roxburghe Club*, pp. 199–201;
engravings of 1739 by Geldart; F Drake,
1736, *Eboracum*, p. 260.
c 1718–20 SIR CHARLES HOTHAM'S HOUSE,
BEVERLEY, YORKSHIRE
Architect: Colen Campbell.
Attrib: Carving, panelling and interior
fittings. By May 1720 his bill amounted to
£116. After his death on 23 September 1721,
Thornton's executors, John Bagnall (q.v.) and
Robert Thornton, received an additional
payment of £64. 13*s*. 0*d*. A piece of the oak
cornice is at Beverley Public Library.
Lit: East Riding CRO, DDHO/15/4, 23
November 1721, cited by K A MacMahon,
1956–58, E. Yorks. Georgian Soc., *Trans.*,
p. 43.

THORP, John (*fl.* 1706–28). Marble-cutter
and Supplier.
Lived at Bakewell, Derbys. Gunnis records
him working at Melbourne, Derbys. (1706),
Castle Howard, Yorks. (1711–12), Knowsley,
Lancs. (1721), and at Bramham, Yorks.
(1727). I have noted the following, and
publish the Castle Howard item in more
detail. The Bramham work for the Lane Fox
family was, I suggest, for their London house
in Cavendish Square rather than the
Yorkshire one.
1711–12 CASTLE HOWARD, YORKSHIRE
August:
Pd him upon Acct of Marble   220. 0. 0.
Pd 2 men to set up ye Marble   13. 0. 0.
Pd for Carridge of Marble   85. 7. 6.
[1700–20, Building Book]
Marble work done Mr. J⁰ Thorp of Bakewell
in Derbyshire.

Aug. 1712:

Marble Chimney Piece in the Saloon	ft.	ins.
In the 2 Out Side Margents	14	0
In the 2 fore alms	27	6
Head	8	11
The Marble Coves	11	4
Side Margents aboe ye Chymn.	9	1
Chymney Mantle	9	9
Black Pannill	22	6
ft in all	103	1

at 4*s*. 6*d*. a yard   23. 03. 06.

Double Doore Case into the dining room		31. 11. 4½
In the Bewfett [Buffet?]		37. 3. 1½
The double doore Case into ye drawing room		31. 11. 0.
Hall doore linings of Marble 50.04 ft at 4*s*. 6*d*. yd		11. 6. 6.
South doore linings of Marble 87.11 at 4*s*. 6*d*. yd		18. 4. 6.
One door in ye dining room 40.10 at 4*s*. 6*d*.		9. 4. 0.
3 doores more		27. 12. 0.

In one Chymney Piece

	ft.	ins.
Palme	5	9
Mantle	13	9
Cornich	12	6
Harth	16	3
ft in all	58	3

at 4*s*. 6*d*.		13. 02. 1½
One more do.		13. 02. 1½
3 Chymney Pieces more		21. 19. 6.
Marble in ye Passige to My Lords Apartment		11. 11. 10.

Passage South Side to Midle of Hall	14. 02. 05.	
the other side	14. 02. 05.	
Ine One Staircase	8. 13. 8.	4. 6. 10.
The other Staircase		4. 6. 10.
Hall Margents		27. 8. 11.

Saloon Floore

216 Square at 7*d*. square		6. 6. 0.
60 Half square 5¼		1. 6. 3.
4 Quarters		1. 0.
		7. 13. 03.

In ye North Passige		12. 13. 0½
the other		11. 16. 10½
		24. 10. 11.
West Passige		9. 7. 0.

Lit: Castle Howard Archives, Carpenters'–
Masons' Book 1702–08, includes payments
1711–12, etc.
1717 BEVERLEY, YORKSHIRE
Sir Charles Hotham's house designed by
Colen Campbell. On 28 October 1717 Thorp
agreed with Sir Charles Hotham to make two
marble chimneypieces 'equal in size and all
other respects' to two 'great chimney pieces'
which he had sold to the Duke of Newcastle
for his London House, 66 Lincoln's Inn
Fields—to cost £50. Thorp also did other
work for Hotham.
Lit: K A MacMahon, 1956–58, E. Yorks.
Georgian Soc., *Trans.*
1727 HARCOURT HOUSE, CAVENDISH SQUARE,
LONDON
Unspecified work. Received £37. 8*s*. 4*d*.
Lit: Bramham (Yorks.), Lane-Fox Archives,
1727–28 Letter-book.
1729 MANSION HOUSE, YORK
'13 Dec. To Mr Thorpe for the Marble Table
in the New House. £2.'
Lit: York Reference Library, Mansion House,
Chamberlain's List.

THORPE, James (*fl.* 1788–89). Plasterer.
1788–89 SOMERSET HOUSE, LONDON
Provided composition ornaments for
chimneypieces at Somerset House.
Received £61. 9*s*. 10*d*.
Lit: London, RIBA, Library, MS, 725.121
(B3); PRO AO3/1244.

THRISK, Henry (*fl.* 1692–1729). Carver (wood and stone).
Of York. A freeman of the City in 1692. In 1729 he worked at the Mansion House in York.
24 July: 'To Henry Thrisk for four Corinthian capitals for the City's House at 15*s.* a pair. £3. –. –.'
Lit: York Reference Library, Mansion House, Chamberlain's List.

TILLSON, John (*fl.* 1809–32). Plasterer.
Of Stamford. Freeman 1795. His son, John, succeeded in 1832 (*Stamford Mercury*, 27 July 1832).
Attributed work
1809 BULWICK HALL, NORTHAMPTONSHIRE
Stairhall. I am indebted to Mr Robert Taylor, RCHM, Cambridge, for this information.

TILSTON, Thomas (*fl.* 1729–72). Smith.
Hawarden Castle, Flintshire, incorporates a classical house called Broadlane, built between 1749–57 by Samuel Turner for Sir John Glynn. The ironwork on the best stairs was supplied by Tilston, who charged £18. 14*s.*; he also supplied the grates and the vanes to the gatehouse.
Tilston also worked as a smith at Eaton Hall, Chester, where his name occurs from 1729–36.
Lit: Information from Ifor Edwards and Edward Saunders; *C Life*, 15 June 1967; Ifor Edwards 1976, 'The Davies family', monograph published by the Welsh Arts Council.
Tilston is, however, better known for the elegant iron balustrades in RA houses, reliably held as his on the strength of the documented example at 20 St James's Square, London. There is, however, seemingly no documentation for his involvement at Kedleston, as mistakenly stated in Beard, 1966, *Craftsmen*, p. 182. In 1767 he worked at Shardeloes, Bucks., receiving £204. 0*s.* 3*d.*
Lit: NLW, Wynnstay MSS, 115/17/23, 115/17/28; Bucks. CRO, D/Dr/5/30.

TIMBRELL, Benjamin (?–1754). Carpenter.
Worked principally for James Gibbs, and, with his partner Thomas Phillips, did the structural woodwork in St Martin-in-the-Fields, London (1722), for £5615. 6*s.* 3¼*d.* They also worked for Gibbs at the Senate House, Cambridge (1724). His bank account is at Drummonds; he also appears frequently in Gibbs's and Flitcroft's accounts at the same bank. With a later partner, John Spencer, and the bricklayer John Barlow, he developed several houses in St James's Square and elsewhere.
Lit: Colvin, 1978, *Dictionary*, p. 828; 1960, *Survey of London*, XXIX, pp. 81, 14; Little, 1955, *Gibbs*, p. 57.

TOOGOOD, Arthur (*fl.* 1650–63). Plasterer.
His son Henry was apprenticed to him and was free of the Worshipful Company of Plaisterers, 23 April 1658. Arthur was Master of the Company in 1663. He took Henry Kidgell (q.v.) as apprentice in 1642.
Lit: London, Guildhall Library, MS, 6122/2.

TOOLEY, John (*fl.* 1702–03). Plasterer.
Official of the Worshipful Company of Plaisterers.
1702–03 Master.
Lit: London, Guildhall Library, MS, 6122/3.

TOWNSEND, Thomas (*fl.* 1751).
Carpenter.
Of Air Street, St James's, Westminster. Mentioned in the will of the plasterer Thomas Betson (q.v.).
Lit: PRO, Prob 11/787, f. 255.

TOWNSON, William (*fl.* 1761). Joiner.
1761 HOLKHAM HALL, NORFOLK
Great Hall, mahogany doors and baluster rail; general joinery.
Lit: Holkham Archives, Building Accounts, 26.

TUCKE, Anthony (*fl.* 1665). Plasterer.
Possibly father or brother of Richard Tucke (see below). May have been the second husband of John Grove's mother.
1665 He worked under John Grove I at Hampton Court, Middlesex.
Lit: PRO, Works, 5/7, September 1665/66; will of John Grove I, PCC, 29 March 1676.

TUCKE, Richard (*fl.* 1668–1700). Plasterer.
Tucke's name appears frequently in the account books of the Office of Works as one of the plasterers working under the supervision of John Grove II. He is noted in 1668 at Whitehall, in 1680 at The Tower, and in 1689 at Hampton Court, and, also in 1689, he was one of the plasterers engaged by Grove to prepare work for the coronation of William III.
Lit: PRO, Works, 5/12, 5/33, 5/43, 5/55, etc.

TURNER, Henry (*fl.* 1712–30). Painter.
1712–14 ST ALPHEGE, GREENWICH, LONDON
Lit: Colvin, 1950, *Arch Rev*, p. 196.
1712–30 ST PAUL, DEPTFORD, LONDON
Architect: Thomas Archer.
Lit: ibid., p. 196.

TURNER, James (*fl.* 1712). Painter.
1712 5 ST JAMES'S SQUARE, LONDON
Lit: 1960, *Survey of London*, XXIX, p. 100.

TURNLY, Thomas (*fl.* 1674). Carver.
1674 ST MARY, ALDERMANBURY, LONDON
Lit: Wren Soc, X, p. 124, pl. 23, XIX, pp. 37, 39.

TUSHAINE, – (*fl.* early 18th cent.). Carver.
c 1706 CASTLE HOWARD, YORKSHIRE
Woodcarving. Received £52. 13*s.* 4*d.*
Lit: Castle Howard Archives, Masons' and Carpenters' Book, 1702–08.

TYLER, William (?–1801). Carver (stone).
1763/64 AUDLEY END, ESSEX
Chimneypieces.
Lit: Stillman, 1966, *Adam*, pp. 47, 56, fn. 102.

VASSALLI, Francesco (*fl.* 1724–63). Stuccoist.
One of a family long settled at Riva St Vitale, near Lugano. Although little is known of him, and while it is difficult to decide if his late work was done by, or in collaboration with, 'John Vassalli', there is little doubt of his talent. There seems to have been a connection with Thomas Clayton. He had a foreman John Johnson in 1755.
c 1715 DUNCOMBE PARK, YORKSHIRE
Lit: See c 1715 entry under Giuseppe Artari, with whom Vassalli worked.
1724 SUTTON SCARSDALE, DERBYSHIRE
Architect: Francis Smith.
Dest c 1919.
Lit: Rising-plate at house; text in Colvin, 1978, *Dictionary*, p. 552; *C Life*, 15 February 1919, p. 171.
1725 DITCHLEY, OXFORDSHIRE
Architect: James Gibbs.
Lit: Oxford CRO, Dillon Archives, I/p/3h.
1730 ASKE HALL, RICHMOND, YORKSHIRE
The Hall and five other rooms.
Lit: Lancs. CRO, MS, DDTO Q/10, letter from Vassalli, 7 December 1730.
1730–31 TOWNELEY HALL, BURNLEY, LANCASHIRE
This example, documented as Vassalli's work, is also in other northern houses and suggests that the stuccoist moved from one house to the other.
Great Hall. Assisted by Martino Quadry. Received £126.
Lit: Lancs. CRO, MS, DDTO Q/10.
1732–33 PARLINGTON HALL, YORKSHIRE
Dest 1950.
Various rooms. Assisted by Martino Quadry.
Lit: Elizabeth Done, 1975, 'Sir Edward Gascoigne, Grand Tourist', *Leeds Arts Calendar*, No. 77, p. 11. (Quadry went on in November 1732 to 'Mr Listers'.)
1736–37 CASTLE HOWARD, YORKSHIRE
Temple of the Four Winds. 'Given to Varcelli for drawing a design for ye finishing ye Temple in Stuco & artificial Marble [scagliola]. £2. 02. 0.'
Lit: Castle Howard Archives, 3rd Earl of Carlisle's Notebook, 1736.
1737 May:

To Mr. Vasally on Acc^t of working at ye inside of ye Temple by recept.	42. 0. 0.	
To Do on the same accot	31. 10. 0.	
To Do	5. 5. 0.	
To Do	5. 5. 0.	

1738–39:

To Mr. Vassalli ye Ballance of his Acct for work done at ye Temple as by Receipt Mr. Vasallei Agre^{mt} for	36. 15. 0.	
finishing ye inside of ye Temple	141. 15. 0.	
Pd at London	21. 0. 0.	
	120. 15. 0.	
Pd at Castle Howard Dec. 1737	84. 0. 0.	
Pd Balance to Vassali by rect.	36. 15. 0.	

1751–52 TRENTHAM, STAFFORDSHIRE
Now destroyed. Work in 'My Lords Drawing-Room'.
Received £57. 2*s.* 0*d.*
Lit: Staffs. CRO, Trentham MSS; *C Life*, 25 January 1968, p. 178.
1753 PETWORTH, SUSSEX
White and Gold Room.
Received £70 (in part).
Lit: West Sussex CRO, Egremont Archives, 626; *Apollo*, May 1977, p. 331.
1758 HAGLEY HALL, WORCESTERSHIRE
Architect: Sanderson Miller.

White Hall. Panel over fireplace, signed bottom left by Vassalli.
Salon, now Dining Room. Ceiling and walls, roundels, swags and trophies emblematical of the interests of Sir George Lyttelton, for whom the house was built and decorated.
1759–61 CROOME COURT, WORCESTERSHIRE
Francesco Vassalli received various sums from 1759–61, some of the work being measured in October 1760. There are three receipts at the Estate Office signed by Vassalli (28 July 1758, £50; 8 October 1759, £50; 30 March 1761, £221. 11s. 7d.). The measured work amounted to £247. 10s. 4½d. and special work in addition, including ornaments in the stone staircase, and 'ye Salon according to my desinge, £47. 15s.'. There is another bill which reads: 'Stucco work by hand & Plaisterers work done for ye Rt Honble Earl of Coventry at Croom, Worcestershire, 1761:

Measured work	247. 4. 7½.
Ornaments by hand:	
ceiling of drawing-room	40. 0. 0.
ceiling of dining-room	36. 0. 0.
wall, ornaments, dining room	44. 0. 0.
ceiling of vestibule, passage	19. 10. 0.
other	159. 10. 0.
	299. 0. 0.'

In all Francesco Vassalli received £643. 17s. 7½d.
This work would have been largely swept away by Joseph Rose junior (1745–99) when working for RA.
Lit: Croome Court Archives, No. 18 (microfilm, Victoria & Albert Museum, Dept of Furniture and Woodwork).
1763 SHUGBOROUGH, STAFFORDSHIRE
Dining Room: Library.
Lit: 'Versalli's Stucco here is twice as good as his Performances at Hagley not to mention the Superiority of the Designs . . .', Philip Yorke, later 2nd Earl of Hardwicke, to his father, 20, 21 August 1763, BL, Add. MS, 35351, f. 406.
Attributed work
In view of Vassalli's work in Lancashire, it is possible that he was responsible for work at: Knowsley; Burrow Hall; Croxteth; The Music, or Muses, Pavilion, Sun Street, Lancaster; and for the vanished Leoni houses, Bold Hall and Lathom, completed in about 1731.
The Ballroom at Lumley Castle, Co Durham, has similarities with his style, but is more likely a work by the Franchinis (q.v.). The Hagley trophies bear resemblance to those at Hatton Grange, Shropshire (*C Life*, 29 February 1968, p. 467), and Highnam Court, Gloucestershire (*C Life*, 12 May 1950).
The late Sir Charles Trevelyan maintained that Vassalli worked at Wallington, Northumberland, but confirmation has now been found that the Wallington work is by the Franchini brothers (q.v.).

VERHUYCK, – (*fl.* early 18th cent.).
Carver.
Elizabeth Verhuyck claimed £136 in 1709 (on behalf of her late husband) from the executors of Ralph, 1st Duke of Montagu, for work at Montagu House, London, and Boughton, Northants.
Lit: Boughton Archives, Executors' Accounts, 1st Duke of Montagu. (I am indebted to Mr P I King for this reference.)

VERRIO, Antonio (*c* 1639–1707). Decorative Painter.
Born at Lecce in Italy. Came to England *c* 1672 and stayed here until his death. Introduced late baroque painting to England. Patronised in particular by the 5th Earl of Exeter. Worked on the following major commissions:
c 1675 EUSTON HALL, SUFFOLK
One of Verrio's earliest commissions.
1675–76 ARLINGTON HOUSE, LONDON
Painted for one of Verrio's first patrons in England, the 1st Earl of Arlington.
before 1677 WINDSOR CASTLE, BERKSHIRE
Worked in Hugh May's north range and in most principal rooms almost until his death in 1702. Very little of his work survived the redecoration of the castle for George IV by Sir Jeffrey Wyatville.
before 1680 CASSIOBURY, HERTFORDSHIRE
Dest in part *c* 1800.
c 1681–88 CHRIST'S HOSPITAL, LONDON
Hall. In collaboration with Laguerre.
1682–83 MONTAGU HOUSE, LONDON
1686 WHITEHALL PALACE, LONDON
James II's Roman Catholic Chapel.
1687–98 BURGHLEY HOUSE, NORTHAMPTONSHIRE
All principal rooms.
before 1698 HAM HOUSE, SURREY
1698 CHATSWORTH, DERBYSHIRE
Great Stairs, State Dining Room, Library, etc.
1700–04 HAMPTON COURT, MIDDLESEX
King's Staircase, King's Bedroom, Queen's Drawing Room.
Lit: Croft-Murray, 1962, *Painting*, I, pp. 236–42.

VITTI, Giuseppe (*fl.* late 17th cent.). Gilder.
Worked at Chatsworth.
Lit: Francis Thompson, 1949, *A History of Chatsworth*, pp. 36, 67, 125, 168.

WADE, Joseph (*fl.* 1712–24). Carver.
Worked at the London churches of St Alphege, Greenwich, St Anne, Limehouse, St George, Wapping, and St Paul, Deptford, 1712–24.
Architects: Nicholas Hawksmoor and Thomas Archer.
Lit: Colvin, 1950, *Arch Rev*, p. 196.

WALKER, Thomas (*fl.* 1705). Plasterer.
Official of the Worshipful Company of Plaisterers.
1705 Master.
Lit: London, Guildhall Library, MS, 6122/3.

WALKER, Thomas and **William** (*fl.* 1823).
Carvers and Gilders.
Of York.
Lit: Baines, 1823, *York Directory*, II, p. 119.

WALTON, Henry (*fl.* 1694). Locksmith.
Lived at the Sign of the Brass, Lock & Key, corner of Newport Street and St Martin's Lane, London.
His trade card (National Trust, Dyrham Park) heads a memorandum dated 1694.
Lit: P Thornton, 1978, *Seventeenth-century Interior Decoration in England, France & Holland*, pl. 102.

WARD, Matthew (*fl.* 1762). Plasterer.
1762 FAIRFAX HOUSE, YORK
'For 9 roses under the stairs. 1762. £2. 0. 6.'
Lit: Leeds, Yorkshire Archaeological Society Library, Newburgh Archives.

WARD, Richard (*fl.* 1755). Plasterer.
1755 KNAVESMIRE RACECOURSE GRANDSTAND, YORK
Architect: John Carr.
Lit: York Georgian Society, 1965–66, *Report*, p. 4; RCHM, 1972, *City of York*, III, p. 51.
A Richard Ward, joiner, worked for Sir Robert Walpole in 1722 at his London house in Arlington Street (CUL (CH), Vouchers 1722).

WARREN, George (*fl.* 1735–72). Carpenter.
1731–37 KEW and ST JAMES'S PALACE, LONDON
Supervised by William Kent and Thomas Ripley.
(Received £582. 7s. 3¼d. for St James's Palace.)
Presumably the same, referred to in 1772, as one of her late Royal Highness's workmen who was to be ready to work at Kew under the direction of Sir William Chambers. He is also mentioned in the architect's bank account (Drummonds).
Lit: Duchy of Cornwall, Vouchers II, 1731–32, p. 287, VI(1), 1735–37, p. 257; Harris, 1970, *Chambers*, pp. 39, fn., 175, 213.

WATERIDGE, John (*fl.* 1770–80).
Painter/Gilder.
c 1770 ALNWICK CASTLE, NORTHUMBERLAND
Gilding ornaments in Chapel.
2s. 9d. per sq ft. Received £665. 1s. 4d.
Lit: Alnwick Castle Archives, U.I. 46.

WATSON, Grace (*fl.* 1775). Plasterer.
1775 BERKELEY SQUARE, LONDON
House of Robert Child.
General plastering. Received £6. 7s. 6d.
Lit: Victoria and Albert Museum (Dept of Furniture and Woodwork), Osterley Archives.

WATSON, Samuel (1663–1715). Carver in wood and stone.
Of Heanor, Derbyshire.
Trained under Charles Okey (q.v.). His main achievement was the splendid woodcarving he did at Chatsworth in the late seventeenth century.
Lit: Francis Thompson, 1949, *A History of Chatsworth*, many references; 'List of charges for carving at Chatsworth, 1702–6' (Central Library, Derby).

WATTS, Thomas (*fl.* 1757–60).
Carver/Gilder.
1757 PETWORTH HOUSE, SUSSEX
King of Spain's Bedchamber, gilding. Ceiling survives of the original decoration.
Lit: West Sussex CRO, Petworth MS, 626.
1757–60 EGREMONT HOUSE, LONDON
Received £97. 17s. 6d. for gilding, painting, and ornamenting in 'papier mache Inriched with Shell work, Foliage, Bands and Flowers'.
Lit: ibid.

WATTS, William (*fl.* 1737). Carver.
Of London.
Left a small legacy in the will of Edward
Poynton (q.v.).
Lit: Notts. CRO, Poynton's will, 1737.

WEATHERILL (WETHERILL), Robert
(*fl.* late 17th cent.–1717). Plasterer.
1682, 1690 St Charles the Martyr,
Tunbridge Wells
Worked with Henry Doogood (q.v.). Together
they received £190.
Lit: Marcus Whiffen, 1952, *Stuart and
Georgian Churches*, p. 143.
Greenwich Hospital, London
Asked to be employed on work there.
Lit: Wren Soc, VI, pp. 31, 56, 58, 62, 63.
Blenheim Palace, Oxfordshire
Lit: David Green, 1951, *Blenheim Palace*, pp.
61, 104, 128.
1707–08 Petitioned for the post of Master
Plasterer to the Office of Works vacant on the
death of John Grove II (given to David
Lance, q.v.). He stated he had been employed
at 'Greenwich Hospital and in many other
eminent buildings'.
Lit: Cal., Treasury Books, XXII, p. 133.
1716 Hampton Court, Middlesex
Submitted proposals with David Lance to
carry out work in certain apartments.
Lit: PRO, Works, 4/1, 6 March 1716.
1718 Mentioned in Vanbrugh's account book
in receipt of £50.
Lit: K Downes, 1977, *Vanbrugh*, p. 195.

WEBB, Thomas (*fl.* 1724–27). Joiner.
1724–27 Houghton Hall, Norfolk
Signed Sir Robert Walpole's receipt book for
unspecified work.
Lit: CUL (CH), Account Book 26.

WELLBELOVED, William (*fl.* 1712).
Carpenter.
1712 5 St James's Square, London
Lit: BL, Add. MS, 22, 254, f. 3.

WELLINGS, – (*fl.* 1775). Plasterer.
Refused admission to the Painter-Stainers'
Company in February 1775.
Lit: W A D Englefield, 1923, *History of the
Painter-Stainers' Company of London*, p. 175,
fn.

WELLS, Henry (*fl.* 1673–74). Plasterer.
1673–74 Ham House, Surrey
'Henry Wells Plaisterer was paid in full of all
Bills to April 10th 1673 on Sepr. 13th 1673.
He hath Recd Since
1673 Janry 13   £15. 0. 0.
His Bills Dated ye
27th July 1674   £71. 17. 09.
Rem. due   £21. 17. 09.
Mr Wells ye Plasterers bill ffor work done at
Ham ffor his Grace the Duke of Lauderdale in
ye year 1674.
ffor 575 yards of plastring at 6d.   £14. 07. 06.
ffor 866 yards of Rendring at 3d.   10. 16. 06.
ffor 3256 yards of whiting almost
all over the old house and new,
& some of it three times done
at 1½d. the yard   20. 07. 00.
ffor 52 yards of cornice in the
west wing of the new building at
4s. 6d. ye yard   11. 15. 06.

ffor 25 yards of frettwork in ye
library at six shill. six pence
ye yard   08. 02. 06.
ffor 34 yards in 3 little cov'd
ceiling at two shill. 6d. ye yard   04. 05. 00.
ffor 45⅓ yards of cornice in
the new east build: at 4 shil. 6d.
ye yard   10. 04. 00.
Measured by me: Jo Lacey'
(Approved by William Samwell, 27 July
1674.)
Lit: Buckminster Park, Lincs., Tollemache
Archives (I am indebted to Mr Maurice
Tomlin for this reference). Wells may also
have worked in the Queen's Bedchamber, its
Antechamber and Closet at Ham House.

WELSH, Thomas (*fl.* 1754). Carver.
1754 Noted as a carver at Hopetoun House
(for RA and his brothers) when he subscribed
to the first edition of Thomas Chippendale's
pattern-book, *The Director*. (Information from
Christopher Gilbert.)

WENHAM, William (*fl.* 1808–09). Plasterer.
1808–09 Clifton Castle, Yorkshire
Architect: John Foss.
Lit: Sir John Cowell's notes about the
building. (I am indebted to Dr H M Colvin
for this reference.)

WEPSHED, Edward (*fl.* 1782). Carpenter.
The architect John Yenn recommended
Wepshed as a carpenter who had worked (with
Thomas Short) at Somerset House.
Lit: London, RIBA, MSS, Cha 2/93.

WESTCOT, Thomas (*fl.* 1766). Slater.
c 1766 45 Berkeley Square, London
Architect: Sir William Chambers.
1766 German Lutheran Chapel, The
Savoy, London
Westcot was one of the architect's reliable
team of craftsmen: Sefferin Alken, carver;
William Chapman, plumber; Thomas Collins,
plasterer; George Evans, painter/gilder;
Edward Gray, bricklayer; James Palmer,
smith; and Benjamin Thacker, carpenter.
Lit: Harris, 1970, *Chambers*, pp. 39 fn., 175,
216, 229.

WESTON, Ned (*fl.* 1738–43). Plasterer.
Assistant to John Woolston (q.v.). Fell from
scaffolding while working on the plaster royal
arms at the 1738–43 restoration of Lamport
Church, Northamptonshire.
Lit: C Life, 10 October 1952, p. 1108.

WHARTON, Thomas (*fl.* 1660). Plasterer.
1660 The Tower, London
Worked under John Grove.
Lit: PRO, Works, 5/1, November 1660.

WHATSON, William (*fl. c* 1728–42).
Plasterer.
1742 Apprenticed at the age of 14 to Thomas
Perritt (q.v.) of York.
Lit: York Reference Library, *Apprenticeship
Register, 1721–56*.

WHEELEY, James (*fl. c* 1760–70). Paper-
hanger.
His trade card indicates that he owned a
paper-hanging warehouse opposite the church

in Little Britain, London, where he
'Manufactor'd & Sold all Sorts of Embos'd,
Chintz & Common Papers, with great variety
of Papier Machee & other Ornaments for
Cielings, Halls, Staircases &c.'
Lit: A Heal, 1968, *London Tradesmens' Cards
of the 18th Century*, pl. LXIX.

WHITE, Thomas (*fl.* 1764–69). Plasterer.
Of London.
1764–69 Manor House, Milton, Berkshire
Entries from surviving account book.
Lit: C Life, 24 December 1948.

WHITEHEAD, John (*fl.* 1748–60). Plasterer.
1748–50 14 St James's Square, London
Repaired ceiling and cornice in Dining Room.
Lit: 1960, *Survey of London*, XXIX, p. 140.
1753 Edgecote, Northamptonshire
Received £581. 17s. 6d.
Lit: Tipping, 1937, *English Homes, Early
Georgian*, p. 298; Jourdain, 1926, *Plasterwork*,
p. xiii.
1754–56 Braxted Lodge, Essex
Received £88.
Lit: Essex CRO, D/DDCA13, f. 118. (I am
indebted to Miss Nancy Briggs for this
reference.)
1758–59 Soho Square, London
Architect: Thomas Dade.
Worked for Sir William Robinson at two
houses.
Received £466. 9s. 0½d.
Lit: Leeds Archives Dept, Newby Hall
Archives, 2785A.

WHITTY, Thomas (*fl.* 1757–80). Carpet
Maker.
The Axminster carpet works, under Whitty,
provided the carpets to RA's design at
Saltram, Devonshire.
Lit: See entry under Thomas Moore (article
by W Hefford).

WICKS, James (*fl.* 1768). Painter.
1768 19 Arlington Street, London
Architect: RA.
Painting.
Lit: North Riding, Yorks. CRO, Zetland
Archives, ZNK X/1/7, No. 76.

WILCOX, Jonathan (*fl.* mid–late 17th
cent.). Carpenter.
Worked particularly under Sir Christopher
Wren and Captain William Winde. He was in
charge for Winde at Combe Abbey, Warwicks.
(1683), and Castle Bromwich, Warwicks.
(1689–90).
Lit: Colvin, 1978, Dictionary, p. 890; Staffs
CRO, Earl of Bradford Archives, Winde
letters, Box 74.

WILDSMITH, John (*fl.* 1763). Sculptor.
1763 Croome Court, Worcestershire
Tapestry Room chimneypiece.
Lit: James Parker, 1964, 'The Croome Court
Tapestry Room', *Decorative Art from the
Samuel H. Kress Collection, at the
Metropolitan Museum of Art*, p. 30; Gunnis,
1953, *Dictionary*, p. 432.
1763 Egremont House, London
Lit: West Sussex CRO, Egremont Archives,
6614.

WILKES, John (?–1733). Locksmith.
Of Birmingham. One of the best known of the late seventeenth-century locksmiths, responsible for fine, decorative and elaborate locks. These may be seen at Arbury, Warwicks., Stoneleigh, Warwicks., and the Victoria and Albert Museum—also one on loan from them at Birmingham City Art Gallery. He provided locks (which are now lost) at Weston Underwood, Bucks., Sutton Scarsdale, Derbys., and Worcester Guildhall; his work is extant at Chicheley Hall, Bucks. Wilkes lived at 9 Old Square, Birmingham, from 1713 until his death. In 1727 he was examined before a Parliamentary Committee in support of a petition about repairing a road which would enable better carrying on of the iron trade in Birmingham.
Lit: Joseph Hill and R K Dent, 1897, *Memoirs of the Old Square, Birmingham*; *C Life*, 63 (1920), pp. 705–07; Worcester City Archives, Guildhall Accounts, entry dated 16 September 1725; Joan D Tanner, 1961, 'The Building of Chicheley Hall', *Records of Bucks.*, XVII, pt. I.

WILKINS, Chrysostom (*fl.* 1700–26). Plasterer.
Was in charge of many plasterers at St Paul's Cathedral. In 1700 he was fined for arrears of quarterage, and in 1709 for bad workmanship, by the Worshipful Company of Plaisterers. In 1707–08 he petitioned for the post of Master Plasterer to the Office of Works, vacant on the death of John Grove II. The post was given to David Lance (q.v.). His name appears in the subscribers' list to the 2nd edition of Leoni's *Palladio* (1721). He worked for Nicholas Hawksmoor at St Anne, Limehouse, St George, Wapping, and St Mary Woolnoth, and for James Gibbs at St Mary-le-Strand and St Martin-in-the-Fields. At the latter he received £593. 4s. 4d. for moulded and other work additional to that by Giovanni Bagutti (q.v.). He worked at St John Horsleydown, gutted 1940, partly demolished 1948.
Lit: Colvin, 1950, *Arch Rev*, p. 196; London, Guildhall Library, MSS, 6122/3, 6126, 8 August 1709; K Downes, 1977, *Vanbrugh*, p. 224; *Calendar, Treasury Books*, XXII, p. 133; Westminster Reference Library, St Martin-in-the-Fields Accounts, 419/311, f. 94 (I am indebted to Dr Terry F Friedman for this reference).

WILKINS, John (*fl.* 1714–23). Plasterer.
Was employed with his brother (?) Chrysostom by Gibbs.
1714–17 ST MARY-LE-STRAND, LONDON
Lit: Colvin, 1954, *Dictionary*, p. 231; Little, 1955, *Gibbs*, p. 37.
1715–23 ST GEORGE, WAPPING, LONDON (ST GEORGE IN THE EAST)
Architect: Nicholas Hawksmoor.
Lit: Colvin, 1950, *Arch Rev*, p. 195.

WILKINSON, Richard (*fl.* 1767). Plasterer.
Subscribed to James Paine's 1767, *Plans . . . of Noblemen and Gentlemen's Houses . . .*

WILLIAMS, – (*fl.* 1726). Plasterer.
1726 CANONS, MIDDLESEX
Worked for James Brydges, 1st Duke of Chandos.
Lit: Baker, 1949, *Brydges*, p. 149 fn.

WILMOTT, Humphrey (*fl.* 1750–73). Plasterer.
c 1750 MANSION HOUSE, LONDON
Worked with George Fewkes (q.v.).
1761 Wilmott was fined 42s. 'for bad and imperfect workmanship in the Cleansing and Whitening of the plaisterers work by him done . . . [at] the Guildhall of the City of London'.
Lit: London, Guildhall Library, MS, 6126, 5 August 1761.
1767 His son John was bound to him as an apprentice.
Lit: London, Guildhall Library, *Boyd's Index to Apprenticeship Registers*.
1772–73 Wilmott was Upper Warden and Master of the Worshipful Company of Plaisterers.

WILTON, Joseph (1722–1803). Sculptor.
Son of William Wilton, plasterer. Worked extensively for George III, for leading architects and for RA at Croome, Osterley and Syon.
1761 STATE COACH, KING GEORGE III
Model, ornaments in wood.
Received £2500.
Lit: Harris, 1970, *Chambers*, p. 220.
1766 CROOME COURT, WORCESTERSHIRE
Gallery chimneypiece. Received £300.
c 1767 SYON, MIDDLESEX
Gallery: bas-reliefs.
Lit: Alnwick Castle Archives, 94; Gunnis, 1953, *Dictionary*, p. 434.

WILTON, William (*fl.* 1722–65). Plasterer.
Father of the sculptor. He died on 27 January 1768, and is buried at Wanstead, Essex.
Lit: Parish Registers; information from Colonel J H Busby.
1722 STANMER, SUSSEX
Architect: Nicholas Dubois.
Entrance Hall.
Lit: Hussey, 1965, *ECH: Early Georgian*, p. 56.
c 1740 FOUNDLING HOSPITAL, LONDON
Lit: L Turner, 1927, *Decorative Plasterwork in Great Britain*, p. 224, pl. 299.
1765 LINLEY HALL, SHROPSHIRE
Worked with Thomas Collins (q.v.), his apprentice.
Lit: Bill at house (I am indebted to Dr H M Colvin and Colonel J H Busby for this reference).
Attributed work
c 1750 FIRLE PLACE, SUSSEX
Library.
Lit: *C Life*, 3 March 1955, pp. 621–22.

WOLSTENHOLME, Thomas (*c* 1759–1812).
Of York. His nephew, John, was a woodcarver who worked extensively at York Minster. Thomas made his name as a maker of composition plaster. His houses at 3/5 Gillygate, York (built in 1797), have ornament in most rooms and on the façade. The composition has been found in several houses in York and district, such as 53/55 Micklegate and Ripley Castle (Francis and John Wolstenholme, *fl.* 1823–52, were carvers).
Lit: David Black, 1968–69, York Georgian Society *Report*; RCHM, *City of York*, III (1972), p. lxxxv, IV (1975), pp. liv, lvi, 60, 63, 72, 74, 85, 90 (I am indebted to Mr Black, the late Major J D Williams, Mr John Harvey and

Dr Eric Gee for sharing the result of their researches, made on behalf of the RCHM); Baines, 1823, *York Directory*, II, p. 110; *Yorks Gazette*, 17 April 1852 (I am indebted to Dr Eric Gee for these two references).

WOOD, John (*fl.* 1782). Plasterer.
1782 COURT HOUSE, NORTHALLERTON
Architect: John Carr.
Lit: R B Wragg, 1955–56, York Georgian Society, *Report*, p. 60.

WOOD, Joseph (*fl.* 1778). Plasterer.
Freeman of York, 1778.
Lit: Surtees Society, 102.

WOOD, Thomas (*fl.* 1717–37). Carpenter.
Carpenter to the Drapers' Company from 1717 and contractor for its almshouses in Mile End Road, London.
Lit: London, Guildhall Library, MS, 14, 334.

WOODROFFE, William (*fl.* ?1636–73). Carver.
A joiner 'Woodroffe' carved the doors of the pulpitum in the Chapel of King's College, Cambridge; one has the date 1636 carved on it. In 1673 he did the Screen in the Brewers' Hall, London.
Lit: Aymer Vallance, 1947, *Greater English Church Screens*, p. 141; H Avray Tipping, 1914, *Grinling Gibbons and the Woodwork of his Age*, fig. 43.

WOODWARD, Francis (*fl.* 1701–03). Carver.
1701–03 CHRIST'S COLLEGE, CAMBRIDGE
Received £145.
Lit: *C Life*, 2 May 1936.

WOODWARD, Thomas (*fl.* 1700). Carver.
c 1700 ST. CATHERINE'S COLLEGE, CAMBRIDGE
Chapel; ornamental carving. The Chapel was dedicated on 1 September 1704.
Lit: Aymer Vallance, 1947, *Greater English Church Screens*, p. 135.

WOOLBRAN, Marmaduke (*fl. c* 1700–15). Carpenter.
Apprenticed on 10 June 1715 to William Etty of York, joiner, for seven years.
Lit: York Reference Library, *Register Book of Apprentices*.

WOOLSTON, John (*fl.* 1738–40). Plasterer.
Of Northampton. Became an Alderman of the town.
1738 LAMPORT, NORTHAMPTONSHIRE
Plasterwork in the Music Hall and over the staircase; Library ceiling.
Lit: Northants. CRO, Isham Archives; M D Whinney, 1953, *Arch Jnl*, CX, p. 205; *C Life*, 3 October 1952, p. 1023.
1740 LAMPORT CHURCH, NORTHAMPTONSHIRE
Interior classicised to designs of William Smith.
Lit: *C Life*, 10 October 1952, p. 1108; M D Whinney, 1953, *Arch Jnl*, CX, p. 206.
Attributed work
EASTON NESTON, NORTHAMPTONSHIRE
Dining Room.
Lit: M D Whinney, 1953, *Arch Jnl*, CX, p. 210.
ALTHORP, NORTHAMPTONSHIRE
Work in the Entrance Hall, *c* 1733.

WORRALL, George (*fl.* 1724–61). Plasterer. Parish of St Martin-in-the-Fields, London. Possibly the son of William Worrall (see below).
Was Master Plasterer, Office of Works, from 17 March 1724/25 to 1761.
DRAYTON HOUSE, NORTHAMPTONSHIRE
Chapel.
Lit: Drawing with attached bill (Coke MSS, Melbourne, Derbyshire) (I am indebted to Mr Edward Saunders and Mr Gervase Jackson-Stops for this reference); *C Life*, XXXI, p. 944; N Stopford Sackville, 1949, *Drayton*; PRO, LC5/105, p. 13.

WORRALL, William (?–*c* 1690). Plasterer. Of St Giles, Cripplegate Without, London. During his lifetime accumulated enough money to purchase estates and endow by will a London charity.
Lit: East Sussex CRO, Add. MS, 2573.

WRIGHT, John and others (*fl.* 1703–77). Plasterers.
A John Wright of Southwark was apprenticed to James Ellis (q.v.) on 2 April 1703 (Guildhall Library. MS, 6122/3), and another of this name was apprenticed to Joseph Rose senior in 1753 for seven years. Rose was then living at Doncaster.
Lit: London, Guildhall Library, *Boyd's Index to Apprenticeship Registers.*
The John Wright who worked at Stanford Hall, Leicestershire, in 1743 and received £270. 12s. 1d. may have been a relative. It is difficult to believe they were the same in view of the apprenticeship dates.
Lit: *C Life*, 11 December 1958, p. 1410.
A John Wright worked for John Thorold at Syston Hall, Lincolnshire, and received £391. 16s. 9d., although he charged £398. 17s. 6d.
Lit: Lincolnshire CRO, Thorold Archives, VI/III/5.
A John Wright also worked under Henry Holland at Cadland, Hampshire, in 1777.
Lit: Receipt, 17 February 1777, Soane Museum, London (I am indebted to Mrs Monica Ellis for this information).
A 'Mr Wright', described as 'the ornament man', 'Ornament plasterer' and 'Stocco', was employed by James Paine at Thorndon Hall, Essex, in 1768, and Thomas Wright was fined for using bad material at the Grocers' Hall in 1771.
Lit: Essex CRO, Petre Archives, D/DPA58 (I am indebted to Miss Nancy Briggs for the Thorndon information); Guildhall Library, London, MSS, 6122/3, 6126, 5 August 1771.

WRIGHT, Thomas (*fl.* 1657–62). Plasterer.
1662 LONDON, WHITEHALL
'Mended the frett ceiling in the Queen's Chappell', etc.
Received £67. 9s. 0d.
Lit: PRO, E351/3276, Works, 5/3.
Wright was fined in September 1657 for keeping four apprentices instead of two, as the Worshipful Company of Plaisterers rules decreed.

Lit: London, Guildhall Library, MS, 6216.

WYATT family (*fl.* 18th cent.). Carpenters. This talented and large family of architects and master builders included some who worked as carpenters. Job Wyatt (1719–?), John Wyatt (1700–66) and Edward Wyatt (1757–1833) were involved in carpentry, woodcarving and gilding. The architect Samuel Wyatt (1737–1807) acted as carpenting contractor on the building of Somerset House, London. The total payment recorded to him was £24 334. 6s. 1d.
Lit: D Linstrum, 1972, *Sir Jeffry Wyatville*, p. 5; J Martin Robinson, 1979, *The Wyatt Family: An Architectural Dynasty*; RIBA, Library, Somerset House Accounts; PRO, AO3/1244.

YEAPE, William (*fl.* 1660). Plasterer.
1660 THE TOWER, LONDON
Worked with John Grove I.
Lit: PRO, Works, 5/1, November 1660.

YOUNG, Thomas (*fl.* late 17th cent.). Carver.
Of London.
Worked with William Davis, Joel Lobb and Samuel Watson at Chatsworth. Young was the master carver. He left Chatsworth in 1692. Lobb, Davis and Watson signed a new agreement on 9 September 1692.
Lit: Francis Thompson, 1949, *A History of Chatsworth*, pp. 149–50.

GLOSSARY

A glossary of architectural terms in a useful format is that by John Harris and Jill Lever, 1966, *Illustrated Glossary of Architecture, 850–1830*. There is an excellent one for cabinet-making and upholstery terms in Christopher Gilbert's, 1978, *The Life and Work of Thomas Chippendale*, 2 vols.

ACANTHUS
Plant with thick, scalloped leaves used as part of the decoration of a Corinthian capital, and in some forms of leaf carving.

ANGLE CHIMNEY
A chimney placed in the angle of a room.

APRON
Horizontal piece of timber in wooden, double-flighted stairs for supporting the carriage pieces. Firmly wedged into the wall.

APSE
Vaulted, semicircular or polygonal end of a chancel, chapel or room.

ARABESQUE
Surface decoration using combinations of flowing lines, tendrils, etc., interspersed in a light and fanciful way with vases, animals, etc.

ARCHITRAVE
The lowest of the three main parts of the entablature (q.v.) of an order (q.v.).

ASTRAGAL
A small moulding of a semicircular profile, applied to the ring separating the column from the capital.

AUGER
A boring tool used by carpenters and joiners.

BACK of a chimney
The recessed face of it towards the room.

BACK of a handrail
The upper side of it.

BADIGEON
A mixture of plaster and freestone, sifted and ground together, used by statuaries to repair defects. Joiners used a mixture of sawdust and glue to similar purpose.

BALUSTER
Small pillar or column, and (in staircases) a turned or carved wood member.

BALUSTRADE
Series of balusters supporting a handrail (q.v.).

BANDING PLANE
A plane intended for cutting out grooves and inlaying strings and bands in straight and circular work.

BASE of a room
The lower projecting part. It consists of two parts, the lower of which is a plain board adjoining the floor, called the plinth, and the upper of one or more mouldings. The plinth is sometimes tongued into a groove in the floor.

BASIL
The angle to which the edge of an iron tool is ground.

BATTEN
A scantling or piece of timber ('stuff'), from 2 to 6 in broad, used in the boarding of floors, and upon walls to receive the laths on which plaster is laid.

BEAD
A moulding whose section is circular. When flush with the surface it is a quirk-bead, and when raised it is called a cock-bead.

BEAD and **FLUSH WORK**
A piece of framed work with beads run on each edge of the included panel.

BEAM COMPASSES
An instrument for describing large circles beyond the reach of ordinary compasses.

BEARING of a timber
The unsupported distance between its points of support.

BEATER
An implement used by plasterers for beating the mixture of lime, sand, hair, etc. Also referred to as 'flails' and 'swingles'.

BEDDING of a timber
Placing it properly in mortar on the walls.

BINDING JOIST
Those beams in a floor which, in a transverse direction, support the bridging joists above and the ceiling joists below.

BITUMEN
A mineral pitch used instead of mortar in early times.

BOARD
A piece of timber of undefined length more than 4 in broad and not more than 2½ in thick. Boards wider than 9 in are called planks. Fir boards were called deal (q.v.).

BRACKET
Small supporting piece of wood or stone (*see* pl. 69) to carry a projecting horizontal such as a gallery.

BRACKETING
Preparing the timber framework ribs to cornices, etc., to carry plaster mouldings.

CABLE MOULDING
Moulding which resembles a twisted cord.

CANOPY
Ornamented covering set above an altar, pulpit, niche, bed, etc.

CANTILEVER
Blocks inserted into the wall of a building for supporting a balcony, staircase, eaves of a house, etc.

CAPITAL
Head or top part of a column.

CARCASE
The naked building of a house before floors are laid, or lath and plastering work.

CARYATID
Stone or wood representation of the human figure used instead of a column.

CAST IRON
The product of the process of smelting iron ores.

CENTERING
Wooden framework used in the construction of an arch or vault, which is removed when the mortar has set.

CERUSE *see* WHITE LEAD

CHIT
An instrument used for cleaving laths.

CHRISTIANA DEALS
Timber from Christiana (i.e. Oslo), Norway.

COARSE STUFF
The first coat of lime and hair in plastering.

COFFERING
The decoration on a ceiling in sunk squares or polygonal ornamental panels (*see* pl. 78).

COLONNADE
Range of columns. Painted occasionally in feigned form (*see* pl. 97).

COMPARTMENT CEILING
One divided into panels, which are usually surrounded by mouldings.

COMPASS
To curve or bend round timber.

COMPASSING
Timber in a circular arch.

CONSOLE
Bracket with a compound curved outline.

CORNICE
In classical architecture, the upper section of the entablature. Also a projecting feature in wood or plaster along the top of a wall or arch.

COVE BRACKETING
The wooden skeleton for the lathing of any cove—the quadrantal profile between the ceiling of a room and its cornice.

CRADLING
The timber ribs and pieces for sustaining the lathing and plastering of vaulted ceilings.

CRAMP
An iron instrument about 4 ft long, having a screw at one end and a moveable shoulder at the other, employed by carpenters and joiners for forcing mortice and tenon work together.

CROWN GLASS
Window glass cut from a sheet blown into a disc form and having a bull's eye in the centre.

CUPOLA
Small circular or polygonal domed turret supported on a drum (q.v.) and often surmounted by a lantern (q.v.). Sometimes applied to the underside or ceiling part of a dome.

CUT STRING STAIRS
Stairs which have the outer string cut to the profile of the steps.

CYMA
A moulding taking its name from its contour, resembling that of a wave. The *cyma recta* is hollow in its upper part and swells below; the *cyma reversa* has the upper part swelled and the lower hollow. Also called an *ogee*.

DADO
The part of the pedestal of a column between the base and the cornice, and applied to that part of a room's panelling representing the pedestal.

DEAL
Usually restricted to the wood of the fir tree cut up into thicknesses in the areas from whence deals were imported, viz. Christiana, Drammen. Their usual thickness was 3 in and their width 9 in. They were purchased by the *hundred*, which contained 120 deals. Yellow deal was obtained from the Scotch fir (*Pinus sylvestris*). White deal was the product of the Norway spruce (*Abies excelsa* or *communis*).

DISTEMPER
Whiting mixed with size or other soluble glue and water with which walls and ceilings were painted. Called 'coloured' when a tint was added.

DRAM-DEAL
Timber from Drammen in Norway. 'Yellow fur (called Dram) being very good' (Sir Balthazar Gerbier, 1663, *Counsel and Advise to all Builders*, p. 64).

DRAUGHT
The representation of a building on paper by means of plans, elevations and sections, drawn to a scale.

DRUM
Circular or polygonal vertical wall of a dome or cupola.

ECHINUS
The same as the ovolo or quarter round.

EGG and ANCHORS/DART/TONGUE
Ornaments used in the echinus in the form of the natural objects.

ENCAUSTIC PAINTING
Ancient classical method of painting with wax colours and fixing these by heat.

ENTABLATURE
In classical architecture the horizontal members above a column (architrave, frieze and cornice). All three vary according to the different orders.

FESTOON
Carved garland of flowers and fruit suspended at each end (*see* pl. 122).

FINE STUFF
The final coat of plastering composed of sifted lime, hair and fine sand.

FLAKE WHITE
A ceruse prepared by the acid of grapes and used in a fine white paint.

FLATTING
Painting in oil in which the surface is left, when finished, without gloss. Nut and poppy oil were often used as good media for the colour.

FLOATED WORK
Plastering rendered perfectly plane by means of using a long rule with a straight edge, called a float, a wood or metal rectangular trowel.

FLUTING
Vertical channelling in the shaft of a column.

FOLIATED
Carved with leaf shapes.

FRAME, FRAMING
The rough timberwork of a house, or any pieces of woods fitted together with mortices and tenons, are said to be *framed*, as doors, sashes, etc.

FRESCO
Wall-painting on wet plaster in which it becomes very permanent.

FRESCO SECCO
Wall-painting on set plaster, wetted just before working on it.

FRETWORK
Ornamental decoration, especially of ceilings.

FRIEZE
Middle division of a classical entablature (q.v.) between the architrave and cornice.

FRIEZE PANEL
The upper panel of a six-panelled door.

FRIEZE RAIL
The upper panel but one of a six-panelled door.

FURRING (FIRRING)
Pieces of wood used to bring a surface to a level with others.

GAUGED STUFF
In plasterer's work, stuff composed of three parts of lime putty and one of plaster of Paris, to set quicker.

GEOMETRICAL STAIRCASE
That in which the flight of stone steps is supported by the wall at only one end of the steps.

GILDING
The practice of applying gold leaf on any surface. Done in oil-size on woodwork and in water-size on plastering. Water gilding can be burnished. The gold leaf was supplied in books of 25 leaves and in various thicknesses designated 'single', 'double' and 'thirds'.

GLUE
A tenacious viscid matter made of the skins and hooves of animals for cementing two bodies together (particularly wood).

GOUGE
A chisel whose section is of a semicircular form.

GROUND PLATE
The lowest horizontal timber on which the exterior walls of a building are erected.

GUILLOCHE
An ornament in the form of two or more bands or strings twisting over each other, so as to repeat the same figure, in a continued series.

GYPSUM
Crystals of calcium sulphate. Subjected to heat to expel the water of crystallisation, it forms plaster of Paris, and when water is applied to it, it immediately assumes a solid form. Alabaster is a form of gypsum.

HALF-PACE
That part of a staircase where a broad place is arrived at, on which two or three paces may be taken before coming to another step. If it occurs at the angle turns of the stairs, it is called a *quarter-pace*.

HANDRAIL of a stair
A rail raised upon slender balusters to assist in ascending and descending.

HANGING STILE of a door
That to which the hinges are attached.

HAWK

A small quadrangular tool with a handle, used by a plasterer, on which the stuff required was carried. The plasterer was kept supplied by a *hawk boy*.

HEADWAY of stairs

The distance, measured perpendicularly, from a given landing place or stair to the ceiling above.

HOLLOW NEWEL

An opening in the middle of a staircase. In the hollow newel, or well hole, the steps are only supported at one end by the surrounding wall of the staircase, the ends next to the hollow being unsupported.

HUNDRED of lime

A measure varying between 25 and 35 heaped bushels or bags. Deals were also sold by the hundred (120).

INDIA PAPER

Hand-painted oriental wallpaper.

INLAYING

Work in which a material is substituted for the surface of another which has been cut away. The inlaying of metal on metal is called *damascening*. Veneering is also a type of inlaying.

JACK PLANE

A plane about 18 in long used in taking off the rough surface left by the saw or axe.

JOIST

The timber to which the boards of a floor or laths of a ceiling are nailed. When one tier of joists is used, the assemblage is called *single-flooring*; when two, *double-flooring*.

KING-POST

The centre upright post in a trussed roof which connects the tie beam and collar beam with the ridge beam (*see* 'roof').

KNOTTING

A preliminary process in painting, to prevent knots appearing, by covering with a coat of red lead, then white lead and oil, and lastly a coat of gold size.

LANTERN

In architecture, a small circular or polygonal turret with windows all round, surmounting a roof or cupola.

LATH

A thin 4 or 5 ft-long piece of wood, 1½ in wide, used in slating, tiling and plastering.

LATH FLOATED AND SET FAIR

Three-coat plasterer's work. The first a pricking or scratch coat; the second floating (q.v.); and the third or finishing, done with fine stuff (q.v.), is the setting one.

LIME

Obtained by exposing chalk and other kinds of limestones (calcium carbonate) to a red heat in a pit or kiln. Carbonic acid is expelled and lime, more or less pure, remains, in which state it is called *quicklime*.

LINSEED OIL

Made from the seed of flax. William Aglionby, 1685, *Painting Illustrated*, I, p. 27: 'The Secret of Oyl Paintings consists in using Colours that are ground with Oyl of Nut, or Linseed.'

LIST, LISTING

Cutting away the sap wood from one or both edges of a board. *Listed boards* are those so reduced in width.

LOCK-RAIL

The middle, horizontal rail of a door.

LOZENGE

Diamond-shape.

MARBLING

Painted work simulating the veining of marble.

MORTICE

A recessed cutting within a piece of timber to receive a projecting piece (*tenon*) on the end of another piece of timber, in order to fix the two together at a given angle.

MOULD

A pattern or contour by which any work is to be wrought. Used by masons, glaziers and plasterers and, in a raised-edge table form, by plumbers for casting lead.

MULLER

An egg-shaped piece of stone 2 to 5 inches in diameter, with one end ground flat. Used to grind pigment and oil on a slab (q.v.) into a smooth paste for painting.

NAKED FLOORING

The assemblage of timbers for the floor of a building, of which there are three sorts: single-flooring, double-flooring and double-framed flooring.

NEWEL

Central post in a circular or winding staircase. The principal post when a flight of stairs meets a landing.

NOSING of a step

The projecting part of the treadboard or cover which stands before the riser. The nosing is generally rounded so as to have a semicircular section.

NUT-OIL

Oil obtained from nut kernels, especially those of the hazel and walnut. Used in making paints and varnish. John Evelyn, 1664, *Sylva*, p. 95: 'For this [polishing] Linseed or the sweeter Nut-oyl does the effect best.'

OGEE

A moulding, the same as the *cyma reversa* (*see* cyma).

PAPIER-MÂCHÉ

Paper rendered to a pulp which, having other ingredients mixed with it, is pressed into moulds, and thus ornaments are formed of it (*see* pl. 77). Also called *stucco-paper*.

PARQUETRY

Inlaid work, made of thin plates or veneers of hard coloured woods, secured to a framing of deal to form flooring.

PAVING

Stone from various sources (Newcastle, Portland, Purbeck, Bremen) used for flooring.

PENDENTIVE

Concave triangular spandrel used to lead from the angle of two walls to the base of a circular dome (*see* col. pl. 4).

PIANO NOBILE

Principal storey of a house, usually the first-floor state rooms.

PLANK

A name given to timber of over 9 in breadth, which is thicker than 1½ in, but not more than 4 in.

PLASTER OF PARIS

A preparation of gypsum procured originally in the vicinity of Montmartre, Paris, but found also in England. When diluted with water into a thin paste, it sets rapidly. Scrim (loosely woven hessian) fashioned in certain forms and soaked in gypsum is the basis of fibrous plaster.

PLATE GLASS

Glass cast in sheets or plates and polished.

PLOUGH

A joiner's grooving plane.

PORPHYRY

A very hard stone, of the nature of granite. It is harder than marble and takes a fine polish. It is found in purple, red, black, green and variegated shades.

PORTLAND STONE

A dull white species of stone brought from the Isle of Portland, Dorset. Used extensively by Wren in building St Paul's Cathedral.

PRIMING

In painter's work, the first colouring of the work, which forms a ground for the succeeding coats.

PURBECK STONE

A species of stone obtained from the Purbeck Hills in Dorset of a very hard texture, and used for paving.

RAFTER

Roof timber sloping up from the wall-plate to the ridge. A roof contains principal and common rafters, the principal usually corresponding to the main bay divisions of the space below.

RED LEAD

Red lead oxide, used as a pigment; resists rust.

RENDERING

The act of laying the first coat of plaster on brickwork.

SCAFFOLD
An assemblage of planks or boards supported by pieces of wood called *putlogs* or *putlocks* placed on others called *ledgers*.

SCAGLIOLA
Cement and colouring matter mixed to imitate marble—in the casing of columns, it is laid on thinly to a plaster coating over a wooden framework.

SCANTLING
The dimensions of a piece of timber in breadth and thickness. Architects gave out the 'scantlings' to obtain estimates from carpenters.

SCARFING
The joining of two pieces of timber together transversely, so that the two appear as one.

SHEET GLASS
Glass blown in a 'muff', which is slit on one side and opened out flat.

SIENNA MARBLE
An attractive yellow form veined with grey.

SINGLE MEASURE
A term applied to a door that is square on both sides. *Double measure* is when the door is moulded on both sides. When doors are square on one side and moulded on the other, they are accounted measure and a half.

SLAB
A square of stone or smooth marble about 18 in square on which powdered pigment and oil was ground with a muller (q.v.) to form a smooth paste for painting.

SOUND-BOARD
The canopy over a pulpit (*see* pl. 125); also called a *type*.

SPRINGING
The level at which an arch rises from its supports.

STAIR WELL *see* WELL-HOLE

STATUARY MARBLE
Pure white marble, such as that quarried in Italy at Carrara, and used by sculptors and carvers for their best works.

STOPPING
Making good cracks or defects in plaster, wood, etc.

STRIGES
The channels of a fluted column.

STRIKING of a scaffold/centre
The removal of scaffolding, or of a timber centre upon which an arch has been built.

STRING BOARD
In wooden stairs, the board next to the well-hole which receives the ends of the steps.

STUCCO
Plasterwork in a mixture containing gypsum, sand and marble powder, or variations thereof. Bastard stucco is three-coat work (render, floating and finishing coats).

STUCCO-PAPER *see* PAPIER MÂCHÉ

STUFF
A general term for the wood used by joiners and the mixture used by plasterers.

SUPERFICIAL MEASURE
Square measure, distinguished from linear and solid.

SURBASE
The series of mouldings forming a capping to the dado of a room.

TABERNACLE
Temporary place of worship. The 1711 Act (*Jnl. House of Commons*, XVI, p. 582) allowed 18 chapels or tabernacles to be capable of receiving as many persons as 8 churches.

TABLE
A circular plate of crown glass in its original form before being cut and divided into squares. Twenty-four *tables* of crown glass made a *case*.

TEMPERA
Painting with colours which have been mixed with a natural emulsion (e.g. egg yolk) or an artificial emulsion (oil and gum).

TENON
A projecting rectangular prism formed on the end of a piece of timber to be inserted into a mortice (q.v.) of the same form.

TERM
A trunk, pilaster or pillar, often in the form of the frustum of an inverted obelisk, with the bust of a man, woman or satyr on the top. Fashioned to a high level of craftsmanship by the carvers of marble chimneypieces.

TIE BEAM
Beam connecting the two slopes of a roof across its foot; prevents spreading.

TOP RAIL
The uppermost rail of a piece of framing or wainscoting, as its name suggests.

TREAD
The horizontal part of the step of a stair.

TRESSEL/TRUSSEL
X-shaped props for the support of anything, the under surface of which was horizontal.

TRUSS ROOF
A roof formed of a tie beam, principal rafters, king- or queen-post and other necessary timbers to carry the purlins and common rafters.

VARNISH
A glossy coat on painting or any surface. It consisted of different resins in a state of solution in essential oils or alcohol.

VENEER
A thin leaf of wood of a superior quality for covering furniture, etc., made of an inferior wood.

VOLUTE
A spiral scroll which forms the principal feature of the capital of the Ionic order in Greek and Roman architecture. The capital of the Corinthian order has one smaller in size (*helix*).

WAINSCOT
The oak, deal or cedar lining of walls in panels.

WALL-PLATE
Timber laid longitudinally on the top of a wall.

WELL-HOLE
In a flight of stairs, the space left in the middle beyond the ends of the steps (also *stair-well*).

WHITE LEAD
A compound of lead carbonate and hydrated lead oxide which, when dried, was used as a white pigment. Also called 'ceruse'. Peter Nicholson, 1823, *Practical Builder . . .*, p. 210: 'the principal ingredient used in house-painting'. It was, however, detrimental to the health of the painters who used it.

WINDERS
The steps in a staircase which radiate from a centre, and are therefore narrower at one end than another.

BIBLIOGRAPHY

Citations to manuscript sources and to specialist articles are given in the footnotes to the text and the Dictionary (Part III). The first section owes much to the generous help of Dr Eric Gee and Mr Paget Baggs. The lists may be supplemented by reference to the catalogues of The British Library and British Architectural Library. A full listing for the period 1600–1840 is given by Colvin, 1978, *Dictionary*. The late Professor Rudolf Wittkower started a comprehensive study of pattern-books, which is being brought to fruition by Dr Eileen Harris. Professor Wittkower's article 'English Literature on Architecture' has been reprinted in his collected essays, 1974, *Palladio and English Palladianism*, ed. Margot Wittkower. *See also* Sandra Blutman, 1968, 'Books of Designs for Country Houses', *Architectural History*, 11, and Michael McMordie, 1975, 'Picturesque pattern books and pre-Victorian designers', *ibid.*, 18. Several facsimile editions of the British Architectural Library's holdings have been issued by Gregg Press Ltd. and on microfilm by World Microfilms Ltd.

The entries for the following bibliography are arranged in two sections. The first section for Printed Sources: Primary (1. Craftsmen's Textbooks, 1660–1820) is in chronological order. The second section for Printed Sources: Secondary (2. General, 3. Patrons, 4. Craftsmen: Biographies and 5. Craftsmen: Trades and Techniques) is in an alphabetical sequence.

PRINTED SOURCES: PRIMARY
1. Craftsmen's textbooks, 1660–1820

1662 SIR BALTHAZAR GERBIER
A Brief Discourse concerning the Three Chief Principles of Magnificent Building.

1663 SIR BALTHAZAR GERBIER
Counsel and Advise to All Builders.

1664 VINCENT WING
Art of Surveying . . . .

1674 ROBERT PRICKE
The Ornaments of Architecture . . . useful for Painters, Carvers, Stone-Cutters, Plaisterers (reprinted 1967).

1677 (4th edn. 1729) HENRY COGGESHALL
The Art of Practical Measuring

c 1680 EDWARD PEARCE
The Art of the Plasterer (issued originally as *Book of Freeze Work* in 1640 by Pearce's father, Edward, *fl.* 1630–58).

1688 JOHN STALKER and GEORGE PARKER
A Treatise of Japanning and Varnishing.

1693 JEAN TIJOU
A new Booke of Drawings . . . Containing severall sortes of Iron Worke.

1722, 1728 WILLIAM HALFPENNY
Magnum in Parvo: or the Marrow of Architecture. (A full list of Halfpenny's publications is given in Colvin, 1978, *Dictionary*, p. 379.)

c 1724 S LE CLERK
A Treatise of Architecture. (Translated by Mr Chambers.)

1725 WILLIAM HALFPENNY
The Art of Sound Building demonstrated in Geometrical Problems.

1726 BATTY LANGLEY
Practical Geometry Applied to the Useful Arts of Building etc. (A full list of Langley's publications is given in Colvin, 1978, *Dictionary*, p. 504.)

1727 BATTY LANGLEY
The Builder's Chest Book.

1728 ROBERT MORRIS
An Essay in Defence of Ancient Architecture.

1728 WILLIAM HALFPENNY
The Builder's Pocket Companion.

1729 BATTY LANGLEY
A Sure Guide to Builders: or the Principles and Practice of Architecture.

1730 BATTY LANGLEY
The Young Builder's Rudiments.

1732 JAMES GIBBS
Rules for Drawing the Several Parts of Architecture.

1733 BATTY LANGLEY
The Principles of Ancient Masonry.

1733, 1735, 1753, 1759, 1765 FRANCIS PRICE
British Carpenter, or a Treatise on Carpentry.

1733 EDWARD OAKLEY
The Magazine of Architecture, Perspective and Sculpture.

1733/34 FRANCIS PRICE
The Builder's Directory.

1734 ROBERT MORRIS
Lectures on Architecture.

1724, 1725, 1736 WILLIAM HALFPENNY
Practical Architecture.

1737 THOMAS MALIE
A New and Accurate method of Delineating all the parts of the Different orders in Architecture.

1737 (2nd edn.) E HOPPUS
The Gentleman's and Builder's Repository. (1st edn. by William Salmon.)

1738 BATTY LANGLEY
The Builder's Complete Assistant or a Library of Arts and Sciences . . ., 4th edn., 2 vols.

1740, 1741, 1745, 1750, 1756 BATTY LANGLEY
The City and Country Builder's and Workman's Treasury of Designs.

1741, 1768, 1787, 1808 BATTY LANGLEY
Langley's Builders' Jewel.

1742 (and 1757, 2nd edn.) WILLIAM and JOHN HALFPENNY, architects and carpenters; ROBERT MORRIS, surveyor; THOMAS LIGHTOLER, carver
The Modern Builder's Assistant . . .. (Issued by Robert Sayer, using the material from Campbell's 1728–29, *Palladio . . .*, section II.)

c 1745, 1750, 1758 ABRAHAM SWAN
The British Architect, or . . . The Builder's Treasury of Staircases. (A selection from Swan's designs was edited by Arthur Stratton, 1923.)

1745 WILLIAM SALMON
The London and Country Builders vade mecum, or the Compleat and Universal Estimate.

1749 WILLIAM HALFPENNY
A New and Compleat System of Architecture. . . .

1751 ROBERT MORRIS
The Architectural Remembrancer.

1754 J AHERON
A General Treatise of Architecture, Dublin.

1756 J JORES
A new Book of Iron Work.

1757 ABRAHAM SWAN
Collections of Designs in Architecture, 2 vols.

1758 (2nd edn. 1762) WILLIAM PAIN
The Builder's Companion and Workman's General Assistant.

1759, 1768 ABRAHAM SWAN
The Carpenter's Complete Instructor in Several Hundred Designs. . . .

1759 SIR WILLIAM CHAMBERS (1st part; other editions 1768 and 1791)
A Treatise on the Decorative Part of Civil Architecture.

1761 JOSHUA KIRBY
The Perspective of Architecture.

1763 WILLIAM PAIN
The Builder's Pocket Treasure. . . .

1765 W and J WELLDON
The Smith's Right Hand.

1765 ABRAHAM SWAN
Designs for chimnies and the proportion they bear to their respective Rooms . . . also a variety of Arches, Doors and Windows.

1766 THOMAS MILTON, JOHN CRUNDEN and PLACIDO COLUMBANI
The Chimney Piece Maker's Daily Assistant, or a Treasury of New Designs for Chimney Pieces.

1767 BATTY LANGLEY
Langley's Builder's Directory or Bench Mate.

1767 JAMES GANDON
Six Designs of Friezes.

1768 S RIOUX
The Grecian Orders of Architecture.

1770 JOHN CRUNDEN
The Joiner and Cabinet Maker's Darling.

1770 MATHIAS DARLY
The Ornamental Architect or Young Artist's Instructor.

1771 N WALLIS
A Book of Ornaments in the Palmyrene Taste.

1772 N WALLIS
The Complete Modern Joiner.

1774 W PAIN
The Practical Builder or Workman's General Assistant.

1774 GEORGE RICHARDSON
A Book of Ceilings, composed in the Stile of the Antique Grotesque.

1774, 1776 THOMAS SKAIFE
A Key to Civil Architecture.

1774 JOHN CARTER
The Builder's Magazine or Monthly Companion for Architects, etc. (Designs by John Carter.)

1774 JAMES PAIN, carpenter
The Practical Builder.

1774 N WALLIS
The Carpenter's Treasure.

1775 P COLUMBANI
A New Book of Ornaments containing a Variety of Elegant Designs for Modern Panels.

1775 THOMAS MALTON
A compleat Treatise on Perspective . . . on the true Principles of J. H. Brooke Taylor.

1776 THOMAS MALTON
The Royal Road to Geometry.

1776 P COLUMBANI
A Variety of Capitals, Frizes and Cornices . . . Likewise 12 Designs for Chimney Pieces.

1777 (and 1792) M A PERGOLESI
Ornaments in the Etruscan and Grotesque Styles.

1778 JAMES GANDON
A Collection of Antique and Modern Ornaments.

1778 JAMES GANDON
A Collection of Frizes, Capitals and Grotesque Ornaments.

1778 WILLIAM PAIN
The Carpenter and Joiner's Repository.

1781 GEORGE RICHARDSON
A new collection of Chimney Pieces ornamented in the style of the Etruscan, Greek and Roman Architecture.

Before 1786 WILLIAM PAIN
The Carpenter's Pocket Directory.

1786 (and 1797) WILLIAM and JAMES PAIN
Pain's British Palladio or the Builder's General Assistant.

1787 GEORGE RICHARDSON
A Treatise on the Five Orders of Architecture.

1787, 1793, 1797, 1800, 1805 J MILLER, architect
The Country Gentleman's Architect. . . .

1789 THOMAS RAWLINS
Familiar Architecture.

1789 DEAN ALDRICH
Elements of Civil Architecture.

1790 WILLIAM PAIN
The Practical House Carpenter or Youth's Instructor, 4th edn.

1792 GEORGE RICHARDSON
New Designs in Architecture.

1792 PETER NICHOLSON
The Carpenter's New Guide, 6th edn. 1814.

1792 PETER NICHOLSON
The Carpenter's and Joiner's Assistant.

1793 J BOTTOMLEY
A Book of Designs (for ironwork).

1793 GEORGE RICHARDSON
Capitals of Columns and Friezes measured from the Antique.

1793 ROBERT CLAVERING
An Essay on the Construction and Building of Chimneys.

1793 WILLIAM PAIN
List of Prices of Materials.

c 1795 I and J TAYLOR
Ornamental Iron Work.

1795/8 (5th edn. 1841) PETER NICHOLSON
Nicholson's Principles of Architecture, 3 vols.

1795 (1804 and 1837) PETER NICHOLSON
The Student's Instructor in Drawing and Working of the Five Orders of Architecture.

1797 PETER NICHOLSON
The Carpenter and Joiner's Assistant.

1799 CHARLES MIDDLETON
The Architect and Builder's Miscellany. . . .

c 1802 P COLUMBANI
Vases and Tripods.

1807 ROBERT SALMON
An Analysis of the General Construction of Trusses.

1807 GEORGE COOPER
Designs for the Decoration of Rooms.

1809 W ATKINSON
Principles of Design in Architecture.

1810 G LANDI
Architectural Decorations.

1811 JOHN BIRD
The Carpenters' and Joiners' Price Book. . . .

1811 W F POCOCK
Modern Finishing for Rooms.

1816 Published by J TAYLOR
The Rudiments of Ancient Architecture.

1818 (2nd edn.) DEAN ALDRICH
The Elements of Civil Architecture.

1819 ANTHONY GEORGE COOK
The New Builder's Magazine and Complete Architectural Library.

PRINTED SOURCES: SECONDARY
2. General

Note: References to biographies and articles about individual architects are given in Colvin, 1978, *Dictionary.*

ALLEN, BARBARA SPRAGUE
1937, *Tides in English Taste, 1619–1800*, 2 vols., (reprinted 1958).

ARCHITECTURAL PUBLICATION SOCIETY
1852–92, *Dictionary of Architecture*, ed. Wyatt Papworth, 8 vols.

ARTS COUNCIL
1972, *The Age of Neoclassicism* (Council of Europe Exhibition).

ASHTON, T S
1955, *An Economic History of England: The 18th Century.*

BOASE, T S R
1959, 'English Art, 1800–1870', *The Oxford History of English Art*, X.

BRIGGS, MARTIN S
1927, *The Architect in History.*

BROWNELL, MORRIS
1976, *Alexander Pope and the Arts of Georgian England.*

BURKE, JOSEPH
1976, 'English Art, 1714–1800', *The Oxford History of English Art,* IX.

CARRITT, E F
1949, *A Calendar of British Taste from 1669 to 1800.*

CHAPMAN, HESTER
1953 *Queen Mary II.*

CLARK, KENNETH
1950, *The Gothic Revival,* 2nd edn.

COLVIN, H M
1974, 'A Scottish origin for English Palladianism', *Architectural History,* 17.

COLVIN H M (ed.)
1976, *The History of the King's Works 1660–1782,* V.

COLVIN, H M
1978, *A Biographical Dictionary of British Architects, 1600–1840.* (The 1st edn. of 1954, *English Architects, 1660–1840* contains many carpenters, etc., excluded from the 2nd edn.)

CONNOR, T P
1977, 'The making of *Vitruvius Britannicus*', *Architectural History,* 20.

CORNFORTH, JOHN and FOWLER, JOHN
1974, *English Decoration in the 18th Century.*

CORNFORTH, JOHN and HILL, OLIVER
1966, *English Country Houses: Caroline, 1625–85.*

CROOK, J MORDAUNT
1969, 'The pre-Victorian architect: professionalism and patronage', *Architectural History,* 12.

CROOK, J MORDAUNT
1972, *The Greek Revival: Neoclassical Attitudes in British Architecture, 1760–1870.*

CROOK, J MORDAUNT and PORT M H
1974, *The History of the King's Works, 1782–1851,* VI.

DICKSON, P G M
1967, *The Financial Revolution in England, 1688–1756.*

DOWNES, K
1966, *English Baroque Architecture.*

DUTTON, RALPH
1948, *The English Interior, 1500–1900.*

FIENNES, CELIA
1947, *The Journeys of, circa 1685–1703,* ed. C Morris.

FRASER, ANTONIA
1979, *Charles II.*

FRASER, P and HARRIS, J
1960, *The Burlington-Devonshire Catalogue of Drawings in the R.I.B.A. Library.*

GILBOY, E W
1934, *Wages in 18th-Century England.*

GIROUARD, MARK
1978, *Life in the English Country House: A Social and Architectural History.*

GLOAG, JOHN
1965, *Early English Decorative Detail.*

GOMME, ANDOR, JENNER, MICHAEL and LITTLE, BRYAN
1979, *Bristol: An Architectural History.*

GREEN, DAVID
1951, *Blenheim Palace.*

HALL, IVAN
1959, *Methods of Decoration and Arrangement of English Greek Revival Buildings,* MA thesis, Manchester Univ.

HARRIS, JOHN
1979, *The Artist and the Country House* (painted views), supersedes title by Steegman, John.

HONOUR, HUGH
1961, *Chinoiserie: The Vision of Cathay.*

HOOKE, ROBERT
1935, *Diary of, 1672–80,* H W Robinson and W Adams (eds.).

HUSSEY, CHRISTOPHER
1965, *English Country Houses: Early-Georgian,* 2nd edn.; 1956, *Mid-Georgian*; 1958, *Late Georgian.*

INNOCENT, C F
1916, *The Development of English Building Construction* (2nd impression 1971)

ISON, W
1948, *The Georgian Buildings of Bath,* and 1951, *The Georgian Buildings of Bristol* (reissued 1976 and 1978 respectively)

JOURDAIN, MARGARET
1950, *English Interior Decoration, 1500–1830.*

KAUFMANN, E
1955, *Architecture in the Age of Reason.*

KAYE, BARRINGTON
1960, *The Development of the Architectural Profession in Britain* (Ch. IV deals with the 17th and 18th centuries).

LEES-MILNE, JAMES
1970, *English Country Houses: Baroque, 1685–1715.*

LENYGON, F
1909, *The Decoration and Furniture of English Mansions during the 17th and 18th Centuries.*

LENYGON, F
1914, *Decoration in England from 1660 to 1770,* 2nd edn. 1927 (covers period 1640 to 1760).

LINSTRUM, DEREK
1978, *West Yorkshire: Architects and Architecture.*

LLOYD, NATHANIEL
A History of the English House (reprinted 1945).

MACAULAY, JAMES
1975, *The Gothic Revival, 1745–1845.*

MARSHALL, DOROTHY
1962, *Eighteenth Century England.*

MINCHINTON, W E (ed.)
1969, *The Growth of English Overseas Trade in the 17th and 18th Centuries.*

MULLINER, H H
1923, *The Decorative Arts in England during the late XVIIth and XVIIIth Centuries.*

PILCHER, D
1947, *The Regency Style, 1800 to 1830.*

REDDAWAY, T F
1940, *The Rebuilding of London after the Great Fire.*

RICHARDSON, SIR A E
1949, *An Introduction to Georgian Architecture.*

SITWELL, SACHEVERELL
1945, *British Architects and Craftsmen, 1600–1830,* 1st edn.

STEEGMAN, JOHN
1936, *The Rule of Taste from George I to George IV.*

STEEGMAN, JOHN
1950, *Consort of Taste.*

STEEGMAN, JOHN and STROUD, DOROTHY
1949, *The Artist and the Country House.*

STRATTON, A
1920, 'The English Interior', *A Review of the Decoration of English Homes from Tudor Times to the XIXth Century.*

SUMMERSON, SIR JOHN
July 1959, 'The Classical Country House in 18th Century England', *Journal of the Royal Society of Arts,* pp. 539–87.

SUMMERSON, SIR JOHN
1969, *Architecture in Britain, 1530–1830* (Pelican History of Art), 5th edn.

SUMMERSON, SIR JOHN
1978, *Georgian London,* revised edn.

THOMPSON, FRANCIS
1949, *A History of Chatsworth.*

THORNTON, PETER
1978, *Seventeenth Century Interior Decoration in England, France, and Holland.*

300   TIPPING, H AVRAY
1921–37, *English Homes*, 9 vols. This set
covers the period from Norman times to 1820.
For the period 1660–1820 it comprises: Period
IV(i), *Late Stuart, 1649–1714*, 1929; Period
IV(ii), *Sir John Vanbrugh*, 1928; Period V,
Early Georgian, 1714–1760; Period VI, *Late
Georgian, 1760–1820*.

WARD, W R
1953, *The English Land Tax in the 18th
Century*.

WARD-JACKSON, PETER
1958, *English Furniture Designs of the
Eighteenth Century*.

WATERHOUSE, E K
Painting in Britain, 1530–1790 (Pelican
History of Art).

WATKIN, DAVID
1968, *Thomas Hope and the Neo-Classical Idea*.

WHIFFEN, MARCUS
1947, *Stuart and Georgian Churches outside
London, 1603–1837*.

WHINNEY, MARGARET and MILLAR, OLIVER
1957, 'English Art, 1625–1714', *The Oxford
History of English Art*, VIII.

WHITLEY, W T
1928, *Artists and Their Friends in England,
1700–1799*, 2 vols.

WILLAN, T S
1936, *River Navigation in England, 1600–1750*.

WILLAN, T S
1939, *English Coasting Trade, 1600–1750*.

WITTKOWER, R
1974, *Palladio and English Palladianism*, ed. M
Wittkower.

3. Patrons
Books and Theses

BAKER, C H COLLINS and BAKER, M I
1949, *The Life and Circumstances of James
Brydges, 1st Duke of Chandos*.

BATEMAN, J
1883, *The Great Landowners of Great Britain
and Ireland*.

BAUGH, DANIEL A (ed.)
1975, *Aristocratic Government and Society in
18th Century England*.

BEATTIE, J M
1967, *The English Court in the Reign of George I*.

BROOKE, JOHN
1972, *King George III*.

CARSWELL, J P
1960, *The South Sea Bubble*.

CARTWRIGHT, J J (ed.)
1882, *The Wentworth Papers, 1705–1739*. . . .

CLARK, SIR GEORGE
1956, *The Later Stuarts, 1660–1714*, 2nd edn.

CLAY, G C A
1965, *Two families and their estates: the
Grimstons and the Cowpers from c. 1650 to
c. 1815*, PhD thesis, Cambridge Univ.

CONNOR, T P
1979, 'Colen Campbell as Architect to the
Prince of Wales', *Architectural History*, 22.

DAVIS, D R F
1971, *The Dukes of Devonshire, Newcastle and
Rutland, 1688–1714: A Study in Wealth and
Political Influence*, DPhil thesis, Oxford Univ.

DICKINS, L and STANTON, M
1910, *An 18th Century Correspondence* (of
architect, Sanderson Miller).

DICKSON, PATRICIA
1973, *Red John of the Battles: John, Second
Duke of Argyll*. . . .

DOBRÉE, BONAMY (ed.)
1932, *The Letters of Philip Dormer Stanhope,
4th Earl of Chesterfield*, 6 vols.

EDWARDS, AVERYL
1947, *Frederick Louis, Prince of Wales,
1707–1751*.

FAIRFAX-LUCY, A
1962, *Charlecote and the Lucys*.

FORD, BRINSLEY
1974, Six articles on eighteenth-century
travellers to Rome, *Apollo*, June, pp. 408–61.

GREEN, DAVID
1967, *Sarah, Duchess of Marlborough*.

GREGG, EDWARD
1980, *Queen Anne*.

HALSBAND, ROBERT
1956, *The Life of Lady Mary Wortley
Montagu*.

HALSBAND, ROBERT (ed.)
1965–66, *The Complete Letters of Lady Mary
Wortley Montagu*, 2 vols.

HALSBAND, ROBERT
1973, *Lord Hervey, Eighteenth Century
Courtier*.

HARRIS, JOHN and HARRIS, EILEEN
Articles on Sir Lawrence Dundas and his
collections, *Apollo*, September 1967,
pp. 170–89.

HATTON, RAGNHILD
1978, *George I: Elector and King*.

HILL, B W
1961, *The career of Robert Harley, Earl of
Oxford, from 1702 to 1714*, PhD thesis,
Cambridge Univ.

HORWITZ, H
1968, *Revolution Politicks, The Career of
Daniel Finch, 2nd Earl of Nottingham,
1647–1730*.

JENKINS, FRANK
1961, *Architect and Patron*.

KELCH, RAY R
1964, *Newcastle, A Duke without Money,
Thomas Pelham Holles, 1693–1768*.

KEMP, BETTY
1976, *Sir Robert Walpole*.

KING WILLIAM (ed.)
1930, *Memoirs of Sarah, Duchess of
Marlborough*.

LEES-MILNE, JAMES
1962, *Earls of Creation*. (The architectural
activities of the 1st Earl Bathurst, 9th Earl of
Pembroke, 3rd Earl of Burlington and 2nd
Earl of Oxford in the first half of the
eighteenth century.)

LEWIS, WILMARTH S
1961, *Horace Walpole*.

MINARDIÈRE, A M
1963, *The Warwickshire Gentry, 1660–1730*,
MA thesis, Birmingham Univ.

MINGAY, G E
1958, *Landownership and Agrarian Trends in
the 18th Century*, PhD thesis, Nottingham
Univ.

MINGAY, G E
1963, *English Landed Society in the Eighteenth
Century*.

MINGAY, G E
1976, *The Gentry: The Rise and Fall of a
Ruling Class*.

NEWMAN, A
1969, *The Stanhopes of Chevening*.

PHILLIPS, C B
1972, *The Gentry in Cumberland and
Westmorland*, PhD thesis, Lancaster Univ.

PLUMB, J H
1956, *Sir Robert Walpole*, I, *The Making of A
Statesman*; 1960, II, *The King's Minister*.

PLUMB, J H
1956, *The First Four Georges*.

ROEBUCK, PETER
1980, *Yorkshire Baronets, 1640–1760, families,
estates and fortunes*.

SEDGWICK, ROMNEY (ed.)
1970, *The House of Commons, 1715–1754*, 2
vols.

The following studies by Simpson and Stone
precede the period covered in this book
(1660–1820), but are essential reading:
SIMPSON, Alan
1963, *The Wealth of the Gentry, 1540–1660*.

STONE, LAWRENCE
1965, *The Crisis of the Aristocracy, 1558–1641*.

STONE, LAWRENCE
1973, *Family and Fortune: Studies in Aristocratic Finance in the 16th and 17th Centuries*.

THOMPSON, F M L
1963, *English Landed Society in the Nineteenth Century*.

THOMSON, GLADYS SCOTT
1940, *The Russells in Bloomsbury, 1669–1771*.

THOMSON, GLADYS SCOTT
1949, *Family Background*.

TRENCH, CHEVENIX
1975, *George II*.

TURBERVILLE, A S
1927, *The House of Lords in the 18th Century*.

TURNER, H D
1964, *Five Studies of the Aristocracy, 1689–1714*, MLitt thesis, Cambridge Univ.

TYACK, G C
1970, *Country House Building in Warwickshire, 1500–1914*, BA thesis, Oxford Univ.

WALTERS, JOHN
1972, *The Royal Griffin: Frederick, Prince of Wales, 1707–1751*.

WATSON, J STEVEN
1960, *The Reign of George III, 1760–1815*.

WILLCOX, WILLIAM B
1971, *The Age of Aristocracy, 1688–1830*, 2nd edn.

WILLIAMS, BASIL
1961, *The Whig Supremacy, 1714–1760*, 2nd edn. (revised).

Articles

CLAY, G C A
1968, 'Marriage, Inheritance and the rise of large estates in England, 1660–1815', *Econ. Hist. Rev.*, 2nd ser., XXI.

DARWIN, K
1950, 'John Aislabie, 1670–1742', *Yorkshire Arch. Jnl.*, XXXVII.

DUNBAR, JOHN G
1975, 'The Building activities of the Duke and Duchess of Lauderdale, 1670–82', *The Archaeological Jnl.*, 132.

GOULDING, R W
1924, 'Henrietta, Countess of Oxford', *Trans., Thoroton Soc.*

HABAKKUK, H J
1939, 'English Landownership, 1680–1740', *Econ. Hist. Rev.*, X.

HABAKKUK, H J
1950, 'Marriage Settlements in the eighteenth century', *Trans., Royal Hist. Soc.*, 4th ser., XXXII.

HABAKKUK, H J
1952, 'The long-term rate of interest and the price of land in the seventeenth century', *Econ. Hist. Rev.*, 2nd ser., V.

HABAKKUK, H J
1953, 'The English Nobility in the eighteenth century', *The European Nobility in the eighteenth century*, ed. A Goodwin.

HABAKKUK, H J
1953, 'The economic functions of English landowners in the seventeenth and eighteenth centuries', *Explorations in Entrepreneurial History*, VI.

HABAKKUK, H J
1955, 'Daniel Finch, second earl of Nottingham, his house and estate', *Studies in Social History*, ed. J H Plumb.

HABAKKUK, H J
1960, 'The English Land Market in the eighteenth century', *Britain and the Netherlands*, ed. J S Bromley and E H Kossmann.

HOUGHTON, W E
1942, 'The English Virtuoso in the 17th Century', *Jnl. History of Ideas*, III.

4. Craftsmen: Biographies

ADDLESHAW, G W O
1967, 'Architects, sculptors, painters, craftsmen 1660–1960, whose work can be seen in York Minster', *Architectural History*, X.

ADDLESHAW, G W O
1971, 'Architects, sculptors, painters, craftsmen 1770–1970, whose work is to be seen in Chester Cathedral', *Architectural History*, 14.

GRINLING GIBBONS (1648–1720)
Carver-sculptor
GREEN, DAVID
1964, *Grinling Gibbons, 1648–1721*.
OUGHTON, FREDERICK
1979, *Grinling Gibbons and the English Woodcarving Tradition*.
TIPPING, H AVRAY
1914, *Grinling Gibbons and the Woodwork of his Age*.
WHINNEY, MARGARET
1948, *Grinling Gibbons in Cambridge*.
Portraits by Sir Godfrey Kneller (Hermitage, Leningrad; versions at National Portrait Gallery, London, Serlby and elsewhere); by Sir John Medina (chalk), British Museum, London.

ANGELICA KAUFFMANN (1741–1807)
Decorative Painter
DE ROSSI, G G
1810, *Angelica Kauffman*, Florence.
GERARD, FRANCES
1892, *Angelica Kauffmann*.
HARTCUP, ADELINE
1954, *Angelica*.
MANNERS, LADY VICTORIA and WILLIAMSON, G C

1924, *Angelica Kauffmann*.
Exhibition of paintings by Angelica Kauffmann, Iveagh Bequest, Kenwood, 1955. Portrait by Nathaniel Dance, 1764, at Burghley House, *repr*: Beard, 1966, *Craftsmen*, pl. 110.

WILLIAM KENT (1685/6–1748)
BEARD, GEOFFREY
August 1970, 'William Kent and the Royal Barge', *Burl. Mag.*
BEARD, GEOFFREY
December 1975, 'William Kent and the Cabinet-Makers', *Burl Mag.*
HODSON, PETER (compiler)
1964, *William Kent: A Bibliography and Chronology*, American Association of Architectural Bibliographers, 27.
JOURDAIN, MARGARET
1948, *The Work of William Kent*.
WITTKOWER, R
1945, 'Lord Burlington and Kent', *The Archaeological Journal*, CII.
Portraits by Benedetto Luti in the Devonshire Collections at Chatsworth; one of the figures in 'A Club of Artists' by Gavin Hamilton, 1735 (National Portrait Gallery, London). A portrait by William Aikman was sold, Wanstead House, 1822, lot 365 (engravings after it are in the National Portrait Gallery files).

DANIEL MAROT (c 1660–c 1752)
Designer
LANE, ARTHUR
1949, 'Daniel Marot, Designer of Delft Vases and Gardens at Hampton Court', *The Connoisseur*, CXXIII, p. 19.
OZINGA, M
1938, *Daniel Marot*.

EDWARD PEARCE (c 1635–95)
Sculptor
SEYMOUR, J
1952, 'Edward Pearce: Baroque Sculptor of London', *Guildhall Miscellany*, I, p. 10.

JOSEPH ROSE Junior (1745–99)
Plasterer
A list of his works is given in Part III, Dictionary.
Portrait: self-portrait in crayons at Sledmere, Yorkshire, engraved, 1799, by F Bartolozzi.

LOUIS FRANCOIS ROUBILIAC (?1705–1762)
Sculptor
ESDAILE, KATHARINE A
1928, *L. F. Roubiliac*.
WEBB, M I
1957, 'The French Antecedents of L. F. Roubiliac', *Gazette des Beaux-Arts*, 6th ser., XLIX, p. 84.

JOHN MICHAEL RYSBRACK (1694–1770) Sculptor
WEBB, M I
1954, *Michael Rysbrack*.

PETER SCHEEMAKERS (1691–1781)
Sculptor
WEBB, M I
1957, 'Chimneypieces by Scheemakers', *C Life*, p. 491.

302   5. Craftsmen: Trades and techniques

ARKELL, W J
1947, *Oxford Stone.*

ÅSTRÔM, S E
1963, 1965, *From Cloth to Iron: The Anglo-Baltic Trade in the late 17th Century,* 2 vols., Helsinki.

AYRTON, MAXWELL and SILCOCK, ARNOLD
1929, *Wrought Iron and its decorative use.*

BANKART, G P
1908, *The Art of the Plasterer.*

BEARD, GEOFFREY
1966, *Georgian Craftsmen and their work.*

BEARD, GEOFFREY
1975, *Decorative Plasterwork in Great Britain.*

BELL, W G
1938, *History of the Worshipful Company of Tylers and Bricklayers . . . of London.*

BENNETT, A F
1950, *Metal windows,* BA thesis, Cambridge Univ.

BRIGGS, MARTIN S
1925, *A Short History of the Building Crafts.*

CLIFTON-TAYLOR, ALEC
1962, *The Pattern of English Building.*

CLIFTON-TAYLOR, ALEC and BRUNSKILL, RONALD
1978, *English Brickwork.*

CROFT-MURRAY, EDWARD
Decorative Painting in England, 1530–1837, 1, 1962, *Early Tudor to Sir James Thornhill,* 2, 1970, *The Eighteenth and Early Nineteenth Centuries.*

DAVEY, N
1961, *A History of Building Materials.*

ENGLEFIELD, W A D
1923, *The History of the Painter-Stainers Company of London.*

ENTWISLE, E A
1954, *The Book of Wallpaper*; 1960, *A Literary History of Wallpaper.*

GARDNER, JOHN STARKIE
1911, *English Ironwork of the XVIIth and XVIIIth Centuries.*

GLOAG, JOHN and BRIDGWATER, DEREK
1948, *A History of Cast Iron in Architecture.*

GODFREY, W H
1911, *The English Staircase.*

GOODISON, W H
1911, *The English Staircase.*

GOODISON, NICHOLAS
1974, *Ormolu: The Work of Matthew Boulton.*

GOODISON, NICHOLAS
1975, 'The Victoria and Albert Museum's Collection of Metal-Work Pattern Books', *Furniture History,* XI, pp. 1–30.

GOODMAN, W L
1968, *The History of Woodworking Tools.*

HARRIS, JOHN
1960, *English Decorative Ironwork, 1610–1836.*

HEWETT C.
1980, *English Historic Carpentry.*

JOURDAIN, MARGARET
1926, *English Decorative Plasterwork of the Late Renaissance.*

JUPP, E B and POCOCK, W W
1887, *An Historical Account of the Worshipful Company of Carpenters.*

KELLY, ALISON
1965, *Decorative Wedgwood in Architecture and Furniture.*

KELLY, ALISON
1968, *The Book of English Fireplaces.*

KNOOP, D and JONES, G P
1935, *The London Mason in the 17th Century.*

LISTER, RAYMOND
1960, *Decorative Wrought Iron in Great Britain.*

LISTER, RAYMOND
1963, *Decorative Cast Ironwork in Great Britain.*

LLOYD, N
1935, *History of English Brickwork.*

MARILLIER, H
1928, *English Tapestries of the 18th Century.*

MARSH, BOWER
1913, *Records of the Worshipful Company of Carpenters,* I. *Apprentices' Entry Books.*

MILLAR, W
1897, *Plastering, Plain and Decorative.*

MORRELL, J B
1948, *York Monuments.*

MORRELL, J B
1950, *York Woodwork.*

MURRAY, PETER
1964, 'Architettura Inglese e Stuccatori Italiani', *Arte e Artisti dei Laghi Lombardi,* II.

NOTTINGHAM UNIVERSITY
March 1965, *The Architect's Vision* (models), Exhibition Catalogue.

OLIVER, BASIL
4 October 1940, 'Stucco, plaster and pargetting', *The Builder,* pp. 328–30.

OMAN, C C
1929, *Catalogue of Wallpapers in the Victoria & Albert Museum* (2nd edn, 1981).

PHILLIPS, H L
1915, *Annals of the Joiners' Company.*

PURCELL, DONOVAN
1967, *Cambridge Stone.*

ROSE, W
1937, *The Village Carpenter.*

RUCH, J E
1968, 'Regency Coade: A Study of the Coade Record Books, 1813–21', *Architectural History,* 11.

SALAMAN, R A
1957, 'Tradesmen's Tools', *A History of Technology,* ed. Charles Singer and others, III, Ch. 5.

SEKLER, E F
1954, *The development of the British Staircase,* PhD thesis, London Univ., Courtauld Institute.

SHUFFREY, L A
1912, *The English Fireplace.*

STRINGER, MICHAEL
1951, *English Facing Bricks: An Historical Outline,* BA thesis, Cambridge Univ.

SUGDEN, A V and EDMONSON, J
1925, *A History of English Wallpaper, 1509–1914.*

THOMPSON, W G
1914, *Tapestry Weaving in England.*

THURSTON, A P
1938, 'Parker's Roman Cement', *Trans., Newcomen Society,* XIX, pp. 193–206.

TURNER, LAURENCE
1927, *English Decorative Plasterwork.*

UNWIN, G
1938, *The Gilds and Companies of London.*

WATTS, W W
12 May 1928, 'English Brass Locks of the 17th Century', *C Life,* pp. 705–07.

WEAVER, Sir L
1909, *English Leadwork, its Art and History.*

WHINNEY, MARGARET
1964, *Sculpture in Britain, 1530–1830.*

WHITWORTH, MARTIN
1951, *Building Stones of Cambridge,* BA thesis, Cambridge Univ.

WILTON-ELY, JOHN
July 1967, 'The Architectural Model', *Arch Rev,* pp. 27–32 (*see also* Nottingham University entry, above).

WILTON-ELY, JOHN
1969, 'The Architectural Models of Sir John Soane', *Architectural History,* XII, pp. 5–38.

WOODFORDE, C
1954, *English Stained and Painted Glass.*

WRAGG, R B
1957, 10 October 'Scagliola', *C Life.*

INDEX OF PERSONS

INDEX OF PLACES

INDEX OF SUBJECTS